STARK YOUNG

A Life in the Arts

STARK YOUNG
A Life in the Arts
Letters, 1900–1962

Volume II

Edited by JOHN PILKINGTON

LOUISIANA STATE UNIVERSITY PRESS
Baton Rouge

ISBN 0–8071–0100–1
Library of Congress Catalog Card Number 73–90874
Copyright © 1975 by Louisiana State University Press
Manufactured in the United States of America

Publication of these volumes was assisted by the American Council of Learned
Societies under a grant from the Andrew Mellon Foundation.

These volumes were designed by Dwight Agner
and composed in Linotype Granjon and Perpetua types.
The composition, printing, and binding were done
by Kingsport Press, Kingsport, Tennessee.

Contents

Volume II

STARK YOUNG
A Life in the Arts

VII

The Sea Gull
and *Belle Isle*
1937-1943

BETWEEN 1937 and 1943, Stark Young's correspondence often seems to originate in a multiplicity of activities that relate somewhat tangentially to his main career. The letters to his friends in Natchez emphasize his desire to help the newly founded Natchez Pilgrimage and, incidentally, to promote the sale of *So Red the Rose.* To his publishers and to Southern colleagues, he wrote about his anthology of Southern literature which Scribner's published as a textbook. In other letters, Young referred to his lectures, book reviews, and negotiations with Hollywood producers. Whenever he had occasion, he wrote to praise the merits of a friend's recently published book, article, poem, or play. The letters from Young to the translators of Lorca's plays show his willingness to help his younger friends with their literary projects, particularly when the work related to the theatre.

Despite these matters, which were, of course, genuinely interesting to Young, the main thrust of his career continued in the drama. His drama criticism, now somewhat shortened at the request of Bruce Bliven, continued to appear week after week in the *New Republic,* though after 1939, World War II and Young's personal despondency tended to decrease the number he wrote. Overshadowing everything else in his life during this period, however, was his association with Alfred Lunt and Lynn Fontanne, first in the translation of Chekhov's *The Sea Gull* and subsequently in the writing of *Belle Isle* or, as it was later called, *Artemise*.

Early in February, 1938, when Young first mentioned *The Sea Gull* in his correspondence, he had already finished most of the tedious work of translating the play. Only the polishing remained to be done under rehearsal conditions. Although he had no knowledge of Russian when he undertook the translation, his lifelong attention to the selection of the precise, effective word to express the nuances of meaning and his years of listening to actors deliver lines across the footlights had taught him the phrasing and speech rhythms that actors could speak effectively in conjunction with their physical movements on the stage. In effect, he brought to bear upon the Chekhov original the combined skills of the director, critic, and scholar. His method was to make, with the aid of a Russian-English dictionary, a literal translation, compare it with seven previous translations of the play, and, finally, refine the lines to produce the correct meaning in speeches that would also be theatrically effective.

After lengthy discussions with the Lunts and Robert Edmond Jones during rehearsals and throughout the trials in Baltimore and Boston, Young continued to polish his translation. On March 28, 1938, *The Sea Gull* opened in New York at the Shubert Theatre, and before it closed on April 30, the Lunts had given forty-one performances. Although Broadway critics emphasized the inherent difficulties in the play, they pronounced it a distinguished, successful revival. Even more important for Young had been his opportunity to show the Lunts that he could collaborate with them successfully in the dramatist-actor relationship. Before leaving for London, they talked about plans for the following year, plans that seemed to include Young. Meanwhile, to the translation itself he added a lengthy preface about the problems of translation and notes for actors and signed a contract with Scribner's for publication. When the volume appeared it received excellent reviews.

In January, 1939, Stark Young returned to Texas to translate other plays by Chekhov and to write a play for the Lunts. With the assistance of a skilled Russian-English translator, who prepared for him a literal version of Chekhov's text, Young rendered *The Three Sisters* and *The Cherry Orchard* into the same acting "speakability" that characterized his version of *The Sea*

Gull. Lengthy negotiations with various producers and actors, however, failed to result in a definite commitment for performance of his work. Young was particularly disappointed when Guthrie McClintic and Katharine Cornell decided not to adopt his translation for their production of *The Three Sisters.* In June, 1941, Samuel French published Young's *The Three Sisters,* but publication of the three plays as a single volume, which Maxwell Perkins had favored, was delayed until 1949, when Random House finally brought out these three plays and Young's translation of *Uncle Vanya* in the Modern Library Series.

For *Belle Isle* and the Lunts, Young borrowed the setting at Grand Isle, Louisiana, and the central situation involving the pirate from Lyle Saxon's biography of Jean Lafitte. According to Saxon, the climax of the famous pirate's career took place in 1815 when he had to choose sides between the British and the Americans. Lafitte's decision to help Andrew Jackson defend New Orleans brought the offer of amnesty but effectively ended his career as a pirate. In the play, Young added emotional tension and romance to the pirate's moment of decision by portraying the pirate as in love with a beautiful French opera singer shot by the British during the negotiations. Had Young written this play earlier, he would have worked with Doris Keane in mind, but, in 1939, he designed *Belle Isle* solely for Lynn Fontanne as the singer Artemise to be supported by Alfred Lunt as the pirate Jean Piteau.

The long, unhappy history of *Belle Isle* may be pieced together from Young's correspondence. By late summer or early fall, 1939, he had finished the manuscript and sent it to the Lunts. Early in December, they had become so enthusiastic about it that they invited Young to join them in Los Angeles to consider Alfred Lunt's ideas about minor changes in the script. Young met them in Los Angeles and toured with them for six weeks. The conferences went well; and when Young returned to New York early in 1940, he confidently expected the Lunts to produce his play that fall. Late in April, however, the Lunts opened in Robert Sherwood's *There Shall Be No Night;* and, in the autumn, instead of producing Young's *Belle Isle,* they took the Sherwood play on the road for a tour that lasted until December, 1941. Young heard no more from them until late in the spring of 1942.

Throughout 1941 and 1942, Stark Young brooded over the failure of his hopes for *Belle Isle.* His contributions to the *New Republic,* less numerous than usual, represented his only serious work. His correspondence declined noticeably. His friends became concerned about his depression, and, more specifically, his drinking. Bowman appealed to Tate and others for assistance, and Julia Robertson came from Texas to help and decided to take him to Austin to get him out of the New York theatre atmosphere. Young was in Texas in May, 1942, when he read in a newspaper that the Lunts were going to produce a new S. N. Behrman play, *The Pirate.* Sensing the possible similarity between his work and Behrman's, Young published *Belle Isle* under the title *Artemise* on June 29, in Austin, Texas. On November 25, the Lunts opened in Behrman's play and performed it until April 27, 1943. Young's play was never produced.

Young's bitterness over the fate of his play arose from several sources. After devoting a year's effort to writing the work, he felt that what he had created was perfectly matched to the Lunts' special talents in the theatre. For this reason, Alfred Lunt's suggestion that Katharine Cornell do the play made no sense at all to Young. So far as he was concerned, the fortunes of his play rested wholly upon the Lunts. It might seem just another stage vehicle to Alfred Lunt, but to Young the play meant a great deal. He felt, moreover, that the Lunts had accepted the piece, fully committed themselves to producing it, and then gradually rejected the work without justifiable or even adequate explanation. More than anything else, Young could not fathom Lynn Fontanne's apparent defection. The disappointment became at once both professional and personal.

After seeing Behrman's play, Young became convinced that the Lunts had betrayed him. Behrman claimed that his romantic comedy about the marital difficulties of a former pirate-turned-mayor had been "suggested" by Ludwig Fulda's *Der Seerauber,* originally produced in 1912 in Vienna. After examining Fulda's work, Young concluded that the most significant differences between Behrman's comedy and Fulda's play had their origin in Young's *Belle Isle* or *Artemise* as it was then called. Young cited as examples changes Behrman had made in time and locale, the use of music, words with specialized meanings, costume effects, and the method of presentation of the heroine in the opening scene. Most important of all, Young thought that the underlying themes of Behrman's *The Pirate* derived not from Fulda's *Der Seerauber* but from his own *Artemise.* Since Behrman could hardly have seen the manuscript of *Artemise,* Young did not blame him; rather, the source of the *Artemise* material in Behrman's comedy, Young believed, could only have been the Lunts, because only they, besides himself, knew his play well enough to transmit these features to Behrman.

Fortunately for Young, he had able, level-headed friends to advise him. William Bowman, Leah Salisbury, John Anderson, and Lawton Campbell listened sympathetically to Young's charges but advised him against making any public statements. They realized, as did Young, that he had no substantial grounds for accusations of plagiarism. They knew also that Young would later regret any hasty action undertaken in a period of emotional stress. Very likely, they foresaw, what Young could not see at the time, that, however important *Artemise* and the Lunts appeared to him then, neither the play nor the friendship was vital to his career. Ultimately, Young reached this position, but the *Artemise*-Lunt-Behrman affair remained a painful memory so long as he lived.

485 | To Roane Fleming Byrnes, Natchez, Mississippi

320 East 57th Street
New York
Thursday [January 28, 1937]

Dear Mrs. Byrnes,

You are a cold hearted fiend not to have answered my note. I only hope that it does not mean that you and Ferriday have had the influenza, like the rest of the world. I had escaped colds et cetera the whole autumn but have been under the weather since I got back here, partly the wild hours of travel, partly the epidemic in town. However I survive. Please send me the Briars[1] lady's name, also the Dixons.[2]

I imagine I was a dull guest. All Christmas I was with my sister and it was sad and forever to be remembered what we have lost. There is a difference when the loss is a young person, as I know by experience. One thing I did not mention while I was there with you all was this weight on my mind. The other was your mother.[3] I missed her very much, and I know you miss her. But there was nothing to say about it. Such is life.

I decided against those objects and now want to put in the museum[4] a Russian ikon painting, on gold leaf, eighteenth century, bought for me in Russia soon after the war—I mean to put this in memory of your mother. I must have a metal plate stamped to go on the frame. Will you please send me the name I should use. The plate would read

1. Sometimes spelled *Briers,* the early nineteenth-century plantation dwelling became during the 1820s the home of William Burr Howell and his wife Margaret Louise Kempe Howell, parents of Varina Howell, whose marriage to Jefferson Davis took place there in 1845. During the later part of the nineteenth century and the first quarter of the twentieth, the house was owned by Walter Irvine and members of his family. In 1927, William Winans Wall and his wife, Emma Augusta Hardy Wall, acquired the property and restored the dwelling. Mrs. Wall is the person about whom Young inquired.

2. Mrs. Joseph Dixon (Harriett Shields Dixon), born in Brandon, Mississippi, moved to Natchez after her marriage in 1920. In 1936 and 1937, she was president of the Natchez Garden Club Pilgrimage; she has also been prominently associated with the Natchez Trace Association.

3. Anna Metcalfe Fleming (Mrs. James S. Fleming, 1861–1936).

4. See above, Letter 435 and n. 4.

Gift of Stark Young
in memory of
—— —— Fleming.

I am planning the framing of the picture now. It is small, and must be well framed, I mean effectively.

I seem to have brought off that Mansfield saucer, well, sooner or later I will give all the pieces to the museum.

The Spanish hanging is much too large, by several feet. I have decided to send only things that I give, not lend. A box will go off soon.

I asked the director of the Museum of the City of New York to give me one of the cards they put by objects. I thought it might suggest a form for you, as to type etc. You can decide on the size you want. Those at Mt. Vernon are smaller cards. I enclose this card. Unlike some museums they say "lent" instead of "loaned." "Lent" is much more elegant English, take note.

On the other hand they have such things as this on various cards, "gown worn by Mrs. Thomas Reynolds etc., *née* Ann Smith." You cannot be born Ann Smith, you are born Smith, *née* Smith.

I was much pleased at your idea of having a So Red the Rose Room. I think some of the things I am sending could be put there in a case or cases and merely marked: "About the period of So Red the Rose."

I am also sending four books that could be put in a case opened, showing dates, under them could be a card, in each case showing the books are, one the time of De Soto, another LaSalle's time, another of the French occupation, another the Spanish governors, another the American territory. I have had the 1540 book glued in such a way that it will stay open. All you have to do is to get some strips of glass to lay across these books, one to a book, to keep them open, or one of those glass triangular rods.

I will send a list and marks for the things, so you can find it all easier.

And now to another point. I was at a musical last Sunday, at a friend's house, two singers from the opera entertained the guests, and afterwards there was talk, and then a marvellous champagne supper, about twenty guests. I heard talk going on and suddenly heard a lady[5] say she thought—I had mentioned Natchez—they should get the gar-

5. Mrs. Lawrence Averett.

den week started etc., she even knew about the museum. At this I chirped up, told her who I was, she was duly impressed, and I so pleasant, blowing the Natchez horn. In view of the row there,[6] it would be a great thing for the museum to get that connection with a prize. So I promised to send her the article in the Times two weeks ago,[7] it has made a great hit, they want—somebody who publishes such things to put it out in a pamphlet—and the enclosed carbon shows what I am trying to do.[8] I want them to decide for Natchez.

I never go to teas, luncheons, banquets etc.—friends here roar at me when they hear of my flying around in Natchez—but they have asked me in two letters already to come to the Southern Women's Democratic something or other, last year the same invitation, I may go just to push this Natchez cause.

I saw your picture in the Memphis paper and I read that account that Ferriday had reprinted. I was very proud of you.[9] I know no prize that was ever more deserved, for work, for tact, for energy, for intelligence and breeding, all expended on this cause. I will sooner or later say so in print.

I will send a reprint of that Times article when it is done. Getting the museum into some shape this year seems to me most important, especially in view of that difference among the ladies, which I mentioned very vaguely to the lady, I merely said the museum was a ven-

6. For a brief period, dissensions within the Natchez Garden Club, which originally sponsored the Natchez Pilgrimage, brought about two separate pilgrimage tours, one conducted by the Natchez Garden Club and the other by the Pilgrimage Garden Club. The two organizations now join to produce the annual Natchez Pilgrimage.

7. Young had written "The South Presents Its Design for Living," *New York Times Magazine*, January 17, 1937, pp. 4–5, 25. He called attention to the elements of Southern civilization which people in all walks of life in the twentieth century sought to identify in an attempt to find permanent values. Young reminded his readers that "the South had a civilization once, the only clearly defined and frankly admitted system that we ever had in this country of ours." He suggested that in view of the fact that the industrial way had "turned into pretty much of a mess," writers, artists, and intellectuals were becoming interested in the South because they felt "that in case there was something in that Southern civilization perhaps some of it still remains."

8. On the preceding day, Young had written Mrs. Averett to express his admiration for Mrs. Byrnes and the museum.

9. Mrs. Byrnes had been awarded a trophy by the City Bank and Trust Company of Natchez in recognition of her outstanding civic service to Natchez during 1936. A picture of Mrs. Byrnes, a news story, and an editorial appeared in the *Natchez Democrat*, December 30, 1936; and an account of the presentation appeared in the paper on January 2, 1937. Later, her husband had the articles reprinted.

ture, and was already an assured and charming addition to Natchez etc.

Pardon this bad typing, I have a pile of letters on hand, all sorts of matters. This letter is close to my heart, however messy in appearance. Remember me to my friends there. Give Ferriday—a remarkable and sweet fellow—and give yourself my love. Yours affectionately

Stark Young

486 | To Caroline Charlotte McGehee, Como, Mississippi

320 East 57th Street
New York
Thursday [January 28, 1937]

Dearest Cousin Cad,

It was a sweet inspiration that you had to write me so soon after I reached here. You knew I would be a bit sunk. So I was. Then this past week came, a year from that Julia and I had in New Haven, Stark has been dead a year last Monday, dear little boy. I would have written you but did not want to pile all I was feeling on your loving shoulders nor yet write an empty letter far from what I felt.

I enjoyed seeing you so much. It would seem to one of these New York narrow persons very strange if they were told that anybody there away from the great full world could be so wise and good and fine, not to say such delightful company. That is where they are provincial and stupid. I have not had the heart to write my troubles, it would be easier to write somebody I do not know or do not care about. Or somebody who knows nothing about me.

I feel grateful for that cemetery lot, it looked better than any I saw out there. All due to you and your trouble, plus your energy. I wish your farm would begin to pay.

Bowman was awfully pleased to have word of you, he admires you extremely. If he did not he would have to say so or have his throat cut.

I saw a purse that seemed very elegant and a useful color and so bought it for you, the other day. It will be posted tomorrow.

It was so nice to see Cousin Wheeler and Cousin Annie, they are each in her own special way such lovely people.

My article on the South that came out two weeks ago in the New York Times had a great success, letters, messages etc. and now a man wants to publish it as a pamphlet.[1] I have consented. I had meant to send you a copy of the Times, but will wait now and send the thing in pamphlet form, easier to read and keep. I hated to write the article, writing on a general subject for a general public is not at all easy, and for me is not an interesting problem or effort. The editor asked me to do it, and I said I would because if I did not some stupid person would write it and make me mad. He was very clever then and said I had given him an idea, if I would not write it he would get that person to, and make me mad. I never thought I would be talking up to the editor of the leading newspaper in America like that, but such is life. I explained to him that it was a labor of love entirely, for the Times does not pay much. $100 for one of those Sunday articles usually. I made him pay me $150, on principle, as I explained, since I was going to put myself into the article, not just do a mechanical thing as so often happens in papers. Of course the truth is I so often feel that I am looking at life from beyond, beyond death, beyond desire for what most people want; and this makes me find a certain advantage—in that it is all one to me whether they do or do not comply with my requests or their own proposals.

I have heard nothing since I got back from Bedford or Beverly Thurman; and I still can't quite decide whether to let them slide entirely. That seems harsh. If Bedford were only living here I might do something for him. As for Beverly I am genuinely afraid to get mixed up with him, for there is no telling what he may do. As I write I decide to send a line to Bedford saying I am sorry not to have seen him, poor boy! it's not his fault. And so there we are and I have enjoyed writing you, dear Cousin Cad.

Lovingly
Stark

1. See above, Letter 485 and n. 7.

487 | To Roane Fleming Byrnes, Natchez, Mississippi

320 East 57th Street
New York
Friday [February 5, 1937]

Dear Mrs. Byrnes,

I had your note, and do thank you for the addresses. I sent you a telegram today, because, in case only a small number of the invitations have been printed, or else others are to follow on demand, there are some emendations that might be of use. I am behind in all my correspondence, but have spent about two hours this morning studying the august sheet you sent.[2] These are my suggestions, and I am an old hand at print and publishing:

I would put it thus

SIXTH ANNUAL PILGRIMAGE
1937
March 28th through Easter Week, ending April 4th.
etc.

On the second page I have made a cut that will give room for a point that helps the effect, since most people know no history. "Louis Philippe, later king of France." On the third page I have saved some room for a mention of Rosedown.

As to Afton Villa I do not know just how pleasantly to put it. It is only the Victorian Gothic, plenty of samples in these parts of that sort of thing, especially in old stables. The owner at present is a common man from Indiana or somewhere—my Cousin Henry Stewart had paid things for him a number of times but is not impressed with him for all that. The house is stupid, pretentious and embarrassing—I always try to steer people away from it. But the drive to the house is pretty, those old trees in an avenue.

Rosedown on the other hand is but a few miles farther. It is more

2. Mrs. Byrnes had sent Young the tentative layout for the announcement of the Sixth Annual Natchez Pilgrimage. His comments below related to this material. The major changes he suggested were the omission of Afton Villa from the featured houses and the inclusion of Rosedown and the St. Francisville Cemetery.

and more famous among the architects, and thanks to me, is getting more and more into the architecture books now being published about America. It is the loveliest place, I think, in all the Deep South, that I have seen. *1831.* Still as it always was, the house. Naturally nobody can keep up such gardens nowadays. And I made a special trip this year to see again, for the fourth time, the cemetery at St. Francisville, what a dream it is!

I suggest you put them in, leaving out Afton Villa or putting it in as you see fit. It is a vulgar mess, alas, (as I have heard tourists say).

You might say

Rosedown, a mile this side of St. Francisville, is the model for Stark Young's Portobello (the novel and the film) in So Red the Rose. Built in 1831, it is in the original condition, the furniture, books, the portraits by Sully and Audubon, et cetera.

The CEMETERY at St. Francisville, with its marbles, old church, vaults, hanging moss, ivy and camellias, is one of the most romantic spots in the South. (Personally I think it's the most romantic thing in the Deep South.)

I strongly suggest that you make these changes in the invitation. *If you can do so, and will send me copies,* I will see that they get to Mrs. Averett by the next mail.

Please answer soon the following queries:

If—after such a success with the article he begged me to write—I send you a copy—it's to be a pamphlet also, such is its success—the editor of the *New York Times* would want an article on Natchez etc., with pictures, would you be able to get pictures of Rosedown, the St. Francisville cemetery, and certain Natchez houses—Rosalie etc.—and send them to me? I mean a fresh lot of pictures, taken now with trees bare. Such an article would be the best publicity in the USA, those hundreds of thousands of people reading the Times. As soon as I know about the pamphlet the man wants to print from the article, I will write you, perhaps he will give us some to use down there. I imagine, with the Times' permission, you could have this article (which I'm sending) quoted at length in Mississippi and Louisiana papers, it has already been in many Southern papers otherwise.

It seems to me most important that these things should come about during this special year, with that split on hand etc. Could I ask you, then, to reply at your earliest convenience? Things here don't wait as they do down home, you are on the dot or are lost. Just this special moment seems to me most important in our future. Please excuse this bad typing etc., I am neglecting dozens of important letters to write this, and I am already so tired I can scarcely sit at the typewriter.

Love to you and Ferriday.

Yours cordially
Stark Young

488 | To Roane Fleming Byrnes, Natchez, Mississippi

320 East 57th Street
New York
Tuesday [March 9, 1937]

Dear Mrs. Byrnes,

Pardon so poor a screed as this. The truth is that I have lately been deluged with all sorts of letters and work, and that Natchez has taken up a lot of my thoughts.

First, thank you very much indeed for that sweet telegram. It greatly set me up.[3] I have had a good many letters and some telegrams. That short piece cost me a good deal of work, trying to get the rhythms so that they would carry easily; I wanted it to be worth something.

This was the first time I ever agreed to talk on the radio. The broadcasting company has made a record. But I will never get into that business. There had been a great deal of hubbub, when I spoke there was a dead silence after the first few words. These are things I cannot understand. All I know is that I wish lots of people could have the things I could get; I want to be apart and quiet, if I have to live at all. But this is our family secret.

3. On March 2, Young spoke on the Texas Independence Day Program sponsored by the University of Texas Alumni Association and broadcast from Washington and New York. The thirty-minute program, ending at midnight, also featured Colonel E. M. House, David F. Houston (former secretary of agriculture, secretary of the treasury, and chairman of the Federal Reserve Board), and Congressman Sam Rayburn. Following the radio broadcast, Mrs. Byrnes sent Young a congratulatory telegram,

I have at last found a picture to put there for your mother.[4] It is a Spanish portrait, artist unknown, seventeenth century, about Charles First's time, in an original frame, old, and perhaps of the epoch. It has to be packed by an expert, and so there will be some delay, but I guarantee to get it there well before *March 30th,* which is what the poster has. I appreciated very much those posters sent me. At first I was worried over the printer's mistake on the it's, which he meant for *its,* but soon I found that the cardboard is so good that a pocket knife easily cuts off that apostrophe and leaves *its* right. In case many of these have already been printed, that is a sheer streak of luck. It relieved my mind.

A great many people after my bit on the radio mentioned the Easter point, as well as asking for autographs. What do you imagine most of them will do with my autograph? Nothing. Or with their own souls, for that matter? Bless us all.

My sister is sending you a lantern, it can at least go in that back court, as a seventeenth or sixteenth century style. It came from Siena. She sends a clock too, about 1840, authentic. Nothing of importance, but might help out, in the kitchen, or a bedroom or somewhere. Later, on a bracket on the wall, when better clocks have been given. When—when!

Thinking over that room and in asking people's opinions here, I find I think I made a poor suggestion. Why not put—

THIS ROOM IS DEDICATED

TO

SO RED THE ROSE

BY

STARK YOUNG

If the other plate has been made already, please let me pay for the new one. My first form for the tablet was too much in the sense that all the things in the room would be around *So Red the Rose.* Your original instinct was much better than mine.

One might think me rich, buying Spanish portraits and all that, but I am not at all. I expect to lead an inexpensive summer, make some little economies and all that as the French say. But I do like this not important picture I got, and am sure it will serve better than the icon, which I will send later anyhow. I wish this were a better letter, but I

4. See above, Letter 485.

am floored with my needs right now, things to be done. Love to you both

S.Y.

489 | To Pauline Goldmann, Austin, Texas

320 East 57th Street
New York
Tuesday [March 9, 1937]

Dear Pauline,

This sheet will exhibit for your diag—or is it og?—yes it is diagnosis, what happens many times a week in my post, as the British say, which accounts for my idiocy where idiocy is not entirely wanted. Hence excuse this note.

My sister wrote that the flowers were very perfect and lovely, and Bowman as well as I is very grateful to you for baiting them—the Austin florists—into fragrant and beautiful flowers.[5] Thank you again. I know only too well how that heroic Texas spirit can charge a first-rate price for a third-rate flower; but you evidently outwitted or bluffed them, and so bless you!

Dear little Stark, there is nothing to say. I think often what a pity it is that he, with his energy and flowering, could not have taken on the mess that I by some sort of hypnotic rot have accumulated in the world. I want none of it, and if I were to be dead tomorrow it would be a privilege,—however unfair to the Austin florists and unassimilable for the Austin faculty—don't repeat that—or if you do, reduce it to what they would understand.

Thank you again, you sweet little cousin. To your mamma remember me, that quite remarkable woman, but do not tell her that, she would only be more remarkable.

Lovingly
Stark

5. Young had requested her to purchase flowers for the grave of Stark Young Robertson, whose birth date was March 3.

490 | To Margaret Mitchell, Atlanta, Georgia

320 East 57th Street
New York
Saturday [March 20, 1937]

Dear Miss Mitchell,

What an irony there can be in things! I did so appreciate your letter about the Virginia Quarterly pieces [6]—they cost me much labor—and I sent it to my sister.[7] There is a lovely, really, little museum in Natchez, an eighteenth century house, just started. I advised them to begin a collection of daguerreotypes. And since your letter in some curious way put that argument of faces and a civilization so perfectly, and elusively, I told my sister to send it to a friend there, to be filed

6. Young's essay, "More Encaustics for Southerners," had appeared in the *Virginia Quarterly Review,* XIII (Winter, 1937), 35–48. Writing in a vein similar to his *New York Times Magazine* article about the South (see above, Letter 485 and n. 7), Young had pointed out some of the loose thinking that has at times characterized the literary criticism of even such astute scholars as Vernon L. Parrington. "The kind of book," wrote Young, "that fares worst is not so much the sharecropper, lynching variety, but a novel that assumes a certain air of old custom, breeding, sentiment, or romance. He will turn on a book like that and lay it out, author and South together. I have sometimes wondered whether it is not that S—— feels instinctively that he could never be a part of the life the book portrays, and this unconsciously is what drives him wild." With perhaps his own *So Red the Rose* in mind, Young added that he felt it would be "worse than useless to try and describe to S—— a kind of society that I grew up to admire, whether I ever saw any perfect expression of it or not."

7. On February 16, 1937, Margaret Mitchell had written Young to tell him "how very fine I thought the article was and how much I enjoyed it." In commenting upon the passage which immediately followed the sentences quoted above, she wrote: "There was one statement that impressed me so very much—'In such a society people value greatly only those opinions that they have put into action or are willing to pay for, sometimes even with their lives, if it comes to that.' This seems so very true to me and so well summed up. It brought back to my mind a conversation I had with my brother some years ago. I had gone through hundreds of daguerreotypes of the fifties and sixties and I was struck by the expressions of the faces of the Southerners in the daguerreotypes. There was a certain expression common to old and young, men and women— an expression which you will not find in many modern pictures. It baffled me for I could not analyze wherein the difference lay. I spoke of this to my brother and he, looking at some of the daguerreotypes, said, 'The reason those people look as they look is because they all believed in something. So few people these days believe in anything and it shows in their faces.' "

After writing across the top "From the Author of *Gone with the Wind,*" Young sent Margaret Mitchell's letter to Julia Young Robertson, who in turn sent it to Roane Fleming Byrnes in Natchez. In 1965, through the courtesy of Mrs. Byrnes and Malcolm Gardner, superintendent of the Natchez Trace Parkway, the letter was placed in the University of Mississippi Library.

with the collection, as a fine expression of the raison d'etre for the whole collection. Mrs. Byrnes there in charge has great taste and sweetness and would do nothing common with your letter. But if you had rather they not have it on file, please be frank and tell me and I will ask them to send it back to me, for I hated to give it up. I have been meaning to write you all this.

Then the other night my Herschel and Norma came over here for dinner and we talked and talked of you. Your ears must have shone with burning, pleasantly too. I said I was writing you in a few days, and had a book to send you to keep as reminder of a friendship, very real, and sight unseen.

AND THEN BY GOD TODAY COMES THE ENCLOSED LETTER. If a year ago I had not been put on to this young man[8] and if I did not know you had sense, I should have burst. As it is, the experience can be taken only psychological, or pathological.

Miss Glasgow told me how she was very decent to him, had him at her house, and he put the whole thing, deafness, years etc. into print, and I think, as I remember her account, brought on much explaining with her old friend Mr. Cabell, and the Lord knows what else, all breaches of hospitality etc. And so last year a rehash of his accounts of people came out in his book, I think the title was *I Live in Virginia.* My copy is in the country. I think Malcolm would have been delighted to use it as a lever for some good Southern roasting. But I outwitted him—he is very lazy—I said I would look through the book and see if it was worth reviewing and if so would review it. I read it more or less—half journalistic talent, half jabber and much malice, perhaps a little congenital nervous defect. So I waited a while, knowing Malcolm would forget it, and then said the book was of no importance, which he believed, since it was about the South by a Southerner, and which is true, the book is nothing.

Mr. Meade does not know my part in all this. No useful review for him in the NR, by some of Malcolm's cronies! Then Emily Clark—not herself without something of his trouble-making quality, wrote a review of it.[9] I had seen his borrowings from her in several spots, she

8. See above, Letter 432 and n.5.

9. Emily Clark reviewed Julian R. Meade's *I Live in Virginia* in "As a Young Virginian Sees His State," *New York Herald Tribune Books,* October 6, 1935, p. 8. After noting that Meade had "violated one of the important ethics of his profession," she declared that he had "quoted freely from books by other writers in his stories about

said he had used the material of others. He through his publishers threatened quite harshly to sue the Herald Tribune, she took it back some way or other to relieve the paper of a suit—telling everybody on all telephones all about it, Jesus God![1]

This is what bothers him in the first part of the letter.

My Times article it was that came out on a Sunday and by Tuesday I had a note from him. I answered politely. And this second letter is a wonder. *Please return it, it will greatly delight Glasgow,* and I must file it against future trouble with him.

Do you know, this is my first encounter with this well known type of literary trouble maker (I wonder if my really insulting letter he will perceive). I go around so little that I don't see his sort, and it is largely since So Red the Rose that I seem to them juicy enough to make trouble with.

Of course the rotten part is that if I had not known about this chap, I should have been all disturbed, wondering what in the world! I must say knowing you had sense was also a good aspect. Someday somebody will knock his head in. How these cases shrink life!

I have a little seventeenth century Ovid that I am parting with, just because I want to give you something as a small record of a fine friendly thing; who knows what years will do, where we shall be, or go, out of this world, or in it, and who knows anything among the darks of life and the mind? So just keep it put somewhere, I am trying to send you something with its own eloquence, not a mere present.

If I go South this summer to see my sister, I will try to come round by your way and see you and Mr. Marsh[2] a day. My sister wrote that

---

public characters in Virginia, even using in certain cases the exact adjectives employed in the books from which he quotes. He does not use these sentences as literary quotations, but repeats them as if they were matters of common gossip in Virginia which have never appeared in print."

1. On October 27, 1935, "A Correction" appeared in the *New York Herald Tribune Books,* p. 9, in which the editors stated: "After inquiring into the matter, we find that the only instance [of failure to give proper credit to the sources of his material] was an anecdote concerning Mr. Cabell which, though originally printed in 'Innocence Abroad,' a book by Miss Clark, has since been told repeatedly in literary circles in Virginia. Consequently, Miss Clark and the Editor of *Books* join in expressing regret for any erroneous impression that may have been created."

2. John Robert Marsh (1895–1952), journalist and advertising executive, married Margaret Mitchell in 1925. He was associated with the Lexington (Kentucky) *Herald,* the Lexington (Kentucky) *Leader,* the Atlanta *Georgian,* and the Washington bureau of the Associated Press before becoming head of the advertising department of the Georgia Power Company from which he retired in 1946. *Gone with the Wind* was dedicated to him.

many ladies and professors had asked her often And what does your brother think of Gone With The Wind? The question does not make her cynical, it makes her laugh at the glint, squint and stint in their eyes—my sister looks well bred, her mask is perfect, and it is marvellous what silly people will bring forth, thinking she takes it for its full bouquet. She goes on feeling so kindly toward them that what she saw they were from the start does not make her resent them at the finish, bless her heart!

Please write me soon, Mr. Meade at least should engage your analyses.

Yours sincerely
Stark Young

491 | To Malcolm Cowley, The New Republic, New York
[carbon]

[320 East 57th Street]
[New York]
March 23, 1937

Dear Malcolm,

It was friendly of you to inquire as to that passage in Miss Porter's review.[3] There is but one logical answer: If we make it a rule not to publish a review of any book by a New Republic [editor], it can only follow that we do not publish the same thing though in briefer form it may appear.

I am confirmed in this by the fact that several years ago a man—I think it was John Chamberlain, but wouldn't swear to it—told me that he had referred to a book of mine complimentarily but was surprised not to see that in the NR proof. On inquiry he had been given the reason for the cutting. I explained to him that there was nothing personal about it with regard to me; it was a New Republic rule.

---

3. On March 22, 1937, Cowley had written Young that in reviewing Caroline Gordon Tate's *None Shall Look Back* in the *New Republic,* Katherine Anne Porter had mentioned Young's *So Red the Rose* in a less than complimentary manner. See below, Letter 492.

I feel sure Miss Porter will understand this; Caroline is devoted to her and has often told me what a fine person she is. Her writing shows as much, of course.

I regard this reply of mine as wholly impersonal; it applies to the slam[4] as much as to the praise; and it is the only logical sequence from the rule. The rule of not having the editors' books reviewed in the paper is an excellent one in certain respects; in others a disadvantage. But that is not the question here, obviously.

Basta.

Yours
[unsigned]

492 | To Caroline Gordon Tate, Clarksville, Tennessee

320 East 57th Street
New York
Wednesday [March 24, 1937]

Dearest Caroline,

It is plain that I shall never get a chance to write you a decent letter, so I may as well knock off something while I can. I could have written easily the other day but used the time writing a newspaper man and setting down some technical points to note in the book.[5] I finished the book ten days ago and have read much of it over, and turned down many pages. As I told Max Perkins yesterday I was delighted with that ad Sunday, it all shows things to the good. You have already made some decent money, he said, as compared with what most novelists get out of a book. I think he feels that the ball will keep rolling. How I wish so!

Sunday

The first thing I must do next fall is to get a part time secretary, I have so many perfunctory letters to write that I never get to the ones

4. Cowley had used this word to describe the reference to Young's work.
5. Caroline Gordon's *None Shall Look Back.*

I want to write. These last few weeks have brought six requests to include me in anthologies, very kind—or am I becoming a part of the standard past?—but I have to take time answering, and there is also every type of letter about lectures and the devil knows what. Spring will ease matters, for everything slows down. Then came Miss Porter's review of your book in the NR. I read it Thursday and wanted to write at once to you, so afraid was I that that passage about my book or me would distress you. I regret it extremely, the tone especially and the inaccuracy, but perhaps had best not go into that, she is a friend of yours. I don't mean to be unpleasant but I won't say that the tone surprised me, after reading her work, good as it often is. The point is I don't want you to feel bothered at all. You and Allen and I know where we stand. I enclose a letter from Malcolm and my reply.[6] It evidently made no difference. . . . I must out of loyalty to my material and country write a note for the NR of next week, since Miss Porter's points are quite inaccurate so far as the "even Mississippi" goes, and "jewelry conscious"—tidy phrase that is at that.[7] When I think that

6. See above, Letter 491.
7. See Katherine Anne Porter, "Dulce et Decorum Est" [review of *None Shall Look Back* by Caroline Gordon], *New Republic,* XC (March 31, 1937), 244–45. The offending portions of her review are included in Young's unsigned carbon draft of his letter to the editor of the *New Republic:*

> Sirs: Doubtless everyone agrees that any book's author worth his salt feels a conscience and a loyalty toward his material—the country, the society, the characters, and all life within which these are seen. In my opinion this conscience and loyalty apply, within various limits, to the criticism of his book. In her review of Miss Caroline Gordon's new novel of the South, "None Shall Look Back," (The New Republic, March 31st) Miss Katherine Anne Porter refers to my book "So Red the Rose" in the following passage, about which I must note the, at the very least, inaccuracies:
>
> "Life for the Kentucky planters was never so grand as it was in Virginia and Louisiana, or even in Mississippi, with its slightly parvenu manners, if one takes Mr. Stark Young's account at face value. The Kentucky planters were down-to-earth men, and the most tenderly bred women were not above taking a hand in the cookery. They much more resembled Madame Washington than they did Mr. Young's jewelry-conscious belles."
>
> ". . . even in Mississippi . . . ." The only Louisiana tradition I know is that in the old days the St. Francisville district was the most aristocratic in Louisiana. Certainly it was one of the most aristocratic—that provocative and threadbare word that I avoided in my novel. This district is, geographically, on the border line of Louisiana and Mississippi; the identical community spread some fifty or so miles up to Natchez and then northward. So many of the houses are still standing—there must be seventy or more—and so many are being reproduced in books on architecture and American history, and were seen by thousands this past week during the Pilgrimage of the Natchez Gar-

that is what she got out of Mrs. Bedford and Agnes McGehee—well that is enough on the subject—when I think that I could have left even the possibility of such an impression about such people, even on Miss Porter!

As to the review I think it will help the book some. To my mind the first thing to mention in your book is the nobility of tone. This is a rare and profound quality. My notion of a right review would be in this case that the tone of the review should in itself convey some of that nobility. I consider your book above that defensive effect that appears now and again in the review. The end of the second paragraph, about men born to die etc. is superb, most worthy of the book.

I telephoned Bruce and said that since no NR editor's book was reviewed in the paper, I thought I would want a short space to take up the few points involved. So I had again to stop writing you in order to go through the book on this jewelry point. They want the letter right off in order to know the space.[8] I enclose a copy.

My God and then when I wanted to come back to this letter to you I had a bolt out of the blue from Mr. Meade in Virginia, had been to see Margaret Mitchell, she had asked if he knew me, etc., he had told her he had heard last fall in New York that I broke into "unholy fury" when her book was mentioned. She said on the contrary etc. I had written her kind letters etc. So he was just telling me, and he had best

---

den Club that to dwell on that "even Mississippi" point would be, rather obviously, ignorant, not to say absurd.

All through my book there is—it seems too plain to remark—an implication of housekeeping, sometimes a list of the dinner served, or drinks, no book of the period could omit that aspect of it.

"Jewelry-conscious" is a tidy phrase. Anyone knows, however, that the Mid-Victorian fashion all over the world required, whenever there were means for them, heavy sets—*parures*—of jewelry. The "belles"—vengeful and revealing word—that Miss Porter mentions shared, doubtless the prevailing mode. Nevertheless, as to So Red the Rose, I may say that there are in the story four main women characters, plus two, if you like, somewhat secondary; six, then, in all. One is said to have some pearl clusters, one some trinkets from her father, one to dislike wearing her ornaments. Otherwise for the six of them, jewelry is not mentioned.

8. After writing the answer, Young decided against its publication. Although quick to resent any remark characterizing *So Red the Rose* as a Southern novel of the moonlight and magnolias tradition, Young probably also sensed that Katherine Anne Porter intended no disparagement of the basic premises of his work and that to refute the "slam" was to tilt at windmills. Probably for this reason and in view of his genuine admiration for her work, Young's better judgment prevailed, even after Cowley had accepted the reply for publication.

not listen to literary gossip any more etc. It happened that I had heard of this young man's trouble making, and his letter was taken up partly with what I must have heard about him from Glasgow and Emily Clark, etc.—I had heard plenty. Otherwise I should have been most uncomfortable. Luckily I was out of New York last year from Easter to late fall, and so saw no literati—how these Meade types people always break down somewhere with meddling lies!—and Mitchell knew that, because she was a few days in the country with the Brickells. But I had nevertheless to write her. Mr. Meade's opening to write me was the fact that I had had a letter from him about the article in the Times, and had replied to it, a very brief note saying thanks, and I knew of him etc., a few lines. This is my first encounter with this sort of person—until So Red the Rose I was not juicy enough material. Miss Glasgow acceded to his request for a visit and he wrote it all up and made a great deal of trouble. How lucky I was to know about him in advance!

To go to the book, I have read a good deal of it twice, much of the latter part three times. The places I have turned down would take all day to mention—I will cite a few: 48, 354, 358, 360–1, 375, 377, 203–4-5, 108, 123, etc.—I am sure this bores you.

That leaving the fort and the scene passed on the battlefield are done better than I know anywhere in English fiction, novels in the English language I mean.

I have read over many times that part you speak of, "going into Forrest's consciousness." My quite considered opinion is that the device is excellent, certainly very moving. I don't agree with you as to there being too much war stuff in that chapter toward the end.

In so far as the book makes trouble or is not always easy reading, and to me it was at times in some curious indefinable way full of an effect of stalling me—I can only say that at present, after a lot of thought—always based on deep affection and respect—it seems to me that this ensues from a lack of blocking in firmly what is in itself a section of life, a part of the pattern. I mean that we are carried on by a certain definity in an image or in a recognizable element, (recurring, perhaps, in many cases through a book, as elements repeat themselves recognizably in the department of life.) I know this is fuzzy talking,— if only I saw you face to face! Another thing that would help at times is a more distinctly discovered or expressed visual quality. And yet now and then the visual presentation is immediate and brilliant. As illustrations of the latter, the hospital scene, the Georgia arrival of the young people, that room upstairs, they all count finely. As an example of the defect, the first sight of Forrest, page 23. I felt that when I first read it and went back to it several times. I don't mean that the effect should be starred, theatricalized. But in my opinion it should be done in such a way that AT LEAST LATER it should flash back into the mind with both visual and character significance.

At any rate when I finished the book the first time I was filled with some complex and lovely elevation—and to get that out of me in fiction, which usually leaves me colder than hell—is a feat. I felt proud of you, and I think your own inner essence is more transfused into this book than into anything of yours that I have read.

I shall be going to the country along toward the end of April, and it will be a good thing to be out there.

I am not working on a novel, I have read and studied a lot this winter, and have done a few of a series of things that will go into a sort of autobiographical book some day, no hurry. Max was talking of Allen's poetry the other day, very handsomely. I said that maybe Allen would not like me to say it—or would not like it if anybody but me said it, because I think he is like me in the sense that if he knows you really love him and his poetry, he gives you free rein, so long as he knows the love and understanding are there—I said it was pretty swell of Scribners to bring out the book—*entre nous* I don't think they feel cheerful about money right now, and most publishers are not too pretty about poetry. Sometimes the whippersnappers are seemingly amiable about publishing poetry, but the thought there is prestige, and unless a certain brand of noise arises they are through with the whole business. One thing Max does really know, genuinely, no bluff or face: that the Confederate Ode is not John Brown's Body. My Jesus, what a comment the run of John Brown's Body—some of it was log rolling here at the start of course—is on many aspects of writing, it makes me sick the very thought!

I have proof to read and must stop.

Love to you both.
Stark

Please send me two or three lines to say that this letter conveyed, dull as it is and rushed, at least something.

Having done the letter for the NR, I find the whole thing seemingly to be a long way from me—I should rewrite some of this letter to you, but have not time—what an irony! So forget it so far as the review goes, and remember my pleasure in your book.

---

493 | To Marian Hall, New York

> [320 East 57th Street]
> [New York]
> Monday [March 29, 1937]

Dearest Marian,

I am stopping in the midst of a boring article to dash off a word with you. You are the only person who ever half valued that Mississippi history I told you of the nigger's cutting the other's head entirely off, with the razor, from a disappointment at cyards [*sic*].

Well, I have been meaning to write you of a Greenwich incident told me solemnly—and I burst into a guffaw!—This Mrs. Cummings watched a man trying to repair a great pump on her place until she could stand it no longer, pushed him aside and would show him how it should be done. The cap blew off and went clean through the man.

I know that you at least won't think me hard-hearted. The poor man's death is one thing. But what I like is the story of efficiency, ego and management, and I am sure she was annoyed and her first thought was: "it just shows there was something wrong with the thing, that's all."

I have tried twice to mention this instance, but the smile was frozen on my lips. You are the last and best who will share it with me.

We want to see you.

> Lovingly
> Stark

494 | To Malcolm Cowley, The New Republic, New York
[carbon]

[320 East 57th Street]
[New York]
Tuesday [March 30, 1937]

Dear Malcolm,

Thank you for your letter, you are always very generous to me.[9]

The cutting out of a reference to me was two or three years before you were on the New Republic—I should have added that. It seemed to me wholly logical.

I do not agree with you about that favorable mention of my work sometime in the future. Let us not do so. It is not to the point just now in our discussion. I think that on the whole our policy is a good one.

Silly as that may seem, I regard the subject matter of my book as important, quite as important as the sit-downs in Borneo, and at least better known to me in detail. And so if anything has to be cut, please let it be my article for the week, on the Critics' Circle. Betty[1] can mark how much I will shorten the article and I engage gladly to do so. Or if the paper needs the space, I need have no article—and no pay—for the ensuing week.

I hope all goes well for you.

Yours sincerely
[unsigned]

9. Cowley had answered Young's letter of March 23 (Letter 491) by suggesting that Young's work be mentioned in the *New Republic* in a complimentary manner.
1. Elizabeth Huling, copy reader for the *New Republic*.

495 | To Allen Tate, Clarksville, Tennessee

320 East 57th Street
New York
Friday [April, 1937]

Dearest Allen,

I made a great mistake this year, trying to fit in my expenses for my aunt, with her doctor, and two nurses and other expenses, and the NR salary reduced: in sum I have no secretary. The result is that with the dozen of letters every morning, plus reprints, books, pamphlets etc., I try to answer those who are unknown to me and obligatory, and I never get to those I love and think of so often. I, also, may send three parcels and a suitcase for the Natchez Museum, and not hear for three months, though the value is over two thousand and I wonder what is lost. On the other hand a columnist from Georgia may send me the clipping and a note, and if I do not reply in three days will write saying I must be annoyed etc. I sent an $8 handkerchief to some sort of charity in Meridian, Miss., one out of a dozen sent from London, and got no answer till I sent an addressed postcard. I am indeed quite sick of it all. Next year I will get a secretary three days a week, whether I can afford it or not, and send off form letters.

Imagine typing to you now—one of the people I love best in the whole world and most admire—a letter that I shall not read over and that is written after a mound of idiotic obligatory replies. You and Caroline always make me smile, making Ransom seem so sublime and Cumaen Zeus—if somebody just lit into those majestic conclusions of his we should have less Ben Jonson if you like but more point. Either one of you are more to the point than he is—if less professorial and bull-balls-like. I am sure I should like him very much, but that means nothing—it grieves me to see the pepee—not semen—that he can cast on Caroline's endeavours. I could not indeed imagine a jabber conference in Nashville just now.[2] I have a horrible feeling that a number

2. During the fall and winter of 1936–37, Donald Davidson and John Crowe Ransom were planning a conference of Southern writers. Allen Tate and Caroline Gordon (Tate) agreed to attend, but in March, 1937, Ransom apparently called off the conference because the principal speakers (Douglas Southall Freeman, Stark Young, and Bernard DeVoto) could not attend.

of quite intelligent people are a bit sick of us not because we are Southern but because we are often silly. For the love of the South we must
correct this—but how?

A conference with Ransom making a short Ben Jonson introduction
—full of male wisdom, unexuded at that, while the speakers make
illogical fools of themselves, is all right, for those who like it. I do not
like it, as things go, though I would like him. Mr. Mims represents
the rich soul of a professorial conference, and that is nothing against
him. It only means that those that think this important should act
importantly. I cling to the idea that a conference is not railroad fares.
Forgive me for all this—I am nothing, nor are most other writers. I
could not have come anyhow!

I read much of F. M. Ford's book, full of complete and perverse rot
and of genuine and exciting point and personality. He is misled by
that belated English idea that personality in itself is interesting, as if
Sit Pulf says he does not care for wood pulp in N.C. I am not thus
interested. But parts of the book's remarkable, and I called up the
Oxford Press and told them how to advertise it in Natchez during
these thousands of tourists, and I promised to mention it somehow.[3]
How sad to see such perversity mingled with such insight and genius!!!!!!!!!!!!!!!! Not that it matters in the general latrinity.

You did not get a copy of the Scribner book [4] for the very good reason that I did not ask them to send it. I hoped to God you would
never see it. That's a fact. I do not complain. This was the issue
:::::::::: when they heard, or Mr. Howe, through the supposed teachers' reports, that the book would have to have modern stuff to be used
in schools, I could have said NO you will print what I have put down.
But why do that if they would use no means to sell it? So I said I
would put in the modern material. I had already spent a lot of money
collecting the other. In other words I could either have (1) withdrawn
the book, (2) given it to another publisher, or (3) turned it their way.
As things had gone the only thing I could hope for was money from

3. Young had also suggested to Mrs. Byrnes that during the forthcoming Natchez
Pilgrimage she display a copy of Ford Madox Ford's *Great Trade Route* opened to a
passage referring to the beauty of the countryside near Natchez. Young reviewed the
book in "That's Latitude," *New Republic*, LXXX (May 5, 1937), 385–86. In his essay,
Young quoted with approval portions of Ford's writing emphasizing the high degree
of civilization in the South and its vulnerability to the ruthlessness of Northern military efficiency.

4. *A Southern Treasury of Life and Literature*, selected by Stark Young.

it. If therefore I did another way I should not complain!!!! I despise people who whine because they cannot have their cake and eat it too. So that's that. I do hope the book makes money—there's nothing dishonest about the performance of it. The preface I am glad you like. I wrote it over several times, and then made Scribners recast the proof of it four times—saying that I had lost money on the original idea of the book and should therefore not pay one cent on the proofs of the preface. I think it is a fine piece of writing—for my own sake at least, as well as the subject's—I did it. Don't repeat. This book is at least worth as many sales as the average textbook.

I can't imagine your spending "an evening" over such a book, and take consolation in the notion that an evening meant an hour for you. I am inclined by nature to read only good literature and have small interest in what the western counties of Alabama may have produced in the first two weeks of March 1854, life is all too short for Dante, Leopardi, Plato, Tolstoi and the various modern interests in philosophers and theologists and poets—meaning you and about ½ of one or two others. It's not my fault if tenth-rate literature leaves my eyes elsewhere.

What is more important is that you are working on your novel.[5] I cannot understand why *June* matters—finish it when you think you have said what you wanted to say, in terms of it—if that's ten years from now.

I expect soon to go to the country, and may not this season see my young cousins in Tenth Street—if they are not more wisely seeing now much noisier people than I am, they ought to leave here and go back South. Every day brings me a list of arrivals in town—and I meanwhile read, write and love those I love—among whom are you and Caroline. I have read her book and much of it several times, and will write her soon.

Lovingly
Stark

How kind you were about it. But, to repeat, please don't hurt the book's sales with the schools by saying I try to forget it. It's all right. But that's that. Be a friend to it.

5. *The Fathers,* which G. P. Putnam's Sons published in 1938.

496 | To Margaret Mitchell, Atlanta, Georgia

[320 East 57th Street]
[New York]
April 9, 1937

Dear Miss Mitchell,

Thank you for your very fine letter. Your astonishment to this sort of business of Mr. Meade's is very much like mine.[6] I can't understand why this sort of thing should interest anybody, I mean so much energy and effort put on what is only half true, or not true, or perfect nonsense. I was hearing lately of some extraordinary mix-ups that he had caused. One concerns Mr. Mencken who denies ever having seen him at all face to face.

There is one thing I feel like saying, which is that when Miss Cole[7] who is a good friend of yours, you say, writes asking you to see him since he was "a very nice boy," you run into a typical New York incident. In the first place she must know he is not a boy by any means; and she must have heard of the difficulties he has made in many places in New York. I imagine that her process of mind is something like this "Margaret Mitchell is a dear, fine person—authors need publicity —she thinks she does not want it—but she should have it—(not to say business should be remembered)—and so she should see this interviewer." This sort of thing goes on incessantly in New York and one's best friends sometimes have a hand in it that may be surprising. The truth is our whole state of mind in this country is confused with regard to privacy, publicity et cetera et cetera. There is no use dwelling on this. I have had many instances arise which one has to take in whatever way enables one to forget them soonest. I have heard lately of four or five more people where Mr. Meade had engaged himself.

I see so few literary people that I trust I am safer than some authors.

I have decided to ask my friend in Natchez to return the letter with the saying about daguerreotypes.[8] Sooner or later some silly reporter

6. See above, Letters 432 and 490 and notes.
7. Lois Dwight Cole (Mrs. Turney Allan Taylor), author and editor, had published with her husband (using the name Allan Dwight) *Spaniard's Mark* (1933) and *Drums in the Forest* (1936). From 1932 to 1945, she was an associate editor of the Macmillan Company.
8. See above, Letter 490 and n. 7.

will mess it up; and they have already had the influence of your re-marks to stimulate them further toward the collection.

I hope the little book came and that it will remind you of happy things in life. Sooner or later I certainly hope to get by Atlanta. Thank you very much.

I enjoy noticing in the Times on Mondays that your book still sails along—its record must almost daze you at times. I am glad you have it.

With cordial regards, I am

Yours sincerely
Stark Young

497 | To Ellen Glasgow, Richmond, Virginia

[320 East 57th Street]
[New York]
April 19, 1937

Dear Cousin,

That is very fine. May thirteenth, then, please put it down on sheets of bronze.[9] I shall be in the country and will be in town that day which I note will be a Thursday and I consider you would be unwise not to join me in a Daiquiri cocktail plus a great deal of conversation.

As to your conception of an insult,[1] I consider it pretty thick, after a young man has written me twice to visit his town, knowing that I know he is in New York fairly often in circulation, for me not even to mention the subject of his coming here. However, I don't agree with you about the passage you quote. If ever such a visitor came to the New Republic and asked me such a question I should say "I am, sir, let me embrace you."

9. Ellen Glasgow was coming to New York to sail for Italy.
1. Young refers to a letter he had written to Julian Meade. In January, Meade had written Young to express admiration for his article "The South Presents Its Design for Living" in the *New York Times Magazine.* Meade wrote Young a second time in April, and again Young, pointedly he thought, refrained from mentioning a possible meeting or interview.

The Scribners that published the book of selections is the same firm but has no connection with anything but education. It would never have occurred to them to send out copies in the way the literary department does. Copies would go only to teachers since this is only a text book. I myself deliberately did not send you one because it is only a text book and they made me put in so many short selections that the whole thing is reduced to undergraduate importance. As to Southern literature, my introduction says exactly what I think.[2] We will talk this over.

Complain as you will you will remain at the end of the volume. It is well known that the most impressive position in a volume of selections is toward the end. The next most impressive position is at the beginning. I wanted to put Poe there at the beginning but Mr. Howe said the teachers would have a fit, so embedded in their minds is the chronological idea. But, of course, this book of mine is arranged for certain effects and only now and then does chronology come in. I must say that I think that the Stribling and Paul Green selections are appalling.[3] But in the case of Paul Green you have to have a whole one-act play or it won't stand up at all. But more of this anon.

All you have to do is to send to Rockefeller Center here, or have your tourist agent do so, to arrange the Italian exchange et cetera. They have a complete and very well organized, and eager-to-serve, bureau right there in Rockefeller City.

I am looking forward then to seeing you the thirteenth and we will say I will come by your hotel at one o'clock.

Affectionately

Stark

2. Young's Preface to *A Southern Treasury of Life and Literature* contained a brief exposition of his estimate of literature in the South. Young argued that "when we concede that the South has not produced too much great literature, we should add that the rest of the United States has not done so either" and that "pre-eminence in the art of literature is by no means any final test of the South."

3. Young reprinted a selection from Stribling's *Backwater;* from the work of Paul Green, Young chose "The Hot Iron," a one-act play which first appeared in *Poet Lore,* XXXV (Spring, 1924), 48–57.

498 | To Irita B. Van Doren, New York Herald Tribune, New York

[320 East 57th Street]
[New York]
May 10, 1937

Dear Irita,

I came back from the country this morning and was so pleased to find your note. The truth is that when I see you I am always filled with the thought of how much sensibility, balanced taste and charming response are embodied in you. This pleases me especially, not only for the personal side of it but because I like to think that popular judgment is always based on something sound. In sum, there is an entirely good reason why the book review section of the Herald-Tribune is the most admired in this country, and very much the most admired.

As for the peon kidskins, the truth is that when I saw the little man standing in the market with it I thought how jolly it would be for you to use in your country place. Sometimes the peons leave the skins in a shape susceptible of returning fragrances, only too natural. Their use in Mexico is almost any old way, but in a dry air. If this piece of yours sometime or other in a damp air seems to breathe out too much of its early soul, all you have to do is to turn it over to let the airs blow softly on it. I ought to confess also that that idea of wedding present came some time after my first thought. At any rate, no one but those Mexicans would ever have thought of popping on those arbitrary—what you call little tails.

Your description of your room sounds very lovely, and reaches a soft spot in me, for in Westchester almost on the Connecticut line I have at least some of these things present or implied. My Greek is long since very bad and never was much in fact, but when I was reading what you said I found coming into my mind the little Greek poem, two lines only, in which the poet says

> Now the rose has come again
> And the little peas are opening— [4]

4. Young has made into two lines the opening line of a poem by Philodemus of Gadara in the Greek Anthology (*Anth. Pal.* 9. 412). Young's translation, *opening,* probably should imply *ripening.*

just that but in its own language perfect with some rhythm and precision that I wonder if we could understand at all without seeing a leaf,
or a tree, or water running, something quiet in nature, something arriving, or final. How absurd I am trying to be intelligent about perfection.

At any rate, I enjoyed so much seeing you and I hope next season we
can have some good talks.

Yours
Stark Y.

499 | To Margaret Mitchell, Atlanta, Georgia

[320 East 57th Street]
[New York]
May 11, 1937

Dear Miss Mitchell,

You are sick by now, I am sure, of receiving notes about winning
the Pulitzer Prize and so please do not answer this one. It is only to
say how very delighted I was.[5]

I wonder if you saw that screaming editorial in the New Republic.
I suppose Malcolm Cowley wrote it. The part about the history prize
is really fantastic, since whoever wrote the paragraph says that he had
not read the book.[6] Can you beat that!

---

5. Margaret Mitchell's *Gone with the Wind* had received the Pulitzer Prize. Replying to this letter on May 17, she denied being "sick" of receiving notes about the prize,
particularly comments from Young.

6. Young refers to "The Lucky Numbers," *New Republic,* XCI (May 12, 1937), 5–6.
The writer of the editorial, preferring John Dos Passos' *The Big Money* or George
Santayana's *The Last Puritan* to Margaret Mitchell's novel, conceded that *Gone with
the Wind* "might have been entitled to third money—or perhaps to a special award
for reducing unemployment in the printing trades." The editorial writer approved
of Van Wyck Brooks' *The Flowering of New England* for the history prize, but
in reference to Allan Nevins' *Hamilton Fish: The Inner History of the Grant Administration,* declared: "We haven't read Allan Nevins' long biography of Hamilton Fish."
Although Young should have written "biography prize" instead of "history prize,"
the mistake is understandable in view of the title of Nevins' book.

In these parts I think you are likely soon to become the world's puzzle. One man was saying to me the other day that you had done nothing to establish your personality. It is obvious what he means. I don't think that to him, at least, my reply was as obvious. I said, "Except to write a book that everybody reads." [7]

Yours sincerely
Stark Young

500 | To Leonidas W. Payne, University of Texas, Austin, Texas

[320 East 57th Street]
[New York]
Friday morning [June 25, 1937]

Dear Payne,

I am in town but leaving for the country in a few minutes. But before I go I want to write so that you will not put yourself to any further trouble about the lecture. I appreciate enormously your interest and efforts, and the dean's cordial good wishes; but for something like fifteen months I have not made a lecture and very few for some time before that. By way of comment I may say that I lately declined an invitation to make the Phi Beta Kappa address at the University of Virginia and for July an invitation to make a speech in London, at some International I don't know what that the English have got up. There have been other offers and a summer school etc. So it is not just Texas that I am not speaking at.

I am trying to be quiet in the country, though there are some articles that I have engaged to write. I have one job of two days for a movie company: they send me the typed copy of a movie and I read it and make some comments, they to use my name in the connection or not

7. Margaret Mitchell was amused at the remark that she had done nothing to establish her personality. She replied, "I still cling to my old fashioned belief that, for good or bad, a writer should stand on his works and not on his personality. Thank you for your reply to his remarks."

as I decide, according to the script's virtues in my opinion. $2500 for this, and I wish more would come my way. As for going to Hollywood, however, that is quite another matter. It does not tempt me at all, and what is the use of scrubbing around and saving a little money if you are going to go on just as if you had none. On this point I have to make up my mind somewhere.

I shall be down sometime in August and am looking forward to seeing you and dear Mrs. Payne. Thank you again.

Affectionately
Stark

501 | To Caroline Charlotte McGehee, Como, Mississippi

Bedford, New York
Wednesday [August 25, 1937]

Dear Cousin Cad,

I find myself entirely without stationery here in the country, though I thought there was a drawerfull down stairs. I was delighted to hear from you, and to know that you were well. I have been well in body at least, look red in the face and squirish. I did not go South this summer, Julia and Ben are in California now, he there to see a famous foot doctor, Dr. Hiss.[8] Ben's foot bones are so small that his weight is not good for them, and he had for years off and on been troubled. The change was fine for both him and Julia.

Your names for the house are good, I suggest the first, I would call it *Boxwood* perhaps, without even the *manor*. It is the home of the real Sallie Bedford but not the home I put her in, so there is a problem. I, however, don't have to solve it, my beloved Cousin Cad has that to do.

8. John Martin Hiss (b. 1891), orthopedic surgeon, author of *Establishing a Foot Practice* (1928), *New Feet for Old* (1933), and *Functional Foot Disorders* (1937).

My summer has been reading, writing, working in the garden, very simple. Bowman goes to town five days a week usually, I about once or not at all. When the theatre opens I may have to go more. We shall stay out here as late as the cool allows. This is my short and simple news.

I took a trip to town yesterday for a present for Bitsy Bemis,[9] my last wedding present for some time. Telegrams will have to serve. I am not working at present on what makes money, and so will not be extravagant. I blew on Bitsy, for several reasons, please note that French purse and the beautiful work on it, the quality. I thought it would be one of those things that can be kept for life. Fortunately the Frenchman who sold it to me was willing at this season to reduce the price.

I wish I were going to be passing through soon, but alas! It seems a long time since I saw you.

Please give my love to Cousin Wheeler and Cousin Jenny, they are both dear people. If you could send me right off Cousin Wheeler's receipt for CORN PUDDING and for CORN CAKES (griddle cake) I should be awfully grateful. Our garden corn is beginning to get older and not good for boiling or frying, and yet good for these other things where grating is done. This would be a Christian act on your part.

Thank you so much for troubling with the cemetery effect and telling me how it looks. When I get to Texas, the next time I will try to send you a picture of Stark's monument,[1] quite an elaborate one, bless his heart. It seems too much to have to face for the rest of one's life, but there is nothing to do about it.

Take care of your dear self, Bowman would send messages if he knew I was writing.

Lovingly
Stark

9. Carrie Mae Bemis was shortly to marry Richard Reynolds Beasley.
1. The monument for Stark Young Robertson, an Irish cross of white Carrara marble surrounded by a marble balustrade, was designed by William M. Bowman.

502 | To Allen Tate, Clarksville, Tennessee

> Bedford, New York
> Thursday evening [October 7,
> 1937]

Dearest Allen,

Max Perkins told me some time ago that he was bringing out a volume of your poems this "fall," he said, but I was greatly surprised not long ago to have a volume from him,[2] I thought he meant somewhat later in the fall. I fell to and was so carried away by the book that I dashed it back into its covers, after an hour of reading and sent it off by the cook to be posted to my sister—he was happening to start for town on his day off. My sister has always liked your poetry so much.

I planned to buy a copy a few days later when I went into town. But when I went to the shop the front was packed with boards as a protection against the Legion, the doors locked.[3] So I had to wait till I got to town a few days later. At any rate yesterday I bought it, and read it through, again or anew as the case might be with the divers poems. The book seems to me very impressive, as I have said so often no poetry that has been written in America is equal to it in quality, in my opinion. I have not my other volume out here to be exact with, but noted a good many changes in lines, without it I should be fatuous taking up points. I do indeed congratulate you on the whole volume thus brought together—by the way the Mr. Pope poem seemed especially ravishing this time, I use the word intentionally just there. None of the poems do I find dimmed by this reacquaintance with them—which can be said of few pieces of writing of any sort.[4]

The little preface is unique so far as my reading goes, a charm and a turn to it, and it succeeds in making poetry sound special in its existence, based on a necessity that justifies its form in contrast to prose.

2. Allen Tate, *Selected Poems,* published late in September, 1937.

3. The national convention of the American Legion was held in New York, September 21–23, 1937.

4. For this volume, Tate had selected poems from his earlier *Mr. Pope and Other Poems* (1928), *Poems: 1928–1931* (1932), and *The Mediterranean and Other Poems* (1936). In the short preface, Tate called the reader's attention to the revisions which he had made in most of the poems.

I have this feeling so strongly that palish thought poetry like E. A. Robinson's in his mediocre phases sets me wild, also most of the MacLeish or Browning kind of stuff. I might be able to endure them in prose. I think this feeling in me is stronger perhaps than should be, and makes me impatient of much poetry; but I don't really care. It may also make me appreciate more the poetry I do take seriously.

That jaguar point of Mr. Winters' might be said to be true in so far as the passage is a little tormented in the image.[5] But I was never troubled by it. It seemed somewhat more *willed* than the lines around it, but that did not hurt. Perhaps the word "jaguar" helps the effect, I always liked it there.

The book as such is attractive and choice looking, I am glad.

I have been meaning to write you and Caroline that a few weeks ago, perhaps two, I went in and asked Whitney Darrow how the novel had gone.[6] He thought encouragingly, and has real hopes that the sales will go on building. At that time about 8000 bona fide sales he said, so far. He has great hopes for the novel to appear this fall.[7] He seems to believe very much in Caroline.

I also meant to tell Caroline that my sister had written me she had at last finished None Shall Look Back—she can read only a very little at a time because of a nervous exhaustion in her eyes and she loathes being read to, as do I if I take anything seriously. She said the whole effect of the book seemed to her to have something "grand" about it. I had never said so to her, but that is exactly the word I used. Caroline is the only writer in fiction these days in America that gives me that special quality. It is something distributed over the book and elusive of course. After my sister's letter I got the book out and reread some of the chapters. Caroline mistrusted that very last part. I don't agree at all, it seems to me very fine. I often wish I could see you both for a talk.

Sunday

5. In his preface, Tate reminded his readers of Yvor Winters' judgment upon the jaguar passage in "Ode to the Confederate Dead." In 1932, when reviewing Tate's *Poems: 1928–1931*, Winters admired the poem as a whole but insisted that the two lines containing the jaguar image were "hopelessly bad." Although Winters objected to what he considered a mixed figure, he argued that the lines fail primarily "because the act of stoning and the act of the jaguar are not perceived poetically." See Yvor Winters, "Poets and Others," *Hound and Horn,* IV (July–September, 1932), 676.

6. Young refers to Caroline Gordon's *None Shall Look Back,* published early in 1937.

7. A reference to her *The Garden of Adonis.*

By the way Malcolm is back from Spain, and I must tell you that if he asks if I have heard from you I shall be saying yes, long letters, but mainly about poetry etc., so he can't catch me on news of you. I do this because I don't want him to have a chance to think his little machinations put a spoke in our relationship, which so far as I am concerned they did not in the least do.

Your request for that message about Ransom got to me so delayed that, as I wrote you, I sent it direct to Nashville, to D. Davidson, so as to avoid if possible its not arriving in time. When you write please tell me if it arrived and in time? It should have been there well before that evening.[8]

I see he has gone to Kenyon College. When I got my degree at Columbia that was the first chance at a job I had, an assistant's job in English, $600, through Trent. But I went to Mississippi instead.

I have some NR proof and must stop. I wish I could see you.

Lovingly
Stark

503 | To Julia Valette McGehee Sledge, Portales, New Mexico

The New Republic
40 East 49th Street
New York
January 26, 1938

Dear cousin Valette:

We talked a lot about you Christmas[9] and about Hugh and Aunt Julia and old times. It is sad to see Aunt Sarah so sick, though she does not look it. She is so weak that she looks merely quiet. She might

8. In June, 1937, Tate was arranging for a dinner to be given to recognize John Crowe Ransom's contribution to Southern literature. Young did not attend but probably sent a congratulatory message for the occasion. Ransom left Vanderbilt in August to join the faculty of Kenyon College.

9. After visiting his sister in Austin, Young returned to New York on January 5. In a letter to Caroline Charlotte McGehee, written on January 7, he described his aunt's condition much as he does here.

go at any time, and again she might linger. So far I think she has very little pain and we hope that she will not hang on to experience it. Julia is lovely to her. The two nurses are devoted and most attentive and Ben as always is remarkably fine about the whole business.

I am sorry Portales is so far out of my route for I could stop off and see you. Time passes and old affections are best. My permanent address you will see at the top of this paper. I wish you would put it down in your address book.

I hope you and cousin Joe Brown keep well.

Lovingly
Stark

504 | To Roane Fleming Byrnes, Natchez, Mississippi

The New Republic
New York
February 8, 1938

Dear Roane:

I am sure that my not hearing from you in the autumn or since I wrote you about two weeks ago,[1] that you feel embarrassed at having to tell me something or other. Perhaps the museum is closed, perhaps they do not want the *So Red the Rose* Room at all, perhaps the ladies have murdered each other. The first of these would be very sad to hear, but you must not in the least feel embarrassed to write me about it all. The portrait is in the way here and is shut up in a storage closet, and if the Natchez plans have exploded all you have to do is to tell me. I am at least one author who has not the egotism that makes things sad and

1. On January 19, Young had written Mrs. Byrnes to ask if she wished to have for the Natchez Pilgrimage museum the portrait of himself by Abram Poole and "a portrait of a lady about 1750 which I bought at auction with a view to adding it to the museum there, to help fill the wall space." For the museum, see above, Letter 435 and note 2. After graduation from Princeton in 1904, Abram Poole (1882–1961) studied painting in Munich and Paris; and during the 1920s and 1930s his portraits received prizes from various museums and academies. His portrait of Young now hangs in the library of the University of Mississippi.

difficult. Meanwhile I will keep the portrait here and the eighteenth century portrait that I promised the museum until I have a note from you.

I am doing a version of Chekhov's *The Sea-Gull* for Alfred Lunt and Lynn Fontanne,[2] under the management of the Theatre Guild, and this has kept me busy, getting up at five o'clock and keeping on till late at night. The version is almost finished now and all I have to do is get it ready for publication. It will open out of town on March fourteenth, here March 21st. It is an interesting adventure.

I hope [you] and Ferriday keep well. Please send me a line at your earliest convenience.

Yours affectionately,
S.Y.

505 | To Roane Fleming Byrnes, Natchez, Mississippi

The New Republic
New York
February 10, 1938

Dear Roane,

I just wrote you Tuesday, because I know you are so nice and I thought you were struggling with some message of some awkward situation.[3] I have so much to do on the theatre situation and Chekhov that I cannot write a letter now. I will call the packer and have the picture sent right off. I am relieved to know that the museum is still

2. For the next several years, Young was closely associated with Alfred Lunt (b. 1893) and Lynn Fontanne (b. 1887). After road trials in Boston and Baltimore, the Lunts opened on Broadway at the Shubert Theatre in Young's translation of Anton Chekhov's *The Sea Gull*. Alfred Lunt had been a star since his appearance in *Clarence* during the 1919–20 season, while Lynn Fontanne had reached stardom a year later in *Dulcy*. After their marriage in 1922, they performed together throughout the next five decades in a succession of outstanding plays. By 1938, they had acted the leading roles in such plays as *Pygmalion, The Doctor's Dilemma, Reunion in Vienna, The Taming of the Shrew,* and *Idiot's Delight*.

3. For the background of Young's remarks in this paragraph, see the preceding letter.

going. Only the other day I was at the home of Mrs. Bliss, whose husband is the head of the Metropolitan Opera House,[4] I mean as a sort of director, who does not throw up when he hears too many sopranos, and she was telling me that she had been in Natchez and had met you and thought you remarkably charming. She is a Maryland woman, which reminds me of what I said to a Boston architect-author, when he volunteered the opinion that he thought the south exaggerated rape and that five years in the penitentiary was sufficient punishment. I said, "I'm afraid rape is more appreciated in Boston than it is in the south."

The way to tell whether the seventeenth century portrait I sent in memory of your mother is in the right condition is very simple. You merely turn it in the light and see if there are any dry spots or discolored specks or blue spaces that look like oil on water, in which case please send it to me and I will get it back to you within two weeks, I guarantee. It was such a lovely thing in its way and your mother was so lovely that I want the combination to be right.

I am sorry indeed to hear of Mrs. Lawrence's death.[5] She was a beautiful person.

You are quite right, I will never come to a Pilgrimage, enclosed though the folders be, but I hope I arrive every few days in the hearts of such people as you and Ferriday—I sometimes think that is all I'm good for, I mean that sort of thing.

I met a lady from Stockholm the other day, she tells me that *So Red the Rose* had a tremendous success in Sweden, Denmark and Norway and that she thought a great deal of the picture was very beautiful.

Your letter just received makes any reply to my Tuesday letter quite unnecessary. I am relieved to know that you have not these things to struggle with that I feared.

Love to you and Ferriday.

Yours sincerely,
S.Y.

Bless you!

4. Cornelius N. Bliss (1874–1949), financier and philanthropist, was a director of the Metropolitan Opera Association and from 1938 to 1946 chairman of the board. In 1906, he married Zaidee C. Cobb.

5. Mrs. Byrnes's aunt, Zuleika Metcalf Lawrence (Mrs. George Lawrence), died September 14, 1937.

506 | To Andrew Nelson Lytle, Monteagle, Tennessee

[320 East 57th Street]
[New York]
March 11, 1938

Dear Cousin,

I have been meaning to send you this line for some time. The publisher sent me that book of Warren's called, if I remember right "A Southern Harvest." [6] I looked over most of the stories and read a number. There was one that impressed me profoundly.[7] It had all the authentic quality, however elusive of the real thing in literature. There was a freshness as if about to be brutal, there was a meatiness and genuine texture, and over the whole thing beat a pulse, so to speak, some kind of ordered vitality that one rarely sees and that remains inexplicable. What an astonishing fact is it—and yet how true even biologically—that a short piece can evince the living character and essence as undeniably as some much longer creations can do! In general, fiction to me is a bore and a waste of time. When it is the real thing it is beyond words compelling. But so far as I am concerned this happens very rarely. The more I thought of it the more I felt that you have the genuine gift.

I suppose as I go on talking I shall sound pompous, academic or patronizing. But my experience with life and with art and the history of those who work in art does indeed assure me that we all need, and are enriched by, the response of others.

Take all this for what it's worth, and go on writing; and don't forget me. When are you coming to New York for a visit, even a few days? Allen and Caroline were here not long ago and it was very fine to see them. They were both really pleased to hear me speak of your story in the terms I have been using to you.

Yours as ever,
Stark

6. Robert Penn Warren (ed.), *A Southern Harvest* (1937).
7. Young refers to Lytle's "Jericho, Jericho, Jericho." Young's own contribution was "Shadows on Terrebonne."

507 | To Alexander Woollcott, New York

[320 East 57th Street]
[New York]
March 12, 1938

Dear Alex:

In the first place, please read this not now, but when you get home—if you read it at all—bless your heart! The other day I happened to be at the theatre when Lynn[8] called the company together and read a letter from you, a very fine and generous letter, and, as I said to Lynn, nobody else around town would have written it or could have written it, for that matter.

The letter reminded me of my old intentions of writing you—they are too old now to go into. When you wrote me that fine note about *So Red the Rose* I replied from a sick-bed—a doctor down in Texas having infected my leg, none of my own fault—and I urged Weber, the publicity man at Scribner's, to quote your letter on all sides and everywhere.[9] He came to it gradually and slowly, that is to say in his own fashion. When my book of stories *Feliciana* came out I went to the office and said I wanted to autograph a copy for you. Weber was not there and his secretary said that the copy had been sent the day before.

So this is the mockery that life keeps up.

About a week ago my sister mailed me from Texas an enchanting little reprint. She said that it had been sent from Vermont, Woodstock, and forwarded to me there in Texas, she didn't know when. It may have been knocking around there a long time. I read it with the greatest pleasure and value having it, and only hope you were the cause of its being sent to me, for which, if so, thanks.

The main point of this letter is to say that I have talked a lot with Alfred and Lynn about your performance in *Wine of Choice*.[1] There

8. Lynn Fontanne.
9. See above, Letter 362.
1. Woollcott played the role of Binkie Niebuhr in S. N. Behrman's *Wine of Choice*, which opened on February 21, 1938, at the Guild Theatre, New York. Young reviewed the play in "Theatre Guild Fore and Aft," *New Republic*, XCIV (March 9, 1938), 132. After observing that "there is not much spine, line, or cogency to the play, and none too much life—much less theatre life—to the writing itself," Young praised the

is a very evident development in the whole thing as acting, a very impressive development in fact. All that first act when you have the telephone to pick up and the connections to arrange among many people and many affairs, the effect is carried off with a seeming readiness and ease that in some way I can't quite analyze, leaving behind it an impression of wit on the actor's part. I was interested the other day to run upon, at the dentist's, a copy of "Stage," and saw in it a photograph of you, very handsome and effective.[2] It reminded me of Balzac or Dumas or some more or less familiar picture I had seen in French. I reflected that we must give the photographer some credit here, for though you often looked like that in the course of your performance, the average photographer would never have sense enough either to perceive or to secure that effect.

We all have our egos and I don't feel too sure that you realize how much you are on the stage during that play. So far as I am concerned it is your presence that keeps the play going as entertainment and as point. I was truly sorry when you were off the stage at all. There is some sort of ironical possibility in the fact that Mr. Leslie Banks,[3] experienced actor as he is, should fade so when he is on the stage with you. Such things belong in the realm of mystery that personality and magnetism involve.

As a general sum to all these remarks I merely ask why you don't sit down and write a play in which the leading part is for yourself, with all the wit, charm, tenderness and headlong power of persuasion that would ensue in portraying such a character in acting terms.

This letter is already too long, but you would laugh if you knew through how many years it has trailed as an impulse and a hesitation within me.

At any rate, I send you the most cordial greetings and appreciation of what you are doing.

Yours,
Stark

---

skill of Woollcott. "Through personal magnetism," wrote Young, "a flair for the stage, and a growing technique of acting, he [Woollcott] gives a very entertaining performance."

2. The photograph appeared in *Stage,* XV (March 15, 1938), 15. The comment below the picture of Woollcott with a paper cutter in his hand called attention to the fact that throughout the play Woollcott scarcely left his chair.

3. Leslie James Banks (1890–1952), English actor, played the role of Ryder Gerrard in *Wine of Choice.*

This letter had been done Friday before I saw you. I just now got round to reading it over. Rather dull, but I'm sending it just the same.

508 | To Leonidas W. Payne, University of Texas,
         Austin, Texas

> The Ritz-Carlton
> Boston, Massachusetts
> Tuesday [March 22, 1938]

Dear Payne,

You can see what I'm about.[4] I dug the words out of the Russian dictionary, straightening into speakable English and following Chekhov more exactly too. Soon to be published by Scribner's.[5]

I'll get about $300 a week so long as the play is played. Here's hoping for some time for the run. But anyway it has been a fine experience. I have learned a lot about the theatre and Chekhov's theatre especially.

New York comes after these two weeks of practicing in Baltimore and Boston. I hope all goes well for you and Mrs. Payne.

> Affectionately yours
> Stark

509 | To Maxwell Perkins, Charles Scribner's Sons, New York

> The Ritz-Carlton
> Boston, Massachusetts
> Tuesday [March 22, 1938]

Dear Max,

I appreciated your letter very much—will say more in detail when I see you next week.[6] Please thank Louise for her note, tell her I'd love

4. Young was in Boston to help with the rehearsals for the Lunts' production of *The Sea Gull.*

5. Young's translation of Chekhov's *The Sea Gull* was published by Scribner's early in 1939.

6. Perkins had written earlier that Scribner's was ready to begin setting Young's translation.

to read her play, but can't come to the performance because I'll be tied up that night with *The Sea Gull.* I'm sorry. Give Louise my love too.

As to *The Sea Gull* I have decided to disregard the agent's entreaties and publish it at the very earliest possible date. For reasons I'll detail to you when I see you. The MS is at the Theatre Guild and I told them to send it to you at once. Do please get it set up at the earliest day possible. The play won't be running long in New York—so the quickest possible publishing is advisable. Of course it's only about 51 pages—at least it is in Russian.

I have some interesting matter to include in the back, which will make it a most unusual volume.[7] Professional notes, as it were, never done for a modern play, so far as I know. I hope the printers can go at this play galley part right off—not waiting on me.

I get back Sunday and hope to see you early next week.

Yours
Stark

510 | To Leah Salisbury, New York

[320 East 57th Street]
[New York]
April 14, 1938

Dearest Leah,

Thank you for forwarding the papers etc.; I am returning them, plus the check due you. As I told you I was leaving for the country last week and I was afraid I would make a mistake if I did the arithmetic. I have been up all night and every kind of business getting this play in shape.[8] I think it will be a very distinguished affair and

7. In his reply, indicating his willingness to publish the translation, Perkins suggested that Young write an extensive introduction in which he would discuss the problems of translation. In the edition which Scribner's published a year later, Young followed Perkins' advice.
8. The reference is to Young's translation of *The Sea Gull.*

you must have the first copy off the press. I was talking to Lynn and Alfred last night; they are going to London but I think they have great plans for next year, so that we shall see what we shall see. I hope all goes well with you.

Love,
Stark

511 | To Julia Young Robertson, Austin, Texas

[320 East 57th Street]
[New York]
Saturday [May 14, 1938]

Dear Sister,

After seven years of using the other I found that it would be better if I exchanged my typewriter and got a new one, the old one went well enough in a way but was constantly getting loose in the action, and having to be straightened out. If I am not to afford a secretary I must make the typing at least endurable, so that I won't dread the very idea of writing at all. This one works so well that it quite puts me out, since the present letter is the first typing that I have done on it after trying it at the sales office. I have a great deal of typing to do on that book, have been getting up at four in the morning, putting touches on that essay that is in the latter part of the volume, about translating Chekhov. Not knowing Russian I have to look up so many things in the dictionary, and can you imagine my calling down these translators who have lived years in Russia. I will not go into the matter now, you will see the essay in the book. I never undertook an effort so endless as this essay, but I think it ought to be a landmark in the case of Chekhov and his English career. It is astonishing what an influence he has had, in spite of those translations that make him sound vague, phoney, or God knows what. I have letters and letters, and the reviews are such as no translation ever had in the American theatre. I think the reviewers will be more astonished when they read this essay on translating and find what Chekhov might really be like.

I won't stay on the point but will merely say that all this would mean more if Stark were here to share it, and go through it etc. Loyalty is a wonderful thing, and when combined with brains and imagination is a life-giving and a life-nourishing and life-creating, thing. Bless his heart. I say this much, because I don't want anybody to think I ever forget him. It is all past my imagination, I just feel stunned and finished when I think of it, which is often enough.

I ought to be thankful, I suppose, for these interesting things coming up—very well, I am thankful. (They come up partly because I often work like the devil.) I had a letter this morning from a professor in Holyoke, whose Ph.D. was on Chekhov in English, had seen the performance, for the first time Chekhov was alive on our stage, and also literature. I suppose it is a pity I don't live again and do some of these things through and through, but in the end it won't make much difference, and I don't want to live again, so that's that. I think Scribner's has a feeling that the book should be out already. I intend to get it the way I want it before it comes out. There is no particular amount of money in it any way, so I may as well have it as distinguished as I can make it. That should be obvious, but is not. But of course they will do as I like. What else could they do?

Lynn and Alfred are going to open the play here in the fall for a very few weeks and then take it on tour. I will make something at least. They want me to study this play and that play, etc. but we shall see. They have been very sweet to me, and I love them both, and appreciate all they feel and say about me. Meanwhile, however, nobody but me can tell what I must do, and none of us are starving, and none of us lives and writes more than once.

Yesterday I went to town, partly to see Scribner's, but more to attend to your rug. Max lives near here in the summer, so I could have seen him at home. I got the measure we agreed on there in the library, recorded in my portfolio. The man was nice about the color, explaining that they were never certain as to what tone exactly. I harangued. The manager-buyer came, everything was very pleasant, they got a sample of color in another type of rug and let us hope the color will come out. If not, we can have that buyer bleach or something. That Texas sun will also do it. The weave went across the rug, like that I gave you.

I mean I had your letter and showed him exactly the drawing of the lines. They were going to do it that way anyhow he said.

I will let the chair stuff wait for a convenient day, when I happen to be in town. I know how the floor is a nuisance, having to keep the dust off etc.

You have been most considerate in the way you put things for Wales with regard to the cemetery sketch, and so must not be annoyed to hear that yesterday coming out from town we were talking the matter over and both of us were vague about just what you and Ben do want. Then when I got home, there was your most welcome letter. Wales is anxious to do something you want. He thinks that with that particular monument the balustrade would not be good, not suitable to the monument's style. He would like you to write the following points. 1. Would you like a solid wall around three sides of the lot, with wrought iron or bronze on the entrance side? 2. Would you want only gates (or gates with flanking panels) of iron or bronze? 3. Is the design that he sent now abandoned? 4. If not abandoned, then what changes do you want made in it? 5. Whether you use stone or marble or bronze or iron does not affect essentially his design, you decide that, the design is his study, etc., this applies also to the pavement. 6. You have not answered his question as to the thickness of the foundation for the wall in relation to the existing monument. (Personally I think moving a monument a few inches means nothing, the grave is not the point, the commemoration is.) 7. Are you to cut the tree, or must it be included in the design for the wall?

This new typewriter mixes me up, I had to have it out here for the Chekhov notes and did not have time to get the same keyboard on it, that has to wait till I don't need a machine, so pardon please the mistakes.

I had a letter from Margaret, a note really, saying she might run up to New York for a change, about a week or ten days, seeing the Sea Gull etc., so dropped her a note saying it had closed two weeks ago. She said some nice things about the music club.

When you see her tell her I forget to mention in my note that I saw Norman Geddes in a restaurant the day I was in town and he stopped and patted my face as if I were his little cousin, and said that his wife had developed TB. Been in bed two months. I was sorry. Norman is a genius, and the world loses him and he the world. Makes money, but wonders about it all. I rarely see him, but he is a reality always. Sometimes I am compelled to think the imbeciles blessed.

I must get to that Chekhov proof.

The razor came today, looks interesting and quite cute too. I never expected a razor when I opened the box—wondered what on earth it was. Thank Ben heartily for me.

Sorry I didn't see Dan,[9] but glad to miss that function, it sounds pretty sad.

We are having some rain, after weeks most bright though too dry for fields, garden, etc.

Lovingly
Stark

Can you send me some of that delicious meal? The new cook—better so far than any person we have had out here, has let meal get down to a quart without telling me. Please send parcel post, Bedford, New York. If, however, express is a great deal cheaper, send to Bedford Hills, N.Y. That we have to call for—8 miles away. The parcel post is delivered at door.

The points about the monument seem clear. I got Wales to tell me them one by one.

It's likely you have covered some of these points, or have retracted [?]. So we won't be delicate—just you and Ben write answers to these six points and Wales is ready to start at once. The Crane house is finished. As for me I am well—feel all right. Will be settled when I get this Chekhov book off my hands entirely.

Love,
Stark

9. Dan Moody.

512 | To Maxwell Perkins, Charles Scribner's Sons, New York

[320 East 57th Street]
[New York]
Thursday [May 26, 1938]

Dear Max,

I expect to have the proof of the long essay back, plus the half page on Chekhov, plus a few more notes, and in your hands Tuesday morning. After that no more to be written.

The play will be here again in the autumn and in Chicago etc., so the delay is not so bad as it might be.[1]

It's an unusual volume if I do say it myself.

Thanks for your help, etc.

Yours
Stark

513 | To Margaret Mitchell, Atlanta, Georgia

610 West Lynn
Austin, Texas
Sunday [August 7, 1938]

Dear Margaret,

That might as well have been Gabriel's horn—I found that unfinished letter and what days have passed since I wrote it there in New Bedford—a good many miles from your Bedford. Meantime your very nice letter came and I was delighted to have it, such a good friendly one, and not without some suggestion that you will come our way again or that I can stampede your house some day en route somewhere.

1. In reply to this letter, Perkins suggested that publication of the translation be withheld until the fall when the play was being performed once more. Evidently, Young agreed, for he left for Texas without returning the proof. Early in September, Perkins acknowledged receipt of the material. See below, Letter 515.

I came rather unexpectedly down here—for various reasons. My aunt has been the same for some months. Can't lift her hand or speak. But she has moments when there is lots of life in her eyes, and there is the old shine, intelligence, gallant gracious spirit. It's marvellous to have been like that. My sister profits in some ways from my being here —she's more or less tied here.

Well, for the present here are many genuine good wishes and appreciations of you. It's fine to be able to tell people who ask the author of *So Red the Rose* about you that I've seen you in the flesh and can assure them you're a swell guy, so to speak.

Yours sincerely
Stark Young

514 | To Allen Tate, Woman's College, Greensboro, North Carolina [2]

610 West Lynn
Austin, Texas
Sunday [August 7, 1938]

Dear Allen,

I came off rather suddenly down here, and have been meaning to write you. I am of some use to my sister, who is more or less tied here —my aunt is about the same. We hope she will just stay asleep, without pain. But she has been this way for some months—poor lovely thing!

Yesterday I was called away in the midst of this, but am starting again. I hope your novel is all fine now,[3] and must try to forgive it for taking up those first two weeks. I shall hope, however, to be back North before August is over.

Life has its ironies—I heard that Ransom is here and was planning to ask him to cocktails at my sister's, when last night some lady supervisor or something called my sister and asked us to lunch today to see

2. In February, 1938, Tate had joined the faculty of the Woman's College of the University of North Carolina.
3. Tate's novel, *The Fathers,* was soon to be published by Scribner's.

Dr. Mims, who is here lecturing, has asked for me, etc. I didn't know he was here. I'm glad I had that talk about Ransom, asking your judgment. I was really puzzled about him and his mind, in case you didn't agree with me about the holes in it. It's odd for him and Mims to be teaching here at the same time, after the past crises.

I hope you and Caroline are enjoying the season up there. Till just before I left, it was rain, rain, rain. The Cape was a good deal of a mess. Sorry your house is so far from Bedford, but you probably wanted the utmost seclusion or possibility of it at least. The two young ladies ought to be happy, there's no heat to prevent their unbroken activity.

I saw John Bishop on the Cape, many fine things to say of you. I shall hope to see you later on. Love to you all.

Stark

515 | To Maxwell Perkins, Charles Scribner's Sons, New York

[Bedford, New York]
Wednesday [September 20, 1938]

Dear Max,

I was disappointed yesterday that we couldn't go out for a drink. I'll be back in town next week, and will telephone. Now I'm off to a damned matinée and then to the country for the rest of the week.

These enclosed are pretty final—so if I could have proof sheets for the whole book—page proof—I'd think you'd have me at last off your hands.[4]

People at the theatre ask me about the date of the book, etc. And I have some plans to help it, I hope.

I was deeply sorry about Tom—and anxious to talk with you about it.[5]

Yours
Stark

4. Young refers to his translation of *The Sea Gull*.
5. Thomas Wolfe died on September 15. Although Young knew and admired Wolfe, the two letters from Young to Wolfe published above (Letters 444 and 449) appear to be all of their correspondence that has survived.

516 | To Allen Tate, Woman's College,
Greensboro, North Carolina

Bedford, New York
Tuesday [October, 1938]

Dear Allen,

My brother-in-law had to go to Mayo for some tests so I stayed on
in Texas with my aunt. What my surprise to see in a *Times* review
section of a week before, left here in the house by some one of the
Bowmans, a review of your book.[6] I expected it to appear this fall, but
later. When you were here in the spring you spoke of my reading it,
but since you didn't mention the subject again, I thought you'd had a
sudden spurt of finishing up and then rushed it off—and so I didn't
mention it either.

I ordered a copy at once and have read it with the greatest satisfaction, as well as admiration. It sounds as expert as if it were your tenth
novel instead of your first. The handling of the little boy is more profoundly and diversely original than most critics or readers will ever
see; but a triumph. It's a man's job essentially, not a matter for sweet,
adopting, possessive pens. There is never in your paragraphs a sense of
cutting or obvious elimination, and yet the economy is remarkable
very often.

Obviously, it seems to me, the great triumph in the book is its
picture of men in relation to each other—Southern men, I mean. I
never saw the elusive, warm, formal, etc. relationship that Southern
men of our class have with each other really created before—not that
I recall—in a novel. To try to explain this in a review of your book
would be a hard job.

By the way I try to tell myself that I may have helped a little. You
remember, I reduced Donald Adams to tears by my remarks on his
not looking after your book of poems—etc. And I said he should know
that what you published he should *seriously* assign for review. What's
more I have dilated a number of times about you to H. H. Brickell.
Not that you would be indebted to me—how could you be?—in any

6. Herschel Brickell reviewed Tate's *The Fathers* in the *New York Times Book
Review,* September 25, 1938, p. 2. Brickell characterized the novel as "a beautifully
written and profoundly searching story of the Old South."

sense—but that I may feel set up and warmed, I'd like to think I gouged them up a little—even subconsciously—But as like as not they've forgotten my goings on.

I got a cold on the train coming back and have been here shut up a good deal, trying to be rid of it before cold weather comes. How sorry I was not to get back in time to see you and Caroline. Give her my love, she must be much pleased and proud over the book.

John Ransom and I had some good talks in Texas.

Affectionately
Stark

517 | To John Mason Brown, New York

[320 East 57th Street]
[New York]
Thursday [November 17, 1938]

Dear John,

I have had so much what with moving permanently into town, articles to be written, and an Italian book—endless—to be read,[7] that I don't know whether I have written you or not. I meant to do it, and I am curst by having words come into my head so clearly and roundly that I don't always know whether I have thought them, written them, said them, or dreamed them—or whether it was all of these together.

I meant first of all to write you—and perhaps I did—what a fine lunch and visit with you that was, and to say I kicked myself five minutes after leaving you because I had been too stupid to get out what had been on the tip of my tongue several times, which was to ask how the little niece was after that operation. I asked John Anderson on the telephone and he said the operation was severe but he thought she had come through satisfactorily. I hope so. And so forgive me. I try to ease myself by telling myself that big cities make us thus thick.

7. Young may refer to his review of Tommaso Antongini's *D'Annunzio* in "Impasse on Parnassus," *New Republic*, XCVI (September 28, 1938), 214–15. In his essay, Young called attention to the "amiable inclusiveness" of "these almost six hundred pages."

And I wanted to take up the final essay in your book[8]—Brooks Atkinson. A justifiable estimate, touched with gilt as it should be, so intelligent, generous and luminous—and very sweet and warm—a lovely thing to end the book with. Congratulations.

What I said of your book was truly meant.[9] I wish there had been more space that week. I am your debtor, sir. These notes published sometimes may be of use to the best of books—in this rushing world.

I expect Monday to have proof of the play from Scribner's,[1] and will get a copy—marked up—to you. I have been thinking a good deal about you lately. Your distinction and charm as a lecturer and your great success at it. You could do much for Chekhov and be the only lecturer who knew much about him. I'll not be lecturing, and you are welcome to any notes I have or anything I may have acquired on this subject, and I'll check up the printed pages of the play with notes and cross-reference that you could find advantageous. And with so much pleasure—first of all for Chekhov's sake—getting him into such good hands. In a few days I'll write some dates with the design of pinning you down for lunch. Thank you again. Love to you both.

Stark

518 | To Allen Tate, Woman's College, Greensboro, North Carolina

[320 East 57th Street]
[New York]
Friday [November 18, 1938]

Dearest Allen,

I have just got back from the country and am hastening to reply to your nice telegram, bless your heart, it made me want to see you and Caroline this very week!

8. John Mason Brown's *Two on the Aisle: Ten Years of the American Theatre in Performance* had been published in October.
9. Writing in "Characters," *New Republic*, XCVII (November 16, 1938), 45, Young mentioned Brown's brilliant essays and "richly charged phrases" in *Two on the Aisle.*
1. *The Sea Gull.*

However, I have lived here at 320 four years almost and nobody has ever spoken of sending me a letter or a book that never reached me, nobody but you. Either the thought of this house gives you hallucinations or the devil sets out to bring me bad luck. Let us begin to think of exorcising this spell, this is about the fifth time you have spoken of writing or sending books and no result at my end of it. I never heard from you about coming there in March. That's that. But I was delighted to have your invitation, mostly the visit to you and Caroline.

All I can do is to leave it open. I am asking for a leave from the NR, after Christmas, shall be in Texas or perhaps Mexico, have some writing to do, and no plans as to when I will start North again. You will think I am wise I know in asking for the leave. They laid me off last summer and this will save money again. The thought of an article every week, the theatre stuff, the cutting to a page, which makes many subjects impossible, etc., and my need to get some other writing done have all led me to this resolution.

So as far as March 3 goes I should greatly appreciate your leaving it open and that is all I can say. A Mr. Axley[2] had written from Savannah inviting me to Savannah the week before Easter, said you and Caroline would be there. I must answer it today.

I have wished often of late that I might have a talk with you. I know you will think my decision right about the leave from the NR. I must leave for Texas December 18, some family matters to attend to in Mississippi and will have to drive myself here to get away so soon.

Lovingly[3]

2. Lowry Axley (1890–1960), then head of the English department of the Savannah High School, organized the Savannah Writers' Conference, which was held in Savannah, Georgia, April 6–8, 1939. In reply to Axley's invitation, Young wrote on November 21 that his plans were presently too uncertain for him to commit himself. Although Axley held the invitation open, Young eventually declined; see below, Letter 524. Allen Tate, Caroline Gordon Tate, Andrew Lytle, John Peale Bishop, Samuel Gaillard Stoney, and George Stevens, however, did participate in the meeting. For an account of the conference, see Ben C. Toledano, "Savannah Writers' Conference—1939," *Georgia Review,* XXII (Summer, 1968), 145–59.
3. Young failed to sign the letter.

519 | To Mary Goldmann, Austin, Texas

[320 East 57th Street]
[New York]
November 19, 1938

Dear Mary, you nice cousin,

I have had to wait before replying to your very kind letter, my own plans have been made uncertain by the course of The Sea Gull on tour. You may have seen in the papers about the sensation in Washington, an extra matinee necessary, nearly $30000, etc. Chekhov never went like that before. If they kept that up I should be getting two or more thousand a month from my tiny share of it all. And what my translation does for that play !!!!! But now the ingenue is bedding a young actor in New York and is cancelling her contract after the Chicago run, so who knows what the play will do?[4] They may let it drop and play other things—so life goes, so the stage goes.

As to the lecture, I realize we are too late to do anything but pester the poor president. So just tell him that, I feel sorry to have bothered the scene there, thus late as I am. $250 would be the lowest rate, and plenty of the lecturers must be cheaper and no less dull. I should be free till January 15. But my own opinion is that this could drop for this year at least.

The Dallas News as usual manages a little diaper work for me[5]—

4. In Chicago, from December 5, 1938, until the end of the first week in January, 1939, the Lunts and their company played *Amphytrion 38*. On January 9, the same company opened two weeks of performances of *The Sea Gull*. For this production, Uta Hagen (b. 1919) came from New York to play the role of Nina, in which she had made her New York debut when the play opened on March 28, 1938. Born in Germany, Uta Hagen had been educated at the University of Wisconsin. On December 8, 1938, she married Jose Ferrer; the marriage was dissolved in 1948. On April 11, 1939, she opened in the role of Edith in *The Happiest Days*. Subsequently, she has appeared in many plays and has taught acting in the studio owned by Herbert Berghof, whom she married in 1951.

5. Young probably remembered two articles in the Dallas *News*. On March 27, 1938, Ira Wolfert wrote that "the Theatre Guild production of 'The Sea Gull' is to bring an entirely new version of Chekhov to Broadway. That does not mean the Stark Young version which is being used. He insists his is a translation, and a more or less literal one and not a version at all." A week later, on April 3, the Dallas *News* printed a picture of the Lunts and cut lines beneath which read: "They Do It Again—The steady parade of successes for Alfred Lunt and Lynn Fontanne continues with the Theatre Guild's production of Chekhov's 'The Sea Gull' in a Stark Young adaptation."

I did no adaptation but a translation from Russian. Scribners is shortly bringing it out, with notes and a preface, endless labor by SY. It has already had such amazing reviews that more may happen. These were reviews of the stage event of course. Your mama has ordered me to order one for your birthday just past, your sixteenth I mean.

The list of entertainments at the college is something yet again.[6] Elissa Landi [7] has no more idea of acting than a chicken, does not even know what the problem of her scene is. She is not a bad actress, just no actress at all, in the same sense that a turnip is not a poor orange. I never saw her in the movies. That Barrymore Colt girl [8] falls flat at every moment she ventures New York, no talent, plenty of nerve. All the Barrymores, whatever their talent etc. may be and their face, are ignorant. John had never read "Hamlet" till a friend of mine, Mrs. Hapgood, suggested he try it.[9] Mrs. Carrington, another friend of mine, taught him how to read the lines phrase by phrase.[1] But he came out

6. Young's reference is to a list contained in a letter from Mary Goldmann; in 1938, the usual list of entertainments did not appear in the campus newspaper.

7. Elissa Landi (1904–48), author and actress, began her career on the London stage during the 1920s but achieved greatest prominence in the 1930s for her work in such films as *The Sign of the Cross, The Woman in Room 13, I Love You Wednesday,* and *After the Thin Man.* In 1930, she made her Broadway debut in *A Farewell to Arms;* later she played in *Apology, Tomorrow the World,* and *Dark Hammock.* On November 5, 1938, Elissa Landi lectured as the first speaker in the "Celebrity Series" at the University of Texas.

8. Ethel Barrymore Colt (Mrs. Romeo Miglietta, b. 1911), daughter of Russell Griswold Colt and Ethel Barrymore Colt, made her stage debut in 1930 as Seraphine, the daughter of Scarlet Sister Mary, in the play of the same name adapted from Julia M. Peterkin's novel. Her mother, Ethel Barrymore, played the lead role of Scarlet Sister Mary. Ethel Colt subsequently appeared in such plays as *Come of Age* and *Highlights of the Empire.*

9. Young refers to Elizabeth Reynolds Hapgood (Mrs. Norman Hapgood, b. 1894), lecturer and translator from Russian, known for her translation of Constantin Stanislavsky's *An Actor Prepares,* Alexandra Tolstoy's *Tolstoy: A Life of My Father, Stanislavski's Legacy,* and others. In Gene Fowler's biography of John Barrymore, his sister Ethel is credited with first giving him a copy of *Hamlet* to read; Fowler's account, however, does not necessarily invalidate Young's remark. For Fowler's comments, see his *Good Night, Sweet Prince,* pp. 190–211.

1. Margaret Huston (d. 1942), singer and teacher, sister of the actor Walter Huston, studied singing abroad and performed on the London concert stage prior to World War I. In 1915, she married William T. Carrington, prominent grain broker and music patron. Two years after his death in 1931, she married Robert Edmond Jones, the scene designer. After her death, Young wrote a tribute to her in which he praised her as "one among the half-dozen most distinguished and brilliant figures in the theatre of the last two decades." He referred to her contribution as an expert on voice culture and cited her tutelage of Lillian Gish and John Barrymore. Young gave her credit for much of Barrymore's success in *Hamlet.* "Week after week," wrote Young, "she stuck him in a corner and ordered the reading for Shakespeare's lines, Jack, say this, and Jack, say

well, so there you are. I can't say the same for the young shoot you saw. Proud that you saw it was funny. These people all think Texas easy money and joke. Pous vainee [?]. John Mason Brown is a smart fellow, bless him!

I am glad you still think next summer possible. Thanks and love to you.

S.Y.

Pardon this typing, your cousin is worn with labors.

520 | To Leah Salisbury, New York

The Driskill
Austin, Texas
Friday [January 6, 1939]

Dear Leah,

I sent you a wire last night. All in all it would be a good thing to do Three Sisters. I telegraphed a Russian friend and will make a collaboration, she can save me months of dictionary use, and she has seen me work on things and knows my methods.[2] She wired she would be de-

---

that, which evidently he did with equal willingness or indifference, who knows which and when? His 'Hamlet,' finally, lacked inner poetic content, which he had not within him and which no teacher could implant of course; but otherwise this Barrymore Hamlet was the finest of our time, admittedly so." See Stark Young, "Distinction and Theatre," *New Republic,* CVII (August 24, 1942), 227–28.

2. Young refers to Catherine Alexander Burland (Mrs. E. G. Burland). Born and educated in Moscow, she studied ballet and had a brief stage career before coming to the United States with her American husband. She assisted Young with his translations from Chekhov. In translating *The Sea Gull,* Young, whose knowledge of Russian was limited, had laboriously prepared an English text with the use of a Russian-English dictionary and comparison with existing translations. With the help of Mrs. Burland, Young corrected his translation and in conferences with the Lunts further polished it for stage performance. For his translations of the other Chekhov plays, *The Three Sisters, The Cherry Orchard,* and *Uncle Vanya,* Young used as the basis for his work a literal translation made by Mrs. Burland. In the preface to the published translation of *The Sea Gull,* Young paid tribute to her contribution by asserting that "to show her a list of problems was to have it answered, both immediately and with remarkable literary tact where one language seemed to challenge the possibilities of another."

lighted. You don't have to mention this to Crawford[3] at the moment.

I hope you can come to a settlement with them[4] soon, because if I do the translation I want to do it now, for I have other things in mind. I could get it ready in three weeks or less. For the published form I could retouch. I could begin sending acts in two weeks, perhaps two acts, in case they wish to begin rehearsing. It is not as if they had no translation already with which they may begin the consideration of many points in the play. The terms etc. I leave to you.

Please make clear that I have one stipulation. THIS: The word "adapt" shall be strictly kept out of print. I will make a TRANSLA-TION, as with The Sea Gull. For one thing I will not have my name associated with a suggestion of messing with Chekhov, improving etc. They can cut where they please, but I want to be consulted if a word is to [be] changed. I think Lynn and Alfred will tell you that I am not stubborn about these changes, I merely want to be consulted. In some cases I can gain much from the actor's or director's suggestion. "ADAPT" no and be Jesus! Your letter has the word—hence!!!! You fool with me and I'll heil Hitler!

The enclosed speaks for itself. I should [think] Peterkin's titles[5] might be fine for movie uses. I wrote her at once about you, and I hope she writes you and meets you. Black April has some of the authentic genius in modern writing, I think, unequal though the whole of it may be. There are things elsewhere in her writing that take your breath.

Thank you for your interest, dear Leah. I hope one way or the other you can get these people pinned up, I want to think of other things, as I said. I have two things buzzing in my wuzzy head.

Tell Miss Dalrymple (her name has something rippling and dimp-ling like a stream with the nymphs looking into it, that suits her face

3. Cheryl Crawford (b. 1902), producer, one of the founders and directors of the Group Theatre (1930–37), has been associated with such theatrical successes as Sidney Kingsley's *Men in White,* George Gershwin's *Porgy and Bess,* Allen J. Lerner and Frederick Loewe's *Brigadoon,* Tennessee Williams' *The Rose Tattoo* and *Sweet Bird of Youth,* and others.

4. Young's reference is to Cheryl Crawford and Margaret Webster (1905–72), ac-tress and director, best known for her acting in Shakespearean roles opposite John Barrymore and Maurice Evans and for her direction of revivals of Shakespeare's and George Bernard Shaw's plays.

5. Julia Peterkin wrote Leah Salisbury about her management of the film rights to *Bright Skin,* published in 1932. Peterkin's *Black April* had appeared in 1927.

and style) tell her thanks, the idea for a book about Mrs. Jefferson is a fine one. She could be made to represent and disseminate a great many essential ideas and qualities. But it would mean endless work and time, and I [have] other things I prefer. Thank her nevertheless. The idea is, as I said, really a good one.

If Scribner's does not send you the copy of The Sea Gull, please let me know. It is out January 16.

I am glad you and Tony and Phil [6] had the cruise, it must have set you up, and you deserve it.

Affectionately
Stark

I have a room here at the old hotel, very nice for a while, trying to write, go to my sister's in the afternoon and to dine. I told the NR I would take off till September. I know you wish me luck.

Do you know this story?

SOVIET CONSCIENCE
(meeting maiden in forest)

"Do you or don't you?"
"Oh, well, all right. You've talked me into it!"

521 | To Caroline Charlotte McGehee, Como, Mississippi

The Driskill
Austin, Texas
Monday [January 23, 1939]

Dearest Cousin Cad,

As fate deals out life and death, I might be seeing you any time, Aunt Sarah does not know me, but she goes up and goes down, and may live a while and may not, bless her heart! I had a ticket bought,

6. Young refers to Philip Salisbury (1892–1967), husband of Leah Salisbury, editor, and publisher associated with business and marketing publications, and their son, Anthony Salisbury.

Pullman and all, through Como and New Orleans, but at the last day changed it and came here direct. Then I went from here to Natchez to arrange some matters about the museum—at much more expense— but could stay only that night and had to rush back here. It is all very hard on Julia and the very thing Aunt Sarah would not want to happen. Ben is wonderful about it, but it prevents his getting some trips and changes that he needs after working at law. Poor everybody! You know all about these things, for who is finer or more loyal than my darling and beloved Cousin Cad? My hat is always off to her!

Thank you for the words about The Sea Gull. It has been a phenomenal triumph as a translation, nothing ever before had that sort of attention in the American theatre They are playing it again, in March in the Middle West and then in New York.

I hope to write again soon, am somewhat devastated with things to be finished up before I begin some longer pieces, have taken off till September from The New Republic, no salary. We shall see. We live only once.

Lovingly
Stark

522 | To Leah Salisbury, New York [telegram]

Austin, Texas
January 25, 1939

Have been hoping to hear further information.[7] The translation is already started any how, regardless. Hope for letter from you. Love to you all.

Stark

7. In response to Young's request for "further information," Leah Salisbury reported the progress of negotiations with Cheryl Crawford: "While she and Peggy Webster are entusiastic and certain about wanting to produce it, they are still trying to convince Maurice Evans that it can be properly adapted and made attractive to the American public. Unless she can get Evans, Crawford doesn't want to do it, and she thinks she cannot convince Evans they are right unless they are able to show him an act or a scene properly adapted."

523 | To Leonidas W. Payne, University of Texas, Austin, Texas

[The Driskill]
[Austin, Texas]
Saturday [February 11, 1939]

Dear Payne,

I was sorry the San Antonio people broke in yesterday on your most welcome visit. But he is a touchy and half-sick person is Buford Walker[8]—you punctuate that, please.

As it turned out, I had to sit up till one last night and get up at six this morning, but The Three Sisters is all done! ! ! !

As for that information—Dallas etc.—it could be made up briefly perhaps from the following:

I have taken a leave of absence from The New Republic till September, want to do some non-critical and longer things.

Have had so many calls and praises and requests about Chekhov that I have planned to do The Three Sisters and The Cherry Orchard, thus covering the three important Chekhov plays, to make a volume along with The Sea Gull already published and to be done again in the North by the Lunts, during the World's Fair and next season. The Three Sisters is finished at this juncture because of a proposition from New York where it may be produced this spring or next season.

I am also on a book of more or less autobiographical material that I have not used and shall not use in my novels. Not my autobiography but material I think of interest and value and social content, plus some account of various people I have known.

FINIS

I wish you would let them publish about your speech in London, many people would be as interested as I was—and the Hudson MS given you.[9]

8. Buford Walker (b. 1900), prominent Austin real estate broker, interested in painting, literature, music, and travel, had known Young while he was a member of the faculty at the University of Texas.

9. On June 29, 1938, Professor and Mrs. Payne attended the unveiling of a memorial tablet erected by the "Hudson's Friends Society," Quilmes, Argentina, to W. H.

I am sending Mrs. Payne a few flowers, with much love. This written in haste, I have to catch the stenographer.

Stark

Am staying on quite a while in Austin at the Driskill.

524 | To Lowry Axley, Savannah, Georgia

The Driskill
Austin, Texas
February 13, 1939

Dear Mr. Axley,

I have delayed writing you for the simple reason that my plans here are so uncertain and, from the last analysis, seem likely to remain so. I took a leave of absence from The New Republic and am here at the hotel in Texas, blue sky, Greek air and all, and doing a good deal of work. Family matters prevent my making plans, and time will settle what my own mind shrinks from. As a Southerner you will know that I am talking of old people who have stood by us and of death. My dear aunt who brought up my sister and me, is now past eighty-five, lying there with shut eyes—there is no need to go into it. So my sister and I make no plans.

This personal matter you will understand and pardon. I am writing to say that I know finally that I shan't be coming to Savannah this

Hudson on the London residence at 40 Saint Luke's Road, where he spent the last forty years of his life. Arrangements for the erection of the memorial had been made through the Royal Society for the Protection of Birds, which Hudson had endowed in his will. Because of the sudden departure of Don Manuel Malbran, the Argentine ambassador in London and the principal speaker for the occasion, Professor Payne was unexpectedly called out of the audience to make an extemporaneous lecture. As a memento of the occasion, Miss Linda Gardiner, editor of publications for the society, presented Payne with six pages of Hudson's manuscript of chapter one, entitled "Earliest Memories," in the first edition of *Far Away and Long Ago* (1918). For an account of the occasion, see "A Memorial to W. H. Hudson," *Bird Notes and News* (London), XVIII (1938), 74–75.

spring,[1] and to express my thanks for the invitation nevertheless. The idea was interesting to me, and the lure of Savannah, with its beauty and its thoroughbred people, was very strong.[2] I find myself thinking sometimes that the South takes for granted such critics as Miss Judge[3] just as it takes for granted the camellias and gardenias and cornmeal. Well, let it go at that.

I hope to have the pleasure of meeting you at some time not far off. With renewed thanks and regrets, I am

Yours sincerely,
Stark Young

N.B. Make allowances for this typing, please. I have no secretary with me. My fingers are poor agents.

525 | To Margaret Mitchell, Atlanta, Georgia

The Driskill
Austin, Texas
February 17, 1939

Dear Margaret,

I had your very nice note and was mighty glad to see it. As a matter of fact, it is in my files now just to warm my heart on some great day —one of those days authors have, as you well know, when the heart sinks, when it sinks indeed straight down through the brain like a plummet—to be Shakesperian.

I don't know when Fortune will bring me through those parts, but

1. Although, as Young writes, the serious illness of his aunt made definite commitments hazardous, probably the most important factors in his decision not to go to Savannah were the negotiations for the production of his translation of *The Three Sisters,* his plans for future translations of Chekhov, and perhaps the prospect of writing a play for the Lunts who had just arrived in Austin. See below, Letters 527 and 532 and notes.

2. See above, Letter 518 and n. 2.

3. Jane Judge (1871–1948), critic and literary editor, was associated with the Savannah *Morning News* from 1899 to her retirement in 1944. Although during her career she performed virtually every editorial assignment on the paper, she is best known as the literary editor of the book page which she originated in 1926.

some day it will and I will see you and John and have a good talk. You, yourself, have an extraordinary way of clarifying life and moments; and if it means anything to you, I will say that I have the greatest faith both in your qualities and in your future.

Thank you for sending me that hilarious clipping. It looked like an exercise sheet for a phonetic lesson. There was an article once in the paper in Amsterdam in which I was referred to as Om Young. I don't know what the lady term of this would be, perhaps you would be Fraw Mitchell.

I have told The New Republic that I would take off until September and so I am here. Hope to get some longer writing done; I am sure you wish me luck.

I send you affectionate greetings and hope your own work comes on well.

Yours as ever,
Stark

526 | To Margaret Mitchell, Atlanta, Georgia

[The Driskill]
[Austin, Texas]
February 22, 1939

Dear Margaret,

I had your lovely note and the clipping from Warsaw—very killing it is! I'll write anon.

This is a letter of introduction or at least an effort to stir up harmony between you and the Lunts.[4] I have told them about you, and you will find them, before ten seconds have passed, to be the darlings of your heart, as they are of mine.

Greetings and love to you and John.

Yours sincerely
Stark

4. The Lunts played in *Idiot's Delight* and *Amphitryon 38* in Atlanta on February 22–24.

527 | To Leah Salisbury, New York

> Hotel Heidelberg
> Baton Rouge, Louisiana
> March 1, 1939

Dear Leah,

The *Three Sisters* was being bound up [5] when I left—rather suddenly, for Natchez—am spending Thursday, Friday, Saturday, with Lynn and Alfred in New Orleans [6]—they insisted—I am guest—railroad, hotel etc.—I'll send the MS when I get back Monday or Tuesday.

Meanwhile please do me a favor—either write or telephone Lewis Isaacs Jr., Gibraltar Mortgage Co., 475 Fifth Ave., the amount of Sea Gull money you paid me in 1938—deducting the 10% of course. He wants it for tax purposes.

Julia Peterkin wrote that she hadn't yet heard from you.

> Love to you
> Stark

528 | To John Mason Brown, New York [fragment]

> Jung Hotel
> New Orleans, Louisiana
> March 5, 1939

Dear John,

We have just been talking you over—sweetly—in Lynn and Alfred's room. You came out very little behind glory—shall we say? At any rate you know already much of what I think. You may even—partly—know how much I value that review of the volume of *The Sea Gull.* [7]

5. Young's remark suggests that by this date he had already completed at least a draft of his translation of Chekhov's *The Three Sisters.*

6. Among the matters Young discussed with the Lunts may have been his plans to write a play for them. He may even have approached them about it during their earlier visit to Austin in February, 1939; see above, Letter 524 and notes.

7. Young refers to John Mason Brown's "Stark Young's Translation of 'The Sea Gull,'" New York *Post,* January 26, 1939, p. 16. After praising Young's "illuminating

It made its point so very well, it moved along so well, and it had that flair under it, in it and over it, that you can display or evince to so great an extent. I felt too something personal and rich in it—and of all its elements—I valued that most. And I do thank you.

As for Lynn and Alfred they think you are brilliant, and also very handsome and wish they had known you better or seen more of you. I told them about Cassie[8] too.

They are having an enormous success in the Southwest and South. In some ways as careers they suffer because they have no side and marked egotism. Lynn always astonishing by the extent to which she has no ego-elevations. As Ellen Terry said of her in those letters, she is certainly intelligent,[9] but she has so little self-complacency that at times it's startling. I miss that comfort of padded egocentric cellism by which actors titillate the moments.

This is really to thank you for that review. I'm going back to Texas in a day or so, and then [end of fragment].

529 | To Margaret Mitchell, Atlanta, Georgia

The Driskill
Austin, Texas
March 17, 1939

Dear Margaret,

I saw the Lunts in New Orleans and they were saying every sort of delightful thing about you. I knew they would love you and that you would enjoy seeing them. They said they wanted to bring you on to

---

and fair-minded preface," Brown wrote that Young "gives us more than the lyricism and the mood of the play. He makes clear its wit, too. He achieves, in other words, such a fusion of lyricism and wit that his text possesses that 'trembling clarity' which Mr. Young describes as having been Chekov's purpose. Mr. Young produces this clarity by refusing to twist Chekov's meanings, or lengthen his sentences, or complicate his thoughts with ornaments of his own. By the very precision of his word choice, his eloquent literalness, he gives us a new sense of Chekov's bold simplicity as a stylist."

8. Mrs. John Mason Brown.

9. Young probably had in mind a reference to Lynn Fontanne in *Ellen Terry's Memoirs,* edited by Edith Craig and Christopher St. John (1932), p. 191. Ellen Terry noted in her diary with reference to Lynn Fontanne's early difficulties in making a living from acting that she must have more money and added "she is so intelligent."

New Orleans with them, but you could not come. This was meant quite sincerely. They had an immense success in New Orleans and have all sorts of plans about another tour. Lynn, being English, found herself often very much at home among our kind of people.

I have been intending to write you with regard to a personal matter, and want you to feel completely free in reference to it. Some months ago the producers of "Gone with the Wind" asked Mr. Owen Davis— on the basis of his having done Jezebel,[1] which they heard was a Southern play—the language of it was completely impossible—if he would like to take a hand with the script of Gone with the Wind to inspect the "Southernness" of it. He was busy with other things and besides, had sense enough to know this was not up his street.

Somebody connected with the film company spoke to my agent, Miss Salisbury in New York, about my reading over the script for the same purpose, but I think the whole thing has wandered along and got lost sight of. What put the matter in my mind was that last summer some company planned to produce a film that was to get ahead of the date of "Gone with the Wind"—I don't know what title they were using, but the film was based on the Kantor book about Gettysburg,[2] etc.,—I more or less read the book once—the proposition was that I was to read the script over, checking it for any mistakes or details that would go wrong with Southern audiences. They were very handsome about the whole thing and agreed that if I liked the script they would use my name, and if I did not like it I was not to be mentioned, one way or the other, but was to be paid for my opinion. This short piece of work was to be paid for at $2500. The film fell through for some reason and I was sorry, for I could have used the money very well—my aunt's expenses keep up—four years of two nurses, doctors, etc., so money is not to be scorned.

It occurs to me that a mere hint from you to the producers that I would be a good person to read over the script for this same reason as

---

1. Owen Davis (1874–1956), actor and playwright, wrote the play *Jezebel,* which opened December 19, 1933, with Miriam Hopkins in the leading role. Young reviewed the play in "Jezebel," *New Republic,* LXXVII (January 3, 1934), 224–26. Young found "the basic rhythm of the writing is not Southern at all." In 1938, Warner Brothers produced the film version prepared by Clements Ripley, Abem Finkel, and John Huston, starring Bette Davis.

2. In the spring of 1934, MacKinley Kantor (b. 1904) published *Long Remember,* a novel dealing primarily with the Battle of Gettysburg. As Young writes, the film adaptation was never completed.

the last summer plan from that other company—might turn down again in my direction or bring an offer for a short piece of work that would pay well.

On the other hand, I know very well the skill with which you have avoided connections, and I was charmed with the astuteness and told people about it—of your comment when they chose the English actress for Scarlet. What you said could never be used, one way or the other, with regard to the actress—whether she proves successful or unsuccessful in the part. I got quite a thrill out of your getting up that reply. Meanwhile, however, I don't want you, for any friendly reason, to connect even slightly—in case you do not want to connect—in this Hollywood matter. Nevertheless, I feel no hesitancy in bringing it up for we are friends on such a good, sound basis.[3]

Since I have been in Texas, I have been interviewed by a number of newspapers unavoidably, and the same in New Orleans. I avoided this in New York but got off on the wrong foot here through my intention of being useful to Alfred and Lynn and to the Curtain Club here. I have sprinkled around, however, a few blossoms that did no harm. The literary editor tried to get some choice bits out of me about your book, but alas, it turned out all brotherly love. I don't believe we have acted in a way that would give the most pleasure to our observers. I have told some of the interviewers about the wonderful things the Lunts said about you and told others what wonderful things you said about them—this spreads good news at any rate, and is better than a lot of cheap, personal publicity. I really feel mean sometimes when newspaper people ask me about you. It seems a shame not to give them a little, at least, of the cat and dog act instead of beaming and laurels.

My news is that I took off from The New Republic until September and I am now on three different ventures that I have long had in mind.[4] In addition to that, I did an article of translations from a new

3. Because of her illness at the time, John R. Marsh, Margaret Mitchell's husband, answered Young's letter. Marsh pointed out—what Young had already recognized—Margaret Mitchell's reluctance to become in any way involved in the production of the film version of *Gone with the Wind* and suggested that, if newspaper reports of the various Hollywood revisions of Sidney Howard's original script were to be believed, Young might want to reconsider his own wish to be associated with the film production. Upon receiving Marsh's letter, Young immediately telegraphed his acquiescence in the Marshes' point of view.

4. The three ventures were probably the play for the Lunts, the translations of Chekhov's *The Three Sisters* and *The Cherry Orchard,* and the play *Alto Rhapsodie* for Maria Ouspenskaya. See below, Letter 541.

book on Duse,[5] in which are records not hitherto published, so far as I know. I also did an article on an El Greco book that I wanted to have some promotion in The New Republic.[6]

I have finished now the translation of Chekhov's "The Three Sisters" and it is going off to New York. Several people there wish to see it and it will be published in the course of time, along with "The Cherry Orchard," the three plays in a volume, and that will be the last of my Chekhov labors. "The Cherry Orchard" is not begun yet, but I will do it in odd times as exercise and amusement, as well as for more solid reasons.

I wish I could see you and John and talk it all over and hear your plans too. I hope you are both well. I was somewhat tempted to accept the Savannah and Greensboro invitations to those literary conferences, particularly to get by Atlanta and see you. But my aunt's condition makes dates and engagements uncertain, and also I had better stick right here on what I am doing, which I know you will be glad to learn is coming along quite well indeed.

With all good wishes, I am

Yours affectionately,

S.

Dictated public stenographer—please make allowances. Bless you!

5. The review of *Eleonora Duse* by Olga Resnevic Signorelli in "Sense about Duse," *Theatre Arts Monthly,* XXIII (April, 1939), 279–88, gave Young another opportunity to analyze the essence of Duse's extraordinary artistry. "Through the quality of her conception, plus of course her natural endowments," concluded Young, "Duse was a great artist as well as a great actress. Artistic here implies the essential source, or basis, or region, that lies beneath all the arts and each particular art, beneath acting for instance. And through this it could be said that Duse of all the actors of our time was the greatest influence: she affected not only actors and theatre artists in general, but also . . . poets, painters, musicians, and so on."

6. Young refers to his review of *El Greco,* edited by Ludwig Goldscheider, in "The Phaidon Press El Greco," *New Republic,* XCVIII (March 15, 1939), 166–67.

530 | To Shepperd Strudwick,[7] New York [carbon]

Austin, Texas
March 17, 1939

Dear Mr. Strudwick:

I have come back from New Orleans where I was a guest of the Lunts for four days and I found your letter here. I was delighted to have it.

With regard to "The Three Sisters" it is a pleasant coincidence that I have recently finished a translation of it. You know my opinion of the work done by your company—its sincerity, thoroughness, and fine intentions. "The Three Sisters" translation, however, was spoken for a month or so ago by New York producers and they will be considering the matter just now, I suppose. I am sending a copy of this letter, however, to Miss Salisbury, who is my agent and one of the streams of good fortune that New York has sent me, and she will communicate with you. Whatever is to happen to New York about next season—she knows what there is to know about that and I don't. I should like very much to have the translation used by your company in the summer, for the sake of things in general. You and Miss Salisbury will have to talk that out.

The Lunts also want to see "The Three Sisters" but I am writing them that I don't think it is suited to their purpose. They had an immense success in Washington and Chicago with The Sea Gull and are playing it at the World's Fair in repertory, in case they do that World's Fair season, and are taking it on tour next year, very likely in repertory. They have already had an overwhelming success in Texas, Oklahoma, Arkansas and the Old South. There has been no success

7. Sheppard Strudwick (b. 1907), actor and producer, was then associated with the Surry theatre company in Maine. From the early years of the 1930s, he has enjoyed a distinguished career on the stage, screen, radio, and, later, television. Although negotiations with Young to use his translation of *The Three Sisters* were unsuccessful, Strudwick played the part of Vershinin in the Surry Players' production which opened at the Longacre Theatre, October 14, 1939. Young reviewed the performance in "New and Old," *New Republic,* C (November 1, 1939), 368–69. Although observing that the acting version, prepared by Samuel Rosen from the translation of Bernard Guilbert Guerney, represented "a great advance over the usual English versions," Young upheld the general verdict of the newspaper critics that the production was a failure.

like it down here in many years, and they plan other tours in this part
of the world.

I hope you will see the volume of The Sea Gull with the preface and
notes. The agency has sent me 70 or 80 reviews, many of them a
column long and all full of praise. This is in addition, of course, to the
reviews that came at the time of the play's production. I suppose there
has been nothing like it in our theatre history when it comes to the
publication of a dramatic translation. I am glad for Chekhov's sake,
for my own, and for the theatre's. He has had a bad deal.

Meanwhile, please do me the favor to correct anybody you hear
speaking of that volume as an adaptation. It is a much closer translation than any hitherto, as most Russians will tell you, who know. And
the same is true of my translation of "The Three Sisters."

Please remember me to Mrs. Strudwick.[8] I enjoyed seeing her very
much at Lucinda's[9] party. For reasons not tactful to go into, she seemed
to me to stand out very happily, or for me at least, she did.

Thank you for your letter, and with best wishes for your plans, I am

Yours sincerely

[unsigned]

8. On March 10, 1936, Strudwick had married Helen Wynn; the marriage was dissolved in 1946.

9. When Young wrote this letter, Mrs. Lucinda Ballard (b. 1908) was already
widely known for her success in designing scenery and costumes for such productions
as *As You Like It* and *Great Lady*. Later, she designed costumes for *American Jubilee,
The Three Sisters,* and *Morning's at Seven.* In 1940, she became technical director for
costumes at the Ballet Theatre and continued to create costumes for Broadway plays
throughout several decades. In 1951, she married Howard Dietz, prominent lyricist.
Among the most famous plays for which Lucinda Ballard designed the costumes are
*I Remember Mama, The Glass Menagerie, Show Boat, Annie Get Your Gun, Street
Scene, Cat on a Hot Tin Roof,* and *The Sound of Music.* Mrs. Dietz writes that Young,
a distant relative, was not only an affectionate friend but also a "critic who was a great
help to me in my own career of designing for the theatre." In his review of *I Remember Mama, New Republic* CXI (December 18, 1944) 836, Young praised her understanding of costume design. "She knows the difference," wrote Young, "between
theatre costumes and clothes. As clothes her work is capital, as theatre costumes it is
top-grade. Costumes for the theatre are clothes that have been recreated in the light
of the dramatic moment in which they are a part." See below, Letter 618, n. 5.

531 | To John R. Marsh, Atlanta, Georgia

[Austin, Texas]
April 1, 1939

Dear John:

I sent Margaret a telegram expressing my reaction to your letter.[1] It was a very nice letter, and I appreciated it. I was far more interested in it as an indication of what her life and yours may be like at present than as any involvements of my life and purposes. As I said in the telegram, I would never have sent such a request if I had not known that Margaret would be free to answer it justly. She is a remarkable person, and if a relation between character and talent has a decisive importance, I should say that we may well expect more and more extraordinary things from her.

What you tell me about Hollywood has the usual fantastics, and even more. A general break-down there would probably do good.

This letter sounds stuffy, but really proceeds from a most generous and cordial response and appreciation.

I send you both cordial regards, and for that matter, I send you my love.

Yours sincerely,
Stark Y.

1. For the circumstances surrounding this letter, see above, Letter 529 and notes.

532 | To Leah Salisbury, New York

The Driskill
Austin, Texas
Thursday [April 20, 1939]

Dear Leah,

This is only a note to catch the airmail—no Monday letter from Crawford.[2]

I'm saying this now—I have great respect for her, think she has for me. No reason we could not agree, as to changes, however, I'm not stubborn, but can't answer at all till I get her letter and see the sort of things she wants—

(By the way, *entre nous,* now—that is by no means a first draft. And I had a girl and two men read aloud the first 2 acts to me—it sounded wonderfully right.)

Tell Crawford to read carefully the *preface* and *notes* of my *The Sea Gull,* before she has too many ideas about repetitions etc. I trust her genuineness—but she must read this stuff. And send me the letter you spoke of.

I have a wonderful letter from Lynn—they are waiting in May for me to come by with play[3]—is what they have in mind, if we can make it.

Love to you—thanks

Hastily
Stark

2. Negotiations were still going forward with Cheryl Crawford for the production of Young's translation of *The Three Sisters;* efforts were being made to secure Franchot Tone for the leading role.

3. Very likely, during the Lunt's visit to Austin in February, 1939, and again early in March during his weekend with them in New Orleans, Young began to discuss the prospect of his writing a play especially for them. This inference gains strength from an item in "Gossip of the Rialto," New York *Times,* April 23, 1939, p. 1: "While his colleagues of the Drama Critics Circle were proving nothing much the other day, Stark Young was down in Texas batting out a play for them to see next season. . . . For its leading players he has in mind Alfred Lunt and Lynn Fontanne. . . ." A few days later, April 29, Lynn Fontanne wrote Young that she and Alfred had not told anyone he was writing a play for them, though she was not surprised that the news had spread. On April 29, the Lunts ended their road tour in Pittsburgh and abandoned their New York engagement so that Alfred could have emergency dental work. Lynn Fontanne wrote Young that in their home at Genesee Depot, Wisconsin, they would eagerly await his coming with his new play, which he was then calling *Belle Isle,*

533 | To Leah Salisbury, New York

[The Driskill]
[Austin, Texas]
Tuesday [April 25, 1939]

Dear Leah:

My poor aunt [4] died at last on Wednesday, though without any pain at all—just fell asleep as we were sitting there with her—it was so like her to die in a way not distressing for us to remember, and so justly, we miss her, more so as of a few years ago, but from now too. But there is nothing to say about all this—or for one's friend to say—We went to Mississippi to bury her—the cousins and old friends were wonderful to us, an ancient tie and a sense of sweetness in a certain continuity within living. So this is why your letter did not reach me sooner.

I have no suggestions to make as to names for Central City.[5] Mildred Natwick [6] is fine—so is Russell Collins.[7] I wrote Franchot a letter, but not—as he theatrelike probably thought—to try and persuade him into this play, but for much deeper inner reasons. Also I'd like to know if he got the copy of THE SEA GULL I sent him when it came out. No answer so far.

I don't know what to say about THE THREE SISTERS. From a certain professional angle, there would be very little prestige for the manuscript through the Surry Players bringing it to town—though I believe in many ways they would do it very well.[8] Without some

4. Sarah Gilbert Starks.

5. Young appears to be referring to a play in manuscript being handled by Leah Salisbury.

6. Mildred Natwick (b. 1908), stage and screen actress, appeared first on Broadway as Mrs. Noble in *Carry Nation* in 1932. Later, she appeared in *The Distaff Side, Night in the House, Candida, Blithe Spirit,* and others.

7. Russell Henry Collins (1897–1965), stage and screen actor, began his career as a member of the resident company of the Cleveland Playhouse from 1922 to 1932. In New York he acted with success in such plays as *Both Your Houses, Men in White, Waiting for Lefty, Paradise Lost, Juno and the Paycock,* and others.

8. See above, Letter 530 and n. 7. The Surry Players performed in Bar Harbor, Maine, during the summers and at times brought their best productions to New York. The group acted under the leadership of Samuel Rosen, Dwight Deere Wiman, and

striking names Cheryl Crawford's bringing it to town won't have any vast prestige either. But, provided you think it best, I suppose the wise thing to chance would be not to give it to Mr. Strudwick but make the excuse that we feel more or less obligated to Crawford. That will be an explanation worth crediting, I trust. This is about all I can say on the subject. I console myself with the fact that I will in time publish the play. I don't, however, feel blue, blissful or anything else about this matter.

They read me the rest of the translation one night last week. It sounds mostly very right, very say-able, very fine. Will you give Crawford this message for me—"Read aloud sounds nearly always fine and moving. I have about 20 to 25 words changed or to change from the copy as sent you. Otherwise the translation is remarkably close to Chekov's words and even his order of words. The impact of THE THREE SISTERS is considerably different from that in the SEA GULL—I mean scene by scene, line by line, as well as the whole play." There are also a few passages that come over rather too tiresomely— we could easily cut or fix them up—in an hour or so that could be done. I don't think she would have any trouble on that score.

Nothing in this situation therefore, could be said to hang on *me*.

So I have covered the main points of the subject—The Surry Players—in the text (changes, etc.). The Surry Players seem set on bringing the play to town, which means that Crawford will put it off—if she ever does it at all. People seem to think Judith Anderson [9] will be doing it—I don't know anything about that. There's a wonderful role for her. You do whatever comes up—so far as I'm concerned—or to hell with it. I'll send you the corrections soon. Perhaps you would like to do some sort of advance and thus hold on to it—whatever you say.

I may be back by June 1st or may not—it doesn't seem very interesting as a subject—save for seeing a few sweet people.

The Africa clippings are from a Ft. Worth interview some time

---

Shepperd Strudwick. Among the acting stars of the company were Strudwick and his wife, Helen Wynn; Anne Revere (Mrs. Samuel Rosen); Katherine Emery; John Boruff; and Robert Allen.

9. Dame Judith Anderson (b. 1898), Australian stage and television actress, has appeared in many plays on Broadway since the 1920s. Before Young wrote this letter, she had been seen in *Strange Interlude, Mourning Becomes Electra, The Old Maid, Hamlet,* and others. She did not appear in the Surry Players' production of *The Three Sisters.*

ago, a sort of spiel. I have had to spend too much money here already. Besides I want my time for writing.

Thanks and bless you.

Love to you,
Stark

534 | To Leah Salisbury, New York

The Driskill
Austin, Texas
[May, 1939]

Dear Leah,

This will be a hasty letter—I'm due elsewhere—got your nice letter—I can't quite be sure—you say lunch with Crawford Tuesday—you prefer—"to one with the Surry Players. But in the meantime I have given them my only script"—I don't know whether *them* means the S. Players or Crawford's group—

My only fear is this—*The Three Sisters* has so many short speeches that it will not be as different in translation as *The Sea Gull* can be from other translations. It is a more diffused excellence that my translation has. (The same would be true of *The Cherry Orchard*.) It's in many of the longer, more lyric and reflective speeches in my *Three Sisters* translation that I have sounds and constructions that speak wonderfully and that will not be in any other translation, because none of them can do it as I can. Peg Webster would see what is done in such passages by me, for she is very intelligent. What bothers me is that by the time they have all pawed it over well, they'll have gleaned the important effects etc.—after that, any of the ordinary translations can be fixed up by the producer—and mine will be left aside. There are few theatre people I'd trust in a case, for after all, one can tell oneself that the Russian was so and anybody therefore had the right to those English words. I hope Crawford has settled about it by now.

And another thing—the enclosed speaks of *The Cherry Orchard*

Search. You can tell Crawford I have *The Cherry Orchard* ¾ done and could send her—*guaranteed*—a pretty good draft of it—by June 1st. But not submitting it—hurrying up myself and then just messing around with her. This draft would be rather less final than *The Three Sisters,* in which latter I'll make a good many alterations—some during first rehearsals—I'd do the same with *The Cherry Orchard.* At any rate it's easily ¾ and more done, as an initial version—already written out but not polished.

I'm, however, not hoping much if The Surry Players have my script in hand and she fiddles around—for as I say it would be easy to "remember" the subtle echoes and effects I have—and to use otherwise any old commercial translation available without much cost. In that case fiddles too long, I'd just *give* my script to the Surry Players to substitute for the one they were using—and I'd ask no royalty at all—Love to you

Stark

Sorry you should have so much trouble with this silly business. I'll be back in New York by the middle of June or earlier, I think. Cheryl seems to be the hardest person in New York to reach—a poor sign!

535 | To Caroline Charlotte McGehee, Como, Mississippi

The Driskill
Austin, Texas
Friday [May 5, 1939]

Dear Cousin Cad,

How often have I thought of the sweetness and goodness you all showed us in Como! Of course the first one as always with me is my Cousin Cad. I told Julia there was one person who would never let me down. You might in time decide I was very wrong and very silly about many things, but that would make no essential difference. After all when everything sails smoothly and sits pretty, almost anybody might stand me conceivably.

I got back here Sunday afternoon and went off to Dallas that night, got there at 8.15 and was trotted steadily about all day, breakfast, luncheon and then the lecture,[1] not to speak of a visit to the museum where I had to be introduced to every man of importance there, and then a sort of lawn sitting after the lecture, and then a dinner party and then about fifty guests invited in to shake my hands. It was all right but not conducive to the peace of the spirit. The lecture seemed to go all right, but I should have been more comfortable in it of course if I had not had all that strain and distress.

We miss Aunt Sarah more than we did when she [was] lying there asleep. We now go back to the time when she was her own lovely self. I will say for her that she made death and dying less horrible and sickening just as she made life gentler and wiser and deeper. She is with us now a great deal, gracious and tender and blessed. Well, such is life and the world passes. I think sometimes we live a long time, but suppose that is rather ungrateful.

I mean when I can get the time to write some notes to a few people in Como. They were all very lovely and loyal. It was Aunt Sarah's due but then people do not always remember such things.

It was so very nice to see all of you, Cousin Wheeler I am writing to. Cousin Annie was lovely. I was glad to see her so alive.

I wish we might have stayed on a day longer or more. Something always seems to push me to somewhere else, and yet not so much seems to come of it. We dream of a kind of peace, but I suppose after all we don't want it or we could surely do something about it. Perhaps life is never single, all of us bound together as St. Paul meant when he said brethren, we are in one flesh, though I don't remember his exact word, I know the Greek word means flesh or body.

I am indeed grateful for all the trouble you took with the cemetery lot. I made the wrong impression about the ivy. I had only objected to the Memphis prices. If now we could start some slips of ivy here and there and then let it creep over the lot and then pretty much let the whole thing alone. I should [like] nothing better than ivy over it all, and cannot expect work to be done indefinitely on the lot. So let us

1. Dallas newspapers did not carry an account of Young's lecture appearance on May 1.

have some ivy out and then you rest from it all. You have been lovely about it. I enclose a check to cover expenses in those past few months or whatever and for the ivy slips. If it is not enough please let me know.

This letter has not by any means expressed my gratitude and affection or what I feel always about my dearest Cousin.

I want also to add another thanks for Aunt Sarah for that lovely floral you and Cousin Annie and Cousin Waller sent. It looked as fresh as perfection the last time I saw it and she would have liked it very much, bless her heart!

Lovingly
Stark

My new photographs are pretty fair compared to all previous ones—the only one I'll give away—I don't want people to see such a face!—is that to you. I'll send it when the photographer has it ready—you brought it on yourself.

S.

536 | To Ella Somerville, Oxford, Mississippi

The Driskill
Austin, Texas
May 9, 1939

Dear Ella:

I have been meaning to write you and thank you for everything, for such fine hospitality and for that good supper and for all the cordial and sweet feeling that you showed us. The truth is I had never intended to be in Oxford again in my life. The strain and sadness of it is a useless ruin for me, but going there so late in the afternoon made it simpler and I could almost believe that some day I might return for a brief visit in those parts. I have to ask you to believe that I am one of the people for whom a mask of words is the only means by which they can survive—I was so worked on by my aunt's death and by the remembrances therefrom to cover these last few years that I merely had to go on talking to exist at all when I was there in Mississippi. Accordingly, I remember only the cleverness of your management of the tea room, the great sweetness of Mary Hartwell's children, and how beautiful your mother is now. These are general matters with very little to be said around them, and the love and admiration I feel for you all comes faintly through at present.

Will you tell Mr. Bishop that I am going to write him soon, when I get myself together and when some other matters are dispatched?

I was delighted to see him again, though as I said, everything for me at that time was completely veiled with the immediate thoughts of the occasion. Sometimes I think we live a long while indeed—but there is nothing to do about it.

I was glad to see Mary Hartwell as beautiful as ever—I appreciate very much your rushing us to Memphis for the train—your reward was slight in entertainment—but you enabled us to make connections that worked out perfectly.

I took a train for Dallas Sunday night and delivered a lecture there on Monday—so that's that.

I hope that Commencement will prove to be a fine thing for your business. If ever you intend to visit New York, I wish you would let me know. If my apartment at the time is vacant, you are more than welcome to it. My address is always The New Republic, 40 East 49th St., New York City.

Thank you all so much for your goodness and understanding—both my words and my face were no indication to what I was really feeling, but that may be just as well.

Please show Mary Hartwell, Mr. Bishop and Somerville and Nina too this rambling letter, and give yourself and all of them my love.

As ever,
Stark

537 | To Alexander Woollcott, New York

The Driskill
Austin, Texas
May 9, 1939

Dear Alex:

I have thought of you so often and wanted to write you a letter. But one minute I hear you are in California, another that you are in Cincinnati, another in Vermont or New York—it reminds me of the ubiquity of the Apostles and of the spinster's remark in Balzac: "Why, you cannot be in two places at once unless you are a bird." [2]

Thank you very much for checking on that date with regard to Mrs. Campbell. I knew she had acted some before she went into the Pinero plays, but the phrase I use about walking from the drawing-room on to the stage is from Shaw somewhere, and I can see from your letter that it gives the wrong impression. [3] My idea of the date—1895—is also

2. The source of Young's quotation may be found in Balzac's *La vieille fille* (1836). The spinster is Rose-Marie-Victoire Cormon who, desiring to stimulate a languishing conversation, "would let out strange propositions, as this one: *no one can be two places at once at the same time, except a little bird,* by which, one day, she awakened, not without success, an argument about the ubiquity of the apostles of which she had understood nothing." See *La comedie humaine,* edited by Marcel Bouteron (1952), IV, 267–68. The passage may glance at the sixteenth-century controversy over Ubiquitarianism which relates to the doubt that Christ's body can be in the Eucharist, since the Eucharist is everywhere and a body may not be in two places simultaneously. Earlier, in *Eugénie Grandet* (1833), Balzac had expressed the same idea but without the reference to the ubiquity of the apostles; see Bouteron, III, 565. A similar remark is often attributed to Sir Boyle Roche (1743–1807), who is said to have declared that "he regretted that he was not a bird, and could not be in two places at once." Fond of the quotation himself, Young used it in a letter written from Spain to the editors of *Theatre Arts Magazine,* IV (April, 1920), 169, and again, years later, in letters to Ruth Ford (see below, Letter 560) and to Anne Sharkey and Jane Wasey (see below, Letter 872). Young had the quotation and the theological controversy in mind when in chapter XIV of *So Red the Rose* Mrs. Bedford asks: "'Do you think you're one of the apostles . . . and can be in two places at once?' Ah, well, bird or apostle, it's only once in this world."

3. Young is responding to a comment made by John Corbin in a letter to Young, January 17, 1939, about his preface to *The Sea Gull.* Corbin had written: "I have read your fine pundicial preface with pleasure but I must speak to you seriously about one lapse. Mrs. Patrick Campbell did not step out of drawing room into Pinero. She had had several punishing seasons in the provinces of something like two pounds a week out of which emolument she had to furnish her own costumes. And whatever she stepped out of, she didn't do it in 1895. She first played Paula [in Pinero's *The Second Mrs. Tanqueray*] on May 27, 1893." John Corbin (1870–1959) began his career in 1897 as a member of the editorial staff of *Harper's Magazine.* Subsequently, he became

vaguely deduced from Shaw. I will hope to make some sort of correction in the next edition of my volume of "The Sea Gull."

You are right about the preface being punditical, but I made up my mind that at the risk of bad taste, I would try to put the point over. Sometimes I think that I have used a great deal of good taste with a very small reward, and neglected to use some good old bad taste that might have worked wonders; but of course, that is not the subject.

Mr. Turner,[4] of the Dixie Bureau in Dallas, came in to see me the other day. A decent man. He is most anxious to get you to do a few lectures. He said he was going to write you.

I was with Alfred and Lynn in New Orleans the first week in March, and I had been hoping that you would be there too. They love you very much, as do I. If anyone asks me where I should like you to be more in evidence, I don't think I could make an intelligent reply—I should just say, "Well, more of Alex everywhere in this world." Please do take that as a compliment.

Affectionately yours,
Stark Y.

538 | To Elma Meek, Kate Skipwith, Ella Somerville, Oxford, Mississippi

[The Driskill]
[Austin, Texas]
May 9, 1939

Dear Ella, Elma and Kate:

This is only a line to three sweet people from whom we had a telegram that we very much appreciated. I had thought that never again

---

drama critic for *Harper's Weekly,* the New York *Times,* and the New York *Sun.* In his articles and books, Corbin dealt with such diverse subjects as the drama, government, education, and public affairs; his most notable books include *The Return of the Middle Class* (1922), *The Unknown Washington* (1930), and *Two Frontiers of Freedom* (1940).

4. Maurice Clark Turner (1878–1953) was owner and president of the Dixie Bureau. During a long career as a lyceum manager, he arranged lecture tours for many celebrities.

would I be in Oxford—for the distress and nostalgia of such a return might be far more painful than the pleasures it might afford.

Ella and Mary Hartwell, however, told us of Mrs. Somerville's grave illness and we decided we would go over and see her. We got to Oxford after dark and left for Memphis fairly soon. Though I should have loved to see my dear friends there, I was glad to escape the sad moment that a sight of the town earlier in the day would have brought to me. In the life I lead, there is about all I can stand already coming in. I have to avoid other things that might destroy me completely. I mean reminders of happy or sad things in the past, or invitations to the renewal of memories half lovely, half painful—etc. You'll understand.

How well I remember the goodness and friendship and generosity of our friends there in Oxford and how I should like to sit down with you all and pass the time—old friends of the past!

Thank you again for the telegram and with affectionate greetings to all three of you, I am

Yours sincerely,
Stark Y.

539 | To Leah Salisbury, New York

The Driskill
Austin, Texas
Wednesday [May 10, 1939]

Dearest Leah,

I seemed to get a bite of the wrong food or something last night, slept badly, etc. so can't write a decent letter.

I wrote you not long ago and left *The Three Sisters* in your hands and God bless you etc. But—

I have a long telegram from Mr. Rosen—sent yesterday and I got it yesterday an hour later but have not answered. Says "Surry Players have been ready two months to contract for fall production your version of Three Sisters under Wiman Sponsorship—" hopes for immediate reply—must set fall schedule— [5]

Well, to reconsider the whole matter—

The Three Sisters could scarcely have a long run anyhow—it belongs rather in repertory.

Without some very drawing name—who could there be?—the run would be short anyhow.

Cheryl Crawford has no renowned company, etc.

Is she willing to sign some paper or something—or give an advance?

The case might be altered if the MS. were some surefire piece we were waiting to sell at a good moment, etc.

In general it may as well become the standard translation and be played here and there.

Would Rosen under Wiman give an advance?

In sum, unless Crawford has something in names or to advance us, I think you might reopen case with Rosen and Strudwick.

At any rate it would be a phenomenal break if The Three Sisters had any run anyhow to speak of.

What this comes to is only to tell you about Samuel Rosen, 26 East 35th St., and this urgent request. And that I will wire him tonight thus:

"Thanks for your interest. Miss Salisbury has had complete charge and I have not kept in touch with her decisions. Have written her air mail asking her to go over whole matter, with check up on all details, and communicate with you."

So now I've told you and will be in Austin for a while yet, if there's anything you want me to think about etc.

Excuse this messy scrawl, written in such haste, Leah, etc.

Love to you
Stark

5. See above, Letter 533 and n. 8.

540 | To Leah Salisbury, New York

The Driskill
Austin, Texas
Friday [June 16, 1939]

Dear Leah,

What with my aunt's funeral expenses, I could use the Crawford check [6]—my coupons are locked in the deposit box—NYC and the details of anybody's getting into that box would make your hair turn white. I haven't the face to ask anybody to do the sweating hours, etc. —Bowman tried it for me unawares and they broke his spirit quite.

Would you make two checks (simpler for taxes and for personal reasons), half to me and the other half to

Richard L. O'Connell. [7]

Thanks.

I expect to be at the villa sometime before July 1. Am sending the play to Alfred and Lynn then going by a few days—I will be sending you a copy at the same time. BELLE ISLE is the title—It seems to me a find for something in the theatre. A letter from Paris—Fresnay and Printemps want to see it. She of course could sing it too.

6. On May 26, 1939, Cheryl Crawford paid $100 to Leah Salisbury as agent for Young and agreed to pay an additional $200 before August 1 for an option on the production rights of Young's translation of *The Three Sisters;* additional payments were to be made later to the amount of $500 for a six months' option.

7. Richard Leo O'Connell, Jr. (b. 1912), playwright, director, and translator, after graduation in 1938 from the Yale Drama School accepted a position as instructor in drama at the University of Texas. Early in the summer, O'Connell met Young at the home of Elaine and Zachary Scott. O'Connell and Young immediately discovered their common interests, and O'Connell helped with the translation of *The Three Sisters* and *The Cherry Orchard;* and when Young began to write *Belle Isle* for the Lunts, O'Connell acted as a sympathetic listener, critic, and, at times, contributor. According to O'Connell, his direct contribution consisted of an occasional suggestion about lighting, scenic effects, and stage directions. Young, however, readily acknowledged his friend's assistance and later formally stipulated that O'Connell should have rights to the production of the play without royalties. After leaving the University of Texas, O'Connell taught at Syracuse University, served in the army during World War II, and became associate director of the Pasadena Playhouse, Pasadena, California. Since 1950, he has been a member of the faculty of the New Mexico Highlands University, Las Vegas, New Mexico. With James Graham-Luján, O'Connell has translated a number of plays by the Spanish playwright Federico García Lorca.

I'll shortly have *The Cherry Orchard* in your hands—it sounds very well indeed. A strange dialogue!

The play for Ouspenskaya[8] is partly laid out. I have to find the *tone* for it. (Something most drama never even remembers.)

I hope all goes well for you and Phil and Tony—

Love to you
Stark

541 | To Lavinia Gadsden Dimond, Cedarhurst, Long Island

The Driskill
Austin, Texas
Friday [June 23, 1939]

Dearest Lavinia,

I have had a number of letters written to you—in my mind's pen, Horatio[9]—but writing so hard has left letter writing far from my lean desires for further exercise in that same field. I was in Mexico for three days Easter—got you a tiny present, you sweet Lavinia.

Down here I seem to have drifted out of time somewhat—when you think I've been gone from New York a full six months! I have, besides two NR articles due, and an article for Theatre Arts on a Duse book[1] —Italian and much of it hard—considered in English. Then I set in on Katia's[2] and my version of *The Three Sisters,* on which I have put endless work—made a third revision lately—at great labour—also now is finished *The Cherry Orchard*—and my own play *Belle Isle* (BELLE ISLE). Its fortunes are not yet clear, since the MS has not yet been retyped completely and sent off. I have drafted part of another play— not written—called ALTO RHAPSODIE. God send us good fortune.

8. The play was called *Alto Rhapsodie.*

9. Young has in mind line 185 from *Hamlet,* act 1, sc. 2.

1. Young refers to his review of *Eleonora Duse* by Olga Resnevic Signorelli in "Sense about Duse," *Theatre Arts,* XXIII (April, 1939), 279–88; see above, Letter 529, n. 5.

2. Catherine A. Burland.

I hope the boy and Doug[3] have kept well this spring and that your summer will go on happily. I'm leaving some time before very long—and will look forward to seeing you.

Love to you all—

Lovingly
Stark

My dear aunt died a few weeks ago—it was all necessary—but she stays with us now more as her old self—such a darling! I'll tell you when I see you. No need to sadden you with these things.

542 | To Mary Williams Goldmann, New York

Bedford, New York
Monday [August 21, 1939]

Dearest Cousins,

Thanks for your sweet words. I mean to telephone you soon—and get into town. Have a good time. You deserve it. At the corner you can buy *CUE,* and see what's going on—stage-theatre revues—films etc. The *Planetarium* is, doubtless, wonderful—I've been meaning to see it for three years (see *Sunday Times ads*), Betty Batter (1st Avenue, just below 57th) is by far the best (and most reasonable) food I know in the neighborhood. Mrs. W. K. Vanderbilt,[4] Mary Canfield,[5] D. Fairbanks Jr.'s mamma,[6] Lily Pons[7] etc. live right by you. You may prefer

3. Douglas M. Dimond.
4. Young probably refers to Anne Harriman Sands Rutherford Vanderbilt (d. 1940). Born Anne Harriman, she married Samuel S. Sands, Jr., in 1880, and after his death in 1889, she married Lewis Morris Rutherford. In 1903, she became the second Mrs. William Kissam Vanderbilt. Active in social circles, civic enterprises, and philanthropy, she lived in a house on 57th Street near Young's apartment.
5. Mary Cass Canfield (1894–1966) wrote literary and drama criticism for the New York *World* and the New York *Evening Journal* and contributed essays to the *New Republic*. In 1927, she published a volume of essays on modern actresses, *Grotesques and Other Reflections.*
6. The reference is to Anna Beth Sully Fairbanks (Mrs. Douglas Fairbanks, 1886–1967). After her marriage to Fairbanks was dissolved in 1918, she married Jack Whiting (1901–61), musical comedy star.
7. Lily Pons (Mrs. Andre Kostelanetz, b. 1904), opera singer.

lunching with them. I, of course, would prefer it with you. Cobina Wright[8] lives upstairs, but I believe she and her she issue are in Colorado. Prince Matchiabelli lived there too, but came home drunk, went into pneumonia, never came to, and so went on to heaven—so that what you smell in those bottles—well—

Charlie Knickerbocker (M. Paul)[9] was there, but has moved out. Clara Kimball Young's husband (3) Mr. James Young,[1] is in 10-D (bore). His wife Countess [?] a dancer once—pleasant. There were last year also a number of actresses and whores—they were in the paper, but as the papers said, I was away and could not be reached for my opinion.

About what?

George Cable's daughter[2] lives there on your floor. Deaf husband.

So what?

That west (small) window cools the apartment at any time. Any-

---

8. Cobina Wright (Mrs. William May Wright, 1888–1970), born Elaine Cobb, singer, columnist, and lecturer, began her career as an opera singer and later became a columnist for the Hearst newspapers. Her first marriage, to Owen Johnson, ended in divorce, and, in 1920, she married William May Wright. In 1921, her daughter, Cobina Jr., was born. In 1939, after her debut, Cobina Jr. was said to have been the most photographed girl in America. She became a film actress in Hollywood and in 1941 married Palmer Beaudette, then an army corporal.

9. Maury Henry Biddle Paul (1890–1942), society editor of the New York *Journal-American,* who wrote under the pseudonym of "Cholly Knickerbocker," coined the phrase "Cafe Society" to describe those who frequented night clubs and exclusive restaurants.

1. Clara Kimball Young (1891–1960) and her husband, James Young (b. 1878), left a Salt Lake City stock company in 1912 for New York to act in the Vitagraph pictures. Her first role was probably that of Anne Boleyn in the one-reel picture *Cardinal Wolsey.* By 1916, she was a star whose popularity largely accounted for the success of Lewis J. Selznick's World Films Corporation, sometimes called the Clara Kimball Young Corporation. Under Selznick's management, she became an international star. In 1918, the Youngs moved to California, and a year later their marriage ended in divorce. Her popularity declined rapidly; and when, in 1928, she married Arthur S. Fauman of Hollywood, her career was nearing its end. Several years after his death in 1937, she attempted to revive her popularity but met with little success. Since she was married only twice, Young's "3" probably should have been "2."

2. Probably Young refers to Louise Cable Chard (1870–1956), eldest daughter of George Washington Cable. In 1894, she married James Alfred Chard (1869–1942), a partner in the firm of Chard and Howe, oil merchants. Louise Cable Chard, an artist, exhibited paintings in a number of cities and at her death was the eldest member of the New York Paint and Brush Club. In the 1930s, Marie Louise Chard, a physician and member of the Board of Trustees of the New York Infirmary for Women and Children, and presumably James Alfred Chard's sister, lived at this address until her death in 1938. The Chards may have been living in her apartment when Young wrote this letter.

thing going wrong can be at once repaired by calling (from kitchen) downstairs.

I'm looking up theatre dates etc. to see if you can't stay three days longer—will know soon. No extra expense—if you lie low. I'll telephone soon.

Love
S.Y.

Please forward all 1st class mail to Bowman or me to Bedford, N.Y.

543 | To Charles Scribner, Charles Scribner's Sons, New York

[320 East 57th Street]
[New York]
Friday morning [September 22, 1939]

Dear Charlie,

I was so tied up yesterday that I couldn't get by; and really there's no reason for my sailing in on your time with divers palaver. The whole point, request, and lamentation is simply to get *The Three Sisters* into page proof.[3] About three weeks have already passed—or almost, and I'd not be surprised to see Odets' version appear. French[4] would jump at it, I'm told, and they rush plays right out. But failing

---

3. Young had been exerting pressure upon Maxwell Perkins to publish the translation of *The Three Sisters,* because Young had been told that Clifford Odets was about to produce and publish a translation of the play for the Group Theatre. Maxwell Perkins pointed out to Young the high cost and probable financial loss in publishing a single play. Perkins, who did not believe that the appearance of Odets' translation would adversely affect Young's chances for success, wanted to bring out a single volume containing Young's translation of *The Sea Gull, The Three Sisters,* and *The Cherry Orchard.* As a stopgap measure, Perkins offered to mimeograph the translation of *The Three Sisters* and bind it in a stiff cover. Young had appealed to Charles Scribner for help in the matter.
4. Samuel French, the leading American publisher of plays.

this, they'd rush out Odets if the idea strikes Mr. Clurman [5] and company.

The enclosed letter [6] could never be explained outside of the theatre, and is rather unusual there since Equity came in.

Please keep it for me.

And can't the proofs begin? The play is not long. And the Odets has been for some time in rehearsal.

It's fairly sure that later on, my version will, as I told you, be done on a good radio list (four plays for the season).

Sorry to bother you with all this—I'm glad it's no great venture, just advance proof—I mean not a volume, $$$ et cetera.

Thank you again for such a nice letter [7]—

Yours
Stark [8]

5. Harold Clurman (b. 1901), director, critic, and lecturer, began his career in 1924 as an extra in the Provincetown Players' production of Stark Young's *The Saint*. Clurman became associated with the Theatre Guild and in 1931 helped to found the Group Theatre. Since that time he has become one of the leading directors in the contemporary theatre. He has contributed drama criticism to such periodicals as the *New Republic*, the *Nation*, *Theatre Arts*, and *Tomorrow Magazine* and written several books, including *The Fervent Years: The Story of the Group Theatre* (1945) and *Lies like Truth: Theatre Reviews and Essays* (1958). At the memorial service for Young at the Morosco Theatre in 1963, Clurman was one of the speakers who paid tribute to Young's contribution to the American theatre.

6. The precise content of this letter which reached Young through Leah Salisbury cannot be known, but Charles Scribner's comment that "it is certainly an amazing document and it makes the publishing business appear to be child's play as compared with the theatre" invites speculation. Probably the letter related to dissensions among members of the cast of the Group Theatre then rehearsing Odets' version of *The Three Sisters*. These difficulties seem eventually to have influenced Clurman to abandon the production.

7. Scribner had responded earlier to Young's request for an opportunity to discuss the publication of his translation.

8. After mailing this letter, Young telephoned Scribner and asked him to disregard it. Subsequently, Young, Scribner, and Perkins decided against issuing the translation as a single volume. Ultimately, Samuel French published the translation in 1941.

544 | To Maxwell Perkins, Charles Scribner's Sons, New York

[320 East 57th Street]
[New York]
December 5, 1939

Dear Max:

I have found among my papers here a copy of the play Louise sent to Mr. O'Connell.[9] He left it with me in the country but in some way I misplaced it. I am really very sorry indeed for not sending it to Louise. I wish I had had a chance to read it but I've been deluged getting some other work ready.

I have just had a telegram calling me South and am leaving unexpectedly, so am very sorry not to have a chance to see you.[1]

With this goes a manuscript of a novel sent me from Boston by an old friend, and a very clever person.[2] I was asked to hand it in at Scribner's. I haven't read this particular manuscript but there is a very good chance of good things being in it.

The little box I am also sending is for Louise, and wishing her a merry Christmas. She's a remarkable person, as we all know.

I wish I might have seen you again before I left. This will convey, I hope, some degree of affection and an old pleasure in your company.

Yours,
Stark

9. Probably a play by Mrs. Perkins still in manuscript.

1. The Lunts were on tour in California. On November 30, Lynn Fontanne acknowledged receiving Young's *Belle Isle* and expressed a wish that he would meet them in Austin. In a postscript, she added that Alfred was reading the play and called the scene between Cassin and Artemise "the most beautiful scene he has ever read." From San Diego, December 2, Lynn Fontanne telegraphed Young that Alfred had finished *Belle Isle* and found it "extremely beautiful." She urged Young to join them in Los Angeles, at their expense, to work on the play. He met them in Los Angeles, traveled with them for a number of weeks, and returned to New York in February, 1940.

2. Dorothy Glaser (the former Mrs. Otto Glaser, 1890–1952), whom Young had known while he was teaching at Amherst, had sent him a manuscript. Earlier, she had published a collection of Gothic stories entitled *Brother Anselmo*. The manuscript which Young was asked to submit to Perkins was probably an antiwar novel entitled *No Memorials,* though Mrs. Glaser also wrote a novel set in the Middle Ages to which she seems not to have given a title. In February, 1940, Scribner's returned the manuscript without accepting it for publication.

545 | To Margaret Mitchell, Atlanta, Georgia

Henry Grady Hotel
Atlanta, Georgia
Wednesday [January 9, 1940]

Dear Margaret,

I wasn't sure I'd be here till yesterday. I do want to see you and John. The Lunts want to invite you two to the play—tonight or tomorrow night or tomorrow matinee. If you let me know I'll connect with them.

Can I see you sometime tomorrow—when? Please let me know here at this hotel.

I had to rush on ten hours' notice off two weeks before Christmas to Los Angeles—so got off no cards, letters or anything. I hope you are well.

Affectionately
Stark

546 | To Roane Fleming Byrnes, Natchez, Mississippi

320 East 57th Street
New York
Sunday [March 24, 1940]

Dearest Roane,,,,,,,,,,

You can see by those commas, which are meant to say it, how distracted and silly I am. I have just got back from two days in the country and that at least was a help. For weeks and months I have been working on a play and on other things, and my brain is empty and filled with a certain phobia against writing letters. It is as if a hotel cook got home and had to make tarts for his social occasion.

This, then, is only a note to say that I am at least sending you that coral rose. I thought I had sent it long ago but found it this morning in a box of items, etc. I toured with the Lunts for their whole tour after Houston and was so absorbed in the play I was writing that everything else went loose and crazy. I used, however, to talk to them a lot about you and my dear Ferriday, I am so proud of the charm, aristocratic breeding and felicitous warmth that pours from you both as fragrance does from a flower.

I sent about ten days ago some more copies of So Red the Rose, charging them to myself as I did before. All I want back is the whole-sale cost, $1.65 a volume, the rest can go to the museum or whatever it can help on.

I saw Natalie Hammond a few days ago—she says she can now send some of her mother's things there—a bed for example. Wisely accept EVERYTHING and with time the various things can be assorted etc. I think, too, I may get an item or two from Mercedes De Acosta[3]— Victorian grander matters etc.

I must close and get over to Scribner's, am due now. I will write again soon. I have telegrams and invitations to thank you for, fully appreciated whatever my seeming response may have been.

Love to you and Ferriday, and give my love to the Adams cousin[4] five feet from your front door.

Affectionately
Stark

I hope Cousin Pierce Butler[5] is flourishing.

---

3. Mercedes de Acosta has written an account of her life in *Here Lies the Heart* (1960). The youngest of eight children descended from a family of noble Spanish ancestry, she knew most of the artistic celebrities of the first half of the century. On May 11, 1920, she married Abram Poole. Her published writings include *Moods* (1919), *Wind Chaff* (1920), *Archways of Life* (1921), *Streets and Shadows* (1922), *Sandro Botticelli* (1923), *Until the Day Break* (1928), and *In New Mexico* (1931). In her autobiography, she records her admiration for Young's stimulating conversation and the brilliance of his drama criticism. She knew him from the beginning of his career with the *New Republic*.

4. Mrs. William A. Adams, Mrs. Byrnes's cousin and closest companion.

5. Young refers to Pierce Butler (1873–1955), associated with Sophie Newcomb Memorial College, Tulane University, from 1906 until his retirement in 1938, as professor of English and dean of the college. The author of scholarly articles and books on Shakespeare as well as an historian of Southern literature, Dr. Butler enjoyed the admiration and friendship of Mrs. Byrnes. The term *cousin* is here a mark of affection and not a sign of kinship.

547 | To Margaret Mitchell, Atlanta, Georgia

[320 East 57th Street]
[New York]
Friday [April 19, 1940]

Dear Margaret,

I wrote so hard on that tour and have had so much to do since I got home in February that I have taken a perfect phobia against writing letters. And yet how also is one to keep in any sort of nearness with the friends one loves. Of which you are one. I am very proud of you generally, and still hope you will begin a broad deep book in a sort of Balzac tradition. You are the only writer in English who could even hesitate at not doing it. The only talent of that kind of any importance. This is a simply sincere remark, and fortunately I have already made it to you.

After escaping a year and over, I took the influenza when I got back, with about three relapses, the kind this season that returns and is accompanied by vomiting. I had nothing in me to bring up and could not imagine what these racking retching spasms were. Enough of that. I am about recovered. Quite recovered from that. But the doctor is pushing me into idleness of sorts and wants me to get on out to the country as soon as I can. That depends on the weather. The spring is very late.

I wanted to send you and John something to remind you of my visit there with you two and how much it meant and what good it did me. I feel marvellously warm and natural with you and anxious to talk and to listen. So I bought from a Polish dealer's collection of Mongolian objects a piece of lacquer I thought you might like. Its date is about 1750, it is a book end from those rolls the sages are shown reading. The dealer had the base for it made in China while he was there buying. At least the piece seemed something I took pleasure in getting for you, and finally it got mailed to you.[6]

6. In reply to Young's letter, Margaret Mitchell wrote that when the piece of red lacquer arrived, she was unable to read the return address which appeared to be "C. Young." Just before Young's letter arrived, her secretary had suggested that the "C. Young" must have been Stark Young.

I have a quite good print of Erasmus, the Holbein, for John, but haven't seen quite the frame for it. I think one I saw the other day may work out. I got the print some time ago at a sale, so don't think I was extravagant and so go bothering about me. Besides, what if I had been. I trust John had some of the kind impression of me that I have of him. He is a fine creature all through, I think. I can understand how you might come back to him again and again and never find him wanting, never go away empty in your deepest self. What a thing to know about a man, about what I'd like to count a new, solid friend for myself. Please remember me to him with every gratitude.

So far as I know the Lunts plan to do my play in the fall. Let's hope for the best in every sense. It is all still entre nous.

I met an Atlanta lady the other day more or less by chance. She naturally brought up Gone with the Wind. If you ever hear anything rotten I said about the book just try to believe that I didn't say it. I wondered afterwards—I had said nothing against it, but what did I seem to say? I mean in silences, or letting remarks pass. There was nothing else to do, unless one started a lecture, and that would be wasted. She was not especially harsh on the subject, but still—It is not worth your thinking about, except for the fact that I cannot learn the technique of how to act where talking would seem futile. I can't jump up and leave the room, especially when nothing very bad has been said. One of the elements involved is half remarks which one must either ignore or go to mat with. I am afraid you and I have been great disappointments owing to our lack of cat work mutually; for some reason many people would like us to scratch each other as authors of two books.

At any rate I enjoyed so much being with you and John, and please don't forget me.

Affectionately
Stark

548 | To Alexander Woollcott, New York

[320 East 57th Street]
[New York]
May 27, 1940

Dear Alec,

This is only a note to say that I was delighted to see by the paper that you are home again and better. I would have sent you a telegram to San Francisco but I thought it might frighten you and make you think you were on your last legs. I am one of your friends who would hate very much to see anything happen to you. Lynn and Alfred are magnificent in their new play and we can be prouder of them than ever.[7]

I hope you will be able to pay this town a visit before too long and I send you lots of love.

Yours,
Stark

549 | To Margaret Mitchell, Atlanta, Georgia

Bedford, New York
Tuesday [June 4, 1940]

Dear Margaret,

This is not a letter, I'll be writing you soon. That letter of yours was welcome and very fine and warming to my heart's cockles—! Lynn

7. On April 29, 1940, the Lunts opened at the Alvin Theatre in Robert Sherwood's *There Shall Be No Night.* Reviewing the play in "Starry Night," *New Republic,* CII (May 13, 1940), 641, Young characterized the performance of the Lunts as "fine acting, shrewd, deep and rich, too rightly felt for any falseness, and too flowing and full for any loss of line." Young found the play possessed "a genuine emotional appeal and beauty." He added: "Its humanity is basic and moving; its aspiration and spirit are high." He concluded that "this is a superb and encouraging theatre experience." The tremendous popularity of the play and the wide acclaim for the Lunts' performances, as well as those of Richard Whorf and Sydney Greenstreet, fully proved the soundness of Young's reaction.

asked me to send you the enclosed, with the request that if such was in accord with your opinion and mood, you send a telegram to President Roosevelt (or to your Congressman) that the U.S.A. act accordingly. Not to go to war, but to suspend our own preparedness for the sake of sending material aid to the Allies—whose cause, *since we must now choose between the two,* is in line with our own.

If you don't feel like doing this, then don't do it. Such is life. And nobody will know the difference. Stark is tired and too full of knowledges about Europe and the nations and our own souls!

Love to you and John.

Stark

550 | To Julian Huxley, London, England

[Bedford, New York]
June 10, 1940

Dear Julian,

I received the photograph of you and though I think it does not do you justice it nevertheless brings you vividly into the room. I have meant to write for a long time, but I have no idea what to say. This is partly because the censors might delete much of it, and partly because with the world going on as it is anything I might say could easily seem vapid and superfluous.

I have not had a picture taken for two years and have but gradually recovered from the shock of that result, though it was not so bad as some of the previous efforts to record my charms—may God help us! (For that matter, the only time I saw his face—perhaps—which reminds me of what the London cabbie said to the American tourist who was arguing about the fare: "And I'd tell you to your face, if it is your face—") Well, to go no further, I may say that I have no photograph at present but divers people are drawing me and snapping at me through one lens or another, and if any of it turns out passable at all I will send you a copy.

I have written Miss Greenwood [8] and had Mr. Courtney, the secretary, telephone two or three times and doubtless the day will come when we shall meet, plus the photograph of her drawing. But this living in the country draws me so infrequently into town and the tarnished elegance of these pre-arranged New York meetings, as much a matter of schedule as of sentiment and of punctuality as of passion, brings this all to such flatulent delay as consumes great sections of time or eternity. (As a matter of fact, that overdone sentence was put in to make you smile, in the midst of your horrors there.) So insistent a titulation of words lasts a very short while in the mind and suggests nothing very long except a moment's excuse or explanation. On the other hand I do hope, and intend, to have this picture from Miss Greenwood, despite her engagements—and I shall treasure it. I also look forward to the pleasure of meeting her.

I must tell you that no piece of 16th Century embroidery or brocade ever elicited so charming a letter as that your Juliet wrote to me—a lovely turn to the lines, a sweet and enchanting accent in the writer's quality, and a deep appreciation on my part of so rare a person as Juliet is and as her letter doubly shows her to remain. Please give her the most affectionate greetings and response from me—I wish I could see you all. How far it all seems, how lasting and yet elusive, how satisfying far down in us!

We have radio announcements constantly and we have the newspapers several times a day. To both of them of late I have been what must be human but not wholly profitable in any direction. The sentiment here in America turns steadily in the direction that you would expect—only time can tell.

I hope you have good news from Aldous and that all his family and affairs otherwise go well. At least there are certain things that he is

8. Sir Julian Huxley mentions in his *Memories* (1970), pp. 211 and 260, that during a visit to New York he met Marion Greenwood, "a charming and talented artist, who lived in the Bohemian downtown area of Greenwich Village," and that she painted a portrait of him. Young's reference is to this portrait. Known for mural painting and lithographs, Marion Greenwood (1909–70) executed commissions for the Mexican Government, the New York Housing Authority, the University of Tennessee, the United States Post Office at Crossville, Tennessee, and the University of Syracuse.

spared. I wish I could do something that might afford you pleasure. This letter is a wet bore, but it carries to you and Juliet and the boys many things deep enough that you will understand without my saying them.

Affectionately,
Stark

I have read this dull letter over. Its intentions at least are from the heart.

551 | To Agnes Bangs Morgan,[9] Paper Mill Playhouse, Millburn, New Jersey

[Bedford, New York]
June 14, 1940

Dear Agnes,

It was very nice indeed to have a line from you and I am sorry for the delay. You had the address right but the post-office mistook the "seven" for a "one," evidently. Leah Salisbury, 254 West 44 Street, is my agent, as well as being a great friend of mine, and I am sure will be glad for you to see the copy of "The Three Sisters."

I have also done "The Cherry Orchard." I hope you saw that version of "The Sea Gull" that the Lunts did. After all those good reviews of the translation when the play was produced, the book came out a year later and had more attention all over the country among literary reviewers than any translation of a play that I have heard of.

I don't think I want to do any directing myself—though you were nice to think of even the remote idea—but I should love to see one of these Chekhov plays done at your theatre.

9. Agnes Bangs Morgan, stage director and playwright, was graduated from Radcliffe College in 1901. From 1915 to 1927, she was director of the Neighborhood Playhouse and from 1927 to 1939 was associated with Actors-Managers, Incorporated, in New York. In 1940, she joined the Paper Mill Playhouse. During her career, she has written a number of plays for various theatrical groups.

Not to dwell on the subject—but I must say that I often think of you and of Miss Arthur[1] and of how much you must miss her. We have had so much death in our family and among our close connections these past years that the whole subject has become a horror for me. Such is life! I send you my good wishes for all your plans.

Affectionately,
Stark Young

552 | To Maxwell Perkins, Charles Scribner's Sons, New York

320 East 57th Street
New York
Monday [September 9, 1940]

Dearest Max,

I appreciated your note very much.[2] I meant to reply at once, but the country and town mingled have made something of a mess for me. Our nigger man left after four days' notice, four weeks ago,—no unpleasantness, just a sort of chauffeur whore job for the winter—and since he left things have been mostly transferred to town and transit.

My news is slight. The Lunts were supposed to do my play.[3] Nazimova has written asking to do my translation of *The Cherry Orchard*.[4] Such is the stage that we may figure that none of this will ever

1. Helen Arthur (1879–1939), executive director of Actors-Managers, Incorporated, had been closely associated with Agnes Morgan since 1915, when Helen Arthur left her law practice to help organize and direct the Neighborhood Playhouse. She managed the careers of such persons as Mrs. Patrick Campbell, Agna Enters, Marion Kerby, and Ruth Draper.

2. Perkins had written about Young's royalties for *So Red the Rose*, which continued to sell, and invited Young to visit him in New York.

3. Young was disappointed that the Lunts had not produced his *Belle Isle*.

4. Allah Orleney Nazimova (1879–1945), Russian-born actress of stage and screen, gained fame playing with Richard Barthelmess in *War Brides* in the Keith vaudeville circuit. In 1916, Lewis J. Selznick is said to have paid her $1,000 per day to appear in the film version of her sensational act. Afterwards, she made a number of silent movies with Charles Bryant and later became successful in the talkies. On the stage she appeared in plays by Ibsen, O'Neill, and Chekhov. In 1928, Nazimova played the role of Madame Ranevsky in Eva Le Gallienne's production of *The Cherry Orchard,* which used the translation of Constance Garnett and starred Nazimova, Eva Le Gallienne, Sayre Crawley, and Donald Cameron.

happen. I return you to Columbia Broadcasting Company, New York
—Bulova watches—that is about the level of the whole thing—and
even then the curtain rises late very often.

I hope to see you soon. Please don't drop me from your affections
and interest.

Yours
Stark

553 | To Richard L. O'Connell, Austin, Texas

[320 East 57th Street]
[New York]
Monday [September 9, 1940]

Dear Dick,

I had yours and Jimmie's [5] very nice notes of thanks for the books,
and also that set of notes on the plays.[6] This is about my first chance to
write a reply to your inquiry as to publishing etc. The notes are ex-

5. James Graham-Luján, who collaborated with Richard L. O'Connell on the translations of Federico García Lorca's plays. Born in Fuentevaqueros, Granada, in 1899, and
executed by a Fascist firing squad in 1936, Lorca was the most brilliant Spanish poet-
playwright of the century. Although he received a degree in law and philosophy from
the University of Granada, he was primarily interested in music, poetry, and drama.
His early volumes of poetry, including *Impresiones y paisajes* (1918), *Libro de poemas*
(1921), *Primeras canciones* (1922), and *Canciones* (1927), brought him critical attention and established his reputation in Spain. In 1928, he achieved the highest critical
acclaim for his *Romancero gitano*. A year later, he went to New York as a student at
Columbia University, and, before his return to Spain in 1930, he wrote his *Oda al rey
de Harlem,* which reflected the influence of the Negro spirituals he had heard in
Harlem. With the help of his friend and former teacher, Fernando de los Rios, Lorca
and Eduardo Ugarte established a traveling theatre called La Barraca which toured
Spain and later Argentina and Uruguay. Among Lorca's best-known plays are *The
Shoemaker's Prodigious Wife, The Love of Don Perlimplin, If Five Years Pass, Blood
Wedding, Yerma,* and *La casa de Bernarda Alba.*

6. During the summer of 1939, O'Connell had read with great enthusiasm the
recent Oxford University Press publication of the English translation of Federico
García Lorca's *Poems* by Stephen Spender and J. L. Gili. Upon his return to the
University of Texas, O'Connell and his colleague, James Graham-Luján, began to
translate the plays of Lorca. Unable to find a publisher for their work, they had sought
assistance from Young. The "set of notes on the plays," mentioned by Young, refers
to a three-page prospectus prepared by O'Connell and Luján.

cellent and make one wonder how any publisher could let this venture alone. So far as Scribners goes, my reading *two* pages of the MSS would count the same.[7]

I am sorry to say that I have not the mind or the time to read the translation with any intelligence. Many people would ask for them, go through the motions of having read them, etc. and that would be the usual New York thing to do. What I mean by reading them is quite another matter, and that you know well and what is meant by this remark. I should be unwilling to insult such work by the sort of reading I could give to it at present.

Our colored man, on three days' notice, left about four weeks ago. The farm since then has been blessed with only part-time service—never good—and that has made the daily physical aspect of life less accessible to human interests—though nothing very tragic. I have not had a car when Bowman was absent, and this has cramped my style in various plain respects. I had a warm nice note from Max Perkins, saying he must see me, talk, etc.; but I have not had a chance to follow that up easily—nothing seems to matter much these days in most cases —I don't care very much for that matter.[8] But what I meant about a book was simply that my recommendation of your book would count with him, which means with Scribners. Alors:

I am selfishly keeping your notes on the Lorca plays; they file well as to information sympathetically stated. But the thing to do would be for you to send me a simple statement of what you want of a publisher, the book or books you mean to do. (You might include a quote from the Oxford Press as to its interest or its experience with Lorca.) I will show this to Perkins, with regard to Scribners and publishing. I feel pretty sure they would not think of any plans for this fall, however, such things have been settled a month or two ago. I doubt if they would make any advance at all. The publication of the book is another matter; I would do my best for such an enterprise. But you should state the exact plan—the number of volumes, or the size of the

7. As the subsequent correspondence shows, Young's recommendation "counted" with Maxwell Perkins, and in the fall of 1941, Charles Scribner's Sons published *From Lorca's Theatre: Five Plays of Federico García Lorca,* in the authorized translation by Richard L. O'Connell and James Graham-Luján, with a foreword by Stark Young.

8. The statement reflects Young's intense disappointment at the failure of the Lunts to produce his play, *Belle Isle*.

one volume etc. One volume is more persuasive so far as a publisher goes. If your page of statement interests Perkins enough, he would ask you to come and talk it over with him.

Fortunately you have met him etc. and he will have a personal connection to go on—so much for your visit at his house last summer.

I think, then—to sum matters up—that there is a very definite chance for a Lorca volume. But not right off. It might be arranged for the spring. Publishers don't just throw books off into the air. Time is needed to lay the ground, and so on. If I had seen you in the spring we might have got something for the autumn. But of course the work had not been done then. In my opinion the work you and Jimmie have done is most unusual and important. And on an important subject—just now in history especially. (I should not expect the Oxford Press to know that too well.)—(*Entre nous.*)

As I see the matter, there is no hurry then. At your leisure get the page ready, stating your plans. I will convey it at once to Perkins. He seems to be your best bet at present. The publishers, like the theatre producers, are up a tree—But Scribners wants something distinguished, and that's that. A part of which is merely the racket's requirement today—

I must close. Give my love to the family. I regret your trouble about the telegram. It was a week old when I received it.

Love to you.

Stark

554 | To Lawton Campbell, New York

[Bedford, New York]
Monday [September 16, 1940]

Dear Lawton,

I suppose Wales told you again of how much Mr. Badham[9] inconvenienced us by the sudden announcement of his departure, the following Sunday at that! For a winter job! So he said.

9. Perhaps a pun upon the name of the man employed by Young and Bowman to help with their country house.

As I told you on the telephone I am not asking you to do anything crooked as regards to the letter.[1] It is just that I saw when I quoted John Anderson's highly enthusiastic opinion of the play, she took it more or less as an answer to Noel.[2] Noel himself meanwhile *remains the author of his works*—and his reading of the play consisted of the ACT I, earlier version with many stage-directions, of it. And he got no further and was taking the clipper next morning to die for Britain. (For the death, you may have noted, he has now re-edited the locale.) He will die for Britain in Hollywood or at the St. Regis—in the midst of the well-known people he has known well—like Napoleon by the Seine via St. Helena. If I enclose the letter from you, when I send in that copy of the revisions you and I were talking about, the effect may be less combative or repetitive.

I had a sweet note from Lynn F, written to the country Friday. So in sending her your letter, the date to me would better seem Friday, so that I don't seem to be forwarding an argument or debate to her. THURSDAY might be even BETTER.

I am not doing this entirely for myself. Lynn adored the play in its fairly complete form—when they were in Los Angeles—wired me to come—then evidently the Sherwood piece came up—they used their unfortunate caginess and said they were sworn to secrecy—why?[3]

1. Throughout the summer of 1940, Young, helped by his friend Lawton Campbell, polished the romantic comedy *Belle Isle* to make it appeal to the Lunts as an ideal vehicle for their talents. As he wrote this letter, however, Young was beginning to believe that the Lunts had lost some of their earlier enthusiasm for his comedy. In particular, Young feared that Noel Coward's remarks about the play, made after only a very cursory reading of the first act, had unduly influenced Lynn Fontanne's judgment. The Lunts had a financial interest in Transatlantic Productions, the English company which they had formed with Noel Coward in 1933. Hoping to diminish the impact of Coward's criticism, Young asked Campbell to support the play in a letter, addressed to Young, which he, in turn, could send to Lynn Fontanne. In an enclosure, Young went so far as to suggest several points which he would like for Campbell to emphasize.

2. Noel Coward (1899–1973), British playwright and actor, came to the United States on April 29, 1940, presumably to report to the British government on the likelihood of American intervention in World War II. His visits to the New York World's Fair, the Lincoln Memorial at Washington, Chicago, and Hollywood were subjects for considerable comment in newspapers both here and in England which Young's remarks reflect. Upon his return to London, Coward was fined for violating Britain's finance laws. To raise money for the Red Cross, Coward visited Australia, where he wrote a book, *Australia Visited, 1940*. In August, 1941, his new comedy, *Blithe Spirit*, opened in London. Coward wrote a number of highly successful plays, including *Sirocco, Bitter Sweet, Private Lives, Cavalcade, To-night at 8:30, Present Laughter*, and *Peace in Our Time*.

3. For an account of the Lunts' reaction to *Belle Isle* in California, see above, Letter 544, n. 1. Young hoped that the Lunts would produce his play in the spring of 1940;

They had not said they would do my play in the fall—as Lynn reminded me. They would do it this fall, she then said. So why the
caginess? On the other hand, with things as they are, they are right to
go on with this Sherwood play—especially since Lynn has got herself
to think it excellent and Alfred has begun to like this solemn self-
abuse that he was at first afraid of in The Sea Gull. Now he finds it is
less work really to be serious and deep and rightly platitudinous. That
takes less physical exertion, less dieting, less exertion, less everything
but timeliness and fuddled audiences plus serious gaps in any approach
in our stage's approach to the present·crisis in the world. What a thing
it is when a playwright of Bob Sherwood's depth and capacity has to
be the spokesman of all that should arise in this moment's American
soul! (An actor of course can never tell applause for himself from
historical rigor and row and applicability and banality and spirit in a
better sense.)

Lynn in Los Angeles told me she thought the play surefire, and she
said that "with modesty" she had shown herself "a good picker," and
so wonderful that it should be worked at till it got to the "little girl at
Gimbel's" as well as at the choice people in the audience. That I know
is true and proper aesthetic principle, I agree. I agree doubly when I
remember that Lynn thinks a choice audience must be something like
that first-night crowd at the Guild [4]—Pirandello [5] told me he thought

---

and during December, 1939, January, and into February, 1940, he traveled with them,
constantly polishing and revising the play. Suddenly, however, the Lunts postponed
Young's play and decided to produced instead Robert Sherwood's *There Shall Be No
Night*. They were probably influenced by their liking for the play and their enthusiasm
for raising funds in behalf of Finnish war relief. The leading character in *There Shall
Be No Night* is a Finnish scientist. On April 29, the Lunts opened in the Sherwood
play. At once it became a smash hit. During the summer of 1940, however, the Lunts
continued to talk with Young about *Belle Isle;* and, as this letter indicates, he was
greatly surprised to read in the New York *Times,* July 9, that the Lunts planned to
take the Sherwood play on a road tour after the close of its Broadway run on November 2, 1940. Young's disappointment and fading hopes for his play lie behind his appeal
to Campbell for help. The Lunts took *There Shall Be No Night* on the road, and before the tour ended in December, 1941, they had traveled thousands of miles and given
hundreds of performances of it. In May, 1941, the play was awarded the Pulitzer
Prize for the best play of 1940. For Young's review of the work, see above, Letter
548, n. 7.

4. Since 1924, the Lunts had been associated with the Guild Theatre.
5. Luigi Pirandello (1867–1936), Italian novelist and dramatist, whose work Young
greatly admired. In 1934, Pirandello had been awarded the Nobel Prize for Literature.
Among his best known plays are *Se non cosi, Sei personaggi in cerca d'autore, Vestire
gli ignudi* (translated by Stark Young), *L'Amica della mogli,* and *Non si sa come,*

they were the most horrible audience he had ever seen! Amour propre would lead her toward that thought. For one thing.

I have a certain tender feeling of wanting to give her support and to get it for her from people who might count. She had kept Alfred from seeing the script till it had nearly got itself completed, she was thrilled that he liked it. And she has helped me greatly on it. On the other hand, their method of caginess has to [be] met somehow and I am not going to keep in this business much longer as to the play. In our sitting-room Lynn says to me "this part I'm going to do—" she means it and wants to. In the kitchen Alfred says to Wales that one thing is certain and that is he won't go on any more tours—and a week later the Times announces that Finnish tour.[6] What is one to make of that? Not deception, no, no, just a method they have evolved, and a process that would be most uncomfortable for any single person but is more comfortable when there is a partner to share it with and talk it over, especially a partner like Lynn who shares his opinions, has a stronger will, and is still sexually in love with him, and—ultimately—intelligent enough to know that [to] keep the relationship right—and erect —is more important than any issue in theatre, drama or what not— especially these days.

In your letter please rub in the Hollywood chances—

It is really a sincere remark when I say that I want Lynn to come off well in this matter of opinion of the play. She lets her hair down once in a while—just as it turns grey again on her once in a while— and on one of those occasions she told me not to think she did not know the bad taste in "Idiot's Delight," the lapses in quality, the commonness at those moments, etc. It took fifteen weeks for them to get the performance and the lines to where the audience could see that the woman was a fake Russian. And then later Bob Sherwood admitted that he had propounded her first as a Russian so as to provide a bait for Lynn to urge acceptance of the play—in which the *shine was really for Alfred's* role. If one thought it shining.

That was a sweet evening at your house, tell your mother that too! Warm, human, Southern, helpful in one's art too! Much beloved of me. I have asked little help in my art ever, partly because the way we are brought up down South in the British country tradition one is

6. See above, note 3.

nervous about being in art, and partly because in time one's sense tells one that few indeed can help at all ever, however kind, interested, officious, or egotistical their intentions. And so thank you again.

I am sending the books, since you said you wanted them. Most of them were for my nephew. There are times when I think life was kind to him, taking him away in all the midst of that vitality, mind, sweet glamor of life, faith in people, flower in response. But it is not fair to him to say that—he felt a full, strong front and male acceptance of all human issues, passions and intellectual marriages of thought and fire and inspiration. And that's that.

This letter of yours may be of real use to Lynn as well as to the play. I want her to think of you as a person of importance, not as a mere friend of mine. She tried—though she never got it done quite—to slide around John Anderson's enthusiasm that way. But that of course was just before Noel sailed to die for Britain.

Thanks, and love to you all.

Stark

555 | To Leah Salisbury, New York

[320 East 57th Street]
[New York]
[October 7, 1940]

Dear Leah,

If you will go over this,[7] with suggestions and send it to me, I will copy it and get it to Lynn before they sit down to their dinner alone, as every night.

Thank you for being so nice yesterday. You certainly did a wonderful thing for Doris.[8]

Love to you,
Stark

7. Young enclosed a draft of a letter to Lynn Fontanne dealing with his *Belle Isle*. Since the draft remained in Leah Salisbury's files, she may have advised against sending it.
8. Probably Doris Keane.

I have at once notified Mercedes that it is not an adaptation.[9]

[Enclosure]
Dearest Lynn:

I have been away again, at Hyde Park and on the farm,[1] came back Saturday night.

I am writing to ask you to help me now, as you have so often before.

We both understand the case and have talked about it so now instead of going to the theatre and engaging you with talking it all over again, I feel that it is more considerate and too, easier for me—to write you this request:

If you and Alfred will only tell me that you will do the play—tell me again now as you have before—but so that it expresses the way you both feel—I am entirely willing to wait so long as you want me to. (You know already how profoundly I wish it done by you.) But somehow I need to have again a gesture—almost a literal expression from you both—that will end this occasional fear that possesses me that you just might be wanting to let me down—and being your gentle selves not know quite how to do it.[2]

Lynn dear—I will wait so long as you want me to—because I wrote it for you and Alfred and I can take no delight in thinking of anyone else in the parts—but suddenly I realize that this unrest—this nervous detachment of the past months is something I can lose only by some clear statement from you. So I put myself in your [hands].

I need not remind you what beautiful, deep and fruitful things I had out of working on the play with you.

9. Young refers to Mercedes de Acosta and his translation of Chekhov's *The Cherry Orchard*.

1. Young had recently visited President Roosevelt at Hyde Park and returned to the Young-Bowman summer home near Bedford, New York. See below, Letter 556.

2. The sentence recalls Young's remarks in Letter 554.

556 | To Pauline Goldmann, Austin, Texas

320 East 57th Street
New York
Monday [October 28, 1940]

Dearest Cousin,

You were a dear to remember so happily my birthday[3] and so generously putting in almost as many pickles as I now have years. So much more delicious than candles—another reason I never fell in love with an Eskimo maiden! I ate one jar right off, with no fatalities, and the others are here in our new apartment, 10 E.[4] The painters' strike, then the Jewish holiday and then various other matters have made moving and October a horror, and that combined with the fact that Bowman had to be away week-ends to direct certain jobs of buildings, and I could not go to the villa in the country. Now the season has reached almost the November cold days.

Did my sister tell you what a delight the President took in Bowman's designs for a house up there at Hyde Park, for a friend of the President's, near his dream cottage, on land she had bought from him.[5] Not a scandal at all, just friends and the President's delight in architecture, about which he knows a great deal and for which he has a fine talent, several times expressed in buildings.

I have some books put aside and will express them down to you soon.

Love to you all, I hope all keep well, and if not well at least delightfully disagreeable, that is almost most [*sic*] as enjoyable as invalidism. I think you yourself have done so very well in your teaching positions—in fact that little Pauline is pretty fine. (Well, not my fault!)

---

3. October 11.

4. Formerly Young and William M. Bowman occupied separate apartments in the same building. Young's reference is to their decision to move into a single apartment which they shared until Young died in 1963. Having now less space for his books, Young gave a number of them to friends.

5. Bowman was designing plans for Dorothy Schiff (then Mrs. George Backer, b. 1903), publisher, vice-president, and treasurer of the New York *Post*. Later, she became publisher and owner of the *Post*. In 1953, she married Rudolf Sonneborn.

Give Cousin Mamie all words of fine messages and when you write Mary tell her my greetings etc.

Affectionately
Stark

557 | To Richard L. O'Connell, Austin, Texas

[320 East 57th Street]
[New York]
Friday [November 15, 1940]

Dear Dick,

I believe this note carries good news to you, and to a considerable extent releases you from having to bother with considering the negotiation of affairs through me, I mean in regard to that Lorca book.

I saw Max Perkins finally, and had a long talk with him. I told him what a distinction this Lorca work of yours and Jimmie's would be to Scribners', etc.

His first reaction was in a vein characteristically intelligent—the more so the more I think of the matter. He said he thought a single volume would be wrong. That the plays were automatically separate from the poems, etc. He had known, too, of the volume of translations by R. Humphries.[6] A flop.

Your opportunity, then, stands thus: (and you are very lucky to have even that opportunity just now, these days) I imagine Scribners would really CONSIDER the publication of all Lorca's plays in a single volume—ONE volume—

If that goes well at all—EVEN FAIRLY—well, there would then be a good chance to publish the poetry book, as Volume II—Perkins has sense enough to mistrust all translation of poetry whatever. (To me the chances are that people who think they have translated a poem

---

6. Young refers to *The Poet in New York and Other Poems of Federico García Lorca*, translated by Rolfe Humphries (1940).

either do not see the point in what they have read or else in what they have written . . . there are exceptions perhaps.)

The next step would be to send Maxwell E. Perkins, Charles Scribner's Sons, 598 Fifth Avenue the complete MS of the plays. If that is not ready, you had best write him as to when he may expect that MS. I am afraid I may have erred in leading him to think it was ready now. Perhaps it is.[7]

So far as my part in it all goes, you need not thank me at all. I can never forget my indebtedness to you for many fine and elevated moments there in Austin, things for which there are no thanks and no compensation outside the mind of the other person involved. It is a privilege and a pleasure, also, to be of any service possible to such work as you and Jimmie have done on such an author. Forget me, please, and put your energies on that Spanish source, much more worthy of your attention.

I have a very strong expectation that Perkins on my urgency will publish the volume of plays. I am sure that should that arrive you may count yourself a most fortunate writer just now, conditions being what they are.

I regret to say I let the prospectus form—that first part as separate from the play list—get into Perkins' hands. It was combined with the other, and I failed to remember that fact till after I left him. But since I had urged the plays—after he had made that point about the error of putting the whole stuff into a single volume—as a venture, I think the volume of plays has a good chance to come off.

*

NB   It is possible that in a few footnotes you could indicate the main facts important to each individual play.

About the last service I can be to you with respect to this Lorca venture is to say that I trust I did not give Scribners a false impression as to the play translations' being already completed. My advice is, in case these translations are not completed, that you rush them forward, dropping everything else—PROVIDED, that is, Max Perkins writes you in an encouraging manner. The thing to do is to send whatever

7. O'Connell replied immediately to Young that the plays would be completely ready to send Perkins within the next three weeks, probably in two weeks. Four of the five plays to be published were "completely ready now."

plays are ALREADY translated. OR EVEN BETTER, TO WRITE HIM AND SAY THAT YOU WILL SEND THE WHOLE SET OF PLAYS***TUTTA OPERA SUA***SOON etc.

I have told you and told Perkins all I can say in this whole matter— I have no will or life left to do more, especially since nobody but the publisher and the authors can do more, and I can only hope that I have been of real use where use, these days, is needed. A few seasons ago all this would have been different.

Please give my love to everybody.

Stark

Sorry this letter is so repetitive and mussy, but I have so much on hand.

558 | To Julia Young Robertson, Austin, Texas

[320 East 57th Street]
[New York]
Wednesday [November 27, 1940]

Dear Sister,

Since writing you I have been in Cornell[8] and what not—so— When I wrote the apartment house carpenter was here making some

8. On November 16, 1940, Young went to Cornell University to see the Michael Chekhov Theatre Studio players' performance of *Twelfth Night* at the Willard Straight Theatre. The Chekhov Theatre Studio had been founded in 1936 at Dartington Hall, in Devon, England, under the sponsorship of Dorothy Straight Elmhirst and her husband Leonard K. Elmhirst. Michael Chekhov (1891–1955), nephew of the dramatist and cofounder in 1911 of the First Studio of the Moscow Art Theatre and founder in 1923 of the Second Moscow Art Theatre, was selected to direct the organization. In 1939, the studio was moved to Ridgefield, Connecticut. The occasion of the group's visit to Cornell was the fifteenth anniversary of the opening of Willard Straight Hall, given by Willard Straight's widow, Mrs. Elmhirst, for many years a friend of Young. Beatrice Straight, Willard Straight's daughter, played the role of Viola. Members of the Elmhirst and Straight families were honored at a reception held the following day. On November 19, in New York, Young saw the Theatre Guild production of *Twelfth Night* which starred Maurice Evans and Helen Hayes. In his review, "Or What You Will," *New Republic,* CIII (December 2, 1940), 755–56, Young preferred the youthful enthusiasm and overall concept of the play as presented by the Chekhov company to the "banal, unromantic and pedestrian" performance of the veterans.

bookcases for the windows and all was confusion, I wrote you and .
Allen Tate—that was Friday—but think the letters were confused by
Lucille[9] into the pile of trash that was going out—papers of all kinds.
There has been a very genuine clearing since Wales and I have so
much less room. (I think, since Allen has not yet replied—from Princeton, an hour away, about getting some books, out of here, that the letters probably never got off at all—it would be a miracle if they had
done so in all this hurly burly.)

If, therefore, in this letter and the next, I should happen to repeat,
you will kindly make allowances. I am not drinking these days,
though I must confess to being stupider than usual even—everybody
is wondering where he is, and no denying the fact.

One thing—tomorrow is Thanksgiving—Wales and I dine with
Lawton Campbell's family—in the country nearby. Sad memories, but
what can be done?

The Lunts on my request sent the MSS back on their departure.[1]
The play is no good for anybody else, so much is their quality etc.
woven into the scenes. But perhaps they will do it some day. They had
said they would do it this autumn, but there is no poking at them
when all the world is so disturbed with the war, and Lynn is half
crazy with it, and who could blame her? That is my personal bad luck
from the war and nobody can say anything about that.

Things go not at all for me, bad or good, since nothing goes anyhow
just now. So I make no complaint. I hope to manage Christmas there
with you and Ben and then back here in NYC. Quietly. Wales has
some openings, but he does not know yet what will happen about any
job involved.

I sent some boxes of books the other day, please put them by—some
are for other people when I get there. The box marked W was for
Professor Wharey[2] but none of that is important.

In one box I put a lamp from Hill's, for little Sue[3]—in case you and

9. The cleaning woman.
1. Early in November, the Lunts left New York to take *There Shall Be No Night*
on tour. From Pittsburgh, November 12, 1940, Alfred Lunt sent a telegram to Young
urging him to offer *Belle Isle* to Katharine Cornell.
2. While teaching at the University of Texas, Young had known James Blanton
Wharey (1872–1946) as a colleague in the English department.
3. Probably Julia Young Robertson's niece, the daughter of Susan and Zeno Ross.

Ben think she would like it. It seemed to me quite effective. That coloring inside the vase is by the designer, not by me, to cut the light to a softer value. I also put in a box with a flower spray brooch and a bracelet—they were bought a good many months ago at a sale. They are for Alice [4] to be given as you think best and most impressive. They were from one dollar to three at the sale when I bought them. Long ago. If you think the spray would be good, present that. Or whatever you think. Both, or either one.

I may have told you in the last letter—if it got posted at all—that Charlie Chaplin is in town again. He was here for the opening of the Dictator film, with Goddard,[5] then went back to California, then is here at The River Club.[6] I saw Constance Collier [7] at the theatre and she said that he was always talking about me and could not understand why I did not call him up—would I come to her house when he was coming, etc., so I went, he ate me up—so much so that they finally just gave us seats together—then he brought me home, and said we were to have an evening this week etc. Also that if I got tired of NYC why not come out there and have a guest house of his and stay as long a time, the rest of my life if I liked, as might be. So we go. He is a marvellous being at that—poor high-strung devil—he mentioned Stark's death three times in that short while—said he wished he might

4. The Robertsons' maid.

5. Charlie Chaplin's finest film, *The Great Dictator,* in which he played the dual role of the appealing tramp in baggy pants and the bombastic Führer, opened on October 15, 1940, at the Astor and Capitol theatres in New York. Paulette Goddard (b. 1911), his third wife, played with Chaplin in *Modern Times* and *The Great Dictator.* For Chaplin's own account of the filming of *The Great Dictator* and its reception, see *My Autobiography* (1964), pp. 398–400. Two days after Young wrote this letter, a writer for the New York *Times* asserted that "Paulette Goddard of the films disclosed publicly today that she was the wife of Charles Chaplin. . . . He introduced her a few weeks ago from a New York stage [at the opening of *The Great Dictator*] as 'my wife.' " See New York *Times,* November 29, 1940, p. 24.

6. An apartment house on the East River at 52nd Street.

7. Constance Collier, stage name of Laura Constance Hardie (1880–1955), English actress and drama coach, first gained prominence near the turn of the century in London. Taught by Sir Herbert Beerbohm Tree and Eva Le Gallienne, Constance Collier became one of the leading Shakespearean actresses of the 1920s and 1930s, and she also achieved great success in such plays as Somerset Maugham's *Our Betters,* S. N. Behrman's dramatization of *Serena Blandish,* and Edna Ferber's and George S. Kaufman's *Dinner at Eight.* She appeared in a number of motion pictures with Greta Garbo, Katharine Hepburn, Fred Astaire, and Paulette Goddard. In 1929, she published *Harlequinade: The Story of My Life.*

help me. Sometimes I almost think I amount to something—I do when a man like that says all that—there is nobody else in our time or for a long stretch of years on the same plane with that genius that Charlie Chaplin is. Fortunately we are all equal and the ass is as good as the rider—so does Plato speak of a democracy.

I had a sweet letter this morning from Miss Hallie.[8] All of thanks for a book. What lovely people they are!

As to you and Ben in voting for Wilkie, more anon. The newspapers did a job for him, through the control of the advertising. They are all furious in Wall Street because they expect or hoped to make millions from this European war trouble, as they did before. The last thing the Rep. party really wants is Wilkie, they are worried by him. That endorser of his Kenneth Simpson[9] I have known for about fifteen years, and have seen him several times when he was not too drunk to talk, a bright phoney fellow. Wilkie is honest I think however in his own style. The papers fixed it all up in a handsome vein. If there had not been the radio Roosevelt might have had a harder contest. The same was true of Landon—the votes were almost the same in Landon's case as in R's, though I did not know that till lately.[1] The Times had an editorial, most instructive, about changing the electoral system.[2] Wilkie's connections with industrial kings, slugging, etc., tear gas, spies, etc., would not stay hidden, though he is a good enough man himself I imagine. But the newspapers buttered it all over very nicely. At that, he missed. Who knows when the war will end, so there is no knowing anything. I often wonder what I could do that would be of genuine use to the world—nobody can tell us anything. Europe is much more wrecked than we could guess from the controlled press reports coming

8. The reference is to Mrs. Hale Houston.

9. Kenneth F. Simpson (1895–1941), Republican representative from New York, active in politics in the Republican party since 1922, became congressman in 1940 shortly before his death.

1. Although Franklin D. Roosevelt's total popular votes in 1936 against Alfred Landon and in 1940 against Wendell Wilkie were very close (27,751,597 and 27,243,466), Roosevelt defeated Landon by almost 11 million votes and Wilkie by only 5 million (16,679,583 and 22,304,755).

2. Although the New York *Times* had recently printed several editorials dealing with the electoral system, Young probably refers to an editorial that denounced the electoral college and called for reform; see "Electoral vs. Popular Vote," New York *Times,* November 5, 1940, p. 24.

often via London. No matter what happens finally there the ruin on all sides.

Well, that is that.

Lovingly
Stark

I sent Niles [3] some first editions, and some books to Villie.[4]

559 | To Caroline Charlotte McGehee, Como, Mississippi

320 East 57th Street
New York
Saturday [November 30, 1940]

Dearest Cousin Caroline,

You will see the enclosed letter to Mr. Bailey[5]—I think you said Chester Bailey—that was months ago and if I am wrong you can explain it all gracefully, I am sure. My financial affairs get neither better nor worse, nobody knows up here what will happen about money etc., so I may as well put the monument now. Bless Aunt Sarah's heart, she if anybody did, deserves it all, and I am not of much importance in this world just now. Who is?

If Mr. Bailey could start matters at once, we should see what we should see. I want the same marble for the top slab as in Auntie's, the same deep concrete foundations. You know all about all that. Tell him to pull his thoughts together and write me at once.

3. Niles Graham, friend of the Robertsons in Austin.

4. Ernest Joseph Villavaso (1874–1971), Professor Emeritus of Romance Languages at the University of Texas, received his B.A. from Tulane University in 1894 and his M.A. degree in 1896.

5. As the context of this letter suggests, Young had been negotiating with Chester Bailey of Como, Mississippi, about the erection of a gravestone for Sarah Gilbert Starks, Young's beloved aunt, who had died April 19, 1939. A flat, marble monument was eventually placed parallel to that of Frances Scott Starks, her sister. In the space between, William M. Bowman placed a matching monument for Young after his death in 1963.

What do you think—my sister and Ben voted for Wilkie—much money was spent making the newspapers paint him as the people's boy—his friends are all among the rich—I know many of them quite well—and he has never been a business executive in any real sense, he has merely represented the big boys. They are raging at the election of Roosevelt—they had been hoping that as in the last war—when a thousand NEW millionaires were created through the profits—that they were going to clean up. What a joke on them! They were bursting with rage. I was at a supper while the election reports were coming in. They were black with despair over it all. The supper etc. meanwhile cost several thousand. These Yankees make me laugh. One of them said that he thought the FDR administration was too much interested in AGRICULTURE. He never thinks there is anything beyond a bit of paper and bond juggling. One told me that night that his firm had picked up—that was a trifle too—a million dollars on Chinese dollar exchange. Well, Cousin Stark eats their caviar, and thinks their invitation to revolution is frightening.

I hope you are all right. Please give my love to Cousin Wheeler and her house, she is a saint. Kiss Cousin Annie for me.

Lovingly
Stark

560 | To Ruth Ford,[6] New York

[320 East 57th Street]
[New York]
[Winter, 1940–41]

Dear Ruth,

For the first time this winter I have almost started a cold, but have been in today and careful yesterday, with fair medications and so on,

6. Ruth Ford, actress, born in Hazlehurst, Mississippi, received her bachelor of arts degree from the University of Mississippi in May, 1932, and returned to the University of Mississippi during the following academic year to take graduate work in philosophy and history. After holding several jobs in New York, she made her Broadway debut

and the devil take it. But it is not time to bring even that much cold to the mother—lovely new friend, new friend and valued—of Cather, Dylon, Sedge, Lucius, Bobo, Toto, Upton, Sandro, Chico, Michael, Ambrose, Alexander, Julian, Urban, Borgia, Cesare, Greco, Licheff, Parian, Gorgias, Phaon, Charmides, Leon, Hymnis, Limon, or whatever name will sweeten his little divinity.

In a few days I hope to be hale again, I want you all to come and see me. Lucille, the maid, said you called and asked me to come over Tuesday, she said I had people, etc. By a fluke I did—though they meant well. I was sorry not to be in two places at once like the holy Apostles.[7]

I got a box from a country town in Mexico today, mere loving nothings, I send some over to you. Those handkerchiefs last forever and AFTER THE SIZING is washed out are really lovely.

I hope to see you Monday or Tuesday.

Love to you both—I hope your mother is well, remember me to her as becomingly as you and she decide to make a Southern author sound. I enjoyed very much seeing Mr. Tt–ff [8]—I'd be sure to misspell it.

Yours

S.Y.

---

early in 1938 as Jane in the Orson Welles production of *The Shoemaker's Holiday;* and subsequently she has appeared in a number of successful plays, notably as Deborah Pomfret in *Clutterbuck* and Temple Drake in *Requiem for a Nun.* She married Peter Van Eyck (1913–69), song writer. She explains the circumstances of this letter in the following comments: "I met Stark Young at a party given by Mr. and Mrs. Eustace Seligman the later part of 1940 or early 1941; I was pregnant. Stark Young and I became immediate friends and that friendship lasted until his death. I hadn't set on any name for the baby and I asked him to help me name it. And all of the names in this letter are the names he suggested. At this time we had all assumed that the baby was going to be a boy." The baby, born early in 1941, was a girl; she was named Shelley. After Ruth Ford's marriage to Peter Van Eyck was dissolved, she married Zachary Scott in 1952.

7. See above, Letter 537, n. 2.

8. Young refers to Pavel Tchelitchew (1898–1957), Russian-born painter and scene designer. In 1918, he was forced to leave Russia with his family. After designing sets for a traveling Russian theatre, he opened a painting studio in Paris. Encouraged by Gertrude Stein, Tchelitchew exhibited his paintings in Paris, London, and New York. In 1934, he came to the United States and in 1952 became a citizen. Among his friends were Edith Sitwell, Cecil Beaton, and Ruth and Charles Henri Ford. Young wrote a review of Tchelitchew's retrospective exhibition at the Museum of Modern Art in "Metamorphoses," *New Republic,* CVII (November 16, 1942), 640–41; and Edith Sitwell included a chapter about him in her autobiography, *Taken Care Of* (1965).

561 | To Pauline Goldmann, Austin, Texas

320 East 57th Street
New York
Sunday [March 16, 1941]

Dear little Cousin Pauline,

I am sending the check for you to fill in and pay for the flowers.[9] My sister wrote that they were very beautiful indeed, but they sounded like a huge bouquet, so perhaps the five dollars is not enough. You can fill in the check.

I am mailing you too a book by Ellen Glasgow,[1] a copy she sent me —I have another—but think you will prefer this one. It appears March 29. The manner at the start is a bit old-fashioned but the book as a whole is a solid fine book full of a sense of life and values. I went to Richmond to see her the other day, she is shut up in her room with her heart—almost died this past summer, on two occasions. She is far in the sixties, but a marvel of life.

I am sorry to hear that Cousin Mamie has had such a hard time. I hope she [is] about well by now. I am sure you and Mary have been very lovely to her, she is indeed fortunate to have such daughters, though she deserves them of course. Love to all three.

Lovingly
Stark

9. Each year, Young sent flowers to his sister on March 3, the birthday of his nephew, Stark Young Robertson.
1. *In This Our Life.*

562 | To Malcolm Cowley, New York

320 East 57th Street
New York
Monday [March 17, 1941]

Dear Malcolm,

I have been meaning to write you about Miss Glasgow's new novel, which I am told you have for reviewing.[2] I have read it, she sent me a copy from her sickbed. The surface manner is a bit old-style now, but the book grows with reading and is a solid piece of work. How she got it done with her age and her heart threatening to bring her to death's door at any time, and twice this year has all but done so, is a wonder to me. She is going on toward seventy, and what vitality and force remains for this book!

I am writing to ask you, if it does not disturb your conscience, not to dash it aside and then take it for a "Southern" novel. There is nothing Southern about it, merely some town somewhere and no matter. The subject deals with people and destiny and characters etc. All the people in it have been clearly seen, and the basis of the whole has something in it solid about life. I am telling you this in the hope you can turn something out that will not break her back, for this her last, very last, novel.[3]

I am sure you will know how I mean it and won't take this for an intrusion. After all, we are very old friends by now.

2. During a recent visit to Ellen Glasgow, Young had agreed to attempt to get her new novel, *In This Our Life,* into the hands of a sympathetic reviewer for the *New Republic*. At the offices of the *New Republic,* he learned that the book had already been assigned to Malcolm Cowley for review.

3. Cowley reviewed the book in "Miss Glasgow's 'Purgatorio,'" *New Republic,* CIV (March 31, 1941), 441–42. Although Cowley began by writing "I have managed for the last fifteen years not to read any novels by Ellen Glasgow," his comments were generally favorable. According to Cowley, she presented "a whole world in limbo, the helplessness of people engaged without guidance in a search for individual happiness" in a novel that was "neither parochial nor old-fashioned." He concluded by saying, "One feels, however, that she has chosen rather decorous incidents and commonplace people to express her vision of despair and utter chaos. Though her purgatory is real, not much happens there; and it is as if we peeped out at it from behind the curtains of a Richmond parlor."

I was glad to see you the other day and looking so well, and so elegantly turned out—oh, authors of wealth!!

Love to you and your lady.

Yours
Stark

I hear Caroline Gordon thinks very highly of the novel.

563 | To Richard L. O'Connell, Fort Niagara, New York

[320 East 57th Street]
[New York]
[ca. April 10, 1941]

Dear Dick,

I have thought of you often and wished I might have a talk with you, though I should be too tired and dull and finished up to be of any interest or brains for anybody. I meant that when I declined the invitation to lunch. I had no intention that you should think of never writing again at all. Jimmie, however, dropped in, and gave me your news. I hope the army experience proves not too bad.[4] It might even turn out a blessing in disguise. Everybody is at a loss these days which way to turn anyhow.

I had already intimated to Max Perkins that I could do something at the first of the Lorca volume; but since it was not absolutely certain I did not tell Jimmie about it. Thinking it over, I went on and said in the note to him that I would do something about this.

I am writing you to say that I have seen Max Perkins and talked the matter over in some detail. You are very fortunate to get such a book published just now, the publishers are in a somewhat desperate state of mind. Max is really pleased over this volume, and is sending me the proofs. I will look through enough to feel better grounded for my as-

---

4. On March 14, 1941, O'Connell had been inducted into the army and sent to Fort Niagara, New York.

sertions. I feel sure, though, that it is beautifully done—I told Max that.

I am writing this to you and you hand it on to Jimmie. It would be best if you and he made a list of a few points you think might be stressed about the contents of the volume. That would save trouble all around and might get a better result. Also a copy of my article on the Lorca play at the Neighborhood[5] would be useful, indeed. I have not one on hand.

I am enclosing Jimmie's letter for the titles he suggests.[6] As business titles or even bookshop titles they do not seem to me good or promising. Max Perkins has quite a sense of that. Their poetic connotations are good, once we know what passages, etc. they refer to. You will doubtless find some fine title in Lorca.

I have told Max Perkins that I will try to see that something is done about the book in TAM and NR. That ought to help some. All this is a pleasure to do, though my store of energy does not rush to it or anything at present. But I hope it helps. I remember your great kindness in Texas, and can never repay it of course.

I found from D. Wolf that I was close to uremic poisioning, which is indeed a malady—it seems escaped after injections, etc.—and it tended to brainstorms of words and excitement of that type. I regret ever inflicting any of that on anyone. Meanwhile I realize more and more that while I frequently regret not being all I should be to other people, considerate or imaginative and helpful, and while I say so, it is rare indeed that I am able to hear from others that they are in any way wrong. Only lately for example, I regretted deeply being about twenty-five minutes late to dinner, and I was allowed to sweat for it. These same people are always late from half an hour to an hour with me, but that aspect of the matter never came up. Just the same I wish I were always as decent and considerate as in my inside I should like to be. Basta. Now that a uremic stroke seems averted, I may improve.

I had the enclosed paper[7] sent me some weeks back and thought I had sent it to you, but it turned up in the file, so I am sending it now.

5. Young refers to his review of Lorca's *Bitter Oleander,* produced at the Lyceum Theatre, February 11, 1935; see "Spanish Plays," *New Republic,* LXXXII (February 27, 1935), 78.

6. Luján had sent Young a page and a half of tentative titles for the translation.

7. Young enclosed a copy of Edouard Roditi's "Why and How Lorca Is Translated," *View,* I (October, 1940), 2, 6.

If you glean a note from it that might be good in my foreword, let me know.

I shall perhaps see the proofs soon of your book.

I saw Lincoln Kirstein at Martha Graham's event[8]—a triumph for her it was—he wants to come over next week—something of importance he said—no more than that.

I hope your family all keep well, and that you are finding your present life interesting—what a change it represents in one's plain habits of the day!

Love to you,
Stark

564 | To Lawton Campbell, New York

320 East 57th Street
New York
Monday [April 14, 1941]

Dear Lawton,

I looked through the play[9] today and decided that in its present state so much of it implies Alfred's participation that it would have to be thoroughly gone over. I can't say that I feel the least inspiration for that just now. I don't in fact think anything I did now would be of value—no inspiration, and a confusion still hanging over the play from the effect of the Lunts, etc.

So you had better tell that nice Miss Landis[1] that. But tell her how much I admire her and that I appreciate her even possible interest.

---

8. Young refers to a program of modern dance compositions which Martha Graham had presented at the Guild Theatre, April 7, 1941. Young reviewed the performance in "Three and One," *New Republic,* CIV (April 21, 1941), 532–33.

9. Young's *Belle Isle.*

1. Jessie Royce Landis (1904–72), actress of stage, screen, radio, and television, made her New York stage debut in 1926. In 1930, she played the leading part in Campbell's *Solid South* and subsequently appeared in many successful productions both on stage and in motion pictures. In 1954, she published her autobiography, *You Won't Be So Pretty.* After the Lunts did not produce Young's *Belle Isle,* Campbell suggested that she appear in the play.

Some day I may get back to the play. Just now it represents painful and hopeless things for me.

I appreciate, too, your thinking of it with regard to her.

Wales said last night he planned to go to the country Saturday. We stayed at Mrs. Adams' this past week-end and worked at the farm, with a farm hand's assistance, and got the house pretty well toward being settled. We have found a servant, who will begin work two weeks from yesterday.

I was wondering how your plans for this week-end are developing. We look forward to tomorrow, tell your sweet mother.

Yours,
Stark

565 | To Lawton Campbell, New York

Bedford, New York
Tuesday afternoon [May 27, 1941]

Dearest Lawton,

I will work out tomorrow morning a report of those pieces we were speaking of. They are, so far as I have read them—the *many* I have read—*theatre* writing—not RADIO at all. Nor could they be rewritten as such.[2]

I have learned a lot about radio, thanks to you—and I wish I could have a talk with Lynn and Alfred about it.

What the Bismarck's sinking[3] did to Lynn God alone knows.

I will send the letter tomorrow to your apartment special delivery, so that is that.

Yours
Stark

2. Presumably Young refers to material which Campbell was considering for a radio program in which the Lunts might be interested. See below, Letter 570.
3. The German battleship *Bismarck* was sunk on the day Young wrote this letter.

The letter is for your eyes *only,* as we agreed. It very well illustrates the special situation that I told you Lynn and Alfred create. Lynn loves me, if she loves anybody, so we may start our interpretation from there.

566 | To Richard L. O'Connell, Fort Niagara, New York

Bedford, New York
Tuesday [June 3, 1941]

Dear Dick,

I have your letter and all you say about the Jones book [4] is true. The point, however, is that it must be seen also in perspective with the stuff around it and in the current theatre. For that reason, though I agree with all you say, I made only favorable points for it—for the most part —in my review. Compared to the stuff in the air now, that book was enunciated by an archangel. However great his faults, Robert Edmond Jones is what he is as the light and seed, etc. Basta. But you are right too.

I sent Jimmie off a letter this morning, saying that if there was anything I could do about John Bishop I would gladly do it. I think, myself, that nothing at all would come of any of it. [5] Perhaps Jimmie has already seen John. At any rate John is an old friend of mine, and he is a very fine person. He has also a wife, a son of about fifteen, and twins, identical, none of them stupid or uninteresting.

Max has written for the words I shall say as a foreword, says everything else now is in shape. I asked him to send me some proof. Your

4. Young had reviewed Robert Edmond Jones's *The Dramatic Imagination* in "To Paint What Then I Saw," *New Republic,* CIV (June 2, 1941), 759–60. Young took the occasion of Jones's book and the twenty-sixth anniversary of his first production to estimate his contribution to the American theatre: "His triumphs, his encounters with lack of comprehension of his work, and his failures make up a case history that parallels that of any fine artist; but his good fortune, and his rewards too . . . have been that his sum remains intact of luster, fresh application and advancing spirit."

5. Luján and O'Connell hoped that John Peale Bishop, then publications director of the Office of the Coordinator of Inter-American Affairs, would find employment for them as translators. Through Bishop's help, O'Connell became one of the translators for the *Anthology of Contemporary Latin-American Poetry,* edited by Dudley Fitts (1942, 1947).

preface is a very important part of the impression the volume will make. After I see the copy I will take the matter up with Mrs. Isaacs and TAM as you suggest more or less.

Love to you

Stark

567 | To Maxwell Perkins, Charles Scribner's Sons, New York

Bedford, New York
Tuesday [June 10, 1941]

Dear Max,

Eighteen galleys of the Lorca translation have come. It seems a remarkably good translation, really unusual. I thought you might be interested to hear that. I am sending O'Connell two or three of the galleys with suggestions for the change of a word or so. That ought to be useful to the cause, to the publishers and to the translators.

Now is the time for some decent translating from the Spanish—as Washington might say. I will say so at least in a review of the volume when it appears.

At the party Elsie Adams gave and I was obliged to attend, Mrs. Frothingham[6] or something came up most cordially, she always likes to talk about you and since she will never understand anything about either you or Louise but admires you both most generously, no harm was done. As for you and Louise I admire and love you both, and that's that.

Yours
Stark

6. Young refers to Mrs. Lawrence Potter Frothingham, a close friend of Mrs. Huntington Adams and the mother-in-law of Perkins' eldest daughter, Bertha Saunders Frothingham. On June 12, Perkins replied: "I always was puzzled by Mrs. Frothingham's account of interviews with me. She is a very nice person, but sometimes gets impatient with me. I have read in many novels about a woman shaking a finger under a man's nose, and to my delight it happened. I made some remarks that she didn't approve of, and she came across the room and actually did it. I supposed it only occurred in fiction."

568 | To Richard L. O'Connell, Fort Niagara, New York

Bedford, New York
Tuesday [June 10, 1941]

Dear Dick,

I have a letter or note from Jimmie saying that he was on the way to the boat, but wanted to tell me that he had seen John Bishop that day —Friday—and that John was interested in the translating. I had seen John the day before, Thursday, and told him what you said about his poetry, and that you had done a fine translation of Lorca. He said that was just what he was interested in, especially in people who might translate poetry, either from Spanish into English or vice versa;[7] let it rest therefore until I see the proofs and see John again. He will be coming out here to have dinner and spend the night some time next week, I think. A sweet fellow and good and talented, his wife rules the roost perhaps, but who knows in this world? He is Virginia, she Buffalo or thereabout, a railroad king's daughter, the money now mostly vanished, these last few years.

Max wrote saying all that was needed was the preface or foreword by me, I replied that I should like to see the proof first, etc. He has sent now 18 galleys. I have several slight suggestions to make, to mend things. On the whole the translation seemed to me remarkably good. I have written him that, and that I was sending the galley suggestions to you. But he did not send the introductory matter. You had best send that to me direct or else have him send me the proofs of it. I am anxious to give any help I can in that matter of the introductory matter, since that does much toward the success of the volume. In so far as seems fit, follow all this up at once. These things are what count often. I will then get Irita Van Doren's ear for the book's having a chance in the Herald Tribune, etc. The publishing world of books, alas, is not the cushioned affair that college life is, and that is a plain hard fact. As you of course know.

The thing now is to put you over—for the time at least—as a brilliant translator. I have not forgotten some of your kindness and sweetness to me nor some of the music you played—that second part of the

7. See above, Letter 566 and n. 5.

Bach for example—and if any of this I am trying to do now will be of use to [you] I am glad.

Love to you

Stark

569 | To Richard L. O'Connell, Fort Niagara, New York

[Bedford, New York]
Tuesday morning [June 17, 1941]

Dear Dick,

I have done about eleven galleys of the proof, a *remarkable* translation, but there are phrases and places where the effect is so foreign that the excellent results *otherwise* would be nullified. For a very simple example—in Latin languages *lauro* yes, in English when you cook with it it is *bay leaves*—bay rum we know etc.[8] Many people in the audience would get that point so fixed in their minds that they would undervalue the fineness and beautiful fluency of the translation otherwise.

I enclose a letter from Max,[9] and tomorrow I will post to you the galleys with the suggestions I have made. This can be a great spot in our theatre and in *your career*. I expect neither thanks nor indebtednesses on the part of you and Jimmie. He was as relieved to hear that this operation on my part was not due to an infatuation for you as he was distressed to hear that you might, as a good Catholic, someday marry,—but what has that to do with translation of fine theatre? Count me out therefore—and study well the proof.

Tomorrow I shall be posting about fifteen galleys to you—

Yours
Stark

8. The passage to which Young refers occurs early in *The Shoemaker's Prodigious Wife:* "And that she wishes she knew how to season a good dish with pepper and bay the way my husband knows how to repair shoes."

9. One June 12, 1941, Perkins had written Young, "I do think Richard O'Connell and James Graham have done an excellent piece of work." Young enclosed Perkins' note with this letter to O'Connell.

570 | To Lawton Campbell, New York

Bedford, New York
Wednesday [June 18, 1941]

Dear Lawton,

I sent you a message by Wales to say that the check had arrived and how ornamental it appears on this desk and in my heart. Thank you very much.

I was sorry not to be of use with regard to Alfred and Lynn. The arrival of her letter was a fortunate coincidence. Allowing for their customary oblique approach, it is quite revealing and, for you, useful. Some years ago their reaction would have been much simpler, just as their performance for radio purposes would have been much better, much. But now the war, the Siddons, the international, the profits and solemnities have come into the situation. As a continuous program—repeated, etc.—I can't imagine any that could be written for them at the present time—(that, moreover, would hold a public). One or two readings or scenes might be a different matter.

If you still have Lynn's letter, please keep it for me.

Wales says you might come out some night next week. I hope you do—he'll telephone you.

Please give my love to my dear Cousin Myrtle. And thank you again.

Stark

571 | To Richard L. O'Connell, Fort Niagara, New York

[Bedford, New York]
Monday noon [June 30, 1941]

Dear Dick,

I'm sending you some more pages. The translation is most remarkable, resolves most difficult passages—(which I can often foresee in the Spanish). That makes all the more astonishing such phrases as *she turns rapidly,* etc. The notes I made are rather inescapable, will probably enrage you at first, then convince you. If Miss Mildred Adams[1] passed some of them, she is not only weak in the English and Spanish idiom but also in plain grammar at times. However, we shall get the whole works in order and have a wonderful book, and for God's sake don't let the credit for it touch me. Only, if I'm to write the preface, we can't say *Silver rusts, place* a flower in your *lapel, eyes become extinguished,* etc.

Could I ask the favour of your sending back the proofs to me too. I'm going to do a small book on translating plays some day, and it might all in some way be of use. After all, a small favor I am asking.

Many of the lyric passages are authentic and brilliant rendering. I was very proud of you. In every case my advice and suggestion is long considered. After all, my whole involvement could only be an interest in the artistic outcome. I'll send more soon.

Yours
Stark

572 | To Maxwell Perkins, Charles Scribner's Sons, New York

Bedford, New York
Tuesday [July 1, 1941]

Dear Max,

Thank you for your note.[2] This is only to say I hope to see you and Louise and that the delay in Dick O'Connell's proof is partly due to

---

1. Mildred Adams (b. 1894), author, translator, and economist, who had known Federico García Lorca in Spain and New York, assisted O'Connell and Luján in obtaining the Spanish texts of Lorca's plays and made suggestions about the translation. Besides writing for the *Economist* (London) and the *Nation,* she has published *Getting and Spending: The ABC of Economics* (1939), translated Jose Ortega y Gasset's *Invertebrate Spain* (1937) and Germán Arciniegas' *The Night of El Dorado* (1942), and edited the *Memoirs of Malwida von Meysenbug* (1936).

2. In a note to Young, Perkins had said that he was writing O'Connell to hasten his return of the proofs for the Lorca volume. The delay was actually caused by O'Connell's desire to consider Young's suggestions before releasing the proof. Young sent O'Connell a carbon copy of this letter to Perkins.

me. This chore is quite a sizable one, and unfortunately it is much against the grain with my state of mind at present. But I am on it again, and have only some twenty galleys to send him. I am sending some today. Don't hurry him too much or it will only be costing him for the corrections.

The larger part of my markings are rather incredible errors in English idiom.[3] Many of these are quite superficial, but the irony is that in a page of no matter how remarkable translation, such a phrase as "breathe strongly"—a Latin tongue form—instead of our "breath deep" would make the average critic or reader discount the rest of the page. The lyrics are triumphs in translation indeed. I have asked O'Connell to give me no credit for this hand I am taking in the book. That would only confuse the issue and cut down his deserved credit for the work in general. The finest things in the work are elusive and real achievement on his part. I know enough Spanish, Italian, French and Latin to see what the original very likely was in most cases—more or less that is.

> Greetings—Yours
> Stark

573 | To Richard L. O'Connell, Fort Niagara, New York

> Bedford, New York
> Monday [August 4, 1941]

Dear Dick,

This is only a line to say that I am sending the brief introductory words into the Scribners' office in a few days now, and am then going on a trip to take a short trip to the Cape, seeing John Bishop perhaps. It has turned out rather foolishly difficult this meeting, what with John

3. Young continued to read the proof of the Lorca volume and in letters to Maxwell Perkins repeatedly praised the translation. On July 9, Young wrote: "As I expected it to be, this translating is most remarkable. The places to change are in words or idiom and come, I think, from Mr. Graham's closeness to the original language, by which things seem natural to him that are not natural to us, he transfers them to what he has always known and been accustomed to. Only in the first play do these corrections seem evident and fairly numerous, the rest of the work goes much more easily. The mood of a play is involved in these cases."

saying he would like to come out here any night. He is a most unusually nice person, you will find when you meet him.

As to that Lunt Fontanne venture with Lorca [4] I have thought it
might be of some sort or other of economy to you, with regard to
time and thought and the verities, to know that nothing could be
farther from them than this quality of Lorca's. If Lorca were where the
Theatre Guild would find him paying well and seeming novel, the
Lunts might be bold enough to read, at least, the plays, or get that
done. A very simple proof of that is to tell you that Lynn thinks the
Alice Duer Miller poem very fine poetry—she was telling me what a
poet Alice was—one evening in her dressing room, long before the
piece was printed.[5] Mrs. Miller offered it to Max, he told me he
thought it might sell, but that after all there was a limit—etc. Which
only contributes one more mite to his judgement as a critic.

And so—alors—love to you

Stark

Thank you for the returned proofs.

574 | To Richard L. O'Connell, Fort Niagara, New York

Bedford, New York
Thursday [August 5, 1941]

Dear Dick,

I am returning the poems, and was glad to see them. They are
beautiful lyrics, I think, and the translation unusually good.[6] I have

4. O'Connell had suggested to Young the possibility that the Lunts could be persuaded to produce one of Lorca's plays, perhaps *The Shoemaker's Prodigious Wife.*

5. Alice Duer Miller (1874–1942), poet, playwright, and novelist, wrote a number of
novels which were successful both as fiction and as plays. Among her best known
works are *Come Out of the Kitchen* (1916), *The Charm School* (1919), and *Gowns by
Roberta* (1933), which became the basis for the libretto of Jerome Kern's musical
comedy, *Roberta.* In 1940, she achieved her greatest popularity with her poem, *The
White Cliffs of Dover,* in which she eulogized England for the British defense against
the threat of Nazi invasion. Young's reference is to this poem. In 1941, she published
I Have Loved England.

6. O'Connell had sent Young a number of translations, including several lyrics from
Romances y villancicos Españoles del siglo XVI, compiled and arranged by Jesús
Bal y Gay (1939). Among them were "En la fuente del rosel" by Juan Vasquez and
"Si la noche hace escura" by Diego Pisador.

not the energy to make the discourse you dreaded, but merely say one point, which is that it is good to keep the order of the original so far as possible. When, for example, you put the little girl first instead of the boy, in En la fuente—you change the Spanish character, i.e. male first. I made a few other notations.

The one page of the translations that seems to me astonishingly off grade are the No te pude ver from Yerma and the Mariposa del aire from The Shoemaker's etc. They seem to me extraneous and literarish versions of the original—no te pude ver is insufferable as hard to find, my belle, and so is the midnight's bell. The line seems to mean *twelve strikes*. The whole poem as Lorca has it is straight and profoundly lyric. The repetitions added in the mariposa seem almost as bad. And is "by the candle light" the translation of luz de candil here? It seems to me the sense is that there is candle light, the candle is lit, etc., to warn the butterfly to stay there, away. Save for these two, the lyrics go beautifully. The mariposa translation in the play is far better.

I note in a letter your query about respectable public. All I can say again is that respectable sounds like translating that knows English tradition poorly—in a Latin country the idea of respectable is quite different. I doubt even calling them public to their faces—the tradition is people. The point is largely important because it falls at the very beginning of things in the volume. Basta.

I have two final favors to ask you. One is for the nice Miss Adams' address, I have a Texas clipping that will make her laugh, if I can lay my hands on it again.

The other is to beg you to try to keep the legend from getting started that I made corrections mostly toward stage ends—while others tended to be literary and so on. A very small percent of the suggestions I made were for the usage of the speaking stage. The suggestions I made that were of most use had to do with English meanings that tended to distort the impression of such excellent translating otherwise. For example, bay not laurel [and] shepherd's conchs shells or horns, not just shells. Not metallic for the moon's horns. All the contrary, which is not English. Mute story, meaning dumb show or pantomime. Citron forest meaning groves of fruit citron. Garland, not English, for braid lace or galloons. St. Joseph's wand, we say staff. Fairies have wands. Wooden soap for soap bark, etc. etc.

A further point is not to let yourself get off the key about "literary." Whatever is most alive and expressive of the sense has the highest claims to being style. Whatever has the highest claim to style has the highest claim to literary. Otherwise the terms make no sense.

The "upon the identical column embraced go dreams and time" does not involve the "literary" problem. It simply is not English but jargon —like the Medieval Latin written by British monks, which is merely not Latin. The *identical* might do, that is usage of course, whether advisable here or not, but the word order is not English for *embraced* go etc.

(By the way cleanses would be better than cleaning with the eclipse's blood; the tone is better and the figure the same otherwise.)

Some of the suggestions I made were confined to word economy for clarity, or for clarity per se, the sense intended.

The translations in general, forgive my repeating it so often, are certainly remarkable. Max Perkins writes that though we may have put trouble on the venture, the Lorca original seems to be worth it.

Well, this ends our conferences. I do wish the book every success, and hope not to see any proof, even such fine stuff, of anything again for a long time. I don't know why I hate proof and type and revising print so much. Et cetera. Good luck to the poems.

Love to you

Stark

P.S. I hope you changed the last paragraphs of the introduction as I suggested. I seriously prefer to be left out of the last sentence, largely for the book's good fortune with reviewers. And the sentence about the version and the authorized are most important. Your statement did not get the two points separated enough.

575 | To Richard L. O'Connell, Fort Niagara, New York

Bedford, New York
Friday [August 15, 1941]

Dear Dick,

My state of mind and affairs would only make this letter tiresome, so I will just say that I hope to hear from you today, that my last letter with the poems, suggestions etc. arrived, and that you have sent the copy to Scribners. I talked with Max yesterday and am getting the foreword in right off.[7] He will send it to press Monday. It all sounds very fine, this venture, and I think Scribners is pleased.

I will try to get it planted for a review in the Times. I spoke of the introduction to the Isaacs but we did not seem to get far.[8] I thought that it might be best to let matters wait for a notice there. Hermine[9] seemed interested, I enlarged on the fine qualities of the translation. Let's hope this all leads to something of great future interest.

Tell me how you are faring with John Bishop. Love to you

Stark

576 | To Richard L. O'Connell, Fort Niagara, New York

Bedford, New York
Thursday [August 28, 1941]

Dear Dick,

Today I had the proof of my foreword to the book. I added a line or two. At least what I said means something—and I hope it is worthy of such a distinguished volume. I feel very proud of this work you and Jimmie Graham have done, and have helped to puff it with theatre people and editors—definitely.

I have marked the proof on page xxii of your *Notes on the Playwright,* and sent it to Max, with a marking that asks him to wait till he hears from you as to your agreement. He felt the same as I did about the Miss Adams passages in the earlier proof—one thought less

7. Young did not finish the foreword as he hoped; after writing several unsuccessful drafts, he sent the manuscript to Perkins on August 21.

8. Although Young was unsuccessful in obtaining a review in the New York *Times,* Edith Isaacs, editor of *Theatre Arts,* printed a very favorable article by Frederick Morton in "Five Lorca Plays," *Theatre Arts,* XXV (December, 1941), 920, 923. See below, Letter 581.

9. Hermine Rich Isaacs (Mrs. Robert Popper, 1915–68) was associate editor of *Theatre Arts* from 1936 to 1948.

of Miss Adams and more of the question of "just who is she and what did she do for these boys?" But that is not up either to Miss Adams or to this book. The way I have it gives a much finer impression. It reads thus.

"To Miss Mildred Adams we owe more than gratitude. Her knowledge of translations and insight into Lorca's theatre were always at our command. By reason of her suggestions this book is better than it otherwise would have been."

This avoids that amateurish mention of "proof"—and that distracting reminder of the question of just who this kind person may be and what exactly did she do?

I don't always feel sure of my conclusions, but here because of the glow and greatness of the material—I know I am right. And professionally right (expedient) at the same time. Miss Adams would certainly tell you the same.[1]

I hope you will feel that you can write Max at once to do this correction (mention page proof xxii—*Notes on the Playwright*). The sheets will then go forward. Max will meanwhile hold that page proof.[2]

Again congratulations on a fine job—A communication with the bishop the other day—lovely fellow—if you are in New York go to see him. Love to you.

Stark

N.B. This was written in haste. I am in *Town* (*NYC*) today for the first time in many weeks.

S.Y.

1. Mildred Adams had already expressed the same opinion. On July 2, she wrote O'Connell: "You'll find that I've mostly taken myself out of the very generous introduction . . . because I thought it wasn't wise from many points of view for any one person to figure so heavily in an introduction. . . . It is lovely to know that you and James feel that sense of my really being of assistance, and I have left in the last fine acknowledgement, but I had a queer hunch that the rest made me sound as though I was claiming far too much credit, and that it threw other acknowledgements out of balance. There was a passionate lover of New Mexico and its civilizations named Mary Austin, who always spoke of the natives there as 'my Indians,' and I would rather hesitate to appear claiming that Federico was 'my Federico'!"
2. O'Connell approved the change suggested by Young.

577 | To Maxwell Perkins, Charles Scribner's Sons, New York

Bedford, New York
Monday [September 8, 1941]

Dear Max,

Bowman has been away so much, and I do not drive the car, or else I should have been to see you and Louise. Next week, let's hope.

Please send me a line as to whether Dick O'Connell returned the change I suggested and the work thus goes forward.[3]

I have lately some working ideas as to a book of reminiscences and people and all that.[4] But not to be published till times look better and the public is more in line with literature and news and despair and to hell with it and so what et cetera. More about my little plans when I see you.

Could I beg of you a copy of your Nostradamus book,[5] reprint of the book years ago? I have read a borrowed copy. It is much better at least than the book got out by the Creative Arts Press,[6] very much better. I have some of Nostradamus in the original, but have lately been trying in vain to get the standard French edition, edited by Pelletier[7] —Nostradamus is really disturbing as to time, space and the ONE MIND. More when I see you.

Yours
Stark

I am out of New Republic stationery—hence this effect.

S.

3. Young refers to the changes in the introductory section of the translation of Lorca's plays; see above, Letter 576 and notes.

4. Young had been considering such a project since the early summer of 1936; see above, Letter 465.

5. The reference is probably to *Oracles of Nostradamus,* by Charles A. Ward, published by Scribner's in 1940.

6. *Nostradamus: The Man Who Saw through Time,* by Lee McCann (New York: Creative Age Press, Inc., 1941).

7. Young probably had in mind *Les oracles de M. de Nostredame . . .* par A. le Pelletier (2 vols., 1867).

578 | To Julian Huxley, London, England

[320 East 57th Street]
[New York]
September 13, 1941

Dearest Julian,

I wrote you early in June, thanking you for the photographs—they are nice to have but are not nearly so distinguished as you look—and also asking what sort of tea you would like me to send you, if any, or what? There are some baskets put up and guaranteed to reach their destination—one way or another—but the contents look so patchy that I can't imagine Juliette wanting them.

Out of twenty parcels sent friends in Broadway, Doris Keane tells me that five have been received. She thinks that is doing quite well, but she has money in plenty and is naturally extravagant. But shops here will send tea for me on pretty good security and please tell me what you think of it, China or what?

Not having heard from you, I fancy you never got the letter. I have seen in the Times that a lot of mail was lost during the first half of June—or perhaps you did get it and have let me know, a letter on the way.

If you never got my letter you missed very little. I know nothing to write, nothing of the censorship, and I feel like all thumbs trying to write while the world around you there is what it is. Scarcely a day passes that I don't think of you, of course. I feel very futile in general. In the New Republic, for example, it seems silly for me to be jabbering about the war and world affairs, there is too much patter about it as things stand. I can at least shut up. This whole country is now deluged with every sort of stuff, news of every nature or purpose, and radios going constantly. Commissions, emissaries and refugees are everywhere, and in the main they do the Allied Cause very little good, they merely tend to build up prejudice or skepticism in the minds of many people. I need not tell you that of course.

I mentioned in my other letter one item regarding you and yours—which is to say I always intended $1000 for my godson, either when he was graduated or of age or I died, or whatever. The idea still stands, naturally, and though I am not laden with riches, I shall be well, quite well, to manage. The item is written on a paper and clipped to my will. But it is a good thing for you to know of it, in case something happens to me. In due time even that sum may come in well.

A week ago your democracy book arrived,[8] I read it [with] much pride and admiration, and it is now lent out. I have promised it to another person as soon as it is returned. It is admirably careful and patient, doing all possible to keep the outlines simple and well stated. That resumé device at the opening of some of the chapters serves splendidly. The chapter on Democracy between nations is the most difficult—since something that does not yet exist has to be figured for the reader's imagination. The drift of it is of course in many people's minds over here. I don't see how we can expect certain nations we intend to make behave, even if they will some other system, to applaud this Anglo-Saxon idea. But there is nothing to be done about that. In this chapter and all through the book you use the threat of chaos as an alternative very tellingly.

It is also very clear what you mean by the democratic system in relation to human beings. What is done there by you is needed here, where as we might expect the word democracy is being dragged about, messed up, used by the cheap etc. not to mention all the banality. That is the kind of thing that comes with war, but the process is sickening. What's more this messing and mottoing of the word is not natural to the Americans who are most Americans, most rooted, and most profoundly tied to their country and next to the English race.

I hope you will write me soon about the tea etc. And thank you again for the photographs and the book. It would be wonderful if you came over on some business for Britain this winter.

As to my play, the Lunts were to do it last fall, but the Sherwood war play came on, did well, and they naturally go on with it. Lynn Fontanne thinks it helps the cause—Alfred finds it a success at any rate and gives a good performance. When a thing is sidetracked in the theatre, nobody knows what then, if ever? My misfortune, in money, etc., obviously. I am not whining, and feel absurd mentioning a pri-

8. Young refers to Huxley's *Democracy Marches* (1941). In the opening paragraph of his review of Frederick Hazlitt Brennan's play, *The Wookey*, Young endeavored to "plug" Huxley's book by summarizing his comments upon the nature of democracy. Young explained that Huxley's statements could be taken as the text of *The Wookey*. See "War Winnings," *New Republic*, CV (September 29, 1941), 404.

vate woe like that to you. I am only explaining what happened—you would like to know.

Give Juliette my love.

As ever

Stark

I should have mentioned how your scope and travel etc. appears in the proportion and cosmopolitan or international scale of values that so quietly appear in these articles.

S.

579 | To Richard L. O'Connell, Fort Niagara, New York

320 East 57th Street

New York

Thursday [October 23, 1941]

Dear Dick,

That first paragraph of your letter, about the direct and Lorca etc. was so good that I meant to cut it out and return it to you, to be used in an essay about him. But the letter has disappeared with the cleaning of our new Finnish maid, Rosa, who has not yet got quite clear about throwing papers away. And so on. You probably remember what you said, however, and while you remember it thus, you had better write it down for future uses.[9]

9. Later Young found O'Connell's letter containing the paragraph about Young's review of the Lorca volume in "Theatre Song," *New Republic,* CV (October 13, 1941), 477–78. O'Connell's paragraph follows: "This is tardy thanks for your beautiful review of the book in the New Republic! It is characteristically generous and exact even down to the careta dormida—or rather con una expression dormida.—Again—I say how impossible it would be to find anyone else to appreciate the values in Lorca and state them so exactly—it is a great pity that these values—generous, honest and from the heart truly—seem not to be readily appreciated by those for whom they should be as simple as breathing—some dire comment on our whole concept of living and of art seems to become involved when you try to point out the clear happiness and vigor of Lorca to almost anyone whom you might think would have some sense about him and theatre."

This isn't a letter, it is merely carrying out my intention of some days ago to tell you about the review in the NR. In the first place I had to fight to get that much space, and was obliged to cut twenty-six lines as it was. The expression of slumber business[1] was merely used technically, it is a great help to produce the effect of knowing the original from which the translation is made. I was glad to have that easy handle. So that is that, it was not malice, just technical convenience. I had to mention something in that line. And I was distressed to be obliged to cut the prose passage I had, after that wind speech. But space is space, and you see what the professional world involves.

Meanwhile the article appears to be a great success. An Oxford editor, Mrs. Elmhirst who supports the NR, and numerous other people have been going on about it—so it may have been of use. I am grateful to Lorca and to you and Jimmie for supplying me with good and beautifully radiant material to write about.

Thank you for the nice letter about the party at Lincoln's[2] etc. I look red, and let it all rest at that, thank you—nobody is on tiptoes as to when I may tip over, and certainly I am not.

I have been hours with the Chekhov people over readings in LEAR, and am very tired, so please forgive whatever incoherence this letter exhibits. I wanted most to let you know that the article I wrote seems to have gone far.

Would you mind writing me the detailed items as to Mr. Blev[3] whatever it is and his address, in FULL—I mean soon to take the play up with him, Rosa has thrown your letter out. Thank you for this trouble—just his full name and address—I remember what he wanted.

S.Y.

1. In his review, Young had mentioned "examples of that impulse in translators where they mess things up not so much through any ignorance of their original as through some hypnotic pull this other language may exert or else some wayward judgment of their own, mixed, perhaps, with a certain blur in their usage of our own English. For instance, '*Se pone una careta de expresión dormida*': 'puts on a mask with an expression of slumber,' which could scarcely claim to be English, much less a proper rendering. The number of such cases, however, is wonderfully small."

2. Lincoln Kirstein had invited Young, Martha Graham, Glenway Wescott, and others to a party to celebrate the publication of *From Lorca's Theatre*. Young had not attended.

3. Blevins Davis (1903-71), producer, known for such productions as *Rhapsody* (1944), *Hamlet* (1946), and *Porgy and Bess* (1952) and for his association with the American Ballet Theatre as organizer and president.

580 | To Pauline Goldmann, Austin, Texas

[320 East 57th Street]
[New York]
[November 9, 1941]

Dearest Pauline,

Thank you all so much for those divine little jars of your chef d'Oeuvres. I ate the onion jar at once and sweetly survived. The others are still in my deposit box at the Corn Exchange Bank. Again I thank you. One's thirtieth birthday [4] is always a bit—

The Lunts write me that they will be in Austin December 2. They have difficulties with this venture, the USA has decided that Finland is something else from what it was when the Russians were tearing it to pieces. And now Noel Coward has been tried twice and fined twice —$800 plus dollars and then $6000 to 7000 for cheating the British government on securities, etc., he the patriot. [5] He, Wilson, Fontanne and Lunt have a partnership and that too is awkward for Lynn and Alfred, patrioteering as they are now. Constance Collier says they have "adopted" the war. That is good theatre malice all right.

I am writing on these cards so that my dear cousins may be drawn back to New York and use the apartment next summer, why not?

Thank you again for that remembrance.

Affectionately,
S.Y.

581 | To Richard L. O'Connell, Fort Niagara, New York

[320 East 57th Street]
[New York]
November 27 [1941]

Dear Dick,

I had meant to write you a decent letter but the world thwarts me. So I am sending these lines on to you anyhow. [6]

4. Young was sixty years old on October 11, 1941.
5. See above, Letter 554 and notes.
6. Young wrote this letter on the back of a letter to him from Jerome Mellquist (1906–63), art critic and historian, who was then reading proof for his book, *The*

We got ourselves a pretty handsome notice in Theatre Arts Monthly, didn't we?[7] It ought to be of use to the book.

I have a few lectures in Atlanta, Charleston etc. after Christmas, and will bring it in, recommending its study for certain qualities, certain uses.

Did you hear Joan Bennett in So Red the Rose Monday night?[8] A 23 minute version, rather skillfully sticking to the theme of a girl and the men in relation to war. They paid me $500 to use it thus. Good for me, though Salisbury gets $50. Of course they would never have paid me the sum anyhow.

I hope all goes well for you. I paint a great deal.[9] Max and Louise Perkins came over to see the paintings, were much impressed it seems and very lovely about them. I have some offers from purchasers but think better to wait, for the sake of my mind—if it is my mind.

I hope all goes well with you. Max has a very fine opinion of your abilities, and he has really a second sight in such matters.

Give my love to Jimmie.[1] There must be times when that Jimmie Parke[2] in Austin writhes to see such a distinguished form of attention as your book got in the NR and TAM.

Love to you

Stark

Emergence of an American Art (1942). Young wished O'Connell to see Mellquist's comment: "I did read your review on the Lorca volume. . . . Why don't these New York producers wake up and do one of his plays?"

7. See above, Letter 575 and n. 8. In his review, Frederick Morton praised the translators for keeping remarkably well "both the Spanish feeling and the folk feeling in these plays, an exceedingly difficult task, especially in the matter of the songs which interlard most of the plays." Morton agreed with Young's remark in the foreword that "Lorca's theatre has only its own reality; it is never seen as anything but theatre, and it uses the theatre medium as frankly and directly as an artist uses paint."

8. Joan Bennett, who had been acting in stage, screen, and radio productions since 1928, appeared in a radio version of *So Red the Rose,* broadcast over WEAF, New York, on November 24, 1941. The program was entitled "Cavalcade of America."

9. An early reference to Young's painting. Although throughout his life he had occasionally painted pictures, he would devote himself increasingly during the next several years to painting as an activity which helped to relieve his disappointments in the theatre.

1. James Graham-Luján.

2. James Hambright Parke, chairman of the drama department at the University of Texas when O'Connell joined the faculty in 1938. See above, Letter 431 and n. 9.

582 | To Ellen Glasgow, Richmond, Virginia

[610 West Lynn]
Austin, Texas
New Year's [1942]

Dearest Cousin,

I didn't stop enroute to Mexico, joined my sister and her husband in Monterrey for Christmas—very Latin and quiet and gentle. We just got back here, and I am sending off to you a tiny box I got for you in Mexico—it is just to say good wishes for your New Year. I have often thought what an appalling guest I made for you in New York— but my whole inside cosmos was very much depressed at the time.[3] The world is a way indeed. I have no desire to be twenty-one again. You seemed as wonderful as ever, in New York when I saw you. What a divine creature my cousin is.

Remember me to Miss Ann Virginia.

Lovingly
Stark

583 | To Leah Salisbury, New York

610 West Lynn
Austin, Texas
Wednesday [May 13, 1942]

Dearest Leah,

I have just today rented this machine and am not used to it.

The telephone conversation was a great comfort, and has settled my naturally perturbed thoughts.[4] There is nothing to be done, I can only

3. Ellen Glasgow had been in New York early in the fall of 1941 at the time that Young was depressed over the Lunts' failure to produce his play.

4. Young, who had fully expected that the Lunts would eventually produce his play *Belle Isle*, a story of a pirate modeled after Jean Lafitte, had been shocked by the following item which appeared in the New York *Times*, May 7, 1942, p. 22: "It is now

hope their memories will be bad and that they have put their foot into it, and we can bleed them as they deserve. I am shocked even at the T Guild. Besides, Wilson,[5] Terry,[6] and Gassner[7] have all read that final version.

I wrote John A that you would telephone him. He is as good as myself in my own interests, better. A real friend. Wi 2 3782.

I am asking another favor. Please telephone Bowman, and tell him about my talk with you. Tell him I knew he would want to hear what you would say.

I have inquired again about the Mexican painted chairs with the beautiful seats. They have gone up some and after the present lot the store is not going to carry. They have at present THREE at 1.98, crude painting, the same fine seats.

They can give you SIX with the much more elaborate and pretty decoration, same seats, 4.98. They are of course very cheap at that. But if you want them you had better let me know by air mail, for they might be sold out. I would get the extra three, the cheap ones too, for

definite for Alfred Lunt and Lynn Fontanne to appear in S. N. Behrman's play, temporarily called 'The Pirate.' Contracts were signed yesterday for the presentation of the work under the auspices of the Playwrights Company and the Theatre Guild. Also financially interested in the venture, opening out of town in September before coming to Broadway, is the Transatlantic Productions, which consists of the Lunts, Noel Coward and John C. Wilson. Both Mr. Lunt and Mr. Wilson will participate in the direction. The play, first suggested to the author by Mr. Lunt, is remotely based on the old play of Ludwig Fulda. During the unfolding of the story, set in Santo Domingo early in the nineteenth century, there will be incidental music by Kurt Weill. One-third of the cast, numbering thirty, will be Negro performers. The settings will be designed by Jo Mielziner."

5. John C. Wilson (1899–1961) abandoned a career as a Wall Street stockbroker to become an actor, director, playwright, and producer. With Noel Coward and the Lunts, Wilson became a partner in Transatlantic Productions and produced such plays as *You Can't Take It with You, Idiot's Delight, Amphitryon 38,* and *The Pirate.*

6. Theresa Helburn (Mrs. John B. Opdyke, 1887–1959), stage director, producer, and author, began her career in 1918 as drama critic for the *Nation.* A year later she became associated with the Theatre Guild as executive director and remained throughout the 1930s and 1940s as one of the producers and directors for the organization. She was associated with the production of such plays as *The Philadelphia Story, Oklahoma!, Carousel, Come Back Little Sheba,* and others.

7. John W. Gassner (1903–67), theatre historian, critic, playwright, lecturer, was then chairman of the playwriting and theatre history departments at the New School for Social Research, drama professor at Hunter College, member of the New York Drama Critics Circle, and chairman of the play department of the Theatre Guild. From 1940 to 1956, he was a lecturer at Columbia University; in 1956, he became Sterling Professor of Playwriting and Dramatic Literature at the Yale School of Drama. Gassner wrote and adapted numerous plays and published extensively in the field of drama criticism.

chairs to stick here and there. They are very strong. They would go either freight or express, as you desire. You can pay me back when I see you.

I hope my cousins there at 320 sent over the two trays I left for you. They may be nice for cocktails in the country. The painting is fun. I got them for you Christmas in Monterrey.

I cannot express to you how grateful I feel that I have as agent a friend in whose affection and fine judgement and brains, all three, I can put so much entire trust.

> Affectionately
> Stark

584 | To Leah Salisbury, New York

> [610 West Lynn]
> [Austin, Texas]
> [May 16, 1942]

Dear Leah,

A carbon of my letter to John [8] will explain about the telegram. And don't think I am worrying my head off. Doubtless my subconscious mind had long since got used to something of the sort.

My young cousins wrote me they were charmed with you and that you were so nice to them.[9] He speaks French so well that he is the propaganda announcer for Columbia to Paris and all France. That is fine for a boy from Norfolk. His great-great grandfather was that Malcolm Bedford—real name Ben—in So Red the Rose. He has much charm and his wife is a darling, and no fool.

I will see to the chairs, hope they are still there, they probably are.

8. The carbon copy of Young's letter to John Anderson is printed below.

9. Young refers to Beverly Reid Thurman (1909–62) and his wife, Elizabeth Farrar Thurman. During World War II, he was head of the French section of the Voice of America. After the war, he was an editor on the world services desk of the Associated Press and in 1961 became an interpreter at the United Nations.

They are not as fully decorated as that I gave you. That type now is the 4.95. If we drive to Mexico I may be able to pick you up something there and tie it on the back of the car. I don't know what the gas business will do to that trip, perhaps kill it.

As for the play, all that can rest till the proper time, if ever.

Please give my love to Phil and Tony and yourself. Yours as ever

Stark

[Enclosure, carbon]

610 West Lynn
Austin, Texas
Saturday [May 16, 1942]

Dear John,

I have used this machine so little that I am not sure what will come out when I go at it. However—

The message from here was reread to me and was all right, but evidently, from Wales' letter, the people at the other end got it wrong. I said please not let the matter get talked about there in the country, it would then via Mrs. Rogers[1] get to Peggy Wood,[2] her niece, and via Peggy Wood to Jack Wilson, and then to the Lunts. Wales got a message saying I was trying to connect with Wilson. I have done nothing at all, and soon was able not to worry too much about the whole business. Very likely what will appear in the Lunt result will be in some general ways of clothes, music, etc. what I started them on—elusive of course, but they had not been in that vein. I asked Miss Salisbury to talk it over with you, so that you would know I was doing and saying

1. Identification has not been established.
2. Peggy Wood (Mrs. William H. Walling, b. 1892), stage, screen, and television actress and author, has been active in the theatre since her New York debut in 1910 as a member of the chorus in *Naughty Marietta*. During the 1941–42 season, she played the role of Ruth in *Blithe Spirit* directed by John C. Wilson. She has served as a member of the Actors Equity Association council and as president of the American National Theatre and Academy. Author of several books on the theatre, in 1941, she published her autobiography, *How Young You Look*. She lived in Stamford, Connecticut, not far from Young's summer home in Bedford.

nothing about it. In other words her involved advice I wanted you to know about. Thank you for your interest. The whole matter rests of course until later on and doubtless forever. The less talking about it the better in general.

There is rather an irony in the fact that it was from Behrman[3] that I was warned. After a meeting of the Critics you and I were walking along with Gilbert Gabriel,[4] who was to see you on some special matter. Before I left you he said to me, "You are working for those people? Berry says they are the kind [who] get you out there and work you to death and then let you down," that last very I am not sure of, he may have said "sting." I remember defending them on this score, and Gilbert then talked of Ina Claire[5] and "No Time for Comedy." He said he wrote it for I. Claire, which Lynn afterwards said was not true, he wrote it for them.

Well, the matter rests.

I hope you and Margot[6] are beginning a happy summer, with a fine season.

My sister sends cordial good wishes, as ever.

Love to you both

[unsigned]

3. S[amuel]. N[athaniel]. Behrman (1893–1973), playwright, had written a number of plays for the Guild Theatre with which the Lunts were closely associated, and they had had outstanding success in his adaptation of *Amphitryon 38* by Jean Giraudoux. Behrman's other plays include *Serena Blandish, No Time for Comedy, The Talley Method, Jacobowsky and the Colonel,* and *Jane.* In 1972, he published a volume of memoirs, *People in a Diary.*

4. Gilbert Wolf Gabriel (1890–1952), critic and author, wrote drama criticism for the New York *Telegram-Mail,* New York *Sun,* New York *American,* and *Cue* magazine.

5. Ina Claire (Mrs. William Ross Wallace, b. 1895), stage and screen actress, began her stage career in vaudeville. From 1909 to 1911, she toured in vaudeville on the Orpheum Circuit. In 1915 and 1916, she appeared in *The Ziegfeld Follies.* In the 1920s and 1930s, she became known for her roles in *The Awful Truth, The Last of Mrs. Cheyney, Biography, End of Summer,* and *Barchester Towers.* Most recently, she had appeared as Enid Fuller in *The Talley Method.* S. N. Behrman's *No Time for Comedy,* mentioned here by Young, opened at the Ethel Barrymore Theatre on April 17, 1939, and starred Katharine Cornell. The play was staged by her husband, Guthrie McClintic.

6. Margaret Wilbur Gaines Breuning Anderson (Mrs. John Anderson, 1875–1965), art critic, married John Anderson in 1920. She wrote art criticism for the New York *Evening Post, Art Digest,* and other journals. Her books include *You Know Charles* (1921), *Exploring New York's Art Galleries* (1928), *Maurice Prendergast* (1931), and *Mary Cassatt* (1944).

585 | To Leah Salisbury, New York

> 610 West Lynn
> Austin, Texas
> Saturday [May 30, 1942]

Dearest Leah,

But for the let-down quality of the theatre and the Lunts etc. I might be quite excited about The Three Sisters. But—

As to John Anderson, I have just decided to write and ask him to put in a word if there is a chance. John is devoted but chronically busy, poor dear!

One point—(rub in that) this is not an adaptation but a close translation, far closer than any published. Also that The Sea Gull got marvellous reviews all over the country when published as a book, and that Scribners is eventually to publish this play plus the T Sisters and The Cherry Orchard, in a volume.

Also that I could go over the speeches with Guthrie[7] and rewrite anything that he thought needed a better form for speaking. If they read mine aloud and then the others they will see the difference in the dramatic speakability.

Again, this is not an adaptation but a translation.

I remember Guthrie's rather scoffing at the idea that I had done a translation not an adaptation of The Sea Gull.

I feel very proud of Kit and Guthrie for doing The Three Sisters, whether they use my translation or not. She will be magnificent in it. I would do anything to be of use to such a venture, no matter what they do about the translation used. That is an inspiration, the idea of her doing that part.[8] Tell her from me that she should do the Cherry Orchard next.

7. Guthrie McClintic (1893–1961), producer, director, and author, directed many plays for his wife, Katharine Cornell, including *The Barretts of Wimpole Street, The Dark Is Light Enough, Candida, The Doctor's Dilemma,* and *The Three Sisters.* In 1943–44, he lectured at the Yale School of Drama, and, in 1955, he published *Me and Kit.*

8. On December 21, 1942, Katharine Cornell presented *The Three Sisters,* directed by Guthrie McClintic, at the Barrymore Theatre. Instead of using Young's translation, the company used a text listed as prepared by Alexander Koriansky and Guthrie McClintic. *Theatre Arts,* XXVII (April, 1943), 212–15, printed an article in the form

I enclose some notices of the Sea Gull. You might use or not use them at your discretion. Perhaps the Lunt association might seem to them to steal a little of Cornell's thunder.

I enclose a letter from Bennington.[9] Please do what you think best, say I have referred the letter to you. You might go easy with them, since Mrs. Elmhirst is interested in the School[1] and the Lewisohns' daughter is there and I imagine mixed up with this venture.[2] But they ought to pay some sort of minimum little royalty at least.[3] You do what you think best however.

As to the other letter, I don't know who this is. Use your own judge-

---

of a letter to Rosamond Gilder from Guthrie McClintic entitled "Directing Chekhov." In his account of the production, McClintic wrote that "I found myself dissatisfied with the translations I read." He selected Koriansky, a Russian drama critic, to help with the preparation of a new text. "We spent endless days and nights working at it," wrote McClintic. "At long last our script emerged and it seems to me to have the great advantage of not seeming a translation!" McClintic later elaborated his account of the preparation of the script in *Me and Kit* (1955), chapter 17. Young reviewed the production in "'The Three Sisters,'" *New Republic,* CVII (December 28, 1942), 857. Young wrote that the text "appears to be based on the version by Julius West, of some twenty-five years ago" and added that "however much or little it follows that text is not so important as the fact that a good deal of the daring of Chekhov's combinations, with their emotional springs of surprise, is misconstrued, omitted or slurred over. The combination of the cutting with the reading method finishes off one of the two main characters, Vershinin [Dennis King]. And Miss Cornell does not attack those dangerous repetitions of Masha's poetical quotation of the oak on the curved strand, she mumbles and evades them. . . . Doing that to Chekhov is too bad for his work or worse for the role and the actress." Young concluded by remarking that "I never cease to wonder as to how translators, producers, players, and what not, feel free to improve upon those whom they apparently consider great."

9. A request from the Bennington Theatre Studio to perform Young's translation of Chekhov's *The Sea Gull* on June 4 and 5, 1942.

1. Since 1935, and perhaps earlier, Mrs. Dorothy Elmhirst had been interested in the educational program of Bennington College and contributed to its financial support. Young may also have recalled that the library of Herbert Croly had been given to the college shortly after his death. See above, Letters 82, n. 6, and 294, n. 5.

2. Young refers to Joan Emma Lewisohn (Mrs. John L. Simon), daughter of his friends Margaret S. and Sam A. Lewisohn. She was graduated from Bennington College in 1943. She was not a member of the cast and seems not to have been associated with the production.

3. Strangely, in suggesting that his agent "go easy" with the royalty matter, Young seems to have ignored the fact that his friend Francis Fergusson (b. 1904), director, critic, and author, was directing the play. Professor of humanities and drama at Bennington since 1934, Fergusson had earlier served as drama critic for *The Bookman* and lecturer and executive secretary of the New School for Social Research. In 1948, he left Bennington to become a member of the Institute for Advanced Studies at Princeton, and since that time has been associated with Princeton, Indiana, and Rutgers universities. His books include *The Idea of a Theatre* (1949), *Dante's Drama of the Mind* (1953), and *Poems, 1929–1961* (1962).

ment. But one thing—I imagine I never finished the copy for French. Perhaps they have the play [4] in MS however. What to do about protecting us, you will know when you know about who Mr. Lewis [5] is and his plans. I don't imagine you will be throwing a MS copy for him to pick over. As to the MS copy—I feel pretty sure French and I have never got to it—I meant to when I got that influenza—which you might explain to Mr. Leverton [6]—you may have a copy there. At any rate if not, you can telephone my cousin Beverly Thurman, 320 East 57th St., to tell his brother Bedford,[7] who is vague, to get the MS he has to you. I left it with him, saying that as soon as I recovered, I would communicate with French and perhaps get him to carry it down to them. You will have no trouble getting it, though I fancy you have a copy there in the office.

I went to the shop, those three chairs are gone by now. The others are so much dearer and are not really as prettily painted as that I gave you. I very likely will get to Mexico some way or other and will see what there is there, provided the car of the family is along and the chairs can be tied on the back and escape shipping and duty. We shall see. I will return your check next time, or even now. There!

Thank you for your help and interest.

Affectionately
Stark

4. Perhaps Chekhov's *The Cherry Orchard.*

5. Efforts to identify Lewis have been unrewarding. Robert Lewis, whose successful acting and recent production of *Mexican Mural* had made him known in New York, writes: "Had I heard of a play in manuscript in 1942 written by Stark Young, whom I greatly admired, I would certainly have tried to read it. I must say, however, that I cannot at this point actually remember the incident."

6. Garrett H. Leverton (1897–1949), teacher and theatrical editor, was head of the speech and drama department at Northwestern University until 1937 when he became the senior editor for Samuel French and Company. From 1946 to 1948, he taught classes in playwriting at Columbia University.

7. Bedford Thurman (b. 1914), director, actor, and professor of speech and theatre, received his first theatrical experience with the Little Theatre in Norfolk, Virginia. After he was graduated with a bachelor's degree in dramatic art from the University of North Carolina in 1938, he acted for several years in Paul Green's *The Lost Colony,* Roanoke Island, North Carolina, served in World War II, and continued his drama studies at the University of Iowa. In 1954, he received his doctoral degree from Cornell University, submitting as his dissertation a bibliography of the writings of Stark Young. Since that time, Thurman has taught and directed at Kent State University. Thurman's great-grandmother and Young's grandmother were sisters.

586 | To Maxwell Perkins, Charles Scribner's Sons, New York

Bedford, New York
Monday [August 10, 1942]

Dear Max,

I am really in New York for the day, due to the tailor's demands on clothes cut out in April—can you blame him?

I came back from Texas two weeks ago about, and stay there in Bedford all the time, no gasoline and no guests, and so life goes. I do hope, however, to see you and Louise.

And also pretty soon I shall have a play to show you and ask you whether or not you think it would make a sort of picaresque or romantic novel of the early part of the nineteenth century. I shall go by your advice,[8] you poor Maxwell Perkins of the authors' dash and kill! Why were you not stupid then?

A friend of mine, a Russian and well-read and talented, writes me asking that I give the name of some publisher to her sister for a translation, well done, she says, of a modern Russian novel.[9] So I am giving her your address, she may send the MS. to you. You can have it looked over. It may prove to be of interest. My correspondent thinks it is. Quite.

Please just file this in case the MS. comes to Scribner's.

I hope to see you and Louise soon. Please send me a line to Bedford, New York, saying how you all are. I think of you not seldom—these times throw us back on the permanence and solidity of human affections.

Yours in haste (or New York)
Stark

I have two quite interesting pictures almost done—to show you and Louise.

8. Young had changed the name of his play *Belle Isle* to *Artemise* and had it printed by the Von Boeckmann-Jones Company, Austin, Texas, June 29, 1942. Young dedicated the play: "To Lyle Saxon, author of *Lafitte*. The play was first suggested to me by the reading of this remarkable volume, a rich source." When Perkins finally read the play in November, he was dubious about rewriting it as a novel. He wrote: "It would have to be so differently done in time and order of events, and in respect to all its elements, that it is hard to judge."

9. Perkins' subsequent correspondence implies that the translator was a Mrs. Weber; Scribner's did not publish the work.

587 | To Ellen Glasgow, Richmond, Virginia

320 East 57th Street
New York
Tuesday [November 3, 1942]

Dearest Cousin,

We have at last moved into 320 East 57th Street, catching the autumn cold in the process, and are at last about settled.

Ever since lunch that day I have been meaning to write you—how nice it was to see you and to feel the vibration—as the modern bores would say—of your presence.[1] You were the first author I had spoken with, even on the telephone, since last February, and I must say you began a standard that the authors I may speak with this season are not likely to live up to.

At that, you must have found me flatter than, as they say, hell, though of course you would never admit that. I am too small a mite in human cosmoses to be able to resist the pressure of our time. Things we love are going by the wind, and that is all there is to it.

This, however, is only a note to tell you that I have just posted the letter that votes the gold medal of the institute to YOU. I should say so indeed, to whoM else?????? That is as Pseudo-Correct as Hollywood—and meant to be witty.

My cousin Carrie Dukes' face told a story, the war goes antiquely well; but your face knows the tragedy of the world. Cousin, cosmic worm that I am, infirm and indifferent journalist, child of flat stars, et cetera et cetera, I know something of what is going on. Just the same, the gold medal to you, for what it is worth—we know what you are worth.

Lovingly
Stark

1. Ellen Glasgow spent the week of September 28–October 5 in New York on her way from Castine, Maine, where she had spent the summer, to her home in Richmond, Virginia.

588 | To Bedford Thurman, U.S. Army Air Force, Miami Beach, Florida

[320 East 57th Street]
[New York]
Sunday [November 29, 1942]

Dearest Bedford,

I was glad to hear that the book reached you.[2] The chap that wrote it is [a] fine fellow, he is entirely self made, and some of his judgements are off the scale, the defect that is largely cultural in a writer he is apt to miss and to get off on the social import—in Mrs. Wharton's case especially, the part I read. The chapters on Faulkner and Wolfe have much point. The book's finality suffers from the fact that the author is one of these young Jews in New York who have never seen anything of this country but have decided what America is. What they think America is does not include a great deal of the country I know and love, here and there, far and wide. I told Kazin this, he was impressed. He is completely without side or pose of any kind. He and I became very good friends at once and had hours of talk. I am told he has great admiration for me, thinks me better than Edmund Wilson, etc. Well, as I told him, little of that came out in the book, but such is life.

I am not a go-getter, and I deserve some neglect for my remote attitude, but it is better for me to keep my own mind, whatever happens. At times I get sick of hearing how this person or that of eminence thinks me the best, et cetera et cetera, I mean people who have a different position in all planes than Alfred Kazin. He is a touching and fine fellow, says his mother still can't read, and he is simple about that, not effective. If you were here I would ask him here with you.

Thank you for that delicious glacé fruit, we have enjoyed it, and all thank you, sir.

The Lunt play is appalling,[3] but Behrman cannot have the buck all

2. Young had sent Thurman a copy of Alfred Kazin's *On Native Grounds.*

3. The Lunts opened at the Martin Beck Theatre in S. N. Behrman's *The Pirate,* on November 25, 1942. Young reviewed this play and *Yankee Point* by Gladys Hurlbut in "Two New Productions," *New Republic,* CVII (December 14, 1942), 792–93. After noting that the play program described the work as "suggested by an idea in a play by

passed to him, Alfred had him fixing it up the way he wanted it, Lynn has a poor part and plays well. Alfred has the whole show, is very campy. I am sorry, for many unkind things will be said, partly deserved and partly the price of success. Basta. In my play they both had a remarkable chance. They have taken Fulda's seventeenth century Spanish story and brought it to the date of my play, with the idea of reality and romance that I had infused through mine, have used music as I urged them to do, and even open the play with Lynn not seen in the face, as I did. But it is never tangible plagiarism at that. Too bad. Please don't TALK about this to people, it might get back to them. I just don't talk on the subject. You know the malice of the theatre of course.

I am glad you had a crack at dramatics down there—ruling passion strong in death.

Beverley and Betsy seem well enough, a few colds, they are as usual very sweet. The little boy steams ahead.

I think it would be nice if you send Bowman a card, he liked you and was delighted to have you in the country. Entre nous, but just a card of remembrance. We have to pay for everything no doubt.

Pardon this typing, I would not read over this drool, that would mean the wastebasket.

Love to my cousin

Stark

Ludwig Fulda," Young summarized the plot of the Spanish play and then dealt with Behrman's changes. "Mr. Behrman, plus whatever suggestions or collaboration he may have had, uses the same story essentially," wrote Young. "What happens in this operation is that Manuela, Miss Fontanne, is demoted from her rank as the principal interest in the situation, Pedro, the husband, has most of his lines taken away from him—thus wrecking the story as such—and Serafin, the juggler, Mr. Lunt, is most of the show." Despite the effective use of music to heighten effects, *The Pirate,* he argued, "turned out a hodgepodge of style and theme." Although he merely implied that he considered Alfred Lunt gave a creditable performance, Young outspokenly praised Lynn Fontanne, who, he wrote, "has for us [in the final scene] that sense of a measured and boundless presence that fine acting must afford." At the conclusion of his article, Young admired the settings, costumes, and property designs.

589 | To Leah Salisbury, New York

320 East 57th Street
New York
January 10, 1943

Dear Miss Salisbury,

You will see the enclosed to Mr. Leigh. He is a most intelligent man and I have great gusto for him. I will write, in accordance with his request, this following reply and agreement:

I do not want to make any lectures at all this season, even if the chance arises, which is most unlikely, given the travel and war commitment generally.

I do not wish *any* lecture *tours,* meaning a series, and don't expect any offers in that direction—lectures, concerts, etc. are all in a mess so far as engagements go. I should like to see any paper that Mr. Leigh sends to you before I agree to anything. He is a fine man and things ought to turn out all right.

Thank you for the bother with the play yesterday. John Anderson called me at length today and thought we were most mistaken. Said he would talk it over with someone and call me again tomorrow.

Excuse this unread note, it is easier than forty rings on that telephone. You are always nice to me, and I don't net you much money which is a situation that dogs me in New York, which is about little else—poor fi chi!

Yours sincerely
Stark Young

(You might send Mr. C. Leigh a typed copy of this)

590 | To Caroline Charlotte McGehee, Como, Mississippi

320 East 57th Street
New York
January 18, 1943

Dear Cousin Cad,

I wanted to write you from Texas but my typewriter had to be left behind and I am sick of writing things by hand. A poor author gets about as much pleasure from that as a baker would get baking tea cakes after he gets home at night.

I got back here last Sunday and found that nice box from you. Those Mississippi pecans have a fine taste, better than the big papershells people brag about. And the pralines are delicious. Thank you very much. I like that much better than fruitcake, which soon palls on me.

I wanted to tell you about Waller Taylor's visit.[4] He came early in the morning, with a very nice boy, a friend of his from Massachusetts. Waller Taylor wanted to see some kin folks. I appreciated very much his coming by. It was too bad I was leaving for Texas. Even with flying around all that day I just made my train, and I could not put off the trip because the reservations had been made six weeks ahead and with a lot of trouble and delay. Waller Taylor was here only till evening of that day, they had to travel that night back to the camp. I gave him fifteen dollars to spend that afternoon, go to the movies, have lunch, take his friend to dinner or whatever. It did not seem to be much money to give such a nice young cousin, but we all have to be thrifty this year. I try to save money by just staying at home in my apartment. My Texas trip was paid for by a lecture engagement for $200 in Corpus Christi. At that I had to decline an invitation on the radio, from Columbia here, for January 3, and so missed that money. However, the people to worry about are the men in uniform. I am ashamed not to be of more use to my country than I am at my age. I could pull wires and get one of those desk jobs in Washington, but would be ashamed to be one of those of the many sponging on the Government. There are thousands at it.

Waller Taylor looked very trim and handsome in his uniform. His

4. Young refers to Waller Taylor Lipscomb, Como, Mississippi.

hair was well cut and looked stylish. He talked well and was very attractive and cordial. I was very proud of him. Bowman came in and thought the same as I did. Waller Taylor spoke of his family with great affection, said he would rather see his grandma than get to be a general.[5] I have always been fond of him among my young cousins and it made me very proud and happy to see him turn out so well. He is a fine fellow and I am sure the men in the camp like him.

With me things go slow. There is little use for writers or artists during such days as these. Perhaps one of the best things I can do is to try to understand things in the world and not talk like a fool, for my country's sake.

I am glad you liked the purse. It looked useful. Ladies carry around everything from money to pillows and can openers nowadays. I don't fancy you have as many bottles, powders, jars and pots as some.

I will not read over this dull letter. It brings you thanks and so many loving good wishes. I had a great desire to go to Mississippi this Christmas, but travel conditions made it impossible.

I am making a carbon print of this for Cousin Wheeler, so you needn't trouble to mail her this to you.

Lovingly
Stark

591 | To Allen Tate, Monteagle, Tennessee

320 East 57th Street
New York
Thursday [January 28, 1943]

Dearest Allen,

I am back in New York after a vaguely Homeric bit of travel. The problem of travel had best be left unsolved just now, of course, but I wanted to be with my family. Enough is heaving away from us, going past, without losing the small human matter that is left. This too is a

5. Waller Taylor Lipscomb's grandmother was Sally Wheeler McGehee Tait (Mrs. Watkins Minor Tait). She reared her grandchildren after their parents' deaths.

bad time of the year for me, for it is the time of my nephew's death. The whole thing seems as near as ever, that week in Yale, and my sister. I don't know how she ever lived through it; she knew she had to live and she developed a strong sense of the survival of his being, not dead. True or mistaken, it is something I can never be thankful enough for its presence in her mind.

But there is nothing to say about it all, or to pile on you. It is just that you and Caroline always seem right in whatever is touching me.

I read the poems[6] the other day and then twice again, three or four times in fact, today. My judgement must be fairly worthless in such cases, for I find myself less and less able to keep my attention on most of our verse today. I really don't try to read it any more. I think what it is that I require must be a certain, constant texture of passionate energy. I am sure I have a good ear and a sort of organic sense of style, if that means anything when said thus. At any rate I have been held by these poems of yours and am very happy that you have gone back to writing poetry. Of all the poems I think perhaps the first sonnet has less grip on me than the others, especially the fifth and sixth lines.[7] The octave of the second sonnet is dazzling, doubly so if read aloud, I find. In fact it read itself aloud. I found myself returning to stanzas in the ode and reading them again with that great feeling of remembering and yet not remembering exactly and yet convinced that it is too fine not to have it exactly as it stands. I hope that is clear. It is one of my strongest and dearest feelings about your Confederate Ode. I memorize very readily but in this case something makes me hold off from memorizing and keep on returning to it.

The final stanzas of the Ode just sent are very fine, I think. The very end one is wonderful, and to cap it with that swan image is the real thing—something not to be guessed at as to source or invention or volition and then suddenly there created. For that air of the miraculous the last stanza of this Ode seems to me—or at present at least it does—as fine as anything you have written.

Well, I do not put myself very happily, I fear. I hope the thought comes through.

6. The poetry Allen Tate sent Young included "More Sonnets at Christmas" and "Ode to Our Young Pro-consuls of the Air" published in *The Winter Sea* (1944).

7. The passage Young had in mind begins in line four: "I feared / The belly-cold, the grave-clout, that betrayed / Me dithering in the drift of cordial seas."

And I send so much affection and appreciation to you and Caroline. I hope my little niece flourishes. That letter to Lytle is still not written. I am balked by what I really want to tell him and think it useless to say. I can't promise to write anything for the Sewanee Review. And alas I have nothing around that could be used.[8] I find that the article as such is a great labor to me, unless there is some immediate urgency or call for it; when it becomes almost like a mere letter. And that kind I feel no inclination to write either. On the NR the long state of things has taken the life out of the writing impulse down there, as you know too well.

I have your lovely letter here and mean to read it again from time to time.

Lovingly
Stark

592 | To Andrew Lytle, Monteagle, Tennessee

320 East 57th Street
New York
Tuesday [February 23, 1943]

Dear Cousin,

You will forgive me I am sure for not answering your letter sooner, as to the article et cetera for The Sewanee Review.

One reason for my delay, truly, was that I had nothing to say. As to the Review I feel most kindly, that goes as a matter of course. And my interest in the Review is further, and much further, strengthened by the fact that you are connected with it. I consider—though my opinion is of doubtful value, since [I] cannot endure most American or British modern writing at all—that your NARRATIVE talent is one of the finest and rarest that has appeared in modern times. I read again your story in that Southern prose book—in which some professor or

8. Andrew Lytle, managing editor of the *Sewanee Review,* had written Young to ask him to write an article for the magazine.

historian had his operations listed while I had about half the space, thanks to provincialism in the collegiate vein and the silliness of professors, these being at Vanderbilt [9]—and what I thought, practically, was that you were too good for the volume, just as Allen's Confederate Ode makes me ashamed to see geese like MacCleish [*sic*] in the same book—or even in the same world.

Time passes and we shall all be dead, after some divine meditation, some dream of great art and scope of creation, some jolly fucking and some sweet music. My own opinion is, that after, the war anarchy will lift its head—no glands required for that, pardon Rabelais—and we shall all see what we shall see.

As for me, it costs me a great deal of effort to write essays and articles, unless the invocation is occasional and brief. I long to be like John Ransom, for example, he who blesses himself as he confuses the issue. That no doubt is a good crusader in criticism, the answer being not to read criticism, which I don't.

Well, then, Cousin, the answer to your request is that I shall have to leave the whole thing open and not promise anything. But that I believe in you and think your great talent is one of the bright spots in American writing. The one thing I could never forgive the Sewanee Review—I have forgiven it vast dullness and moss on the balls long ago—is that it might cut down so fine and brilliant a talent. In this case, as in all genuine cases, what I wish to see happen is that something shall be created. In the four hundred years, almost, of American life, the amount of creation has been pitifully small. The electric bulb is a cute masterpiece, but then—?

If, to return to the answer to your request, I should have an impulse to state something, I should be delighted to be of use to you. IF YOU THINK, YANKEE STYLE, that announcing me as a probable contributor to the Review would be of any use, just announce me. Just as they announce any quadroon at a New York night club. Just as I say I wish Andrew Lytle would write stories, what with that very unique

9. In *Contemporary Southern Prose,* edited by Richard Croom Beatty and William Perry Fidler (1940), Young was represented by "Encaustics for Southerners" (pp. 33–48) and Lytle by "Jericho, Jericho, Jericho" (pp. 384–96). Although identification of Young's reference to "some professor or historian" is not positive, very likely he had in mind Walter Prescott Webb's essay "Everywhere in Chains" (pp. 226–55). Beatty was professor of English at Vanderbilt; Fidler taught English at the University of Alabama.

and wonderful talent he has, just that, for I have seen him and read him. But I have neither raped Mary Pickford, or Martha Washington, and therefore am, alors, I say alors, am not of much use to you. I am not loud enough, yes?

Cousin, bless you, for you are as near a genius as our writers are likely to come. No indecency intended either. Sometimes I have a horrible thought, lest all American effort be merely sold or lost, not passionately used and ending in intense creation.

Affectionately yours
Stark Young

593 | To Allen Tate, Monteagle, Tennessee

320 East 57th Street
New York
Saturday [February–March, 1943]

Dear Allen,

I hasten to thank you for the poems and am very glad indeed, as you know, to have them. I suppose the Jubilo poem [1] is more astonishing and full of the surprise I have before spoken of to you, in your work. The Dejected Lines is more gripping and infectious. The last two lines sound fine but I am not sure I understand them. [2] Coming after that colon do they mean that the damnation consists in being drowned, though not by the sea, and that to achieve death it is even worth having lived? At any rate it is the office of a friend to serve as laboratory, even if you feel like knocking my head off.

These new poems do move on and out into their due regions. But I was troubled that you seemed to dismiss so cavalierly the others you sent. There may be some central thread needed for that ode, [3] which you will with time discover and work into the whole poem, but I still

1. Tate's "Jubilo" was published in his volume *The Winter Sea.*
2. Young's reference is to the last two lines of Tate's "Winter Mask," published in *The Winter Sea:* "The drowned undrowned by the sea, / The sea worth living for."
3. Presumably Tate's "Ode to Our Young Pro-consuls of the Air."

think it gets somewhere and I think the end is dazzling—I have just read the poem over.

As for my beginning a book of memoirs, I have notes going away into the file, fairly often, and I think I know the key now that I would write the book in. But I cannot say I feel disposed to write on it. The impact of the war is more than I can easily throw off, and I am not even sure how much I should try to throw it off. I am going to try to refrain from reading as much about it and the related subjects, like India for example, than I do now. I am so suggestible that things go round in my head. I have started well on painting again, and that does make a region where a certain degree of free life can go on even today. Whenever I do actually start writing pages for a memoir—I really have a pile of stuff now but not in any final shape, because I don't want to freeze it into a final shape that may hamper me—wherever I do start, I shall think of myself as talking to you, and that will be a help.

Of course one of the things that enrages and bursts me about the NR is that it should be taking advantage of your great distinction and taste, etc. I think for your poetry's sake that it is a good thing you are not taken up thus, but that does not alter the situation. As for me in some subtle way I am almost hamstrung when the thought of writing for the paper arises. Nevertheless I stay on it, though Bruce [4] has tried indirectly and directly enough to get me off. You see my point. It remains to be seen whether this will prove good or bad for me, but with things so torn up, it will do no harm to let the matter rest a while longer.

The war and the strain on the Elmhirsts partly explain the way in which Bruce has managed. He has about—really—cooked George and Malcolm—they don't even have office space there any more. I went to one conference, George was there, Bruce presiding at the desk, etc. But George would have been the last man ever to bother over what was being done to anybody else there, so I am not sad about all this. And you know Malcolm's gentle ways. So there.

Thank you for mentioning the letter from my nephew. He was certainly a wonderful, free, fresh, generous and brilliant creature, still adored by the young people who knew him.

I hope Caroline is entirely well now. Bless her heart.

---

4. Bruce Bliven, editor of the *New Republic*.

I am glad you have each other. I don't think I could stand living down there in the country like that, not these days. That is because I could not throw off the personal pressure of everything. I love people and am sensitive to them, and for that very reason the impersonal protection of a city helps me out greatly. It is all partly a way we were brought up, my sister and I, with people at the back of our minds, be considerate of so and so, tell so and so this, etc. Don't hurt so and so. You know the variety.

I had given me, Christmas, Harmonium, by Wallace Stevens. I have read perhaps ten pages in all. There seem to be some good images. But I don't have to read, in the course of a short life things like the opening poem, Earthy Anecdote.

Every time the bucks went clattering

Over Oklahoma

A firecat bristled in the way.

So finally the firecat bristled in the way every time, later, the firecat closed his bright eyes and slept.[5]

Thank God I am not a professional poetry critic and had to read all these matters. I had rather look in my book from Paris of the El Grecos in Spain.[6] Also I am memorizing some of the Greek anthology.

I am glad you are in the world, and Caroline is in it.

Lovingly
Stark

I crashed off a letter finally to Andrew Lytle, not at all drunk, for I had had nothing to drink and am on the wagon pretty much, but the letter sounded drunk, since I found the whole issue distressing. I am sure you are right about the whole review. We may as well face the facts in such Southern or academic cases as that.

---

5. After quoting above the first three lines of "Earthy Anecdote," Young's paraphrase of the concluding passage is virtually a quotation. Wallace Stevens' *Harmonium* was first published in 1923; a second edition was issued in 1931.

6. Young refers to *Les oeuvres du Greco en Espagne,* by Christian Zervos (1939). In 1940, Young had reviewed a reprint of it in "A New Book on El Greco," *New Republic,* CIII (October 28, 1940), 601–602.

594 | To George Jean Nathan, New York

320 East 57th Street
New York
Tuesday [March, 1943]

Dear George,

Beverley Thurman, a cousin of mine, knowing about the pirate play I wrote for the Lunts and this shift Alfred Lunt made to the Fulda play, more or less, caused him to think I might be interested in what the Fulda play was about. He got a German girl student down there at the University of North Carolina to make a sort of scenario of it, to send me.

I fancy you have read nearly every play ever written on the Continent, and are our sole critic really entitled to speak of drama in German. But let us hope from the scenario that you escaped this one. I have had the secretary run off a copy for you and for John Anderson. I thought you might like to look at it in connection with the Lunt-Behrman event.

The play I wrote for the Lunts had too much for Lynn and not enough for Alfred, who will very likely be the prima donna camping away in the new piece.

The history of my case is that they telephoned from Wisconsin along in March that they were about to do a highly contemporary play by Sherwood, and would do my play "in the fall." The war went on with Finland suffering and the box-office on the road was good, so naturally they went on with the play. In the course of time it was Alfred who finally decided to let mine go by the boards. Lynn knew it was the best part she ever had, and Sydney Greenstreet [7] was eager to do it, but

---

7. Sydney Greenstreet (1879–1954), stage and screen actor, born in England, made his debut in America with the Ben Greet Shakespearean Players and appeared with such famous actors of his time as Sir Herbert Beerbohm Tree, Margaret Anglin, Julia Marlowe, Viola Allen, and Lou Tellegen. With the Lunts he played in *The Taming of the Shrew, Idiot's Delight, Amphitryon 38, The Sea Gull,* and *There Shall Be No Night.* After reading Young's *Artemise* (earlier called *Belle Isle*), Greenstreet thought that with the exception of some scenes from Shakespeare the death scene at the end— the role of the decadent French nobleman Cassin was written for him—contained the most beautiful part ever composed for a character actor. In 1946, when Richard L. O'Connell wished to produce the play at the Pasadena Playhouse, Greenstreet was eager to perform the role, though he had virtually retired because of ill health. Despite O'Connell's and Greenstreet's enthusiasm, the play was not produced.

she is too loyal and shrewd to express her regrets, I mean Lynn is. She even had her clothes figured out.

Well, such is life. Dear George, please don't mention to anyone that I sent you my play. I had it printed last summer in Texas for a song, and like to have it at least thus for the present. You and John are the only people besides my sister that I have given a copy to, and I have not mentioned having it printed.

Bruce Bliven kicked up so about libel that I had to pare my Theatre Guild article down greatly, but it may be of use.[8] You will do the job much better than I can, you know so much more theatre record, for one thing, and too—I will spare you the compliments.

All this mess about the debacle of my play for the Lunts has made a hole in me, but no need to whine.

Talking on the telephone with you yesterday was very warming and good.

Yours
Stark

595 | To George Jean Nathan, New York

320 East 57th Street
New York
Saturday [March–April, 1943]

Dear George,

I have got a decent copy made of some of the points to be noted about my play and *The Pirate*—as you say—that's a good crack—well named.[9]

8. Late in 1942, the Theatre Guild celebrated its twenty-fifth anniversary. In his article, "Twenty-fifth Year for the Guild," Lawrence Langner, one of its founders, reviewed its accomplishments in the New York *Times,* November 15, 1942, Sec. 8, pp. 1–2. In the New York *Journal-American,* November 22, 1942, John Anderson disputed many of Langner's claims; and Young, in his essay "Theatre Guild Anniversary," *New Republic,* CVII (December 7, 1942), 745–46, continued the discussion. Young argued, contrary to Langner's assertions, that many excellent American actors had been acting in "literary" plays before and during the Guild's existence, that the production of foreign plays by the regular commercial producers far overshadowed the Guild's productions, and that "the most provocative and profound experiments in our theatre . . . have been outside the Theatre Guild." While conceding the "valuable work" of the Guild, Young protested against what he considered Langner's extravagant claims in its behalf. See below, Letter 595 and notes.

9. Young had pointed out to Nathan some of the similarities between *Artemise* and Behrman's *The Pirate.* In his column, "First Nights & Passing Judgments,"

I have now got the copies of *Esquire*—that article seems to me a masterpiece in every aspect.[1] Nobody else in town could write it in the first place; and in the second place no other theatre writer would ever know all that authoritative data. And in the third place, nobody else would defy chatter, threats and libel suits as you have done in it. I'll see that Bliven is confronted with it.

Yours
Stark

596 | To George Jean Nathan, New York

320 East 57th Street
New York
Saturday [March–April, 1943]

Dear George,

This note was to have gone off yesterday but I got myself heavily embroiled in a painting I am calling the Valley of the Pertonalis— probably misspelled so far—but at least located in Southwest Texas,[2] to account for the design and color.

Thank you so much for returning the letter. I will copy out those points more becomingly and less alcoholically [sic]—on my part— and return them to you, for I should like you to have them.

Your remark about the appropriateness of *pirate* made me laugh.[3]

Esquire, XIX (March, 1943), 80, Nathan had already mentioned *The Pirate* as having been "culled by S. N. Behrman from a German play written some thirty-odd years ago by Ludwig Fulda." Behrman's title seemed doubly appropriate.

1. Like Young, Nathan resented Langner's extravagant praise of the Theatre Guild. The subtitle of the monthly column in *Esquire*, April, 1943, indicates Nathan's attitude: "Puncturing Mr. Lawrence Langner's inflated claims for the peerless discoveries of the Theatre Guild." Making essentially the same points that Young had made in the *New Republic*, Nathan provided impressive documentation. Again the basic objection —this time phrased in Nathan's words—was to Langner's claim that the Guild "alone had been responsible for the advancement of American theatrical and dramatic art" (p. 76).

2. When finished, Young called the painting *Valley of the Pedernalis* and noted that it was "one of the rivers that Coronado gave names to when he passed through Texas northward in 1540." Today usually spelled *Perdernales,* the river is a short distance west of Austin.

3. See above, Letter 595, and notes.

But that pirating in itself—by friends, one thought—is an awful point with me. Doubtless both Alfred and the Theatre Guild got somewhere the notion that I am a gentleman—in their minds synonymous with imbecile—and so would do nothing about anything done to me.

That meeting of ours this week—please let me know when it would be convenient for you. I am mostly at home. The telephone is Wi.2.6493. It would be fine to see you.

Meantime, that article of yours about Langner's piece—I have so far four copies—one reserved for my own use. That is my idea of writing about the theatre. There are the facts, there are the possibilities for adventure in production and in creative art, and there is a brilliant overtone that comes from you as George and not as encyclopedia—useful as that part of the article is. It astonishes me that you who once did so much for an obviously living American theatre can still do so much for a theatre that just now spins around here and there and threatens to die on us. Though I suppose nothing dies. At any rate you show signs of nothing but life, and I am all for you.

> Yours as ever
> Stark

597 | To Allen Tate, Monteagle, Tennessee

> 320 East 57th Street
> New York
> Tuesday night [April 6, 1943]

Dearest Allen,

I have read the poem with my usual excitement over your work. As you say we can better discuss it when you are here.

I have to go to the farm and attend to some matters with an agent but will be back Sunday night, the 11th. We should like you to come here any time Monday or Tuesday for dinner or afternoon or lunch. I don't see why you can't come in the afternoon and stay to dinner Monday. Do try to. I won't make any engagements for those two days. You could send a note that would be here Monday morning. Or telephone Monday morning—I get up at seven. Wi.2.6493, in book under Bowman's name, you can remember that if you forget the number.

I have no doubt Stephen Benet was a nice fellow, he was vice-president of every group it seems, or something in causes. Perhaps some of his work is fine, I never read anything but JB's Body—I don't remember that any of it was poetry at all to my thinking. I saw the Literary Review—greatly aided by his family and connections he certainly got a hand there.[4] And the editorial in LIFE.[5] The quotations seemed not poetry to me. I have not talked about it. The people raving would turn out to have forgotten the thing they are ranting about, so what is the use.

I wish Caroline were coming to New York too. I am looking forward so much to seeing you here in the apartment. Bowman does too and sends regards, he is a great admirer of yours and Caroline's.

By the way I didn't mean to insult you but I proposed your two names for the American Institute of Arts and Letters, and then when the list of proposed or suggested names came I voted only for the two plus some one else, I don't remember who. It seems to me it was somebody who wrote music or painted. Odd I should forget it, the list was absurdly long, and many of the present members seem to me absurd. I have never so far been to a meeting or a dinner or a funeral, I always send word I am out of town. Mr. Damrosch is still president,[6] I think, if you can imagine that.

Lovingly
Stark

4. Young used the original name of the magazine founded in 1920 by Henry Seidel Canby. In 1924, Canby and William Rose Benét, brother of Stephen Vincent Benét (1898–1943), replaced it with the *Saturday Review of Literature,* which, in 1952, became the *Saturday Review.* Throughout his career, Benét published extensively in it, and after his death on March 13, 1943, the editors published a Stephen Vincent Benét memorial issue; see "As We Remember Him," *Saturday Review of Literature,* XXVI (March 27, 1943), 4–14.

5. The editors of *Life* called Benét "the leading poet of his generation"; mentioned as his principal works *John Brown's Body* (1928), *Ballads and Poems, 1915–1930* (1931), and *The Devil and Daniel Webster* (1937); and quoted the Lincoln monologue from *John Brown's Body* and several brief passages relating to Benét's concept of the significance of America. See "Editorial: Stephen Benét," *Life,* XIV (April 5, 1943), 22.

6. Walter Johannes Damrosch (1862–1950), composer and opera and symphony orchestra conductor, was president of the National Institute of Arts and Letters from 1936 to 1941. Young's comment would have been valid for the American Academy of Arts and Letters, of which Damrosch was president from 1941 to 1948. Young had been a member of the National Institute of Arts and Letters since 1938; Tate was elected to membership in 1949.

VIII

Painting
1943–1947

ON OCTOBER 11, 1941, Stark Young reached his sixtieth birthday and with it a low ebb in his career. During the next two years, his mental outlook would become worse instead of better. World War II would have an increasingly depressing influence upon him. He believed, almost intuitively, that the war had already marked the end of the great flowering of the American theatre that had begun in the 1920s. His personal ambition to create for it was being submerged in the unhappy conclusion that was gradually unfolding for *Artemise.* Even the *New Republic,* once a source of pride to him but now a melancholy subject, seemed to be in the grip of men who cared little or nothing for the arts and whose editorial policies no longer resembled Croly's. Finally, alcohol, once a pleasure, had now become for Young both a burden and an obstacle to creative activity. He looked for a new field of endeavor which would divert his mind for the present and perhaps eventually renew his creative energy. He found it in painting.

Stark Young's ventures into painting resulted from a lifelong interest in the art. Even as a boy he had wished to learn to paint, but his father had refused his son lessons for fear he would become a painter. The desire to paint, however, persisted and manifested itself in an occasional sketch or painting begun as a relaxation from the tensions of daily work. During his travels abroad, Young acquired an extensive knowledge of painting which he used in writing articles about special exhibitions in the New York museums and in preparing for the *New Republic* reviews of books about painting. In addition, his friendships with such painters as Margaret Boroughs, Robert Edmond Jones, Maurice Sterne, and Pavel Tchlitechew kept the subject of painting constantly in Young's mind. Consequently, his decision to learn to paint seems more an outgrowth of a sustained interest than a sudden entrance into an entirely new field.

Although Stark Young was largely a self-taught painter, he did receive instruction from Margaret Boroughs, who, with her husband, Wayman Adams, conducted an art school in Elizabethtown, New York. Herself a painter widely respected for her rendering of flowers and other still-life subjects, Margaret Boroughs helped Young to master the technique of painting flower arrangements in oil so that they exhibited a remarkably lifelike appearance. Having learned what he could from her, Young refined his technique through study and experiment until he created a style of his own. The typical Young canvas featured in the foreground a large, formal arrangement of white or pink, waxy peonies or roses. In the background and at a distance, the picture included an indistinct landscape, religious statue, or horizon of a medieval city. Critics often called attention to a nostalgic quality in the composition, as if the painting were executed from memory and not in the presence of real flowers. Young's poetic titles, which often reminded the reader of lines from the Greek Anthology, Dante, Spencer, Leopardi, Racine, Keats, Francis Thompson, and other literary classics, reflected the literary or religious inspiration for his work. Admirers of his paintings considered such titles as *Garland of the Garland, Still Wouldst Thou Sing, Votive,* and *Ave Maria,* with their accompanying quotations, appropriate both to his subject and his technique of painting.

Under the circumstances, Stark Young achieved remarkable success with his painting. His first exhibition of seventeen canvases, under the auspices of the Friends of Greece in May, 1943, brought high praise from Louis Kronenberger, Margaret Breuning, Robert Edmond Jones, and others. In November, 1945, Young's one-man show at the Rehn Galleries, consisting of twenty-five paintings, resulted in favorable notices in the leading art journals. The recognition of his work brought invitations to exhibit at the Pennsylvania Academy of Fine Arts, the Whitney Museum, the Dayton Art Institute, and the Chicago Art Institute. Three of Young's paintings were selected by the American Artists Group for reproduction on Christmas cards. In addition, he sold a number of his paintings through the Rehn Galleries and presented others as gifts to his friends. As a painter, Young's record did not make him an important figure in American art, but his achievement was respectable and certainly personally satisfying enough to help him through the unhappy and trying period in his life. As he regained a more cheerful outlook, he would turn back to his writing career.

Meanwhile, the situation at the *New Republic* was not promising for Young. He realized, of course, that his influence as an editor of the magazine was diminishing year by year; and, late in 1946, when Henry A. Wallace became editor-in-chief, Young sensed that his position would become even more difficult than it had been under Bliven. In assuming the editorship, Wallace announced that he would use the journal to promote his political views and left the day-to-day work in the hands of Bruce Bliven, Michael Straight, who had joined the staff during the preceding year, Robert Hatch, and others. Wallace manifested slight interest in articles devoted to the arts, while Bliven and Hatch, Young thought, were actively opposed to his contributions. When ordered to cut his article to a single column, he knew that his connection with the *New Republic,* which for more than two decades had been the outlet for most of his drama criticism and much of his other writing, was rapidly becoming more and more tenuous. As he looked backward upon his career, Young thought that the *New Republic* had traveled a great distance from its position in Croly's day, and he doubted that the direction had been upward. The order that he limit himself to a column merely emphasized the pattern events had been taking in the last several years.

Other events reminded Stark Young of the passage of time. Within a single year, he felt keenly the deaths of Doris Keane, Ellen Glasgow, Beatrice Chanler, Mary Lasater, Valette Sledge, Lyle Saxon, and Edward Sheldon. Doris Keane, for whom he had felt more affection than for any other woman, and Edward Sheldon stirred memories of the theatre that went back to the early years of the century, while for Ellen Glasgow he had long felt the sincere admiration of a colleague in fiction and the attraction of a strong, sympathetic personality. Their deaths increased Young's desire to write a book of memoirs.

598 | To Julia Young Robertson, Austin, Texas

[320 East 57th Street]
[New York]
Sunday [April 18, 1943]

Dearest Sister,

It was fine to have your letter first thing this morning, it made good time indeed. I was so glad to see that your arm was well enough to write, though I imagine the effort is not pleasant.

The check knocked me over. As a matter of fact I had thought of that flying up. Then in addition to the money I thought what if it did not go so well, then how fallow and flat we should all feel.[1] Since the play, for one thing, I am accustomed to the idea of things not going off. John Brown[2] was in. Allen Tate was the last to see the pictures for the first time. If what they feel and say is true, then I may expect a good opening. Then if some pictures sell I may invest the money in yours and Ben flying up, it would not tire you so very much. Nothing compared with the train. Well, time will tell, and I will honestly put that extravagant gift into one of the frames, and let you know exactly which one. The man who did that fine plaster work all over Hampshire House is doing them, then they are to be gilded, etc. He has that large old frame of mine to go by and I am to see Tuesday what progress will be made. He would not make single frames; too much mess with a mold for the trouble and money—so I have five of each design, taken from frames I supplied, not made there—that would be a fortune. Then the gilding. The ten plaster frames, not all one size, are $350. The gilding is ten to fifteen each, but I would be a fool to economize at such a really vital juncture.

I have just come back from an hour and a half at the radio, Columbia. Very tired, the strain. The strain is partly getting John[3] to stick to planning the thing. Miss Hamilton[4] was in distress, her first time, and

1. Young was making plans for an exhibition of his paintings to be held under the sponsorship of Friends of Greece, Inc., to open May 18, 1943. Originally, the exhibition was scheduled to last two weeks, but the closing date was extended to June 12.
2. John Mason Brown.
3. John Anderson.
4. Edith Hamilton (1867–1963), classical scholar, born in Dresden, Germany, but reared in Fort Wayne, Indiana, received academic honors at Bryn Mawr and the University of Munich. After serving for twenty-five years as headmistress of the Bryn

it was all I could do to get John to go on and stick through that making out an order. The result proved better than deserved, considering
that recklessness. The Columbia people thought it one of the most
successful programs they had had. I had written some outline words a
few minutes before we began, and at points I would stick my finger on
them and get Miss Ham back to the point, otherwise, she would have
made a pacifist lecture for the whole hour. A lovely lady and fine
scholar, but about 72, retired, and used to holding the floor without
interruption in classrooms. So everything I said was entirely extraneous. I thought I was pretty good at that. There were some new Columbia managers—they told John some quite grand things about me, who
was this man who made everything so exciting, etc. I must have some
sort of gab or something. Of course there was a great deal I could have
said in developing the point, but there was never any time. And John
though he is a dear fellow, intelligent and a true friend, just can't
seem to pull himself or the thing together. If I had not been there
Miss Ham would have gone mad and also would have wandered entirely off the subject and the amount of time.

Yes, the exhibition is settled. The editor of the NY Times [5] has
agreed to be a sponsor, Mrs. Harrison Williams,[6] I believe the Greek
Ambassador,[7] and so on. There is the opening with my talk and then
the varnishing—the audience making up the seers that first afternoon,
plus any press people if any want to come. They tend to avoid exhibitions for causes, since they have enough anyhow and like to stick to
the seemingly professional. Well, maybe it will get over as news. I

Mawr School in Baltimore, she resigned in 1922 to write articles about Greek drama for
Theatre Arts Magazine which became the basis for her best-known book published in
1930 as *The Greek Way* and republished in 1943 with additional material as *The
Great Age of Greek Literature.* Her other writings include *The Roman Way* (1932),
The Prophets of Israel (1936), *Three Greek Plays* (1937), *Spokesmen for God* (1949),
and *The Echo of Greece* (1957).

5. Charles Merz (b. 1893), editor of the New York *Times,* was one of the patrons
for the exhibition. Merz began his career as correspondent and associate editor for the
New Republic from 1916 to 1921. After writing for the New York *World* and *Collier's,*
he joined the staff of the New York *Times* in 1931 and edited the paper from 1938
until 1961.

6. Mona Bush Williams (b. 1897), wife of Harrison Williams (1873–1953, executive
of electrical utilities companies and patron of the Metropolitan Museum of Art), lived
much of the time in their villa in Capri. At the time of their marriage in 1926, Williams
was said to own the largest private yacht afloat. Later, Mrs. Williams lived in New
York where she gained a reputation as one of the best-dressed women in America.

7. Cimon P. Diamantopoulos (1887–1946) came to the United States in 1940 as the
Greek minister and subsequently was made ambassador.

went to dinner at the Colony Club with Elenor, the Countess Palffy,[8] and Mrs. Chester Nurder[9] was there and told me she had heard the paintings were remarkable, so something must be going round.

Well thank you and Ben again for that dazzling check, and for the thought behind it.

Wales sends his love. We are going to Easter lunch at Gertrude's.[1] My picture with the two figures seems to be a special success with people. I am glad because I was afraid of it.

I think I told you all that about the exhibition already. At any rate you can tell anybody, newspaper people and all.

Stark

599 | To Julia Young Robertson, Austin, Texas

[320 East 57th Street]
[New York]
Monday [April 19, 1943]

Dear Sister,

I have not cashed my check yet, like to look at it and think what a lovely family I have. I hope, as you said once you did, we will all die close together in time, not stay in a lonely world where we have not really much point anyhow. I just love my family, you and Ben and Stark as few people can love and as few are therefore loved. The "therefore" is not entirely to the argument.

8. Eleanor Jenckes Roelker (1890–1952), socialite and author, in 1914 married Harrison Tweed, New York attorney. After her divorce in 1928 and marriage to Count Paul Palffy in Paris, she lived much of the time in Europe. In 1948, she used her own experiences in international social circles as the basis for the book, *Largely Fiction;* and, in 1951, she published *The Lady and the Painter,* in which she gave a fictional interpretation to the life of Isabella Stewart Gardner (Mrs. John L. Gardner, Jr.).

9. Identification not established.

1. Gertrude Macy (b. 1904) began her career as a stage manager in 1928 and since that time has served at times as general manager or producer in a number of successful Broadway productions, including *Wingless Victory, No Time for Comedy, The Doctor's Dilemma, The Barretts of Wimpole Street, The Lark Is Light Enough,* and others. From 1941 to 1947, she was executive producer of Martha Graham's Dance Company.

I have been reading the Greek anthology lately. We have not so long to stay in this world and should try to be with the treasures of time like that—somehow I feel that I am being guided to make a speech at that Greek place of my pictures and *conference* such as has not been heard in this town.[2] I was so touched with those people wanting to do this for me. I wish I could give back the wonder and sweet humanity that I feel in certain people. That is one reason why I should be well and rested, but who these days is well and rested.

Countess Palffy called me this morning about my radio words. What she said would please my sweet sister. I could take the whole thing away from John Anderson, but I don't want to because he is a fine man and a true friend, and because he suits this great city sloppy way of doing things. Even if I were the sort that would take it, I would not want the results. I am afraid we are citizens of a very silly, dear country. But no other race can say that to me!

Lovingly
Stark

600 | To Julia Young Robertson, Austin, Texas [carbon]

[320 East 57th Street]
[New York]
Thursday morning [May 20,
1943]

Dearest Sister,

It was fine to talk with you and Ben over the telephone yesterday and I would have written yesterday but had to be at the gallery about all day seeing how the ladies in charge were running the lighting and who was there for me to see.[3] There were some newspaper people,

2. At the preview of the Friends of Greece exhibition of his paintings, Young delivered an address entitled "Marathon Looks on the Sea." Henry McBride summarized the lecture as "a rhapsody upon the theme of the 'Miracle That Was Greece' and which still continues in these tremendous days upon miraculous heights comparable to Thermopolae." See "Attractions in the Galleries," New York *Sun,* May 21, 1943, p. 23.
3. After the preview opening on May 18, at which Young and the Greek consul general addressed an audience of invited guests, the exhibition of Young's paintings was formally opened to the public on the following day. Young exhibited paintings

though the war news and the weddings take up all the space in the papers. Considering that fact it is remarkable how much space the show has gotten and there will be articles tomorrow and Sunday.

Margaret Lewisohn who knows painting and has that great and famous collection came yesterday, she asked me to meet her there. She was delighted and called Sam Lewisohn and told him he had to come by that very afternoon and see the show. I had to meet him at five and was astonished at his wholesale endorsement. He knows painting and writes on it, as well as owning the famous collection. Also Lintott came, the first flower painter in the world and so recognized.[4] I was terrified but he said wonderful things, and I have been told on the telephone this morning by Mrs. Winthrop[5] and by Marie Sterner,[6] who has been so famous for her gallery and her introduction of new painters, that he has been saying this picture or that was a "masterpiece," etc. She said the most remarkable things when she was at the gallery and Mrs. Winthrop is so overcome that she won't take the small flower painting at the price they said but has written insisting on paying more. She has done so much for the exhibition that I begged her to let me give her the picture but she will not accept it. She had asked if I would take $100, which is all she felt she could afford just now. I said of course, and I wish she would not insist on paying more.

Mrs. Sterner, who ought to know, said it made her sick that I sold

with the following titles: *Peonies, Childe Harold to the Dark Tower Came, Presidio Range—West Texas, Feather Flowers, Rehearsal in Red, Of Every Sort Which in That Meadow Grew, Sketch for Six, Valley of the Pedernalis, The Chambers in the House of Dreams Are Fed with So Divine an Air, Flowers over San Antonio, Votive, And over the Sad Land, Ode, To Romance, Three Vases, Long Ridge—Westchester,* and *Garland of the Garland.*

4. Edward Barnard Lintott (1876–1951), British painter who lived much of his life in the United States, achieved a widespread reputation for his flower studies, still-life paintings, and portraits of such well known persons as Leslie Howard, Lady Diana Duff Cooper, Mrs. Theodore Roosevelt, and Frank Lloyd Wright.

5. Emmeline Heckscher Winthrop (Mrs. Edgerton Leigh Winthrop, Jr., 1874–1948), served during World War I as Manhattan chairman of the Committee on Volunteers of the Mayor's Committee of Women on National Defense. In World War II, she was active in war relief projects, one of them being the Stark Young art exhibition for Friends of Greece, Inc. From 1906 until his death in 1926, her husband was a prominent New York lawyer in the firm which included his brother, Bronson Winthrop, and Henry L. Stimson.

6. Marie Sterner Lintott (Mrs. Edward Barnard Lintott, 1880–1953), prominent art dealer, established an art gallery in 1912 while married to Albert Sterner; and after their divorce and her marriage to Lintott in 1932, she continued to operate the gallery under the name Marie Sterner. An art critic as well as a dealer, she helped to introduce to this country the work of Paul Cezanne and Jacob Epstein.

the pink peonies for $150, I should have said $450 and the dealers would be getting $1200 for it. I have finally settled on prices and given the list to the attendants at the gallery.

Mrs. Sterner said $450 was about right for a man showing for the first time especially, that means the larger landscapes. The Dream has come out beautifully.

Mrs. Chanler[7] is delighted with the way the opening went off— first about the most distinguished audience you could get up in New York, really people, not newspaper celebrities. The hall seated 80 to 90 —which would be $400 to 450. The sale was 665, and people had to stand outside the door. Mr. Ogden Hammond[8] read the telegram from the Greek Ambassador.[9] The Greek Consul General[1] made a really very tasteful and poetic presentation speech. I spoke about thirty minutes, and it seemed to go well. Then people stayed on, many of them for over an hour looking at the pictures. There were three or four people interested in buying several pictures, I mean for each picture. The Greek Ambassadress[2] came up from Washington especially for the occasion. A beautiful and chic woman of about 38.

So it is all somewhat overpowering. But I hope many people will hear of it and come to see the pictures.

The frames after working us to death came out very well indeed. I

7. Beatrice Ashley Chanler (Mrs. William Astor Chanler, 1886–1946), actress, sculptress, and philanthropist, was president of the Friends of Greece, Inc. Born in Virginia, she began her acting career with the name of Minnie Ashley and achieved recognition for singing such hits as "I'm a Naughty Girl" and "Rhoda Had a Pagoda." In 1903, she married William Astor Chanler, African explorer and Democratic congressman. She studied sculpture and executed a number of portrait busts before ill health forced her to abandon her work. She published a volume of French verse, *Le péan du nouveau monde* (1927) and *Cleopatra's Daughter: The Queen of Mauretania* (1934). During the first and second world wars, she served in a number of relief agencies and received decorations in recognition of her work from the French and Greek governments. After her death, Young wrote a tribute to her in which he said "she had something almost like genius in her power of moving others to outdo themselves in what they found they rightly delighted in and worked for. She constantly moved outward, and carried others with her, from some beautiful spirit and enthusiasm within herself, something both secret and shining." See Young's letter to the editor of the New York *Times,* dated June 28, 1946, published July 2, 1946, p. 24.

8. Ogden Haggerty Hammond (1869–1956), diplomat and civic leader, began his career in the real estate business in New Jersey, served in the New Jersey legislature from 1914 to 1917, held various state offices, and from 1925 to 1929 was ambassador to Spain.

9. Cimon P. Diamantopoulos.

1. Nicholas Lély.

2. Madame Sapho Diamantopoulos.

put one of those carved Mexican frames on to a flat board frame and had that cast. The ten frames cost me about $365, and then I had to do the gilding and painting.

Robert Edmond Jones has written me three letters about the pictures. Since I have heard him say that easel painting did not interest him, I was much pleased that he should be so moved.[3] James Reynolds[4] was there yesterday and was going on at a rate. He has just had an exhibition himself.

One of the oddities of the situation with all those high top swells for sponsors was that the pictures were carried over from here to the gallery in Lily Pons' very elaborate station wagon. Her music librarian is a friend of the electrician and mechanic for this building and so arranged this.

We are going to the country tomorrow till Monday morning and both of us need the country indeed after this strain. When the gilder called up a few days before the opening and said he could not take on the job of the five frames—at $35 each—I thought the world had ended, but we got it all done nevertheless. Then of course I had to look up all the Greek stuff for my talk.

Mrs. Harrison Williams sat up in front and was awfully nice about the show and the speech. Mrs. Delano was full of praise.

Mr. Delano came, frail as he is.

3. Young had just received a letter written by Jones on May 19 in which he had said: "It is surprising that you paint so well technically. . . . What is interesting is the content of each picture. Your flowers, for instance. You see them so beautifully and so strangely, with a kind of sad contemplation. There is no 'Go, Lovely Rose,' no flame of spring. They take their place as a cosmic manifestation, one of the myriad happenings in the universe, bits of eternity. This is odd, and different, and appealing. The finality of flowers. . . . Your eye sees them and places them in time as well as in space. Here is the point of view you speak of in relation to the art of Duse. In a way they are like the Greek epigrams you love and quote. But it is your skies that mean most to me, the relation of the Heavens to the earth. (I can't say this!) What seems to me is that— whether you mean it consciously or not—you have indicated with a great deal of precision a sense of a presence that is purposeful. I don't mean a mystical presence in the yearning Fiona Macleod [pseud. William Sharp, 1856–1905] sense we use the word—not a brooding, lamenting thing, but a sense of activity, movement, influence, a spirit *moving* over the waters. There is a spiritual pattern. This again is odd, and peculiar to you. And again it is most appealing." Jones published several of these comments in his flattering article about Young's exhibition, "Filled and Pervaded," *New Republic,* CVIII June 21, 1943), 829.

4. James Reynolds (1891–1957), artist and author, gained recognition as a painter and scene designer before he became a writer. His work included paintings of horses, murals, and illustrations for his books on Spain, Ireland, England, Italy, and Austria. In 1948, he wrote and illustrated *Ghosts in Irish Houses,* which was followed by *Ghosts in American Houses* (1955), and *More Ghosts in Irish Houses* (1956).

I must stop and get some things done.

Thank you and Ben for the telegram and for the flowers. Doris got back by chance the morning of the opening and I kept wishing you and Ben could be there too.

This is a dull letter, but I feel like a rag, but well.

Lovingly

[unsigned]

601 | To Julia Young Robertson, Austin, Texas

320 East 57th Street

New York

May 25, 1943

[Dear Julia]

I sent Eddie's letter answering this.[5] You note he does not mention what happened to the first asking him to be a patron. He is bound to have gotten it because it would have been returned otherwise to the NR. Mrs. Chanler thinks this is a great joke on him. He thought it was an amateur event and he was to be used for it. Then there is this list of patrons that knocks people backward and is said to be the last word and vast surprise etc.—all Mrs. Chanler—and some of them people Johnson could scarcely meet—he runs with messes like Grace Moore[6] or else people he thinks might be useful or is impressed by, such as poor Mrs. Belmont.[7]

5. Young wrote this letter on the back of a carbon copy of a letter he wrote to Edward Johnson, then general manager of the Metropolitan Opera Company. As a very young man, Young had known Johnson before he attained widespread fame. See above, Letter 12 and notes.

6. Grace Moore (1901–47), opera, radio, and screen actress and singer, spent her childhood in Jellico, Tennessee, and attended Ward-Belmont School in Nashville, where she abandoned her plans to become a missionary to study singing. She had her first musical success in such musical comedies as *Kitchy Koo* (1921), *Up in the Clouds* (1922), and the *Music Box Review* (1923). After studying in Europe, she made her opera debut in 1928 as Mimi in *La Bohème*. Rapidly she became a favorite with audiences for her singing in opera, motion pictures, and radio. In 1931, she married Valetin Parera, a Spanish actor. Although critics at times objected to the quality of her performance, she became one of the most popular artists of her day. In 1944, three years before her death in an airplane crash, she published her autobiography, *You're Only Human Once.*

7. Eleanor Robson Belmont (Mrs. August Belmont, b. 1878), actress and civic leader, made her debut in 1897 as an actress in a San Francisco stock company. She appeared in a number of New York productions before her marriage to August Belmont in

It was stupid of him, but such is human nature and the sting of early years etc. I was determined not to let him get away with it, and so sent the second letter, enclosing too the program with the patrons, and putting it all on the friendly basis. They say the French people at Columbia radio even are raving about this show. What a joke on Johnson and poor retrograded fellow he is, though he deserves credit for according to his lights he has done the best he could.

I should like it if you would put this letter aside—in the Florentine casket in the library—I want to keep the two letters as a historical item of modern art NYC life.

Lovingly
Stark

[Enclosure, carbon of letter from Young
to Edward Johnson, May 25, 1943]

Dear Eddie,

I am sorry my first letter to you, asking you to become a patron of my preview etc. did not reach you; but I still want you to know that I should have liked your name on the enclosed list of patrons.

The occasion went well, more people than the gallery held, a telegram from the Greek Ambassador, read by Mr. Ogden Hammond, the Greek Ambassadress came up especially for the event, and the presentation, or introduction, a very happy one, was by the Greek Consul General.[8] People stayed on after the chairs were removed, and a long time. When I left six paintings of the seventeen had the red stars of sold on them. The reviews have been remarkable—you may have seen the Friday Sun or the Sunday Times.[9]

1910. During World War I, she became a member of the central committee of the American Red Cross. Subsequently, she was involved in a number of civic activities in New York, and, in 1933, she became the first woman elected to the board of directors of the Metropolitan Opera Association. In 1935, she founded the Metropolitan Opera Guild to raise financial support for the association.

8. See above, Letter 600 and notes.

9. For Henry McBride's review in the New York *Sun,* see above, Letter 599 and note. McBride observed that after Young's lecture, "a criss-cross of questioning arose demanding an explanation for the lack of primitiveness in these new pictures—for it had been given out that the artist had been self-taught—and flatteringly disbelieved. Certainly they had all the sophistication in the painting that one could desire. 'That one has all the poetry of a Ryder,' said Harry Bull, who was present and who is never

I know you will be glad to know of all this. Bee[1] would have been delighted and so will Fiorenza[2] be. Give her my love when you see her.

With affectionate greetings
[unsigned]

602 | To John Benjamin Robertson, Austin, Texas

[320 East 57th Street]
[New York]
Friday [May 28, 1943]

Dear Ben,

I have been standing most of the time since ten this morning seeing people who came to look at the exhibition. People telephone or there is some photographer or newspaper man or some arrangement, etc. So I am too dead to write a decent letter—it is six forty five now.

All sorts of people have been there today, not such a great number of course but interesting people. Constance Collier, Charlie Scribner, Mildred Natwick, the English designer and artist, Robs-John-Gibbings,[3] a very distinguished British family and that is just the fam-

---

deceived in anything, indicating a particularly desirable landscape. Poetry and romance were rampant in all the pictures. 'Rampant,' perhaps is not the word, for the romance was controlled and not at all frightening. Even the delightful flower piece, dedicated 'To Romance' openly, turned out to be peonies rather than camellias—sacred, therefore, rather than profane romance." Edward Alden Jewell, writing in the New York *Times,* May 23, 1943, Sec. 10, p. 10, remarked that Young has "evolved a paint manner subtly adapted to the intimation of his thoughts and reveries. Several of the flower subjects are charmingly brushed. The imaginatively wrought fantasies, sometimes reminding one a little of Greco, sometimes a little of Ryder, are irradiated with a revealing and yet eluding, an always haunting and intensely personal, mysticism."

1. A reference to the Portuguese viscountess, Beatrice da Verga d'Arneiro whom Johnson had married in 1909. She died in 1919.

2. Johnson's daughter, Fiorenza d'Arneiro Johnson (1912–65), who had been born in Florence and named for that city. In 1936, she married George Alexander Drew (1894–1973), Canadian high commissioner to Britain and former premier of Ontario.

3. Terance Harold Robsjohn-Gibbings (b. 1905), interior decorator and designer, born in England, came to the United States in 1929 and became a naturalized citizen in 1945. Known primarily as a designer of contemporary interiors and furniture, he has written *Good-Bye Mr. Chippendale* (1944), *Mona Lisa's Mustache: A Dissection of Modern Art* (1947), *Homes of the Brave* (1954), and *Furniture of Classical Greece* (1963).

ily name, the three. A Greek sculptor came yesterday and had much to say. The photographer said the values and pigment were so good that the photographs were extra good.

It already seems a week since I was talking to Julia this morning, Gerta surprised me when she mentioned if I had telephoned you or not. I hope you are going to be decent and take me up on the offer about that check. It would be best used that way, and the exhibition looks really quite thrilling.

I would rather be there longer Christmas, as compared with summer—evidently I can't seem to paint very successfully there—perhaps it is the unaccustomed light. So you can see how there would be only one fare, and I should like to spend the money that way. By the way I wore the tie you gave me for the preview and was complimented on it by several people more or less in the family.

Of the fifteen pictures for sale now eleven are sold, I hate to see them go away.

Betsy is anxious for you to use the apartment, the people move June 1, and the apartment is next to the Fairfax, so you would have no expense. Gerta will cook for us. Since the preview there is nothing personal about going to the gallery—Julia mentioned not having a spring dress or something. Bosh, at that, I fancy.

I cut out the Times clippings for you. The other might amuse Miss Hallie or the Goldmans. At the end of next week I will disappear. I have had more now than I ever underwent for the sake of my books. But I did want this go to well. Town and Country is also going to have pictures. Or one at least.[4]

I hope to hear you and Julia can come up, though that long trip is a mess.

Love to you both
Stark

4. Photographs of Young's *Garland of the Garland* and *Votive* (purchased by Gertrude Newell) appeared in *Town and Country*, XCVIII (July, 1943), 78.

603 | To Julia Young Robertson, Austin, Texas

320 East 57th Street
New York
June 3 [1943]

Dear Sister,

You can see I began this letter yesterday but I was called to the gallery, anon. I got your telegram last night about nine thirty when we came home. Gerta stuck a small tack in her foot at the farm and the doctor told her to keep off it for two days, etc. So we had to eat out. Then this morning, after such delightful and surprising news last night I had the letter about your tooth. What a rotten shame. Two weeks ago one of mine started up but for the present seems suspended. I imagine it will come back on me. I do hope yours can be quickly healed. It is a shame.

I had planned to take you to the exhibition and then to the train [*sic*] for Saturday night and Sunday till Monday morning, then we had arranged here to use a bed of Betsy's that she had in her dinette —David Hugh is still in Carolina—and put it in the dinette here, it would have been fine for all of us, you could have had my room. Wales was so pleased that you were coming, and I more than pleased, though I was worried about the train trip without Ben. Well, they have extended the exhibition still another week, which makes four instead of two, a compliment. Then after a bit it goes to Boston. So maybe you can get here next week. I hope you take reservations on receipt of my telegram and can make it yet.

The news could not be better. It seems that New York is really interested. There have been the papers, then the Art News [5] and Town and Country,[6] then Time Magazine [7] sent their critic Tuesday—seeing

5. A picture of Young's *Flowers over San Antonio* appeared in *Art News*, XLII (June, 1943), 38.

6. See above, Letter 602, n. 4.

7. A review of his exhibition, entitled "Stark Young, Painter," appeared in *Time,* XLI (June 14, 1943), 42. "Stark Young," wrote the *Time* critic, "takes a view of art which is warming to those tired of abstruse and cerebral esthetics. Says he: 'In my opinion a picture should be nostalgic with all we love and follow after in life; but . . . it should have finally within it a calm and harmony as if it had arrived at a completeness in itself and its own peace.' Young's work in no way suggested that he

seven exhibitions. He evidently liked mine, they telephoned yesterday and sent their interviewer for data for a real article about me and asked for photographs of the paintings. Nothing could be better or wider publicity for them. Mr. Jewell on the Times is the best and most important of the critics and he has also written me a fine letter besides his articles.[8] And to cap the climax—or so I am told—Bessie Beatty[9] or however you spell it—who has had many distinguished people on her program, has asked me for June 9, WOR 11.15 AM. I don't like doing it, but am told it is a wonderful chance, etc. So everybody is delighted. I am holding two of the paintings for myself, and of the fifteen for sale eleven have already sold. That is another language and knocks people over. The sales of recent pictures this year is said to have been almost nil, so that's that. I can't say I take it all in.

I have to stop and dress and go to the gallery. The famous Russian painter Tchelichew is coming, has telephoned and Martha Grahame.[1] Maurice Sterne came, is very blunt, but was relieved when he saw the pictures. Said they were a reproach to most painters, were painted as only a great master can technically, etc. I was overwhelmed indeed,

---

had been painting for only two years. His solid, slightly impressionistic flower pieces indicated close study of the still life masters by a man who loves nature as well as art. That Stark Young also loves literature and history was somewhat fruitily evident in his precious titles and subtitles lifted from Francis Thompson, Racine, Leopardi, etc."

8. See above, Letter 601, n. 9, and below, Letter 607, n. 9.

9. Bessie Beatty (1886–1947), radio commentator, lecturer, and author, began her career early in the century as a newspaperwoman in Los Angeles, San Francisco, and Washington. She wrote articles about Russia for *McCall's Magazine, Hearst's Magazine,* and *Good Housekeeping* and lectured on Russia and woman's suffrage. At the time of Young's letter, she was conducting a forty-five-minute daily radio program for WOR, New York City.

1. Martha Graham (b. 1902), dancer, choreographer, and teacher, made her Broadway debut as a dance soloist in 1923 and shortly afterward began her career as teacher of interpretative dancing at the Martha Graham School of Contemporary Dance. Young, who recognized her talent from the beginning of her career, contributed significantly to her success by his perceptive reviews in which he recorded the development of her art. So early as 1931, Young noted that "there has come something lately . . . into Miss Martha Graham's work, a certain freedom and relaxation, you could almost say spiritual generosity or flowering, a fresh happiness or discovery, something which no one can describe, but which is like some inner possibility of light and the way ahead"—"Town Melange," *New Republic,* LXIX (December 23, 1931), 163. The following year, Young wrote an extensive critique of her artistic growth in "Miss Graham and Mademoiselle," *New Republic,* LXXIII (December 14, 1932), 127–29. In 1941, he reaffirmed his admiration and enthusiasm for her art in "Three and One," *New Republic,* CIV (April 21, 1941), 532–33. In 1945, he wrote that her "compositions offer the most creative, as well as the ultimate, most strict and most nobly designed, manifestations of our theatre today"—"Martha Graham," *New Republic,* CXII (June 4, 1945), 791.

and really, since he is not only the best painter in America but very learned etc. He stayed an hour and a half, looking at them very solemnly. I still think that is a sort of trance I got into. If he thinks nothing of somebody's painting he just says so, and that combined with his fame makes painters want to murder him, though all have a great respect for him. As a draughtsman they all admit he is the greatest in the world. So there.

Well I know you want to hear all this, though it seems egotism when you have that damned tooth to contend with. I certainly hope you got it fixed up, they probably took it out. Mine last summer—the one that made me nearly faint there in Austin from infection—was all over in half a day after it was out. I had before that another of the dizzy spells. Just poison.

Those Goldman cousins sweetly sent me a telegram and I am making a copy of this for them carbon, for there is not time to write anything but notes. The telephone rings all morning nearly. Sergava[2] the Russian ballerina prima at the St. James Theatre came yesterday and nearly expired with pleasure, bless her, and a lovely creature, I never saw her before off the stage.

I must stop, I wish you and Ben were here.

Lovingly
Stark

2. Katharine Sergava (b. 1918), Russian-born ballerina, was then being featured in the dances created by Agnes de Mille for the production of *Oklahoma!* at the St. James Theatre. Young had praised her performance in his review of the musical in "Oklahoma with Details," *New Republic,* CVIII (April 19, 1943), 508–509.

604 | To Harriet Hendrickson,[3] Jamaica, Long Island

320 East 57th Street
New York
Thursday [July 15, 1943]

Dear Harriet,

I had the check [4] and a lovely letter from you, and have been meaning to write. But the two weeks extension made a month of the exhibition and there was a great strain not only of people but of interviewers,
critics, photographers, and so on. Then when it was all over there was
great an accumulation of letters, thanks, telegrams etc. from all over
the country. At last I got a case made for the two paintings going to
Gloucester,[5] and will soon have a case for yours, one I already have
among my stores, though the Gloucester case has not been picked up
by the express yet.

I am doing another peony picture, larger, with water and sky, very
dark, behind the flowers. The flowers around white and cream and a
few pink. I have been using your painting to teach myself the method
of finishing the flowers.[6] It is really astonishing how the treatment
goes out of one's head. So I should like immensely to have the picture
for about another ten days, then Wales and I will bring it out and see
it hung and we can all have an old time party.

3. Harriet Bevin Hendrickson (Mrs. Arthur Ward Hendrickson, b. 1898) met
Young about 1924 shortly before he became drama critic for the New York *Times*.
Born in East Hampton, Connecticut, she moved to Long Island after the death of her
father in 1900. Soon after her graduation from Smith College, she married Arthur
Ward Hendrickson. Mrs. Hendrickson recalls that Young had sent her mother a
painting depicting a kneeling figure of St. Peter to be placed over the mantel in the
living room of her mother's French Provincial house which had been designed by her
brother, Newton Bevin, shortly after his return from a European trip with William M.
Bowman in 1923. In transit, the sleeve of the blue robe of St. Peter had been damaged;
and after Young had skillfully repaired it, members of the family urged him to take
up painting. He replied that "one day I shall."
4. The Hendricksons had purchased Young's painting *Peonies*.
5. Young was sending to Gloucester *Feather Flowers,* purchased by Alice Lewisohn
Crowley (Mrs. Herbert E. Crowley), and *Flowers over San Antonio,* bought by
Natalie Hays Hammond.
6. Mrs. Hendrickson explains that "the 'teaching' was his own experience and he
did keep our paintings for several weeks while he made a 'replica' for Sam Lewisohn.
He would have bought 'The Peonies' for his own collection, had we not seen it first.
That was, no doubt, the larger painting to which Stark referred."

I love the fact that Chick [7] just went up and picked out one of the two paintings there that Sam Lewisohn, who really has gone in for collecting and modern art, and that the famous Marie Sterner of the galleries had so much to say about. I don't know any people that I would rather [the] picture went to live with than you and Chick. One of the nice things about the exhibition was the fact that nearly every picture went to a darling person—the others may be so too. I just did not know them. The small landscape that Mrs. tightish Ryan [8] bought she never came to see and evidently went off to Bar Harbor and forgot it. I had asked Edna—Elizabeth's sister [9]—to buy it so I could say the person I had [sold] it to in case after so long Mrs. Ryan turned up. But she never did so I have the picture and want it. Diane Tate could have sold it, she said, but Maurice Sterne told me to keep it.

Your picture was the only picture there that that buff in the walls did an injustice to. You will see how much better it looks without that tan near to dull the amount of tannish tone in the picture.[1]

I will telephone or something before very long and then we can all get together and hang the painting too.

Affectionately
Stark

605 | To Julian Huxley, London, England

Bedford, New York
August 16, 1943

Dearest Julian,

I had a very fine letter from you today—it did me good indeed— and my mind has been low. I will wait to reply when I get back to

7. Arthur Ward Hendrickson (1899–1968), designer and manufacturer of architectural lighting, executed lighting designs for the restoration of Williamsburg, the Planetarium in Chapel Hill, and the National Gallery of Art in Washington.

8. Precise identification of the object of Young's witticism cannot be established.

9. Young refers here to Miss Edna Hopkins and her sister, Elizabeth Hopkins Bevin (Mrs. Newton Bevin).

1. Mrs. Hendrickson notes that " 'The Peonies' did look much better on our own walls, which were 'off white' and showed up the delicate shades of pink, to better advantage."

town and my typewriter next week. I'll do a mucho palabras on some of the many points of your pages. But meanwhile congratulations on your lecture going well. The special nature of the occasion must have broken you into fragments.[2] The whole sequence of the grandfather connection, etc. and the complexities of the modern scene, ethical and scientific, could work at the back of your mind till you broke down into nervous prostration. The lecture occasion probably derived a certain communicable and splendid tension from the very same, however —if that is any comfort. It is to you—I know, but half of you is artist.

I did—partly the results of your push and excitement over the paintings—have an exhibition which turned out—so regarded in print too —as one of the art events of the year—I was overwhelmed—not that I didn't think well of the pictures, but still—more of that when I write. I have some photographs I'd like to send you, but—tell me—would they ever be likely to reach you, do you think?

The main point of this advance—as they say in Hollywood—short of a letter is to congratulate my godson on his wedding dreams—I hope he finds due happiness. If you can do me a favor I'd be glad. Please advance him the equivalent of a hundred dollars for a wedding present and send me a line saying the best and surest way to get it to you. I can't cable it from out here in the country and I don't know but that some kind of draft is easier for you to manage. If you'd let him have it to use for the occasion, I will send it in whatever form you say as soon as I hear from you. Just a line. I won't be back in town soon enough to get it there in time for the wedding—no matter in what form I send it. I wish it were a larger sum but incomes here—and with me certainly—are getting very dubious. About all I can do about it is try and live very simply.

Give my love to dear Juliette and to yourself. I hope you are all right —you don't sound the least moribund, believe me.

Affectionately
Stark

The Good address is still 320 East 57th St.

2. On June 11, 1943, Huxley delivered at Oxford University the Romanes Lecture, subsequently published as *Evolutionary Ethics*. In 1893, his grandfather, Thomas Henry Huxley, had also delivered the Romanes Lecture with the title "Evolution and Ethics." Both lectures were reprinted in *Evolution and Ethics, 1893–1943*, by T. H. Huxley and Julian Huxley (1943) and *Touchstone for Ethics, 1893–1943*, by T. H. Huxley and Julian Huxley (1943).

606 | To Ellen Glasgow, Richmond, Virginia

320 East 57th Street
New York
Thursday [September 30, 1943]

Dearest Cousin,

I got to town Tuesday afternoon to see the dentist, and found your book [3] in the apartment. I at once telephoned the NR—Mr. Mayberry, [4] whom I have not met—and said I had read a lot of the book already and would like to write about it. He said the copy had not arrived but Malcolm had asked to have the say about it. He would communicate with Malcolm in the country. My heart sank. But today he telephoned and said Malcolm said for me to go ahead and do it for the literary supplement in October, a good place, 1500 words.

That took a great load off my mind. I am going back to the country tomorrow and will take the book with me. My piece has to be in October 10. [5]

Now then, Cousin, this is entre nous and we both clear-headed and are old friends. So if the short piece does not say something you want to have said that will be your fault. Please think this over and just write me some of what you do want said, the NR is a good place to have the record of such a distinguished book. The book is indeed distinguished, and please tell the wide world I said so with a resounding flourish. I am so proud of you, that you should be able in these mad, shaken days to assemble such pages. The things you say about me mean as much as could possibly be imagined. I need just that at the moment.

Cousin, please do not hesitate just to write out whole sentences. I can't imagine people like you and me being coy about a thing that is necessary and right—what other purpose could my review serve. You

---

3. Ellen Glasgow's *A Certain Measure: An Interpretation of Prose Fiction* (1943).
4. George Mayberry (b. 1913), after teaching at Harvard and Radcliffe from 1936 to 1942, became a member of the editorial staff of the *New Republic* in 1943. He was associate and literary editor of the periodical until 1948; presently he is professor of English and coordinator of American studies at Point Park College, Pittsburgh.
5. Young reviewed the book in "Beautiful Apologia," *New Republic,* CIX (October 24, 1943), 588–91.

cannot admire your book more than I do, so that clears the field at the start.[6]

Thank you for the interest in my exhibition.[7] It is regarded as a vast and amazing success. The criticisms were remarkable, the people came back two to four times to look again at the pictures. I did wish you could be there. I can't tell you how much I wished you could be there. Some remarkable photographs were taken, the man who did them is a goose, but if I can get him to do them I will send you some. There is no telling what he will do.

Please remember me to Miss Ann Virginia. I wish I could drop in and see you all and have some of that incredible dinner you toss off so lightly and divinely.

This is a foolish letter in effect but don't think I fail to appreciate both the book and your opinion expressed of me. And even more your affection for me. It is just that right now everything is so distracted that my brain will not cling to a letter even as I am writing it. I am not reading this over.

I append a sentence in case you can use it anywhere. It is the first time in many years that I have made such a gesture. But there may be some place where it will prove useful.

Lovingly
Stark

In these days, so vast and confused, when most books are at best only good material half completed, it is a notable experience to find a book so profoundly unified, so brilliantly quiet and distinguished.[8]

6. On former occasions, Ellen Glasgow had suggested to Young points which she wished him to emphasize in reviewing her books. A passage in a brief note which Young wrote to her on October 7, 1943, however, suggests that in this instance she made no suggestions.

7. Ellen Glasgow had been one of the patrons for Young's lecture at the preview of his painting exhibition sponsored by the Friends of Greece.

8. Young used this sentence, virtually unchanged, in his review of *A Certain Measure*.

607 | To Julian Huxley, London, England

320 East 57th Street
New York
October 5, 1943

Dearest Julian,

I have a limited mind when it comes to suggestibility, with the result that vagueness of address or other form of uncertainty leaves me hamstrung and completely undesirous as it were. As I write I feel that the censor may not like what I say about my own gizzard—which like everything else, does have a certain relation to the all out war effort—and so a letter to you whom above all people I feel drawn to in conversation, gets quite sick and falling away. I force myself to write these dull words.

Your letters were very interesting lights on the problems of empire and all that. I feel that any opinions I may have would not be welcome to the censor or censoress, and so do not take up the subject. Perhaps they will let me say one thing: the democracies have got themselves into a sad mess, what with denials, affirmations and international jargon. What is the use, however, of saying, writing, even that if I cannot say just what I mean.

I went to the bank and my director said they thought the best way to send the money for Anthony would be direct to your home address. I have the receipt, so that there can be no loss, and I hope the account arrives safely and performs in the way intended. Tell my godson I wish him a great deal of happiness. I am sorry his wife is rather a dull proposition—as I gather she is—but such women are often a rest—or at least a lack of impediment—to men who are interesting. The longer I live the less I think of marriage in general, in these modern times. But the social machinery is still geared to it, and noble examples are still thrilling and noble. Fortunately the women have not written our fiction or we might have quite a shock.

I am going to inquire shortly as to the photographs. Your seeing them means a lot to me. It was your pleasure in it that made me complete the Dream—that young man and landscape—and that was the painting that Mr. Jewell of the Times was so moved by.[9] The exhibition I had not intended but when they proposed it for the Friends of Greece I finally said yes. The opening, with a talk by me about modern Greece, Old Greece, and the War, went too well for words, the Greek ambassadress, all sorts of swells etc. Six pictures were sold the first day, and out of the fifteen paintings for sale, eleven were sold. That broke all records for the season, and the magazines were duly aware of it. The page in Time was considered kindness itself for Time and I am still getting letters about it.[1] Since the exhibition was extended after the two weeks to another week and then to a fourth and then wanted more, I was about dead when it was over.

Please give my love to Juliette. I hope all goes well for you both.

Affectionately
Stark

I'm not reading this over—had to write an article today—the mere aspect of type sickens me.

9. Edward Alden Jewell had been impressed by Young's painting, whose title, *The Chambers in the House of Dreams Are Fed with So Divine an Air,* was suggested by the opening line of the third stanza of Francis Thompson's "Dream-Tryst." In a letter to Young, May 28, 1943, Jewell had written: "I took to them [Young's paintings] as the proverbial duck, etc. I understood them at a glance because they 'clicked' with certain adventures from my own interior experience. Some day when we meet I'll tell you, if you'd be interested, about a remarkable dream I had years and years ago, a dream irradiated with the most intense spiritual happiness, which instantly came back to me when I saw your remarkable 'Chambers in the House of Dreams Are Fed with So Divine an Air.'"

1. On July 9, 1943, John Anderson wrote to Young: "I must say Time gave you the works. Though I did think they were more scrupulous in their humorous distortion than they often are, and preserved a tone of high regard for the rare qualities they obviously found themselves in the presence of, which is a hell of a sentence but loaded." See above, Letter 603 and notes. In addition to serious praise of Young's work, the writer for *Time* referred to "florid, balding, loquacious Stark Young" and remarked that, like most events in his life, his exhibition was "a shooting of the most fashionable rapids." But the same writer concluded by observing that if Young's "painting matches the quality of his dramatic criticism, it will be something."

608 | To Julian Huxley, London, England

320 East 57th Street
New York
October 25, 1943

Dearest Julian,

I wrote you a stupid letter not so long since but fear the mail stamped it not airmail and heaven knows when it will get to you. The bank itself attended to sending the money and that will probably be all right. They preferred to send it direct to you for some reason.

I have just reread your two fine letters, about your plans and all. It was for the sake of feeling that I was having a good talk with you. I could discuss a bit the whole idea of imperialism and of what the United States can do a good turn to the international perfecting of other races even if they don't want to be perfected. I must say the thought of little English church in the midst of an opalescent plain and brilliant cloudless sky, plus some tea does not thrill me at all. The introduction of general bores among raucous savageries has not great lift for me, despite our Vice-President Wallace with his quart of milk for everybody everywhere, though some races detest milk shall we say. That of course is all superficial and high-handed as I word it, but I can't go into a discussion that would take me fifty pages, even to deal with Italy, the only foreign country I know much about, though after eighteen visits I don't always think I know much about that.

I am not even sure what I think of the Northern races, though being a member of them I naturally love them most, at least the British Isles people. All of which remarks make me blush for being a part of the over amount of jabber and second-rate writing that is going on, while we walk about under the huge legs of the few great Government colossi —colusses sounds more fun as to them—who are not without temperamental resemblance to tenors, and are arbitrary enough as to what we are allowed to share by way of plans and thoughts. It happens that I have long known a good many of our planners and heads of things— I mean known them personally—and I am afraid the prospect of their ideas and works is far from encouraging. But since I am serving their causes in no constructive way I feel it not too apt—even *decente, vero?*

—in me to remember too closely what third-raters they are. They have the great faculty of yessing—basta. I cannot go into any of these things for I don't know what the censor wants said.

I hope the war may end as soon as possible and that some profound guidances will be ready to construct the peace. What fine banalities I am uttering! Forgive me.

Your African remarks are quite thrilling and I think the experience will be.[2] I hope you will keep close notes. And then make a volume, partly with the aspect of notes, that would seem more promising and more significant than a book that assumes a kind of completeness, such as most of the half-baked and padded books about war topics etc. manifest and are made half contemptible by. I have no patience with print as such and print thus without completeness or import or distinction makes me nauseated literally, the mere thought of them. You have far more tolerance and patience and habit for second rate books than I ever had. It is a part of your wonderfully cosmopolitan and alive mind. Even at that I don't envy you the reading for the most part—the mere thought of reading through a book by Mr. Wells, Mr. Laski and most others makes me want to throw up. One thing I would do if I were rich, that is employ an intelligent person to go through most books in English and make me a paragraph or so about them, and then read me the paragraph aloud. One thing I have decided, that most of these New York people who talk of having read this and that book, every weeks' parturition, have only run through them, in order to be ready for the profound matter. Either that or their reactions and their gift of words are most elementary.

Your eyes see so much and your response is so remarkable that even from the notes in your letter I can see that you might write a quite dazzling book about that African country—leaving the book frankly fragmentary.

My painting seems to come along. It is astonishing what an impression it made in New York, but you said it would at your first sight of

2. Young refers to the appointment of Huxley to the British commission of inquiry into higher education in British West Africa under the chairmanship of Colonel Walter Elliot. The commission, appointed by Colonel Oliver Stanley, secretary of state for colonies, was established to investigate the facilities of present centers of higher education in British West Africa and to recommend future university development in that region. As a member of the commission, Huxley spent three months traveling in West Africa.

the pictures. So that is for this Julian, whose interest ranges so marvellously.

Tell that sweet Juliette I am sorry if Anthony's choice is not too interesting, but if she turns out to have at least solid virtues that will be something. A brilliant so called modern mind or what you will might be a thorn in your side. Most of my friends don't know what to think of their own choices in marriage much less of that of others. Some of my friends about whom I have worried seem to have stopped worrying —whatever else they have stopped too—about themselves. But the human heart is so screened that only in wonderful moments or in true art does there seem to be any real glint of anything accurately true. The longer I live the more remarkable I think human beings are and the less I feel able to cope with the infinite stretches of their natures or get any outline of what their special countries are, their continents and wastes and intensities. Since I can't do anything about such an attitude or idea on my part—so genuinely seated is it—I can only go on developing it to more meaning and application, always remembering the role fate plays—meaning partly the kind of person one is born— in each life.

I have used so many words about that that even if it is a platitude nobody could be sure about it.

I have some radio invitations and am urged to do the script for some producers doing two of the great hits of the town, revivals of The Merry Widow[3] and of Fledermaus—is that the spelling—it is playing as *Rosalinda*[4]—quite wisely, the other title would be spoiled by other theatre associations, melodrama and chauve souris[5]—and the one offered me is that celebrated Russian piece about the Fair at S-some-

3. *The Merry Widow,* by Franz Lehar, Victor Leon, and Leo Stein, was revived by Yolanda Mero-Irion for the New Opera Company at the Majestic Theatre, August 4, 1943. One of the most popular of the many revivals of this comedy, it closed on May 6, 1944, after 322 performances.

4. Adapted from the Max Reinhardt version of Johann Strauss's *Die Fledermaus, Rosalinda* was produced by Lodewick Vroom for the New Opera Company, at the 44th Street Theatre, October 28, 1942. Still being performed when Young wrote this letter, the operetta finally closed on January 22, 1944, after 521 performances.

5. Young refers to a kind of Russian cabaret entertainment originated by members of the Moscow Art Theatre and made famous in Paris, London, and New York by Nikita Balieff, who created for it a number of short, burlesque scenes often sentimental and frequently based upon old ballads or folksongs. A version entitled *Chauve-Souris 1943* based upon Balieff's work opened on August 12, 1943, for a short run at the Royale Theatre.

thing[6] or other. The Punts [*sic*] stole the main theme of the play I wrote for them, the place, the musical pattern and use, the time, the open effects and about twelve other points, thus wrecking my play, the one I wrote for them, for any other future use. They cleverly avoided using any direct phrase. I don't know I shall have the plagiarism suit or not. They were friends you see and the shock was double. The man they got to put this together for them did not know what they were having him do, not having known my play himself. I think Lynn Fontanne has been very unhappy about this, has written me etc., but I have not gone to see them. The whole business was done by Alfred, I think, and he counted on my affection for Lynn and hers for me to get away with it. Fortunately I had sense enough to have my play printed the day I read in the paper that they were to do a pirate play. All ugly, I have mentioned it so far to but two or three people. Well, we shall see. I don't intend to let this betrayal embitter me, that would be defeated in a worse way than having your work stolen and nullified as theatre use.

I will send this air mail and hope it reaches you. The censorship and the war dangers make me feel that no letter ever arrives. My love to Juliette.

Affectionately
Stark

609 | To Allen Tate, Monteagle, Tennessee

320 East 57th Street
New York
Sunday [December 5, 1943]

Dearest Allen,

For two people who love each other we don't do very well with conversation.

6. *The Fair at Sorochinsk* by Modest Petrovich Musorgski, based upon the story by Nikolai Vasilievich Gogol.

At any rate I hope you got my endless and endlessly tedious letter about the translation.[7] There was the message here that you were at Paul Green's or Fanny Hurst's [8] or somebody—of course I know it was P. Green but the other names will make my distinguished Caroline laugh—but it was about two hours later than the time you said to call —when I got home—and so I missed you. I was sorry. I had also a painting up here I wanted you to see, but it is now going off to the Whitney Museum and then see what all happens to it.[9]

I hope everything goes well with you, including Archie MacCleish [*sic*]. He was born a problem for me, for no reason.

I often think of you, and you and Caroline remain with me always, distinguished, loved and no qualifications.

Bowman would ask to be remembered if he knew I was writing. Out of a clear sky he had a cable from London asking whether he would be interested to come over and do some designing, various American plans. The matter has not been settled. It was a warm compliment. I waited to see what his plans would be but finally had to go on and get my tickets to Texas, to see my sister, after a year, and was able to get reservations for the 19th.

I have had a number of notable compliments lately, all about the level of Life magazine—and so—?

I hope all goes well for you and Caroline.

Lovingly
Stark

7. The letter to which Young refers has not survived in the correspondence file.

8. Fannie Hurst (1889-1968), novelist, playwright, and radio celebrity, whose works were applauded by millions of Americans, attained her first widespread recognition with her short stories, *Every Soul Hath Its Song* (1916). Among her many volumes of popular, sentimental fiction, the best known include *Star-Dust* (1921), *Lummox* (1923), *Back-Street* (1931), and *Hallelujah* (1944). In 1958, she published her autobiography, *Anatomy of Me.*

9. So early as October 30, 1943, Young had been working on a flower painting for an exhibition early in December. On November 19, he wrote his sister that "I am at work on the Madonna for the exhibition, but though it seems to be coming on well I will not show it unless it has by then arrived at something that suits me." On December 3, he wrote her again, "I have just a week or six days on the Madonna and will try like blazes to get it right. Gertrude [Newell] has seen it and thinks it very beautiful. I have not finished the lower half at all and will get at it now. The frame I have is a very good one for it." Presumably, this is the painting that Young was sending to Whitney Museum. Although the Whitney Museum did not accept the painting for exhibit, Young evidently exhibited it during the Christmas season; see below, Letter 619 and note.

Perhaps you saw my review of Miss Glasgow's book.[1] I long since settled that I would never review another novel. This book gave me a chance to foister a service to her on the NR. She wrote a nice letter but was not, I imagine, satisfied. I should have said she was better than Sappho, but there are so few authentic remains of the Grecian author that I don't feel justified in urging this point. Dr. Wolf says women are never satisfied with anything. . . . I can't decide that but God lets me think about it. Well, thank God I am not married to Peg Bishop.[2] Poor John looks to me as if he might have a stroke, that breathing and strain—he is a sweet fellow, I wish he might recover his stronger state of health. I asked Dr. Wolf about him, but the answers were somewhat vague. We have always to remember that Dr. Wolf is always most interested in the *diagnosis* of *new* cases rather than the nursing of old ones.

610 | To Lawton Campbell, Bronxville, New York

[En route to Austin, Texas]
Sunday [December 19, 1943]

Dear Lawton,

I had much to do to get away, but this is a line to you before you begin your great voyaging.[3]

It was lovely to be at your house and to see you. I kept thinking what a sweet thing in a room it is to take for granted all you think and feel is understood. To *make a rendezvous in true communion*. Think that phrase over deeply in your heart.

Lawton, you and I have an ever-growing, sweet relationship that nothing can harm. I am very proud of you and I wish everything right for you to come to you. Meanwhile you do your part in it all—which keeps the respect going. It's very necessary that we all give life to one

1. See above, Letter 606 and notes.
2. Mrs. John Peale Bishop.
3. Early in March, 1944, as a lieutenant colonel, Campbell was sent on a special mission to inspect civilian feeding in the occupied areas of Algiers, Sicily, and Italy.

another and give it more abundantly. Jesus said that, taking it out of Greek of course.

Love,
Stark

611 | To Rosamond Gilder,[4] New York

320 East 57th Street
New York
Tuesday [March 14, 1944]

Dear Roz,

You were lovely like yourself to think of writing me. I'm getting on my feet, now it is the fruits of the new strong drugs that weight me somewhat.[5] Thank you for all those good wishes and friendly concerns. And thank you for taking the trouble to recount your interest in the articles. If there were more space in the New Republic, more scope in the theatre and perhaps more altitude in me I might hope to do better —et cetera.

I have not half expressed my appreciation and for that matter can only indicate my old affection and admiration.

Yours sincerely
Stark

P.S.

Please thank the editors for those grand copies of Theatre Arts— a real treasure, really valued.

S.Y.

4. Rosamond Gilder began her career as a writer in 1916. She has achieved widespread recognition for her work from 1938 to 1948 on the editorial board of *Theatre Arts* as drama critic, associate editor, and editor. In 1945, she became a director of the American National Theatre and Academy. Her published work includes *John Gielgud's Hamlet* (1937) and *Enter the Actress* (1960).

5. Since returning from Texas in January, Young had been ill with influenza.

612 | To Mary Carter Rice,[6] Natchez, Mississippi

320 East 57th Street
New York
Thursday [April, 1944]

Dear Mary,

The things came—and intact. I can't thank you enough for all the trouble. Packing in itself is a sad bore.

I meant to write to Austin, but entre nous the flu still leaves me very flat and out of order. This is complicated by the fact that a sculptor [7] has to finish my bust before I leave for Texas May 1st. Long afternoons of this sitting, taking up my feeble time till I curse.

I am delighted that the things were shown at the library. The delay was all right once the things were out of Natchez. Mrs. Byrnes still has not got a letter written to me, though she sent two telegrams about the objects I wanted. (No mention of the brooch)

I have a number of items (of the epoch) connected with *So Red the Rose*—one a full newspaper account of burning the house. Has your library any place for things like these? If so I'd love to present them *through you.* You can let me know at your convenience.

Thank your friend for her interest. I'll be in Austin about a month and hope to see you all. *Please don't write Austin, anybody,* that I'm coming. It gets things mixed up and stirred up. My sister is still in bed trying to recover from the flu—what a mess!

I hope you have escaped. Thanks again and love to you.

S.Y.

6. Mary Carter Rice (b. 1902), librarian of the Austin Public Library from 1944 to 1967, was a child when Young came to Austin in 1907. Young and his sister lived on Salado Street next door to the Rice family until he built a house down the street a block away. She recalls that the neighborhood children helped Young in his garden and "later he would entertain us with stories he made up as he went along. Once when the Ben Greet players were here he got permission for the children to play in *The Tempest* and *A Midsummer Night's Dream*." When Young wrote this letter, Miss Rice, then a teacher of library science at Louisiana State University, had gone to Natchez to supervise the return of items he had loaned to Mrs. Ferriday Byrnes for the museum associated with the Natchez pilgrimage.

7. Jane Wasey (Mrs. Jane Wasey Mortellito, b. 1912), sculptor, was executing a bust of Young. The work is now in the library of the University of Mississippi.

613 | To Maxwell Perkins, Charles Scribner's Sons, New York

610 West Lynn
Austin, Texas
May 10, 1944

Dear Max,

I missed seeing you these past spring months, but the last of February I had that virus flu and in March it turned to bronchial pneumonia. The last of April I was able to get to the country and from there here in Texas, where I'll be till the end of the month—then Bedford.

I wanted especially to show you my copy of the Santayana that you sent me.[8] I wanted you to see the marked places page after page—showing how I went into it. I read it for days while I was sick, many passages over and over, etc. An unequal book but very distinguished and at times brilliant and profound. I hope the next one comes out soon.

Carolina Gordon's book[9] came the day I came in from Bedford and left for Texas. I have it along and will begin it soon. I hope it is good, for everybody's sake.

On the train down I read the NR with a review by Lincoln Kirstein of those Latin American books—the first I had heard of Graham's and O'Connell's book.[1] If you could send me a copy here I'd write them. I wish I had known long ago of it. I might have got George Mayberry to give that book more space in the NR. It was stupid of Dick and Jimmie not to write me long ago that it was coming out. Too bad, and not too well-bred, considering my exertions over the Lorca. However, that does not really affect the case, the new book is not a personal matter after all, and I'd have been glad to be of use. At least I'll be glad now to write them.

8. Perkins had sent Young a copy of George Santayana's *The Background of My Life,* the first volume of his *Persons and Places.*

9. *The Women on the Porch.*

1. Lincoln Kirstein began his review of "Recent Latin American Novels" with the assertion that "it is no easy matter to accept the responsibility of trying to say something illuminating and at the same time gracious about such books as these. Here they are, lumped together, six recent novels about different places in Latin America." In reviewing the group, Kirstein wrote a brief paragraph about *The Horse and His Shadow* by Enrique Amorium, translated by Richard L. O'Connell and James Graham Luján. For Kirstein's review, see *New Republic,* CX (April 24, 1944), 574, 576, 578.

I hope you and Louise are having a good spring—send you lots of love. I wish you could see my latest pictures—

Yours
Stark

P.S.

Could Miss Wycoff[2] have a copy of *Heaven Trees* charged on my bill and sent to

Mrs. Charles F. Neergaard[3]
Mead Road
Waccabuc
New York

Would Miss Wycoff look up this place—it is right near Cross River and South Salem and Katonah—in New York (not Connecticut).

614 | To Ellen Glasgow, Richmond, Virginia

Bedford, New York
Thursday [July 20, 1944]

Dearest Cousin,

Your note some way or other was delayed about two weeks getting to me here, but I was surprised and delighted to have it. It's wonderful you were able to get to Maine. The air and the whole change ought to work miracles, I do hope so.

I went to Texas in April—found my sister recovering too slowly by far from bronchial pneumonia—and left her June 1st not so well at all as I want to see her. Since then I have been at the farm—but in a

2. Irma Wyckoff, secretary to Maxwell Perkins.

3. Alice LaForge Mead Neergaard (1877–1961), wife of Charles F. Neergaard (1876–1961), hospital consultant in the New York firm of Neergaard, Agnew, and Craig, and author of technical articles for architectural and hospital periodicals. The house at Waccabuc, New York, which Young and Bowman were purchasing, had been the summer home of her parents, Mr. and Mrs. George Washington Mead. Mrs. Neergaard was active in little theatre groups, various charity organizations, and artistic projects.

new house across the street. The other house was needed by the owners —and now we have bought an adorable small house—90 years old with Victorian additions, on the Mead properties, the most tied up and restricted land in all this part of New England.[4] We were looked over and sold to at a good speed, my Stark ancestress Jenny Mead—b. 1760 —married David Stark makes me the same distance from the original William Mead—came to Stamford 1635—with a wife, son, and six servants.[5] Forty-four members of the clan are banded into a company and are to sell at vastly restricted terms some of the 2000 acre tract they have held together. It is quite an interesting bit of Americana. They are nice, real and distinguished people—no Long Island to their idea of life.

I have the oddest ancestral roots—my great grandmother McGehee came from the first Page—he owned the Williamsburg tract—his daughter married Mr. Childs. You spoke of not hearing of these McGehees of mine. They came in Cromwell's time. See Burke's *Peerage* —he was the younger of the two sons of the McGregor and his mother was the daughter of the MacDonald, the Earl of Antrim who led Charles First's armies. But my people left Virginia in 1783 and went to Georgia. The wife was the daughter of James Scott, who had married Collier's daughter of Portobello, near Williamsburg, who had married Miss Eppes I believe. My father's family came from Michael Cadet Thomas Young second son of Sir Francis Young, a colonel, who fell at Blenheim. Thomas was taken prisoner and to France, from which he escaped and came to Isle of Wight country. The Youngs married

4. The eleven children of Mr. and Mrs. George Washington Mead of Brooklyn, New York, settled in Waccabuc, and at one time virtually all of the property around three sides of Lake Waccabuc was owned by members of the Mead family. Despite the sale of houses recently to "outsiders," Mrs. Robert Murdock, Mrs. Neergaard's niece, writes that the area remains "a beautiful country place. No stores, nothing commercial. The property around the lovely natural mile-and-a-half long lake is still unspoiled by houses and will hopefully remain that way, as it has recently been given over to the Nature Conservancy, so that the border immediately adjacent to the lake, for half its length, at least, will remain in its natural wild state."

5. In a memorandum in the Murdock collection, Young writes that William Mead was born in London in 1600, married in 1625, emigrated to Stamford in 1635, and died there in 1663. His descendant, Jane or Jenny Mead (1766–1834), married David Stark (1765–1805). Their son, Stephen White Stark (born 1786), married Sarah Gilbert, and their son, Stephen Gilbert Stark (1816–1859), married Caroline Charlotte McGehee (1821–1861). Their daughter, Mary Clark Stark (1858–1892), married Alfred Alexander Young (1847–1925), and they became the parents of Stark Young. The name *Stark* was also spelled Starks. Young and Bowman decided to call the house at Waccabuc, Jennymead.

Douglass, Hal, Cabell, Baytop etc., and went before the Revolution—the ancestor of mine—to N.C. then to Tennessee.[6]

This Mead property stuff started all these memories in my mind. They may make you smile at least.

The state of the world probably does not prevent you from writing I feel sure. I paint a great deal but have no impulse to write. If only the war would end and things not be worse than before. Some awful people in our country are having a picnic out of the war, alongside the real people who are doing so well.

So I run on and on—it makes me think for a moment that I am chatting with you. Remember me to Miss Ann Virginia. Bowman sends messages. What a great cousin you are.

Lovingly
Stark

You can't imagine how much good it did me to have a word from you.

615 | To Alice Mead Neergaard, Waccabuc, New York

Bedford, New York
August 10, 1944

Dear Cousin,

I forgot to show you how, except for the blackberry patch behind the tool shed, it was all cleared out, all but the desired trees, up to the very terrace of the house. This information might have made you even nicer about our efforts, if that were possible. You can't imagine how you lifted our tired hearts.

We are going into town Monday to arrange about the money, so as to get the whole thing paid up, cash, and settled. I always feel more content when any affair is swept together and the slate is clean. Perhaps Mr. Leonard[7] will need one more flash from your eyes.

6. The account of Young's ancestors given here is virtually the same as the genealogical record he later included in chapter six of *The Pavilion*.
7. The local surveyor.

I am enclosing a list of the things in the house that we'd like to buy if we can afford them and the owners care to part with them. You can take the matter up at your leisure. Some of our effects are usable but rather on a large scale for the cottage and would look better in the apartments to be established in the barn. You will smile at the names of those apartments, *the loggia* in the outside open section, the *sala d'oro* is the large room with the concrete floor. The guest room (now stalls) the *hospice*. Now you won't lose your way when you climb the great stair.

Those things set aside in the tool shed and the laundry we don't need very violently. It's only, as I told you, we could employ them at the barn if they are going to be thrown away, and could let the owners own them as possessiveness ruled their bosoms. There is a gloomy Morris chair in the laundry that I could move to rest in my barn studio and find useful. But please do whatever is convenient in these matters.

Did you ever get kin to such a garrulous old party? So I'll close with thanks and regards to you both.

Yours sincerely
Stark Young

616 | To Ella Somerville, Oxford, Mississippi

Bedford, New York
Monday [August 14, 1944]

Dear Ella,

I would never let such a lovely letter go unanswered. Thank you so much for writing the information about the museum[8] and about the family.[9] I certainly hope some of the troubles have begun to mend. It seems hard that one person should have so much of it come down on her head. I often think the women war workers have a snap of it compared to those—some of them—who are at home.

8. Young had written earlier to ask about the Mary Buie Museum, Oxford, Mississippi. He referred to it as the Skipwith Museum.
9. The family of Katherine A. Skipwith.

My friend Bowman and I, having been ousted from the house we have had in the country for ten years—the owners have decided to live in it themselves—have at last had to buy a house—a lovely little old place about ninety years old, with two bathrooms, six acres, a brook, small wood, great old barn etc., in a restricted region—and at a very modest sum—so we have been struggling to get it in shape for next spring. I came to town today only to arrange for the payments and then go back to the country.

My painting comes on well, some good commissions, etc., but I don't think now I'll get much more done till I get back into town settled. I hope some day you can come up again—use the apartment some in town and pay us a visit in the country.

Julia has been feeling run down but writes she feels better after some Battle Creek style static massage. It has helped her nerves. She and Ben are great blessings for me.

Please give my love to everybody—I wish I could get by Oxford—travel has become almost impossible.

Thank you again for such a sweet oldstyle family aristocratic letter.

Affectionately
Stark

617 | To Maxwell E. Perkins, Charles Scribner's Sons, New York

320 East 57th Street
New York
[November 16, 1944]

Dear Max,

I have waited a long time to thank you for sending me the Rome Hanks.[1] As you know I can't read novels, but I read this one. Full of real talent, full of real variety. Some of it does not come off, of some the intention is vague to me. But real gifts.

1. Young refers to Joseph Stanley Pennell's *The History of Rome Hanks,* which Scribner's had recently published.

Thinking back over Caroline's book[2] it seems solider and solider. A genuine mind she has.

We must lunch together soon. I am anxious to hear your news, to tell you about some paintings and so on. The summer for me has been very busy in the country, trying to get settled in a new little house, just bought, with all that goes with such a move. But I have to get settled and houses for rent are scarce and uncertain and so—It is at the restricted end of Lake Waccabuc, not far from South Salem, eight miles from Ridgefield. Bowman and I hope to get it finished in early spring and to see you and Louise there. The amount of reinforcing and the like was pretty heavy, and getting help from workmen now is not easy. If Bowman had not his architect connections, we could not have attempted it at all.

I will telephone soon, am back to town at last.

> Yours
> Stark

618 | To John Van Druten,[3] New York

> 320 East 57th Street
> New York
> December 1, 1944

Dear John,

I returned from the country last Sunday for good and must write you about my not reviewing "I Remember Mama." I was absent from town, then the tickets were all sold and I expected anyhow to be going in a theatre party. That fell through, however, and I was away from

2. *The Women on the Porch,* by Caroline Gordon (Tate), published by Scribner's in 1944.

3. John William Van Druten (1901–57), playwright, novelist, and director, born in London, began to write plays in the 1920s. His best-known work includes *The Distaff Side; Leave Her to Heaven; The Voice of the Turtle; I Remember Mama; Bell, Book and Candle;* and *Cabaret.* In 1951, he directed the production of *The King and I.*

town again. They were kind enough to promise me seats for tomorrow matinee, a very nice young lady at Mr. Mok's[4] office talked with me on the telephone.

Certainly the play needs no help from the New Republic or from anywhere else, but knowing that with you such is not the whole point, I want to explain this silly delay on my part.[5]

Curiously enough we have never seen anything of each other, but we have for all that a solid friendship.

I recall that when you first came to America your mother had just died; and I have often thought how much if she were still here she would enjoy your wonderful success, never cheap and increasingly secure.

> Yours very sincerely
> Stark Young

619 | To Ellen Glasgow, Richmond, Virginia

> 320 East 57th Street
> New York
> Sunday [January 7, 1945]

Dearest Cousin,

I have had a mild attack of flu—not bad this year, thanks to taking many precautions etc. and so don't really know whether I have written

4. Michel Mok (1889–1961), reporter, literary agent, born in Amsterdam, began his career as reporter for the Philadelphia *Record* and the New York *Post*. In 1940, he left the *Post* to serve as business agent for Billy Rose and Jed Harris. In 1944, he joined Richard Rodgers and Oscar Hammerstein II in the production of John Van Druten's *I Remember Mama*.

5. Young reviewed John Van Druten's *I Remember Mama*, adapted from Kathryn Forbes's *Mama's Bank Account* in "I Remember Mama," *New Republic*, CXI (December 18, 1944), 836. After noting that a "combination of circumstances" prevented him from seeing the play earlier and that "a review in a weekly journal can be of no practical use to the enterprise," Young remarked that there were persons involved in the play "who would not see the matter quite from that angle." His verdict on the production was that although the theatre form of "a set of one-act plays or sketches, or shall we say short stories, that enjoy the human projection that the stage affords" had been employed many times, he considered *I Remember Mama* "a lesson and a monument to this season and to our theatre."

you or not. I think of you so often and the words are in my head, but I don't know whether or not I have written them down. That's the truth.

I wanted for one thing to tell you about the card. There was an exhibition from about thirty professional painters—Christmas a year ago, and I was asked to contribute.[6] The American Artist's Group asked if they could make a card from it, on a royalty basis. 38,000 sold right off to the trade, then the paper gave out. I'm told there will be a fine sale next year and the next, if paper is on hand again. I have had letters from everywhere about the card—and various people have written about buying the original. It was too bad about the paper. Otherwise I'd have written you or given your name to the Group. I spoke of some names of people I knew would be interested, but they said it was no use—no paper available, and the 38,000 sold right off.

The times are terrible. I paint a lot, but try to have no escapism in my painting. I wish I could see you. I'm sure you are as shining as ever. Wales sends you his love. Remember me to Miss Ann Virginia.

Lovingly
Stark

620 | To Pauline Goldmann, Austin, Texas

320 East 57th Street
New York
Sunday [January 7, 1945]

Dear Three Cousins,

Thank you so much for the table set. It will be fine and hearty for our dining terrace in the country. The cloth spread out looks so gay and strong. So thank you again and I hope some day you will be here again and dine off it there under our tulip trees.

6. See above, Letter 609, n. 9. Young's *Madonna,* which depicted an arrangement of flowers in the foreground of a madonna and child, was reproduced first as a postcard and later as a Christmas card. The painting is now owned by Lawton Campbell.

Thanks, Miss Pauline, for the etching card. It is very pretty. I hope Bendel got your right gift to you, three soap mits, with good smells. I adore that shop above all in New York, but the mink coats are so thick there at this season that you feel like a drunken trapper having a dream of whole forests of million dollar pelts. However, poor as I am and ragged, I manage to get to speak with Mademoiselle Hortense at the perfume counter, with about ten other beauties assisting her.

My card sold around 35,000 right off to dealers, then the paper gave out. Dirty works like Forever Amber get paper meanwhile.[7] I made about $450 but next year, the company says, the sale will go on and the next. There was a lot of attention for the card in the papers, to my surprise. The company is the best in the country and they are now asking to do two other of my paintings, though they would not be Christmas cards.

Bowman got back, ten hours late from the storms, last Wednesday. He asks to be remembered to my charming cousins, etc. He has a new job in Washington, a Mr. Landa,[8] partner of the Davis[9] who was Ambassador to Russia.

I hope all goes well with you this year, and give my love to the Harris Williams.[1]

Affectionately

S.Y.

7. Kathleen Winsor's *Forever Amber*, first published in 1944, had reached its eleventh printing by 1945. The demand for paper during World War II had produced a paper shortage for commercial printing.

8. Alfons Landa (b. 1897), lawyer, had become a partner in the law firm of Joseph E. Davies, in 1935.

9. Joseph Edward Davies (1876–1958), lawyer, diplomat, and author, was United States ambassador to Russia from 1936 to 1938 and during World War II had been President Roosevelt's special envoy with the rank of ambassador to Marshal Joseph Stalin.

1. Dr. Judson Harriss Williams, who had treated Young and become a friend; see above, Letter 428, n. 9.

621 | To Maxwell Perkins, Charles Scribner's Sons, New York

320 East 57th Street
New York
Tuesday [March 20, 1945]

Dear Max,

If some copies of So Red the Rose are being printed,[2] don't bother to read the rest of this letter. If not, then please read this letter very seriously.

About three weeks ago I went with a list of five names, people in the South who wanted me to have signed copies of So Red the Rose sent for various uses. There was only one to be had, and I went in vain to several bookshops.

The Granville-Barkers wanted a copy but I had to tell them I could not find one, they got it from some lending library club evidently, and have been telling people how they admire it. Their opinion may well be valued.

I had a telephone message the other day asking if I would be interested in letting records be made from it to play for blinded soldiers.

I have heard from a good many sources that the book has been read considerably by the soldiers.

Last Wednesday night a man came to my seat, it was Theatre Guild and he knew I would be there the second night. He said he had not been able to get a new copy of So Red the Rose, had a second-hand copy for me to autograph, he was giving it for some special person. All I know is his name he said was Morison, with one r. I did not say you had let the book get out of print, I said I would inquire.

Well, the point simply is that this is not like my other books or most other books. The book is about a society in a war, and it is built on a great deal of thinking about war, the life of the affections, etc. If we believe anything at all we have to believe that such a book should be

---

2. On the following day, Maxwell Perkins replied that *So Red the Rose* had very recently gone out of stock and had been immediately placed upon a list of books to be reprinted "at the first moment possible." Perkins remarked that the record of sales of *So Red the Rose* had been remarkable, "never less than 750 to 1,000 copies" annually since its publication in 1934. Perkins also encouraged Young to continue writing his memoirs.

available now of all times. I am sure paper can be got for printing up some copies, it can be shaved off other books that are not so applicable to the time or they can wait a little. If all this means nothing then I don't see why we ever should talk seriously about books in any way ever.

Speaking of books, I am making a start on memoirs which I think are going to be good, but time will tell, it will be quite a while before I know what tone and content are to be. It seems good however.

Quite a number of people have telephoned me about So Red the Rose, and I hope you write me that some copies are to be made, so that I can tell them. Even a theatre agent telephoned the other day saying what about another movie, this time in Technicolor. Probably a pipe dream that. But copies to be sent soldiers seem to me a really serious subject and I feel very seriously about it.

All good luck to you.

                    Yours,
                    Stark

622 | To Allen Tate, University of the South,
        Sewanee, Tennessee

                    320 East 57th Street
                    New York
                    Thursday [March 22, 1945]

Dearest Allen,

I have to write an article for the NR, in that short space I now have, and about two not important plays.[3] So this letter will be dull and brief.

I had your note about sending me your new book and am so glad you didn't blow any money on those special copies. The one I have is

---

3. Young reviewed *Dark of the Moon* by Howard Richardson and William Berney and *The Deep Mrs. Sykes* by George Kelly in "Varieties of Legend," *New Republic,* CXII (April 2, 1945), 447.

as pretty as could be wanted and the paper is very fine so far as I know anything about that.[4]

The times are so confusing that one does not remember as well as of old, but so far as I can tell I have seen all the poems before. I cannot say what has been changed exactly, where you have worked them over. But I have read the book and then read some of it several times, and its strange and bracing distinction and uniqueness among our poets— a ridiculous remark from me, for I can rarely get more than a few lines ahead in their works, and am not responsible for them or myself in relation to them so what the hell?—have meant a great deal as I read on and reread. In the II Autumn, at the bottom of the second page, that passage

I will leave this house, I said

etc., that is one of those places in your writing where I give up, the rhythm is wonderful and unpredictable, the thought is unexpected and haunting, the whole aspect is of profound, almost biological, creation. I am glad I am capable of saying to myself, that is the real thing, there is wonder, the elusive marvel—

Stanza VI of the Yeats piece has that same thing, and much of the verse otherwise constantly evokes and surprises at the same time.[5]

However, I have an article to write, and I don't suppose you want to hear a lecture on your own works.

I had such a good letter from Caroline, and have kept it here in the file to thank her for troubling about telling me about Mrs. Lambert.[6] We can just let that rest. I have had reactions from the Philadelphia Academy, really dazzling, the good painter Watkins,[7] the Boston Modern Art people, the Aubudon Society exhibition here at the National

---

4. Young refers to Allen Tate's *The Winter Sea: A Book of Poems* (1944).

5. The reference is to stanza VI of "Winter Mask to the Memory of W. B. Yeats." See above, Letter 593.

6. Grace Lansing Mull Lambert, wife of Gerard Barnes Lambert (1886–1967), then president of the Lambert Company. Earlier he had helped to sponsor the flight of Charles A. Lindbergh, publicized the word *halitosis* in connection with Listerine mouthwash, and served as president of the Gillette Safety Razor Company. Lambert had been an advisor to the federal housing administrator and had originated a plan for inexpensive public housing which he had demonstrated by building low-cost housing developments in Princeton.

7. Franklin Chenault Watkins (1894–1972), painter, received prizes for his work in exhibitions at the Carnegie Institute, the Art Institute of Chicago, the Paris Salon, and the Pennsylvania Academy of Fine Arts, where he was a member of the board of directors.

Academy Galleries, and now some praise indirectly from the director of the Chicago Institute, Mr. Rich.[8] Meanwhile Rehn,[9] who has most of the good people, has taken me on, and it remains to be seen. Something has to happen, for I am too far along in life to wait forever, and the treatment at the NR has considerably dashed the verve of my ego. Such is life.

Well, bless you and Caroline, nobody loves you both more than I do. By the way Max told me the last time I saw him that they were bringing out Caroline's stories.[1] I said merely that it was a distinguished thing to do.

Thank you again for the book, dear Allen.

Lovingly
Stark

623 | To Caroline Charlotte McGehee, Como, Mississippi

[320 East 57th Street]
[New York]
June 1, 1945

Dearest Cousin Cad,

I so often think of you and wish I could see you. Cousin Jennie wrote me that you are better, and I am glad of that. I suppose we are all

---

8. Daniel Catton Rich (b. 1904), director, critic, and art editor, has been associated throughout his career with the Art Institute of Chicago. In 1927, he joined its staff as editor of the *Art Institute Bulletin;* in 1929, he became the assistant curator of painting and sculpture, and in 1938, curator, and in 1945, director. Since 1958, Rich has been director of the Worcester Art Museum. He has served on various advisory committees concerned with artistic matters in this country, Europe, and Latin America and contributed articles to art journals.

9. Frank K. M. Rehn (1886–1956), art critic and gallery director, was the son of the noted landscape painter Frank Knox Morton Rehn (1848–1914). After a brief career as a writer of fiction and as an art critic for newspapers, he established his own gallery with the help of his wife, Peggy Wrenn. Confining his exhibitions to the work of American artists, his roster of artists included such men as Eugene Speicher, Edward Hopper, Reginald Marsh, and Henry Mattson.

1. In 1945, Charles Scribner's Sons published Caroline Gordon's volume of collected short stories, *The Forest of the South.*

getting old. At any rate there are often times when I am so tired I could just lie down and quit. And there never seems to come a time when we can just lie down and give up.

A few years ago I started on an old ambition and began to paint. I have had a good success. Lately a painting of mine was shown in an important exhibition among twenty established artists. My picture was one of four nearly every time picked out by the critics.[2] To begin after sixty and get that far is not bad. I have a large one-man exhibition on Fifth Avenue in November, considered the prize month.[3] I hope the gods will be kind to me, I need it.

Bowman and I had to give up to the owners the country house we have had for ten years, and since there are none to rent, except enormous houses that nobody wants, we had to buy a little house. Six acres, a wood of our own, a barn, a servant's house, a tool house, wood cellar etc. We paid only 9000 for it, cheap for these days, but have to spend several thousand on it to pull it into shape. I had to borrow $7000 for my share of the total cost, so tell Cousin Jennie I have no money to give that boys' home in Memphis, she sent me the paper about. It is a fine idea and I wish I could help. But I have never been in debt and the first thing I have to do is to get this all paid up. Living costs so much, and the materials up there on the house are three or four times their old price. The carpenters cost of $16 a day to begin with. The painters 14. The yard digger gets 7. When I think of the old days down home, my me!

Julia writes that she keeps pretty well. Ben too. I wish I could see them but won't try it this summer, too expensive by far and the Government does not want us to use the railroads anyhow. The traffic to the West Coast is going to be heavy, carrying our men over there. It seems awful that the Japs cannot be finished off [and] the war ended. Then begin the hates and struggles all through Europe, and we are certainly into it all.

It seems ages since I walked up that front walk with my Cousin Cad. Life passes, and so we go. I hope you hear good news from the boys away from home. Give my love to Cousin Jennie and Cousin

2. In the 140th Annual Exhibition of the Pennsylvania Academy of Fine Arts, held January 19 to February 25, 1945, Young exhibited his painting entitled *Votive*.

3. See below, Letter 627 and n. 3.

Wheeler and all who ask about me. I hope you are a lot better. Bow-man sends his love.

Lovingly
Stark

624 | To Ellen Glasgow, Castine, Maine

320 East 57th Street
New York
Friday [August 3, 1945]

Dearest Cousin,

I wrote you a letter some time back just to send you my love. And now I hear you made the journey successfully to Maine. I hope it is doing you much good. The summer in these parts has been humid and vilely rainy. Our cook quit at least for the summer and we have been able to be in the country only week-ends. So far we have had two really clear days. Let's hope the autumn will be better. Last summer we had a devastating drought. Our garden started brilliantly, then just stood still and dried up.

I did not try to go to Texas this summer for many obvious reasons. Wales and I lost the house we had rented for ten years and had to buy one. It is very attractive, Victorian, about 100 years old, six acres, a barn, servants' house etc. We have had to do a great deal on it however.

Except for some short NR things I have not tried any writing.[4] Life is too confused to find a starting place for writing, it seems to me. I have painted a good deal, have been taken over by about the best dealer in New York—Rehn, 683 Fifth Avenue, and he is giving me a one-man show in November—which is considered the best month for New York exhibitions. The Whitney, Chicago, Carnegie and Pennsylvania Acad-

---

4. Since the middle of June, Young had contributed only a few short pieces to the *New Republic*. On June 25, he reviewed Bertolt Brecht's *The Private Life of the Master Race;* on July 9, he wrote about Ralph Nelson's play, *The Wind Is Ninety;* and on July 30, he reviewed Lionello Venturi's *Painting and Painters* and *Marc Chagall* by the same author. He published nothing more until September.

emy—the four most important in the country, have asked for paintings of mine to be in their show.

That's about all my news except that the war and the state of the world leaves me more or less numb and in a fog. The state of our country is certainly puzzling. I think the New Deal is well on the decline. We need a real change now.

Bowman would send his love if he were at home, and will you please remember me cordially to that fine Miss Ann Virginia.

I hope your summer is really beneficial. I think of you often.

Affectionately
Stark

625 | To Huntington Cairns,[5] National Gallery of Art, Washington, D.C.

320 East 57th Street
New York
August 31, 1945

Dear Mr. Cairns,

It was very nice to hear from you. Your letter and the photographs were waiting here when I came back from the country.

I didn't expect you to return those photographs. I meant to give them to you. But now that they are here, Mr. Rehn no doubt can put them to good use.

He tells me that the Chicago Institute and the Carnegie have both selected pictures for their next exhibitions.

5. Huntington Cairns (b. 1904), lawyer, art critic, editor, and author, has had a distinguished career in a number of fields. Among the many varied positions he has held are legal adviser and counsel for the Department of the Treasury, secretary and treasurer of the National Gallery of Art, lecturer in political science at the Johns Hopkins University, and chairman of the radio program "Invitation to Learning." Cairns's publications include *Tax Laws of Maryland* (1936), *The Theory of Legal Science* (1941), *Invitation to Learning* (1941), *Masterpieces of Painting from the National Gallery of Art* (1944), *The Limits of Art* (1948), *Legal Philosophy from Plato to Hegel* (1949), and *Great Paintings from the National Gallery of Art* (1952).

I do indeed appreciate your efforts in Mr. Phillips' direction and hope something will come of them.[6]

When you are in New York this fall do let me know. It would be such a pleasure to see you again. And I wish in your letter you had told what fortunes befell that Titanic manuscript you showed us at lunch that day. The idea for the venture seemed to me highly interesting.

Some day I hope to be in Washington again and it would indeed be something to see you in your habitat of masterpieces.

Meanwhile I send you very cordial good wishes. Your visit bucked me up no little, and this is a solitary world, we all need each other.

Yours very sincerely
Stark Young

626 | To Huntington Cairns, National Gallery of Art, Washington, D.C.

320 East 57th Street
New York
October 11, 1945

Dear Mr. Cairns,

It was very good to have your letter. My beloved Allen had even a better time in New York than I thought—inventing a new scheme by which one works in town week-ends and spends the week in the country.[7] It is doubtless well suited to Seraphim.

I went out Friday and came in Monday night, as usual.

Please keep me informed as to your book's date. I am asking our review editor, George Mayberry, to hold the review for me to do. *I*

6. Cairns had shown pictures of Young's paintings to Duncan Phillips (1866–1966), trustee and member of the acquisitions committee of the National Gallery of Art; and Phillips had expressed his intention of viewing Young's work at the Rehn Gallery.

7. Young here responds to a comment in a letter to him from Cairns on October 5: "Allen Tate is a rascal. I had dinner with him on Monday night, and told him I hoped to see you on Tuesday. He said that he had just learned that you would not be in the city until the end of the week. I therefore did nothing about getting in touch with you on Tuesday."

will wait and ask him after I have heard the title from you.[8] Otherwise we are likely to get into one of those confusions that happen in a review department. (Do I know!)

I saw your Mr. Finley's picture in the *Art Digest,* as a Carnegie judge.[9] What a fine face! Like a true Southerner I glowed with pride. Please tell him for me. (Poor backward South, the New Republic so longs to improve it, and has no way of even approaching it. Circumcised nobility on the NR's part, as it were.)

Mr. Rehn is really interested in my exhibition, and what a pity it is that paintings selected by the Carnegie and Chicago directors can't go this year—the dates overlap with this first show in New York. Boy, am I on the tenterhooks about this first show—! "There is no name, O Rhodope, with whatever emphasis of passionate love repeated—"[1] You remember the incredibly beautiful rhythm of that, and the fatalism behind it.

Thank you so much for your letter—what a shame I missed seeing you—and I do hope you will see my exhibition in November.

Yours very sincerely
Stark Young

8. Cairns replied on October 16 that the title of his book would be *The Limits of Art.* Not published until 1948, the work was not reviewed by Young.

9. See "Museum Directors Award Carnegie Prizes," *Art Digest,* XX (October 1, 1945), 9. David Edward Finley (b. 1890), born in York, South Carolina, began his career as a lawyer, served in World War I, and entered government service in Washington. From 1927 to 1932, he was special assistant to Andrew W. Mellon, secretary of the treasury. In 1938, he became the first director of the National Gallery of Art, a position he held until retirement in 1956. From 1950 to 1963, he was chairman of the Commission of Fine Arts.

1. Young quotes a passage from "Aesop and Rhodopè" in the first series of *Imaginary Conversations* by Walter Savage Landor. In Landor's text, Aesop declares: "There are no fields of amaranth on this side of the grave: there are no voices, O Rhodopè, that are not soon mute, however tuneful: there is no name, with whatever emphasis of passionate love repeated, of which the echo is not faint at last."

627 | To Helen C. Ellwanger,[2] Rochester, New York
[fragment]

320 East 57th Street
New York
October 30, 1945

Dear Helen,

You wrote me such a lovely letter, and thank you. Your painting has been a great success at Mr. Rehn's—he shows things to people on occasion. I have at last found a title for it, which was difficult. It seems to me beautiful. From Keats's *Ode to a Nightingale*—the picture's atmosphere and setting have always reminded me of that poem. I suppose the poem, at the back of my mind, helped me to paint it. The title is: *Still Wouldst Thou Sing.*

It made quite a sensation at Mr. Rehn's—they are getting the catalogue list ready[3]—the opening is November 12—for three weeks. May the gods prosper it—he is taking such pains with the whole event and is so intensely interested.

I hope Margaret[4] is all well again, and that we shall see you both [end of fragment].

2. Helen Cresswell Ellwanger, member of a prominent family in Rochester, New York, and long a friend of Young. Her grandfather, George Ellwanger, founder of the noted horticultural firm of Ellwanger and Barry, distinguished himself as a horticulturist and pomologist, while his son George Herman Ellwanger (1848–1906) had a distinguished career as horticulturist, editor, and author.

3. The catalogue of Young's paintings exhibited at the Frank K. M. Rehn Galleries, November 12 to December 1, 1945, listed *Presidio Range, Rehearsal in Red, Ode, Still Wouldst Thou Sing, The Garlands, Peonies, Rehearsal for Spanish Pageant, Romance, The Dream, Landscape with Rocks, Morning Flowers, Promontory, Sweet Land, Flowers over San Antonio, Red Mountain, Votive, Not China but West Texas, Ave Maria, Swans, Valley of the Pedernales, The Saint's Statue, Study for Twenty-three, Of Every Sort Which in That Meadow Grew, Flowers That Their Gay Wardrobe Wear,* and *White Roses.*

4. Margaret Ellwanger, sister of Helen Cresswell Ellwanger.

628 | To Robert Downing,[5] New York

320 East 57th Street
New York
November 2, 1945

Dear Bob,

Of course, of course—and I was entirely sober—can you imagine not knowing you were you.

You get one thing at least out of your nice note, I said to Bowman, the friend with me, I never saw Orson Wells but once without make-up, and years ago. I didn't remember that he was so handsome, no wonder Rita Hayworth married him.[6]

It was very good to hear from you. And while I am writing I may as well tell you that the Rehn Gallery—the best in town for American artists—at 683 Fifth Avenue is giving me a one man show the best month of the year—it opens November 12 and runs till December 1st. You may not know that I turned painter. The Chicago Institute, the Pennsylvania Academy and the Carnegie—the most important museum exhibitions in this country—have all asked to show my pictures —beat that! The point of which is to ask you to come to the opening or to drop in during the run of the show, I think you would like them.

Thank you again for your charming letter.

Yours sincerely
Stark

5. Robert Downing (b. 1914), actor, stage manager, playwright, director, collector, and editor, has participated in virtually every phase of dramatic activity. Young's association with Downing probably dates from his performances during the early 1930s, but certainly no later than Downing's tour in 1938 and 1939 with the Lunts in *The Sea Gull, Idiot's Delight,* and *Amphitryon 38.* Downing also toured with the Lunts in *The Taming of the Shrew* and *There Shall Be No Night* in 1939 and 1940, when he acted as their secretary and edited the weekly backstage paper, *The Luntanne Tatler.* When Young wrote this letter, Downing was production stage manager for Maurice Evans' production of *Hamlet,* which opened on December 15, 1945. Since that time, Downing has continued to be active in the drama both in the theatre and on television. With regard to this letter, Downing has observed that "a few nights earlier he [Young] had mistaken me for Orson Welles in the lobby of the Empire Theatre."

6. Orson Welles (b. 1915), director, producer, actor, and author, married Rita Hayworth (b. 1918), motion picture actress, in 1942; the marriage was dissolved in 1948.

629 | To Mary Williams Goldmann, Austin, Texas

[320 East 57th Street]
[New York]
Friday [November 16, 1945]

Dear Cousins,

I have been up an hour already and I won't get things half finished by midnight. But I must thank you for that heavenly box of good things. I ate the corn jars the first two days and never told Bowman about them, lunch solo you see.

But both of us have been enjoying the pickle, so very delicious. It must be an old recipe, it does not taste like the new things.

Would you mind calling up my sister and asking her about the opening of my exhibition? It went better than my fondest hopes, a triumph I may say. I have not time to write you about it in any detail because I have a New Republic article to write and deliver before noon.[7] What a world!

But I will live through these next two weeks till the exhibition ends, so long as it shines like that.

Bowman sends cordial regards. I hope to see you Christmas if I survive.

Thank you again for being so sweet to me.

> Love to all three
> Stark

[November 26, 1945]

Dearest Cousins,

You see what went wrong.[8] With two of my oldest friends dying[9]—

7. Young refers to his article "Plays and Plays," in which he reviewed Viña Delmar's *The Rich Full Life*, Robert E. Sherwood's *The Rugged Path*, and Howard Lindsay and Russel Crouse's *State of the Union* in *New Republic*, CXIII (November 26, 1945), 711–12.

8. The letter, addressed by Young to New York City instead of Austin, Texas, had been returned to him by the postal service.

9. The deaths of Ellen Glasgow, on November 21, 1945, and Doris Keane, on November 25, 1945, profoundly affected Young. As a writer of fiction dealing with the South, he had felt both an intellectual and emotional kinship with Ellen Glasgow; and, as a critic of the drama and intimate friend for more than thirty years, he related much of his professional and private life to Doris Keane. The depth of his affection

Miss Glasgow and Doris Keane and all the reviewers [1] etc. connected with my exhibition, it's no wonder I'm witless.

Seven or more of the pictures have sold, two into fine collections.

Love and thanks again for that wonderful pickle. Bowman raves about it.

---

and his critical estimate of her place in the theatre find expression in the brief essay that he was writing about her at the time he wrote this note. In "Doris Keane," Young reminded his readers of her contribution as an interpreter of a playwright's work and thereby defined what he considered the attributes of superb performance in the theatre. Wrote Young: "She brought to it [Edward Sheldon's *Romance*] the fruits of a secret life, lived often in solitude, concerned with art and with a study, prolonged through years, of English and Indian philosophic writing, and with literature. Those interests, plus generosity, intuition and elements of greatness, were what went into this creation of hers. What people felt about her had, then, its source in these deep elements as well as in beauty, perfection of stage movement and an unusual degree of intensity in stage projection"—*New Republic,* CXIII (December 10, 1945), 798.

1. Reviewers of Young's paintings continued to be as impressed with his second show as they had been with the earlier exhibition for Friends of Greece. Edward Alden Jewell, in the New York *Times* (November 18, 1945, Sec. 2, p. 7), called Young "one of our most charming and elusively romantic painters" and added that "his skies are wonderful; his flowers fragrant and special. Now and then the two themes will be brought into mysterious confluence, and he becomes openly the mystic—just as he is at times the poet of imaginative nuances." Noting that Young's best work dealt with flowers, the reviewer for the New York Herald *Tribune,* November 18, 1945, Sec. 5, p. 7, wrote that "still-lifes, garlanded with flowers, seem to hold a very pure, almost a religious devotion for the subjects, whereas flowers in landscape and simple flower forms are dreamlike apparitions, remote and intangible." In *Art Digest,* XX (November 15, 1945), 41, Ben Wolf characterized the show as "notable for understanding and love for paint per se," praised the "paint quality," and found a "haunting mystery" in many of the paintings. In *Art News,* XLIV (November 15, 1945), 25, the critic wrote: "A single canvas like *Ode* tells you volumes about the sky, its enormous thoughts, its slow procession of vapors which dwarf the earth, man, and his works. In *Rehearsal for Spanish Pageant, Marfa, Texas,* a sky like bright curds climaxes the defiant gesture of the small foreground figure. Flowers are another preoccupation. Gathered into formal bunches, they seem alive, almost breathing, the most personal of offerings from the artist. The setting for all this is a low land, dark, wet, and green. . . . The flowers are stroked into life, the land is laid on in long, flat, glistening strokes, the sky is dabbled or trailed or skimmed. . . . One new *Landscape with Rocks* is outstanding, its richness evoking Poussin."

630 | To Huntington Cairns, National Gallery of Art, Washington, D.C.

> 320 East 57th Street
> New York
> Saturday [December 1, 1945]

Dear Huntington,

This is my first chance to thank you for that luncheon—so warm and friendly and interesting—and for your concern about my paintings. And for the pleasure I had in finding a new friend in Mr. Finley. I sometimes think it is almost a curse that I have so strong an apperception of the real thing—and am thus forever bound to it. That's a fine, delicate, flexible mind and a lovely spirit, and a great gentleman, of course I mean Mr. Finley, not me.

The Fragonard book seems to me a great success. I will do a note on it for the New Republic.[2] One-tenth of one-hundredth of our violent subscribers might be interested in such a thing. Well, *we* are at any rate.

My exhibition ends today, but Mr. Rehn is delighted all through at the response. Seven or more pictures have sold, but some of these could have sold several times. He seems quite indifferent to that, so certain does he feel. I know you'll be pleased to hear that.

I will write Mr. Finley tonight. With cordial regards, I am

> Yours as ever
> S.Y.

2. Young reviewed *Fragonard Drawings for Ariosto,* with essays by Elizabeth Mongan, Philip Hofer, and Jean Seznec, in "Drawings," *New Republic,* CXIII (December 24, 1945), 874-75.

631 | To Huntington Cairns, National Gallery of Art, Washington, D.C.

320 East 57th Street
New York
January 10, 1946

Dear Huntington,

I got back from Texas[3] only Monday and found your very nice letter. I hope this delay will not be of any inconvenience to you. I tried to telephone but they said that was "indefinitely delayed," then I tried in vain to telegraph.

Perhaps I have missed in Texas a note from you. At any rate I know you spoke of events there in January but I don't recall anything about February 2nd.[4] If there is any special reason I could come down then, or else later on in the season. If I am to come, could you engage a room for me somewhere. I don't mean it to stick you—Washington must be a burden on that score—I mean I just don't know how to secure some sure accommodation. If I came I'd come on Saturday morning and spend the afternoon in the great gallery.

At that time or later on, either, I could be free for a Sunday lunch, it is awfully nice of you and Mr. Finley.

The Saintsbury book[5] has come, I am looking forward to it as soon as I catch up on my delayed chores due to my absence from town.

I am glad you thought well of the Fragonard review.[6] The book inspires awe. It would be much easier to write about it in a technical journal. But writing about such a book for *general* readers, however intelligent, is a problem that is enough to do anybody in. In the first

3. Young had spent the Christmas holidays in Austin and in Mexico with his sister and brother-in-law, Mr. and Mrs. J. Ben Robertson.

4. David Finley had invited Young to a dinner at the F. Street Club in Washington on February 2 in honor of the opening of new rooms in the National Gallery of Art for the display of more than a hundred additional paintings and sculptural works in the Samuel H. Kress Collection. Finley had also rearranged the entire collection into a series of galleries which could be viewed in sequence beginning with thirteenth-century Italian art and concluding with the nineteenth-century French School. Before Cairns could reply to this letter, the invitation arrived.

5. *French Literature and Its Masters,* by George Saintsbury, edited by Huntington Cairns, had just been published by Alfred A. Knopf.

6. See above, Letter 630 and note.

place one can't be academic, but one has to show one is literate so that whatever opinion is expressed will seem worth noting. I realize, that, in the main, this latter is an old-fashioned necessity. Everybody has a right to every opinion—what a mess our culture is in!

The only news I have had from Allen and Caroline was when she telephoned and said they had "made up," were they "not silly"? and would I come to dinner. I could not go at that last moment's notice. Since then I have heard indirectly that they have parted again. I hope not. After calling Sewanee five times and never finding Allen and after talking Caroline's head off on the telephone to Princeton, I feel that I ought not to put my finger in again. Bless their hearts, I do think it would be a shame for them to lose each other. Poor humanity!

You can let me know about February 2nd or some future date, as suits you and Mr. Finley. Remember me to him. Happy New Year to you.

Yours
Stark

632 | To Ella Somerville, Oxford, Mississippi

320 East 57th Street
New York
Friday [January 11, 1946]

Dear Ella,

I am back from my Texas visit, Julia and Ben as well as most people are these days. It was fine to see them.

I have so many things to make up that this is a blunt poor note. I merely wanted to thank you for your lovely letter about the card and the books etc. The painting is quite large and was in my exhibition. It got a lot of praise. The reason it seemed not in my catalogue was because the company who made the card had to change the name to something right for a card. The title is really Presidio

Range, but on a card that would sound like a travel card not Christmas.[7]

The two good plays this year are State of the Union and The Glass Menagerie.[8] The latter I have a copy of and am sending it to you since you won't be likely to see the play. T Williams is from Mississippi and a cousin of the John Sharp Williams family.[9]

You don't have to thank me for this. I wrapped it so fast I only hope it gets to you safely. I was glad I had this copy to give you, the author sent it to me.

Love to you all, I wish I could drop in and hug the whole family.

Affectionately
Stark

633 | To Maxwell Perkins, Charles Scribner's Sons, New York

320 East 57th Street
New York
January 17, 1946

Dear Max,

You have always been a lot in my work and have helped me toward it—I remember how you bucked me up on So Red the Rose and I went

7. Young had sent a Christmas card produced by the American Artist Group from his painting *The Dawning of the Day*. Originally, the title had been *Presidio Range*.

8. Young had reviewed both plays. He characterized *State of the Union* by Howard Lindsay and Russel Crouse as "unbrokenly entertaining, stirring, virile and a credit to our theatre and all of us"—"Plays and Plays," *New Republic,* CXIII (November 26, 1945), 711-12. In one of his most admired essays on the theatre, Young praised the performance of Laurette Taylor and the writing of Tennessee Williams in *The Glass Menagerie.* "The play," wrote Young, "gives every one of the four characters that it presents a glowing, rich opportunity, genuine emotional motivations, a rhythm of situations that are alive, and speech that is fresh, living, abundant and free of stale theatre diction"—"The Glass Menagerie," *New Republic,* CXII (April 16, 1945), 505-506.

9. Although Young understood the relationship of cousin in a broad and, at times, vague sense, Tennessee Williams has claimed a kinship with Senator John Sharp Williams (1854-1932). Tennessee Williams' assertion appears in his biographical note to "Landscape with Figures," in *American Scenes,* edited by William Kozlenko (1941), p. 174.

ahead with it, and how your letter to me about the story, Beatus Rex,[1] set me at its followers, etc.—and so I want you to help me again.

The enclosed clipping from a letter[2] is only one of many inquiries about my books. People have telephoned, bookstores have written— one lately from Mobile—a letter even came from Holland. A man named Glover Thurman[3] in North Carolina wrote asking me to autograph five copies of So Red the Rose and have them sent to men in the service, he sent the list, and have Scribner's send him the bill. All this has been very embarrassing to explain, with books pouring out in every direction, and what's more it has been very discouraging.

In my case it is more than discouraging. It creates a subconscious effect that has made it impossible to write. I think of something and then feel it is all futile. I have notes for the book of reminiscences, The Reader's Digest, the Virginia Quarterly and the Sewanee Review asked about them, etc. and I can't get myself to do anything about it.

All this combined with the fact that the Lunts stole a good deal from the play which I wrote for them and which they had promised to do, and used it in Behrman's *Pirate,* which was not only plagiarism but betrayal by trusted friends—well all this has considerably plugged me. In spite of the success of my exhibition, I have not even put paint on the palette since December 1, when it closed.

For anybody doing creative work you can see how all this is fatal if it goes on. It is much easier to write you about it than to talk about it. If you can, would you find out what is being done or has been done about So Red the Rose[4] and Heaven Trees, and tell me tomorrow?

1. Apparently a reference to Young's story, "Beatus Rex," originally printed in *Scribner's Magazine,* LXXXIV (August, 1928), 216-23, and reprinted in *Present-Day American Stories,* by Ernest Hemingway, Thomas Boyd, Stark Young, and others (1929), and in Young's *The Street of the Islands* (1930).

2. Young enclosed a portion of a letter from a newspaper writer in Suffolk, Virginia, January 10, 1946, beginning, "I hope you won't mind my writing to remind you that scores of your fellow Southerners are wondering why we haven't seen one of your delightful stories of the old South in the bookstores, or libraries, recently. 'So Red the Rose' still holds first place in my mind and heart. . . .'"

3. Young had received a letter from his cousin, Glover Bedford, High Point, North Carolina, requesting autographed copies of *So Red the Rose.* Either Young did not wish the request to seem merely a family matter or he inadvertently wrote the last name of Bedford's sister.

4. Scribner's ordered a reprint of *So Red the Rose* in December, 1945, but the book did not reach the market in time for the Christmas sales. Perkins wrote that "under normal conditions we would never have been out of it."

At any rate I am looking forward to seeing [you] at Pierre's tomorrow, at 12.30.

Best to you
Stark

634 | To Huntington Cairns, National Gallery of Art, Washington, D.C.

320 East 57th Street
New York
Thursday [January 24, 1946]

Dear Huntington,

I have had this clipping [5] and the envelope addressed, and the introduction twice read, since two days now, but waited to get in touch with George Mayberry. He was not in the office whenever I tried to reach him, but yesterday afternoon I got him. I wanted to ask him if he had done anything about the Saintsbury book. I carefully said it was not that I was wanting to write about it—I am, though I did not say so then, saving my Cairns thunder for the art book. He said he was no great admirer of S.—that was partly a hangover from university opinions, I imagine, and said—but that he had sent the book to one of his men, Levin, [6] I suppose at Harvard, and asked him to decide what was or was not to be done about it. I thought you would like to know about whatever had happened at the NR.

The Bates review you saw of course. But I thought an extra clipping might be useful perhaps. He knows everything about French literature, I gather, though several of the allusions are from your preface. The Christ sentence, [7] marked, I don't think I follow very well. I have been

5. Young refers to Ralph Bates's article "The French Genius" (a review of *French Literature and Its Masters,* by George Saintsbury, edited by Huntington Cairns), which appeared in the *New York Times Book Review,* January 20, 1946, pp. 4, 32.

6. Harry Levin (b. 1912), author, editor, and critic, has taught English at Harvard University since 1939.

7. After suggesting that Saintsbury's remark that Racine used only a fraction of the whole world subject to the poet was "an astonishingly defective judgment," Bates continued: "As well say that the Agony in the Garden is only conventionally important to a believer in Christ, or that the sense of abuse of the individual is merely a side-thought to the conscientious revolutionary!"

reading Bertrand Russell and Plato too much lately, perhaps; it dulls one's perceptions. It takes so much to know so little, I find it so at least, that an attitude like that of Mr. Bates leaves me at sea.

This morning the letter and address etc. thank you, and thank you for that catalogue, it is interesting to have and to inspect before the opening. I am getting very solid with the five-and-tens. Frasier McCann, grandson and Woolworth heir is a friend of mine in the country [8] and now Mr. Kress and his passion for beauty looms on my horizon.

Best to you
Stark

Not dictated but not reread.

635 | To Julia Young Robertson, Austin, Texas

[320 East 57th Street]
[New York]
Saturday [February 9, 1946]

Dearest Sister,

This is Saturday morning. I have had three plays to go to this last week but none next week. Last night we went to dinner with the Sobys,[9] he used to be painting director at the Modern Museum. The Charles Laughtons [1] were there. I met them years ago with John

8. Since 1935, McCann had been operating a dairy farm in Bridgewater, Connecticut. Young and Bowman saw the McCanns frequently at the home of Mrs. McCann's mother, Mrs. Sydney Lawton, at Pound Ridge, New York.

9. James Thrall Soby and his wife Eleanor Howland Soby. Art critic, editor, author, Soby (b. 1906), was director of painting and sculpture at the Museum of Modern Art from 1943 to 1945. Since that time, he has continued to be prominently associated with the museum, published a number of books about painters and painting, and, beginning in 1946, written a monthly column of art criticism in the *Saturday Review of Literature.*

1. Charles Laughton (1899–1962) and his wife, Elsa Lanchester Laughton. He had been a motion picture star since the early 1930s, appearing in such films as *Henry VIII, The Barretts of Wimpole Street, Ruggles of Red Gap, Mutiny on the Bounty, Hunchback of Notre Dame,* and *The Paradine Case.*

Anderson, but last night he was much more intelligent and interested in real matters than I had had a chance to observe before. John was quite a friend of his. She was very pleasant, about painting, glass etc.

I may have given an ungraceful turn to my sentence about the title matter.[2] I meant that if the title had been accepted by a man like Ben, you would think the same stuff could be read over and serve in this instance. It was the same with Jennymead. They have owned the place for several hundred years, but it took some months to go over the title. These are mysteries beyond me as a layman. I am not in any great hurry for the money. The interest at the bank is just $2\frac{1}{2}$.

I am about to write the Lasaters,[3] meant to do so earlier but seemed to have so much to do generally. Mrs. Stravinsky[4] asked why everybody she saw in New York looked sick. I said they were all worn out. I don't look sick at any rate, though I will be glad when the season ends.

My eye fell on the enclosed sentence and I burst out laughing, thinking what it would sound like to someone who had no idea what we were referring to.

It is good that Baby Ann[5] is moving away, I can't think you delight in her company at the expense of doing other things you want to do.

I have not yet heard what Mr. Watkins' sister[6] means to do about the little painting. Mr. Rehn wants 600 for it. As smallish pictures go

2. The reference is to the sale of lots owned by Young and his sister and brother-in-law. On February 1, Young had written his sister: "Hope the title to the lots is accepted, I should think it would be all right, it was good enough for us to buy, why not the new man?"

3. Young refers to the death of Mary Gardner Miller Lasater (Mrs. Edward C. Lasater, 1880–1946), whom he had earlier characterized in a letter to his sister as "a remarkable person and a real friend with a gift for being a friend when needed most." Mrs. Lasater lived at La Mota, in Falfurrias, Texas, a city founded by her husband, a pioneer land developer and prominent Texas cattleman. In the years before her death on January 27, 1946, she was closely associated with the Falfurrias Creamery Company, the Falfurrias Mercantile Company, and her family's ranch interests in the area.

4. Vera de Bosset Stravinsky, born in St. Petersburg, Russia, of French and Swedish parentage, married the painter Serge Sudeikine in St. Petersburg, shortly before the Russian Revolution forced them to flee to Yalta in 1917. Her brief acting career ended at the outset of the Russian Revolution. She went to France with her husband in 1920 and during the next two decades assisted in designing costumes for ballet and opera. In April, 1940, she married Igor Stravinsky and during World War II founded the gallery "La Boutique" in Hollywood. Since then she has enjoyed success as a floral and landscape painter.

5. Probably the reference is to Ann Townes, daughter of a friend of Young's sister.

6. Shirley Watkins Steinman (Mrs. John Frederick Steinman), novelist and sister of Franklin Chenault Watkins, decided against the purchase of the painting.

at the galleries that is a very high price, but I leave it to him. He knows his business, or certainly better than I could.

Wales sends love to you both. The tile man thinks of taking on an agent in New York, but not to use Wales's designs of course, for one thing the clients would be furious to have their designs around like linoleum. Wales has stipulated both that and that he will himself deal direct with Mr. Lozarno there in San Antonio.[7]

I don't seem to have any more news. I hope your valentine gets safely to you.

Love to you both
Stark

No wonder you bothered and were confused about the UNO site.[8] If it should be extended as they have sometimes talked it very likely would hit Jennymead. The chances are now that if it comes to that country at all it will buy a much smaller piece of land than talked about. The public will object to so much spending. It is so idiotic of talk about ponds and hills etc. as if a resort were planned. Also to pick a thickly settled place. Four miles further than Stamford, from NYC, in another direction is the Bear Mountain region, sparsely settled or developed, 40,000 acres already belonging to the Gov. The idea of the UNO being near New York is also a great mistake and will cause debate, already has. The pressure groups for different countries and causes will bear down on the delegates. No telling what the end of it all will be, but it is mostly unlikely they will get near Jennymead. Poundridge is at present a limit to the site, that is six miles from us. If at all, I imagine they will cut down the whole size of things, the smaller nations won't want the expense, for one thing. And Congress will debate it.

7. The passage cannot be satisfactorily explained. Possibly, Bowman had been approached about the use of designs which he had created in 1928 for the Robertson house in San Antonio.

8. A large number of possible sites was considered for the headquarters of the United Nations, but the final decision upon the location was not reached until December, 1946, when John D. Rockefeller, Jr., offered to give $8,500,000 to purchase a site on the East River in New York City.

636 | To Huntington Cairns, National Gallery of Art,
Washington, D.C.

> 320 East 57th Street
> New York
> Wednesday [February 13, 1946]

Dear Huntington,

I keep wishing for a line from you to tell me how Florence[9] is
getting along. She managed it well, but plainly did not eat any lunch?
She has to eat, so what about it? I certainly hope she is mending
steadily.

I still remember with so much pleasure my visit to Washington, but
also how much trouble I put you to, all that taxi work you had to do
on me. I should think that living in Washington you would think
hard before making a new friend. However, I profited and so greedy
was I at that delicious luncheon that—I don't know what was going to
follow.

Well, as my grandmother doubtless wished to say often but never
allowed herself to do it—I'll be God-damned! Mrs. Austin Strong[1]
called me on the telephone, and in the midst of it I heard the elevator
man drop a letter at my door. It was from you, and such a nice letter.
I was glad to get it, though I see my question at the start of this letter
still remains to be answered.

I was talking about you to James Soby, formerly of the Modern
Museum painting department, as you know, and he was saying fine
things about your ability etc. and I told him I had spoken with you
about his book on Rouault,[2] and that you admired it very much and
so on. He was much pleased. Afterward I suddenly wondered if I had
been right; it was more likely somebody at the gallery that evening
with whom I had spoken about the book. I felt like telephoning Soby
and saying that, but to do so seemed verily the Puritan sin of what the
Catholics call scrupulosity, not to say lacking in a sense of humor. So I
let it stand, faintly hoping that it was you after all. You lose nothing

9. Florence Butler Cairns (Mrs. Huntington Cairns).
1. Mary Holbrook Wilson Strong, wife of Austin Strong, the playwright; see below,
Letter 641, n. 4.
2. In 1945, James Thrall Soby published *Georges Rouault: Paintings and Prints.*

by it, for it is an excellent book, I think. I only wanted you to know, in case you run into him. You have probably read the book anyhow, and approved of it. Mr. Soby said he had met you once but did not know you, but he knew your reputation etc. as a man of great perception, he said. So that's that.

I will write Allen asking him to come by when he is in New York will say I won't discuss matters if he'd rather not. I hope so much he has not landed in a mess for his life, he is one of my loved friends indeed. It is remarkable and tragic how we poor human creatures throw away what is dear in the long perspective for something that very soon after is of no importance, however strong it may have seemed in its appeal for the moment. I am talking like a badly translated Greek chorus.

You are a great though kind fraud to talk about my knowledge and penetration. I have some penetration and just about enough knowledge to be embarrassed by my lack of it. I am fortunate in one thing, which is to be born in the era of the columnists: then the quarter wits are promoted to half wits.

I said at least one thing the other day to a theatre designer, it pleased both him and me. I said one didn't expect the actors to read the *New Republic,* it looked too much like a book. Tell Florence that, and tell her also to eat something.

Love to you both

Yours sincerely
Stark

637 | To Julia Young Robertson, Austin, Texas

[320 East 57th Street]
[New York]
Sunday morning
[February 17, 1946]

Dearest Sister,

My Valentine came yesterday morning and much impressed me. I know how handsome and how expensive that silver bit was at the shop. Someday I may give it back to you, since I have already enjoyed owning it. It is in the hall cabinet with the rarities at present. The box was so pretty. I showed it to Wales, saying see what a sweet sister I have. He brutally said yes, and that I should paint it. I may be able to, it would be like a group by Toulouse Lautrec,[3] he uses book etc. with flowers. So I cut the ribbon at the bottom and slit the paper at the bottom and slipped all off the box. I can easily put it back, now that the contents are seen and out. Asked Wales if he was trying to torture me making me keep the box till I had painted it, not knowing the contents, I don't love art that much I said.

Thank you very much and for the trouble.

I got Christmas socks from Margaret,[4] very welcome and will write her later today. I want Wales to mail this on his way to the office.

I didn't tell anybody I was to be on the radio last Tuesday, had nothing to say and didn't know what was going to be talked about. But Bessie Beatty was so kind about my first exhibition that I had to accept, either now or later on, so I went on and accepted. We talked the program over for about three minutes before the 10.15 came. Afterward people came up from another floor of WOR, and kind remarks, and I have been stunned by the number of people who heard it. It was partly because the Mayor had closed all shops that day for fuel—to fight the strike more, I imagine, of the harbor tugs.[5] And now I keep getting letters, cranks and otherwise, and a telegram etc. More things to answer even if with a short note. Even the liquor shop man we used to see in Stamford five or six years ago wrote me at once. The editor of Broadside,[6] a theatre society national more or less wrote me. What it is all about is not very clear to me. I rarely hear radio, but evidently most of it must be very stupid indeed. Mr. Rehn was at home, gallery closed by Mayor, he heard it, his housekeeper nearly had fits over what I said about him, his assistant he called and told to listen and next day telephoned me, somewhat overpowered, said he had tears in his eyes listening, that all sorts of friends had telephoned him that night about

3. Henri de Toulouse-Lautrec (1864–1901), French painter and caricaturist.
4. Margaret Robertson.
5. On February 4, 1946, members of Local 333 of the United Marine Division, International Longshoreman's Association, struck against the harbor tugboat owners. The strike had caused Mayor William O'Dwyer to ration fuel oil; and, on February 12, he issued an unprecedented order closing all industries, business houses, schools, libraries, bars, and amusement places in the city. On the following day the order was rescinded.
6. Sarah Chokla Gross has edited *Broadside,* a journal devoted to theatre records, issued at irregular intervals since 1940 by the Theatre Library Association.

it. It seems the curator or guest hostess at Knoedlers heard it too, told Wales compliments. The framing place heard it. Well, well, well, it was only answers about Lincoln, painting, reading, the house in the country etc. It comes out and I don't know what I do say. Mrs. Beatty and her husband manage it so expertly that it is very easy indeed, just like a conversation, plus a bit of strain.

Zack [7] and Elaine called me twice, asked us to dinner, went to Rehns beforehand. Mr. Rehn impressed with their manners etc., was much impressed by Elaine's taste in painting. She has greatly improved in looks and all. They are among the few who have gone to Hollywood and not been made fools or silly. We went to a quiet restaurant they used to know, but I heard of them at other places, crowds wrecking everything for autographs. Warners put them up at the Sherry Netherlands—which put out Stravinsky at the end of the allotted time but not a Warner star—and they had a big Warner car and chauffeur, etc. I must say I was proud of the way they took it all, liking it frankly but not silly. Zack is really devoted to me and grateful for my frank criticisms. People speak of him in the movies, always mention his good acting before his looks. He has lost some of his looks, seems older, as he is. That is what I didn't understand in the films of him.

Your letter looked very elegant, I wish you would buy a pad and scratch with a pencil, that is what the great ladies often do. It simplifies matters.

I wrote Garland and Lois and Tom last week.[8]

The clipping[9] is for Ben. What taste that family permit themselves. Selling the stamp collection—for a fortune was dubious enough, since

7. Zachary Scott (1914–65), born in Austin, Texas, married Elaine Anderson in 1935; the marriage was dissolved in 1950. Scott played in English repertory companies before appearing on Broadway as Neil Harding in *The Damask Cheek* in 1942. After performances in *This Rock* and *Those Endearing Young Charms*, Scott went to Hollywood in 1944 to appear in a succession of Warner Brothers motion picture productions, including *The Mask of Dimitrios, The Southerner, Hollywood Canteen, Her Kind of Man,* and *Whiplash,* before Young wrote this letter. In 1952, Scott married Ruth Ford.

8. Friends of Young in Austin, Texas.

9. Recently the New York *Times* had printed several stories about the auction at the Parke-Bernet Galleries of the late President Franklin D. Roosevelt's stamp collection. Very likely, the clipping Young sent was the article by Kent B. Stiles, February 5, 1946, p. 25, in which Stiles commented upon the objections of philatelists to the die proofs, which, they contended, had been given Roosevelt in his official capacity as president and should have been regarded as property of the nation. The collection was sold in two parts, the second auction scheduled for April. According to a story in the New York *Times,* February 6, 1946, p. 25, the sale of the first section amounted to $134,500.

they expect other people to donate to that Roosevelt library at Hyde Park and since many of the valuable stamps were given to FDR as President of the USA, from foreign ambassadors etc., who of course got them free. Alice Roosevelt will relish this tax bad taste,[1] though it is against NY law to publish the figures for taxes.

Roger[2] called the NR, of course the girl could not give him my number, he left his hotel place, I called him. Since I suppose I had to do something I preferred asking him to the Gripsholm to lunch rather than here with no Gerta to clean up and a longer visit. So from the G I went on to the NR with my proof. About 3.25 for lunch. I trust he enjoyed it. Somewhat times down and more Hancock being here on a visit to his father and doing the right thing, as he said of his step-mother, she wanted him to do the right thing and meet the right people, etc. I hope it came out all right, it was no treat for me. Not boring, just not what I would plan for a day.

Tell Marjorie[3] he looked well and anything else that would give her any satisfaction. He does very well, all things considered. Will get tamer and tamer as he tries to get on in the world.

Thank you again for the lovely Valentine, Wales sends you all his love.

I hope you and Ben are all right.

Lovingly
Stark

1. Presumably, Young means that Alice Roosevelt Longworth (b. 1884), daughter of President Theodore Roosevelt, would use the incident to continue her criticism of the administration of President Franklin D. Roosevelt.
2. Roger S. Hanks, Austin realtor.
3. Marjorie Hancock Hanks, mother of Roger S. Hanks.

638 | To William Lewis,[4] Oxford, Mississippi [carbon]

320 East 57th Street
New York
February 18, 1946

Dear Willie,

I was very much pleased to have your nice letter, and certainly appreciate the remarks about my works and the museum there.[5] I have been intending for some time to write and ask you about your wishes for the museum and the accommodations there for various things of various kinds.

First, as to the paintings—to have an exhibition there at present would be difficult. My dealer has entire charge of such matters, they usually fall in groups, places near enough to share expenses. The mere packing of the paintings here costs about two hundred dollars or more, not to speak of other expenses. I am to have a one-man exhibition in Dayton in June,[6] but of course the museum there is rich and if they sell any pictures will get that percent too. Let us hope they do sell some. I have not too many on hand, it takes time to paint them. Mr. Rehn, my dealer, gets 33 percent. He expects to have higher prices later, but for my first show he asked higher than most painters get—my smaller pieces—around 16 by 20 were $450, the larger 1200 to 1500.

As to objects for your museum, I have some things now and intended to will some or give them later on. I thought various things connected with *So Red the Rose* and *Heaven Trees* might be of interest in my native state among my own beloved people. I have two beautiful old dolmans—cape like wraps, one of moiré, one gros-grain trimmed with seed pearls and chenille.[7] Has the museum any way of

4. William Lewis (b. 1897), Oxford merchant and banker, known throughout the region as "Will Lewis," has served for many years as chairman of the board of trustees of the Mary Buie Museum (see below, n. 5). After the death of his father, when Will Lewis was a young man, Dr. Alfred Alexander Young acted as Lewis' "unofficial guardian."

5. The Mary Buie Museum, Oxford, which was opened in 1939, was established by the gift of Mary Skipwith Buie (Mrs. Henry T. Buie, 1856–1937) and her sister, Katherine Adair Skipwith to the city of Oxford to preserve the Skipwith and Buie art collections and to further interest in the fine arts.

6. See below, Letter 640 and n. 2.

7. These items are now in the Mary Buie Museum; see also below, Letter 661.

presenting such things? They would make no sense hanging sidewise or folded up. Please let me know about this.

I have my father's fraternity pin—Sigma Chi—and then my own, the same but so different with the epoch. Also his old literary society pin, I forget the name, but people there would know.[8]

Later on, certainly when I go to heaven, I shall have quite a number of interesting Southern things.

I hope Marie[9] and all your house keep well. It seems a long time since I saw you all. Even the kin at Como I have not seen, what with travel being so disrupted by the war, etc.

Thank you for your good letter.

Yours affectionately
[unsigned]

639 | To Huntington Cairns, National Gallery of Art, Washington, D.C.

320 East 57th Street
New York
Sunday [March 3, 1946]

Dear Huntington,

I took the Navy injection against flu—my one enemy—and it dazed me for several days, else I would have written to say how nice it was to see you but especially to thank you for listening to my tales of woe.[1]

8. In 1867, as a student at the University of Mississippi, Alfred Alexander Young was a member of the Eta Chapter of Sigma Chi. At that time, there were two literary societies, the Phi Sigma and the Hermaean societies, which met "during the forenoon of every Saturday for the purposes of improvement in debate, declamation, and composition"—*Catalogue of the University of Mississippi, 1869–1870.* Young was probably a member of the Hermaean Society. In 1870, he enrolled in the Medical Department of the University of Pennsylvania, from which he was graduated during the same year. Early in 1948, on his return trip from Texas to New York, Stark Young lost his father's literary society pin.

9. Young perhaps intended a reference to Marjorie Tankersley Lewis (Mrs. Will Lewis).

1. Although the specific nature of Young's "tales of woe" cannot be determined, Young had been depressed by both personal and public events; see above, Letter 633.

I did not mind in the least troubling you, and knew you would be glad to do anything you could. In general it is not my habit to ask things of people, and I would not profit by the act if I did, not very often. God knows, I have enough favors asked of me, but they are not usually by people whose work I should be only too delighted to do anything I could for, or whose quality is such that I want to stand by and fight for in this world. I would go to the stake for the real thing, but am not fond of being tracked down by people who are trying to work something. Moreover, they are nearly always people I scarcely know if at all.

I felt certain you would be ready to stand by me, and that is a compliment from my heart.

I sat by George Nathan the other night at the theatre, that is to say his young lady sat between us. I have not seen him in so long that I almost gave a shout. He spoke at once of having met you and I told him the fine things you said about him. His face glowed like a sweet little boy's hearing that. Then when I did my solo number about your prodigious accomplishments, he said, "And do you know he is just forty!"

You evidently appealed to the very nicest side of George, and that is very nice indeed. I count very genuinely on George's friendship, and I know he feels sure of mine.

I am painting on some new things, and hope they are going well. It is a solitary world in which art is born, and I envy various people who are wholly without creative impulse. They just flourish about in artistic waters and never lack a word or splash. Everything has its price, and I am getting philosophical and had better quit. Allen and I were talking about Florence, he said such fine things about her, really fond of her. We both think she is a rare and wonderful-looking person. I am glad you found her. When I see the sad centauresses that some of the men I know took on! (And of course vice versa.)

The gods give us joy—I am longing to get to the country.

Love to you both

> Yours
> Stark

640 | To Huntington Cairns, National Gallery of Art, Washington, D.C.

320 East 57th Street
New York
Tuesday [March 5, 1946]

Dear Huntington,

This is not a belaboring screed, it is just to say that I think I told you Toledo for my one man show in June, I should have said *Dayton,* which is a better museum is it not?[2]

Also it might be ammunition for your kind works sometime for you to know that I found my painting hung in the main gallery at the Pennsylvania Academy show, which was hung with "canvases by those of undisputed standing in the art world."[3] At that I do hope to God I am a good painter and will be so.

Bless you, Huntington

Yours sincerely
Stark

641 | To Julia Young Robertson, Austin, Texas

[320 East 57th Street]
[New York]
Tuesday morning [March 12,
1946]

Dearest Sister,

I was glad to have your letter yesterday. That sounded interesting about Ur. I have read of the excavations. In your Britannica there you

2. During June, 1946, Young exhibited the following paintings at the Art Museum of the Dayton Art Institute, Dayton, Ohio: *The Garlands; Landscape with Rocks; Rehearsal for the Pageant, Marfa, Texas; Presidio Range; Ode; Votive; Apparition of Flowers; Romance; The Saint's Statue; Sweet Land; Bouquet; Study; From Haley's Ranch;* and *Far and Near.*

3. At the 141st Annual Exhibition of the Pennsylvania Academy of the Fine Arts, January–March, 1946, Young exhibited *The Garlands.*

will find, not up to date on excavations of course, a good account of the great vanished Sumerian Empire, one of the phenomena of history. I read it while in Austin some time or other.

I am sorry your drama group did not have my review of Deep Are the Roots.[4] I was among the few critics who knew it was largely Broadway rubbish. The Jews and Colored people like the oppression theme and also the rather gory sexy implications and the snappy theatre tricks. The introduction to the published volume is absurd in many points.

I had a copy of the Koestler Twilight Bar, which is only so so but is going to [be] done by Luther Adler—a rather common Jewish actor —it is only a passable play.[5] I seem to have thrown or given my copy away. Not worth your bothering. The only other thing I have is Tennessee Williams' book of one act plays.[6] I don't fancy that would do at all, very broad, neurotic, often dirty, etc., and the ladies would not care for its talent, which whatever else is said is genuine. He wants me to write about the book for the NR, wrote me from New Orleans, but I am not going to do it. I don't even intend to bother with reading it all. I don't think any other plays have been published, I am sent them all as they come to the NR. Sorry. All I can suggest is that [sentence unfinished]

I am glad you are reading in So Red the Rose, if you will read some of the places aloud you will see that the tone is one of its chief points, also the speech rhythm. I was so pleased to hear of Granville Barker's raving about it last year. He is the soul of the critical and was a brilliant figure in the theatre and writing. He said among other things that most books were largely holes, this had scarcely a one. Delivered himself at length I heard to a company at the Century Club, where his

4. Young reviewed *Deep Are the Roots,* by Arnaud d'Usseau and James Gow, in "Serious Efforts," *New Republic,* CXIII (October 15, 1945), 499. Young regarded the play, which dealt with racial problems in the South, as a "third-rate drama" in which "grave matters are turned thus into theatre trash."

5. Luther Adler appeared as Glowworm in the pre-Broadway tryout of Arthur Koestler's *Twilight Bar,* which opened at Ford's Theatre in Baltimore, March 12, 1946, and closed at the Walnut Street Theatre, Philadelphia, March 23, 1946. Adler (b. 1903), actor and director, began his career as a child actor in the Yiddish theatre and later became a member of the Group Theatre. In 1938, he married Sylvia Sidney. Among the plays in which he has appeared are *Street Scene, Night over Taos, Men in White, Waiting for Lefty, Awake and Sing,* and *Tovarich.*

6. Young refers to Tennessee Williams' *Twenty-Seven Wagons Full of Cotton, and Other One-Act Plays* (1946).

name means a lot. I wouldn't go through with writing such a book again for anything, in fact I could not stand it physically. Stark and Doris and Allen Tate and Caroline Gordon seemed really to understand it. I have heard of people who still read it over. It still sells modestly after ten years. This country and the world is in such a mess however, so muddled and harassed, that nothing counts very much, and I have never cultivated the publicity side, which is what Americans at large understand. Every year they hit a masterpiece and every next year forget it and hit another. It is a true pity that most of them were ever taught to read. Those ladies in the reading circle there, they neither have an intense church feeling, nor the old frontier culture nor any real literary modern culture, their culture is about on the level, or below, that of The Reader's Digest, which as a rule aims at about such a public.

By the way at Archie Roosevelt's [7] at dinner not long ago I met the White who wrote that candid book of Russia last year.[8] Sections of [it] appeared in the Digest and were most interesting. He rode me home and was very likable in general.

Yesterday on Mrs. Winthrop's and Mrs. Crane's [9] so urging I made a talk on the Greek theatre and style in general at Mrs. Crane's, that group, about as good as could be found in New York. They had the largest attendance of the year, even Lady Ribblesdale [1] and Countess Mercati [2] and the Iselins [3] turned out. People went on with much kind-

---

7. See above, Letter 414, n. 7. Roosevelt was then serving as assistant military attaché in Tehran, Iran.

8. William Lindsay White (1900–73), writer, editor, and newspaperman, published in 1946 *Report on the Russians*.

9. Frances A. Crane (1888–1954) married Jan Masaryk, Czechoslovak patriot and political leader, in 1924, after her marriage to Robert W. Leatherbee ended in divorce. After the annulment of her second marriage in 1931, she became known as Mme. Frances A. Crane. In 1954, she was killed in an automobile accident near Falmouth, Massachusetts.

1. Ava Lowle Willing (1869–1958), member of a socially prominent Philadelphia family, married Colonel John Jacob Astor in 1891 and lived much of the time in England until her divorce in 1910. After Colonel Astor's death in the sinking of the *Titanic* in 1912 she divided her time between London and Newport. In 1919, she married Lord Ribblesdale (1854–1935). In 1940, she returned to the United States as a war refugee and regained her American citizenship. Although she renounced her title, she continued to be known as Lady Ribblesdale.

2. Countess Marie Manice Mercati (1869–1951), wife of Count Alexander Mercati. She was first married to Newbold Leroy Edgar. A year after his death in 1925, she married Count Mercati. The count and countess were prominent art patrons and active in committees for war relief in both world wars. She was a patron for Young's exhi-

ness and the attention was absolute. But I don't see why it was all that good. Austin Strong who wrote that hit some years ago Seventh Heaven,[4] came and stayed on afterward. He said I seemed to have a thing like lightning around my head while I was talking there. Doris [5] thought something like that. They are kind but I can't remember right afterward anything I said that was so much, just some searching things here and there, and some sort of fluency or magnetism or projection. I have promised to do one more talk. $50 each, these ladies consider that a mere gesture, but I can buy plants with it. This does sound flighty.

While I was writing a book has just been delivered at the door, a play that was done last fall and had some praise from good men. Perhaps last spring. It is based on Darlan.[6] So I am posting it right off without cutting the inner wrapping, perhaps that will help you.

Your yard sounds lovely.

The enclosed drawing seems funny if you live in Westchester.

Wales sends love. Love to you both.

Stark

---

bition at the Friends of Greece, Inc., and active in support of the Philharmonic Symphony Society, the Metropolitan Opera, and the Ballet Associates of America.

3. The Iselins were descendants of Isaac Iselin who came to the United States in 1801, from Basel, Switzerland, and became a prominent, wealthy New York merchant. Although Young's reference cannot be established beyond doubt, he may have referred to Eleanor Jay Iselin (1882-1953), wife of Arthur Iselin, textile executive and banker; Madeleine L'Engle Iselin (1896-1961), wife of Adrian Iselin II, real estate broker and yachtsman; and Dorothy Hyde Iselin (1891-1949), wife of Oliver Iselin, merchant and textile executive.

4. Austin Strong (1881-1951), architect and playwright, born in San Francisco, wrote his best plays during the first three decades of the century. He is now remembered primarily for a one-act play, *The Drums of Oude* (1906), and for *Seventh Heaven* (1922). In "Notes," *New Republic,* XXXIII (December 20, 1922), 97-98, Young reviewed *Seventh Heaven* and characterized it as "good, honest theatre, with bells, vice, hardships, heroism and true love."

5. Doris Keane who died November 26, 1945.

6. Young refers to Irwin Shaw's *The Assassin,* which opened at the National Theatre, October 17, 1945, and closed ten days later. The events of the play closely parallel the circumstances of the assassination of the French admiral Jean Louis Xavier François Darlan on December 24, 1942. Reviewing it, Young called the production "boring" but remarked that "some of the speeches are far above the usual run of plays and the dramatist has created an intelligent hero who can express himself and whose motives are both complex and intense." Young seemed to think *The Assassin,* as effective theatre, inferior to Shaw's earlier *Bury the Dead.* See Stark Young, "Assorted Murders," *New Republic,* CXIII (October 29, 1945), 573.

642 | To Francis Fergusson, Kingston, New Jersey

Bedford, New York
Friday [Spring, 1946]

Dear Mr. Fergusson,

I must ask your forgiveness for having delayed so long in writing you about the plays,[7] which I have read with genuine attention, interest and admiration. (Imagine that applied to plays!) I read the Greek play long ago and somehow the other got delayed et cetera—

I should tell you that I loathe things in manuscript and, for perhaps violent visual reasons, am a poor judge of writing in that shape. In fact one of my arrangements with the *New Republic* is no reading or consideration of MSS. I'm mentioning this fact partly too for the sake of expressing my great personal interest in you and your work, which is why I did not demur at the prospect of reading your two plays. Believe me, dear Mr. Fergusson, it was no chore—the two plays are both highly readable and have a curious gift, or technique, that holds the interest—a strong quality and a notable one. Both deal with subject matter already known and yet each of them holds the eye and leads the reader to a greed for the final conclusive bait of the dénouement. I congratulate you on this very rare talent or aptitude in structure or plot building.

The only suggestions I have to make for the Greek piece is a line or so in the very first part stressing the relation of Eumaeus to Odysseus, and my feeling that "you asked for it" does not improve the effect you are seeking—it's somewhere in your hero's mouth—your idiom in the modern vein comes off well nearly always, but I don't think this particular phrase keeps the tone of your scene. But the whole piece really goes along, and a certain breathless time, day, night, old passion and old song is truly present in it.

The other play I read with much interest—it is really a musical show

7. Francis Fergusson identifies the plays to which Young refers as *"Penelope,* a dramatization of the end of the Odyssey, and *The King and the Duke,* a sort of minstrel show based on the episode in *Huckleberry Finn."* Both plays have been performed at Bennington College. *Penelope* has been published in Fergusson's *Poems* (1962), and *The King and the Duke* has appeared in Eric Bentley's *From the Modern Repertoire,* II (1952).

in the same school as *Oklahoma*. Its great liability, speaking quite practically, is that no producer could achieve the right general tone for it as a whole. Otherwise its atmosphere and characters are engaging, violent and theatric in the good sense of the term—all to the good that is.

You know these things already of course, but I say them just the same.

Will you please remember me most cordially to your lady—nel occhio la mia donna porta amore—(not quite Dante's line) [8]—and if you think of it when you see him give the President my regards.

With all good wishes and appreciation I am

> Yours most sincerely
> Stark Young

Not dictated and not reread—as they say—so make allowances.

643 | To Huntington Cairns, National Gallery of Art, Washington, D.C.

> 320 East 57th Street
> New York
> Tuesday night [April 9, 1946]

Dear Huntington,

I have not written earlier about your coming to New York and about the Leopardi mask because the navy flu injection some while back was not only a fizzle; it gave me the flu and the toxin from it settled in the nerves of my right side and has given me hell. I can stand and paint but writing at the desk is still anything but pleasant. Forgive this brief scrawl therefore.

We have secured for Saturdays only some workmen and I have been [in] the country directing etc. Bowman, the architect who lives with me, shares the labors—mine has to be mostly standing about with them. We have to go again Thursday morning—they are coming again

---

8. Dante's line, *Ne li occhi porta la mia donna Amore*, is found in *La vita nuova*, 21.

and we have a digger for two days. I get home at bedtime Sunday or early Monday morning and hope you will be staying over, and will lunch with me Monday or Tuesday. Let me know on the enclosed card.

The sculptor has been sick but at last brought the Leopardi.[9] I'm much delighted with it—it is even more beautiful than the Italian one because the plaster is a finer grade. I prefer this white finish, for the values, but if you want the toned look just give it two coats of *white* shellac *thinned* well with wood alcohol. You can try it first on the back. The tone is like alabaster—as you of course know.

My ills have kept me from trying to see Caroline—also my black mind has had little brightness for others. I have some new paintings at least that seem to have come off.

By the way the sculptor said keep the mask in the open for a week at least, before wrapping and packing—so I'll express it next Monday.

Love to you and Florence.

Stark

644 | To Julia Young Robertson, Austin, Texas

[320 East 57th Street]
[New York]
Thursday [May 2, 1946]

Dearest Sister,

Ben has been very nice writing me your news daily, and I am so glad to hear you are getting really better. One of the worst things about this kind of flu is that it is so depressing. But let's hope time will soon help all that.

Ben said you said no flowers, no. So next week I'll see if Mary Chess has any of the mimosa bath powder yet.

9. Jane Wasey had made a new cast from the original. On April 19, Cairns wrote: "The Leopardi is lovely. It is now at the Gallery, in the hands of Mr. Stephen Pichetto, our Restorer. We are both of the opinion that the mask will have to have a coating of white shellac or some other substance. Otherwise, it will absorb the dust and grime of Washington and in a relatively short time take on the hue of a blackamoor."

Our new man [1] seems so far very good indeed—it seems hardly possible these days, but I can tell you we got enough of cooking, cleaning, beds, floors, garden etc. and finally just let the beds go unless somebody was coming in—which was rarely—everybody is worn out these days. We are going to the country tomorrow—have to be in town most of next week—theatre etc. After that we hope to be in the country pretty constantly. Things are ready to begin spring out there—the apple trees, lilacs, etc. I hope May doesn't act up with too much cold, wind and rain. June is likely to be all right.

Gertrude sails [2]—perhaps—this week. She is going into an adventure indeed, with things as they are in France. Wales is busy and tired— two of his bigger jobs are shut off till the priorities are changed. He says he is delighted—could ask nothing better. He had about $200,000 work to do. Not bad, I should say. He's to pay his draughtsman $100 a week. He asks each mail if I have heard how you are, is very sorry you have been having a rotten time.

Please thank Ben for his letters. Love to you both.

Stark

645 | To Ella Somerville, Oxford, Mississippi

Waccabuc, New York
Thursday [June 6, 1946]

Dearest Ella,

This is four o'clock in the morning—so many things happen I can't sleep. But I do want to explain that I'd have written sooner about Mrs. Somerville's death [3] if I had not been sick. I have had bad flu from

1. The "new man," named Patton, had recently arrived from Nassau. A week later Young wrote that the new man had developed problems with the immigration authorities and was returning to Nassau.

2. Gertrude Newell was returning to Planterose, her home in Moumour, France, which had been occupied by the Nazi army during World War II. In a letter to his sister written the following day, Young remarked that "Gertrude sails Saturday, by present signs. Has fourteen trunks and goodness knows how many cases. It seems a mess to be attempting France just now and she feels the strain of it. Her English butler is there straightening things out, the Germans left the house at least and a good deal of the furniture. Ruined much of it, took away all books and various things."

3. Mrs. Ella Vasser Somerville (Mrs. Thomas Hugh Somerville) died on May 14, 1946.

taking the *navy* injection against it. The virus went to my vertebrae—a special brace—belt—nine nights sitting in a chair instead of going to bed. No need to talk about it—I'm getting all right but slowly.

Dear Ella, would you and Mary Hartwell and Nina therefore forgive the slow coming of this letter and believe that I love you all and that I know the value and depth of old affections and old friendships.

I am an ancient and a bore, but somehow not finished at all, and my heart in its gentle impulses seems to me as full and warm as ever. (I may be mistaken.)

This month I have a *one-man show* at the Dayton Ohio museum.[4] That is fine no doubt. But it all seems silly, the world is so shot up, inside and outside.

In the country Bowman and I have a lovely house—Your comfort, the longest, best made and most elegant I ever saw, helps us out at a rate. I always like to recall that this comfort is a present from a very, very dearly loved person—one of the world's best—

Stark

Written lying down. Please, if you write my sister, don't tell her I've been sick. This is a poor letter. I have not even said what a wonderful person Mrs. Somerville was, and a great lady. So many of my friends have died this year—two of them among my very closest—Doris Keane and Ellen Glasgow—that I don't seem to have words left. Life goes by, and that's about it.

Lovingly
S.Y.

646 | To Julia Young Robertson, Austin, Texas

[Waccabuc, New York]
Monday [June 24, 1946]

Dearest Sister,

We have been working so much that I am dulness itself, and at last today is warm summer. Perhaps the garden will grow now. The cool nights have kept things almost at a standstill all but the weeds.

4. See above, Letter 640 and n. 2.

Mrs. William Astor Chanler died in her sleep last Tuesday, on the train to her summer place in Maine.[5] She was a remarkable woman, remarkable looking too, and with talent and a fine spirit. She was a genuine and very loyal and warm friend to me, and I am really sorry. Quite a year—close friends like Doris and Miss Glasgow—friends like Mary Lasater, Lyle Saxon,[6] Ned Sheldon,[7]—Cousin Valette[8] too—etc.

I haven't any news but often think how nice it will be if you and Ben get up here.

Wales sends his love.

Love to you both
Stark

647 | To Julia Young Robertson, Austin, Texas

Waccabuc, New York
Monday [July 15, 1946]

Dearest Sister,

I had to come to town for my paints and to attend to several things. It was suddenly cold at seven this morning in the country but today has got hot here and I am too sleepy almost to get to the train.

I hope Ben had a good birthday. I sent him a telegram, to get there that morning.

I met at the Campbells' two weeks ago a young man named Mike

5. Her death occurred on Wednesday, June 19. In a letter to the editor of the New York *Times,* Young characterized her as "a dreamer, with the consistency and the un-defeatable purity of dreams about her very presence." See above, Letter 600, n. 7.

6. Lyle Saxon had died on April 9.

7. Edward Brewster Sheldon (1886–1946), to whom Young dedicated *The Theater,* died on April 1. Young's friendship with Sheldon dates back at least to 1913 when Sheldon wrote *Romance,* which has always been associated with Doris Keane. After participating in George Pierce Baker's "47 Workshop" at Harvard, Sheldon wrote a number of plays, including *Salvation Nell* (1908), *The Nigger* (1909), *The Boss* (1911), and *The High Road* (1912). He collaborated with Sidney Howard on *Bewitched* (1924) and with Charles MacArthur on *Lulu Belle* (1926). Stricken with progressive paralysis, Sheldon became blind in 1931 but continued to play an influential role in theatrical activities.

8. Julia Valette McGehee Sledge (Mrs. Joe Brown Sledge) died January 11, 1946. See above, Letter 322 and n. 9.

Brown who went to that camp with Stark.[9] He said one day at the University he felt blue and went out to walk, it rained, you picked him up, were so lovely and sympathetic, turned out to be Stark's mother. This fellow is trying to do a sort of Cole Porter career. He has astonishing talent in that boogie woogie music. He could easily get them on the radio. Lawton said he was the pet of Palm Beach when they were there. Was in the army, could not be paid, but people sent him checks and presents after he had sung for their parties.

Wales asks now and again do I know when you all are coming up? We would like to know ABOUT the time whenever you can estimate it. I told him August, I was not sure just when. The country club—ours —is open, if Ben wants to play golf, but of course there is not much playing except week ends for the most part. I don't know whether Ben would think it too much bother to drag his stuff up here for the brief spell. It is only half a mile or less from our house, looks like a good field. We pay club dues anyway.

Our garden is slow but healthy. We have now four kinds of lettuce, young beets, radishes and green peas. Black raspberries. Will soon be having snap beans and later cucumbers and tomatoes and corn and lima beans and those Mexican chaluppas. All ages of young onions now, and very good. It looks as if we would have bushels of tomatoes. Some of the corn is planned for your visit, it is marvellous taken right off the stalk and young. Big black berries will soon be in, the vines are loaded this year. The deer got in twice, so we have a sheet in thirds, that is to say a quarter of a sheet hanging in three places, two of them on one cross waving, and under them every night hangs a lighted lantern. The deer so far have kept away. They can ruin a whole garden in a night. One day last year we saw as many as twelve in one field, on the hill in a Mead oatfield. The women's clubs defeat all efforts to change the law against killing them, absolutely idiotic, imagine a poor

9. Stark Young Robertson and Michael Brown (b. 1920) became friends at a summer camp near Kerrville, Texas. The incident Young relates took place in 1937 while Brown was a student at the University of Texas. After being graduated from the University of Texas in 1940, he served during World War II in the Air Force as a cryptography officer. In 1950, he married Joy Williams, a ballerina with the Ballet Russe de Monte Carlo. Primarily a songwriter, Brown's first work on Broadway was done for *New Faces* (1952). With Harold Arlen, Brown wrote "Indoor Girl" for Pearl Bailey (*House of Flowers,* 1954). During the New York World's Fair, he produced, directed, and wrote the music, lyrics, and script for the *Wonderful World of Chemistry,* sponsored by the du Pont Company. Brown has also produced shows for a variety of industrial companies and has written children's books.

family with children unable to have a vegetable [garden], out of this sloppy sentiment, and then people killing lambs. In the winter when we were away they ate some of the lilac tops and some of the apple tree. Last summer next door they sat and watched deer eat the cabbages and then the window box flowers one moonlight night. I think, certainly hope, this lantern and scarecrow business will work. I put the idea together from various things people have said in despair. Frances Mead says they walk right up to their dogs or at least don't mind them. The first day I saw them I was reading—about two weeks ago—in the loggia behind the barn and a fawn walked right up the bank near me to eat the lilies and zinnias, his mother was a few feet away. They merely float over fences etc. and look quite wonderful I must say. But when you have worked a lot and paid for diggers too and got things going, it is far from tender sentiment to have them eaten off like nothing. We had four hundred feet of chicken wire around the garden for wood chucks, then had to put that much again of finer wire against the baby rabbits, and then the deer turn up.

I hope your ankle is about all right. Do begin to be careful, evidently you must do so or end in being a cripple. Papa banged into things, I hope to goodness I can watch and try not to break some old bone now, I am just at the age to begin it.

I was serious about Ben and that fine Dr. Blake.[1] The first visit is 25, the others ten each, so his position makes him no more expensive than the others in town.

It took me ten days to get an appointment at all, and they created that. So let me know something about this if you can. Dr. Wolf has been away on vacation but was expected back today.

Wales would send love if he were here. Arthur Sachs[2] has cabled

1. Identification not established.

2. Arthur Sachs (1880–1975), banker, art collector, and philanthropist, became a partner in the New York banking firm of Goldman Sachs and Company after his graduation from Harvard in 1901. In 1928, he retired from the firm, moved to Paris, and after the death of his first wife, Alice Goldschmidt Sachs, in April, 1930, married Georgette Boyer in December of that year. Sachs spent most of his life in assembling one of the world's greatest private art collections and in contributing to various philanthropic activities in France. Among his principal interests were the French Musées Nationaux, the American Hospital in Paris, the American Library of Paris, the Eisenhower Fellowship Fund, the Arthur Sachs Scholarship Fund (for Harvard), and the Conseil des Amis du Louvre. During World War II, he purchased Featherhill Ranch at Montecito, near Santa Barbara, California. William Bowman, with Diane Tate and Marian Hall, assisted with alterations and interior decoration for the house. While living in Santa Barbara, Sachs served as trustee of the Santa Barbara Art Museum and, in 1946, loaned his art collection to the museum for an exhibition. After

from Paris about a house in California and Mr. Landa in Washington has bought a house and wants him to start working it over. So his success—all right—is about to leave him no rest this summer, which he needs. I wish you would see the room he has done for Mrs. McBride,[3] the mother of that young woman who lived in a shack there in Austin. A large bedroom, some entrance closets, under the room an open room for a sun room, with the Texas tile floor. It is the finest work I have seen in a long time. Cost 25000 and shows it. The baths etc. were already there, he merely did the closeted entrance to the bedroom and the bedroom with sun porch beneath. The rest of the house is stupid but cost a lot once, the grounds are elaborate, walks dropping down to a body of water, avenues, some marble benches from Italy, orchards, gardens etc. Tell the Houstons, they will enjoy the contrast of it all.

I must go to the train.

Love to you both
Stark

648 | To Gladys Coates Hamilton, New York

[320 East 57th Street]
[New York]
October 8, 1946

Dear Gay,

I don't want to have that beautiful poem of Ham's[4] without thanking you for sending it to me. It must be a comfort to you, just rereading it. I have made several copies for friends.

---

the war, he sold the Featherhill estate and returned to Paris. Sachs, Bowman, and Young continued their friendship, and, in 1955, Bowman and Young visited Sachs in Paris.

3. Identification not established.

4. Gladys Coates Hamilton, wife of Clayton Hamilton, had sent Young the first verse of a poem entitled "Morituri," which Hamilton had written just before he died of a heart attack on September 17, 1946:

> Sea-gulls sidelong circling
> Over the turbulent sea
> Promise the peace of a great release
> From to be to not to be.

Young's letter relates to this poem.

It would be a happy hope if there were a next world for us all, but in case there is not, people like Ham leave something so rich behind them that they are always present.

Affectionately,
Stark

649 | To John Mason Brown, New York

Waccabuc, New York
Wednesday [October 9, 1946]

Dear John,

Thank you for your adorable letter—of course as old Mrs. (General) Custer (83) told me once "I said to my dear husband, those Virginia gentlemen—I tremble before them but I don't believe a word they say." Just the same what you said warmed my heart.

Sooner or later the cold will send me and Wales back to town permanently, and then we will impinge on you and that lovely Cassie.

Meanwhile now that the war is over and the theatre starting up, with you, Brooks and others returned, I think it would be advisable for me to return to the Critics Circle. My reason given for leaving was that "the disruption caused by the war, among critics and theatres," made the functions of the Circle for the time being—not fully working etc. If the Circle thinks that once out I should stay out, that's all right too. I wish it success at any rate and I entirely, and very much, agree with the recent decision that a prize should be given every year, willy nilly—otherwise the question of standards that arises is insoluble.[5]

Love to you both
Stark

5. Brown replied that he was delighted to hear of Young's decision to return to the Critics' Circle and agreed with Young's comments about the "willy nilly prize arrangements." At Young's suggestion, George Jean Nathan also expressed interest in returning to the group.

650 | To Julia Young Robertson, Austin, Texas

[320 East 57th Street]
[New York]
Wednesday [October 16, 1946]

Dearest Sister,

Mrs. Wolf kept me so long the other day that I had to tear off the letter to you, long but badly typed, and not reread it since we were getting the train for Harrison and the Mezzulos,[6] without whom there would have been far less of Jennymead. We have put them off several times and at last got there.

I have written Hallie, and I would send something else and will, but there is not time to get anything there by the 19th anyhow.[7] In case I insured the parcel for a fair sum, perhaps that can be used by Hallie to buy something she wants, but I don't think the Houstons would like that. I didn't fuss over the sum in the insurance for it never occurred to me that so strong a box, so well packed, would be thrown. You need not blame yourself, the affair sounds as if one of those heavy cartons would have been smashed just the same. I was very proud of the way the parcel looked, and so there we are.

I enclose the Times piece about Wallace.[8] I have heard nothing more

6. Young and Bowman were going to visit Mr. and Mrs. Arthur F. Mezzullo, who lived near Harrison, New York. The firm of Marcello Mezzullo, Inc., general contractors, had been founded by Arthur F. Mezzullo's father, Marcello Mezzullo (1876–1942) in New York but had been moved to Port Chester. Although best known for such buildings as the Victory Arch in Washington Square, New York, and the residence of Governor Herbert H. Lehman in Purchase, New York, the firm had also built many of the largest homes in the vicinity of Port Chester.

7. Young refers to the wedding of Hallie Bremond Houston, daughter of Mr. and Mrs. Hale Houston, Austin, Texas, and John Simeon Burns, on October 19, 1946.

8. Young refers to a news story, "Wallace Will Edit the New Republic," in the New York *Times,* October 13, 1946, p. 1. Henry Agard Wallace (1888–1965), former secretary of agriculture and vice-president, had recently resigned from President Truman's cabinet as secretary of commerce because of a dispute over foreign policy. According to the *Times* account of the reorganization of the *New Republic,* Wallace was to begin his editorship on December 16, and Bruce Bliven was to remain as senior editor of the board of editors consisting of Bliven, George Soule, Michael Straight (see below, Letter 653), and Stark Young. When Wallace assumed the editorship, however, the masthead revealed Straight as publisher, Bliven as "editorial director," and the "senior editors" as William Harlan Hale, Robert Hatch, Penn Kimball, and James R. Newman. Young was listed among the "staff contributors," while Soule's name did not appear in the masthead. Wallace edited the magazine until January, 1948, when he resigned to campaign for the presidency on a third-party ticket, though he continued as contributing editor for several months thereafter.

and Dan Mebane couldn't lunch with me till Friday, then I will know some details. It is odd that Mr. Wallace should have bought a place last year at South Salem, about six miles from me, and here the NR brings us together. Sorry I can't tell you more now.[9]

Thanks again for your lovely letters. I treasure that birthday letter. Yesterday the presents were all sorted out, my goodness I certainly cleaned up. Wales said he felt we must go and get me some MORE pajamas. That wrapping and the blue flower stickers and the ribbons was a work of love and duly appreciated, but work at that.

Wales says give you and Ben his love. At present he is to go with Arthur Sachs to California to advise him about some alterations in a house, Arthur is flying over from France. But it may fall through.

Lovingly
Stark

651 | To Julia Young Robertson, Austin, Texas

[320 East 57th Street]
[New York]
Tuesday [October 22, 1946]

Dearest Sister,

I don't seem to feel very energetic, I think the injections for that artery business—the third came today—make me feel a bit shot. Dr. Wolf says two more, then another test to see if I have entirely got rid of that bacillus. I took the same treatment for those eye hemorrhages five or six years ago and it worked all right.

I suppose the wedding has about laid you and Miss Hallie out. Hope to hear about the doings. The postmaster was very nice at Waccabuc,

---

9. A week later, Young wrote his sister: "Great storms are going on at the NR, all sorts of plans, struggles with the new budget and making ends meet etc. I have written Mr. Wallace a welcoming letter but otherwise keep out of it and am not consulted anyhow. For the present at least they are cutting all the department writers, movies, theatres and books I suppose to a column. That is not very encouraging, a far cry from the times I wrote authoritative things at length to Croly's delight that went far and wide. But the paper has grown stale with no central faith, and I am **glad** something is going to be tried."

said he remembered noting how well packed the box was but went on and marked it fragile just the same, since I had asked him to, he volunteered this remark about the packing. I have not found the record on just how much I valued the figurine at but he has it in the PO and will take it up he said. He was very nice about it.

Arthur Sachs has arrived and Wales is to go to California with him, it seems for two weeks in all, it will do Wales good perhaps but he says it is a most inconvenient time and that he wants to be away less time. He will probably enjoy a lot of it, though Marian Hall will be there also and though one is fond of her she is dominating and tiring. She and Diane are giving Arthur a dinner tonight at the Pavillion, which is a fine and ruinous place. I am going but don't look forward to it. I will not be drinking anything and some of the guests will drink much too much, and the combination is not a delight. But both Marian and Diane and the Sachs have been most kind to me and doubly so to Wales, throwing him jobs etc. Black ties.

Wales may have to go Saturday, in which case no Jennymead, or he may go Sunday. Arthur has a whole row of compartments reserved for them but is trying to change to Saturday. Doubtless Wales will see the Stravinskys,[1] and that will be fun.

He thought it awfully nice of you to send him the Dandy.

I hope you and Ben are all right.

> Lovingly
> Stark

652 | To Julian Huxley, London, England

> 320 East 57th Street
> New York
> Friday [October 25, 1946]

Dearest Julian,

I saw so little of you and thought it so fine of you to plow over here; this is a line to tell you so. And to say I feel proud of the way you go

1. Igor Stravinsky (1882–1971) and his wife, Vera de Bossett Stravinsky, whose friendship Young greatly valued as he did Stravinsky's music and Mme. Stravinsky's painting.

at UNESCO,[2] and as to your frail body I begin to think you have a Renaissance vitality and in your old age will be turning into one of those indestructibles.

Bowman thought you looked very sharp and fit. He is leaving Monday with Arthur Sachs (Goldman Sachs) who cabled over from Paris to ask him to go with him to California about a Santa Barbara house, to plan and advise. Taking architect and decorator—ah, the rich! Just got here on the Queen Elizabeth and now off to more acquisition in the West. He had Bowman over to Paris to design a house at St. Cloud, but only the foundations were dug when the war drove the Sachs family to this side—Jewish etc. It was interesting and very surprising to me that he paid $60,000 for two acres at St. Cloud, near the golf club. He plans now to cut that house down a bit and go on with it. I think he already has two smallish houses in France. The world is too much for me.

You were nice to ask about the painting. Your liking the pictures has meant a great source of encouragement for me. People have responded wonderfully but I am disconcertingly out of line with what is being pushed these days. Such as the enclosed. They say that a romantic return is due, let us hope for something like that. I had a fine letter lately from the director of the Chicago Art Institute, said he liked my pictures and coming to see more of them when he gets to New York, and that as a writer and critic I had long been an idol of his. I have heard remarkable things about him—Daniel Rich—but never saw him. Well, we shall see.

Give my love to Juliette, I did love seeing her and how she has steadily grown in so many senses, and am glad to hear she did not find me too much going backward like the crab of Hamlet fame. Juliette wears her clothes so well, and I think she is prettier than ever.

That was quite a breeze of a man who came in, seemingly a person indeed. If I spoke French he would astonish it out of me for a while. Nous sommes quelquefois aussi differents de nousmeme que des autres is one of the best things in La Rochefoucauld.[3]

As to Wallace, whatever way that turns out in the end, it was an

2. Since 1945, Huxley had been provisional secretary general of the United Nations Educational, Scientific and Cultural Organization.

3. Young has slightly altered Rochefoucauld's "On est quelquefois aussi different de soi-meme que des autres."—*Reflexions ou sentences et maximes morales,* 135.

inspired idea to get him, I think. The paper needs new life and a more strong faith or source of action, something more of belief at the core of it.

Take care of yourself, and knock the Zimmerns in all directions.[4] You have remarkable qualifications for what you are doing, and life and experience have prepared you for it.

Affectionately
Stark

Excuse haste, I wanted to get Bowman to post this. Love to you.

S.

653 | To Julia and John Benjamin Robertson, Austin, Texas

320 East 57th Street
New York
Monday morning [October 28, 1946]

Dear Julia and Ben,

There was no need to write yesterday even if we had not been outdoors planting endless bulbs that Wales had bought, and paid for himself I am glad to say. We had an understanding that we would not go fifty fifty if he wanted this and that, 150 of shrubs and all that. He is making money and if this gives him pleasure he is welcome to it. I should like the place quite as well without so many varieties etc. I have not that sort of feeling about a garden. An enclosure with bare dirt and some oleanders etc. is good enough for me. But Jennymead is certainly beginning to look lovable.

4. Young refers to Sir Alfred Zimmern (1879–1957), who was executive secretary of the preparatory commission established to organize UNESCO. Zimmern had resigned from the post because of illness, and Huxley had been appointed in his place. In the fall of 1946, the British delegation to the organizational meeting in Paris was strongly supporting Huxley for the post of director-general. On December 6, Huxley was elected for a two-year term. Young's comment, of course, was merely an expression of his eagerness for his friend to win the office.

I was much pleased and touched about the painting and Wales said it was one of the loveliest things he ever heard of.[5] Without meaning at all to be snippy I said right off yes it was, very wonderful, but you were that kind of people all the time. I was not surprised. That was a fine compliment at any rate.

Well, over the telephone it was hard to express appreciation but of course you knew I felt it. I will ask Mr. Rehn and see and then write you. He would make a special price to a museum and then there would be only the cost of his third of the price, so it would not be too horrible. I must confess I was disappointed about Dorothy Elmhirst and am sure she was too, Dan Mebane told me that with the new arrangement at the NR their budget was driving all mad, since the British government won't let them take money out of there. Dan and the office are about a wreck but I am not involved or consulted. I lunched with him the other day and he told me all this.

I gave Wales your message and he sent you his love and thanks. He leaves this afternoon with Arthur Sachs and Marian Hall, I have three plays this week[6] so that will break things up a bit and I intend to go to the Metropolitan a good deal, and see if I can't get some new inspiration about painting.

That one column idea at the NR gives little opening there. I will wait and see what happens, it would be foolish to be hasty. I wrote Mr. Wallace a letter of welcome, they say he is a very nice man and I would see him rarely. It is an irony, perhaps, that his house should be right near me, and that might do good or not as things turned out. At my time of life this is not exactly the thing to have a[7]

Lord knows the NR has been much unpleasanter and more hampering to me since Croly died than I ever told you about. No use worrying you, since you could do nothing about it. It looks as if Bruce might

5. The Robertsons had offered to donate to the Chicago Art Institute the money to purchase one of Young's paintings. The painting eventually selected and presented to the museum was his *Apparition of Flowers*.

6. Probably John Synge's *The Playboy of the Western World*, Noel Coward's *Present Laughter*, and Anita Loos's *Happy Birthday*. Young reviewed the first two plays in "Synge and Webb," *New Republic*, CXV (November 11, 1946), 628, and the last in "Return to Comedy," *ibid.*, November 18, 1946, p. 662.

7. For some reason, Young did not finish the sentence but went ahead to the next paragraph of his letter.

get some of his innings, I hear he is [in] a jittery state indeed, and I imagine Michael Straight[8] thinks poorly of him.

Poor Gene O'Neill has palsy so he can hardly talk, is white haired and looks seventy five. I had a note the other day saying do come and see them, I would buck him up. I don't suppose Gene ever tried to buck anybody else up but he is a remarkable fellow and has always blown my horn besides. If you see TIME for 21, the article on Gene, it is almost, or in many ways, very accurate.[9] A friend of mine, Louis Kronenberger[1] is on Time and wrote it I imagine.

Well, thank you again about the painting, we shall see. I appreciate such a thought far more than I could tell you or you would want me to try to tell you. But as I say it is so in character that I can be calm about it.

Love to both
Stark

8. Michael Whitney Straight (b. 1916), editor, author, publisher, administrator, son of Willard and Dorothy Whitney Straight, held posts in the department of the interior and the state department from 1938 to 1941, when he became Washington editor for the *New Republic*. From 1941 to 1958, he served the magazine in several capacities, including contributing editor, publisher, editor, and editor-at-large. Straight has been associated with various educational, artistic, and theatrical organizations; and, since 1969, he has been deputy chairman of the National Endowment for the Arts. His publications include *Make This the Last War* (1943), *Trial by Television* (1954), *Carrington* (1960), and *A Very Small Remnant* (1963).

9. Young refers to "The Ordeal of Eugene O'Neill," *Time*, XLVIII (October 21, 1946), 71–72. O'Neill's picture appeared on the cover.

1. Louis Kronenberger (b. 1904), drama critic, historian, poet, novelist, and editor, was then drama critic for *Time*. He had begun his career as an editor for Boni and Liveright and Alfred A. Knopf, Inc. From 1940 to 1948, he was drama critic for *PM*, and, since 1950, he has lectured at various universities including Columbia, Brandeis, Harvard, and Princeton. Kronenberger's publications include *The Grand Manner* (1929), *Kings and Desperate Men* (1942), *The Thread of Laughter* (1952), *Company Manners* (1954), and *Marlborough's Duchess* (1958). In 1940, he married Emmy L. Plaut.

654 | To Eric Bentley,[2] University of Minnesota, Minneapolis, Minnesota

320 East 57th Street
New York
Tuesday [November 5, 1946]

Dear Mr. Bentley,

I saw your theatre article in VIEW,[3] in which by some alchemy not altogether clear to me, I am a fellow editor. The spirit of the times is that nothing should, perhaps, be clear, and so we are all right. Charles Henri is an able piece[4] and that dear Pavlik[5] is an artist regardless of the inner organs that he loves to smear his ladies with, and there we are.

I am writing to say that I think your article on the theatre is out of the usual run, I respect it and you. You have a certain high innocence that I think most important in the realm of our future theatrical criticism. You are still quite capable of complaining that a porpoise could not make the full sound of a triton. That is as it should be really, and bless you for it. What perhaps you don't know is that Broadway does not give a damn what you think, so long as the tickets sell. And when the tickets do not sell, then Broadway is for something else again. Deep thought, at this moment, arises, great theories as to the theatre's soul and solubility. (Your remark about Kit Cornell's unwillingness to be

2. Eric Bentley (b. 1916), drama critic, teacher, editor, and translator, taught courses in the drama at Black Mountain College (1942–44) and the University of Minnesota (1944–48) before becoming drama critic for the *New Republic* from 1952 to 1956. In 1954, he became Brander Matthews Professor of Dramatic Literature at Columbia University and since that time he has also lectured at Harvard. His drama criticism includes *The Playwright as Thinker* (1946), *Bernard Shaw* (1947), *In Search of Theatre* (1953), *The Dramatic Event* (1954), *What Is Theatre?* (1956), and *Theatre of War* (1972).

3. Eric Bentley, "The 'Old Vic,' the Old Critics, and the New Generation," *View*, VII (Fall, 1946), 31–34.

4. Young may refer to Charles Henri Ford's poem *"Chanson pour Billie,"* in *View*, VII (Fall, 1946), 17, or to his work as editor of the periodical. Ford (b. 1913), painter, photographer, poet, editor, born in Hazlehurst, Mississippi, began his career as editor of *Blues Magazine* (1929–30). During the 1930s, he edited several collections of stories and wrote poetry; from 1940 to 1947, he edited *View* magazine; and since that time he has published additional volumes of poetry and made two films. Throughout much of his career, Ford has been closely associated with Pavel Tchelitchew.

5. Pavel Tchelitchew.

anything but a princess, with the ensuing implication of vulgarity, was very brilliant indeed.[6] It is, in acting terms, another way of saying that as a stage medium she cannot graduate her effects. The bourdon stop, or the voix celeste, is pulled out all the time.)

Your remarks about me and the nostalgic eye toward the past are all right,[7] partly right but largely waiting for a veritable suggestion. This is the point; twenty years ago, in Croly's time, I had columns to turn things over in; my articles were quoted entire here and there over this country, and abroad. Since Croly's death, since nobody but the Elmhirsts, who happily supported the paper, thought either I or art was of any importance, I have been put off with shorter and shorter space. And so later has come the instruction that while the Wallace regime is being adjusted, the departments will therefore stick to a column.

Considering the fact that I was much excited by the thought of a chance to see *The Duchess of Malfi* on the stage, and had spent some two days entire, plus nights on the restudy of it, plus notes, I thought I did very well in my treatment.[8] With more ignorance I might have done worse. With more pertinent despair I might have done nothing at all. I could have written several columns, of use to some people at

6. Writing about the Old Vic Company's production of Chekhov's *Uncle Vanya,* Bentley had observed in parentheses: "Miss Cornell will never consent to be anything less than a princess in any role, thus glamorizing, vulgarizing, destroying Chekhov's 'scenes from country life.'"

7. After surveying the criticism of the plays presented by the Old Vic Company in its tour of the United States, Bentley concluded: "So far as I could discover, the only accounts of the Old Vic that were thoroughly worth reading were Stark Young's. Mr. Young has standards and he describes acting better, perhaps, than any other critic of this century. It is hardly necessary to say he likes Chekhov. The point is that he brushes off the Old Vic's Chekhov in a couple of paragraphs. The point is he seems bored nowadays not only by bad performance but by the theatre itself. Now a critic is not entitled to dislike his medium. Nor to be wholly reminiscent and nostalgic. 'Things were different in my day' is the unwritten corollary—well, not always unwritten—of nearly every statement Mr. Young makes about the theatre. Let us grant Mr. Young's corollary. What follows? That every performance is to be matched against the Moscow Art Theatre, every actress against Duse? By no means. A dead actress is very dead and should be left to rest in peace. One must see present-day performances in the context of the present day. One must be interested in the future more than in the past of acting."

8. Young reviewed the production of John Webster's *The Duchess of Malfi,* adapted by W. H. Auden, at the Ethel Barrymore Theatre, October 15, 1946, in "Revivals," *New Republic,* CXV (October 28, 1946), 556–57. The performance convinced Young that "the drama of 'The Duchess of Malfi' is the drama, often high in import and power, that belongs, for us at least, to the printed page rather than to the stage of a theatre."

least, about the Old Vic's *Oedipus*,[9] there was no room for that. This is the side of things, if I may say so, dear Mr. Bentley, that you seem entirely oblivious of in the theatre or in any art, like a God damned PROFESSOR, which, alas, you are not. I imagine my heart is warmer toward you than is your colleagues. My confession of my situation accrues from a great respect for your opinion and a desire for your friendship, and so on the strength of this I ask you not to quote any of this I have said, in print. In private please explain my handicaps.

That last judgment of yours on the Old Vic Players is, to my mind, entirely admirable. The center was lacking, and you hit the point exactly.[1] The question that at the moment is very close to me is how could all that intelligent summation happen in a single column etc. Of course it could not happen. There could merely be a chance for what you call, in regard to TIME, verve. If I myself get to the point of verve, look out! I may be cheaper and livelier and commoner than the cherubim of Broadway could ever have hoped for.

Since you mention the subject, I am shocked to think how rarely I refer backward to the twenties, alas. It was better than what we have been having these last few years, everybody admits that, but not much of it was any good. There were shining personal performances, shining single artists, and a few—at that time—geniuses like Robert Edmond Jones.

9. Young reviewed the Old Vic's production of *Oedipus Rex,* in the English version by W. B. Yeats, on May 20, 1946, in "The Old Vic: II," *New Republic,* CIX (June 3, 1946), 805–806. In the same article, he also discussed the production of Chekhov's *Uncle Vanya* at the Century Theatre, May 13, 1946. Young sharply criticized the costumes designed for *Oedipus Rex;* and although conceding that Laurence Olivier's performance had "sincerity, intelligence and a certain degree of semi-projected intensity," he felt the actor did not have the voice for the role. For Young, *Uncle Vanya* turned out "pretty much a character piece."

1. In his article, Bentley admitted that the Old Vic revivals lacked "coordination," which he explained as a "lack of a leader and a lack of a philosophy." The audience, he argued, "craves a more complete theatrical experience. Some critics have located the deficiency in a particular spot—in the feeble music, the characterless decor, the merely decent costumes. All these are part of the same trouble. [Ralph] Richardson and Olivier are playing a double concerto for a middling orchestra with no conductor." In the Old Vic's productions of *Henry IV* and in Olivier's film of *Henry V,* Bentley could praise "the virtues of forth-rightness and respect for the playwright." But at the conclusion of his article, he found that these productions likewise felt "the Old Vic's lack of mature and comprehensive interpretation. They made nothing of the civil war, which after all is the chief subject of the play. They spoke their lines and left the rest to Shakespeare. In short the Company is still in an inchoate state as an artistic ensemble." With this verdict, Young strongly agreed. For Young's review of the *Henry IV* plays, see "The Old Vic," *New Republic,* CIX (May 20, 1946), 731.

My telephone is Wickersham 2,6493, if you are in town.
You can see by the typing how I hate writing such a letter as this is.

Yours sincerely
Stark Young

655 | To Richard L. O'Connell, Pasadena, California

320 East 57th Street
New York
December 2, 1946

Dear Dick,

Thank you for the two letters, one direct and one through Leah Salisbury.[2] I have had so much to do today that this typing will be faulty, but please forgive it. Of course I'll never forget you, naturally. And I shall always be grateful to you for making the days, in a trying time, more trying than I ever told you, more rich and right, and so forever thank you, Dick. Life goes on, and that is that.

As to the play, I should be delighted to have it done there, and think that under your hands it might come out well. You have great facility, insight and brains, I should never be surprised at anything by way of success that you might have.

I could not come out, but that will not matter much. The New Republic at the moment is in a state of flux, what with Michael Straight coming on, and Wallace chosen for the head. Some new birth was needed, let us hope it will be wonderful, or at least fresh in spirit.

Do anything you like with the play. This is all I can say, the rest of the matter concerns Leah Salisbury, a very fine person. Ask her anything you like, she will connect with me.

You will presently run into the fact that my play is in some ways like *The Pirate,* which Mr. Behrman cooked up for the Lunts. The

2. O'Connell, in his first year as associate director of the Pasadena Playhouse, had written Leah Salisbury to ask permission to produce Young's *Belle Isle,* which he had printed under the title *Artemise.*

answer to that is simple. The Fulda play which he is supposed to have adapted is not at all like mine. It is a story of an eighteen year old young woman married to an older husband, and the husband is the central hero of the plot. He has been a pirate. Fulda laid it in Andalusia in the 17th century. The Lunt play moves it to my region, the Mexican Gulf, to my time, the early nineteenth century—the time is placed in the first two scenes as in my play, by references to NAPO-LEON, the central motif of my play—ILLUSION etc. is used, sometimes almost in the same words, etc. etc. It is a shameless steal, but Mr. Behrman insists that the Lunts did not even tell him that I had written a play about a Pirate. (It had been announced in the Times and Herald Tribune.) Etc. But all this does not concern us, since my play was printed as soon as I saw the Lunt announcement, and so was in print in June where the Behrman effort did not reach Broadway and the light till that autumn. That is that.

One thing I want to tell you. Sydney Greenstreet was really mad about the play, so much so that his part—the French ruined General—he said was the finest role in or out of Shakespeare, that he had ever had. So he had the part typed out, in case the Lunts did not do the play. Lynn was crazy to do the play, Alfred not, he was not *It* and she was.

The point of all that is to say that if you could get Sydney to do the part it would be one of the marvels of the theatre of our time.[3] His performance in The Sea Gull was recognized as one of the world's events. It ranks with my four or five greatest performances I have ever seen in the theatre. Sydney Greenstreet's address is 1279 Ozeta Terrace, Hollywood.

I am glad you see Zack and Elaine. They were in New York a year ago. I was very proud of them. They have moved forward and forward, bless their hearts! I am so very much delighted with Zack's progress. I will write them tomorrow.

If you want to see the original Fulda play, I can send it to you at any time. Mr. Behrman ruined it and I, without meaning to, contributed to a bastard effort. . . . It really surprised me. More or less.

This is a very dull letter, but we have had so much confusion at the New Republic with the new adjustments for Wallace, and life in gen-

---

3. Although Greenstreet was very enthusiastic about the proposed production, he could not take part in it because of ill health; and eventually O'Connell had to give up the project.

eral is so wild these days, what with the passions and plans of the nations, that I as a small gnat cannot get anywhere by way of expression.

Mr. Moe[4] of the Guggenheim sent me a request not long ago for a confidential opinion on Jimmy Graham. I said I had seen two works of his, the Lorca and the fiction book, and said they showed ability, sympathetic understanding and enthusiasm. I think those were the words, and what more could a translator ask by way of praise?

If I read this over I would tear it up perhaps, so please forgive all faults etc.

Love to you
Stark

656 | To Leah Salisbury, New York

320 East 57th Street
New York
Monday morning
[December 2, 1946]

Dear Leah,

I was in the country or would have written you yesterday. Thank you for that sweet note, so like you, about the young man.[5] He may turn out to be something. At least you can size him up and ease him out if need be. I must say you are lovely to see him. But you have such a turn for stimulating people who want to be something that maybe there is a reward even for you somewhere in it.

As to the play, it seems that Richard O'Connell ran into Zachary Scott right after writing you, and Zack gave him this address. So I had already sent him a copy of the play, which he had asked for. I have very few left, alas. I should be glad for them to try it. I wrote him that,

---

4. Henry Allen Moe (b. 1894), foundation executive, professor of law, and trustee of the Guggenheim Foundation.

5. On November 24, Young had written Leah Salisbury: "This is to ask if you would see a nephew of Sallie Benson's—the playwright—his name is Wharey, his mother is the girl Esther in Meet Me in St. Louis, if you have seen that movie. He does not want to be an actor!—he wants other work in the theatre. . . . I do not know him, but friends of his and mine are concerned to get him started." In her reply, November 25, Leah Salisbury readily agreed to see him.

and said the rest of it would be between him and you. That was right, was it not?[6]

I am going to Texas in two weeks, leaving a couple of MSS. to be used at the NR. There have been so many distractions in the world around us, and such a confusion and vagueness at the New Republic, that alas I have no paintings finished, only several begun. Mr. Rehn has a few new ones, since my exhibition. When I get back, perhaps you would lunch with me and we could go by there. At any rate I am looking forward to seeing you as soon as I get back, and hope you are entirely well now.

The NR is to come out in a new form and new policies, and I can only hope all that will be successful. When all is a little better under way, I will have some talks down there as to the drama reviews. At present the space is greatly limited and everybody there is so occupied that there is no chance for a quiet discussion of any policy, etc. Michael Straight is taking a great interest in the whole venture, with many plans for expanding, and so on. All that has to be worked out. He is a fine fellow, and would have to be with his mother.

I hope your Christmas is a good one. Love to you and Phil and Tony —I often think of you, Leah, what a friend you are and a remarkable and sweet person.

> Affectionately
> Stark

657 | To Caroline Charlotte McGehee, Como, Misissippi

> 320 East 57th Street
> New York
> Tuesday [December 10, 1946]

Dearest Cousin Cad,

I wish I were going to see my most beloved cousin this Christmas, but I will be lucky to get even to see Ben and Julia. The expenses here are fantastic. We pay the cook, who does a bit of cooking, mending and slopping, $35 a week and then cook for ourselves on Sunday. That was the price in the country. Here we pay $5 for a half HALF day

---

6. See the preceding letter and notes.

and cook our meals on Sunday. Food in the market is a joke, three small half green tomatoes for twenty five cents—so what.

I wish I could send you something lovely that would serve to express a little of my great affection and my appreciation of the fact that you are one of the finest people I ever saw. As it is I send a small cheque which may, and may not, buy two hairpins and a small mousetrap, and little else. If not, you can buy one lump of sugar.

Well, no matter about all that, the great and fine things of life concern money very little. What I value above all things is that I have had in life a great deal of affection, of noble and sweet relationships and of gentle acquaintance. Among all these assets many have come from knowing such people as my darling Cousin Cad. And there are not many like her, more is the pity.

I am leaving December 20 for Austin and will enjoy seeing Julia and Ben. I am indeed a lucky man to have such a brother-in-law. We may ride down across the Mexican border to Monterrey, and that would be a pleasant change.

New York is crowded and brutal. Bowman and I have bought a little house in Westchester and work there like dogs in the garden. But it will be the end of April before we can stay there again.

He always says the finest things about you and would send you his love if he knew I was writing.

I hope you will write me some time as to how you are.

> Lovingly
> Stark

658 | To Julia Young Robertson, Austin, Texas

> [320 East 57th Street]
> [New York]
> Monday [January 13, 1947]

Dearest Sister,

It was lovely to have you call up last night. We could have talked much longer if we had asked the operator to tell us when three minutes was up.

I hope you really are well from your cold. What a world.

The slippers followed your letter today. Wales will be pleased, his have the heels out, that kind, and so need socks. I think you said 1.96, so am putting in the $2. You should not pay for them.

I wish I could tell you more about the painting.[7] Mr. Rich certainly said definitely that he wanted it, told Mr. Rehn he was coming back, that was Thursday. Telephoned me Friday evening how much he liked the pictures, and said he was going back to Chicago Saturday. Mr. Rehn was expecting him about other business also. He evidently is still here but has not been in. I imagine he is on a bit of a binge, he seemed to like his cups. But he was a most remarkable man, very delicate and fine and right. I will write when I hear something about it.

The Friday I left Austin Natalie[8] had a dinner for that Polish pianist at El Morocco. Wales went. The Windsors[9] sat near them. The dinner was superb. The pianist a horror. Had told various friends to drop in and get some of the champagne. Natalie was disgusted. Said she had carried a slum to dinner, said that yesterday when we went to see her. Said her friend the pianist Schmetterling introduced her to the woman, said she had invited her up after being overcome with her playing, had given her a Portuguese antique brooch of garnets and old paste. Said the woman telephoned later that her Polish jeweler said it was false and in her family they wore nothing false. Did not return it. Natalie did not send anything real. Then the woman got Natalie to go to select a cigarette case for her fiance, they went to Tiffanys, she said she had no account, charged it to Natalie. Also later a marriage bed covered with pink satin and the sheets etc., something under a thousand. Also the fiance worked it so that the engagement ring was charged to Natalie. It is all supposed to be paid back after 24 concerts and money, which of course is rubbish. Natalie says she does not know why she did all this, except for the fact that the woman is a genius. After two concerts here the third was a marvellous hit. Natalie had asked us to it, in a box, but I was in Texas. Odd you should have seen that particular person and were talking about it. Natalie wants to ask the pair up so that I can see how horrible she is. But I don't think so. I

7. See above, Letter 653, n. 5.
8. Natalie Hays Hammond.
9. The duke and duchess of Windsor; the identifications of the other persons mentioned in this paragraph have not been established.

will go to the concert in two weeks or whenever it is. Natalie says she is a gaseous stinking manhole, whatever that means, it means of course the sewer family. But a genius. I thought this wild news would amuse you. Trust Natalie for making life whizz. She is devoted to me on the most serious gentle scale, and so life goes.

Your letter about the party sounded most grand. Austin can go it, as Byron said quoting Horace, quandoque Homerus dormitat

Homer sometimes nods

and added

Wordsworth sometimes wakes.[1]

That is a marvel about 22½ after eight.
I will write John Gracy[2] a little letter soon.
I hope you and Ben are all right.

Lovingly
Stark

659 | To Norma Long Brickell, Jackson, Mississippi

320 East 57th Street
New York
January 23, 1947

Dearest Norma,

I cannot ever thank you for bringing me into contact with Dan Rich. He is one of the most intelligent, distinguished and fine people I ever saw. And in addition to that, he has what these New York people in art have not, namely his own opinion and stand.

---

1. Young has in mind a passage from Byron's *Don Juan:* "We learn from Horace, 'Homer sometimes sleeps'; / We feel without him, Wordsworth sometimes wakes" (Canto 3, lines 98–99). Horace had written in the *De arte poetica,* "quandoque bonus dormitat Homerus" (line 359).
2. John Gracy, Austin realtor and businessman.

He was wonderful about my pictures and put new life into me. There is so much fad and so much semi-insincerity all around me here that I was beginning to get very much the sense of futility. One can see how such a man has gone as far as he has, and he certainly has a superb position in people's opinions. This does not express his great gentleness and insight. He spoke of you so beautifully, and that warmed my heart. We both agreed that you were pretty much a genius and a saint.

He chose a large painting—Apparition of Flowers.

I went to Texas Christmas and found my sister and brother-in-law pretty well. It was wonderful to see them. I was glad to get a card from you when I got back here. I wanted to write you Christmas but had only the old address in Washington before you gave that up.

I wonder if you and Herschel are staying in Mississippi a while. I should so like to see it again, but at Christmas time it is impossible to go by there on the way to Texas—I am always sick with grippe etc. after even the Texas trip. It takes me about a month to recover. It seems a shame not to see more of my own people and own country. I am going to see if Wales won't take a trip down there in April, we can't do it in summer, the house in the country keeps us. You were at your house near Ridgefield, but Wales was away and I had no way of getting there, and did not know how to write or telegraph, and you said you had no telephone. I called Frances Tinker finally and asked how to connect with you but she said you had gone. I should have loved to see you and to have you see our place.

How life throws us around! I have to whistle a great deal to keep my courage up. Have begun a book of memoirs, hard to find the right tone. I want it to be fine. It will be my last book. I shall not have enough vitality for another of value, provided I ever get this to suit me. Things done solely by the will have no real quality or life, but I think I have enough to light me to one more summit.

How I do wish I could join you there. I was thinking so much today of the abla plena—those white lovely forms on the dark leaves. And here I sit very stupidly, with only what I can make flower in my own self.

Well, I am so delighted that I met Dan Rich at last and that he is such a deep, right person.

I wonder what HH[3] is about. Is he resting up? He makes me proud of my little pupil. Mr. Chinese Wan came to see me before he left, said good things about HH and was most charming to me.

I wish I might have a line from you. Wales would send love if he were here. He has many jobs and is sick of a lot of it, but successful.

Lovingly
Stark

660 | To Maxwell Perkins, Charles Scribner's Sons, New York

320 East 57th Street
New York
January 23, 1947

Dear Max,

I have been meaning for some time to write and thank you for the copy of the Scribner record book.[4] I saw Charlie at the Newport and talked about it but was too tight to make sense, and my recollection is that he was not as sober as William Penn. At any rate the book as a job seems to me in bad proportions and pretty poor, but the record of Scribner's is very impressive and made me feel proud to be connected.

The finest thing in the book is you. Your letters to various authors are rich and warm and distinguished, in fine taste, highly personal at the same time, and very stimulating. I don't think there is any other man in America who could evince what you evince in these letters. I felt much set up by them, that such a quality could be in the world we live in today.

The enclosed letter[5] was sent me and I want you to see it. The point

---

3. Henry Herschel Brickell.

4. Young refers to Roger Burlingame's *Of Making Many Books: A Hundred Years of Reading, Writing and Publishing,* published by Scribner's in 1946.

5. Although the letter has not survived, it must have dealt with the writer's inability to purchase copies of Young's books. Perkins replied by saying that *So Red the Rose* had been reprinted.

is that I don't know how you are but I am getting on in years and getting, in spite of my conscious resistance to the thought, to feel touchy and not needed. Something of vitality fades from me, and I find myself not feeling that I will ever do anything again. I have not even been able to paint for several months. I have begun the book of memoirs and it seems good indeed, but when this sort of thing comes up, the feeling that my own publishers and friends don't think my work worth keeping in print, even though it sells to some extent, I am slowed down to an absurd degree. It is a problem how to live out the rest of one's life in style and spirit, and I often feel I am not going to manage that. So if you can only truly stand by me a year or two more then it won't much matter what happens to me. I have always counted on you and I need you now more than ever. I trust that does not sound maudlin, but so I find it, so life seems. That *it* refers to life for me.

I think you will be pleased to hear that the director of the Art Institute of Chicago has just seen my paintings and chosen one of the largest for that collection. Since that is considered the finest modern museum in America and he the leading director, we should be much impressed. I am so, and try to keep reminding myself, in order to keep myself up and feel more fruitful or something.

Best to you.

Yours
Stark

661 | To Ella Somerville, Oxford, Mississippi

320 East 57th Street
New York
January 23, 1947

Dear Ella,

Thank you for that lovely letter, and thank you for the card you sent, I appreciated it.

What you say about Hubert Creekmore[6] seems to be what my impression is, though I have never seen him but a very few times. I read some of his verse in MS many years ago. The novel[7] I have never seen and I am not a fiction reader in general. I saw a fair notice of it in the Herald Tribune or somewhere.

I am making a list of things to leave after my death to the Oxford museum, a sixteenth century tapestry,[8] a large wall hanging of grospoint, Spanish, 17th century, and some little statues and some quite fine objects. I may send down before long two dolmans,[9] one figures in So Red the Rose, and the other is twenty years later, Paris, cream grosgrain, embroidered with seed pearls and chenille thread, very fine. But I gathered from a letter of Willie Lewis's that there were small arrangements for such things. I wish you would write me about that, as to whether they would be properly taken care of or not. I want to see the musuem if I can ever get by Mississippi since I should like to leave some quite good paintings to it, and if wanted, the portraits of my greatgrandfather and my grandfather and grandmother. If I have any money left by the time I die I want to leave some money to the museum too. I have thought of various places and decided that whatever I could do, would be best done in one spot. And I don't see why these rich musuems up here should get everything. I have also a set of four chairs that belonged to Pauline Bonaparte,[1] and a Charles II globe, small in perfect condition, that cost 465 $ in London, was given to me.

Christmas is an impossible time to try to get by the roundabout Mississippi way to Texas, and things don't seem to work out that I can get down in the summer. By the way if you get East this summer

---

6. Hubert Creekmore (1907–66), poet and novelist, born in Water Valley, Mississippi, attended the University of Mississippi while William Faulkner was postmaster there and later studied drama at the University of Colorado and playwriting under Professor George Pierce Baker at Yale. In 1934, examples of his verse appeared in *Poetry,* and, in 1940, he published a collection of his early poetry as *Personal Sun.* After World War II, his work includes *The Long Reprieve and Other Poems* (1946) and his novels, *The Fingers of Night* (1946), *The Welcome* (1948), and *The Chain in the Heart* (1953).

7. A reference to *The Fingers of Night.* Young may have seen a review of it by George Dillon in the *New York Herald Tribune Books,* May 19, 1946, p. 13.

8. Subsequently given to the library of the University of Mississippi.

9. Now in the Mary Buie Museum.

1. Mary Pauline Bonaparte (1780–1825), duchess of Guastalla, wife of Prince Camillo Borghese, and sister of the Emperor Napoleon. After Young's death, the chairs were given to the University of Texas.

please let me know, I should like to much to see you and to have you see my little house in Westchester.

I wish I could see my Oxford friends. Please give my love to the family, all of them. Time flies, and I don't think we make much of the passing years.

Affectionately
Stark

662 | To Huntington Cairns, National Gallery of Art, Washington, D.C.

320 East 57th Street
New York
Monday [February 3, 1947]

Dear Huntington,

I have read your Hobbes brochure twice, at intervals apart and with much profit and pleasure. That about the judge on page 76 interested me especially.[2] I have just sent the piece to my brother-in-law in Texas, who is most intelligent and has done a good deal of thinking about this latter day business of the judge deciding not what was THE CONTRACT but what he considers right. My brother-in-law's partner is Dan Moody, his first cousin, once the governor, not so intelligent as my brother-in-law but busy and intent with law practice—a different type but a good type.

Allen and Caroline came to dinner just before Christmas, I was glad to see them again and hope they are happy.

2. Young refers to an offprint of Cairns' article "Hobbes' Theory of Law," *Seminar,* IV (1946), 58–83. In the passage mentioned by Young, Cairns writes: "Hobbes states precisely that the interpretation of the law of nature is the sentence of the judge constituted by the sovereign authority to hear and determine controversies, and consists of the application of the law to the case. For in the act of judicature the judge does no more than consider whether the demand of the party is consonant with natural reason and equity; and the sentence he gives is therefore the interpretation of the law of nature. That interpretation is authentic, not because it is his private sentence, but because he gives it by authority of the sovereign; whereby it becomes the sovereign's sentence, which is law for that time to the parties pleading."

You will be very glad to know, I feel sure, that Daniel Catton Rich from the Art Institute of Chicago, was here a week or so back. I had never met him though I know his great reputation. He saw my paintings at Rehn's and could not say enough about them, wrote me two letters.[3] He bought one of the largest for the Chicago museum. That is supposed to be about the finest modern collection in this country, so I was greatly pleased, not to say overwhelmed.

Otherwise, I don't seem to have any news. I have felt very dull and confused, and can't say I see much glitter in most people nowadays. Perhaps the Republicans will save the world, they have had a good rest in the opposite direction.

I hope Florence is well and now and then eats something. Please give her my love.

Thank you again for that reprint.

Affectionately yours
Stark

663 | To Julia Young Robertson, Austin, Texas

[320 East 57th Street]
[New York]
Wednesday [February 12, 1947]

Dearest Sister,

The letter Ben wrote was quite right, exactly, and I will mention the Cotton spelling as the typist when I write Mr. Rich a note, which I have to do soon. I do appreciate all this very much. As to keeping that money, I will write again about that.

Mr. Spruce is a much better painter than most of them. I am glad he

3. In a letter to his sister, written on January 23, Young had quoted Rich's praise of Young's work: "'All that I said about your painting I mean and more. It is most extraordinarily good—which doesn't surprise me since you made it. What does amaze me is its remarkable power and beauty, the latter a word I seldom use about painting today. You will keep painting won't you? I know how much it costs you in emotion—it wouldn't be half as moving otherwise—but it is so very important that you go on.'"

gets the prizes.[4] The nice thing is that once you get a prize you get others, for that puts you in jurors' minds. I will never get a prize, no matter how much they like the painting the jurors want to be on the bandwagon. I am out of line, as I have mostly been with my writing. Well, we shall see what we shall see.

The MS after six days got here from Washington and I am taking The Cherry Orchard down to the publisher tomorrow.[5] I am glad to get it off my hands and that finishes all translating for me. Today is a holiday.

I still have not heard from the postoffice again, but will perhaps. The money will be welcome to little Hallie[6] and it is all settled that way, alas.

Thanks for the pictures, the royal families look better than most of them do in many of the states, which is something. Wales was quite struck with their looking like at least nice people.

Our Nora[7] is cleaning the place beyond anything it ever was. She is quite a good cook and wants to leave us things good and to shop for us. On special occasions she would stay through dinner but as a rule wants to be at home and doing good food for her husband. They are from Galway and have been in this country a year. She takes the initative and really wants us to have something to eat. The restaurants are so poor and so costly that this is a good thing. She also really darns etc. for us, where Phyllis after getting to them merely bluffed, she was so full of her enterprises.

I will write again soon, thanks again for the sweet letter. Love to you and Ben and much appreciation.

Stark

4. Everett Franklin Spruce (b. 1908), painter, born in Faulkner County, Arkansas, since 1940 has been a member of the faculty of the department of art at the University of Texas. He had recently received prizes for his paintings in the Texas General Exhibition (1945), the Worcester Museum of Art (1945), the Pepsi-Cola annual show (1946), and the La Tausca Exhibition (1947).

5. Samuel French was preparing to publish Young's translation of *The Cherry Orchard* by Anton Chekhov. Mrs. E. G. Burland, who had helped Young with the translation, had sent the manuscript from Washington.

6. See above, Letter 650 and n. 7.

7. The new maid and cook. The former maid, Phyllis, operated a beauty parlor business on the side and had been a dressmaker. When her various enterprises kept her from working on Saturday, Young and Bowman decided to get a replacement.

IX

Retirement of a Critic
1947–1949

IN LETTERS to his friends, Stark Young supplied so many of the details about his leaving the *New Republic* that additional introductory remarks would only serve to repeat the correspondence to follow. Taken in context with his earlier comments about the attitudes of various members of the editorial staff, Young's resignation was probably inevitable. Nevertheless, his friends have always lamented the unfortunate atmosphere in which his departure occurred, and, with his colleagues in the Critics' Circle, his admirers have wished that somehow he could have found a way to continue. With all its failings, the *New Republic* had served Young throughout much of his career as a medium ideally suited to the expression of his particular kind of drama criticism. Unfortunately, when he severed his connection with it, he also stopped the flow of that criticism.

Young's decisions to abandon the struggle with Bliven and to decline Michael Straight's offer to publish a monthly article on some general subject cannot be explained easily. Although probably no single reason was decisive, the crisis at the *New Republic* came when Young's patience had been strained beyond its limit by a series of unpleasant experiences that all related directly or indirectly to the theatre or to the magazine. The fiasco of *Artemise* and the rupture of his friendship with the Lunts had left behind a residue of bitterness that his painting, which in itself had taken him away from the theatre, had not fully dissolved. In the years during and immediately after the war, Young came to believe that the theatre was entering a period of decline. With only a very infrequent exception, he thought he discerned a deterioration in the quality of plays being written, in the level of production, and in the skills of the actors. With the standards of the contemporary theatre increasingly disappointing, Young may have been more inclined than usual to resent the treatment he received in the editorial offices of the *New Republic*. Since Croly's death, he had never been completely in sympathy with the political and social philosophies of the other editors, but the differences among them had never directly affected his drama criticism. Now the demand that he cover all the plays on Broadway somewhat in newspaper fashion, the curtailment of the space allotted to his criticism, and the arbitrary "editing" of his copy suddenly produced an intolerable situation for Young. If he remained, he could no longer write the kind of drama criticism that had distinguished the *New Republic* throughout his career. His patience finally exhausted, Young resigned.

At sixty-five, having quit reviewing the plays on Broadway, Stark Young looked back upon his career as a drama critic. At Scribner's suggestion, Young began to select his best reviews of various events connected with the theatre. When published as a volume, he intended that they represent what he considered permanent in the hundreds of drama articles he had published in the *New Republic*. Of the pieces he finally chose for *Immortal Shadows,* the title which his sister suggested for the book, more were written during the 1920s and early 1930s than in later years. In his preface, Young accounted for this preponderance of reviews from the early period by alluding to the high quality of American drama during these years and by noting that the editorial policy of the *New Republic* in the 1930s, after the death of Herbert Croly, severely curtailed the length of his contributions.

The wisdom of Young's self-criticism appears in the uniform excellence of the reviews he reprinted in *Immortal Shadows.* From the 1920s, Young's choices included his reviews of John Barrymore's *Hamlet,* Eleonora Duse's acting in Ibsen's plays, Max Reinhardt's celebrated production of *The Miracle,* Eugene O'Neill's *The Great God Brown* and *Dynamo,* George Bernard Shaw's *Caesar and Cleopatra,* and R. C. Sherriff's *Journey's End.* From his writing in the decade of the 1930s, Young selected his criticism of O'Neill's *Mourning Becomes Electra,* Gertrude Stein's *Four Saints in Three Acts,* Maxwell Anderson's *The Wingless Victory* and *High Tor,* Shaw's *Candida* and *Heartbreak House,* and Maurice Evans' *Richard II* and *Hamlet.* Young's criticism in the 1940s included his analyses of Tennessee Williams' *The Glass Menagerie,* O'Neill's *The Iceman Cometh,* and Katharine Cornell's version of *Antigone.* The volume also contained reprints of Young's articles about the Moscow Art Theatre, the acting of Mei Lan-fang, the Shakespearean productions of the Old Vic Company, and the dancing of Martha Graham. Although Young disclaimed any effort to make a chronicle of the American theatre during these years, *Immortal Shadows* may easily be taken as an anthology of the best criticism of the best plays of the first half of the century.

When Young's admirers read in the preface to *Immortal Shadows* that it was to be his final book about the theatre, many wondered why he chose to conclude his writing about the drama with a reprint of his earlier work, especially because from his vantage point of experience and maturity he might have written a fresh evaluation. Surely, they reasoned, he had more to say. The answer may lie partly in Young's despondency over the termination of his association with the *New Republic.* Presently, he had no enthusiasm for Broadway's glories either past or present. At the same time, he very much wanted to make progress with his memoirs, which he had been planning for since 1936 and writing since 1945. Already he had decided that he would eventually write two volumes: the first would deal with his life in Mississippi, and the second would contain accounts of his friendships with persons associated with the arts, particularly the theatre. Indirectly, Young probably felt that here he would say whatever else he wished to say about the theatre. Unfortunately, Young never wrote the second volume.

664 | To Huntington Cairns, National Gallery of Art, Washington, D.C.

> 320 East 57th Street
> New York
> Thursday [February 13, 1947]

Dear Huntington,

Life is ironical, I got to the Algonquin early last Thursday, about 2.30 and then there was the Critics' Circle from three to nearly four. That night I found your message on my desk but it was already past eleven. I called Friday morning, soon after nine, fearful of awaking you in the big city, there was no answer. The clerk lady took a message for you to call me, but you probably never got it. I was hoping you could lunch with me either Friday or Saturday. Well, come back. It was our new Irish maid from Galway and very nice who talked with you on the telephone. Sometimes her brogue is thick and handsome indeed.

Whether I am to read the reprints or not, I read over the latter part of the Hobbes and sent it to my brother-in-law, so that's that.[1] You are very good to send them to me, but when on earth do you find time to do them?

I was interested to see what you said of the NR.[2] Michael Straight, since they put the money in, certainly has a right to try to make it alive again. I can't make out how things are going. There are a lot of new youngish men. A great swivet there. Mr. Wallace is there daily and works hard. I have been in for a few minutes twice only. Most of the men there don't yet seem to know about what is going on, but it may take time. For a while, when one could learn nothing at all directly, I was made almost sick by it all. Now I just wait and see what will happen. I have no other job, and the small sum I myself proposed to take when the Elmhirsts were stuck for money—I said only 2000 the year, flat, me to write what weeks there seemed any need. Certainly

---

1. See above, Letter 662 and n. 3.
2. On February 10, Cairns had written: "The *New Republic* is a mess. I am completely in the dark about the whole situation there, but I hope its present gyrations are not too burdensome for you."

that is not excessive even if I wrote only 30 times a year. I have to see the play and read the books after all. Nevertheless, since I don't make lectures and since I won't write silly little review pieces at silly prices, and since one does not sell a lot of pictures, especially when as out of line with the moment's fad as I am, there is not a lot of money, and even the "2000" is of use for the rent. So I will just have to wait and see and do what I can in that wretched space the NR works out at present. Back of Michael's mind is such a thing as TIME, with big sales, etc. Mr. Wallace likes to think of it as spreading the gospel I suppose, but Michael thinks around the clock rather, sales, gospel, Wallace and what not. I wish the venture well but so far have not heard a single good word for the changed paper. It may be that I don't know the people who are saying good things. I regard the New Republic from the old standpoint of Croly's time and that means that it is larger than any one person or persons for that matter, a kind of spiritual body in itself. But it has been a long time since those directly running the paper had any such feeling.

George Soule, for a good example, thinks only of himself, to a smooth degree that I have never seen equalled. Long ago Mrs. Elmhirst, who has her insights, told me that nobody there knew what I was talking about. That is true, not since Croly. There have been some strong efforts to get me off, but I would not get off. All this has not been made useful in my spirit, nor added to the quality of my work. The knowledge that the Elmhirsts stood so solidly with me was what kept me going at all. I never go near the office, don't want to feel off-key or whatever it is. I must say that with Mr. Wallace and Michael I feel at least less antagonism. Dan Mebane, the business manager, has always stood by me, partly to offset his case with the others. All this sort of thing is not up my street. I don't like intriguing, I am paralysed by hate. None of all this has done me any good. And of late I have been unable to paint, with all this new mess and uncertainty. I am going back to painting today, and so that's that.

Well, I am indeed lucky to have friends like you and Florence, to pour out this low grade personal stuff to, and know you will see it in relation to less poor values in life and in a good scale. To most people such revelations are, I am afraid, only a form of intimate gossip, and so disgusting so far as I am concerned.

See what you stirred up.

Bless you and Florence, there is no reason I should just stumble on such lovely, intelligent friends. Life can be kind at that.

Yours affectionately
Stark

You can see by the typing what a divine calm the subject of the NR arouses.

665 | To Julia Young Robertson, Austin, Texas

[320 East 57th Street]
[New York]
Friday morning
[February 14, 1947]

Dearest Sister,

I should be beginning a silly little review for the NR [3] but will write a line to you first. Your Valentine came this morning, pretty blue and pink, and the sheets will be most welcome, though I don't see why you and Ben must furnish Jennymead entirely. However, thank you very much. Wales thinks it lovely of you.

I read twice this morning the letter you wrote me right after Christmas, had kept it in my file and now have torn it up. I find you can't keep things forever in this world. But the letter was like having a little visit with you and was most pleasant, besides being a sweet letter.

The Chekhov Ms with introduction and a biographical note and a few notes has been delivered and that is that, the Ms complete finally came from Washington. I had lent it a long while back to Mrs. Burland though I can't remember just when and she had not mentioned having it. [4]

I had a letter from Mr. Cairns at the National Gallery, much

---

3. Probably "Another Patrick Play," a review of John Patrick's *The Story of Mary Surratt* and comments about the work of Ruth Draper and George Kelly's *Craig's Wife, New Republic,* CXVI (February 24, 1947), 40.
   4. See above, Letter 663, n. 5.

pleased by the Chicago affair, says he may be there soon and will try to see the painting there, that will impress the people at the Art Institute. He is author of that big book of colored plates from the National Gallery and is a distinguished man in law, lectures at Harvard, so much learning that it is frightening, only his manner is very simple. He [is] firmly resolved to [be] devoted to me and thinking I am remarkable, but I make no effort to hide my ignorance. I think the other reprint he sent me was on some phase of higher—philosophical— mathematics. His writing is rather hard to read partly because he has no natural sense of the emphasis, so your mind keeps wandering off the sentence. But a fine man. Knows everybody in Washington, is from Maryland.

I am glad to hear Sandy [5] is better, sick animals break you down. She is a fine companion.

There were four friends of Norma's [6] from Mississippi, and I remember the name Lyon without placing him exactly. Garland Lyell [7] has a son [8] here, a big fattish young man, Garland Lyell was finishing law when I entered the university and I think tutored me in math or something for a month or so. There is no waltz club. Theodate Johnson, [9] whose brother used to live next door to us, she is an old friend of Betsy's, got up the idea of engaging Webster Hall several times a year and an orchestra and then inviting various people to subscribe. A considerable number of people are there, varying. No food or party, just people with their groups waltzing, with a few other dances, two or three worked in. It begins about nine and stops at one sharp, so it is

5. The Robertsons' dog.
6. Mrs. Herschel Brickell. The person referred to as "Lyon" in this sentence has not been identified.
7. Gordon Garland Lyell (1874–1961), lawyer and judge, born in Carrollton, Mississippi, was valedictorian of the graduating class of 1896 at the University of Mississippi. Two years later, he received his bachelor of laws degree from the University of Mississippi law school. Lyell preceded Young as editor of the university annual, *Ole Miss*. After teaching mathematics for a year at the University of Mississippi, Lyell began to practice law in Jackson, Mississippi. In 1906, he became chancellor of the fifth chancery district and held the post until 1916, when he resumed his private law practice.
8. In the fall of 1946, Frank Hallam Lyell, born (1911) in Jackson, Mississippi, had begun his career as a professor of English at the University of Texas. Between semesters, he had gone to New York for a brief vacation.
9. Theodate Johnson, opera and concert soprano, made her New York debut in 1934 at Town Hall. From 1935 to 1953, she lived mostly in Europe and sang with various opera companies. In 1954, she joined the advertising staff of *Musical America*.

not a wear and tear. Betsy adores it, so does Wales. Five or six times in a year. I don't think there is anything else to it except not letting just anybody come, they have to be known some way or other. It is a pleasant occasion. But nothing in the nature of a club. Some of the people come in for an hour only etc. A small bar belongs in the hall, not much drinking at all however, just mild sitting to rest at tables with the people you connect with. It is nice to see something in New York not crowded, well-bred but without side or pretense, and not at all self-conscious like the people at the night clubs.

I hope my small Valentine gets there, those lilies really grow well without care, just water. The florists keep sprouting them at intervals to have them for sale.

I must get to the article. I still will think about that $1000—it does not seem exactly fair to stick you so heavily.[1] I wish Mr. Jones would send that [bond].[2] Max Perkins said he had been winding up his wife's father's estate for years and it seemed never to get done. Several millions I think, but Max is sick of it as executor and after the six or seven years.

I still can't believe I have a painting in the Art Institute of Chicago, it has a great reputation that museum. Mr. Rich stands very high in connection with it.

I will telephone Mr. Rehn when he comes in later and see if he has had the final formal statement, then will write you.

Love to you and Ben.

Wales sends his love, is posting this for me.

Stark

1. A reference to the price paid by the Robertsons for the painting by Young given to the Chicago Art Institute.

2. Although the precise meaning is uncertain, Young refers to a bond which he expected to receive from the settlement of an estate.

666 | To Julia Young Robertson, Austin, Texas

[320 East 57th Street]
[New York]
Tuesday [February 18, 1947]

Dearest Sister,

The sheets came yesterday and are awfully nice. Nora was much impressed, said she had hunted for sheets etc. Thank you and Ben for the thought and Jennymead will certainly thank you.

Scribners wants me to do an introduction for a new volume of Sidney Lanier,[3] they say there is a steady demand for them. I am going over to see them about it today. I have agreed to do an introduction, short, to a book of photographs from Louisiana, that region, some beautiful, some just banal or cranky. Scribners is worried about it, has to be a $10 book, and they can't do anything with the young man who makes the photographs.[4] He had a beautiful one of two columns with vines and a connecting balcony, in Harpers Bazaar, last year sometime,[5] but thinks that too romantic or something. I met him last year, he is a captain, announces his views, acts as if he were favoring Scribners and everybody. I think he is a little touched, at any rate he has given the art editor there a sort of spasm, she says she can't stand much of it any longer, he wore Max out so that Max put him on the art editor, Miss Devoy, I wish you could see this young man, about 30, but very gifted. No manners, no taste.

3. On February 14, Thomas Walsh, Scribner's educational editor, had asked Young to write the introduction. Sidney Lanier's *Selected Poems,* with a preface by Stark Young, was published by Scribner's later in the year.

4. Young refers to Henri Cartier-Bresson (b. 1908), who had been making a series of photographs for *Harper's Bazaar.* Born in France, Cartier-Bresson began his career as a professional photographer in the 1930s. In 1937, he married Ratna Mohini, a Javanese dancer. After working with Jean Renoir on French motion pictures, filming a documentary (*Return to Life*) of the Spanish Civil War, and making a series of pictures of the coronation of King George VI, Cartier-Bresson entered the French army at the outbreak of World War II. Captured in June, 1940, he spent three years as a German prisoner and escaped in 1943. In 1946, he exhibited his work at the Museum of Modern Art and since that time has continued to receive international recognition for his photographs. Young did not write an introduction for the proposed volume.

5. Young probably refers to Cartier-Bresson's "Cajun Gamblers" or "Chartres Street after the Rain," illustrating Truman Capote's article "Notes on New Orleans," *Harper's Bazaar,* LXXX (October, 1946), 271.

One of the Roosevelt family, we are not quite sure what kin she is to old Teddy, Wales thinks granddaughter, at any rate she told a funny story about him at the Delano's. Teddy considered that he had learned some Spanish so tried it at a function in his honor somewhere in the West Indies. He replied to the President's or Governor's speech of welcome and one thing he said—he meant to say you are a bachelor and don't know about a family of children, I have four—or rather meant I have four children, you are a bachelor etc. What he actually said in Spanish was I have four children and know about family life but you are a tapeworm and don't, etc. He also explained that he would have Mrs. Roosevelt along with him but she was too tired. What he said in Spanish was that she was too tiresome.

Nora has the place cleaner than it has ever been and really tries to get up food for us, leaves it to be heated. We just pile the dishes on the sink to be washed. She would stay some evening or other if we really wanted to entertain. Is a good creature and always obliging, does not intrude but if you give her the opening she loves to talk like everything, very Galways brogue, impossible to imitate.

The superintendent tells us that a girl who worked for some people in this building just told him her job now is room and expenses and $260 a month. Beat that.

I hope your lilies of the valley arrived and grow. They are very tough, like weeds. At the Murdocks they have spread all out in the grass and they run the lawn mower over them like grass but they come up again.

I hope you and Ben are all right. Thanks again for the Valentines, paper and sheets.

Lovingly
Stark

I still can't believe I have a painting in the Chicago Art Institute. People who have heard it here are much impressed.

667 | To Julia Young Robertson, Austin, Texas

[320 East 57th Street]
[New York]
Tuesday [April 22, 1947]

Dearest Sister,

We have had breakfast and Wales is getting dressed up for his grand jury duty, it ends this week, and he will post this.

I have no news. Have to be busy today on the introduction [for] the new Sidney Lanier collection that Scribners is bringing out. It is hard to write, should not be too exacting critically for a general book, etc. I will be glad when it is done, and hope about to finish it today and to take it to Max tomorrow at lunch, to which he asked me the other day.[6] They pay me $150 for the article, however long or short. They just consider that my name in it will help forward the book in the South. They say Lanier continues to be in some demand, has many admirers. It is out of date from the modern writer's point of view but that means fads and fashions that change anyhow. The worst of it is that the poems have great talent and quality, but he struggled against illness, musical temperament etc. and none of the poems in itself to my taste as good as it might be. However in a book like this that remark would be out of place.

I am glad Ben's eye got all right, it drives you wild when your eyes act up.

We plan to go out to Jennymead about the fifteenth but will go this week end, Friday and maybe stay through Monday. The weather here is divine today and yesterday too, but the week end was bad, Saturday the wind was terrific at Jennymead and very cold too. Sunday much much wind but warmer, we came in Sunday afternoon. The fact that Lou[7] was there forced us to be out Saturday but we pretty much labored indoors Sunday, till three when we left. I had the Critics Circle party to go to whether I wanted to or not.

---

6. Perhaps Young's last meeting with Maxwell Perkins, whose wise counsel and warm friendship had meant much to Young throughout their long association. Perkins died on June 17, 1947.
7. The gardener at Jennymead.

That reminds me, three published plays came yesterday afternoon. They are Years Ago by Ruth Gordon; This Happy Breed by Noel Coward, acted in England but only in film form over here; Another Part of the Forest by Lillian Hellmann. Let me know when you next write if any or all of these would be of use to you in the club, I can send them easily. But let me know, since we will be going to the country.

[unsigned]

668 | To John Hall Wheelock,[8] Charles Scribner's Sons, New York

Waccabuc, New York
Thursday [June 5, 1947]

Dear Jack,

For some reason or another this Lanier piece seemed a chore to do. If you have any suggestions please feel free to make them.

I think I should give the earlier editor, Ward, some credit, if you can suggest the place where I could bring that in.[9]

Greetings to you

S.Y.

8. John Hall Wheelock (b. 1886), poet and editor, had been associated with Scribner's since 1911 as editor, director, secretary, and treasurer. His volumes of poetry include *The Human Fantasy* (1911), *The Beloved Adventure* (1912), *The Black Panther* (1922), *The Bright Doom* (1927), *The Gardener and Other Poems* (1961), and *By Daylight and in Dream* (1970). In 1950, he edited *Editor to Author,* a selection of the letters of Maxwell E. Perkins. After the death of Perkins, Wheelock became the senior editor at Scribner's and edited Young's last books. Young greatly valued his friendship with both Wheelock and his wife, Phyllis de Kay Wheelock.

9. In reply, Wheelock, after noting that Young's introduction was "beautifully done," suggested that "it would be nice to give some credit to William Hayes Ward, the editor of the old edition. It would come in very aptly at the close of your first paragraph and should not be more than a sentence or two." Actually, according to the title page of the edition issued by Scribner's in 1884, Lanier's poems were "edited by his wife, with a memorial by William Hayes Ward." Young's acknowledgment to Ward appears at the end of the second paragraph of the preface. William Hayes Ward (1835–1916), known primarily as an Orientalist and editor of the New York *Independent,* helped significantly to establish the place of Sidney Lanier in American poetry.

669 | To John Hall Wheelock, Charles Scribner's Sons, New York

Waccabuc, New York
Thursday [June 12, 1947]

Dear Jack,

I have been away and received your fine and generous letter only last night.[1] It gave me a great deal of real pleasure and encouragement. The curse of writing is that you never know whether you have hit it right or not, and this was a delicate subject to handle, especially in a book with its purpose, this edition's purpose, I should have said. Thank you very much. Such letters make working on something a very different matter.

The cheque comes in well, in a country garden as much can be spent as may come into the picture.

I should like to have the proof sent here to the above address.

My telephone, by the way, is South Salem 547.

Yours as ever
Stark

670 | To Bedford and Joreta Thurman, Ames, Iowa

Waccabuc, New York
Tuesday [July 15, 1947]

Dearest Cousins,

I wrote you a letter in town last week, but had no typewriter and decided it was too much of a scrawl to send you, out of human kindness.

I thought you very nice indeed to write me about the fine son[2] and the plays, and would have answered long ago but have been messed up

1. See above, Letter 668, n. 9.
2. The birth of their son, Roger Thurman.

with the New Republic trying to decide what I am going to do. I re-signed last Monday [3] but yesterday now Michael Straight has returned from Maine and telephoned yesterday expressing much distress and urging me to have a talk with him. Of course he has been busy this year, but he should have done this sooner. With the present outlay and conditions of work I certainly shall not stay on the NR. I will have to have the talk however.

Giving up that small salary, even that, cuts down my income still more so that I am now living on my modest savings. If that were not the case, I should be sending my new cousin a handsome present, but alas—

Beverly and Betsy and the boys are in North Carolina. Betsy needs the change after a winter in town with three children [4] on her head. I am certainly glad you are so happily established in your college town [5] and I think the college is very lucky to have you both.

I am sending Bedford a new collection of plays,[6] he may find it use-ful in his library. Bowman sends all good wishes.

Affectionately
Stark

3. Young's final work for the magazine was a review of Congreve's *Love for Love* in the issue for June 16, 1947, pp. 31–32. His name was removed from the masthead after the issue of September 8, 1947.
4. The children were David Hugh, Robert Alexander, and John Thurman.
5. Thurman was taking graduate work in theatre at Iowa State University.
6. The Modern Library edition of *Sixteen Famous British Plays*.

671 | To B[ernard]. H. Haggin,[7] New York

Jennymead
Waccabuc, New York
August 25, 1947

Dear Mr. Haggin,

Many things have happened to make me delay in answering your very good note.[8] I have not written about Balanchine for the very good reason that I don't know enough about the subject in general, etc. The theatre-going for the New Republic has prevented my seeing much ballet at all these latter years.

And now I have resigned from the New Republic. Michael Straight urged me to stay on, but the whole system there is impossible for me now. They want all the plays covered, and in a very limited space, then the plays come late, and I saw my proof very rarely last season, which is something I never had before. Then there is "editing" of the copy, which I never had before and will not put up with. I was made to say banal things, sometimes incorrect things and the style was constantly messed with so that I was at times ashamed of it and even had to write explanations to various persons, et cetera. Basta.[9]

7. B[ernard]. H. Haggin (b. 1900), music critic, has written criticism for the Brooklyn *Daily Eagle,* the *Nation,* the Sunday New York *Herald Tribune,* the *Hudson Review,* the *Yale Review,* and the *New Republic.* His books include *Music on Records* (1938, 1941), *Music for the Man Who Enjoys "Hamlet"* (1944), *Music in The Nation* (1949), *The Listener's Musical Companion* (1956), *Conversations with Toscanini* (1959), *Music Observed* (1964), *The Toscanini Musicians Knew* (1967), and *Ballet Chronicle* (1970). So early as 1940, Haggin had written in "records," *Nation,* CLI (October 5, 1940), 310: "I would say Stark Young is the most distinguished critic in this country (though I would not suspect it from the amount of space he has been getting in the *New Republic*); and he is that, not because of what he himself can do in the arts, but because of what he perceives in them—what he brings, astonishingly, to any art he chooses to consider, in sensitiveness to the medium, in quality of mind, in range and depth of experience and emotion."

8. Haggin had written Young to ask why, since he had written earlier about such dance artists as Mary Wigman, Vicente Escudero, and Martha Graham, he had not discussed the contribution of George Balanchine (b. 1904), whose choreography for ballet companies, musical comedies, and motion pictures had received widespread admiration.

9. Years later, Haggin attributed his resignation as musical critic for the *Nation* and Young's departure from the *New Republic* to the harassment by Robert Littlefield Hatch, who served as literary editor of both magazines. Wrote Haggin: "I still have the letter in which Stark Young, in 1947, told me his reason for resigning from the

I tell you all that because I have so much respect for you and your work. I had planned last winter to ask you to come by if you would, but was prevented by the eternal stew and mess in connection with my copy. This coming season, if agreeable to you, do let me see you. I am at 320 East 57th St. and the telephone is Wickersham 2,6493, not in the book, and please write it in your address book. I will write you in any case when I am back in town.

Thank you again for your note. I hope your summer is going well.

Cordially
Stark Young

Forgive the summer day typing. And I liked your putting in an oar for an artist—that is the kind of thing sadly needed in this scattered American life.

S.Y.

672 | To Julia Young Robertson, Austin, Texas

[Waccabuc, New York]
Wednesday [August 27, 1947]

Dearest Sister,

I wrote you when I got to town Monday—the train late—the city being burnt alive. People looked as if they were staggering. So I fancy you could read little of my scrawl. It makes me appreciate your having to write me in longhand, when this typewriter is almost like talking with you straight.

I told you about Mr. Jewell's liking the painting so much, so does Wales.

New Republic—including the messing up of his writing, which he said had never been done before; and for years he continued to speak of this indignantly; 'Why, that man Hatch made me sound like an ignoramus. He made me say things that were so embarrassing I sometimes had to write to people to explain I hadn't said them—!' " See Haggin, "The Editor's Rite," *Partisan Review,* XXXII (Winter, 1965), 122–23.

I don't think I told you Mr. H had written that the frames were done and waiting for my inspection. Mr. Pribble left the first of the month. I was going over to see the frames but had a case to carry, books, olive oil etc., and the thought of dressing and dragging the case over there, so far west and then getting to Grand Central was rather thick, so I told Mr. H I would be to see the frames the next time I was in town.

I told you about the visit to Mr. Wallace. He was out looking over his new strawberry patch, all in muddy boots. Gathered some corn for us and tomatoes and had the maid indoors fix up a bag of tomatoes—ours are just in and very smooth and fine, we often wish you and Ben could have some—then on the porch he took off his boots and socks and sat barefoot all the time in the library, his little toes stuck up over the others, early pointed shoes no doubt.

Then he walked out barefoot to the car with us, all very cordial, reminded me that we are to have some of the prize new variety strawberry plants, in about three weeks now, so we have to have Lou get the bed ready soon. They bought Ambassador Winant's [1] house, and something over a hundred acres. A stupid house, though comfortable, really hopeless to do anything with. The kitchen large and all new, he was very proud of it, freezer, grand enamels etc., cost several thousand Wales said. Perhaps only about two. I know our grocer has had four of those open top freezers put in, and it cost him 6000. Of course Mr. W's was closed, but tall and very deep, full of chickens, strawberries and what not. We said there were no fresh chickens in our stores, not to suit us, he said we could get all we wanted from him—meaning buy of course—but I said we had nobody to clean them. It is a smelly job and gory. So that was the visit and I tell it again because my scrawl was probably too much. We have been warm out here but not uncomfortable at all, all but Helsa,[2] she can't bear New York, too hot, and so far this summer I can't recall any form of weather that suits her, and the letters from Norway say the summer there has been record breakingly hot, so "isn't it terrible!"

We did not get the mail Saturday or Monday and so your letter came yesterday, and I was awfully glad to have it. I wish often that I

1. John Gilbert Winant (1889–1947), United States ambassador to Great Britain in 1941.
2. Maid and cook.

could drop in on you and Ben. Next year I hope you can come up this time of year, the weather is softer, the garden very pretty and the drives around here are endless, there are houses and places in numberless small roads one would never know existed, and many of the houses show many signs of being loved, really con amore, people like having them. Some, hidden in lanes and trees are elaborate establishments.

That was funny and sweet about the waitress and the swimming, it makes me think of the couple in an Italian train explaining to the priest that the little girl they had adopted was the daughter of a street walker, now in jail, "S'imagine, Padre," the little voice kept saying, "Fancy that, Father," delighted to be the center of so much attention. Real politeness in waitress and little girl.

I am still trying to settle into not being attached to any regular job, after twenty five years of it. It takes a good deal of discipline of the mind and habits.

I hope Ben is over his cold. I have not had one since you left—knock on wood—and hope I don't. As Papa said after funerals well I never felt better.

I had a nice letter again from Michael Straight and will send it for you to see after Wales sees it. Thanks for sending back Bobby's letter.[3]

I hope the unit works, not too too like Mrs. Rice's.

I should stop, since I have no news.

> Love to you and Ben
> Stark

Wales would send love—off for the morning on a job nearby.

3. Robert Edmond Jones had written on August 11 to affirm his confidence in Young's ability to reach his public despite his resignation from the *New Republic.*

673 | To John Mason Brown, New York

Jennymead
Waccabuc, New York
Monday, September 29, 1947

Dear John,

I could never let so beautiful a letter go unanswered, and so this is a dull reply to thank you and to tell you that it goes into my lasting files.[4]

I think of myself as a failure and washout in a present-day world where there are too many failures and washouts, but your good opinion, however prejudiced by affection and an old regard, means a great deal to me. I don't have to tell you that. And so thank you again. Basta.

The postscripts were welcome indeed, that you are well again is especially welcome. You must easily be the one brilliant theatre lecturer in America, and it takes physical strength to keep it up.

Love to you and Cassie and the boys. I should like awfully to see them some time this season. The children of one's friends always seem to me a part of a noble and warm continuity in life.

Affectionately
Stark Young

4. After receiving Young's letter of resignation from the Critics' Circle, Brown replied on September 15 that although officially he would accept the resignation, "personally—and critically—I cannot, will not, resign myself to it. You mean much too much to the theatre and to criticism for either to try to struggle along without you. Far be it from me to try to fathom the inscrutable ways of the present *New Republic*. But I know, even if its editors don't, what they have lost in you. More accurately, what we have all lost. No one has written more distinguished criticism in our time. No one has seen and felt with finer perceptions. Understood acting so completely. Revealed with such intellectual comprehension the mysteries of the theatre. Had such an eye for color, for fabrics, for light. Or such an ear for words."

674 | To Eric Bentley, University of Minnesota,
Minneapolis, Minnesota

320 East 57th Street
New York
November 6, 1947

Dear Mr. Bentley,

I am just back from the country, or would have written some sooner.
I saw that fine letter about me that you sent to Theatre Arts.[5] I not
only value your opinion very much as you know; I also value more
than I can tell you the generous spirit that moved you to make the
gesture. You know what the conditions were at the New Republic, so
that I don't have to go into that.

Among the many things I don't understand is the case by which Mr.
Shaw[6] writes these generalized pieces, and only now and then, covering one or two plays, while all last year I was being nagged to cover
almost everything, and in that silly space allowed the arts in the N.R.
I could have fought it out, but saw it was hopeless anyhow. Michael
Straight begged me most cordially to stay on, with the same reviewing
or with general articles longer and more special in the body of the
paper, once a month or so. I would be ashamed to tell you some of the
silly subjects that were thought of at the office for that purpose, though
Michael said they were only suggestions and need not concern me.
Well, that is over, and it all represents quite a change in my way of

5. A reference to Bentley's tribute to Young in a letter to the editors, *Theatre Arts*,
XXXI (November, 1947), 1. Bentley called Young "one of the two or three very best
dramatic critics that America has yet produced" and found it "deplorable that, for
every three people who tell you that Irwin Shaw is the *New Republic's* new critic,
only one observes that this means the retirement of Stark Young. If Irwin Shaw is
half as good as Mr. Young he will be the best critic in New York." After noting that
he had often attacked the " 'theatre arts' " point of view for which Young stood, Bentley concluded that Young was probably the only representative of this school who, "in
any distinguished way, *did* write about acting and design with the skill that a first-
rate literary critic lavishes on poetry. If our latter-day champions of 'theatre arts' are
going to write books like *Theatre Practice* and *The Flower in Drama,* their sins will
be forgiven them."

6. Irwin Shaw (b. 1913), critic, playwright, and novelist, wrote drama criticism for
the *New Republic* from September 29, 1947, to March 22, 1948. Primarily a writer of
fiction, he has lived mainly in Switzerland since 1951.

life. Scribners is now pushing me toward a collection of my reviews, selected of course, and I am going over some old pages of the NR with that in mind. If I don't think I can do a volume that would satisfy us I will drop it.

Dear Mr. Bentley, what I appreciate most in your letter is that you have the will and the ability and range of scholarship to speak out and want to speak out. In New York the great trouble, among others, is that nobody represents anything. Whatever the critic's feeling, dislike or enthusiasm may be[,] the result is the same pussy-footing and lack of center, championship or seed. About six of you could make a great difference here.

My opinion was not asked as to who would follow me on the New Republic, and you would not have the job if they offered it to you. Nor would they have the least appreciation of you anyhow or think of you as their man.[7]

The NR is much disorganized, I imagine. And the circulation, which under the new regime picked up from in the thirty thousands to around eighty, has dropped, I am told, to thirty. It cannot run on that, of course, and unless there comes in money, I don't think Michael can swing it. Perhaps some interested people, in Semitic defense, for example, will come into the field.

I saw a splendid review of yours about Red Warren's play.[8] I read the book with much admiration for its remarkable gifts. The only part that failed, in my opinion, were the long passages about the girl he finally married. So many of the scenes about the Boss were really notable. I admire and like Red Warren very much indeed, I wish you would remember me to him when you see him. I also liked his Italian wife and send her greetings.

I hope to see you and Mrs. Bentley[9] in New York again, and before long. If you will just let me know. And the telephone is Wickersham 2,6493.

7. In 1952, Bentley became drama critic for the *New Republic* and remained on the staff until 1956.

8. In *Theatre Arts* (November, 1947), Eric Bentley reviewed the production of Robert Penn Warren's play, *Proud Flesh,* at the University of Minnesota. The play had been performed in April, 1946, under the title *All the King's Men.* In 1939, Warren wrote the work as the play *Proud Flesh* and later rewrote it as the novel *All the King's Men.*

9. Bentley was then married to Maja Tschernjakow; the marriage was subsequently dissolved.

Thank you again, and especially for your whole spirit in the arts and their place in life. The world is in a hard way just now, and we have to whistle for it.

Yours sincerely
Stark Young

675 | To Hudson Strode, University of Alabama, Tuscaloosa, Alabama

320 East 57th Street
New York
Thursday [November 6, 1947]

Dear Hudson,

I came back to town yesterday morning and found your letter and the book,[1] the book among a lot of parcels and books and magazines. I was very much delighted to have both the letter and the book, and news of you and Therese.

The book I am looking forward to, and will in a few days have a chance to begin. The format is very handsome. The jacket is by about the best man in the field, Ted Kauffer.[2] He is a friend of mine and a warm admirer and trumpeter of my paintings. A lovely fellow too.

I had an awful time on the NR last year. It was all rattlebrained and half baked, nobody knew what was wanted, etc. Michael Straight is a nice fellow, with a fine spirit, ambitious, but not too strong, and he has delegated a lot of things to poor choices among people. I don't mean

1. Hudson Strode's *Now in Mexico* had just been published by Harcourt, Brace, and Company.
2. Edward McKnight Kauffer (1890–1954) was probably the greatest poster designer of the century. Born in the United States, he began his career as advertising artist in 1915, in England, where he lived until 1940, when he returned to America. Known for his application of modern artistic principles, represented by Picasso and Braque, to commercial art work, Kauffer designed during the twenties and thirties for Lund Humphries and Company and for the Nonesuch Press. Retrospective exhibitions of his work were held at the Lund Humphries Galleries, the New York Museum of Modern Art, and the Ashmolean Museum at Oxford. The jacket which Kauffer designed for *Now in Mexico* was reproduced on the front cover and spine of the book.

not too strong physically, I mean he is not very powerful in general. My advice was not asked about anything in the art end of the paper, all sorts of young people were taken on, the space for reviews was very short, the space in the paper wasted with those idiotic and ugly draw-ings and decorations. I was, or seemed to be, wanted to cover most of the plays, and in that short space. And for the first time in my life my copy was messed with, changed, cut etc. This was partly due to the fact that things were rushed so that there was no time for me to see my proofs as a rule. I wasted my time and my state of nerves on it, for poor results. I had long since agreed to help the Elmhirsts out by tak-ing very little pay, the more fool I, so that the financial loss is slight. Some of the new men are getting large salaries, and they are mostly unheard of people who were supposed to get a chance to rise there in prominence but have gotten little by way of a chance. I think the truth is Bruce Bliven, with everybody so busy and scattered, has had much more power delegated to him than he had before as the managing editor, and he is at the root of a lot of the trouble. I usually went, since Croly's time, to the NR about twice a year, so the personal side has nothing to do with it. Mr. Henry Wallace has nothing to do with the matter. He has never mentioned it, my resigning, but made the gesture of calling on me in the country, with Mrs. Wallace—a very lovable gesture and to his credit. Later he has sent me a hundred plants of his famous strawberries, mostly in little pots.

Michael urged me to stay, held the matter off for weeks, insisting on paying me during them, offered to let me do general articles once a month instead of reviews etc. But it was clearly time to leave. His fam-ily are old friends and have a great opinion of my dramatic reviewing, so that is all too bad.

The truth in general is I should have left the NR long ago when Bruce got his hand in, ruined everything, got rid finally of everybody except me, and that was because I told the Elmhirsts I would stay, and when Bruce asked me why I had not resigned, since I did not agree with a lot of the paper, I said why didn't he resign, and nobody with any brains agreed with everything in any paper, certainly the Elmhirsts did not do so as concerned the NR. He backs down at once, being a tricky coward as well as a neurotic liar, so that was that. Now he has a less direct and a better chance to do people in. All the younger peo-ple on the NR past and present hate him like poison. So I just stopped going near the office. Basta, you can see it was time for me to get out.

With living so wild and dear, and things in general so harassed, you can see why this makes a change in my life. I am trying to study over past reviews, since about 1923, with the idea of choosing a volume, Scribners urges and urges me to.[3] And I am slowly beginning a book of memoirs, which I hope to make something if I can get the tone into it that I want.[4] I will also have more time for painting. I have a painting now in the big Carnegie annual[5] and the Art Institute of Chicago —the finest modern painting collection in this country—now owns one of my largest things, with some fine letters to me from the admired director, Mr. Rich. Basta, I have wasted a lot of time and nerves and substance on the NR these latter years, with cramped and meagre results compared to what I did formerly and could still do.

Though I have not seen too much of it I think Mexico is as a country the most beautiful I ever saw, and I like Mexican people very much. The photographs in your book are splendid, and yours as good as any of them. You must be pleased with yourself as a photographer. You were right to dedicate the book to that wonderful, lovely, profound Therese.

Before so long I will write you after I have read the book really. Meanwhile thank you for remembering me with it and for your letter. Your commendation and affection have done a lot for me these many years.

Love to you both
Stark

I can't make myself read all this over—the NR subject is very depressing.

3. Published as *Immortal Shadows* (1948).
4. Published as *The Pavilion* (1951).
5. Young entered *Landscape with Rocks* in the exhibition, *Painting in the United States, 1947*, held at the Carnegie Institute from October 7 through December 7, 1947.

676 | To Ella Somerville, Oxford, Mississippi

320 East 57th Street
New York
Monday [November 24, 1947]

Dearest Ella,

Your lovely letter makes me feel sad and homesick. As I wrote you, I have gone into everything and just cannot work out how to make all those connections, be back in New York and all that. In the spring I am going to try to persuade Bowman to take a motor trip down there, and then you sweet people can just expect to get such hugs from me that your necks will be broken. As time passes one values more and more old friends and old memories. I will say some of that in my memoirs, which I am making notes for.

The lawyer is now drawing up my will—my estate is well over thirty-five cents—and I am leaving a list of things to the museum, and some to Bowman, who is asked when he is through with them to leave them to the museum. That is the best I can do, since he would think it odd if I left the chairs of Pauline Bonaparte right from under him to a museum.

Just writing to you, dear Ella, makes me long to come by Oxford and sit by the fire with you all, toward whom my heart is so full of love and admiration.

It is too bad that Miss Kate is not well, and so I begin to be a plague to you. I should like to ask this: I will send soon a handkerchief belonging to the Empress Marie Louise, the 2nd Mrs. Napoleon, I bought it in her duchy of Parma—and two waistcoats [6] embroidered, 18th century, etc.—but what I want to inquire is this other matter. I have various MSS. memos and daguerreotypes pertaining to So Red the Rose. Instead of leaving them to the University of Virginia Library, where I have a good name, or Washington, or Mississippi, I prefer to have them in your museum. One is a MS. written a month after the house was burnt, as described in So Red the Rose. It is in my aunt's own handwriting,[7] a genuine document. If I send them to your

6. The handkerchief and waistcoats which Young sent in February, 1948, are now in the Mary Buie Museum at Oxford, Mississippi.

7. Young refers to Mary Hines Burruss McGehee, wife of Edward McGehee, and the burning of Bowling Green at Woodville, Mississippi, during the Civil War.

museum, could you arrange a case in which they could be shown so that people could really see them? Otherwise they may as well go to some university as be buried there with you, the universities at least provide a lasting tomb. If you can do a case like this, I can send you a number of real items.

I hate to be a bother, but we are all getting older and there is a lack of character in trying to avoid getting settled these things that ought to be settled.

How I wish I were coming by this Christmas!

Love to you all
Stark

677 | To William Lewis, Oxford, Mississippi

320 East 57th Street
New York
December 1, 1947

Dear Willie,

I had hoped to see you last summer, you said you would be in New York. You doubtless looked for me in Dunn and Bradshaw or whatever it is, and decided I was not financially important enough to bother with. In that respect, you were quite right.

Miss Kate writes me that you are a mainstay of the Museum, and so I am writing you to say what I have already written her, which is that the "Bowie" is not entirely right for name of the museum. The connection for Oxford and Mississippi people is Skipwith. I think the name should be changed at once to The Mary Skipwith Bowie Museum.[8] That would mean the same thing and yet so much more.

I hope everything goes well with you and yours. Old friends are best. Love to you and your lady.

As ever
Stark

8. See above, Letter 638 and n. 5. For *Bowie,* Young should have written *Buie.*

678 | To Eric Bentley, New York

> 320 East 57th Street
> New York
> Tuesday [January 13, 1948]

Dear Mr. Bentley,

I am just back a few days ago from Texas and Monterrey, took your book[9] with me and admired it greatly as well as finding it highly readable as writing per se. I can go along almost entirely with you about Shaw—there are moments when I think him not entirely sincere, not by intention but through lack of imaginative depth or through being heavily set on one theme. But the delight and abundance that we have all had of him should put us on our knees. The whole subject is too complicated to take up in a letter. It was a pity I was just leaving for Texas when Mrs. Bentley [*sic*]. I just made the train. And after all, the piece on that silly Bertita Harding Duse book[1] that I was pushing myself so hard to leave finished for *Theatre Arts*—so that the packing I did was a scandal—proved to be time and effort wasted. *Theatre Arts* is already by now closed[2]—Rosamond Gilder said on the telephone that the back all of a sudden said he was dropping it.[3] That seems a great pity. It had its faults but there is nothing to take its place.

Red Warren has telephoned that he and his wife are coming up next Monday. I am sorry I have no place as a reviewer to be of use to him.

If this letter is hopelessly dull I try to lay it on the fact that with a deadline ten days off I am trying to get some number from my book of memoirs ready for the *Virginia Quarterly*. It is a work in which I am deeply interested, and my brain feels fagged with trying to find the tone etc. At present the results seem good.

9. Bentley's *Bernard Shaw: A Reconsideration* had been published late in December, 1947.

1. Young refers to Mrs. Bertita (Leonarz) Harding's *Age Cannot Wither: The Story of Duse and d'Annunzio*, published in October, 1947.

2. Rosamond Gilder edited the final issue of *Theatre Arts*, February, 1948, before it merged with *Stage Magazine* under new editorship.

3. Late in December, 1947, Robert W. Dowling and Henry Steeger, owners of *Theatre Arts*, notified Rosamond Gilder, the editor, that the magazine was being sold to Alexander S. Ince and that the February, 1948, issue would be the last. Miss Gilder tried unsuccessfully to raise the money to continue the magazine under her direction.

I saw the *Galileo*—a good deal of it most remarkable.[4] Mr. Laughton's exhibitionistic weaknesses limited the effect badly at times, at other times his work was most authoritative. I am grateful to him for giving us a chance to see such a play. The boys and their singing the transitions in the play etc. might be good if done superbly. The result here was pretty wasteful and tedious.

The scene of the peasant monk talking about religion and his parents with Galileo's replies was one of the very finest and most moving scenes I have watched in years.

Thank you again for the *Shaw*. I prize having it. Regards to you both.

Stark Young

P.S. All that last chapter about artist and propagandist is done admirably and con amore too.

S. Y.

679 | To Julia Young Robertson, Austin, Texas

[320 East 57th Street]
[New York]
Friday [February 6, 1948]

Dearest Sister,

Your letter came today and I am glad to hear that you and Ben are all right and the house well protected against the cold. No, Wales thought nothing of the Gibson picture[5] etc., it was in the same letter with the note to him I think. I am returning it now. That collar might be very becoming to you. I don't think Mrs. Gibson is very rich of late years, she sold the house, however, on a good street. I always like her

4. Earlier Bentley had urged Young to see Bertolt Brecht's *Galileo*, translated by Charles Laughton, which opened on December 7, 1947, and starred Charles Laughton as Galileo. The production closed a week later.
5. Identity not established.

and she always holds out her cheek to be kissed, but I don't see her but every year or so. She wrote a lovely letter thanking me for some flowers I sent some time, several weeks, after Mr. G's death. She said how alone she was and all that. They seemed devoted, and for some reason always so nice to me, he would hold out his hand and say, Cousin, how are you? I imagine I would get on well with Lady Astor, though she is both more violent and tanked up with religion, meaning Christian Science, which under the surface always creates something you don't really like, such silly stuff to evade the issues that all other religions face. What good is it except a foolish comfort to sit up and think you don't feel something that human beings are intended to feel, I don't mean just physical pain?

I finished another of the memoir numbers yesterday and sent it yesterday to Virginia, that makes five. I will take notes but have no real design for any others just now. It pretty much wore me out as it was. Now I am going to paint a few weeks, because I have a very cordial letter from Mr. St. Gaudens [6] of the Carnegie, the largest and important show every year in this country, saying he will be here in March and wants to select one of my things for next year.

I send this letter of Lawton's, it does him credit.[7] He is pleased because Miss Trippe has now taken the picture to her Palm Beach house and it hangs there in her drawing room. She has a swank apartment here in New York, a house in Bar Harbor, and one at Palm Beach, and is always asking Lawton to stay with her.

Those pictures were entertaining, thanks for sending them, the man is not as completely effective as Grant Wood,[8] how good GW is as a painter is another matter, opinions differ. He is dead and that helped the prices.

That blouse at Wanamakers whether it would be good or not could

6. Homer Schiff Saint-Gaudens (1880–1958) was briefly associated with *The Critic* and directed several Broadway productions before joining the Carnegie Institute of Fine Arts in 1921 as assistant director. The following year, he became director and held the post until his retirement in 1950.

7. Campbell had written Young to express admiration for the painting of white and pink flowers, entitled *Pink Flowers in a Vase,* which Campbell had commissioned Young to execute for Carolyn Trippe. After her death in 1958, the painting, under the terms of her will, was returned to Campbell.

8. Grant Wood (1892–1942), American painter, known for regional paintings of the midwest. The pictures, presumably newspaper clippings, sent Young by Mrs. Robertson, cannot be identified.

be used as a model that would be very becoming to you, I think. I almost sent it to you as Valentine, but was afraid the size etc. would be off. The price is certainly mild. The blouse business is a well known racket as to prices. Mrs. Stoddard[9] like all the swell places bought many of her things at the same jobbers that a cheap department store does, she told me so.

Wales sends his love.

I hope you and Ben are all right.

Lovingly
Stark

680 | To John Hall Wheelock, Charles Scribner's Sons, New York

320 East 57th Street
New York
Monday [March 29, 1948]

Dear Jack,

I am enclosing about the best data I can supply about the book.[1] I still have no real title for it but will be thinking.

The typewriter I use is a newly rented one, mine is at the Remington repair place, so I make blunders worse than usual perhaps and perhaps not.

You sounded so troubled about Charlie that I wrote him a loving and mournful epistle, and then, bless us, I heard he was already at the office. Please explain to him.

Just do anything you please with the material I send in. But though theatre people and such men as Professor Baker have thought me the leading, or often one, American critic of the theatre, please do not say that I am leading or anything like it. It will ONLY MAKE THE

9. Buyer and dress shop manager who frequently helped Young in selecting gifts for his sister.

1. At Wheelock's request, Young had submitted some material about his collection of theatre reviews (*Immortal Shadows*) for announcement in Scribner's "Fall List."

CRITICS AND REVIEWERS PICK ON ME. As a matter of fact people like George Nathan and John Mason Brown have always been wonderfully generous about me. This point of not saying the leading business is most important.

Thanks for everything.

Yours sincerely
Stark

681 | To Charles Henri Ford, New York

320 East 57th Street
New York
Thursday [April, 1948]

Dear Charles Henri,

I think too much of you to kid you by saying that I have read every page of your manuscript.[2] Scribner's had a dead line ahead of me on my book of selected theatre reviews, and I have been getting up at five in the morning and working all day most of the day for some time. To read all your MS carefully would take many hours.

But I have read a great deal of it—in fact I have indulged myself in reading it when I should be at Scribners' labors. I don't think in all this flurry I could say anything very luminous or helpful about your book except that I think it is original in the general effect and plan, that it has a warm heart, plenty of brains and is full of talent. Well, that is a good deal, isn't it, after all!

It gets steadily more interesting as it goes on. I think almost anybody would suggest cutting some of the childhood letters where the simple statements of things tend to repeat in effect. At any rate I know it is stupid to advise artists, but if I were you I would do a bit of that shortening at the first before showing it to a publisher.

2. Although identification of Ford's manuscript is uncertain, Young may have read an early version of *Sleep in a Nest of Flames*, which Ford published in 1949 with an introduction by Edith Sitwell.

One thing I can say, and from my heart, for I am very fond of you as well as my dear Pavlik,[3] and that is that at any time I will be more than glad to speak of this book at Scribner's and say you are thinking of sending it to them. It is, however, so different from most books and MSS. they see, that I could not even hazard a guess as to what publishers would think of it. The book market they say is very discouraging to them right now, but that may change.

Please forgive this dull, hurried letter, I am really up a tree on my own MS, such is life.

Tell Pavlik that in these drab days lately I have frequently looked at the beautiful drawing he gave me. I do that to touch my mind up and to get some flowers into my heart.

Love to you both

Yours
Stark

682 | To Leah Salisbury, New York

320 East 57th Street
New York
Tuesday [April 6, 1948]

Dear Leah,

Would you please thank Ada for her very nice letter.[4] My reply had better be sent to you and thus settle the matter. I should like you to happen to be the one who will settle with these English suggestions. I don't know who their dramatists are and don't care, not from most of those I have seen in the theatre. But if you think there are possibilities,

3. Pavel Tchelitchew.
4. Ada Ellison, member of Leah Salisbury's staff, had written Young about the proposed production of his play *Artemise* by the Company of Four at the Lyric Theatre, Hammersmith, London. Representing the Company of Four, Judy Campbell had suggested that an English playwright "make an 'adaptation' of the script into a form more understandable for an English audience." Nothing came of the proposals, probably because Young's answer was never transmitted to the Company of Four.

just let them go ahead and rewrite what they please. With the proviso that if it should come to America—which it would not of course—I should have a say in changing what they had done with the script. As usual with these ham theatre people, they know best what the author was only groping toward. I don't care, however. I am through with the theatre and have enjoyed enormously this season not seeing any of it except the ANTA plays, which Lawton made me go to and bought the tickets for, and the only other piece that with Beatrice Straight, which for family reasons I had to see and to which Natalie Hammond took me.[5] Not worth the trouble it took crossing town.

Forgive this messy look, I have a rented Remington—mine is at the cleaner's—and it gums up the paper.

There is an important thing I want to tell you about. Sokolov[6] has approached me about the *Mandragola*[7]—to be done by that organization he directs—in Hollywood?—and he is excited about taking the play and having Stravinsky do the music, and Berman[8] the settings etc. That of course would be a worldwide event. I should like in this case for you to make them the simplest of terms—if they come to you about it. I gave Mr. Sokolov your address as my friend and agent—so long as it is confined to that organization out there of his. If it got on a wider basis, then the terms would have to be revised. That ought to be clear. Stravinsky and the Arthur Sachs and the Sokolovs are probably coming over here next Tuesday for cocktails and the subject will very likely come up. Three years ago I saw the Stravinskys several times a week, but since then they have not been in town to speak of. If this should come off it would really be a distinguished event, with such people interested. So as to terms I don't want to do anything that would deter them at the start.

I wrote you with heartiness a longish letter some time back, and

5. Beatrice Straight was appearing as Lady Macduff in *Macbeth,* which opened on March 31, 1948.

6. Nikolai Sokoloff (1886-1925), conductor, began his career as a violinist but in 1918 became permanent conductor of the Cleveland Orchestra. After resigning from this position in 1933, he became head of the Federal Music Project and later conductor of the Seattle Symphony Orchestra. From 1941 to 1961, he was musical director of the La Jolla Musical Arts Society, La Jolla, California. At the time Young wrote this letter, Sokoloff was married to Ruth Haller Ottaway, his second wife.

7. Niccolo Machiavelli's *Mandragola,* translated by Young and published in 1927.

8. Eugene Berman (1899-1972), painter and designer, born in Russia, became a resident of the United States in 1937. He designed settings and costumes for operas and ballets both here and abroad.

sent two copies of the play,[9] which you evidently got. Leo Lermer[1] seemed much excited about the play. You do whatever you think best, I would not cross the street for any theatre stuff that was popped into the air as a proposition for me. The Mandragola might be another matter.

Soon I shall be in the country. I cannot tell you what a relief it has been to be off the New Republic. I hope you and Phil will come up and see our little place. I will send you the telephone when we get settled. That reviled Henry Wallace and Mrs. Wallace are neighbors and friends—such is life. He sent me a hundred strawberry prize plants and they are flourishing.

> Lovingly
> Stark

683 | To Julia Young Robertson, Austin, Texas

> [320 East 57th Street]
> [New York]
> Thursday [April 29, 1948]

Dearest Sister,

I have been working at my book since about six this morning or earlier and all but one piece is finished. I will do it either in the morning or Monday morning and have promised to take the MS to Scribners sometime Monday. I still don't know in what order I want them to come. I may not stick, and probably won't, to the chronological, especially since I don't want the book to be taken as a record or chronicle, which it could not be anyhow. So this is just to tell you that I am all right and was glad to have your letter, and hope you can be driving your car soon. I am sorry you bothered with sending the books, my instinct told me not to telephone and stir up my dear family, but that stenographer had me so exhausted and suspended that I was desperate. The photostats came out splendidly, cost $6.25 where she

---

9. *Artemise.*
1. Young's reference seems to be to Leo Lerman (b. 1914), actor, director, stage manager, author, and magazine editor.

would have cost about $75, and that also means a much easier handling of the MS for me.[2]

Don't get a mistaken idea about the cornucopias. I had decided to hold them till I saw you, in the hope that you might like them and want them for your birthday. I'd like to give you something you like and that is lovely, not easy these days.

It will be a rest to get to the country tomorrow. I have had about enough of the labor on this book. I hope it is good. To knock us over the Stravinskys are really coming out Sunday and the Sokolovs with them. A Russian company for the Russian Easter. Mrs. Sokolov is on a special diet so that lets us off from trying to have Russian celebration stuff. Fortunately our Warren cleans well and has not to be told to do things, and has the house already after one week end cleaner than it has ever been before, so he will take care of that. But of course everything looks naked yet and few things are out except the bulbs and the tiny leaves beginning. What is more if it rains that will be a mess for the effect of the terrace. By the way Wales has had much of the terrace straightened out and relaid, which with time it needed. We look forward to seeing you and Ben sitting on it.

It is very flattering of the Stravinskys to want to get out of New York and be with us, when they are having so much attention, but I could wish it were a few weeks at least later. They are leaving next week. I must say they are dears. The world premier of this new ballet, Orpheus, was last night,[3] and he had a big personal ovation. He is evidently a legend already. Is 66 in June.

The rabbits are eating up everything but if it does not rain the wire fence will be done Saturday much needed.

Bob could not come to Rehn's, Katherine did not of course buy a painting, but the Votive with the cross and flowers it seems is in some exhibition in Atlanta now, so I told her to go and see it and tell Bob to buy it.[4]

2. To facilitate the preparation of his manuscript for *Immortal Shadows,* Young had photostatic copies made of his essays in the *New Republic.*

3. The first performance of Stravinsky's *Orpheus* took place in New York, April 28, 1948; George Balanchine wrote the choreography and Nicholas Magallanes and Maria Tallchief were the principal dancers. Stravinsky himself conducted.

4. In his exhibitions in 1943 and 1945, Young exhibited a painting called *Votive,* the title being further explained by Racine's phrase, *De quel amour blessee?* The painting was later purchased by Gertrude Newell. Young's friends mentioned in this paragraph have not been identified.

I must stop, love to you both. Wales is not home yet or would send you both his love.

Stark

684 | To John Hall Wheelock, Charles Scribner's Sons, New York

320 East 57th Street
New York
Monday [May 3, 1948]

Dear Jack,

Here is the MS. according to promise. They made the wrong photostat for the *Hamlet*[5] and *Four Saints in Three Acts*.[6] Others are ordered and should reach you in a day or two.

After spending over $300 on this venture, I went in for some less comfortable pages, as you will see. When I get the galleys I may change the order of two or three pieces—but that will be before the page proof. I have put five or six weeks hard labor going over all this, re-writing etc.—so hope it is good.

Thanks for your encouragement.

Yours
Stark

5. Young refers to his review of John Barrymore's performance in *Hamlet;* see above, Letter 116.

6. Originally Young reviewed this play by Gertrude Stein and Virgil Thomson in "One Moment Alit," *New Republic,* LXXVIII (March 7, 1934), 105; see also *Immortal Shadows,* pp. 138–41.

685 | To Charles Henri Ford, New York

320 East 57th Street
New York
Monday [May 3, 1948]

Dear Charles Henri,

Back from the country last night and have a practical idea in my head about your book—you see how well I wish it.

Undoubtedly the interest would be greatly increased if readers knew who you were talking about. Even if you have to change some intimate details, it is more interesting, for people who know of her, to read about Djuna Barnes[7] than about D— if she is D. At least somebody could be D. That general effect of reading about people whose names are withheld is certainly an effect to watch out for. As a rule half of something, if you know who it is about, is more interesting than the whole about somebody you don't know who. There are, of course, certain things complete in themselves and interesting regardless. Nevertheless—

This is a hasty letter, pardon stupidities.

Would you and Pavlik be interested to come out May 15, a Saturday, and spend that week-end in the country with us? We have two guest rooms for you, no social life, just plain sweet country, old clothes, and a warm welcome and being let alone when you wish it. Wales and I both would like very much to have you. Please think it over.

It is easy, just go to Katonah and we pick you up.

Love to you both.

Stark

7. Djuna Barnes (b. 1892) began her career as a reporter and magazine illustrator, but by 1931 she had become a full-time writer. She has lived much of her life in Paris and London where she knew Ford and Tchelitchew. Her best work includes a novel, *Nightwood* (1936); a verse play, *The Antiphon* (1948); and her collected short stories, *Spillway* (1962).

686 | To Julia Young Robertson, Austin, Texas

[320 East 57th Street]
[New York]
Monday [May 3, 1948]

Dearest Sister,

Harold Morris sent me the enclosed.[8] His review bits are impressive. So that's that.

We were granted to a brilliant day yesterday till the later afternoon when it began to cloud up. The Stravinskys and Sokolovs came out, and the visit seemed a great success. They certainly do their part and are sweet about everything.

They were worn out with New York, eternal interviews, photographs for every magazine, paper, etc. The new composition Orpheus, long with ballet, got a fine reception in the press.[9] They are going back home to peace tomorrow. I thought you would be interested to know how well the visit [went]. After lunch—around four, he went to sleep on my bed under the red comfort you sent me, on the pillow you gave me. The white rug looked really very fine in my bathroom, which needed something like that. I wore the white sweater too, so you see—

I am getting the MS in final shape to take to Scribners this afternoon, so must stop. I hope you and Ben are all right. The books have not come yet but they will. That reminds me—without taking any trouble at all will you have those packers come and get the two chairs, crate them and express them to me at Katonah? They are in the attic I think. Just let them do it all, they will charge just as much anyway. And don't you pay the express this time.

I must stop indeed.

Lovingly
Stark

8. Young enclosed newspaper clippings containing accounts of a concert by the Houston Symphony Orchestra, March 13, 1948, devoted to the works of Texas composers. Featured on the program was Harold Cecil Morris' "Amaranth" Symphony No. 3, which had received the Texas Composers Award. With the clippings, Young included a leaflet describing Morris' achievements as a pianist and composer and reprinting selected critical comments about his work. Morris (1890–1964), born in San Antonio, Texas, taught music at Columbia University from 1939 to 1946 and at the Julliard School of Music, Rice Institute, and other institutions.
9. See above, Letter 683 and n. 3.

687 | To Julia Young Robertson, Austin, Texas

[320 East 57th Street]
[New York]
Tuesday [May 4, 1948]

Dearest Sister,

The box came yesterday—thank you for all the trouble. I'll have to store them in the trunks here in the basement or in the barn trunks at Jennymead. A number of items will be of use now, though I have already copies of any reviews themselves that I'll use and that are in the box. Thank you again.

The enclosed is from Charlie Scribner[1] and as nice as can be—he always has to kid, is shy about showing feeling—thinks it's apt to be gush. Mr. Arthur Scribner was even shyer though not as smart as Charlie is.

I am lucky to be with not only the most distinguished and richest firm of publishers anywhere in English, but also with gentlemen and loyal friends and a high-toned ethics. I left the MS[2] by yesterday, and they telephoned later how much they appreciated the fact of being on time, etc. Now later come the proofs, and I can cut or insert as I like, plus paying the cost after a certain allowance for changes has been passed.

House and Garden has telephoned most flatteringly, asking me to do an article for a special issue—America—historic houses in the issue. A terrible subject they said—nobody in the office could handle it. It would mean little credit to me and I imagine not so much money—so I telephoned to say I could not. They were more flattering—said perhaps I'd do something about some house in the Deep South sometime. I said I would. I am tired now from the theatre book—about six weeks of hard work, then the proofs will be coming in, more revisions etc. And I want to finish one more chapter of the memoirs, to make three for the Virginia Quarterly—It's about half written. Planning for those chapters, what to use etc. is an awful job and almost beyond me.

---

1. Scribner wrote to thank Young for sending a copy of his "Chapters from a Book of Memories," *Virginia Quarterly Review,* XXIV (April, 1948), 217–34. Scribner declared that as he read the article he could hear Young's voice just as Scribner could hear the voice of Winston S. Churchill when reading his writing.

2. *Immortal Shadows.*

Wasn't Bobby Jones' letter a wonderful one![3]

We are going to Jennymead this week Thursday instead of Friday. If the weather permits the workmen will come and finish the garden fence. We can't hope for much till it is done and the rabbits out.

We still take pleasure in the thought of the Stravinskys' visit—the sky so bright, the terrace—so much better looking since it is straightened out—so bright with cushions—the Mexican pots, painted white and filled with dirt, looking so well.

I hope you and Ben are well.

Thank you again for the box.

Lovingly
Stark

688 | To Julia Young Robertson, Austin, Texas

[320 East 57th Street]
[New York]
Monday morning [May 10, 1948]

Dearest Sister,

We had a cold but good week end, much done in the garden and the fence around it is at last finished. We were planting nothing else till then, since the rabbits eat up everything as soon as it comes out. The fence cost several hundred dollars but I think Arthur Mezzulo is not going to let Wales pay anything because Wales has done his house for him, repeating to some extent the plan for the father's house in the past and Arthur is planning to pay nothing on that. I told Wales that to even these things up I would write a request that when the house is finally settled, one of us dead and then the other to have it till his death or till he chooses to sell it, that $1000 more will go to his estate. This is about all to do about it, since no sums have been mentioned, and that includes the front door. The fence is wire, double at the bot-

3. Earlier, Young had sent his sister a letter from Robert Edmond Jones; the letter has not survived.

tom with finer and stronger wire, and with iron stakes every eight feet and then wooden posts at the corners and four gates well planted and built. The cost would be about $400 I suppose, but a good deal of that is the labor and no way of computing that if Arthur supplies it. At that he is getting a bargain, for Wales is entitled to more on the work he has done for Arthur's house. These friendly matters are awkward.

Yes, there were some flowers for the Stravinskys, mostly forsythia, cherry blossoms and narcissi of divers colors, with some grape hyacinths and blue myrtles and white anemones. I met the celebrated painter the other day at Knoedler's, his exhibition, I mean Berman.[4] He is a friend of the Stravinskys and every time he sees them he says they tell him what a lovely time they had with us, good food etc. I must say they are ideal guests. I agree with you about Harold Morris, saw him at Wayman Adams' opening,[5] still looks soft and silly and now ugly and gushy. And there is the music evidently, I would have to hear it to believe however.

My sister is awfully smart. I knew you would put me on the track of a title, The Immortals' Shadows of the Theatre or whatever you put it, is not so good, I think, but I grabbed out of it a wonderful title, and that, as Gertrude Stein would put it, is is is is—beat it, I am delighted—!!!!!

IMMORTAL SHADOWS

I telephoned Wheelock at Scribner's who has more or less taken Max Perkins' place, and he said he thought it was a marvellous title. Considering the theatre and its immortality and considering the flitting shadows of the names there. Here is Doris, more adored than any actress in generations, for her moment, and then retired early, and now most of the young people never even heard of her. Of course, however, they never heard of anything.

4. During the first week of May, Eugene Berman's exhibition of paintings of Mexican themes opened at the art galleries of M. Knoedler and Company.

5. Wayman Adams (1883–1959), portrait painter, studied painting in the United States, Italy, and Spain and began his career as portrait painter in 1910. Since that date, his formal portraits and impressionistic sketches have been recognized in competitive exhibits throughout the country. In 1954, his portrait of Young was exhibited in Austin where Adams made his home. In 1948, Adams was awarded the medal of honor at the fall exhibition of the Allied Artists of America. Young's reference to Adams' "opening" may relate to his exhibition of still-life paintings at the Grand Central Galleries late in 1947.

Jack Wheelock said he was going right in and tell Charlie Scribner about this wonderful title. I am lucky in my family, you and Ben, and how lucky I am to have the most famous publishers in the world and them gentlemen, not asking me ever to be cheap.

I hope your weather is mending. By the way it is time for you and Ben to think of when you are coming up into these wilds to see us. It ought to be late enough to avoid as far as possible those hot spells there later in the summer. You will miss the peonies etc. but you will also miss the damp cold and later on the Texas hot. Be thinking of your time and let us know, and then we can plan for it. The apartment will be open here, so that you and Ben can spend a day or so when you like here in town shopping for all the mess for sale. For my part I think the shops are now disgusting. Mrs. Stravinsky said a very fine thing about it all—she and he like to shop around and pick up clever bargains, pretty bits, etc.—she said it was not fun shopping anywhere nowadays, everything so expensive, so few things of any interest. It is obvious, I should have replied, that what is droll for thirty cents is a damned bore for five dollars.

Our place is slowly beginning to flower, though the rabbits and animals wrecked so much during the bitter winter. You are quite right about Warren and trays. That took care of itself, however, after the first two meals. By then he had found the mats, dishes, and so on, and regular service began, done quite nicely with a pride that makes Helga more disgusting than ever. He has washed all the windows, polished all the floors, cooks extra bits and dishes for the meals, on his own, and has painted the fence and done laundry. We are going to have to invent things for him to do if this keeps up. Wales says he must be a typhoid carrier or something, it is too good to be true. Well, we shall see what we shall see.

Thank you again for the wonderful title, cease firing therefore for others, this is exactly what I want and too good to be true. I don't know what fates sent me a sister like that, but it is to my credit that I always knew it.

Love to you and Ben, I hope he really thought, outside politeness, that the candy was good. Thank goodness for the typewriter, I can whack off a letter long enough to bore you to death, in a short time.

Lovingly
Stark

P.S. I can't get over that title. Like all good things it is better than its creator knows—a biological example would be the parents of Beethoven.

689 | To John Hall Wheelock, Charles Scribner's Sons, New York

Waccabuc, New York
Sunday [June 20, 1948]

Dear Jack,

Thank you for your letter. As to the contract I, naturally, follow what you and Charlie, as officials and friends, suggest, and so the arrangement is entirely satisfactory. The 10,000 must be a graceful flourish on your gracious part, for a book of that sort rarely sells, at any time, like that.[6]

I wish you would meanwhile manage to agree that if I put in a few paragraphs—not affecting the text at all, that I won't be charged correction rates on them.[7] I need my allowance for corrections for the text otherwise. However—

Thank you for returning the Frenchman's letter.[8]

If you and your lady are ever passing near here or at Louise Perkins', I wish you would come and see what a sweet little place this is. I should like that very much. It is almost exactly half way between Ridgefield and Katonah, on Route 35. The telephone is South Salem 547.

Best to you

Yours
Stark

6. Young is replying to a letter from Wheelock, June 16, 1948. He had suggested a contract under which Young would receive a 10 percent royalty on the first ten thousand copies of *Immortal Shadows* and 15 percent thereafter.

7. Wheelock replied that Young's request would be made a part of the contract.

8. In a postscript to his letter of June 16, Wheelock had remarked: "The enclosed letter from Jacques Guy, with your pencilled annotation on the back, came with the other letter. I gather that whoever gets M. Guy as cook will be a lucky person. We have solved our problem on this front, for the time being at least."

p.s. Please ask your nice secretary to call the retail department and ask them to send me a copy of The Street Car Called Desire, to Waccabuc, and charge to my account. Thanks.

S.

690 | To John Hall Wheelock, Charles Scribner's Sons, New York

Waccabuc, New York
Thursday [August 5, 1948]

Dear Jack,

I had just finished the last batch of proof when this final lot came through the mail.[9] I don't think there will be any more deletions or additions, but it will be a favor to have the run off of the whole, and settle everything before the page proof starts.

I am trying to write a foreword, or note about the book's not being a theatre chronicle etc.—a hundred words or so, which I will send you for your advice as to its taste etc. I will be sending it soon. The book is dedicated to the memory of Doris Keane, and I have the dedication written, but it will have to wait till I am in town next week and get it out of the files there.

I have an idea about the jacket. Let us have on it somewhere

The Flower in Drama—some critical quote
The Sea Gull—some critical quote.

In this way we can combat the trouble about these books being out of print, and by saying other theatre books by Stark Young we can make it come in all right.

I found the letter from Texas,[1] even at this late date I will go on and enclose it to you.

I am glad you had a good vacation.

Stark

9. Since the middle of July, Young had been reading galley proof for *Immortal Shadows*.

1. Young had received a postcard from a person in Texas who signed himself "E.S." and complained that he could not purchase Young's books from Scribner's bookstore.

691 | To John Hall Wheelock, Charles Scribner's Sons,
      New York

Waccabuc, New York
Tuesday [August 31, 1948]

Dear Jack,

Even if I did not agree at all I would make the change for you, since the third-rate item disturbed you. But on the whole I think the change is better. In Doris Keane's case her creation in *Romance* was like a good many that Duse did: taking a trashy play and putting into it something that was indeed something. But to state this well would take an article in itself, and does not, I see, belong in a dedication. It is ungracious and extraneous to the moment. Doris herself would agree to this, though she would have had no illusions in the matter.

I must, therefore, thank you for the suggestion, and say that I am glad you felt free to make it.

Yours as ever
Stark

692 | To Hudson Strode, University of Alabama,
      Tuscaloosa, Alabama

Waccabuc, New York
September 15, 1948

Dearest Hudson,

I was delighted to have your letter about the memoir pieces in the *Virginia Quarterly*,[2] and had been hoping that you and Therese would like them. In fact I felt pretty sure you would, for when I am writing, or trying to write, matter like that I keep people like you all in mind.

2. Young refers to his "Chapters from a Book of Memories," *Virginia Quarterly Review*, XXIV (April, 1948), 217–34.

It gives me assurance in a faint-hearted contact with an assaulting world these days.

I had meant to write you that I was sending or having sent a copy to you—paid for by me too with a cheque. The Virginia Quarterly graciously allows the author two copies only! So now I have my reward in your letter. Of course I should have written you at the time. But I have been absorbed getting ready for publication in October a book of my theatre reviews that Scribners urged me to do. I have as usual with me done a vast amount of thinking and revising. That will represent my swan song indeed so far as the theatre is concerned. I will send you a copy. Naturally. I think I have a marvellous title for this book:

IMMORTAL SHADOWS

Scribners told me yesterday when I was in town that they heard that a remarkable reaction had followed just that one section of the memoirs —they are greatly pleased and say that if I do a whole book like that it will be wonderful etc. I am glad they feel that way when most publishers with the book market what it is are not anxious for works to print etc. I think I will do the memoirs in volumes, taking the first as far as my finishing college and going to Columbia for post-graduate work. But I have to go on working out a pattern. I don't mean to do the usual narrative affair, tracing the years and so on. It took me about four years to decide how I would do this work—and the result appears in that VA. issue, and I will try to keep that tone.

The tone of the second volume would be different, for that would come to the theatre and my contacts with Duse, Charlie Chaplin and Mei Lan-fang, Pirandello, Benavente and the others—all of whom were quite wonderful to me. I think myself I never came off except indirectly perhaps—though I believe So Red the Rose to be a landmark —but I have on the whole done about the best I could. Many cursed things have lain within me, and many bright angels have called to me. Among these—among the human—are you and my dear Thérèse— how people like her bless and shine on us!

Affectionately
Stark

Don't ask me to read this over—I'd probably never send it.

693 | To John Hall Wheelock, Charles Scribner's Sons, New York

Waccabuc, New York
Thursday [September 16, 1948]

Dear Jack,

I am returning the copy you so kindly sent me. There is also the jacket for Johnnie Brown's book[3]—which was sent me yesterday—at $3.50, which is a mistake, I think, though his radio and lecturing will sell some copies—and the reason I send it is to say I think it is pretty silly but shows how much can be got on a page.

I suggest, then, that you use the Rumanceff and Atkinson about *The Sea Gull*.[4] If you will continue *The Flower in Drama* you could use the first *two* of the quotes you sent under that. If you don't continue it, you could use the material under the heading you now have for it.

I am sorry this nuisance has to fall on you, and I appreciate your understanding attitude. Without meaning to whine, I may say that I have come to the conclusion that it matters very little what happens to what I write; and it seems a pity you should carry the load of the issue. Walter Winchell[5] is on the blest track.

Thanking you again, I am

Yours as ever
Stark

3. A reference to John Mason Brown's *Seeing More Things,* which had just been published.

4. Quotations from Nicholas A. Rumanceff (1875–1948), chairman of the board of directors for the Moscow Art Theatre, and Brooks Atkinson (b. 1894), drama critic for the New York *Times,* had appeared on the dust jacket of Young's translation of *The Sea Gull.*

5. Walter Winchell (1897–1972), drama critic, journalist, and radio commentator, reached the peak of his fame during the 1930s and 1940s through his radio and syndicated newspaper "gossip-columns."

694 | To Edwin Duerr,[6] Pittsburgh, Pennsylvania

Waccabuc, New York
October 19, 1948

Dear Mr. Duerr,

Your letter was delayed reaching me out here in the country and so I am replying at once to say that you are entirely welcome to use the quotes you mention in your letter and as much more of my pages as you like.[7] In case the matter comes up with my publishers you can keep this letter for reference. I will speak to them of the situation.

There are no conditions attached to this, except that you allow me to wish your book great success.

Thank you for your interest in my reviews and the idea of a collection. The book I have with a good deal of thinking and rewriting put together is to be out on November 15. I am delighted with the title I have thought of, especially for this book about the theatre

IMMORTAL SHADOWS

If you have a chance to mention it anywhere, I hope you do. It is my swan song in any sort of writing in the theatre field.

This letter sounds lumpish, but I am somewhat rushed getting packed to move back to town. My address there is 320 East 57th St. Plaza 5.6493.

With cordial regards, I am

Yours sincerely
Stark Young

6. Edwin Duerr (b. 1906) has taught drama and theatre courses at the University of California, Western Reserve University, Carnegie Institute of Technology, and California State College at Fullerton. When Young wrote this letter, Duerr was teaching at the Carnegie Institute of Technology and writing *Radio and Television Acting,* published in 1950. In 1962, he published *The Length and Depth of Acting.*

7. In *Radio and Television Acting,* Duerr quoted frequently from Young's *Glamour, Theatre Practice, The Theater,* and essays in the *New Republic.*

695 | To Julia Young Robertson, Austin, Texas

320 East 57th Street
New York
Saturday 8.30 [October 23, 1948]

Dearest Sister,

We had to be in town last night because Arthur Sachs cabled about dinner. He landed (delayed) Thursday evening. The dinner at Pavillion—cost probably 10 or 15 $ a person—about eight. I was glad it wasn't a large party.

Thank you for your letter. I was glad you liked the pieces[8]—your rum wetnurse point may be right—I never thought of it—I was always told Uncle Hugh's nurse was Uncle B's Mother and always heard him spoken of as a nice field nigger—I remember he had a kind of Gullah accent from S. Carolina. But how the two could go together I don't know. Smart of you to notice it.[9]

The enclosed from Jack Wheelock—who succeeded to Max Perkins' place as head of the literary dept. at Scribners—you need not return.[1] It was enough to knock me over because I never thought I'd live to see my writing compared to this book of Yeats'. His book comes from

8. Young refers to the first installments of his memoirs that had appeared in the *Virginia Quarterly Review:* "Chapters from a Book of Memories," XXIV (April, 1948), 217–34; and "More Chapters from a Book of Memories," XXIV (October, 1948), 558–73.

9. Mrs. Robertson's comments may have prompted Young to revise the passage about Uncle Billy when it appeared in *The Pavilion.* In "More Chapters from a Book of Memories," Young wrote: "In the first place Billy Machedric was a 'rice-field darkey' and had been raised on rum, so how could you expect any great pickin's out of him? But most of all, he was a baby when Uncle Hugh [McGehee] was; his mother had been Uncle Hugh's wet nurse, and that was how it stood." In *The Pavilion,* Young wrote: "In the first place Uncle Billy's mother, before she was brought to Mississippi, had been what was known as a rice-field darkey in South Carolina and raised on rum so how could you expect any great pickin's out of her son? But most of all he was a baby when Uncle Hugh was, and his mother had been Uncle Hugh's wet nurse, and that was how it stood" (pp. 33–34).

1. On October 19, 1948, Wheelock had written Young about the second installment of his memoirs: "You succeed magically in conveying an atmosphere and a world and in making the people in it as real as if I knew them. I'm very much excited about this Book of Memories. It has delighted me more than anything of the kind I have read since *Reveries of Childhood and Youth.*"

1914—plus some a bit later,[2] and has long been ranked by people of judgment as by far the finest memoir writing in modern English, the most distinguished in great style. I ought to be pleased, since Scribner's could scarcely go further.

We are going to the country this morning, will get Lou tomorrow, much to be done—Warren promised to join us, that leaves us free—last Tuesday I couldn't help Wales plant bulbs because I had to clean up, wash the stove etc. If Warren doesn't turn up this time I told him we'd just have to say goodbye—no hard feelings, he did much to give us a pleasant summer.

We went to Sulka's yesterday—after much looking—the ties mostly hideous as well as dear—we chose three for Ben—I pounced on the white and grey black dot one, thought it so dressy etc. Wales chose himself one he liked—the same as the red diamonds one of Ben's. I'm waiting to look around—still have the 7.50—gratefully. Wales sends love and says he's getting around to the cloth next week—has several places in mind.

Love to both of you—

Stark

696 | To Julia Young Robertson, Austin, Texas

[320 East 57th Street]
[New York]
Saturday 8.45 [October 30, 1948]

Dearest Sister,

We are going to the country in a short while, get Lou tomorrow. No news except that my speech at the Doris Keane exhibition opening[3]

2. William Butler Yeats's *Reveries over Childhood and Youth* appeared in 1915 and *The Trembling of the Veil* in 1922. Both works were printed together in 1926 as *Autobiographies*. In 1938, a third work, *Dramatis Personae* (1936), was added and the collection published as *The Autobiography of William Butler Yeats*.

3. Young paid tribute to Doris Keane at the opening of the exhibition, "Doris Keane and Her Art," at the Museum of the City of New York, October 29, 1948. The program also featured the singing of Anne Jeffreys and Lawrence Brooks, who were currently appearing in *My Romance* at the Shubert Theatre. The exhibition of Doris Keane's work continued to be shown until April 1, 1949.

was said to go very well. Several hundred people, seated in entrance hall and marble stairs and a good many standing. A trying thing to do, irregular and brief. I owed it to Doris however. Indian summer here, very mild—not even overcoats for the most part. I hope you had a good time at the wedding—at least the country club sounds fine. Love to both—Wales sends love

Stark

697 | To Allen Tate, Princeton, New Jersey

320 East 57th Street
New York
Wednesday night [November 17, 1948]

Dearest Allen,

I got back today from Ohio where I went to the burial of Wales' only brother.[4] Stayed a night over and returned to New York yesterday, or rather took the train. All very sad but I knew Wales would appreciate it on my part and it was little otherwise that I could do.

Your letter was here when I arrived and was indeed welcome.[5] I value all you say, and depend greatly on your approval. I see a good many native wits, or good sense, but writers, so far as I read them, seem to me mostly outside endurance.

I forgot to mention that last page on Hart Crane, it is remarkable and more than that.[6] We can talk of that when I see you. Monday the 29th will be right for us.[7] Wales returns Friday and we go to the country Saturday to do some closing up on the house, prevented by his absence.

4. Young refers to Samuel Andrew Bowman (1893–1948), although William McKnight Bowman had another brother, Walter Bowman (1900–1965).
5. Earlier, Young had written Tate about his newly published *On the Limits of Poetry, Selected Essays, 1928–1948*. In reply, Tate had praised Young's *Immortal Shadows* and named several essays which Tate considered "little masterpieces."
6. A reference to Tate's essay on Hart Crane's poetry.
7. The Tates had invited Young and Bowman for dinner on that date.

I ordered last week two copies each of the VA. Quarterly and so am sending two to you. If you have some already by now—which I hope you will not have troubled about—you can just keep these for me. If they are as good in the minds of you and Caroline as they are in mine I shall feel all right. At any rate please read them soon, both of you.

I am so glad my dear Caroline is all well again, she is a great woman —how rarely I should ever say that! That phrase I mean.

Ohio, two nights on the train, Scribners today and a broadcast to help the book have left me dull with a vengeance, please make allowances.

Love to you both
Stark

698 | To John Mason Brown, New York

320 East 57th Street
New York
Saturday [November 27, 1948]

Dear Mr. Johnny,

I have been away from town a good deal lately—a family friend died in Ohio etc.—and you may have been away lecturing, but I sent you an advance copy of my theatre book—*Immortal Shadows*.[8] I am very proud of the title I invented for it. I do hope and do believe you will like it. If you like it, please do all you can for it—mention it when and where you can and so on. In return there is this promise of mine— never again in print will I write on the subject of the theatre art in any form. You will, therefore, be as safe as if you were writing of Plotinus.

John, I have been intending to write and thank you for sending that matter to Scribner's.[9] I spoke of you there and my laudations were loudly received—if, therefore, your publishers are ever unsatisfactory,

---

8. Although the book was not published until November 15, Young had been sending advance copies to friends and reviewers since the first of the month.

9. In September, John Mason Brown had sent Scribner's excerpts from his essay on Young in *Upstage: The American Theatre in Performance* (1930) and had given permission to use them on the jacket of *Immortal Shadows*.

you have a standing welcome with us. You would have as aristocratic and well-bred a management as you deserve and were born to have— you old-fashioned thoroughbred under that pleasing facade etc. And so do what you can for my book, and thus salute the dead.

Love to you and Cassie.

Stark

699 | To Huntington Cairns, National Gallery of Art, Washington, D.C.

320 East 57th Street
New York
Monday [November 29, 1948]

Dear Huntington,

Thank you for sending me your astonishing anthology.[1] I have already spent many hours reading it, and am giving a copy or so for Christmas presents. A good many of the things in it are old friends, of course, but there are many I never saw before, and some I never even heard of. It is more overwhelming than even those pamphlets you used to crack my head with. I am wondering where you will break out next.

I don't think it always makes the most interesting or the most stimulating critical writing, but your idea of having practically rave notices, as they say in the theatre, for every selection from some critic or reader, some grateful admirer, is a very happy one. After all if the selection is not good why have it only to point out the fact? But it all does give a different general tone.

How that proof was all read so well beats Hell. I thought I had found one slip—Francesca speaking of Paolo says "questi," [2] I thought it must be questo. But I looked in my Dante and you are right. My Italian is not good enough to know why that is so, but so it is. One,

---

1. *The Limits of Art: Poetry and Prose Chosen by Ancient and Modern Critics,* edited by Huntington Cairns, Bollingen Series, 12 (Washington, D.C., 1948).
2. The word appears in a line from the selection "Paolo and Francesca," in *The Limits of Art,* p. 369: "questi che mai da me non fia diviso." Cairns printed a translation (p. 370) by Byron: "He who from me can be divided ne'er."

the only, mistake is due to old man Matthew Arnold. For years he put me off in this line

e la sua volontade è nostra pace[3]

and I took it as

in his will is our peace.

It is much more profound and beautiful what Dante really says

AND his will is our peace.

It was a lovely idea to put in St. John of the Cross and the Esposo poems.[4] And those touchstone lines at the end of the volume delight all one's inmost pedantry.[5]

I should never have thought of putting in the Saint Simon.[6] It reads splendidly.

There are here many examples of how impossible translations of poetry are. Shelley for instance does an inspired lyric based on the Plato Ἀστὴρ πρὶν μὲν etc.[7] but it is far from the real idea, which is much simpler and deeper but the three words about stars—aster, heos and hesperos make an insoluble problem for us in English.

I suppose everybody will mention at least one poem were in [*sic*]. I think of one especially—the Bianor

3. The line from Dante's *Paradiso* (3. 85) translated by Matthew Arnold appears in the Appendix of Cairns's volume, p. 1394.

4. Cairns included poems from "Canciones entre el alma y el esposo" by Saint John of the Cross, translated by E. Allison Peers (pp. 539–50).

5. Young refers to the Appendix entitled "Touchstones of Great Poetry."

6. The selection by Louis de Saint-Simon was "The Death of Monseigneur" from *Memoires,* translated by Bale St. John (pp. 878–84).

7. Young refers to Plato's "Aster" from *The Greek Anthology* (vii. 670), translated by Percy Bysshe Shelley (p. 170). Young calls attention to difficulties facing the English translator who tries to compress into a very brief passage the Greek allusions and associations of the boy's name Aster (star), heos (morning star), and hesperos (evening star). The Greek poem follows:

Ἀστὴρ πρὶν μὲν ἔλαμπες ἐνὶ ζωοῖσιν Ἐῷος,
νῦν δὲ θανὼν λάμπεις Ἕσπερος ἐν φθιμένοις.

Cairns printed the translation by Shelley:
Thou wert the morning-star among the living,
Ere thy fair light had fled;
But now thou art as Hesperus, giving
New splendour to the dead.

In other editions of Shelley's poetry, the third line appears as "Now, having died, thou art as Hesperus, giving."

Οὗτος ὁ μηδέν, ὁ λιτός, ὁ καὶ λάτρις, οὗτος ἐρᾶται,
κἀστί τινος ψυχῆς κύριος ἀλλοτρίης.

That seems to me one of the very final among love poems or rather poems about love. If you look in the Oxford book of translations from Greek verse you will hardly believe the silly jingle they get out of it.[8]

Well, I suppose, I feel sure, you must have enough of this, and so will leave off. Congratulations anew on such a stupendous achievement. I intend to leave my copy lying around to increase my own prestige.

Thank you for your letter about my book. I don't know what chance such a volume has or has not these days. Please ballyhoo it in conversation when you can.

Love to you and Florence, that fine being.

> Yours
> Stark

700 | To Hudson Strode, University of Alabama,
Tuscaloosa, Alabama

> 320 East 57th Street
> New York
> Thursday [December 2, 1948]

Dearest Hudson,

Thank you for a letter so generous and so full of life-giving thought and heart. Jack Wheelock showed me the letter you wrote him.[9] It was

8. The Greek poem by Bianor appears as No. 364 in *The Greek Anthology,* translated by W. R. Paton (1926), IV.11.242–43. The poem is translated: "This man, a cypher, mean, yes a slave, this man look ye, is lord of some other's soul." In *The Oxford Book of Greek Verse in Translation,* edited by T. F. Higham and C. M. Bowra (1938), the poem is numbered 598 and entitled "Unseen Riches." The translation is by Walter Leaf: "This household drudge, a slave whom all despise, / Is loved, and royal to one pair of eyes." A less poetical but more literal translation would read: "This man, a nothing, a simpleton and a slave besides, this man is loved / And is the master of another person's soul." In the Greek passage it is a man who is loved, but the sex of the lover had been left indeterminate. Young discussed the poem and the translations in *The Pavilion,* p. 142.

9. Strode had written both Wheelock and Young to express admiration for *Immortal Shadows.*

quite wonderful and he is holding it for publicity purposes etc. Dear Hudson, thank you and Therese always for everything.

I put about four months going through the mass of my reviews and combining, cutting, rewriting, so that I am doubly glad that you approve of the result. Now I have two smallish books more to write. One the memoirs up to about twenty years of age and then memoirs of people like Duse and others. They would not go together in one volume, no single tone could be established for such a combination. I should, by the way, have mentioned in that short preface that I had done considerable reworking and so on in the matter of those articles, but I honestly forgot to do so. There are things there now that have come only with the passage of the years.

I hope the days go well for you and that lovely being, Thérèse, it is not easy these days to have any inner peace or even the right kind of tumult. The morning papers are confusing and full of spiritual ruin; the evening papers are better since they are largely dirt and murder close by and more lurid and therefore more exact to a foul moment. Nevertheless, it is silly to gripe vastly against one's time, though to be in a rage against it may have results. I do not feel that I am big enough to be in a rage, and I had best endeavor to make and keep my own quality in a suitable and fecund vein.

I wish I could see you and Thérèse.

Lovingly,
Stark

701 | To John Hall Wheelock, Charles Scribner's Sons, New York

320 East 57th Street
New York
Thursday [December 2, 1948]

Dear Jack,

Thank you for sending me the Strode letter, a fine and generous one. He wrote me also.[1]

---

1. See above, Letter 700.

I have had very good letters indeed from John Mason Brown, Allen Tate, Edmund Wilson, Robert Edmond Jones, George Nathan, Brooks Atkinson, Lawton Campbell—one of the head people in the American National Theatre and Academy—Mrs. Isaacs, former editor of Theatre Arts Magazine, Louis Kronenberger on TIME, and a good many people otherwise. The reviews in the *Times*[2] and the *Herald Tribune*[3] were friendly enough; it was just the lack of interest in anything these days, and the *Times'* Mr. Nichols knows much less than anything about the theatre. It was a very callous move when the paper put him in as dramatic critic during Brooks Atkinson's absence. I hope that at least Scribner's won't lose money on this book, the book itself will hold its own in the years, but that is another matter.

It would be very nice to lunch together soon.

Yours as ever
Stark

702 | To Juliette Huxley, London, England

320 East 57th Street
New York
December 6, 1948

Dearest Juliette,

The envelope to this letter was addressed about a month after you left, and there was a page written. Something interrupted and when I returned to the letter it was so stupid that I tore it up. You were at least spared.

2. Lewis Nichols reviewed the book in "Anti-Caliban Stark Young," *New York Times Book Review,* November 28, 1949, p. 26. After noting that in the foreword Young said that he would write no more about the theatre, Nichols lamented that Young offered only reviews for his final verdict and added: "With a half-forgotten play as the subject, the essay does not carry the air of generality so much as an air of morning-after description." Nichols, who had been drama editor of the New York *Times,* wanted Young to "set down his thoughts without, as it were, yesterday's deadline."

3. Walter Prichard Eaton reviewed *Immortal Shadows* in "Theater in Perspective," *New York Herald Tribune Books,* November 28, 1948, p. 16. Eaton wrote that it is a "great pity that so keen a mind as Mr. Young's, so catholic a taste and so civilized and wide-ranging a background for appreciation, should no longer contribute to the pitifully small body of drama criticism seriously concerned with our current theater."

I had a letter from Julian about the agents et cetera, and the conclusion of his term with UNESCO, and then the trip to the far countries [4] the mention of which for no good reason perhaps always makes
me think of Julian the Apostate.[5] He is one of the people in history
who bind my attention to them, and yet I am sure he had a boring
insistence and a dirty beard—which latter the malicious Greeks or
Byzantines you may be sure pointed out.

The state of the world has us all so mixed up that a great deal of
communication between one friend and another is strained and scattered I have got so that the morning TIMES with its subtle, covered
propaganda for its point of view gives me the horrors. Michael's New
Republic is for the most part unreadable and looks too rotten for
words. Now and then a good article. Losing money, which I am told
Dorothy must make up, since Michael is not rolling in wealth. In that
case it must be only fair to say I ought to amount to something myself,
but that too is a large order. I sent my new book of theatre pieces to
the London address, and I hope you and Julian will find time to read
them some. I don't think they are the ordinary stuff written about the
theatre or the other arts for that matter. I am now on a book of memoirs, the second volume of which will be about remarkable people I
have known—Duse for example. But the first volume—not too long—
will be more personal, getting only to about twenty years old. In that
way I can keep a persistent tone. Two installments have appeared in
the Virginia Quarterly, and if the rest can come out as well and get as
high praise I should be hopeful over the results. But writing, if I get
the tone and the clear movement I want, wears me out. I don't consider most of the matter that is printed to be writing at all. And so—

I don't think this letter is much better than the one I tore up, so I
had better close. I have written the agents on a separate sheet for Julian.
I conferred with Scribner's—the world's leading publishers these days,
I should think—and got the best names I could.

Love to you both
Stark

4. In the summer of 1948, prior to the UNESCO conference in Beirut, at which
Huxley resigned as director general, he made a tour of Turkey, Lebanon, Syria, Jordan,
Iraq, Iran, and Egypt to confer with scientists and politicians.
5. The reference is to Flavius Claudis Julianus (331–363), who made military cam-
paigns in the Middle East and became a convert to paganism.

703 | To Huntington Cairns, National Gallery of Art,
Washington, D.C.

320 East 57th Street
New York
Monday [December 6, 1948]

Dear Huntington,

Thank you for your letter and that needed lesson in Italian. In a note in my Dante I saw a quotation from De Sanctis about that passage,[6] he used questi the same way, but until your explanation I did not know why. I never studied Italian except mostly reading and talking and my ignorance is immense. I do remember being told in Rome that "if one is sincere" would be sinceri.

I think despite the commentators that your French verse is much deeper. The idea of in and an is nearly the same but here is one of those divine differences that bless poetry. It would have been easy for Dante to say the in.

On the Bianor translation I challenge your legal powers—unless the poem is ludicrous the translation cannot be accurate and ludicrous. The sad, beautiful quality "lord of another's soul" is a long way from royal to one pair of eyes.[7]

My book will fall far short of any lists but I value your blessings and opinion, I should say I do.

Love to you both

Stark

I should have liked a few lines from Allen's ODE,[8] but suppose he is so honored with critical quotations that he should be puffed up as it

6. Although Young's edition of Dante cannot be identified, in his essay on "Francesca da Rimini," Francesco de Sanctis calls attention to the significance of the lines "questi, che mai da me non fia diviso, / la bocca mi baciò"—"this one, who never shall be divided from me, kissed my mouth." See *De Sanctis on Dante,* edited and translated by Joseph Rossi and Alfred Galpin (1957), p. 50.

7. See above, Letter 699 and n. 8. On December 8, Cairns replied: "I am not certain how I should express myself about Bianor. The translation is faithful to the words, but the result is, if not ludicrous, flat and tasteless."

8. Tate's "Ode to the Confederate Dead."

is. I have been delighted with the full quantity of such admirable Dryden as you have included. Most people would never even have thought of them.

704 | To Bedford and Joreta Thurman, Lafayette College, Easton, Pennsylvania

320 East 57th Street
New York
Saturday [January 8, 1949]

Dearest Cousins,

I have just got home from a lengthy visit to Texas and Monterrey, and here I find that box of candy which you should not have sent—and have eaten five pieces already. It is delicious and the thought from you is very heart-warming.

I hope life is treating you kindly. You are glad to know, I am sure, that my book, *Immortal Shadows,* is getting notable reviews, even out over the country. That in TIME did a lot of good, the tone was so generous that it surprised people and Time is so widely read.[9] Even Walter Winchell thought he must be on the band wagon and speak of it.

I think Bedford is fortunate to be in a college[1] and not batting at this bad Broadway situation. Television is now taking a crimp or promises to, so that the theatre is even less hopeful for itself.

9. Young refers to "Farewell Appearance," probably by Louis Kronenberger, in *Time,* LII (December 13, 1948), 69. Young had reason to be pleased with the estimate of his work: "Critic Young's theater reviews are probably the last writing of their kind. No periodical is currently printing anything about the theater that even resembles them. His essays, often more critical of the acting than of the play, walk through the field of esthetics, far from Broadway. He berates the doorway of a certain stage set as 'lean and trivial,' and objects to the cut of Juliet's gown. He sees the theater as a complex collection of arts, each to be weighed. His judgments reflect poetic perception, solid scholarship and standards far loftier than Times Square is accustomed to. If his writing lacks the sparkle, and sometimes the clarity, of some of his colleagues, it has a depth and substance as rare in the theater's critics as in the theater itself."

1. Thurman taught courses in speech and the theatre at Lafayette College from 1946 to 1950.

Wales sends messages to you and I do indeed wish you every happy thing this coming year.

Affectionately
Stark

705 | To Leah Salisbury, New York

[320 East 57th Street]
[New York]
Thursday [March 17, 1949]

Dearest Leah,

Thank you for the cheques and for your sweet note. Alas, I am one of those people who if they once love you as a friend are hard to lose. You are a part of my inner life, an old friend, a trusted darling and adviser, and there is nothing you can do about it, in case you wish to clean house among the people you know. Well, in that case, there will be Stark, not budged an inch, just thinking isn't that Leah, my beloved friend?

I am going to Washington—having just returned from Westchester —tomorrow till somewhere around the first—to study at the galleries there. Then back here for two or three days, then to Texas and from there to Mississippi, where on April 22 I am guest of honor at the University and so on. Then back here and to the country—where I will try to make up for the depredations of the deer, the chipmunks and the squirrels. Mr. Henry Wallace sent me a hundred of his prize strawberry plants last summer, we got eight—EIGHT—out of an abundant, fragrant crop—and who did this?—chipmunks—they strolled through our walks, each with a strawberry in his mouth. The point of these remarks is that, with Bowman and me in the country as soon as I return from the South, we are going to want—and urge—you and Phil[2] to come to see us. It's just nine miles from Bedford Village. I will tele-

2. Leah Salisbury's husband, Philip Salisbury.

phone to that effect. We spoke of it often last summer, but the days passed and life seemed to defeat time.

I suppose you have seen the remarkable reviews of my book, *Immortal Shadows*. Well, now one has come from Harold Hobson, critic for the London Sunday Times and the *Christian Science Monitor*—he says, mentioning Shaw, Ivor Brown etc. that they have not, and perhaps never have had, a critic functioning like me.[3] You will, I know, be pleased by such praise for the book.

Dear Leah, I am glad that life seems to be treating you kindly. As for me I have some more painting to do—I don't know whether you have heard that I have now a large painting in the permanent collection of the Art Institute of Chicago—supposed to be the leading modern museum in the USA—and I have had three letters, or notes, from their famous and brilliant director, Daniel Catton Rich, about my picture, and how he admires it. But art is long and life is short, vita longa—ars brevis—and I don't know at all where I am in the scheme of things.

I hope life goes well for you, and as soon as I am settled in these parts I will call you up—

Affectionately
Stark

Tell Ada[4] I think she is a good dear. You are lucky to have her. Dear Leah!

---

3. Harold Hobson (b. 1904), drama critic for the London *Sunday Times* and the *Christian Science Monitor*, reviewed *Immortal Shadows* in "Theater Critic upon Theater Critic," *Christian Science Monitor*, March 2, 1949, p. 2. Hobson wrote: "To an Englishman, the reading of Mr. Young's criticism is an immense refreshment. This criticism proceeds from a clear judgment fortified by an understanding knowledge of many phases of culture, and it is expressed in prose of unusual richness and freedom. Its warmth of eloquence is something to which, in the foggy, restrained atmosphere of London, we are unaccustomed. In London, in fact, we have not, and I doubt if we have ever had, a dramatic critic like Mr. Young, functioning in the same way." Hobson concluded that "in their collected work," such British critics as Shaw, Agate, and Ivor Brown have produced "a body of writing as informed, cultured, and erudite as Mr. Young's . . . but not . . . so sticking-to-the-subject, so vivid a record of things seen, heard, and admired." Young was later to reprint these comments on the dust jacket of *The Pavilion*.

4. Ada Ellison, Leah Salisbury's assistant.

706 | To B[ernard]. H. Haggin, New York

320 East 57th Street
New York
Friday [March 18, 1949]

Dear Bernard,

Your letter touched me and gave me a great deal of pleasure. I am one who appreciates the kind of friendly interest and support, and faith in me, that you show in your trouble about the review of my book.[5] Even without the review, I value the opinion you hold as to my writing; it means more than I can tell you in this crippling world around us now and with the complexities of my nature, which are more than some people might think from my chattering Southern outside, half mask.

I have had on the whole what are considered, I believe, tremendous reviews in New York and over the country, plus some radio and Walter Winchell. Mr. Hawkins in *Theatre Arts* wrote a really capital piece,[6] the TIME little article meant most kindly and went a long way.[7] Mr. Eaton in the *Herald Tribune* tried to manage some fairness or whatever you call it; but the overlong, for the piece in general, quotation gave what he really thinks.[8] He told Mrs. Isaacs once that he could not understand what I meant when I wrote, etc. Lately from the *Chris-*

5. At Haggin's suggestion, Margaret Marshall, literary editor of the *Nation,* had assigned Young's *Immortal Shadows* to Philip Robinson, an actor and director whom Haggin admired. Robinson reviewed the book in "Theater Critic," *Nation,* CLXVIII (March 5, 1949), 666–67.

6. William Hawkins reviewed *Immortal Shadows* in *Theatre Arts,* XXXIII (January, 1949), 79. Hawkins characterized Young's drama criticism as "illuminating, cultured, penetrating and constructive" and added that "his great and rare gift is not only to write about what he has seen, but to create it sensually."

7. See above, Letter 704, n. 9.

8. See above, Letter 701, n. 3. Eaton complained that Young was "not always far from a touch of the verbal excess which is the bane of too much modern literary criticism. Take for example this sentence from his review of 'The Green Bay Tree': 'The tone and taste arrived at in dealing with this play seemed to be unique in our theatre which with its energy, its willingness like a prostitute to oblige by the moment, and its lack of any general meaning, needs above everything (and understands least) this landscaping and subordination within a decision and perspective.'" Eaton found the passage "with some effort . . . intelligible" but a "rather dreary way to write."

tian Science Monitor came a review by a London theatre critic, Harold Hobson, whose work I don't know.[9] He could scarcely have praised the book more highly. If I can get some extra copies of that review— I have only one now—I will send a clipping to you.

It seems only fair that Mr. Eaton should find me a trial, for I have always found him, the little I have read, too flat and too stupid for words, and you probably think even worse of him.

I missed the two Carnegie Stravinsky concerts[1]—he seemed to be trying to tell me at supper after the MASS that it was pretty tame, I mean those two occasions. I wanted to hear the MASS, and Town Hall is more merciful. Mrs. Stravinsky called up that noon to greet us and said if we came to the MASS to join them afterward, with Soulima, his wife and various people. So we were talking till after eleven.

You were very good to think of inviting me to go to the concerts, and I wish you had spoken to me in the intermission at Town Hall. I usually spend little time in the lobby. In this case it must have been Harry Bull's sister[2] I was talking to, inquiring about his book, which she seemed to imply he was not bothering to write.

I hate to hear about your being so what you call hard-pressed. A long life has told me—though I nearly always forget that—one truth: when we are driven it takes much more will and effort to accomplish something that under less strain would come off more easily and often better. That is a platitude, but a sadly true one. If you could only bother with the things you are going to write about—I mean not bother with so many things till you get rested up a little—you might begin to feel better in general. That is not a graceful sentence but the thought behind it is full of grace. You are so full of fine things that are so much needed that you must not break yourself up. I really mean that small lecture. And I also mean to say now that you are one of the very few critics we have or have had who combine fine and delicate feeling with character and guts.

I have a chance to go to Washington Tuesday, in a friend's car, and

9. See the preceding letter and n. 3.
1. Igor Stravinsky had conducted the Boston Symphony in concerts at Carnegie Hall, with his son, Soulima Stravinsky, as piano soloist on February 16; and on February 26, at Town Hall, Stravinsky conducted a program of his own music, which included the American premiere of his Mass for mixed chorus. Soulima Stravinsky was again the piano soloist.
2. Identification not established.

am going for several days' look at the galleries there. I have seen them much too superficially.

Thank you again for your letter and for your interest in getting the book seen to. I only wish there were something I could be of use to you about.

This is a dull letter, but not quite as dull as I seem to feel today. Life can be too much, and this season it has seemed too often so.

I may as well sign this letter Affectionately for that is what I mean.

Stark

X

Return to the South
and Europe
1949–1953

BETWEEN APRIL, 1949, and May, 1953, the most important events recorded in Stark Young's letters are his return to Mississippi, the publication
of his autobiography or book of memoirs, a new edition of *So Red the Rose,*
and his trip to Europe. Diverse as these activities outwardly appear, each of
them relates to Young's strong desire, as he neared the end of his career, to
affirm once more the tradition and culture which he thought lay at the
center of the good life in any century and in any place. The trip to Mississippi sharpened his memories of his boyhood and enabled him to compare
what he had known in the 1890s with the changes visible at mid-century.
The memoirs Young felt compelled to write out of his conviction that "the
very last and ultimate flowering of all human experience is its sharing and
revelation." The new edition of *So Red the Rose* brought before the public
what he had already written about the life of culture and tradition in an historical framework. Finally, he welcomed the opportunity to revisit Europe,
especially Italy, because there had been the fountainhead of the classical
humanities that had been the most enduring element in his continuing
education for living.

In April, 1949, the centennial year of the University of Mississippi, Young returned to Oxford to deliver the principal address at the Southern Literary Festival. Young chose to speak on "Lights from Strange Lamps," a title which, he hoped, would suggest the enrichment that could be brought to English poetry from foreign languages. Throughout his lecture, which he delivered from memory, Young quoted extensive passages from French, Italian, Latin, and Greek literature which he related to well-known selections from English poetry. His primary objective, which became apparent as he spoke, was to document the contribution that the classics could make in the ethical, intellectual, and imaginative outlook of a highly civilized man in the twentieth century. At least for the moment, Young was resuming the role of teacher and presenting the classics as he wished they had been taught to him fifty years before in this same university. Later, in writing his autobiography, he made a similar defense of a classical education as a sound preparation for purposeful living in modern society.

The return to Oxford and the brief visit which he made to Como meant both pleasure and pain for Young. The acclaim he received at the university and his visits with friends of many years afforded him great satisfaction and very real pleasure. As he remarked afterwards, he was proud of the Southern people he saw, and he knew they were proud of him. But he was depressed by much that he observed, particularly the places that reminded him of his father, mother, aunts, and the McGehees who had taken care of him in his boyhood. As he expected, many of those he had known, both in Oxford and Como, had died, and age had made inevitable but sad changes in the faces of others. Often, while responding to the warmth of friendliness, he thought he recognized the limitations of education and talent. Throughout his stay, he sensed that this was his last visit to Mississippi. For many months, Young's letters contain references to the satisfactions he found in seeing again familiar places and faces, but even more they reflect the tension and the depression that these same scenes created in his mind. In the end, nevertheless, what remained as he wrote his account of his early life in Como and Oxford was a conviction that compared to the vulgarity and confusion in New York, the South still had excellent qualities that gave it a great potential for right living.

From Mississippi, Young returned to New York to continue to work upon the volume of memoirs that had occupied him intermittently since

1936. Already, in 1948, the *Virginia Quarterly Review* had published a substantial portion of the initial five chapters, and, in the spring of 1950, it printed what would later become the seventh chapter. The final work, completed after many revisions, contained nineteen chapters. After considering and rejecting a multitude of suggestions, Young took his title, *The Pavilion,* from a passage in the thirty-first Psalm: "thou shalt keep them secretly in a pavilion from the strife of tongues." The subtitle, *Of People and Times Remembered, of Stories and Places,* emphasized the autobiographical content of the book. When Scribner's released the volume in September, 1951, Young declared himself satisfied that his "child of endless memory and effort" was what he had wanted it to be.

In the first chapter of *The Pavilion,* Stark Young recalled seeing, as a boy in Como, a small waterfall made by the drop in the level of a culvert in front of his house. This "small descent of flowing water" became for him a symbol and an essence throughout his life and made the magnificent falls of Niagara, Mexico, Tivoli, and the American West seem merely extensions of what he already knew. The incident and the significance which Young attached to it suggest the roles of place and education as the basic themes to be developed in the book. As the narrative of his youth unfolded, Young repeatedly called attention to the relationship between his educational experiences in Mississippi and his life as a mature writer and artist in New York. In a wider sense, he sought to identify the special contributions which the South could make to a man's preparation for the good life wherever he chose to live. For Young the answer, as he had already written in *River House* and *So Red the Rose,* continued to be the "life of the affections" and the humanistic tradition.

Of these two strains, the "life of the affections" was the most difficult to convey, because it was not a matter that could be reduced to precise terms. To Young, the life of the affections was more an attitude felt but not expressed in his father's family and among the McGehees. They possessed this value system and passed it along to Young without ever speaking directly about the subject. When Uncle Hugh McGehee talked about his family, Young recalled that he had the "sense" of his uncle's "being joined to some continuous life of human affections," while at the same time having an inner, solitary life of his own. For Young, these two qualities, the individual's consciousness of his own separateness from all others and his simultaneous acknowledgment of his role in the succession from a known past into the future, lay at the heart of the Southern tradition which was the "life of the affections." Young had tried to make this point fictionally both in *River House* and *So Red the Rose;* now in *The Pavilion,* he made it explicitly in his autobiography.

Before he entered the University of Mississippi, Young recalled, his education in Como consisted more of personalities and general principles than formal schooling. He remembered vividly the family conversations that without specific mention of "love, loyalty, generosity, kindness, and honesty" led him to the belief that right living was based upon these virtues. Without knowing exactly when, he accepted them as the necessary corollaries to the "life of the affections" and the humanistic tradition that became the essence of his education at the university.

"Not solid and thorough," wrote Young about his studies at his Southern university, though he considered that his education would have been no more solid and thorough had he attended one of the great Eastern institutions. In the East, asserted Young, his education would have been more factual, more prescribed, and certainly more regimented than it was in the South. As an introduction to science, the content would assuredly have been more scientific. But, he continued, an Eastern education would also have lacked any intense commitment to abstract thought or to knowledge without regard to its practical uses. For Young, an education that exhibited these deficiencies or that emphasized psychological and scientific fads and theories contained no real preparation for the experiences that every man must face in daily living.

Young's final judgment upon his own university education was that although his professors had not been so learned, cultured, or inspiring as they should have been and though the instruction had not been so solid and thorough as he would have wished, what he learned had been a preparation for living. The books he read and the faculty who taught him affirmed the continuity of tradition, insisted upon the responsibilities of man to society, and asserted the right of the individual to his own individuality. Perhaps more than anything else, Young realized that the university experience had been the starting point of his love of the classics, his understanding of the principles of art, and his knowledge of Western philosophy. In acknowledging the contributions it had made to his later career, Young linked his Southern inheritance with classical humanism and declared the result equally valuable in Mississippi and in New York. That a writer for the *New Republic,* after reading *The Pavilion,* declared him an anachronism cast no cloud upon Young's convictions about the education that would best prepare a person to live a meaningful life in modern society.

As Stark Young's letters make clear, the writing and publication of *The Pavilion* brought him immense satisfaction. From the first, Charles Scribner and John Hall Wheelock, whose opinions Young greatly valued, had thought the autobiography a beautifully written work that would bring credit both to Young and the firm. After the favorable reception of the book from critics and nonprofessional readers, Scribner and Wheelock decided to issue a new edition of *So Red the Rose* and invited Donald Davidson to write a lengthy introduction to it. Young was doubly pleased at the publication of a new edition of the novel and the opportunity it presented him to offer suggestions about the content of the prefatory material. His letters to Davidson strongly suggest that Young felt that thematically the relationship between *So Red the Rose* and *The Pavilion* was so close that either volume could be read as a commentary upon the other. He liked the idea that, as his career approached its end, his two best nondramatic works should appear separated by only a brief period of time. The success of both helped measurably to relieve the bitterness he felt over *Artemise* and his departure from the *New Republic.*

In view of Young's defense of the classics and his statements about the enrichment that comes to an individual from a knowledge of foreign cultures, his decision to travel for six months in Europe is not surprising. At seventy-one, he thought it would be his last trip. Leaving with Bowman early in October, 1952, Young spent almost two months in Italy before going to France, England, and Morocco, then returning for an additional six weeks in Italy. His letters show how greatly he enjoyed both places and people. Despite the cold and occasional discomfort during the winter, Europe, especially Italy, remained as marvelous and wonderful to Young as it had been to generations of American artists before him who had sought there the stimulus of art, beauty, and tradition.

707 | To W. Alton Bryant,[1] University of Mississippi,
Oxford, Mississippi

320 East 57th Street
New York
April 4, 1949

Dear Dr. Bryant,

Thank you for your letters and for the kind offer to come to Memphis and drive me down to Oxford. I should like that very much indeed and will let you know from Austin, Texas as to the time I expect to reach Memphis.

The round table discussion does not appeal to me, since I don't keep up with modern verse and not much with modern or any fiction. But other performances I should be happy to try, such as conferences etc.[2]

I still think I want to make the address on translating, which to me is a very living subject. I should be talking about other languages as means by which to develop our own and to see the special points in writing, such as emphases, sound, and so on, plus a variety of qualities. I don't think I would be stuffy about all this. I can't think of a promising title. *Translations.* Or *Lights from Strange Lamps*[3] or anything you can think up.

I have asked Scribners to send the photographs, sent them your letter in fact.

Thank you again, and I am looking forward to the pleasure of meeting you.

Yours sincerely
Stark Young

1. W. Alton Bryant (b. 1907), professor of English, chairman of the department of English at the University of Mississippi, and president of the Southern Literary Festival, had written Young to ask him to address the Southern Literary Festival on April 22.

2. Bryant had suggested the possibility of presenting a round table discussion in which both Young and John Crowe Ransom would participate. The program would also include several group meetings with students and classroom lectures.

3. The title finally selected. In his address, which he delivered from memory, Young endeavored to show how a knowledge of foreign languages could enrich the study of English poetry.

708 | To Ella Somerville, Oxford, Mississippi

Waccabuc, New York
Tuesday [April 26, 1949]

Dearest Ella,

I told you my news on the telephone, but this will say again how I enjoyed my visit, and I know how much commotion a guest in the house can be. And to swing a really large party so successfully—my Lord! I have kept house enough to realize these things only too well.

There was a great deal of love and kindness in the air during my visit, and under such things I get fairly decent and sweet myself. I think you are most sensible to live in Oxford, and that you are fortunate in having a pleasant, roomy, open-seeming house. I'd be slow to leave it if I were you. And Willie May[4] is a treasure.

We are moving to the country, with our colored boy, today. Bowman has been out already. Says the ground looks very lovable and diverting, with spring flowers coming on. The inside of the house pretty awful, but the three of us will start trying to get things in place again. And I'll go back on the wagon for a few weeks. But I don't know how I'd even had got through the high-pressured days in Oxford without the benefit of your gracious bottles.

I hope you get North this summer. We'd like so much to see you with us in the country.

Would you ask Phil Stone to send the MS.[5] to me here (Waccabuc, N.Y.) and say how sorry I am to have forgotten it. I put it downstairs to remember it and then rushed off without it.

I am writing a line to Professor,[6] to thank him for the driving etc.

Please take care of yourself—and let me repeat how much I appreciate the loving pains you had bestowed on my little offerings to the museum. Even the night cap looked important. The Empress Marie

---

4. Willie Mae Buford, maid and cook.
5. A manuscript written by Emily Whitehurst Stone (Mrs. Philip Stone, b. 1909) which Young had been asked to recommend to a publisher.
6. James Hector Currie (b. 1917), then associate professor of law at the University of Mississippi.

Louise's handkerchief was beautifully shown. All that means special care and trouble and I do thank you.

Take care of yourself.

Affectionately
Stark

709 | To Julia Young Robertson, Austin, Texas

320 East 57th Street
New York
Monday [May 2, 1949]

Dearest Sister,

We came in town last night and now I have the typewriter to send you some news about Como, Oxford and all. I will make it briefish, for there are a good many items.

Como, we arrived in Memphis almost on time, Cousin Cad sat in the car, Edward, Cornelia and her daughter—who looked like some lady from the New York East side dressed for a matinee, that is Eula of the circus hypnotism—and various children. Then Edward and Cousin Cad drove down to the house. Dee,[7] the wife from Penn., is a perfectly good child, not common, and all right for Edward. They have a year old baby, about whom the whole house is crazy, especially Cousin Jennie, who takes charge of him. She is a shrunken little old woman now, very darling at that, a saint in the maternal aura or direction. Cousin Cad mostly without teeth, still a wonderful person, pleased at your present, said fine things about you and Ben. Next day Cousin Wheeler and Cousin Annie and Waller. Cousin W toothless and repeating everything, 84. Cousin Annie as spry as a cricket, Cousin Waller like a pale monkey, the small face withered, but devoted to Cousin Annie and happy to be with her. Waller Taylor working in a cotton firm in Memphis, lives in Senatobia, commutes daily with other young men, has a wife from Oxford, Sisk, a handsome girl, teaches in

7. Delores Darabod Nelson (Mrs. Albert Edward Nelson, Jr.).

the schools of Senatobia. Then there were Caroline and her husband, harmless enough and Sallie Tait with her husband, a little neat man. Waller Taylor thanked me for the money I gave him in New York, and Cousin Wheeler spoke of how much they appreciated your being so nice to Wheeler when she was in Austin. Ella came for me at three and there were so many cars of cousins at the place that she thought it was a parking lot. Then farewells—to Cousin Cad that was sad for me, I don't think I shall see her again. They said she perked up for me, but at that she could hardly walk even with a stick, though she drove the car and expressed her mind with force. I stopped at Helen Pointer's, a very pretty youngest daughter there, and various offsprings, sons and so on. The cemetery is messed up with the mowing etc. The large bush on our lot killed by fire. But the lot looked well, in general. Stopped by Cousin Mary Taylor's. Gaga at 83, but very gentle and kind. Messages to you. Agnes came up to Cousin Cad's—with Hugh McGehee Taylor his little boy—very sharp and nice—and a plump wife—divorced when he married her—he is a successful farmer Cousin Cad says, and the Methodist preacher from Como—simple enough for Annie and John or Chester—what a world!—Agnes was well dressed, with a pince nez too I think, and grey waved hair and false teeth that stretched her mouth—nice enough looking, very like one of those Great Lakes Club women, modern versions to the girls Grant Wood paints. Asked many nice things about you. Grace and Monroe live near Cousin Cad, but she said it might be well not to see them, a grandson of five lately died in his sleep, a heavenly child it seems, adored by everybody, and they are wrecked, go to the cemetery every day and all that. Poor human creatures, it does seem they might be spared some things. Cousin Cad said she had never seen a young child so engaging and so beloved by everybody.

In Oxford we had dinner at Ella's, then a visit from the Bishops, then Phil Stone would have us there, with a writer from Tenn., whose name hit me wrong from the start and I can't remember it. Next day at ten the poetry reading, John Crowe Ransom, awarding of prizes, etc., then I had to talk half an hour to a drama class, then a great luncheon at the University Cafeteria, with speeches, then a round table discussion of modern writing, from which I absented myself to go home and dress again etc., then at four there was a reception at the Chancellor's, I had to stand in line to 5.45, then go to the Bishops, then to the so called banquet—always table of honor and speeches from various men—then around 8.30 to the hall where there was to be the speech by me. Mr. Bishop introduced me, a long professor speech, familiar and homey, and kind, and it let things settle, warmed my heart and helped make the occasion easy. The hall was soon full, then chairs in the aisles, then in front by the stage, then in the hall outside from the hall, then people sitting in the windows. The hall was easy to speak in, the audience our own people, loved still by me, and attention was remarkable. I really gave them a talk that would have been a compliment to any audience, but I have faith in such things, if the heart is right and one knows the subject of the remarks and feels it inside it can be made to secure itself in the listening minds, often of very simple people. At any rate the attention was heartbreaking—such watching, such listening—so that I was almost at the point of being ashamed of myself for not being better. But I really did the best talk I ever did, and in the place I would most want to do it. I was extra glad for the sake of you and Ben, who would have wanted it like that.

Next morning the museum,[8] really beautifully done, I think you have a place to leave some of the things you and Ben have to leave, and everything there is in fine taste, the cases excellently chosen and arranged, the whole thing well bred and in fine tone, not to say professional fittings. It seems that some of the money came from the discovery of bauxite and other mineral on some land belonging to Mrs. Bowie's husband's estate, in Arkansas, and Miss Kate will leave more. I hope I will die with a little for them to have.

Miss Ella Wright looks as plasterish as ever, mildly common and embalmed, Miss Elma fat in the face and as of the same general superficiality, Mr. Bishop at 79 spry in the mind, an effect of noble mind and spirit, and Mary Hartwell is wonderful with him, watches to see he does not fall, hiding the watching. Therese is in bad shape, I did not see her, penicillin every day, the bones in the jaw wasting away. Ella says she will not stay with her or Nina, only at Mary Hartwell's whose house is large but has few rooms, and it is all very sad and difficult.

The film of Bill Faulkner's new novel just finished so far as Oxford shootings go.[9] The whole thing went off with dignity and good re-

8. The Mary Buie Museum.
9. *Intruder in the Dust.*

sponse all round. The lead of the women is Eliz. Patterson.[1] You saw her in So Red the Rose, where they made her do everything she knew was wrong, but she is a fine actress. Very fine at her best. She had been doing the grandest talking about me, so all the movie grandees came to the lecture, etc.

Nina had me to lunch Sunday before I left. The place is lovely and in great style. I was proud of her.

Many flowers in Austin [*sic*]. The place is huge, more new buildings than I had a chance to see. A long street to the southwest of the Univ. of fraternity houses, the Sigma Chis had asked to see me, etc., so after the speech and greetings and the autographs, I went there. Well bred young men, I was proud of them. They said plenty of intelligent things.

Oxford is so busy with buses, cars, streets and so on that I got no impression of it at all.

It was a good thing you did not try it, though many people said they wished you had come and all that. Ella has a room and bath on the first floor rented to a young professor,[2] very nice, and the only guest room I had. Mary Hartwell's house is crowded with a lot of daughters and grandchildren and Therese and Mr. Bishop's old age etc. The minutes were occupied and nothing made any sense unless you were immediately involved. Even the Friday was jumbled, but I suppose that happened because the terms of the visits often made more than one day impossible. As for Como, Cousin Cad may not live long and I advise you not to visit there. My room upstairs was rather dank, sleep none too good, and things in general chaotic. Mary Hartwell looks still very lovely in the face, only a sagging underchin, which could be greatly helped by a velvet such as I gave Mrs. Rice. The Somervilles are the real thing, and it is a privilege to see them again and to confirm one's memories of them.

You and Ben will be pleased to know that I have a $1200 cheque for two pictures sold to a Tait and Hall client and that Mr. Rehn thinks

---

1. Elizabeth Patterson (1874–1966), actress, born in Savannah, Tennessee, began her acting career with the Ben Greet Players in 1905 and made her Broadway debut in 1910 as Hermia in *A Midsummer Night's Dream*. During the 1930s and 1940s, she appeared in a number of plays and motion pictures, including the screen adaptations of *So Red the Rose* and *Intruder in the Dust*.

2. James Hector Currie.

he has sold the white peony painting for $900. I have to pay a third in commissions but even then it is some money and also the fact of appreciation, and the fact too of the effort or gesture on the part of Diane Tait. That last I value greatly. This kind of thing always reminds me of the thing Ben did in relation to the Chicago exhibition. That has helped me no end. That gesture of Ben's is one of the half dozen things I most appreciate in my whole life. It is not only a matter of kindness, the rare thing that enters it is imagination. Appreciation of kind, profound actions like that is always difficult, and is an example of how many things lie silent or muted in the heart, as life goes on, muted so often and not very articulate. Loathsome people are often proud of what they "cannot say," but I am ashamed only when I cannot say it. Madame de Maintenon [3] said sincerity does not consist in saying a great deal but in saying all. But what a problem.

Betsy looked in the Bendel neighborhood without fruits. I am sending the pages from our directory—from the start to the finish, since sometimes the upholsterers have fabrics on hand—I hope you can find your man.

Please forgive all the typing errors, I have too many letters left to answer and sacrifice neatness to news, which you want to learn I am sure. I certainly miss you and Ben more than if I had not been there at all.

Lovingly
Stark

3. Young recalls a letter from Francoise d'Aubigne, Marquise de Maintenon (1635–1719), mistress and second wife of Louis XIV, to Madame de Saint-Périer, October 21, 1708: "La franchise ne consiste pas à dire beaucoup, mais à dire tout, et ce tout est bientot dit quand on est sincère, parce qu'il ne faut point employer beaucoup de paroles pour ouvrir le coeur"—*Lettres sur l'education* (1854), p. 279. The passage may be translated: "Frankness does not consist of saying a great deal, but in saying everything, and this everything is soon expressed when one is sincere, because it is not necessary at all to use many words to open the heart."

710 | To Ella Somerville, Oxford, Mississippi

> 320 East 57th Street
> New York
> Tuesday [May 3, 1949]

Dear Ella,

I wrote you yesterday but Warren,[4] our Florida luxury, does not know whether he got it posted or mixed it up with the waste paper—two very different things obviously—and so I am writing again. He has not come today at all.

I still feel most grateful for your hospitality, and all that gentle, thoughtful concern and trouble. I thought of sending you a bottle of Tabac Blanc to remind you of my appreciation—if it can still be bought—but then I thought it would be more lasting to paint you a flower picture. I have ordered the frame from one of the two leading makers in New York and hope it will be becoming to the picture and your walls. The picture is now begun and may be finished soon or in quite a long while. I let them rest if they do not quite suit me, and then keep going back to them, and never know just when all that will come out right, if ever. If never, then to the ash can, though I rarely abandon a picture in that manner. So, sooner or later, and I hope it will be beautiful. I told Professor to tell you about the sale of three paintings that was awaiting me here as news. One landscape and two flower paintings.

I sent that darling Miss Spencer[5] a message in the letter yesterday, but in case Warren lost the letter, I will repeat. I have not seen anyone in a long time that I liked so much at once—I mean new people of course—and tell her that it was her eyes so full of wild flights and the glass so full of your bourbon that made me tease her. Please not to think me a fresh old man. After I knew who she was I could see the likeness between her and the photograph on the book I have. But what

---

4. Butler and cook for Young and Bowman.
5. Elizabeth Spencer (Mrs. John Rusher, b. 1921), novelist, born in Carrollton, Mississippi, was teaching English at the University of Mississippi. She had just published her first novel, *Fire in the Morning*. Subsequently, she has written *This Crooked Way* (1952), *The Voice at the Back Door* (1956), *The Light in the Piazza* (1960), *Knights and Dragons* (1965), *No Place for an Angel* (1967), *Ship Island and Other Stories* (1968), and *The Snare* (1972).

a silly mess, for she is many times more charming looking than that rather sulky bit of art. And her book is full of real talent. I wish her well and hope she goes far with her work. You have real friends, Ella, and you deserve them.

Now for a favor—please tell Mrs. Bondurant, if she is still alive, that I was sorry not to find a moment in which I could come and pay my respects. When you realize that I have been forty-two years away from Oxford, it is something that I could remember my own name. And I don't always know who is dead and who is not, though that same is true of the people here I often run into, they themselves are not always sure they are alive—how right they are!

And would you send me the full name of my Sigma Chi brother Napier.[6] I want to thank him for their little sweaty party—men coming in from a dance and blowing hard—and very nice and to the credit of the State. Good manners. Bless our Southern people, I wish I could do more for them.

Dr. Bryant has written me a very fine letter saying in his opinion and that of various others that was the finest lecture he had ever heard. Very kind. If anywhere in the world I'd like my words to go right it would be there in my own country.

Julia writes that she has a wonderful letter from you. I am glad to have her hear these things, because one of the reasons for putting up a fair front is to warm the hearts of those who love us. My dear sister has survived such sorrow as breaks your heart even to remember, and all the while I can do little that would help. Not long ago a letter came from Vienna saying that a great sentence in *So Red the Rose* was that we should in the South think less of what we have lost materially and more of what we have loved. A famous dancer of the Isadora Duncan [7] school has just read that book of mine and has sent me a message that it deals beautifully with all life and is a perfect book. Be that as it may, the novel of *So Red the Rose* will for a long time fortify and reassure Southern hearts, I hope.

---

6. John Hawkins Napier III, president of Eta Chapter of Sigma Chi Fraternity at the University of Mississippi.

7. Isadora Duncan (1878–1927), American dancer, after successes in London and Paris, established a school of dancing for children, near Berlin. In 1921, she opened a dancing school in Moscow and a year later married Sergei Esenin (1895–1925), a Russian poet. Shortly before her death in an automobile accident, she published her autobiography, *My Life*.

Phil Stone has sent his wife's story,[8] which I will read and return today. She has good qualities and is alive, and so may they rest in peace. What is peace? The most touching of all inscriptions on monuments is that often found in Italy.

Maria etc.

Implora pace

She asks for peace.

Instead of a lot of bourgeois stuff on New England Yankee egoists' tombs—usually meagre cheap ones that pass for conservative taste but as often as not are merely thrift, etc.

I am writing Miss Kate, that saint and darling. She is as remote as music, as untouched as roses in a garden, as real and human as the blood, she is an illustration of what I have sometimes said—goodness is the highest form of imagination. In medieval times we would have cut her into bits and put her into reliquaries, but in our times, instead of those objects in which the invitation to worship was implicit, we have substituted silly evasions and justifications of semi-human science, *never proved*—and thus we come out as we began at the loose end of the horn. What horn? (Ask Professor, and explain to him first that it is not the Roman horn, just plain exploitative cornucopia). You have to be careful with professors—remembering the poem in the Greek anthology—

All Cretans are liars except Cryntas, and Cryntas is a Cretan.[9] Think over that poem and consider.

I had the most lovely letter from Mary Hartwell, full of her exquisite wisdom, and making me think of Dante's definition of poetry —the loving use of wisdom. I have been over the world a great deal, as you know, and one of the objectives of my research has been to justify the inheritance I had at the beginning, and if I were right in my energy I would tour the South explaining this cheap thing that the North has to give. Unwillingly the South gives up its dream, and

---

8. See above, Letter 708 and n. 5.

9. Young's translation resembles the version given by J. W. Mackail in *Select Epigrams from the Greek Anthology* (1890), p. 241: "All Cilicians are bad men; among the Cilicians there is one good man, Cinyras, and yet Cinyras is a Cilician." Other versions of the epigram, attributed to Phocylides, include that which Paul appears to quote in Titus 1:12: "One of themselves, even a prophet of their own, said, The Cretians are always liars, evil beasts, slow bellies."

strangely the substitutes create only a Yankee disturbance and despair and silly frustration, despised by the civilized world in Europe and empty of even the comforts of a cheap roadside tavern.

If you want to use any of these remarks in an interview or a Memphis newspaper please feel free to do so. And could you, dear Ella, when you send me the name of the Sigma Chi brother, send me the full name of that fat fellow who represents pleasantly *The Commercial Appeal?* Flower?[1]

And so, till I get that painting done, farewell, and thank you again.

Lovingly
Stark

711 | To John Hawkins Napier III, Sigma Chi House, Oxford, Mississippi

320 East 57th Street
New York
May 10, 1949

Χαῖρε—but I am not sure I should write in Greek—Brother Napier— I want to thank you and your, and mine, brothers in Sigma Chi for your cordial gathering.[2] How patiently the young blood came back from the dance to pay their respects! Alas, my memory is so good that I can recall with what horror we dreaded these returns, with what young pangs we mourned the loss in some brother returning of the fresh morning of which we presumed he had once presented in his soul. That was an impression that was more a credit to our youthful faith than to his adult failure. How dreary the boys are who go out to success in the world! Those who achieve it may have a successful cackle, as it were, the rest fade into the dull nest of everyday hennery and bathos.

1. Paul Abbott Flowers (b. 1905), teacher, reporter, and columnist, had been associated with the Memphis *Commercial Appeal* since 1943 as book editor and writer of a popular literary column, "Paul Flowers' Greenhouse."

2. Young refers to his visit to the Sigma Chi fraternity house after his lecture at the University of Mississippi; see above, Letter 709.

I am sure from your general quality that you have some writing up your sleeve. In my case I remember Plato

Αἱ Χάριτες τέμενός τι λαβεῖν ὅπερ οὐχὶ πεσεῖται

ζητοῦσαι, ψυχὴν ηὗρον 'Αριστοφάνους.[3]

and I should be glad always to be of use to you with my beloved publishers—the most distinguished in the modern world—Scribners or elsewhere if I can.[4] Just let me know.

Please remember me to the brothers, and say I was delighted to observe their unfailing endurance and good manners—rare and undesired in these brave, dirty days. I am through them doubly proud of my State.

With cordial regards, I am

Yours sincerely
Stark Young

712 | To Ella Somerville, Oxford, Mississippi

Jenny Mead
Waccabuc, New York
Wednesday [June 8, 1949]

Dearest Ella,

This paper will puzzle you—the stationery man printed the name of this place wrong. It's one word—*Jennymead*—named for my great-great grandmother, 1760, in Vermont, descended from the same William Mead—he landed in Greenwich or Stamford 1635—that the family owning this land are—we bought from them and I knocked them over telling them more about the Meads than they knew—(I didn't say our Yankee kin had never thrilled us). But I think I told

---

3. J. W. Mackail, in *Select Epigrams from the Greek Anthology* (3rd ed., rev.; 1911), p. 179, translates the epigram: "The Graces, seeking to take a sanctuary that will not fall, found the soul of Aristophanes."

4. Young wished to encourage Napier's interest in writing. Napier replied that despite his desire to write, he had decided upon a military career in the Air Force.

you all this. Thank you for your sweet, generous letters and for the clipping. I belong, or subscribe to a high-priced clipping service, but since the two pieces in the Memphis paper they have sent me nothing —not a clipping that covered my Oxford visit, and there must have been brief ones at least in Memphis or New Orleans.

Your painting will soon suit me, I hope. Mrs. Tinker (of the Chase National—with a huge house on Long Island, another in Vermont, one in Nassau, and an apartment in New York—and what's more interesting a really lovely person—with a nice, peevish retired Wall Street husband) sent me word she'd buy a flower painting in a minute. She is coming by here tomorrow and I may show her yours to see if the general subject, the size, etc. are what she wants hers like. (I'm not selling her yours however).

I appreciate all those kind thoughts of me in Oxford, I do indeed.

Ella, I mailed a box to you yesterday for the museum. I picked up lately a communion set such as the itinerant preachers used a hundred years ago—riding about where there was not much of a church sometime, much less a service. And also to take to the sick or dying. It's the only one I ever saw in this country. The locale for it was Kentucky. It can be stored if need be till the museum is larger. I thought it had real historical point for our part of the world. Tell Miss Kate—bless her heart—not to trouble to thank me.

I had such a sweet letter from Nina—her place, the taste and the way it was run made me feel very proud, of her and of the South.

Give my love to the Bishops and to Therese—remember me to Professor—quite a person—and to that nice Spencer. And forgive a dull letter.

Love to you
Stark

713 | To Charles Scribner, Charles Scribner's Sons, New York

Waccabuc, New York
June 13, 1949

Dear Charlie,

I appreciated your letter and am sorry you were troubled about my disappointment in the sales.[5] Bookstores and people talked as if many copies were selling. But such is life, and I must be satisfied with the most remarkable *succes d'estime* that the book enjoyed. I think it will last as a book. I hope you lost not too much money on it. Max told me once that Scribners had never lost on me.

I hope you saw the most friendly review in The Nation a week or so back.[6]

As to the proof charges, thank you for the offer to split matters.[7] But when I asked to have in the contract a chance for some additions I meant additions, and the cost of them would not come to a half. Some of the other heavy corrections were due to the nature of that sort of book, where there are so many details and so many accessory thoughts coming up. They were due in part, too, to the fact that the the Scribner proof-reading was none too good and mine no better. I think a third and not a half would cover what I really had in mind when I asked for that indulgence of additional matter. I am, therefore, enclosing the

5. On June 3, 1949, Scribner had written to enclose the report of the sales of *Immortal Shadows* and express his apprehension that Young would be disappointed in them.

6. Young refers to Philip Robinson's review of *Immortal Shadows* in "Theatre Critic," *Nation*, CLXVIII (June 11, 1949), 666–67. Robinson praised Young for focusing "on what was taking place on the stage not only a profound and cultivated mind but a specific theater sense, a developed eye and ear for the various arts of the theater, for which he had a deeply felt passion and about which he had acquired vast technical knowledge. He was able to see a dramatic production as a composite of elements of which the written play was only one, and could evaluate the specifically theatrical elements by the degree of their success in realizing the dramatic idea of the written play."

7. In his letter of June 3, Scribner suggested that because of the impossibility of separating time spent by compositors for alterations in the text and time spent by them for additions at the end of paragraphs which Young's contract gave him the option of making, Scribner's would divide the total cost ($292.09) of all changes equally between author and publisher. After making this proposal, Scribner indicated the firm would abide by whatever Young thought was equitable. For the terms of the contract, see above, Letter 689 and n. 7.

cheque for $194.73, deducting 97.36 as one third, and this seems equitable enough.

Meantime I can add to the profits on the book that most happy and understanding contact I enjoyed with you and Jack Wheelock. And Miss Emerson[8] was always most considerate.

Thank you again for your letter, and the only thing I add further is to say not to let the book get out of print.

Affectionately yours
Stark

A dreadful looking page—the country dampens the paper and blotter.

714 | To Allen Tate, Princeton, New Jersey

Waccabuc, New York
July 3, 1949

Dearest Allen,

I have been intending to write you and Caroline to let us know when you'd happen to be in New York and would run out to see us. It would be a happy event in my life, believe me, and in Wales'—who admires you both very much.

Perhaps you have seen the enclosed,[9] perhaps not. Since Mark Van Doren has such a fine, gentle face and since you liked him, I have always held him in excellent esteem. This review seems to me to be written in a soft-minded, easy chair, professor style that is quite disgusting, and some of the points are either from stupidity or pious gullibility. I was the one that started Frost off at University classes. I persuaded Mr. Meiklejohn to that for *six months*. Frost worked tubercular pallor, mussed hair, sensitive feelings to get it all extended—against, I think

---

8. Barbara Jane Emerson (b. 1920) was publicity director for Scribner's from 1945 to 1949.

9. Mark Van Doren's "Our Great Poet, Whom We Read and Love: In His 'Collected Poems' Robert Frost Again Speaks to Us All," a review of *Complete Poems of Robert Frost, 1949*, in *New York Herald Tribune Books*, May 29, 1949, pp. 1, 11.

Mr. Meiklejohn's better judgement. I know very well Frost's poses, his grudging and jealous (and piously admitted) narrowness about other *living* poets, etc. I don't dislike him but this solitary thinker and humorist business [1] makes me laugh, remembering his conversations (for a time he quite loved me). (That was before he came to Amherst to find I had all the good students.) So if I am wrong about those marked lines and about the Van Doren essay it just shows I'd better shut up, and am not a judge of poetry at all.

John Ransom was very nice indeed to see in Mississippi,[2] and made a warm, right, perfect morning talk to the young writers.

Love to you both
Stark

715 | To Eric Bentley, New York

Waccabuc, New York
July 5, 1949

Dear Eric,

I was much pleased to have your letter of June 29. You to me are one of the luminous people, a fine scholar, a warm heart, a rich gift of expression—may it all remain yours and give you a life that lives always more abundantly.

I am sorry to hear of the divorce—but no outsider can pass on such things—Every heart hath its own sorrows, as Jesus knew. I hope things take a turn that will be right and desired for both you and that lovely Maja.

1. Young objected to Van Doren's paragraph about Frost's treatment of the modern themes of "isolation, the world forsworn, the pleasure of being misunderstood, the scorn of folk, and the resolution to understand oneself." Van Doren wrote that "no one else has handled them as he [Frost] has, with humor so that they seemed common, and with drama so that they became exciting. Every great poet has humor in him somewhere." Van Doren concluded: "Robert Frost's isolation is everybody's isolation. And lo, it is not isolation at all. It is terribly and laughably common."

2. John Crowe Ransom had appeared with Young on the program of the Southern Literary Festival at the University of Mississippi.

Your plan for an anthology sounds fine and I hope goes forward well. As to the Chekhov selections, my offer stands of course. You are free to use anything of mine and always without any fees. I will write French & Co.—who now own the translations—that I'd like you to use them free of any fees. What they will say to that I don't know. They have that very fine and warm soul there, Garrett Leverton, as editor of the literary department. Meantime you write them, will you, quoting my saying that so far as I am concerned there are no fees, etc.

I'd suggest Eric, that you do something with my translations of Molière's *George Dandin*. Nobody owns it—you could have it for nothing, and I would be glad to go over that translation and check it. It has startlingly *modern* values and implications. Most French admirers—in Paris—of Molière have, I find, no idea of it, and are thus excited when I expound, etc. If you have some decision—which you could make quite startling about this Molière piece—I'd be glad to go over the translation and *present* it to you as a gift.

John Ransom made a perfect speech for a morning session with authors at the University of Mississippi. I had to leave before he began to read his poems—I was subject to a mistake in the drama department—but I admired what he was doing, my heart rose to him, my mind wished him well.

As to writing about the theatre—for the review—I am through with all writing about the theatre. If what I have written won't help, nothing will help—if I have not shined, I won't again shine. So all ends well—(if you don't care what you say).

The thought of the memoirs gives me much pleasure—I will write John about that. The two published chapters had an astonishing success, a great success. Dear Eric, I hope life is treating you kindly, and that you will continue to believe in great things. There is always Leonardo da Vinci's line—

lo fingo grande cose [?].

Yours affectionately
Stark Young

716 | To Ella Somerville, Oxford, Mississippi

Waccabuc, New York
Monday [July 11, 1949]

Dearest Ella,

I'd not take anything for Willie Mae calling the communion cup a jigger[3]—what a good story! (Did you all work out the screw top of the container for the wine?)

Professor's MS is in Scribner's hands and I am sending him tomorrow the reply from the literary editor—who says he will read it when he gets back from vacation.[4] It keeps going quite cleverly as to certain developments, but the characters and the human interests are never really developed, and the hero and heroine are in bed—*quite, quite indeed,* I may say warningly—without our having any real picture of either—the woman especially. Then we get back to local politics, a newspaper mind, and the book ends. Plenty of brains may be said to lie behind the whole piece, but writing has its necessities, if a response is to be secured, and Professor is innocent of them.

Well I did a kind thing and that's that. Partly because he is a superior man and partly because of his relation to you there in the house. Art is cruel, however we may be kind about it—its necessities and requirements are almost precisely biological. *Ars longa vita brevis* is a terrible Latin saying. Democratically any man has the right to sing at the Metropolitan, if he only has the throat. What a world! The throat!

Now here's a problem you can help me with and I know will be glad to. Is the library at the U. of M. built already, or building, or only in prospect?[5] When you inform me as to this, I will take up with Mr. Bishop, or *whoever you think,* the matter of my portrait there. Abram Poole, a very well known portrait painter, who has done many famous people, *asked* to do mine—not his usual $3000 to $5000—gave it to me, *framed*—what frames cost now!—and I sent it to the Natchez shows

3. See above, Letter 712.
4. Young had requested John Hall Wheelock to read a manuscript by Professor Currie. On July 6, Wheelock wrote that he would read the manuscript upon his return, August 1, from his vacation.
5. Although ground was broken for the University of Mississippi library on November 6, 1948, actual construction of the building did not begin until about the middle of 1949.

or whatever they have. They are the bottom of all ignorance—what a rotten old place!—and I am going to get the portrait back through Mrs. Ferriday Byrnes—a darling, fine person—if only there were more of them in Natchez—can arrange this for me. A man here—Colonel Campbell—head of many leading radio ventures, and one of the heads of the American National Theatre and Academy, wants it very much. I'd rather give it to my own university. If you'll find out about the library and its present state and tell me, I'll take the matter up with Mr. Bishop or the right people. Somebody snugged up to me and said what about a painting of mine for the library? I said yes, et cetera, but of course my dealer at present would be furious and say if your alma mater wants it she should *buy* it—so I merely grinned appreciation.

Your little painting will be sent soon. I keep saving it partly to keep touching at it—I saw yesterday showing it to a leading decorator that a little blue needed to be in a certain spot—but people are moved by it, and I am so glad for you to have it. In about a week I'll get it off to you—and it's not so overwhelming at that—but it has in it a dream supported by some technique. In your picture you can be sure that most of the places that look splashing and fast have been done over many times. I am constantly tempted to try for some extension of the vision or mood. Well, after all, a good number of our very top painters have liked the result, my paintings that is. I will go down to my grave admired by the best, muddled by the many, and sick at my heart. So what?

I hope our Spencer is working on another book. She has real talent and real creative pressure—and will see what torment lies in the path of anyone who means to be really creative. Remember me to her and tell her those starry, Shelley eyes may or may not deceive us.

Finally dear Ella, don't mention Professor's MS. and its case to anybody. Else I'd have wasted my unexhilarated labors—done most because of his relation to you and because he is a nice man and was very kind to me.

Love to you all

Stark—

Not reread, this screed and rubbish. If you can't read this you are lucky.

717 | To Ella Somerville, Oxford, Mississippi

Waccabuc, New York
Thursday [July 21, 1949]

Dearest Ella,

That was such a fine letter, and I am sure your analysis of Professor was both kind and exact. In Waugh and that Aldous—brother of one of my best friends and a sweet, mystical, brilliant man,[6] are in my opinion misleading models for Professor. Even the front line of his chucked little figure shows that. At any rate I enclose the letter from Jack Wheelock, the literary editor and arbiter of Scribners since Perkins died, that wonderful genius in editing and the most famous literary editor in English, and a close and loving friend of mine. You can send the letter or give it to Professor, showing my efforts. That is that. It would be funny if Wheelock found the MS worth publishing, but that I do indeed doubt. All this except the outward form and tone of W's letter is between us of course.

Your painting has finally gone off. The delay has been partly because I keep seeing a form or tone I wanted to change or create and partly because I wanted to show it to various visitors. I am glad to say it met with approval from all of them and I do hope it will give you pleasure.

Don't be discouraged by that extra shiny look. It will soon dim down, and it is necessary to bring the colors to their full light and to keep out the dirt in the air.

Get hold of some POPPY OIL, at any art department and if the painting looks dull do not pile more varnish on it. Just wipe it up with a soft cloth or cotton and poppy oil. The added varnish in time only yellows a painting. You could do this also to the portraits etc. you have already.

Open a corner of the box carefully, the painting faces one side, close to the beaver board. If anything has happend to it, just ship it right back and I will make the reform.

The one thing you can thank me for and pray for my soul because

---

6. Young refers to the novelists, Evelyn Waugh (1903–66) and Aldous Huxley, brother of Julian Huxley.

of the Goddamns I spent on it is the packing. I had the boards and excelsior fortunately, but not the tools, hence the crude look, and it took me several hours to get it done. That is a real offering, believe me. But even that was easier than getting it to New York and packed. Fortunately some frames had just arrived from an expert packer—at a price—and that gave me an idea of how to proceed, as you can see from the marks inside the beaver board covers.

There is a little box for Nina. It has no great value, but is early eighteenth century Venetian. I know because I bought it at the sale of the collection of Mrs. Emily Hapgood,[7] twenty years ago. She always had a heavenly palace in Venice, near Santa Maria Salute, where she went every summer, and used to return home with these things, large and small. Finally she went abroad for good—and died—and hence the sale. Modern Italian faince is quite different from this. Not necessarily better or worse—that depends—but different.

Mrs. Hapgood was a genius in her own way. She put John Barrymore, Robert Edmond Jones and others on the public map of art, and got small thanks for it. And one of the few things I ever did that I like myself for was that I wrote her to Rome, a few months before she was to die, it turned out, and told her how wonderful she was and how

---

7. Emilie Bigelow Hapgood, daughter of Anson Bigelow, Chicago banker, married Norman Hapgood in 1896. For many years they lived in New York but were divorced in 1915. Active in theatre circles as president of the Stage Society, sponsor, producer, and scene designer, in 1917, she produced John Galsworthy's *The Little Man*, G. K. Chesterton's *Magic*, and Ridgeley Torrence's *The Rider of Dreams, Granny Maumee*, and *Simon the Cyrenian*. On February 15, 1930, Mrs. Hapgood died in Rome, and on March 5, 1930, an unsigned editorial in the *New Republic*, which may have been written by Young, paid tribute to her personality and contribution in terms similar to Young's comments in this letter: "Only those on the inside can have an exact idea of the part Mrs. Hapgood played; and it remains to be seen how much we shall hear from the leading actor or so, the diverse lesser lights of our stage, and playwrights, designers, adapters, scene-painting establishments, producers and foreign innovators whom she discovered or believed in, and backed with her influence, her money, while it lasted, and her own great discernments. . . . She was one of those people so rare in the theatre, who care nothing for anything connected with a work of art except that it be beautiful and exalted. There was in her spirit a kind of magnificent blindness to the small or incidental or even practical; a strange, bold mysticism, a sort of baroque richness or soul; and a faith which, once aroused, was like a child's or a mad saint's. In the theatre she saw but forgot commonness, and thought only of how it might have luster, invention, wonder and a high, adventurous power. In an artist she looked to find if there was a necessity present by which the shine and glory she loved should appear in him. In life she loved vision, poetry, oblivion and splendor"—*New Republic*, LXII (March 5, 1930), 56.

wonderful she had been for many people. (Meanwhile the sour fact remains that she got rid of six or eight millions.) I think this is interesting matter for Nina, whose house has such distinguished taste as made me very proud, to remember.

I put in also a Victorian fan for Mary Hartwell that I came by not so long ago. It is no treasure, but is sweet and is full of the taste and choice material of that period when nice people got into it. I hope it gives that sweet, lovely Mary Hartwell a little pleasure, at least as a memento of old times if not as an air cooler.

The truth is—as I wrote my sweet sister afterwards—the Somervilles are my idea—I have babbled about it for some time—of a family of fine people, discreet, loyal, aristocratic and charming. So put that in the family pipe and smoke it. The things in my heart have a strangely old durability.

Please remember me to sweet people there who may happen to ask about me. It is unlikely I shall be there again for a long time, that is the way I live. It will take a good many years to digest that perfect visit to Oxford.

About the portrait, please don't say a word about it to anyone until I get it away from those people. The point is, you see, I did not mention the Beelhoovers or whatever it is in SO RED THE ROSE, and they were on the other side from the people I knew in Natchez, in that famous row, and so my book has never if you please been mentioned even in the report of the Chamber of Commerce. And there is no use sending things there. I gave them some fine things, and they in ALL GOOD FAITH showed them about the way a nigger pressing shop would show them. The 18th century waistcoats for example—not nearly so fine as those last two I had kept for myself and finally sent to Oxford were hung on those black wire frames, showing only the sweaty armholes, exactly like a pressing shop. Those Natchez people, with a few exceptions are a mess. What I shall try to do is to get the portrait back here, then varnish and freshen it up and then talk of it with the University of Mississippi. So till I get it back we will be very reserved and secret. There is nothing dishonest about it, for I only sent it, not lent or gave it, I mean I never presented it at all. The artist, Abram Poole, gets from $3000 to $5000 a portrait, and has painted for various rich persons.

I have no secretary here at all in the country and I am a hater of typing, so will not read this screed over, please make allowances.

Love to you all

Stark

718 | To Julia Young Robertson, Austin, Texas

[320 East 57th Street]
[New York]
Wednesday [July 27, 1949]

Dearest Sister,

This is in town. One of my pictures at Ronda's[8] fell and got a bad scratch, and I said I'd mend it for her—Wales is going there to see after the repairs he had been making—repairs is hardly the word for so much rebuilding etc. Ronda has plenty of money—her father, Howard Gould,[9] keeps giving her this and that. And so we are driving down—about two hours from New York—Doylestown, Pa. Also I want to ask Ronda to give a piece of stage jewelry from Doris' career—to go with some brocade and the tapestry in memory of Doris and *Romance,* at the U. of Miss. I think I'll give the new library there the 16th century tapestry,[1] if they will provide it a good show space. The vandals who broke into the house tore it down and trampled it, but did not know its value and so left it on the floor. So it is obvious it should not be left

8. Ronda Keane, actress, playwright, daughter of Doris Keane, married Carl Muschenheim, physician and educator, in 1951.

9. Howard Gould (1871–1959), socialite, automobile racer, and yachtsman, son of the railroad financier Jay Gould, after his much publicized engagement to the actress Odette Tyler was broken, in 1898 married Viola Katherine Clemmons, an actress, whose English tour in *Theodore* and whose American appearance in *A Lady of Venice* (1894) had been financed by William F. (Buffalo Bill) Cody at a cost of more than $75,000. In 1907, she sued Gould for divorce and successfully defended herself against counter charges involving her with Cody. In 1937, Gould married Margarete Emma Dorothy Fosheim, also an actress, and formerly the wife of Oscar Homolka, motion-picture actor. At various times, Gould lived in England, Irvington-on-Hudson, New York City, and Port Washington, Long Island.

1. The tapestry now hangs in the library of the University of Mississippi.

there to be stolen, and I have not an inch space for it here. They spoke of a painting of mine for the new library, and this will serve the same end. (What a mercy it is I took—against Wales' doubts—that brocade red bedcover to town—since they took the comfort that went with it. Diane,[2] who knows, says a new one would cost her $150 and perhaps more) I am going to give the orange and silver brocade (Catherine the Great performance at St. James for the Russian Ambassador—command) to Miss Kate's museum. (It's a superb gift indeed.)

I have looked everywhere, the massive scissors are nowhere to be found. Perhaps you lost it on the train. The apartment seems quite sad without you and Ben.

The shirt, number L, came, and fits perfectly—I'm sorry you all blew your money for it—but it is a fine color and unusually good material. Thanks very much.

This pen is a small gold one, French, that George Sachs[3] gave Wales. Hard to write with, so I'll stop. I hope you can read it all.

Lovingly
Stark

Ella's painting finally went off last Thursday, as I told you I think.

719 | To Ella Somerville, Oxford, Mississippi

Waccabuc, New York
Sunday [August 7, 1949]

Dearest Ella,

Thank you for writing such a lovely letter about the painting. I hope it gives you much pleasure indeed. You noted the flowers very keenly. The round pink flower is lavatera—lavatera—a flower I never saw at home down there. I pick flowers that will paint effectively, then try not to do colored photographs of them. I never have a flower in sight while

2. Diane Tate.
3. Georgette Boyer Sachs, second wife of Arthur Sachs.

I am painting. Sometimes I do a close likeness to some flower—I can paint them very accurately—then when I use that flower in a painting, I put aside this likeness and try to do something unreal enough to convey a feeling or idea. It is easy to paint a rose that looks like a rose, but took me a long time to handle them as I do in your painting. I learned that partly from Goya, partly Renoir, Degas and my own efforts.

I have a large painting very decorative where all the trees are bright red, the water pink and violet, the city in the distance pale rose and lavender. When people ask what sort of trees they are I say "Red paint trees." That illustrates what I am trying to say about unreality and flowers.

This fall I am going to send down that grand brocade of Doris Keane's for the museum. It can make the back of a case, draped as a background, I mean. I saw her daughter the other day and am trying to get a piece of stage jewelry to sit on the bottom floor of the case with the brocade. Doris had some astonishing stage jewels in those London days. I hope I can persuade a piece out [of] the Museum of the City of New York, to whom Ronda Keane has assigned them.

My name is not in the book—the telephone is under my roommate here—or housemate—William McKnight Bowman—South Salem 547. In New York it is Plaza 5-6493.

I wish I might have seen more of Tom [4]—he looks like an interesting young fellow—an unusual face.

Give my love to everybody in the family and Professor my cordial regards.

Thank you again for such a sweet letter. It's hot here and sticky and I am very dull—but off this scrawl goes just the same. Remember me to Spencer.

Affectionately
Stark

I have word the portrait will be sent. I'll let the matter lie low a while, so as not to offend Natchez. I never really *gave* it to them.

---

4. Thomas Somerville Culley (b. 1928), Miss Somerville's nephew, had been graduated the previous June from the University of Mississippi. After graduation from the Vanderbilt University School of Medicine in 1953, he specialized in orthopedic surgery.

720 | To Ella Somerville, Oxford, Mississippi

Waccabuc, New York
Tuesday [August 16, 1949]

Dearest Ella,

Thank you for such a good letter, and I am indeed delighted that the painting gives you pleasure. Nina wrote so sweetly about it, while she was thanking me for [the] little Venetian trifle. And Mary Hartwell was so sweet about that fan, which was also a trifle but full of its past. The Somervilles are about my idea of nice people, as I have said to many and will go on saying.

Professor wrote and thanked me about the Scribner matter and wishes to know my opinion of the MS etc. I wrote him a simple compliment and a suggestion, and added that I think people would want more done with the man and woman theme. His writing has a certain journalistic talent that helps to keep the interest. Amateurs—between us—are wonderful. There are not six people in the world I would ask to read a MS of mine, any more than I would ask Doctor Culley[5] to take home some of my blood and let me have an analysis—I mean John. So, honey child, if Professor ever gives birth to another work and mentions me just say gently that you had heard me say I never read MSS. It is about the truth. If they are fired at me by people who have no claim on me at all, I just glance through them and write a polite short letter. Even that is a waste of time. They want praise, to be told it is wonderful and that is that. Besides, I am not in the agent business, or editing a magazine or a publisher, in which case reading MSS would be a part of my job and perhaps a pleasure. I even dislike my own things in MS and often let them rest and feel like tearing them up.

You make a highly able sketch of Professor. Not at all unkind, I should say generous in fact. Congratulations. You might help him with some of his passages in the opus he sent me.

5. John Clifton Culley (1886–1966), Oxford physician and surgeon, husband of Nina Somerville Culley, had been practicing in Mississippi since receiving his M.D. degree from Vanderbilt University in 1909. In 1922, he married Nina Wilson Somerville. Although primarily active in private practice, he served the University of Mississippi from 1914 to 1955 at various times as a member of the medical faculty and as university physician.

Now we come to the portrait. I hope you will be careful and help me be tactful. Just don't mention Natchez at all. Let it pass as from here. I never really gave it to Natchez and I fancy they cared little about it. It is scarred in several places, and would cost me a good deal to have it repaired if I could not do it myself. Fortunately I am quite a wizard at restoring and repairing. The fatal thing, one that even professional repairers are sometimes stumped with is a jagged tear. These places on my portrait are more callous and ugly and indifferent than irreparable. Some time or other if the picture is shown in Oxford somebody will remember perhaps having seen it in Natchez, but it will be only vague and soon forgotten. If I wrote anybody in Natchez that I was taking it back for Oxford they might have things to say, merely because of the Oxford not because of the portrait. As portraits go it is effective. Abram Poole has painted a good many notables and beauties and costume portraits and gets from $3000 up, he has exhibited internationally and taken prizes. About the most you can hope from portraits in general is that they are moderately decorative when hung on the wall. I shall have to get the repairing done in time to send it down by October, since I go to town then. It can be put in the basement of the museum and then opened whenever you all see fit and go where you see fit. I should think the new library. Unless you tell me not to I can have it sent directly to the museum. The packing was done by some carpenter and is very heavy and clumsy and about five feet high. It took a long time and a helper to get the boards off the front and the painting lifted out. You can tell me about this. The details are sometimes very good painting by the way, some of them. Poole studied in Munich a good deal and paints after that school at the time, I suppose. There is a certain decorative toning given the whole, by warm glazings and the use of umbers etc.

If you will advise me as to the best person to write to about the tapestry I will do it.[6] It is a sixteenth century tapestry, on the whole the verdure type Flemish about seven feet by ten, in excellent condition. I think I wrote you about it and that I would give it in memory of Doris Keane. It would look very distinguished in a library. But they would have to arrange a good place for it and not stick it anywhere. I should have to communicate with somebody who would have the authority to

6. Upon her suggestion, Young wrote to Pete Kyle McCarter, dean of the University of Mississippi, about both the tapestry and the portrait by Abram Poole.

make an assurance about this. I have seen things get sadly lost in colleges, at Amherst for instance. There were scandalous instances. For instance someone long ago presented Audubon's collection of birds. Not the books, the stuffed birds, a really unique and exciting possession. They had been allowed to fade almost away, till a new young professor of biology came and raised the devil and brought a restorer to the college, and it took the man a whole session, the whole winter to get them back again, such brushing, waxing, glazing, etc. But what a treasure! They also had a fine mummy case, painted well, the mummy inside, and had by the time I got to Amherst let the rats eat the entire mummy. This is a college in New England, where they affect such care and conscience. (You see I did read this part over and find I can take it—I hope you can't quite without nausea.)

Well, I lay the burdens on you, but you always seem to be glad to help us mortals.

You will excuse me from reading this screed over, I'd never send it off. Please give my love to all the family.

Love to you, and give my love to whoever may even seem to love me.

Stark

I want to know about the tapestry before I go to town. It is too valuable to leave in the country, however insured, and I'll either send it to the U. of Mississippi, or store it, or give it to another museum.

721 | To Caroline Charlotte McGehee, Como, Mississippi

Waccabuc, New York
Thursday [September 8, 1949]

Dearest Cousin Cad,

I wrote Agnes the other day, as you seemed to suggest, and would have written you too at the time but had not the typewriter and I [am] sure the letter thus is easier for you than my scrawl. I can write very plain but it bores me and looks even stupider.

That order I told you of was to the Virginia Quarterly to send you the two issues in which some of my memoir chapters were printed. They made quite a hit, my publishers are much stirred by them, nothing like it except Churchill they say, there in their swell office on Fifth Avenue, and I say the whole book will be wonderful if I get it the way I want it. Endless labor and there we are, but I hope it will be good. I have been painting some on an order from a wife [7] in Chase National Bank, a sweet woman and I hope to do something for her that will give pleasure. I have sold six pictures since spring, several thousand dollars, but have some in my heart that are not yet painted. I still think with so much pleasure of my visit at your house, and how I reassured myself all over again that my Cousin Cad is one of the most magnetic, loveliest and interesting people I ever saw. My opinion in this has a bit of authenticity, because after all I did meet the princes, royalties, authors and what nots in Rome and elsewhere in Europe and New York, and I still say my Cousin Cad is more delightful, aristocratic and charming than most of them. So there, put that in your pipe and smoke it. Bowman agrees with me, he still talks of how much he admires you, else I would kill him of course. He is away in Pennsylvania today telling Howard Gould's daughter [8] how to arrange her drawing room, for a price. I meanwhile getting poorer and poorer.

I still think that among my small talents the best one is my gift for appreciating and admiring and loving wonderful people, who at times have responded to me I may say, but the love was in my heart and their goodness has always seemed to me the highest form of imagination.

It is a good thing how gently dwells in my heart all the sweetness Aunt Sallie meant to me and all the dear moments when Aunt Rosie was her darling self, and Cousin Abner was a very charming gentleman, I can still see that smile he had, and Cousin Jennie, is a saint, with never an ugly thought in her mind. When I am flattered by the great, so to speak, and by the press, I think of what I owe to the beloved dead and all their goodness and rightness and pure hearts. But most of all I love my Cousin Caroline the best, and don't mind telling anybody that. It is a shame that I am so far away, but if you saw me more you might see what a mess I really am, a poor mixed up goose, saved from

7. Young was painting several flower pieces in oval shapes for Mrs. Edward L. Tinker.
8. Young refers to Ronda Keane.

being worse largely by my heritage. You would be surprised, darling Cousin Cad, at what cheap rewards I could have, but they bore me at the very thought—Hollywood for example, two offers at a thousand and more a week. Hollywood asses, I said—

I am writing in the garden and a yellowjacket—the only thing it seems that really likes me, is sitting on my nose, not to be slapped at I can tell you, so I had better stop, dearest Cousin Cad—love to you all

Stark

722 | To Ella Somerville, Oxford, Mississippi

Waccabuc, New York
Monday [September 26, 1949]

Dearest Ella,

It seems crude to write a letter of condolence on a typewriter, but I am in the garden without pen and ink and you will understand. I am so very sorry to hear of Mr. Vasser's death[9]—we always called him that. I remember him as a real gentleman and as unfortunately married to a woman not of his own fine quality. But I do remember later on when Julia Compton[1] was in the offing, I knew they had married finally and I am glad to know from your letter that his troubled life settled into peace and form. I am sure he was a dear person and that you will feel his death. I suppose there is nothing I can say that will be of any help. Time alone eases these things, more or less. Will you give Mary Hartwell and Nina my love and sympathy and tell them I think of them and love them. I'm writing them.

I am working on my memoirs and they make me all undone, so that you will have to pardon a very poor letter. The price one pays for life and certainly the price one pays for trying to create life into art comes very high.

9. Vasser Somerville (1879–1949), postmaster, brother of Ella Somerville, died in Paris, Tennessee, September 16, 1949.
1. Julia Compton Somerville, second wife of Vasser Somerville.

The visit from Welty [2] sounds very nice indeed, however gouty. She has great talent. I am almost through her last book. Sometimes I find myself wishing she would study the piece more and get the line, pattern or progression, whatever you want to call it, steadier and more accessible. But there are astonishing passages and flashes and many luminous effects, and sharp drawing. I wish you would tell her from me that when she is in New York, in case it interests her to do so, I should like her to write me a note to 320 East 57th, and give me the pleasure of having her for a drink. I am a real admirer of hers.

I am laboring on Mrs. Tinker's pictures and can't get them to suit me. Also memoirs, and various inner horrors.

I thought of Vasser when I was in Oxford, but did not like to ask about him for fear he was dead. You see I am so far away that all kinds of things happen without my knowing it—for example I knew about my cousin Dr. Lucius McGehee's death [3] only because I was in Como, some months afterward. Such is life. I wrote his wife but she has never replied. I suppose she thought a letter so long after was not to be acknowledged. Again such is life. I can see how after the years one may get enough of it.

I will be sending the portrait soon. People who have seen it seem to think it distinguished. At any rate it is a long way from the average portrait, God help us. Thank you, dear Ella, for writing me about your trouble.

Affectionately
Stark

2. Eudora Welty (b. 1909), Mississippi novelist, and short story writer, had been visiting Ella Somerville. Young had been reading Eudora Welty's volume of short stories *The Golden Apples* (1949).

3. John Lucius McGehee (1879–1949), surgeon and professor of surgery at the University of Tennessee Medical School, died February 16, 1949.

723 | To Nina Somerville Culley, Oxford, Mississippi

320 East 57th Street
New York
Tuesday [September 27, 1949]

Dear Nina,

I am in town for the day, to straighten out some none too pleasant matters with my publisher—and I have no proper paper here on which to write you. Ella wrote me of Mr. Vasser's death [4]—we always spoke of him as that—and I know it means a sad break in your life. Blood is blood, and to try to escape it is only silly—our hearts are traditional and biological, and these deep things are not easily escaped. The fact that your brother has been so long at a distance will soften some of the impact of this sorrow, and then time steps in with its gentle fingers blurring all things.

Dear Nina, I did so enjoy seeing your house and that delicious lunch —though I was exhausted from the day before and quite tight with that day's refreshments—and I thought Tom [5] looked like a young man who might turn out to be something indeed, and John [6] a convincing, fine person. All these things stay in one's memory and stir the heart and warm our thoughts. I must say my Oxford visit did me good, as well as ripping me up with memories both good and terrible, and made me feel a little less common after so many years of a great city. This city has been very kind to me, considering—naming lipsticks and various messes after my books and even allowing me to be of aristocratic background—it has to be just *background,* for Hollywood's sake. Well, as Hamlet says, something too much of this.

Lovingly
Stark

4. See above, Letter 722 and n. 9.
5. Thomas Somerville Culley.
6. John Clifton Culley.

724 | To Hudson Strode, University of Alabama, Tuscaloosa, Alabama

Waccabuc, New York
October 11, 1949

Dear Hudson,

I have now finished your book [7]—You see I really read what I read, not get off this New York guff of six new books laurst week—(to be noted in silly reviews for the most part and on the jackets—in bookshops)—and your book is a good, long dose. But a dose of first-rate and dignified enthusiasm and research. And always entertaining, even when talking of co-operatives, splendid subjects without testicular appeal. It is a pity that such substance cannot be spread in a country like ours, where the bland Lions-Veterans-Rotarian smile is so mingled with low ideals, cheap craft and dirty foods. Your book could well be a shocker, were it not so tactful and well-bred and persuasive that it will have an influence far past anything that a mere shocker could ever have. This book, if we had a press or reviewers worth even a little bit more than our public, could have a most potent and revolutionary an effect—so much tact, charm, patient judgment and appeal. Dear Hudson, I know I can be very tedious in these matters, but I do think such a book could have—if well presented and promoted and culled from— a national effect.

And some of the pages have great charm in themselves. What a noble, rich book of nations, what a gentle, aristocratic book of individuals!

If you can quote any of this anywhere, please feel free to-do-so.

To you and that lovely, lovely Thérèse, with a loveliness that time cannot affect—my love.

Stark

7. Young refers to Hudson Strode's *Sweden: Model for a World* (1949).

725 | To Donald Oenslager,[8] New York

Waccabuc, New York
October 18, 1949

Dear Professor,

The day after I saw you with that very adorable lady you succeeded in marrying,[9] I went to see your show.[1]

You are doubtless tired of praise by now, but it was indeed a beautiful and distinguished display. Poor as I am I was delighted to see a red star on that Number 4—or else—

The variety in the designs was very impressive, and the techniques, so varied and clear, were very engaging in themselves. That exhibition should give you great satisfaction, Professor.

Those small models seemed to me very chic and charming in themselves, and served to recall the originals, most of which I remember distinctly. That very handsome room for *The Eagle Has Two Heads*[2] —(the director has not even one) I recall as most luxurious and noble, most intricate and bold. That set for *Sweet River*—if that is the title— the George Abbott show that folded up[3]—was the most romantic and rich setting for a Southern scene that I ever saw. (The emotion of that

8. Donald Mitchell Oenslager (b. 1902), scene designer, teacher, and lecturer, was associated with Kenneth Macgowan, Robert Edmond Jones, Eugene O'Neill, and Stark Young at the Provincetown Playhouse and Greenwich Village Theatre in 1924 and 1925. During the 1930s, 1940s, and 1950s, he created settings for ballets, musical comedies, plays, and operas. After serving in the armed forces during World War II, he joined the faculty of the Yale School of Drama.

9. In 1937, Oenslager married Mary Osborne Polak.

1. Oenslager's exhibition, "Twenty-five Years of Theatre Scene Design," had taken place at the Ferargil Galleries, September 26 to October 15. Included in the show were paintings and models of sets which he had designed for such productions as *Pygmalion, The Doctor's Dilemma, Born Yesterday, Of Mice and Men,* and *You Can't Take It with You,* as well as sketches Oenslager had made for projected dramatizations of the Book of Job and Goethe's *Egmont.*

2. Oenslager designed the settings for *The Eagle Has Two Heads,* adapted by Jean Cocteau from the French by Ronald Duncan and produced by John C. Wilson at the Plymouth Theatre, March 19, 1947. For the production, Oenslager created a grand staircase down which Tallulah Bankhead, as the tragic queen of a mythical country, could fall to her death. Young reviewed the play in "Wonders Never Cease on Broadway," *New Republic,* CXVI (March 31, 1947), 38.

3. Young had in mind George Abbott's *Sweet River,* adapted from Harriet Beecher Stowe's *Uncle Tom's Cabin,* which opened at the 51st Street Theatre, October 28, 1936, and closed after five performances.

memory has just made me, as I dropped some ink on the other page, swear.) I thought the whole show as such as might have made—if the whole theatre had not decayed into such a muddle and scattered vagary,—would be a center of alive discussion. I came out feeling the impact of warm and varied creative force.

My typewriter is in town at the moment, or I would not inflict this screed on you. Again congratulations and best auguries for your future work. Sherwood Anderson used to say to me that in America the public was not for the artist, it was not against him—it was merely not with him. That's why it might be useful to you to have a letter like this, of living pleasure and commendation.

Yours as ever
Stark

Love to your lady—I never can remember her name and have decided to call her Samothrace.

726 | To Julia Young Robertson, Austin, Texas

[320 East 57th Street]
[New York]
Wednesday [November 9, 1949]

Dearest Sister,

I seem all right again. I am sure the several days of that virus x or whatever it was [were] as uncomfortable as could be. Not dangerous, just trembling and gagging and vomiting—not the stomach so much as the solar plexus, the center of the nervous system, so that nerves are what are attacked. Well, that's over. It seems to be everywhere. Thank you for the phone calls, they warmed the heart at least.

One messy side of the case was that Oliver Messel[4] had arranged

4. Oliver Messel (b. 1904), British designer, had recently designed the settings for *The Lady's Not for Burning* and *Tough at the Top*. Young had long admired Messel's work in designing sets and costumes for Shakespearean and Restoration plays and ballets. Illustrations from his settings for the Sadler's Wells Company's performance of Tchaikovsky's *Sleeping Beauty* ballet, mentioned by Young, were appearing in the November issue of *House and Garden*, pp. 218–19.

largely for my sake a special showing of the fine film—*Pique Dame*—
not to be seen in this people [*sic*] at present, for unknown reasons. I
saw some of the stills—very wonderful. About a hundred people were
invited. How I hated to let him down like that. Please look in the
November *House and Garden* and see his glorious setting for *The
Sleeping Princess*. I hope you can see a copy.

Last night I went over to see a run-through of a ballet John Butler [5]
is creating. Woodie Taulbee [6] and Allen Porter,[7] from the Museum of
Modern Art brought Garbo [8] whom John had invited. There were
about thirty other people, managers, Burgess Meredith,[9] etc. Garbo has
a morbid dread of meeting people. But Woodie insisted on introducing
me. So I sat by her and he stood by me so the audience couldn't see her.
She had some eye make-up and lips, no rouge—looked quite wonderful, and was frank and simple. Looks strong but sensitive, stubborn
but shy. Was very sweet with the young dancers, but escaped as fast as
she could.

I'm glad Vic's [1] visit was a success. She seemed an awfully nice person when I saw her in Oxford.

I'm sending you a copy of *Anne of a Thousand Days* [2]—probably
stupid, but is having a run and your club may not have seen it.

Mary Hartwell [3] said to me in Oxford that she never mentioned her
children to you—the point is obvious, and she never meant you to see

5. John Butler (b. 1920), choreographer, director, dancer, born in Memphis, Tennessee, made his New York debut in 1945 with Martha Graham's company in *Deaths
and Entrances*. Subsequently, he has choreographed such works as *Brigadoon, Lady in
the Dark,* and *Ice Capades* and has been associated with numerous television productions.

6. Probably Daniel J. Taulbee (b. 1924), lecturer and painter specializing in historical Indian and Western scenes.

7. Allen Porter, then assistant secretary of the Museum of Modern Art.

8. Greta Garbo (b. 1906), Swedish actress, whose extraordinary Hollywood career
began in 1926 with *Torrent*. Among her most famous pictures are *Anna Christie,
Susan Lenox, Grand Hotel,* and *Anna Karenina*.

9. Burgess Meredith (b. 1908), actor, director, and producer, directed and acted in
The Man on the Eiffel Tower in 1949. After making his acting debut in 1930, he
played in such productions as *High Tor, Candida, The Playboy of the Western World,*
and *Winterset*. Since 1950, he has staged various productions in motion pictures, radio,
and television.

1. Mrs. Gerald FitzGerald.

2. Maxwell Anderson's play about Anne Boleyn opened at the Shubert Theatre,
December 8, 1948, and closed October 8, 1949. The text of the play, which Young sent
to his sister, was published in 1948.

3. Mrs. David H. Bishop.

her letter. But though it may be painful to you I think its beautiful spirit will more than make up for that. She is a wonderful creature.

I hope you and Ben are all right. Wales sends love.

Love to both
Stark

727 | To Pete Kyle McCarter,[4] University of Mississippi, University, Mississippi

320 East 57th Street
New York
November 11, 1949

Dear Dr. McCarter,

This is only a note—I have been in bed with Virus X—the devil's own torturing malady. I just want to tell you that the portrait and tapestry went off by express Monday last. You must excuse the country packing—there was no other way to get it done. The top lid of the portrait case must be taken off carefully.

The tapestry is a good one—Flemish—16th Century, in good condition. The braid border is, of course, modern. Originally there would have been an elaborate border—but this one is not incorrect. The chances are that this tapestry is a part of a much larger piece; they were used as hangings, door fillers et cetera and were cut often as needed. If it is agreeable to the powers there, I should like a card at the bottom of the tapestry saying

Flemish, 16th century
Presented by Stark Young
in memory of Doris Keane
the immortal actress of *Romance*[5]

4. Pete Kyle McCarter (b. 1910), university administrator, born in Batesville, Mississippi, was professor of English and dean of the University of Mississippi.

5. The tapestry, bearing the inscription, hangs in the library of the University of Mississippi.

Doris Keane willed this tapestry to me—it is obviously out of class with my purchasing powers. She played *Romance* nine years and after New York was the idol of London. The first World War with the bombing and the dying soldiers willing her their helmets and medals finally broke her down and closed the play.

If the canvas seems loose after the shipping of the portrait, just tap those wooden wedges in the back-frame, they stretch the frame a little.

I still remember my visit there with pleasure and with great pride in my own people. It warms my heart—I who have seen a lot, perhaps too much, of the world—to think of their beautiful manners and gentle bearing, along with an impression of plenty of good sense.

I am still rickety from my Virus X, and so make allowances, will you please, for a stupid letter.

Yours sincerely
Stark Young

728 | To Allen Tate, Princeton, New Jersey

320 East 57th Street
New York
Monday [November 21, 1949]

Dearest Allen,

If I had not been under the remains of an attack of virus flu two weeks back, leaving me dull and relaxed, I would have written you sooner about the Johnson essay.[6] I read it almost at once and then again later, and think it most happily done. You clear away when needed any pretense of knowledge where you have not got it, since naturally nobody but one type of critic speaks with authority on everything; and you have many passages that seem to me luminous with a poet's insight. That passage about receiving the discipline of objectivity which transcends the disorder of unacknowledged opinion is really

6. Allen Tate, "Johnson on the Metaphysicals," *Kenyon Review,* XI (Summer, 1949), 379–94.

superb.[7] That about consistency in point of view and lack of it in particular judgements—one reason he is a great critic, is very keen and illuminating.[8] But of course you know all this. Thank you very much for having the review sent to me.

The Koch piece[9] about you may be very excellent but I have never read much in that dialect of poetic criticism and so, though I usually seem to know what the critic is driving at by the inch the ell passes out of mind before I know it. I won't say so much that I feel out of my depth with it as that such waters are strange for me, and hard to keep in mind. The first sentence in your essay, coming right after, makes me jump with its directness. The Koch study of the Confederate[1] is really useful in showing the changes and some of the implications. I still prefer that poem to any since the Prothalamion—an odd pairing no doubt.

I am working at the memoirs. I have little hope of their success. The New York reviewers will dismiss it as Southern sentiment and Scribners will do little to push it. In fact when I have it to suit me I shall be in panic as to whether to publish it all or, or else wait, etc. I want you and Caroline to see some more of it after Christmas, when some rewriting or filling in has been done.

Love to you both. Wales sends his love.

Stark

7. Tate wrote: "If we refuse to see him [Johnson] as a part of a positive culture, in which personal prejudice can at times, in certain persons, receive the discipline of objectivity which transcends the disorder of unacknowledged opinion, we shall the more readily see in our disagreement with him a failure of sensibility on his part."

8. Young had in mind Tate's assertion: "One is constantly impressed by Johnson's consistency of point of view, over the long pull of his self-dedication to letters. There is seldom either consistency or precision in his particular judgments and definitions—a defect that perhaps accounts negatively for his greatness as a critic: the perpetual reformulation of his standards . . . has done much to keep the 18th Century verse alive in our day."

9. Vivienne Koch, "The Poetry of Allen Tate," *Kenyon Review,* XI (Summer, 1949), 355–78. This article immediately preceded the essay by Tate.

1. Tate's "Ode to the Confederate Dead."

729 | To Ella Somerville, Oxford, Mississippi

320 East 57th Street
New York
Thursday [December 15, 1949]

Dearest Ella,

It was very fine to get your lovely letter and to hear news of your fresh palatial surroundings—what a job to get it done! I have almost decided never to have anything done again, to take a chance on things lasting as long as I will or else getting to hell out.

I am glad you liked the portrait and the tapestry.[2] The portrait is far better than most and makes me look passable—you like an angel used the word *handsome,* which nearly knocked me over. In the mirror I always remind myself of what the London cabbie in an altercation over the fare said to the tourist—"And I'll tell you to your face, if it is your face—"

It was nice to hear news of Spencer, and will you tell her from me that I hope she is getting on with her next novel.[3] And that there was a scene in her book that was done so well that I think it has cut a gash in me for the rest of my life, it is unforgettable. That is where the mean boy leads the little dog to his death in the water.[4] It is quite powerful, and therefore full of talent. And, dear Ella, be sure to remember whether that is in her book or not, for I read it a good many months ago. I feel pretty sure it is there, and if not, then don't give her that part of my message. She has real talent.

That's interesting about your house being an art gallery for the University. I should like to see it. I have a very fine Bassano,[5] Titian's time, about 1550, that I will leave the University gallery some day when the Lord snaps me up.

It is a joke about me and philanthropy. Doris Keane left me the

2. Young had given the portrait and the tapestry to the University of Mississippi. See above, Letters 720 and 727 and notes.

3. *This Crooked Way,* published in 1952.

4. Although his memory of the incident is slightly inaccurate, Young refers to a scene in Elizabeth Spencer's *Fire in the Morning.*

5. Jacopo Bassano (1510–92), Venetian painter, known for genre paintings, portraits, and Biblical scenes. Young did not give the work to the University of Mississippi.

tapestry, and Abram Poole gave me the portrait, after it had been in a good many exhibitions.

I saw Bill's picture[6] about a week after it opened. It is at the Mayfair over on Seventh Avenue. The two or three newspaper reviews I saw were excellent, the *New Yorker* and *Time* magazine very bad.[7] I went at the late afternoon performance, and the theatre was all but wholly empty. Doubtless at night there is a larger audience. Most movie addicts of the popular variety would say, I think, that as a thriller, it is not thrilling enough, and most of the more serious observers would say it leans toward being a thriller—in sum it may prove to fall between two stools. I enjoyed it on the whole and Bowman was quite heavily impressed with the way the race question was presented. By far the best scene in my opinion was that in Lucas' cabin, with that old woman—she looked marvellous, and far beyond what mere movies can accomplish, being what she is and looks like. But of course Mr. Brown deserves credit for having chosen her and not messing her up á la Hollywood.

Patterson's role,[8] I thought, should have had a few more lines in it. There was a fine chance for that in the grave digging scene, for which chance Bill had provided in the book some very good details and nuances. They threw her away in that scene, which was making a mistake on their part. The passage of time as recorded in the book was not well indicated, and the mobs as photographed looked like ashcans. The uncle[9] could have had a few more speeches of the excitable-brain type, which Bill had provided abundantly, not to say a little tediously and with some signs of banality—explosiveness and theoretical effusion, not always convincing or distinguished. In so far as any of this might be taken as author cat stuff please don't repeat it to anybody. Things are so distorted in the repeating, and I really thought the picture did the book much credit.

6. *Intruder in the Dust.*

7. John McCarten reviewed the picture in "That Problem Again," *New Yorker,* XXV (November 26, 1949), 84, 86. McCarten found the picture "nowhere near as interesting as the Faulkner novel," though "satisfactory" if regarded as an "elementary melodrama." In "New Picture," *Time,* LIV (December 12, 1949), 98, 101, the reviewer found the movie "not only dead serious but dead on its feet."

8. Elizabeth Patterson played the part of Miss Habersham.

9. The lawyer-uncle, Gavin Stevens, in the novel, becomes John Gavin Stevens in the motion picture; the role was played by David Brian.

I was astonished at the square the way it looked, and when you find time to write me a letter please answer these questions—

Why did the courthouse look so bone white and ghastly and sudden —the place as seen in Oxford looks rather mild. Is it because the pic tures of it were taken at night? I jumped when it came on the screen The little shops and posts and so on around the square looked naked and sharp and common. The square looks plain enough but not this ghostly stick quality. Were any of those shots taken by artificial light? That would produce such an effect.

Bowman tells everybody as a joke on me that when I saw that crowd I said hotly—But there are plenty of people in Oxford that look better than that. He thinks that very funny local pride. Nevertheless I do think the whole point of the picture would have gained if we had had a few more glimpses of people of our better class. All I saw was the mass going to church and you did not see them very well. The lawyer was all right and mother's voice and back all right, the father at the foot of the table did well enough, but had too much of that tacky accent you hear more and more in Mississippi, and I think the point would have gained by that sensitive boy's having a father of somewhat more choiceness.[1]

And that scene in the church—did they rig up the choir boys etc. in the church actually, or was that a built set?[2] I don't remember how the inside of the church looks, and so wondered about this. I do remember the caterwauling there in the name of God, some broken voices and gentle hearts.

These are matters I hope you can tell me about.

Well, this is a banged off letter and I refuse to read it over, lest I tear it up. I am leaving Sunday for Texas, and Julia and I will be talking about you all. Please give my love to all the family.

Love to you
Stark

1. Mr. and Mrs. Mallison were played by Harry Hayden and Lela Bliss. Claude Jarman, Jr., took the part of the boy, Chick Mallison.

2. St. Peter's Episcopal Church was used for the church scene; the choir boys wore their usual cassocks and surplices.

730 | To William M. Kethley,[3] Cleveland, Mississippi

Gran Hotel
Ancira, Monterrey
Mexico
December 27, 1949

Dear **Mr. Kethley,**

I have your note, forwarded to me here, about the photograph, and, what is much more important, the pecans from you and Mrs. Kethley. (How well, I remember you both—two people I knew I loved as soon as I saw you.) I will write my thanks when I get back to New York and open the parcel.

I noted your suggestion of a trip down there in the Spring. I do appreciate the whole idea very much and the sweet endorsement behind it. But it is very complicated for me even to attempt a trip to my own South—in many ways—including a place in the country that violently needs attention. But also there is the tear and tragic wreckage of the return to old scenes and old loves in people and ideas—it took me weeks to get over my visit to Oxford and the University. There are times when I think all of life, in every part, is not worth the deep cost of it. I am not a defeatist or an escapist, but it seems to me I pay very high for all experience that is worth anything. And yet one reaches out for and clings to all that is blessed and beautiful and full of warm life.

I hope the New Year brings happy things to you and yours.

Sincerely yours,
Stark Young

3. William Marion Kethley (1894–1964), educator, was president of Delta State Teachers College, Cleveland, Mississippi, from 1926 to 1964. In 1922, he married Elizabeth Brooke Hunter.

731 | To Eric Bentley, New York

[320 East 57th Street]
[New York]
[January, 1950]

I have cut up a copy of the Review in order to save you bother with the references.[4] This following matter is written off without special pains or formulation, so take it for just a friendly lot of comment.

1. A good deal of concern on your part would have been saved if I had thought to write, what I should have written, that the pieces[5] were selected not with an intention of making a record; many important plays reviewed were left out; the pieces were selected solely as what might embody some idea of the theatre etc. as I see it. I should certainly have done this.

page 141[6] Doris Keane, who for something like nine years had the world at her feet, in New York and London, said many times that I was the only person she knew who so combined intellect with the psychic. This is interesting not because of me but because of her. Few people knew the amount of reading in Eastern thought, the interest in psychic response, in intuition etc., that absorbed her, and it passed into her performance in *Romance* completely transmuted into a marvel of glamor and wit and for most people romantic fascination. I have met people who saw her in that play 65 and 70 times.

Page 144[7] I evidently give the wrong impression of what I think of

4. Young wrote this letter, without date or salutation, to respond to an article written about his retirement from the theatre by Eric Bentley: "An American Theatre Critic! (or the China in the Bull Shop)," *Kenyon Review*, XII (Winter, 1950), 138–47; reprinted in Bentley's *In Search of Theater* (1953), pp. 250–61. Bentley illustrated his remarks with quotations from Young's *Immortal Shadows*.

5. Young refers to the reviews reprinted in *Immortal Shadows* from his writing in the *New Republic* and other journals.

6. Bentley had discussed Young's ability to recognize and define moments of greatness in the theatre. Young's work, wrote Bentley, attempts "to come closer than criticism usually does to the definition of our responses to works of art." Citing his criticism of Doris Keane's acting, Bentley asserted that Young's "ready emotionality is not divorced from his finer feelings or from his intellect."

7. Paragraphs numbered by Young two through seven contain his reactions to Bentley's remarks about areas of disagreement between himself and Young. After calling attention to Young's "blanket preference of what he calls the Mediterranean to what he calls the Teutonic," as "the most limited thing in his criticism," Bentley wrote: "If it sharpens his awareness of Ibsen's shortcomings it blinds him, apparently, to the

D'Annunzio. A genius and an ass, but in ITALIAN at times very dazzling, and the *Figlia di Jorio* something to consider. I am a great admirer of *The Wild Duck,* some of *Peer Gynt* and parts of Ibsen elsewhere, especially for the expositions. I feel sure that in the Archer translations there is about one half of Ibsen's quality. Sometimes, it seems, as in *An Enemy of the People,* the effect he intended is completely lost, so Norwegians tell me.

2. It had not occurred to me to think of Pirandello and Shaw together. I think of Pirandello as using ideas as characters in a kind of commedia dell'arte, played in the brains of us. Shaw takes his ideas sociologically, as important social comment. He cannot resist however, letting his brain have fun at times and thus lessening his serious impact though giving doubtless more zest and pleasure.

3. I should have said that Lorca or Molière are so for our theatre. I am entirely convinced of this, having seen various efforts to put on them. It is partly true as to reading, but nothing like so much of course.

4. It was Duse who told me that Mrs. Alving [8] was a liar, those were her very words. To Duse's kind of mind Mrs. Alving's staying on with her husband and then deceiving her son about his father was not as simple as Mrs. Alving put it or perhaps thought she saw it. Duse would have said you must face the whole thing out, and pay the price. In sum the point at which Mrs. Alving was sparing herself to some extent is a delicate decision. For example, when she caroused with her husband for the noble ends she speaks of and he by chance hopped in bed with her did she never get any kick out of it, not ever? And on the nobler end was it easier not to make the great break—not that Mrs. Alving would have all this quite clear to herself. At any rate that would be the way Duse saw life, though it may have its social limitations that kind of seeing. She lived by it anyway, for good or ill.

---

more disastrous shortcoming of D'Annunzio. It leads him to excuse in Pirandello what in Shaw (a Nordic in whom Mr. Young finds 'British rubbish or Teutonic conception') he roundly condemns. He gives us admirable interpretations of Molière and Lorca while observing that to all of us non-Latins, presumably including himself, they are inaccessible. When looking, as he must, for the supremely modern as well as the supremely good, he has to leave too much out. For the Nordics are excluded from the start. Ibsen is rough-handled (an Italian actress told Mr. Young Mrs. Alving was a liar). The whole succession from Strindberg through the Expressionists to Brecht is ignored. If the reason for such omission is that Mr. Young is reporting on Broadway where these authors have not been performed, what about Odets and Marc Blitzstein and the social theatre of the 'thirties?"

8. The leading character in Henrik Ibsen's *Ghosts.*

5. I admire lots of Strindberg, for example *The Father* excited me like Shakespeare. Too bad I have nothing about him in the book.

6. I wrote some about the Expressionists, it seems a long way back, and the articles must not have been what I wanted to preserve. At the time I thought I had some insight into that method. The Brecht plays I am ignorant of, I have seen two but so badly done that there was little to do about them. One of them was in an admirable translation by you.[9]

7. I wrote some about Odets and he admired me and George Nathan among the critics, he told me, but he was much annoyed at my review of his last play, which seemed to me to lack taste and to be quite banal in its upheaval. That was a good many years ago. I did not see his last play here. The only Blitzstein I ever saw was rendered into such a mess that I can't recall anything but the hideous chaos and vulgarity of the players. If I had been interested and conscientious I doubtless would have looked more into him. There is a certain kind of insistence and bad taste that make the going very hard for me. I tend to leave the crusade to somebody who is more human and active about it. Not to my credit perhaps.

8. As to the aristocrat[1] I will turn Southern for a moment and I hope not bore you—it would most people these days. I was brought up on constant stories of the family, not boasting, just family tradition handed down. My father not so much, so I can go back only to Sir Francis Young, a Colonel who fell at the Battle of Blenheim, 1704. His older son was said to have been killed some years later hunting with King William. The younger son Michael escaped from a French imprisonment to Virginia, and so on down to me. Out of one house in the fam-

9. Young reviewed Brecht's *The Private Life of the Master Race,* translated by Eric Bentley, in "Nazi Privacies," *New Republic,* CXII (June 25, 1945), 871. See below, Letter 820, n. 5.

1. Bentley wrote: "Mr. Young is a Southerner and, by instinct at any rate, an aristocrat. . . . He shares that blind animus against the whole world of liberalism which is the most limiting factor in, say, Robert Penn Warren's thinking. One must explain his failure to make more effective contact with the main stream of modern theatre—so largely liberal and libertarian in inspiration—by this fact. It is a pity to be dead set against 'problem plays' and 'dramas of ideas' and the like if these are almost the only intelligent plays going. On the other hand, what has given Mr. Young his special place among dramatic critics is precisely that he was never in the swim. The dull, undiscriminating, sentimental liberalism which has taken such a beating from writers like Lionel Trilling still persists on Broadway, which is not aware of Mr. Trilling's existence. If for Lee Shubert it is enough that a play make a lot of people laugh, for the Broadway liberal it is enough that it be in favor of Negroes, that it be against fascism, and so forth."

ily nine Douglas men went off to the Revolution. My mother's father was the Revolutionary Stark family in Vermont. Her mother was Mc-Gehee, for the name was taken when Cromwell cancelled the whole name, and this younger son came to Virginia with Cromwell's permission. His father was the Macgregor, head of the clan. His mother was the daughter of the Macdonald, her father the Earl of Antrim who headed the armies of Charles the First. They go into the royal Stuarts, and so back to Richard le Clere signing the Magna Carta 1215, and back from that. My great grandmother McGehee was a White, the tradition in the family was that she descended from the governor of the Lost Colony, White. She descended from the first Page in Virginia, who owned most of Williamsburg. I could tell you a long spread of other people, some of them interesting like Sir Francis Eppes, Gentleman of the Bedchamber to Charles the First, who came later to Virginia and is said to have fought duels with everybody right [and] left. ETC. ETC. I hope you are not laughing at me. At any rate it gives you an idea of the kind of what is now called nonsense that I was raised on. My great-uncle that I lived with after my mother's death used to tell me these things not from papers but from what his father had told him, and I have seen some of it since in Burke's Peerage and elsewhere, books he never heard of. Please don't show that to anybody, lest they mock me. I had rather not write it to you, but I think it does bear in its own way on (8).

9. Innocence[2] is a sweet way to take this. Arrogance as to a certain kind of people and things, partly inherited, partly from my experience with great art, had much to do with it. I never even thought as a rule what Broadway would think of what I wrote. In fact I was three years in New York before I knew what paper Percy Hammond was on. It was not all arrogance of course, not really—seriously speaking. It was also a cultivated separation from all that world in which I had no share and little interest. Once when I had written a review of *Peleás and Melisande* I went by chance into the Theatre Arts office and Mrs. Isaacs

---

2. Bentley had expressed his admiration for Young's "innocence" in commenting upon Anouilh's *Antigone* in terms of the "profound and hidden ties of family devotion and its loving mystery, plus the recoil from a sense of outrage done to our deepest instincts—in this particular case the reverence for the beloved dead and their souls' peace." (See below, Letter 755 and n. 7.) Bentley concluded: "These are profound thoughts but more remarkable is the innocence it takes to hand them on a platter to Broadway, the platter being *The New Republic.*"

told me Kenneth Macgowan had said I had answered point by point all the criticisms and critics of the play. The truth was I had not read a single criticism, I had merely tried to think out what various types would say of the occasion and covered their points as I felt sure they were to be found. I meant no harm. Croly, Editor of the New Republic, had something to do with all this, he delighted in my work and attitude and wanted *The New Republic* to take with regard to all the arts just that position and high faith or whatever you call it.

10. You may be right about being set against the "drama of ideas" and "problem plays." [3] I never knew I was. I asked only that the "ideas" and the "problems" be an organic or created part of the play. Euripides wrote a problem play in *Hippolytus* and Molière in *Tartuffe,* but the whole substance of each play is so one and complete and created that most people would not apply the terms to them. I must say I have had a vast amount of pleasure and excitement out of Shaw, though most when his ideas and problems are most created, as in *Caesar and Cleopatra*. I once admired *Heartbreak House* but when after years I returned very seriously to it I found it completely boring. In my salad days I confess to having great pleasure out of *Mrs. Tanqueray* and *Ghosts*. I still like much of *Ghosts,* despite its limitations. *The Doll's House* is a slick French play larded very obviously with a "problem," and finally wrecked with an ending attached to the problem, though most of the play before that was very entertaining. It might be more nearly exact to say of me that I am dead set against TAGS of all kind in the arts. This too, however, may show a limitation in me.

11. I was four years on the *New Republic* before Mr. Van Anda, the real head on the *Times* asked me to come on. [4] I was none too good because at that time the advertising was different, the managers brought pressure etc., and I was supposed to write about plays that on the NR I would never even have used the tickets for. Once in a while I did

---

3. See above, n. 1.
4. After remarking that Young stands out among American critics and theatre lovers because he always took the theatre seriously and refused to lower his critical standards, Bentley continued: "As critic of the *New York Times,* Mr. Young lasted exactly one season. A niche was then found for him (would it be today?) on *The New Republic*. The distinction of his pieces, their negative relation to liberalism good and bad, made them look very odd in this context, but it was not till *The New Republic* fell into new hands that he threw up the sponge. What is the opposite of a bull in a china shop? Stark Young was it. In the *New Republic* office, on Broadway, in 20th Century America."

pretty well, as in the two Sunday pieces reprinted. But on the whole I
was not suited to it. There was, to be honest, a tacit understanding between Croly and me that I'd be back on the NR, and so all I did was to
call up and say I was coming back, and he raised my salary by a thousand. Croly was a wonderful editor, he wanted the men, once they were
chosen to be there, to do their own thing and he had a remarkable
power of filling in the life of you, making you want to be what you believed in. I feel that I ought to quote some passages from his letters,
which I have in my file. You will not believe from what you have seen
of the NR that it was ever under the hand of such a man. I wish he
could read your article. Of course if he were still the NR you would be
on it and writing with the greatest happiness within yourself. (By the
way Bruce Bliven was City Editor on the *Globe* and Croly took him on
mostly to help in that general line, he had a poor opinion of his quality,
and afterward I fancy BB's feeling toward me was not unaffected by
Croly's feeling about him and me.)

"Dear Stark . . . I hope you will not think because I write to you
less often that I value any less the articles you are contributing to the
New Republic. They do more to make that publication worth reading
than any other part of our contents. It seems to me that you are growing steadily in your ability to give luminous and beautiful special ap-
plications to a sound group of critical ideas. I know of no criticism
which is being done anywhere which is so likely to be at once so serv-
iceable to the artist and yet so illuminating to the intelligent reader
and theatre-goer. It is of unique value to me personally."

(From a letter about my going to the *Times*.) "During the last two
years what you have done for the paper and what you have done for
me has meant more to me as an editor and as a human being than anything else which has been happening to me. When you go it will mean
an absolute loss to me for which there will be no compensation. But I
agree you cannot afford for many reasons not to take it, and I shall
assume that you have taken it. . . . I shall go ahead in the hope that
some day you will come back to the New Republic and I shall look
back on my association with you as the best gift the New Republic
ever presented to me."

I wanted you to see this, both in Croly's glory and because it supplies
a comment on whatever excellence or light I achieved in the reviews
I wrote under his editorship. Edmund Wilson will tell you the same

thing. I think a good deal of my independence of Broadway's opinion was due to this backing and faith from Croly.

After his death the paper steadily declined. Mrs. Elmhirst, who supported the NR, thought little of Bruce, but he was on hand, schemed and was willing to work hard, so there he is still and I am told Michael Straight leaves a great deal to him and stays himself oftenest in Washington.

I trust this long screed does not smack too much of author-egotism. It is by no means my habit either to write or to talk about my work. But since you put so much care and detail on your article I thought these points might be of interest to you.

I am thinking of taking up the matter of the memoir chapters with the Kenyon Review soon, since you and John R. both mentioned it. There are various things to explain etc. Shall I write to you about it or to Mr. Rice? [5] I see John is absent.

I am sure you work like a beaver, I hope it is all going to suit you.

Yours
SY

Forgive this typing.

732 | To Charles Henri Ford, New York

320 East 57th Street
New York
January 5, 1950

Dear Charles Henri,

This letter was written in heart long ago, but I have just returned from a three weeks' absence with my sister and brother-in-law in Texas

---

5. Philip Blair Rice (1904–56), philosopher and editor, was then teaching philosophy at Kenyon College and serving as acting editor of the *Kenyon Review*. Young's remark here is somewhat puzzling in view of the previous publication of two installments of his memoirs in the *Virginia Quarterly Review* and his agreement for the publication of a third part in the April issue of the magazine. Also perplexing is Young's comment in a letter to Tate in August, 1950, that Ransom had written "some time back" about the manuscript and that Young would soon send it so that Ransom could "choose anything he likes out of it." See below, Letter 739.

and Mexico, and failed to take my address book with me, so that I could not write and thank you for the poems. Oddly enough the same mail brought your card inquiring as to the book's reaching me and the book itself.[6] I sat right down and read the poems through, and then next day read it all through again. That is indeed going it for me, who don't read things all over the place. I am not a born reader of books generally—they have to mean something for me, else I can pass the time better otherwise. I wish very much that the volume contained the poem that darling Miss Sitwell says so much about. Perhaps I have it in former volumes of yours. You have a most remarkable talent, full of unexpected brilliances and glowing fascinations. I do wish you everything, dear Charles Henri.

I hear that Ruth looks very wonderful in *Clutterbuck*[7] and gives a fine performance.

Thank you again and love to you.

Stark

733 | To Ella Somerville, Oxford, Mississippi

320 East 57th Street
New York
Saturday [February 4, 1950]

Dearest Ella,

As usual I plague you with requests. I have tried to buy the *Kenyon Review* for the *Winter issue 1950*—they are all sold out at the bookshops, so would you stop at the University library and read that wonderful article about my book, written by Eric Bentley,[8] who knows more about the modern drama than anybody in this country? I'd like for you to see it. If Mr. McCarter hasn't had the article written (about me) for the alumni paper, he might like to know of it. I'm sure Mr.

6. Ford's *Sleep in a Nest of Flames* (1949), with an introduction by Edith Sitwell.
7. Ruth Ford played Deborah Pomfret in Benn W. Levy's highly successful comedy *Clutterbuck*, which opened on December 3, 1949.
8. Eric Bentley, "An American Theatre Critic! (or the China in the Bull Shop)," *Kenyon Review*, XII (Winter, 1950), 138–47. See above, Letter 731.

Bishop would like to see it. I tried at several shops to get one to send you, but failed. I have a memoir chapter coming out in the Spring Anniversary issue of the *Virginia Quarterly Review*[9] and will put in an order for one to be sent to you. The proof is due now, but I don't know exactly when the issue appears.

Bill's movie[1] has not been on any of the lists I have seen here—I think the list I saw was from the Memphis paper. I don't think its run was very long. But I see today that it has come to some of the distributing lesser theatres. Its misfortune in so far as it had any, came I suppose from its not being slick enough at the popular end or quite distinguished enough at the other. They got, for example, neither what Bill had or what a melodrama would have, in the grave scene. The cabin scene with the old woman seemed to me remarkable. Red Warren's Huey Long movie is having a top success—*All the King's Men*.

I was glad to know the courthouse was, as I thought, falsely lighted —I couldn't believe my eyes. All your points in your letter about the picture were very interesting indeed, and I am grateful.

Love to all the family and tell Spencer I do hope her book comes on well. I heard several people praising it—I had given them a copy— a few Sundays ago. Remember me to the Professor.[2]

Love to you
Stark

734 | To Ella Somerville, Oxford, Mississippi

320 East 57th Street
New York
Wednesday [March 22, 1950]

Dearest Ella,

Thank you for the clippings.[3] I hadn't time left to call on Bill[4] in Oxford and he didn't look me up here, but I'd have been delighted to

9. Stark Young, "From a Book of Memories," *Virginia Quarterly Review*, XXVI (April, 1950), 261–67.
1. The film version of William Faulkner's *Intruder in the Dust.*
2. James Hector Currie.
3. From the Oxford *Eagle*, relating to the film version of *Intruder in the Dust.*
4. William Faulkner.

try to do something agreeable for him. I have tried but learn nothing about his movie—I have never seen it in any other lists up [here] or in California. Too bad, it was certainly better than many movies, though quite unequal in its achievements of the various parts. My friend Robert Penn Warren has had a huge success with *All the King's Men.* I'm hoping he'll be in to see me in April—a very fine person. I haven't yet seen the movie, though it's been all over the country and New York.

Will you tell Mr. Bishop I sent a cheque to the *Kenyon Review* for a copy [5] to be sent him. A handsome article about me, I hope you see it. I'm sending soon a copy just sent me from Europe of the German copy of *So Red the Rose.*[6] I heard it got an excellent reception over there. I intend it for the U. of M. Library but have lost the Librarian's name [7] —very silly of me—so sometime when you are out there will you hand it to the right personage? No hurry. Thanks for the Commercial Appeal clipping—very kind—perhaps I'd better speak Greek all the time.

Tell Spencer I hope she is getting on well with her novel—a real talent she has.

I wish I could see you Somervilles—it's nearly a year already—I am duller than ever.

Lovingly
Stark

735 | To Ella Somerville, Oxford, Mississippi

320 East 57th Street
New York
Monday [April 3, 1950]

Dearest Ella,

I wrote you, I think, that I would be sending the German translation of *So Red the Rose,*[8] begging you to leave it by some time when you

5. See above, Letter 733 and n. 8.
6. Entitled *Leben in Bluten und Sturm,* translated by Edith Mugdan (1950).
7. John Sykes Hartin, director of libraries, University of Mississippi.
8. See above, Letter 734, n. 6.

passed the library. The truth is I can't recall the librarian's name[9] and don't want to be untactful. I do thank you for the favor, one of many you have done me.

I finally saw Warren's *All the King's Men.*[1] The whole treatment is more realistic than that of Bill's book. The book itself is more tangibly full of events. The photography is a great deal better. Those pictures of crowds in Mr. Brown's film were smudgy and poor, unusually so. The Oxford square looked ghostly and unreal. The acting in the Warren picture is also much better, far better. There is no scene as touching and choice as that single scene in the cabin that Mr. Brown created. Otherwise the other picture is out of class with Brown's. The director is out of Hollywood and well-known, but I am poor at such knowledge —Rossen—doubtless you have seen the picture. It certainly got the palms—voted the best film of the year, its star as the best performance, and the woman lead the best supporting performance.

My colored boy, who professed to know exactly what to get, went out and bought the wrong ribbon, hence all this smutting. I will get another this afternoon, so had better stop. It is one thing after another unless one waits on oneself and is thus half shot most of the time.

If you want to brag a little about the painting I sent you, you can say that Mrs. Marie Sterner in assembling a very distinguished exhibition, very handsomely presented, of flower paintings from over the world, had my name on the list with Fantin-Latour,[2] Van Gogh,[3] Augustus John,[4] Lintott and others at the top. The painting she had in mind was the size of yours and a good deal like it. I was vastly pleased and you will be no doubt.

9. See above, Letter 734, n. 7.

1. In the following paragraph, Young refers to the motion picture versions of Robert Penn Warren's *All the King's Men* and William Faulkner's *Intruder in the Dust.* Clarence Brown produced and directed *Intruder in the Dust,* which was filmed in Oxford during the spring of 1949 and released in October. Robert Rossen produced and directed *All the King's Men.* The picture won the Academy Award for 1949, and Broderick Crawford and Mercedes McCambridge received Academy Awards for their performances.

2. Ignace Fantin-Latour (1836–1904), French painter of portraits, flowers, and allegories. Much of his fame arose from widespread popularity of his flower paintings.

3. Vincent Van Gogh (1853–1890), Postimpressionist painter, spent much of his most productive artistic life at Arles where he decorated his studio walls with sunflowers and painted in bright colors portraits and still-life subjects.

4. Augustus Edwin John (1878–1961), British painter, established his reputation as a painter of gypsies, romantic landscapes, and portraits.

The enclosed drawings [5] have just come in a letter from Julia; Ben likes to cut them out and have her send them. Their humor varies in quality. I like that of the one little kiss [6] and the one with the fireman. [7] Give my love to everybody.

Love to you
Stark

736 | To Leah Salisbury, New York

Jennymead
Waccabuc, New York
July 17, 1950

Dear Leah,

Thank you for your sweet letter—the Lee Black address [8] is just what I need.

I wish I could be the least use for that nice Tony—and your Tony as well—but I never even heard the names you mention except Sarnoff and don't know him. [9] My world has indeed swung away from the theatre.

I wrote Ina Claire today about *The Sea Gull* [1]—She has always been

5. Young enclosed a group of six cartoons from the *Saturday Evening Post*.

6. A drawing of a man standing below a woman climbing a house column and pleading "Oh, come on! Just one little kiss!"

7. The drawing depicted a man and woman in bed and a fireman at the window pouring water on them from a fire hose, saying: "Place down th' street afire—thought I saw a spark fly in here."

8. Young had requested the address of Lee Black, who did typing for Leah Salisbury.

9. On July 11, 1950, Leah Salisbury had written that her son, Anthony Salisbury, who had recently been graduated from college, was seeking to find a position in radio journalism. Young was replying to her remark that "if by any chance it should turn out that you are on even turned-up-nose acquaintance with David Sarnoff, Bill Paley, or anyone within seven-eights of the way down the ladder and would care to give Tony a letter of introduction I would be personally very grateful."

1. Leah Salisbury mentioned that Ina Claire was "seriously considering" using Young's "adaptation" of *The Sea Gull* and that she suggested that a reference to her plans be made in the paper so that "some other little actress wouldn't come along and anti-climax it by another poor production." A brief announcement of her interest in the play appeared in the New York *Herald Tribune*, July 6, 1950, p. 18.

most kindly disposed toward me—I did *not mention him* but only that I had seen this in the papers (I had not in fact) and that I had been written to by two agents about it—a friend of hers was called by her last week and went for a visit to the Sherry Netherlands and found her with a copy of *The Sea Gull*—mine, (and for God's Sake try to stop its being spoken of as an adaptation!) and heard that Tennessee Williams liked my translation very much etc.—and there was much talk about it. He came out to spend the week-end and urged me to write her at once—Mrs. William Wallace—1000 Mason Street—San Francisco—said she'd be glad to have a letter from me on any account. So I wrote no propositions but just that I'd feel sure she would be very wonderful in it—etc. I am sure she would—She has had a considerable rebirth and wants to do something with some "beauty in it"—so she told her friend and mine. I carefully *did not mention* him or his report of her when I wrote. So we will see what happens.

Bless you, Leah—Wales sends his love.

Stark

737 | To Julia Young Robertson, Austin, Texas

[Waccabuc, New York]
Thursday [July 20, 1950]

Dearest Sister,

I am back—this morning at 7.20—after two strenuous days at Williamsburg.[2] They put us up at Brafferton Hall—the college guest room—had us to juleps the first afternoon—dinner that night. But meanwhile working my head off. Conferences with students—the talk from 2 to four—more conferences. Next day conferences and meeting with a class in play writing at 12.30–1.30, then at 2–4 another talk, many questions etc. I was proud of the quality of the college and of

2. On July 18 and 19, Young conducted seminars in "Producing Foreign Plays" at the William and Mary Institute of the Theatre directed by Althea Hunt, professor of drama in the College of William and Mary department of fine arts.

the students I met. A good many brought copies of *Immortal Shadows* to be signed and they applauded quite thunderously at the end of each of the seminar talks.[3] Then there was the *Symphonic Drama*[4] at the amphitheatre by the lake, among the trees. The place marvellous, the music good and *some* at least of the show good. I asked Wales not to bother with the talks—on the contrary, so he saw the sights, the new things etc. Meanwhile he enjoyed a good many privileges, invitations, etc.—places not seen by tourists, because of me. I was glad of that. The head of the Fine Arts [5] took us around to see all the Page portraits.[6] etc. You'll see the results on these papers. Impressive only in a provincial sense, and he made no bones about that.

I do hope you and Ben are happily settled and will benefit by this trip.

I have some clippings in the country, about the war, for you and Ben to read, will send them tomorrow.

I have a lot of letters to answer—however stupidly, for that academic jaunt has left me rather limp, and so will stop. The Tinker paintings are really finished. Love to you both. Wales is having a time of it with the restriction controls threatened. Is at his office now or would send love to you.

Lovingly
Stark

3. In a letter to Professor Hunt, written the following Sunday, Young remarked: "As usual after any speaking I lie awake thinking of what I might have said better and what I could have been more clear about, and what I should have left out. That's the main reason why I do almost no speaking or lecturing at all any more. I tried to treat the meetings rather as classroom, and the young people made a delightful audience. I try to seem to take it all lightly but am really very dead in earnest about what I am trying to do."

4. Paul Green's *The Common Glory,* produced in the Lake Matoaka Amphitheatre.

5. Professor Thomas E. Thorne had been head of the fine arts department since 1943.

6. Sixteen portraits of the Page family of Rosewell in Gloucester County, Virginia. The collection includes paintings of John Page (1627–92), the founder of the family in Virginia, and Thomas Nelson Page (1853–1922), the novelist.

738 | To Norman Dello Joio,[7] New York

> Jennymead
> Waccabuc, New York
> Monday [August, 1950]

Dear Norman,

It seems to me that your music could make this a beautiful song.[8] At any rate I wrote it for you and your music, out of a deep affection and admiration.

That dear Grace asked us to dinner Wednesday and we are coming, so there you are.

> Love to you both
> Stark

739 | To Allen Tate, Princeton, New Jersey

> Jennymead
> Waccabuc, New York
> August 15, 1950

Dearest Allen,

Wales and I have spoken several times of you all's saying that you would come to see us again before the season ended, and I hope you intend to do so. He is always enthusiastic about both of you, which shows the good sense and understanding that he has. As for me you

7. Norman Dello Joio (b. 1913), composer, began his musical career as an organist but as a young man turned to composition. After study at the Juilliard Graduate School and with Paul Hindemith at the Berkshire Music Center, Dello Joio played briefly with jazz bands. From 1941 to 1943, he served as musical director of Eugene Loring's Dance Players, a ballet company, and in 1944 and 1945 received Guggenheim fellowships. In 1944, he became a member of the faculty of Sarah Lawrence College and subsequently the Mannes College of Music in New York. Dello Joio has composed ballets, chamber music, choral music, operas, and piano and orchestral music. Shortly before Young wrote this letter, Dello Joio's opera, *The Triumph of St. Joan,* had been performed at Sarah Lawrence College. In 1942, Dello Joio married Grace Baumgold, a dancer.

8. Young had written a poem which he called "The Dying Nightingale." For a slightly revised text of the work, see below, Letter 745.

know how much I love and admire and depend on you and Caroline.

I have brought my MS.[9] to as far as I can carry it at present, it is typed by the professional typists and seems good. I am going to let it rest a few weeks before showing it in this form to Scribners. It was a great relief and benediction for me that you and Caroline seemed to commend it.

Considering what a fine poet you are I keep hoping this book will be good enough to be dedicated to you—and so I ask permission from you to dedicate it so, without further comment on the printed page than

To
Allen Tate

but with a full heart of thoughts of you always. From the beginning of my friendship for you and Caroline I have had an unbroken delight and blessing and a rich and happy fecundation of my mind and purposes.

I had a very nice letter indeed from John Ransom about sending him the MS.—some time back—and I will do so soon. He can choose anything he likes out of it. The brief glimpse of him I had in Mississippi and his letters have made me see how one may easily have an affection for him. I wrote John Palmer [1] at last, in answer to a letter from him, but have had no answer and fancy he is somewhere with the war—what a grotesque war it is, in my opinion!

Please let us know when you think you can come to visit us and not for just a night—if one or both of you want to have flushes—wasn't that your word? this time—we have a room for each, instead of both in the same room. Please think well on this and let us know something about dates. October 6, that week-end, is the only *fixed* date we have at present—this week-end excepted.

I hope the trip West was happy for you and Caroline.

Lovingly
Stark

9. As yet untitled, the manuscript for *The Pavilion.*

1. John James Ellis Palmer (b. 1913), editor and administrator, had been associated with the Louisiana State University Press, the *Southern Review,* and the *Sewanee Review.* He served as an officer in the U.S. Naval Reserve during World War II and in the Korean conflict. In 1954, he became editor of the *Yale Review* and in 1963 dean of Silliman College, Yale University.

N.B. I thought Mr. Schorer's review of *Two Adolescents* (Moravia) in the *Times*[2] was very soft, considering the book—it seems to me a pretentious book and largely made up.

S.

740 | To Caroline Charlotte McGehee, Como, Mississippi

Jennymead
Waccabuc, New York
Tuesday [August 15, 1950]

Dearest Cousin Cad,

I really have nothing to say except that I talked a man's head off about you Sunday, saying how wonderful you are, and aristocratic, and elegant and high-minded—all of them qualities that I love most. I do wish I could see you.

I made two lectures in Williamsburg lately,[3] at William and Mary —the $350 fee was most welcome these days when we seem likely to be skinned to the bare bone—steak is $1.10 etc.—our laundry about forty-five a month—etc.—and that has been my only adventure into the South since I was at your house and in Oxford. I could not buy special clothes for two days, and since I have been so long North I almost perished of the Virginia heat. But they were most kind to me, had my ugly face pasted here and there—and made me think I was almost somebody, while in the meantime the Washington papers wrote up me and my visit. As far as I am concerned it is all thin soup. I belong to these times when nobody amounts to anything—if you don't believe it look at the faces of those in Washington who are running our country.

If Bowman were at home he would send you his love—he has got the

2. Mark Schorer, "To Grow up Means to Be Born Again" [review of *Two Adolescents: The Stories of Agostino and Luca*, by Alberto Moravia], *New York Times Book Review*, July 23, 1950, pp. 1, 20.
3. See above, Letter 737.

habit of beaming and nodding agreement, when I begin to talk about my darling Cousin Cad.

Please give my love to that sweet Cousin Jennie and to Cousin Wheeler and Cousin Annie and Cousin Waller and Edward and Dee —She is a nice young matron—I wish you could send me a line as to how you are. I have about finished my memoirs up to twenty, my distinguished publishers say they are very fine—I myself can only hope they are good. A number of pages are about Aunt Sally and Uncle Abner's house—The publishers—Scribners—the leading publishers in the world—want to bring it out right off, but I will hold it a little and see if I can't make it better. This is my last book except one—I will write a book of people, the world's great or wonderful that I have known. Then I am through—I will study Greek and philosophy. During this last year I have studied a good deal about the Old Testament —much of it stinking Jewish stuff, some of it beautiful, and I have gone through the New Testament in Greek, studying especially the belief in spirits, demons and astrology that held people's mind in the first centuries of our era. I am constantly puzzled by the fact that so many Christians who believe everything in the Bible rarely read a word of it. I can quote them passage after passage which is very wonderful but is as new to them as what my awful friend Walter Winchell will say tomorrow. There is one person I can think of who could understand me in what I am saying and that is my darling Aunt Sallie. When my book does come out you will like the things I say of her.

I do wish I could come in and see you.

Lovingly
Stark

Did you see that Mr. Henry Wallace had dropped his party etc.? So I've asked him and Mrs. Wallace over to dinner next week. He is a very nice man indeed when he sticks to the soil and growing things, about which he knows and loves a great deal.

741 | To Ella Somerville, Oxford, Mississippi

Jennymead
Waccabuc, New York
Tuesday [August 22, 1950]

Dearest Ella,

You will smile at my egotism in sending you a copy of a new poem I have written.[4] Norman Dello Joio—our leading figure among the American composers now—has asked me to write words for an opera he would compose. I don't know what I can do about that, but I have got so far as a song to go into a short opera form of Oscar Wilde's fable of *The Nightingale and the Rose.* Even if we get no further, I think he could do something beautiful with this song I have written. Don't bother to return it, but show it to a few sweet people there. I have been sorry you didn't go to Europe this year and so could stop by here for a little visit. (I sound [like] the lady who ordered a cocktail in order to get the cherry.)

Julia and Ben are in California—they are coming up here in September or October for ten days—I look forward to seeing them.

I have just finished two oval, Louis XV baroques for a rich lady who is also a darling. And I just did two days of lectures and conferences at William and Mary, Williamsburg.[5] That's all my news—otherwise a summer here in the country—strange weather—many many flowers —and Mr. and Mrs. Henry Wallace are coming to dinner next week and I'll hear what he thinks of this war. We are ending by getting the entire Orient against us, I fear, and for what exactly? Well, you ask the gods about that. Please let me know your news—Love to all the family—

Lovingly,
Stark

4. For the poem, see below, Letter 745. Young's poem is based upon Wilde's fable of "The Nightingale and the Rose."
5. See above, Letter 737 and notes.

742 | To Charles Munro Getchell,[6] Oxford, Mississippi

> Jennymead
> Waccabuc, New York
> August 28, 1950

Dear Mr. Getchell,

I did appreciate and value your too kind and gracious letter [7] more than I can tell you. It is in my files to stay with me a long time. It is I who remember all that gentle cordiality and friendly response in that world of my old University, and I recall that visit to your class with a warm heart. It was delightful to me to see that the new men on the faculty are of the calibre they are. One could see at one glance that your class was not taught by anything mediocre, anybody without wit and theatre practice and wisdom.

Scribners finally came to the end of the edition of *The Sea Gull* and French has brought it out in an agreeable little volume. I am sending you a copy, with the most cordial regards.

I can recommend *The Sea Gull,* alone out of Chekhov's plays, as a gold mine for amateur or college production. The parts are soundly scored and distinct, and the feeling is close to young perceptions; the plot is marked enough to carry along.

I hope you are at the beginning of a happy season—there are times when I miss the life in a college profoundly.

> Yours sincerely,
> Stark Young

6. Charles Munro Getchell (1909–63), born in Gardiner, Maine, was chairman of the speech and theatre department at the University of Mississippi from 1946 until his death in 1963.

7. Getchell had written Young late in June about his visit to the University of Mississippi. "I wanted to write you all this sometime ago. I wanted to write it when I saw the portrait and the tapestry that are to remain with us, as a talisman, I like to think, until you return again. But, to repeat, I was slow to action and then delay was implemented by the unnerving thought that such a letter might seem, if not a little ridiculous, a shade presumptuous. And so I did not write."

743 | To John Hall Wheelock and Charles Scribner, Charles Scribner's Sons, New York

[Waccabuc, New York]
August 28, 1950

Dear Jack and Charlie,

The only title I can think of to cover these years of mine up to twenty-one is *Perchance to Dream*—but the connotations there spoil the impression.[8] We will get a title, however, before we leave off. I will study this MS and doubtless add minor variations—this autumn—at present I have gone as far as I can go. But perhaps we *can prepare the way* for some spring publication—if you think best of the whole matter.

I regard it as a great privilege to be writing for civilized publishers, who are also friends in the great style.

S.Y.

Lea Black is a theatrical typing concern, and did not do so good a job as I should like on this MS. But I can't better it now.

S.Y.

744 | To Robert Penn Warren, Random House, New York

Jennymead
Waccabuc, New York
Tuesday [August 29, 1950]

Dear Red,

I wish I had asked you the last time we met whether you liked to be called that or not—and so we go, I had heard it and meant to make a

8. Young seems not to have objected to the Shakespearean connotation but to the substance of Hamlet's phrase, "To die, to sleep / To sleep—perchance to dream" (*Hamlet,* 3, 1, 64–65).

friendly gesture. Well, the point now is that I have been in Williamsburg on a seminar mission and at home have been trying to get a MS. to the point where Scribner's could see it, and so the time flies.

I was delighted to have a copy of your new novel,[9] and read it with absorbed attention, though in general I am a poor reader of fiction. Your book has been reviewed to the point of strangulation and I am sure you don't want an exegesis here from me. But what struck me most was the sense of a mind that is rich, poetic and based in tradition and culture. That is a fine compliment indeed, or so I should take it.

The narrative interest succeeds in holding us—that means a lot— and that device of Jerry's *Journal*[1] allows for some beautiful writing in a style not permitted by the surrounding text. Some of his passages are sweeping and intricate and grand, like a fine poet's. Basta—but thank you very much.

Please remember me to your lady. I have never seen her name written, but it always sounds like Cenina.[2] At any rate she is very distinguished and *molto simpatica* in my opinion, I always think of her with a warm and happy enthusiasm.

When you all come to New York please let me know. Thank you again.

Affectionately yours
Stark Young

9. *World Enough and Time: A Romantic Novel* had been published by Random House early in the summer of 1950.

1. Warren used extensive quotations from his primary source, "The Confession of Jereboam O. Beauchamp," published in Bloomfield, Kentucky, 1826.

2. Young refers to Emma Brescia Warren.

745 | To Norman Dello Joio, New York

[320 East 57th Street]
[New York]
[September, 1950]

THE DYING NIGHTINGALE [3]

Come, sweet Death,
Come with thy sweet darkness!
I have given my blood for love,
I have given the blood of my heart,
I am fading into the heart of thee.
My voice grows faint.
Does the white moon hear me?
Does Echo, where she dwells amid the gentle slopes,
And wake the sleeping shepherds from their dreams,
Or the river reeds carry it to the sea?
O Death, thou art the daughter of Night,
I will go with thee, I am with thee,
I, the nightingale, who sang of love,
I sang unto the rose of love.
In my days' silence I was lost and sad,
Only in the shadow of darkness I sang,
Under the moon or the stars,
And now in this thy night
I will sing forever.

Dear Norman,

I was delighted at what you said of those two places. I knew all along that for a song they could be better with the changes you saw needed. As poetry to be *read* I think the lines are better as they stand—pro-

---

3. In a letter to Julia Young Robertson, August 30, 1950, Young enclosed the poem with the following comment: "Note, this is written for an opera of one-act by Norman Dello Joio, our leading composer among the young Americans. The theme is to be based on a fable of the nightingale, who, when the lover must have a red rose to be loved by his beloved, pressed her bosom against a thorn until her blood made a red rose, lovelier than was ever seen, and when the blood was done and the rose thus red, the nightingale was dead." Young thus summarized Oscar Wilde's fable of "The Nightingale and the Rose." See above, Letter 741.

vided the question mark is removed after *dreams* and the four lines are grasped by the eyes as a group together.

As it stands if you read it with the voice making the question mark after *Echo?*—you get quite an effect.

But for a song the new form is much better.

It is very sweet to have somebody you love come out at just the right place in a point of view or agreement, as my dear Norman did in this.

Please give my love to Grace. Wales sends messages.

Best to you, dear Norman, bless you—

Stark

"Does Echo, where she dwells amid the gentle slopes,
Wake the sleeping shepherds from their dreams,
Or the river reeds carry my voice to the sea?"

746 | To Lawton Campbell, Bronxville, New York

[Waccabuc, New York]
Wednesday [September 6, 1950]

Dear Lawton,

Wales and I both appreciated very much your writing us about the changes in the play.[4] They sound good. But I always thought the cast of characters was from the start a brilliant opportunity for the right actors. That mask idea will be fine if a good actress plays the part—the reasons for Cassandra's putting it on have to be created deeply from within the mind of the actress and the character. I wish Miss Barrymore would play it, she would knock us down.

It already seems a long time since you sweet people were up here with us, and now the cold nights are coming and the season will be over before we know it. Cousin Nell[5] wrote us a very graceful note. Of

---

4. Young refers to Campbell's *Foolish Sunset,* which was never produced.
5. Mary Ellen Booth Parker (Mrs. William L. Parker, 1882–1965), Campbell's aunt, known to close friends and her family as "Nell."

course Cousin Myrtle[6] stands first in my heart, but Cousin Nell and Cousin Margaret[7] are awfully nice.

You will be glad to hear that both Jack Wheelock and Charlie Scribner are greatly delighted with my book, they can't say enough about it; and want to try and do something special for it. They think a spring publication is best, and that means early spring, and they want to get the book printed so that copies, not review copies, should go to the right people a month ahead of publication. For this they want the MS. by the middle of this month, this month, and I have been making some additions and what not, and so we shall see what we shall see. I still have no title. I would like to call it

Perchance to Dream

as a picture of a young man's mind up to twenty and over, but the *Hamlet* connotations of that are all wrong, and it goes overboard.[8] I thought of

The Chambers in the House of Dreams[9]

from Francis Thompson, but that is very likely too long, May the Lord help me, though he seems slow about it.

Thank you again for your sweet letter, very like Lawton. Wales sends his love and so do I, to you all.

Stark

747 | To Caroline Charlotte McGehee, Como, Mississippi

Waccabuc, New York
Tuesday [September 12, 1950]

Dearest Cousin Cad,

I have been typing on a MS. all day for my publishers—it will be a book like those chapters in the Virginia Quarterly, and brought up to

6. Myrtle Gertrude Booth Campbell (Mrs. Charles Lawton Campbell, 1872–1963), Campbell's mother.
7. Margaret Booth; see below, Letter 823 and n. 7.
8. See above, Letter 743, n. 8.
9. Francis Thompson, "Dream-Tryst," stanza 3, line 1.

my twenty-first year. My publishers profess to be much excited about it. It will be in print before long but not released for public sale till the early autumn of 1951.[1]

I am sorry to hear you feel broken up, bless your heart, you still seem to me my favorite cousin and a wonderful person, witty, brave, aristocratic, loyal and many other beautiful qualities.

That is news about a new baby boy,[2] the blessings of life are often tied up in the children we love. I sent your letter to Julia, she will enjoy seeing it.

We have many vegetables and flowers here now but it all is to end, for the air begins to be sharp with fall. I hate to see the summer pass and to go back to New York, in the midst of the general horror that is in people's minds and their fears about what a war may do and all that. I wish I could feel we have wise men in Washington to handle the situation as is best possible.

Bowman is bothered of course because so much building has to be called off. He has made money from the plans he has done, about $17000, but the building would have brought in more money as well as giving him the satisfaction of seeing his work carried out. I had saved enough money to live modestly on but now with the prices of things a dollar is worth less than fifty cents. We like to use a country place partly to have friends out for week-ends, and every time we do so it costs us about forty dollars extra for the two days, which is of course absurd. So life goes.

I will not read this dull letter over or else it might be torn up. Please give Cousin Jennie and everybody my love. Bowman sends very cordial messages.

Lovingly
Stark

1. Both Charles Scribner and John Hall Wheelock had written Young to express enthusiasm over the manuscript and to suggest possible titles. After advising postponement of publication until the "early autumn of 1951," Wheelock remarked: "The symbol of spring or stream runs through the book as a sort of unifying under-current. I suppose you might build a title around that: *The Sparkling Stream,* or *Youth's Sparkling Stream,* though the latter is a little bit hard to say."

2. Young refers to the birth of Peter Darabos Nelson, August 10, 1950.

748 | To Eldon J. Hoar,[3] Oxford Eagle, Oxford, Mississippi

320 East 57th Street
New York
November 25, 1950

Dear Mr. Hoar,

My old and dear friend, Phil Stone, has just sent me a copy of THE OXFORD EAGLE for November 16, devoted largely to honoring Bill Faulkner. It is an excellent issue and will prove highly useful to future biographers and writers on American literature.

There is one point, however, that for the sake of fairness all round I should like to point out in this letter, which I hope you can find space for in your columns.

IN PHIL STONE'S valuable personal record of Bill he states that nobody in Oxford except Phil and Mack Reed and Bill's mother cared anything about his writing.[4] I was not in Oxford but I was from Oxford and every summer I was in Oxford to visit my father. And, Phil Stone having brought us together, I would see Bill Faulkner and often read things he had written. Finally it seemed to me highly desirable that so remarkable a young writer should try a change to New York.

I proposed this and said that a friend of mine, Elizabeth Prall, who directed an important bookshop, would be able to give him a job there that would tide him over till he found something better suited to his needs, and that meanwhile he would be more than welcome to stay with me. He agreed to come. Miss Prall not very long afterwards married Sherwood Anderson, and through Sherwood Bill Faulkner was put in touch with Horace Liveright, who published SOLDIER'S PAY and gave him the usual three-book contract with a publisher. I am

---

3. Eldon J. Hoar (b. 1906), editor of the Oxford *Eagle* from 1950 to 1955. He published this letter from Young in the *Eagle*, November 30, 1950, p. 13. Young's letter was occasioned by an article by Phil Stone which appeared in the *Eagle*, November 16, 1950, pp. 1, 3, one of several articles honoring Faulkner for winning the Nobel Prize for Literature. Announcement of the award had been made on November 10. Young's letter was again published in the *Eagle*, April 22, 1965, Sec. 2, p. 2.

4. Stone had written: "Nobody in Oxford cared . . . nobody but his mother and myself and Mack Reed." In a headnote to Young's letter, when it appeared in the Oxford *Eagle*, Hoar explained that "Phil Stone said Tuesday morning that he apologized for neglecting Mr. Young in his story about the Faulkner career."

anxious to have this long belief on my part known in Oxford; since it is only natural that there will be some people, some of them friends of both of us, who may wonder why I as an Oxford man and a fellow writer should never have shown an interest or admiration for William Faulkner. I am already touching on this point in certain New York quarters; on numerous occasions various critics and authors have said to me as taken for granted that of course I did not care for Faulkner. I have always tried to convince them how mistaken they are, though I have never seen my way exactly to telling them in my opinion Bill has more of the real thing in his little finger than all these New York writers put together.

I AM WELL aware that when a man has a great success such as the Nobel Prize there will be many people who have always known, who have thought all along, who have often said—et cetera—on the basis of the Spanish proverb that he who wins is always likable. But after more than thirty years that can hardly be laid at my door.

My visit to Oxford a year and a half ago after so long an absence, and seeing old friends and making new ones, and feeling so much pride in the wonderful development of our old University, brings all this even closer to me.

With regards and best wishes for the continued success of the EAGLE I am

Yours sincerely,
Stark Young

749 | To Julian Huxley, London, England

320 East 57th Street
New York
November 27 [1950]

Dear Julian,

After three relapses I seem rid of my Virus X at last—I ought to be, considering the number of infections I had.

It was a great disappointment not to see you, even on one of those few days you wrote you were to have in New York. I was in the country, a lot of the time in bed. On the 17th, your last day, I called up at the Lamonts', to hear your voice if possible, but even more to learn whether you had picked up this intestinal flu, which was all over New York. I hope not, for it is the very devil to get rid of, and is apt to strike you down again if you get tired, etc.

I wish I might have heard directly from you Juliette's news. I have often thought what a strain it must have been for you to adjust yourself from all that Unesco business and return, as it were, to private life. I don't doubt you managed, but what a problem. Of course you do have that wonderful and intelligent and sympathetic Juliette to be alongside of you at such times.

I was glad to see that William Faulkner got the Nobel Prize.[5] I started to read his Mss. when he was about eighteen, when I visited my father every summer in Oxford, Mississippi. Then finally one summer I urged him to try changing to New York and staying with me till he could find himself. Through me he came to know Sherwood Anderson, who persuaded Horace Liveright to publish *Soldier's Pay,* his first book, and give him the usual three-book contract. The first two books did very little, then *Sanctuary* came and went extremely well. Bill told me at the time that since they would not read the other two books he put the dirt into *Sanctuary* to make them read it. Such is life. If Pearl Buck got the Nobel award,[6] I think Bill should have a round dozen of them.

Goodness knows when I'll see you. I hope you have a lecture tour over here on your list. Oliver Messel is here with his décor for *The Lady's Not for Burning*[7] and Edith Evans in *Daphne Laureola*[8]—both have urged me to come and stay with them in London next spring, but there is no chance of it. The place in the country for one thing would hold me here. It is a marvellous refuge from April to November.

I hope you and Juliette will find time to write me your news.

Bowman would ask to be remembered if he were at home. He has

---

5. Newspapers carried the story on November 11.
6. Pearl Buck (1892–1973) received the Nobel Prize in 1938.
7. The play opened November 8, 1950, at the Royale Theatre.
8. Opened September 18 and closed November 4. Edith Evans (Dame Edith Mary Booth), actress, began her career at Covent Garden in 1912 and subsequently has had a distinguished career both in London and New York.

about $400,000 in commissions on hand (at 10% my God!) and is very busy at his office.

Love to you both

Stark

750 | To Lawton Campbell, Bronxville, New York

320 East 57th Street
New York
Sunday [December 10, 1950]

Dear Lawton,

Not as an egotist author but because you have been so sweet about the memoir pieces, I am sending you the new form for the last page of the book.[9] It has taken me several days to think it out and to work it out from Leopardi's very difficult style.

Love to you all—bless Cousin Myrtle.[1]

Yours
Stark

[Enclosure]

house, Thou all my hours of happiness. These and many passages came to me; but at the same time I found myself tortured by one recurring doubt; might it not be that I was nothing and was only moved by the power and persuasion of great words? I tried to think not, and remembered Dante's saying: Poetry is the loving use of wisdom.

But speaking, meanwhile, for the classic tradition and for the clear, lovely daylight of the classic thought and its avoidance of the murky, ethereal and turgid, I could put my small mind and timid wonder

---

9. Young enclosed several pages of rough notes and a typescript of his most recent draft of the final portion of *The Pavilion*. This draft is printed below. Before the volume was published, however, Young made additional revisions.

　　1. Myrtle Booth Campbell.

against the unknown and the confused shadows of mystical desire. I did recall a line of Tibullus'

qua nulla humano sit via trita pede

where no path groweth trite with human feet, and could say to myself where are the voices now, the songs and the pipes blowing upon the hills?

More than thirty years have passed since that time these pages write of. And it saddens and perplexes me to think that most of what was passionately lived or rich in hope at least may have been lost to me long since with the years, and that the effort indeed to return to what no longer exists may be only vain. I recall to mind Leopardi's poem where he imagines boundless spaces and immortal silences in which for a moment the heart is not afraid. And as he hears the wind rustle in the trees he goes comparing that infinite silence to this voice, and remembers eternity, and the dead seasons, and then the season that is present and alive, and the sound of it—*e il suon di lei,* against the immensity of time and space, like a breath of wind.

751 | To John Mason Brown, New York

320 East 57th Street
New York
Thursday [December 14, 1950]

Dear John,

I have read and then Wales read aloud, for the second time, your *Macbeth* article [2]—indeed Macbeth shall sleep no more.

2. John Mason Brown reviewed Edith Sitwell's recital of *Macbeth* and the production of Christopher Fry's *The Lady's Not for Burning,* starring John Gielgud, Pamela Brown, and Richard Burton, in "Seeing Things: Poets and Players," *Saturday Review,* XXXIII (December 2, 1950), 44–46, 68–69. Although Brown conceded Edith Sitwell's devotion to Shakespeare and "her poet's insight into his technical devices," he held that both she and Glenway Wescott were insuperably handicapped by their lack of training in acting. Wrote Brown: "A lecture is one thing, a play another. The two do not mix. No drama can be expected to survive if it is cut up into canapes, and if critical comments are always interrupting the line of its action and destroying its sus-

I have nothing against Miss Sitwell,[3] I think she is a game old war horse, part fraud, part muddled, partly haughty, and part high nosed. I must say I cannot make the same statement about some of the weak fish that attach themselves to her sides, and make themselves look silly and pretentious and false enough. (You will kindly note that I avoided the natural bottom.)

However—

As to this article of yours I have not seen anything in several years in American journalism that came within a mile of it. I will also say that nobody I can think of but you could have written it. This is partly due to the double nature of that piece. In the first place it is homey and human and witty, full of sharp and clever observation, all based on the facts of life and Sitwells.[4] But the wonder is that all the underlying inference is based on real education and on sound aesthetic principles, or whatever the Modern Museum will let us call them. There are reverberations of a profound understanding of the things involved, the theatre art, the nature of poetic readings, the reading by poets, the absurdities of bombastic pretense, the visible scene as contrasted with the deep elements involved. I congratulate you and all of us in fact on a brilliant—a word I rarely use—and complete presentation; I know the problems of such a piece, I marvel at your competence and lovable go. That beautiful and admired Cassie of mine, as an old friend, must be bursting with pride.

I have only one suggestion to make, to be thought of when the article is to appear in a book—I hope it does, I should say so! That is when you speak of Miss Edith's bunko analyses of certain lines, you

---

pense. The supposed justification of this hodge-podge treatment of Shakespeare's tragedy was . . . to let us hear his poet's words spoken by a poet. That Dr. Edith has an arresting voice, no one can deny. But that she has scant knowledge of how to use it dramatically seems equally incontestable. Reading with an ear for assonance rather than an eye for character, she succeeded chiefly in reducing Lady Macbeth to a lesson in prosody."

3. Edith Sitwell (1887–1964), English aristocrat, achieved an international reputation for her poetry and criticism of Alexander Pope and Jonathan Swift. On November 16, 1950, she presented at the Museum of Modern Art a recital of scenes from *Macbeth*. She was assisted in the performance, which emphasized the poetical qualities of the play, by Glenway Wescott, the novelist, and two actors, Bernard Savage and Gertrude Flynn.

4. A reference to Miss Sitwell's brothers, Sacheverell Sitwell (b. 1897) and Sir Osbert Sitwell (1892–1969), both prominent men of letters. Sir Osbert Sitwell was present for the New York recital of *Macbeth*.

mention that they were so far as Shakespeare goes written by "instinct." [5] In my opinion the word just there is highly unfortunate. I think I understand what you mean; you mean that Shakespeare based this passage not on theory and stale British snob assertion but on a certain inherent compulsion of impulse in which what some people might call inspiration played a part. Your word *instinct* would certainly produce a false impression among many readers. The author of those violently baroque passages in *Lucrece*—

For example

Her cheeks—but look up those lines in the 1400's of *Lucrece*—nothing could be more exotic, more baroque—

and certainly the word *instinct* is misleading, even if a half of one's public are half-wits. You can remedy that very easily.

Dear John, I do congratulate you. The quality remaining from your essay is pure delight and perfect commonsense recognition.

As Pascal said in the seventeenth century, and Shaw, Yeats, Oscar Wilde and who knows who are reported to have said, according to the narrator, please excuse this long letter, I didn't have time to write a short one. I am packing to go to Texas and Mexico, with my sister.

In the heat of my enthusiasm over that article I sent it off to my beloved Edith Evans, since she had spoken with warm enthusiasm about what you wrote of her, and so if you think of it when you are at the office will you mail me a copy for my files—where few articles of any kind are retained—? Evans came out to the country for two week-ends. I had met her two or three times on her last visit, and so sent her word through a common friend that if she would like the country for a change it would be delightful. To my surprise she said she would come that week-end. I mention this because it is a comment on her—it was not so much my remembered charms that brought her; it was a desire evidently to get away from the Broadway and theatre strain—this was the night before her opening. I tried for the article at the news places but in vain. I want to read it aloud from time to time to guests. What

5. Brown had written that "so overintellectualized was Dr. Edith's approach to what Shakespeare did instinctively that in all probability he would have been befuddled by her prating about 'schemes of tuneless, dropping dissonances,' 'a thickened, darkened assonance,' and his 'placing of double-syllabled and treble-syllabled words and quick-moving, unaccented, one-syllabled words.'" Miss Sitwell had discussed these matters in her article "'Macbeth,'" *Atlantic Monthly,* CXXXV (April, 1950), 43–48. On December 20, Brown replied to Young: "I see your point about 'instinct.' It suggests something I had in mind but not all."

a really heavenly piece of writing that is! And most writing is so sloppy, baseless and rotten, as well as being extraneous.

Give my love to that dear, beautiful Cassie—and no fool at that. I wish you all a good Christmas and a year ahead that will not be too involved with wretched things in this world.

Yours as ever
Stark

752 | To John Mason Brown, New York

320 East 57th Street
New York
Monday [January 8, 1951]

Dear John,

I am just back from Texas, and your letter and the clipping[6] are here waiting for me. Such a lovely letter, and you and that dear Cassie so lovely as friends! As for the article it is even better on this renewed adventure into it. Most wit and perception of the incongruous front of ambition and push are marred by being smarty. This of yours is not, just as your final judgement comes off in some genial but not sour solution, and your true taste is evinced in subtle plunge and revelation.

I enclose an Evans Christmas message[7]—ashamed to say that in my departure for Texas and my virus X there I did nothing about her. I'm not sure I told you what pleasure she took in your article about her. I thought it one of the few things I happened to see about her worth reading at all.

My new book[8]—the child of endless memory and effort—is with Scribners, they think so well of it that they scare me—no title—out of hundreds considered—has come off yet. Early in the fall of 1951.

Thank you again—

Stark

6. See above, Letter 751 and notes.
7. Young enclosed a cable from Edith Evans: "Affectionate good wishes most happy Xmas dear Cousin Stark and Cousin Wales."
8. The manuscript of *The Pavilion*.

753 | To Charles Scribner, Charles Scribner's Sons, New York

320 East 57th Street
New York
January 9, 1951

Dear Charlie,

Thank you for your good letter. I am returning the contract and have no suggestions.[9] I hope to get a title soon. Went over about fifty or more during the holidays.

As for any advance, I appreciate your mentioning it. I won't want any. I thought I had saved a modest sum for my declining years, but with the dollar dropped to almost nothing things are a bit different. However, I think that with modest living I will get by if I don't live too long. Nevertheless, thank you, and feel assured that I would not hesitate to call on you at any time.

Bowman and I both enjoyed so much having you and Vera[1] here. He admired you both greatly, and sees why I have so often told him about you.† I am sorry he had no photographs to show you; one of his houses for example had forty-two pictures from it in the Architectural Forum. He was President of the Triangle Club in Princeton and loves the place still but never seems to go there any more.

I hope you hear good news from Little Charlie.[2] Please give Vera my love. I just had a card from another charming Vera: Mrs. Stravinsky. So life goes.

Affectionately yours
Stark

† This is an illustration of a place where our smiled at Southern "you all" comes in very usefully, Yes?

---

9. Scribner had sent a contract for *The Pavilion* which specified the royalty at a "flat" 15 percent, and he asked Young for suggestions. Scribner also offered an advance payment.

1. Mrs. Charles Scribner.

2. Probably Charles Scribner's grandson.

754 | To Myra Champion,[3] Asheville, North Carolina

[320 East 57th Street]
New York
February 17, 1951

Dear Miss Champion,

I have your letter about Tom Wolfe and am glad to hear of the collection you are making in his honor.

I never saw much of Tom but admired and liked him very much, and felt always sure that we were good friends. There is a very fine letter from him to me that is to be included in Scribner's volume of his letters.[4]

Tom and I had Max Perkins as a very close friend to each of us and that made our relation somewhat more of an intimacy than circumstances might otherwise have brought about.

We shall not have many writers as gifted as Thomas Wolfe and I am honored to have this opportunity to speak of him, however briefly.

Yours sincerely
Stark Young

755 | To Eric Bentley, New York

320 East 57th Street
New York
Sunday [March 4, 1951]

Dear Eric,

That was an unusually pleasant experience this past week: your book[5] came, I went right at the notes you had written for the various plays. I saw the list of plays chosen, adapted, translated and otherwise —what's the use of taking only the regular standbys? Your scheme is

3. Myra Champion, librarian of the North Carolina Room, Pack Memorial Public Library, Asheville, North Carolina.
4. See above, Letter 444.
5. Eric Bentley (ed.), *The Play: A Critical Anthology* (1951). Bentley dedicated the volume: "To Stark Young from whom I have tried to learn."

much better, and with great skill you often put teeth into the question of the play chosen, congratulations—and then innocently and suddenly I saw the dedication page. I was immensely pleased and honored. I cannot express my appreciation, though I don't quite swallow my teaching you much. The range of your experience in reading drama stuns me.

Your book sins in the right direction: it really asks for and expects brains from teacher and student and the casual reader of plays.

Have you ever seen anything sillier than my dear old friend Bunny Wilson's remark on Antigone's brother fixation.[6] In the first place when does, at what point, this fixation become a fixation? In the second place what if it is so?—though that only lessens the dimension of the situation and problem. It is only human for a sister not to want her brother left to be eaten by dogs, whether she loves him or not. It is Greek religious to believe that if he gets no burial he will forever be etc. etc. But as I say, in the lines you kindly quote,[7] there is, deepest of all, the outrage to an immediate human—with us in the West at least —instinct. All the rest, as mentioned above, in editors and so on can easily follow on this.

Once Mrs. Isaacs, who is a very swordswallower when it comes to points in psychoanalysis, going into committee and seeing subtly and complicatedly—while I sweat to get anything and everything not complicated but clearly—the complication as a part of it if necessary but not as the end to reach—well, when I first knew her she did a bit of the subtle—"Were you," she said with an almost bedside manner, "very fond of your mother?" (*S'immagine!*)—as the Italians say. "Why yes," I said, "and I love garlic too, so what?" Health ensued.

Your review selections for the *Salesman* are very astutely chosen.[8] I have read so little in editorial writing and explanations and theories about plays like *Othello* that the idea of the final eloquence coming from self-dramatization, self-deception,[9] astounds me. His not being

6. In the notes to *Antigone,* Bentley referred to Edmund Wilson's interpretation of the "brother-fixation" in *Antigone* advanced in Wilson's essay "The Wound and the Bow" from the volume of that title published in 1931.

7. In the notes to *Antigone,* Bentley quoted the same passage from Young's *Immortal Shadows* that Bentley had quoted earlier in his article about Young's retirement. See above, Letter 731 and n. 2.

8. Bentley included reviews by Brooks Atkinson, Ivor Brown, John Mason Brown, Eleanor Clark, and Frederick Morgan.

9. Bentley mentioned two interpretations of Othello's final eloquence: that it confirms Othello's achievement of self-knowledge and dignity in death, or that it represents the height of his "self-dramatization, self-deception."

easily jealous plays quite a part in the headlong violence of his jealousy when it does rise. I have always thought of that last eloquence as a carrying and overwhelming flood, which to varying degrees is its essential nature.

Most eloquence analyzed in our approach to it tends to become foolish, especially in English, whereas folly if expressed with eloquence may take on a certain amount of force or persuasion. Othello, as he speaks or spouts might easily dramatize himself, just as everything and everybody around is dramatized by the elevation and intensity. To dramatize himself and then spout takes away the very thing that Desdemona most loved in him. It was Epictetus, wasn't it, who said that the grammarians set the very letters of the alphabet quarreling together?

I once heard Walter Hampden[1] speak Othello's passages as if in deep thought—he could not have got the power anyhow—and Othello sounded like a perfect fool.

It is evident that Shakespeare meant Othello to be *black,* that is said straight, and thick-lipped. The Italians whom I have heard use *moro* always meant a Negro, whom they often find beautiful—I remember Harrison Rhodes'[2] nurse, a big black, gentle-faced creature, who whenever he went around the streets of Venice, kept hearing, *Ah, che bel moro!* A lot of ink has been spilt on this question. A good many Arabs like a good many Hindoos are very dark indeed, but I never saw a black one in Tunis or Algiers. You must have enough by now of my screed, and you can see by the mistakes that this is not one of my typing days.

Eric, can you send me a line at your early convenience as to where you will be, I want to send you a book—not one of mine.

Thank you again.

Affectionately
Stark

1. Walter Hampden (1879–1955), actor, began acting Shakespearean roles in New York in the first decade of the century. In the 1925–26 season, he appeared with Ethel Barrymore in *Hamlet* and *The Merchant of Venice* and played many roles in repertoire theatre during the 1930s and 1940s. One of his last appearances was in *The Crucible* in 1953.
2. Probably Harrison Rhodes (1871–1929), author and playwright, best known for *Ruggles of Red Gap* and other plays which he wrote with collaborators.

756 | To Allen Tate, Princeton, New Jersey

320 East 57th Street
New York
Friday [March 30, 1951]

Dearest Allen,

My typewriter is at the cleaners etc. so I must deliver this scrawl on your head. I heard from Mrs. Wheelock that you have a chair at $8000 in St. Louis.³ I'd like to hear more details of it. I hope it is good, but Mrs. W. seemed to think you were going to keep the Princeton house. Well, I'll hear more of this. I hope you and Caroline won't be farther off for most of the time.

I have decided on a title.⁴

The Pavilion—(on the opposite page would be this from the 31st Psalm—) "thou shalt keep them secretly in a pavilion from the strife of tongues."

The sub-title to help the person interested to know a little of the contents—

Of People and Times Remembered, of Stories and Places.

I like the idea of keeping secretly in a loved place the loved things I write about. I hope you and Caroline like the title. The enclosed Bishop clipping is an extension of the Miracle mess about which you wrote such an excellent letter to the *Times*.⁵ I'm glad you did. Sometimes I

3. On April 3, Tate answered that he was going not to St. Louis but to the University of Minnesota as a replacement for Robert Penn Warren, who had accepted a place at Yale.

4. Tate replied that he thought the title good but not perfect, since it needed the quotation from Psalms to explain the meaning. Earlier, Tate had approved his wife's suggestion, "The Summer Is Ended" (Jeremiah 8:20), which seemed to suggest the end of youth.

5. Tate had written a letter to the New York *Times* (February 1, 1951, p. 24) to protest Cardinal Spellman's attempts to obtain suppression of the Italian film *The Miracle*. Tate wrote that there is no institution in the United States that has the "legitimate authority to suppress books and motion pictures, however disagreeable they may be to certain persons on theological grounds." Books and plays, "bad as literature and bad as morality, in the long run suppress themselves." Young sent Tate a clipping of a news story, " 'Pastures' Boycott Is Asked by Bishop," from the New York *Times,* March 26, 1951, p. 24. The article related to an open letter from the Right Reverend Decatur Ward Nichols, bishop of the African Methodist Episcopal Church, to Cardinal Spellman and other religious leaders, urging the boycott of the current Broadway revival of *The Green Pastures*. Calling the play a "travesty on the folkways of religion,"

think the book is good and sometimes I think it pretty poor. It all remains to be seen.

It would be very fine to see you and Caroline.

Lovingly
Stark

757 | To John Hall Wheelock, Charles Scribner's Sons, New York

Waccabuc, New York
[April 8, 1951]

Dear Jack,

Thank you for the letter [6] and the suggestions about the jacket cut, which would be all right, since the other things mentioned might imply that education had been quite a subject for me to consider.

Have patience with me, please, but the more I think of the Glasgow quote the more unhappy I think it is. She said something better for the jacket, but could not stick it as a rival author and so changed to Deep South novels during the Civil War.[7] This is plainly silly, since there were none on that subject or field that are worth rivalling. I will find another sentence in her article.[8] We could use that on the jacket of *So*

---

but denying that he wished to advocate censorship, Bishop Nichols wrote: "Rather, I merely ask for good taste, dignity and truthfulness in the dramatic presentation of religion. Like its late counterpart, 'The Miracle,' any such distortion of things spiritual should be condemned to the scrap heap."

6. Wheelock had written to discuss the material for the jacket of *The Pavilion*.

7. The following comment by Ellen Glasgow appeared on the jacket of *So Red the Rose:* "There has never been a novel of the South in the Civil War that can compare with it." In her review of the novel in the *New York Herald Tribune Books*, July 22, 1934, p. 1, she changed slightly the wording: "It is . . . in my judgment the best and most completely realized novel of the Deep South in the Civil War that has yet been written." The sharpness of Young's comment suggests the possibility that Ellen Glasgow had originally written to him a stronger statement but rewrote it when she sent it to Maxwell Perkins for use on the jacket. See above, Letter 353.

8. From Ellen Glasgow's review, Young selected the following passage: "The penetration is unerring; the light falls straight on the subject . . . it contains the essential qualities of imaginative literature: simple fidelity to truth, the strong quiet pulse, like the pulse of life itself, and the sudden light that brings a deeper understanding and an enlargement of vision."

Red the Rose, but it could not be as if from the *Herald Tribune,* and so would be different in value or class or whatever.

I have from letters two other points for your consideration, not as to the jacket. Tomorrow I go off to Exeter with Bowman and his young nephew[9] but will be in New York on Friday and will call and see when I can drop by a moment or so.

All good wishes,

Yours
Stark

758 | To Julian Huxley, London, England

320 East 57th Street
New York
May 21, 1951

Dear Julian,

I just came back from the country today and am packing to go and settle for the summer. Your good card was waiting here for me.

I was so done in that what you told me of your address I was blind to. I wrote Juliette an air mail and she sent me the address. Meanwhile you have sent it to me.[1]

I had looked forward to seeing you and that Tuesday when I got pretty bad I thought I would go to lunch and get a cocktail and with the pleasure of seeing you be all right. But I went from bad to worse, was in bed several different times, thought I would go to heaven. I am about all right now, just a bit rickety. Ptomaine poisoning, to which I am very subject, but this last I really caught it. It made a pressure on my heart that was pretty bad at times. I do indeed regret giving out on you, dear Julian.

My book at Scribners is all in page proof and is being held till an advantageous date in the early fall.[2] I hope it is anything like as good as

9. Samuel Andrew Bowman (b. 1936), then attending Phillips Exeter Academy.
1. Huxley was lecturing at the University of Indiana at Bloomington.
2. Publication of *The Pavilion* was scheduled for September 10.

they say it is, at least I hope the right people will like it. On the lap of the gods.

I had the most lovely, witty and sweet letter from Juliette and will answer it soon.

Edith Evans, Oliver Messel and John Gielgud have all urged [me] to come for a London visit; but I shall probably never get there. The state of the world is at present overpowering, it seems to me. The newspapers and the incredible amount of military and Government babble are appalling. This is a time when not to know anything about history would leave the mind more comfortable.

If you are around these parts and have the time and inclination it would be delightful to see you in the country. It is about forty minutes on good trains, many of them, the New Haven Hartford to Yale, then we meet you and drive you forty minutes through pleasant scenery to the house. Unless we know well ahead week days as a rule are better, since somebody is apt to be there week-ends. If we knew a little ahead that would be another matter. We have a good man and much quiet, and it might be pleasant for you.

> Affectionately
> Stark

759 | To Ella Somerville, Oxford, Mississippi

> Jennymead
> Waccabuc, New York
> [May 23, 1951]

Dearest Ella,

It was very fine to hear from you and to know that life treats you kindly. I have been hopping around partly because the American National Theatre and Academy, who have been giving a number of productions this season and arranging things for outside town, insisted that I close the season for them with a lecture. They have been so kind about me and my little reputation that I had to do it. I chose Duse as a subject. I don't make lectures any more. Except for a kind of seminar, nicely paid, at Williamsburg last summer, the talk at Oxford was the last one I did. Luckily the theatre last Sunday was packed, and it seemed very pleasant, since I don't write in anything here in town and don't get around and advertise myself in the public eye. I am glad to say the attention was wonderful, and when I let forth with a quotation from a D'Annunzio play that Duse used to do, a round of applause. So afterward the Italian end of the Voice of America came around and urged me to make something like that in Italian, yesterday five of them came, the mechnists [*sic*] or whatever you call them, the director, and a man who had made a translation for me to read on the tape, there was much rehearsing and they nearly worked me to death. I hear from the outside that they were much pleased with our outcome. I hope I don't have to do it again soon, but I owe it to Italy and to Duse. God bless us.

I think Phil's last letter will entertain, more or less, you.[3] I never offered to read Emily's play—you can see what that brings on in all cases—but gave them the name of my agent, about the best in New York. I never spoke of it to the agent, and said it would be better for Phil not to mention me, since I had not read the play. I think I have written five or six letters to Phil—I have no secretary and all he has to do is to rear back and dictate. The agent sent it back with a courteous professional letter thanking him for sending it and saying she did not feel possibilities in it for handling or production. Phil then wrote me to ask her why, was it the subject matter or the play? I was obliged to write that the agent's letter would have to stand, she would think it very strange of me to ask her to give a longer opinion. I explained that hundreds of scripts for Broadway and Hollywood are submitted. You see his letter. He won't bother me to do more; he has thought all along that the subject matter would scare any producer in New York. If the agent had thought the play was any good she would have said so and suggested some modifications in the theme, etc. But I am glad Phil feels that way, it is much more comfortable to think you were too bold a playwright than one the agent is indifferent to. The non-professional

---

3. Phil Stone had written Young to thank him for his efforts in behalf of Mrs. Stone's play. Stone wrote that they had merely wished to test their belief that the theme of the play would frighten any New York producer.

world can be astonishing so far as the arts go. I think you had better not mention my mentioning this matter.

That lovely Professor Robinson sent me a sheet about a memorial pair of volumes about him,[4] ten or twenty thousand to be raised, with $5 and $20 a volume mentioned in an easy way that made what hair I have stand on end. I was sorry to write him that since I resigned from the New Republic in 1947 I have had no salaried income, was obliged to cash in some of my modest savings to get by, and with the dollar worth nothing I don't know how long those savings will last. I don't want to be obliged to do jobs in writing, it is a waste of time and I need my time for other things. Scribners thinks very highly indeed of my book that is to come out, much about the fine quality etc. but unless some chance arises it is not the kind of book that would make much money. Nevertheless I prefer to have written it, it was worked over and over, and it is what I wanted to write. Nothing else is worth anything about a work of art except this. New York is full of writers writing trash, and saying that when they get together some money they will write what they long to write. Appalling rot. My answer to that is yes, be a whore till you have saved up enough money to be a virgin. I am proud of that one.

The title of my book—after endless thought, suggestions and searching is

The Pavilion

(subtitle, to give an idea of the contents)

Of People and Things Remembered, of Stories and Places.

The title is taken from the Psalms: "thou shalt keep them secretly in a pavilion from the strife of tongues."

I want the book to be the pavilion that keeps loved things and places secretly contained away from the strife etc.

People seem to like the title, I hope you do.

Be sure I will send you one of the first copies. The whole thing is in

---

4. *Studies Presented to David Moore Robinson on His Seventieth Birthday,* Vol. 1, edited by George Emmanuel Mylonas (1951), and Vol. 2, edited by George Emmanuel Mylonas and Doris Raymond (1953). David Moore Robinson (1880–1958) taught Greek and Latin at the Johns Hopkins University from 1915 to 1947. From 1948 to 1958, he was professor of classics and archaeology at the University of Mississippi.

print now, paged, but not bound. They are holding it for early autumn, the best time for any book to appear.

It has been very warming to the heart talking things over with you, but don't ask me to read it over for mistakes, I'd never send it off in that case. Please tell the Bishops and Nina about the book and title. Bowman sends admiring greetings.

Love to you.
Stark

Remember me to Spencer.

760 | To John Hall Wheelock, Charles Scribner's Sons, New York

Jennymead
Waccabuc, New York
Saturday [June 2, 1951]

Dear Jack,

The binding[5] came yesterday afternoon and I am returning it at once—In a sadly depleted same envelope, the nearest envelopes to buy are seven miles away. Thank you very much for your trouble, well rewarded. The effect is excellent, the gold is a great addition and a good color of gold—not always true. A smallish and less expensive book like this may appeal, let's hope so, to Christmas tastes.

I have to come in for a treatment Tuesday and will call and see if you are free for lunch. I'm in town only for the day. I'd like to see you of course.

Thank you again.

As ever
Stark

5. For *The Pavilion*.

Have I ever seen those first pages of title, etc. I forgot whether I have or not. Scribners still has the MS.[6] have they not? No hurry. It can be sent not here but to 320 any time.

761 | To Caroline Gordon Tate, Bloomington, Indiana

Jennymead
Waccabuc, New York
Wednesday [July, 1951]

Dearest Caroline,

I have now read the St. Catherine,[7] some of it several times, and have marked passages all through it. *The Dialogue* has many remarkable places in it, but what I like especially is the Purgatory. I don't know anything about Purgatory, but I do know this wonderful soul and feeling when I see it. The whole idea of enveloping love is set forth more wonderfully than I have ever seen it before. It is all one of these things that if they are not proofs are marvellous evidences of God. I do thank you and will treasure this little book, you may well believe. I have sent it down to my dear sister and she will read it and return it. Bless you, Caroline.

If you see Santayana's *Dominations and Powers*[8] you will find some very fine paragraphs on Protestant morality, procedure and commercial mediocrity, plus a certain romantic egotism in the individual, etc. It is in the middle part of the book, in the two hundreds. What a man!

I am happy in the thought of what you and my dear Allen are getting out of the Church. After all few Americans have had as much contact with it as I have and feel as easily at home in it. I have had friends in Texas, seeing them often, one of the dearest friends I ever

6. Young gave the manuscript to Lawton Campbell, who has given it to the library of the University of Mississippi.

7. Caroline Gordon Tate had sent Young a copy of *Treatise on Purgatory* [and] *The Dialogue,* by Saint Catherine of Genoa, translated by Charlotte Balfour and Helen Douglas Irvine (1946).

8. George Santayana's *Dominations and Powers* had been published earlier in the year.

had was Frate Ventura Dei, in Fiesole, gentle saint and editor of the scholarly Franciscan Review, and I was three times in San Girolamo, the last for five months, and Mother Edith loved me and I her, a holy woman, an aristocrat, niece of some archbishop or other in England, and I was a friend, a daily, almost, companion of Archbishop Orth,[9] who lived there pretty much as Santayana is spending his last days in the same order's house in Rome. I spent many an afternoon in the monastery of San Francesco, in Fiesole, where Ventura got a special dispensation for me to have the freedom of the convent and the gardens and often for the brief intervals that were allowed sat with me. Duse used to come up sometimes just to greet him and see his face, though she could not frequent most of the convent. The sum of all which is to say that the one thing I could never forgive the Catholic Church is that it takes or might take you and Allen farther away from me, that is to say that you will love me less. I have loved you both and appreciated you and depended on your feeling about me so long that I don't want to readjust it all over at this late date. After all if you for your delight just go on to Heaven I should have at least the right address and might assert a nuisance value. You could regard me as the Purgatory that takes the rust off, painlessly, as St. Catherine says.

Please forgive this typing, I am writing in the loggia at the barn and have no erasers etc., here.

Thank you again for the book. I hope your jacket got to you. It was insured.

Lovingly

Stark

9. Bertrand Orth (1848–1931), born at Algert, Germany, was ordained priest in 1872 and became a missionary in the diocese of Vancouver. In 1900, he became bishop of Victoria, British Columbia, and in 1903 archbishop. In 1908, he resigned his see and became titular archbishop of Amasée.

762 | To Hudson Strode, University of Alabama, Tuscaloosa, Alabama

Jennymead
Waccabuc, New York
July 20, 1951

Dearest Hudson,

Not so long ago I saw a piece in *Newsweek* with a picture of Mr. Bowen, author of a new novel, and quite an account of your work there with budding novelists.[1] I knew you had seen the page but, nevertheless, I cut it out to go with this letter, and now I can't find it. But I was greatly pleased with this recognition, though of course it is not at all new. It does no harm just the same; your local lights will play more easily into your hand and give you fuller rein. Also it does not harm to speak of that great talent that you evidently have to straighten people out in their efforts to write novels. The novel in general is to my mind a poor and bastard form of the literary art, but when it does come off that is another matter. I do indeed admire what you have done there in this field; it is unique so far as I know.

When I was at the University of Mississippi in April a year ago— some centennial or something, I as honor guest speaker and what not, —I met Elizabeth Spencer, whose novel with some bad title I can never remember—*Light in the Morning* or something—it had lots of talent, I thought, and she was an adorable young woman, all the signs of talent.

Scribners professes to think very highly indeed of my new book, and I hope there will be readers for it. It is all in page proof, the jacket settled and all that, and they say they are saving a good date in the autumn for its appearance, let us hope so. It goes to my twenty-first year, though some of it moves forward into later years. You saw the things in the *Virginia Quarterly* and so may have some idea of what

1. Young refers to a review of Robert O. Bowen's *The Weight of the Cross* in *Newsweek*, XXXVII (April 23, 1951), 99. Bowen (b. 1920) had been Strode's assistant and a member of his writing class at the University of Alabama. The reviewer mentioned a number of Strode's students who had become successful writers; the group included Catherine Rodgers, Prewitt Semmes, Aubrey Carney, Thomas Hal Phillips, Alice Fellows, and Caryle Tillery.

the effect is. It cost me endless labor, trying for all sorts of perfections in style and also in the choice of what is to be included. If anybody reads it and likes it I have one more book to write, that will be in the nature of the autobiographical but will deal with people largely, Duse, Mussolini, Benavente, Pirandello, Doris Keane, Eugene O'Neill, Sherwood Anderson and so on. If I never write it that will be no great loss perhaps. It is very hard to make out what people are interested in these days. Dirt and sour sex, yes, and some sort of half-baked fuddle and bad taste about modernish matters for discussion, plus adolescent brains and interests—witness all the novels about homosexualism, fairies, lost mothers, and what not. The trouble with all subject matter is that in the end, *eventually,* it stands or falls by the amount of brains and distinction brought to it by the author.

I often think of you and that lovely Therese, a great person and a beautiful lady, and a true and loyal friend. I daresay that even with the passing years she is beautiful still, for she has "that within which passeth show."

Bowman asks to be remembered to you.

Affectionately
Stark

The title of my book is

The Pavilion
Of People and Times Remembered, Of Stories and Places

the title is from the Psalms, "thou shalt keep them secretly in a pavilion from the strife of tongues."

And this is what I have tried to do with loved things, loved people and so on. The book has a certain strong connection with *So Red the Rose.*

763 | To Allen Tate, Princeton, New Jersey

Jennymead
Waccabuc, New York
Sunday [August 11, 1951]

Dearest Allen,

When I got back from New Hampshire [2] I found in town on Tuesday some advance copies of my book—the actual publication date is September 10. So I sent you a copy.

Since I got my copy I have read the volume through five times. I can say that good or bad it is what I wanted it to be. I hope you take some satisfaction in it, since it is yours,[3] out of inmost heart, a belated payment of an old, very old debt and delight in you, your quality and affection.

You doubtless have your own matters to attend to before your leaving for Minnesota,[4] your poem [5] et cetera, but if you all are in these parts or want to come to see us it goes without saying that it would [be] a fine thing here. Please, of course, consider your own interests and pleasure. Thank my darling Caroline for her letters.

Wales sends messages.

Lovingly
Stark

2. Young and Bowman had been visiting Robert Edmond Jones in Union, New Hampshire.

3. Young dedicated *The Pavilion* to Allen Tate.

4. Tate had accepted a position on the faculty of the University of Minnesota.

5. Tate was composing a long poem in *terza rima*. Although still unpublished in its entirety, two parts of the work have been published as "The Swimmers," *Hudson Review*, V (Winter, 1953), 471–73, and "The Buried Lake," *Sewanee Review*, LXI (Spring, 1953), 177–80. Both poems have also appeared in Tate's *Poems* (1960).

764 | To Julia Young Robertson, Austin, Texas

[Waccabuc, New York]
[August, 1951]

Dearest Sister,

This is from a wild bird[6] they sent down from Memphis for that centenary occasion. The newspaper mind is a special kind of mind, all to itself. I saw him but once. He wrote several times, I see from clippings, of my reciting Greek!!!

The Wallaces last night at dinner were very nice indeed. I hope you and Ben will meet them. He is two or three people, all mixed up, silly in sections and in heart rather grand.

Lovingly
Stark

765 | To Allen Tate, Princeton, New Jersey

Waccabuc, New York
Sunday [August 19, 1951]

Dearest Allen,

Your lovely letter came Saturday—yesterday, and I was very happy to have it. That book is as good as I can make it, at least, with endless notes over time and endless rewriting and so on, and if it [is] even approximately good enough to be dedicated to you I am grateful indeed to life.

6. Paul Flowers of the Memphis *Commercial Appeal*. Young enclosed a letter, dated August 17, from Flowers in appreciation of the autographed copy of *The Pavilion* which Young had sent. Flowers wrote: "I am happy to testify in open meeting, that of the hundreds of spellbinders, waxworks exhibits, men with messages etc., I have encountered in the last fifteen years, there are only a scant few I would go to hear again. At the top of the list I submit Stark Young, reciting Greek poetry. I recall that delightful evening . . . at Oxford, when you convinced me that one does not need to be able even to identify a fraternity key to enjoy Sappho."

I wangled a copy out of Scribners for Francis Fergusson on the basis of a professorship in Princeton drama study. He is a very superior person, vastly studious and informed. At the center of him there is some sort of knot that interferes with the pressure and direct impact of his writing, sometime even when the content is admirable. A generous, fine spirit certainly.

I hope Nancy's wish comes true as to a girl.[7] In these times I'd stick to boys if it were left to me. Give her my love and Percy too—they are very lovely and unusual young people, and very sweet together. It means a great deal to have the children of people you love turn out so beautifully. When you think what a calamity children can be and the people they marry even worse hazards and sodden to boot. That mirror place I go to successfully is on Second Avenue—the Sutton Mirror Company—around 53rd–56th St. I think I have already written you this.

I have been reading a good deal about Thomas Aquinas, with Averroës, Abelard and other Arising [?]—I wish I might have seen your Thomson [?] article.[8] Were you disappointed in it?

Caroline's book I can hardly wait for. Jack Wheelock says it is good, very. Of course, but may good fortune attend it—so much in this business is luck and hit and miss, as you know.

The dampness here makes the paper like pulp, and this scratch paper is because my good stationery is exhausted. I have to go in to see Scribners tomorrow and will bring some of mine out.

All this scrawl ad infinitum is largely to give myself the illusion that I am having a visit with you.

Wales sends love to you both. I hope the terza rima poem comes on.[9] I do most heartily hope so.

Love to you
Stark

7. In 1944, Tate's daughter, Nancy Tate (b. 1925), married Percy Hoxie Wood (b. 1921), then a student at Vanderbilt University and later a graduate of the University of Tennessee Medical School in psychiatry. In 1953, he joined the staff of the Carrier Clinic, Belle Mead, New Jersey.

8. The two questionable readings in this sentence do not provide sufficiently clear material for documentation.

9. See above, Letter 763 and n. 5.

766 | To Caroline Charlotte McGehee, Como, Mississippi

Waccabuc, New York
Tuesday [August 21, 1951]

Dearest Cousin Cad,

You can see by this paper how damp it is here. I had to go to town yesterday to see my publishers and on my return found your sweet letter. The book is out September 10th—but they gave the author six copies—after that he buys what he needs, with ⅓ percent off. Such is life. So I am sending you one of the six early copies before the book is really out for the public. Some of it will touch your heart,[1] I know, dear Cousin Cad.

You should not speak of Edward or Dee as "handicapped with old folks." In so far as they have any sense, which I am sure they have, they know what a blessing it is to have you all, with your lovely characters and your memories and your sweet ways. Otherwise they would have largely the cheap mess in the magazines and those poor over-promoted wretches that one usually sees in the movies or hears on the radio. I was recently asked to do a television series with good money I suppose, but I'm only too sure it would be silly. So I declined. I may be on the radio soon about my book—Mary Margaret McBride—a great favorite—she has telephoned Scribner's about it. She says I have a perfect radio voice etc. and that people love me—she does, she says. Be that as it may I will let you know when anything is decided about that occasion.

I wish I could see you. Bowman not only listens to what I so often say about you, he really agrees. His brother[2] died two years ago and his two nephews[3] have been with us here this summer. They think they own their Uncle Stark and I love them.

Affectionately
Stark

1. In a letter written to her August 9, Young had already suggested that there were "many things in the book about Aunt Sallie and Uncle Hugh and the hours on that porch with the columns going up and the magnolias. I hope it does them all credit."
2. See below, Letter 771, n. 8.
3. The reference is to Samuel A. Bowman and John Elden Bowman (b. 1938).

767 | To Paul Flowers, Memphis, Tennessee

Waccabuc, New York
[August 21, 1951]

Dear Paul Flowers,

I was delighted to have your cordial letter and to know you were glad to have the copy of my book I sent you. It was sent to you personally from me, to recall the pleasure I had in meeting you that time, already long ago, at the University of Mississippi.

You were one of the attractions I encountered there. Many years ago that dear place seems, and going home again did me good and reinforced my morale. I was very proud of my own people, seeing them again like that—their fine looks, their very good manners and so on. In my time I have seen a good deal of the world, the humble and the grand, so that I have a scale of values that is at least not founded on ignorance. To see in my own people the splendid qualities and to feel a surge of love for them in my heart is a blessed experience.

I have a special feeling for the *Commercial Appeal*. Years ago, before anybody was born, there was a member of your Staff—Mr. John Liesk Tait [4]—who read my pieces and published them and encouraged me no little. As Catullus wrote to his friend Cornelius—out of an old gratitude—*nam que tu solebas meas esse aliquid nugas* [5]—because he used to think my trifles something.

I went over many titles in my mind for my book. *The Pavilion* comes from the Psalms. The idea, of course, is that my book is intended to be a pavilion in which loved things shall be kept: "thou shalt keep them secretly in a pavilion from the strife of tongues."

Notebooks running through many years served this book, and two years on and off went to the writing of it. To get the right form,

4. John Liesk Tait (d. 1935) for many years held the Sunday editorship of the Memphis *Commercial Appeal*. He left Memphis about 1913 to enter the advertising business in St. Louis, established a daily newspaper at Columbus, Mississippi, for a short time, and then moved to Denver. In 1931, he went to Santa Ana, California, where he lived until his death on December 26, 1935.
5. Young quotes the lines from the poems of Catullus (I, 3-4): "Corneli, tibi: namque tu solebas/meas esse aliquid putare nugas. . . ." F. W. Cornish has translated the lines: "To you, Cornelius: for you used to think that my trifles were worth something"—*The Poems of Gaius Valerius Catullus* (1913), 3.

length, tone for all those divers matters, those stories, people's feelings et cetera is a great problem. I worked endlessly on the MS. and the proofs, trying also for a style that has the right emphases but at the same time should seem effortless and relaxed and inevitable.

I can only leave it all now on the lap of the gods, and can only hope it will not be as case of

> Ἀστὴρ πρὶν μὲν ἔλαμπες ἐνὶ ζωοῖσιν Ἑῷος,
> νῦν δὲ θανὼν λάμπεις Ἕσπερος ἐν φθιμένοις.

the accents on that are sketchy, but you seem to like the sound of Greek poetry and this of Plato's has always seemed to me marvellous. It is not possible to translate, because the word *star* would come three times when in Greek it comes once—

> Star, who when alive shone as the morning star of the living
> now being dead shinest the evening star of the dead.

If we used Eos and Hesperus—the morning star and the Evening Star naturally and familiarly all this would be different.[6] At any rate I do hope I will not in this book turn out to be a star, being dead, for the dead. The American memory is very short, though less so in the South I really believe.

It seems a pity that so many Southern writers should make all that part of the world seem so rotten and common, to bring in our good old Southern world of words. The true Southern quality, though it is easy to disgrace is very hard to define. That has to be done *creatively* and with much tact.

Not so long ago I told Mr. Henry Wallace that he knew nothing about the South etc. Why didn't he have colored servants, since he was such a friend to that subject. So the last time I was at his house he said look, Stark, I have followed your remark—etc. Last night he and Mrs. Wallace—a darling—came to dinner, and I said how are your darling servants and they said—Oh my God—they are gone—they were too good to work—I said that's fine—I hoped they'd prove to be awful— "but even that won't teach you anything, Mr. Henry" I said. "You'll go right on talking rot just the same." But as a person he is a very lovable man, and I always enjoy being with him and "sassing" him and he must like it or he would not keep on coming here to see me,

6. See above, Letter 699 and n. 7.

bringing plants, flowers and so on. Mrs. Wallace is a darling—lovely looking, sensible etc.

I have the feeling that I can never express the Southern quality more aptly and deeply than in *The Pavilion*—it is the best I can do—I know that—infinite labor and thought have gone into it. My publishers think it is the best thing in its field since Yeats [7]—That is high praise indeed. They are now talking of when I will have another volume ready for them. I don't know—this business of tearing your heart in twain and working for such a perfection of style as to be almost invisible is something to consider.

I am belaboring you, dear Paul Flowers, with too many of my thoughts and author-woes, but your lovely letter and the recollection of meeting you have seemed to melt my mind into ink.

If you come to New York I shall hope for the pleasure of seeing you. 320 East 57th St—I am here in the country from April till November, in a lovable house, with a garden—a good cook, and lots of books.

Yours sincerely
Stark Young

768 | To Caroline Gordon Tate, Princeton, New Jersey

Waccabuc, New York
Wednesday [August 29, 1951]

Dearest Caroline,

I began your book but had to put it by for a bit because of an attack of intestinal something or other plus its effect on my heart, so that I was in bed a good deal and in no shape to read anything of any importance. But finally I was all right and since then have read through *The Strange Children* and have reread several parts of it more than once. I must say I think it is a very remarkable novel. At the start, however, I should say that though in my time I have read *through* Balzac, Fielding and much of the Russians and some of the French,

7. See above, Letter 695 and n. 1 and n. 2.

Spanish and Italian, I am not really capable of comparing modern works together. I perhaps in the last twenty years have read thirty novels of our time. I am trying to say that my opinion as to great originality of your book may not be too reliable. But it seems to me original in a most impressive sense, and real and intricate and based on a very sound mind.

The wit underlying much of the book is wonderful and very heartening because it is neither obvious nor full of punches in the American smarty manner. That portrait of Uncle Fill is as brilliantly done as Hogarth plus some of our latter realists. That description of how the little girl saw her parents' friends torn to pieces, put together again or left lying around in parts is delicious.

Many of the small details are so finely observed, many such rich tiny lights and shadings and items are to be found when one reads as closely as I do—well, I'm damned, dear Caroline.

The characters when one is through with the whole book are very distinct in a subtle way, an effect accomplished by various manipulations and transitions. The vague portraits remain vague, the distinct characters are distinct, which of course gives the right scale to the drawing as a whole.

The intensity and interest of the story gain definitely as the conclusion approaches until those quite spell-binding final chapters. The very last paragraph has a strange grand sound and impression of tragic seriousness without heaviness. It is an idea but first a mood, which gives that sense of reality and profundity in the author's intention.

To my mind the most remarkable chapter in the book is Chapter Eleven. What happens and what is said and not said, what is dramatized between those two people, plus the child and her passionate inclusion, is one of the most remarkable chapters I ever read in a novel anywhere. I have reread it slowly, trying to see how you got so many of the things that are contained. It makes me feel that if you were interested and studied dramatic structure somewhat you could write an astonishing modern play about a man and a woman. I wish I could see you and ask you if you agree with me about this chapter and feel that you have done something masterly in it.

I should like also to ask you how the novel started, what was the first germ for so complicated and involved a state of characters and things, which you end by making live so well or rather with such a strange completeness as if [it?] left in my mind.

Often in the book there is a degree of realization achieved and with such elusive means the while that the result is highly impressive and at the same time very moving.

Doubtless the most notable thing of all is the creation of the child. I have seen some good efforts at creating children from some abstract motif or idea as a base—pathos, loneliness, eagerness and so on. As generalized children, so to speak, the most satisfactory I ever came on was with Tolstoi in *War and Peace*. Your Lucy, of course, has a far more intricate and complex intention. It seems to be a real triumph. And I noticed constantly how the physical detail of her scenes is varied and also made to seem necessary to the moment. I was very much struck with that.

I appreciated your letter and Allen's letter, since you are among the people whose opinions I value most and whom I love the most.

Wales if he were here would send messages to you. My love to all four.

Stark

769 | To Julian and Juliette Huxley, London, England

Waccabuc, New York
September 9, 1951

Dearest Julian and Juliette,

I sent you my new book the other day and do hope you will find it something—*namque tu salebas meas esse aliquid nugas,* as Catullus wrote for his beloved Cornelius.[8]

Notes back over many years have gone into it, and I have been two years, off and on, trying to achieve a style for it and working out the many transitions involved in presenting the many varieties of the material involved. There was also the problem of finding patterns for

8. See above, Letter 767 and n. 5.

divers stories, chapters, motifs, ideas and so on. I hope all that is well concealed in the general effect.

Some—about five—of these chapters appeared some time back in *The Virginia Quarterly* and met with a remarkable response. I only hope that good fortune will continue for the whole book. And I hope you will feel something toward it.

Except for a brief return of the ailment that Julian saw me felled with, I have been very well indeed. The summer has not been perfect as weather or climate, and the state of the world has everybody strained and uncertain, to put it mildly.

I have just read for the second time Hoyle's *Nature of the Universe.*[9] Not only the ideas are absorbing, or if you like often dazzling, but the personality expressed with so much openness and lack of the scientific pulpit is one that leaves a joyous taste in the mouth. There is a great deal about it that seems to me essentially English; I doubt if an American could handle himself with that secure and clean revelation—and that lack of tedious academic caution. I was delighted to see how thoroughly Julian commended this book.

I hope you are both coming over before long.

Lovingly
Stark

770 | To John Hall Wheelock, Charles Scribner's Sons, New York

Waccabuc, New York
Saturday [September 15, 1951]

Dear Jack,

Thank you for your note and the clipping.[1] I'm glad they gave it space and am sure Irita Van Doren[2] wanted good done by the book. I

---

9. Fred Hoyle (b. 1915), British astronomer and philosopher, published *The Nature of the Universe* in 1950.

1. Wheelock had written a brief letter about the forthcoming reviews of *The Pavilion* and enclosed a clipping of Richard Sullivan's review of the book in "Of Times Remembered," *New York Times Book Review,* September 9, 1951, pp. 4, 26.

2. Editor of the *New York Herald Tribune Books.*

have a sweet note from her saying she is looking forward to reading it. When she does she'll see what a dull missing most of the quality Krutch did.[3] You'd think it a social study, not a work of art. I'll see Irita and ask her if some more notes or a letter from some one can't be managed in order to fill out the outline—that's the way I'll say it.[4]

Monday is now the day for Mary Margaret McBride—I hope it goes well.[5] I'll come by a moment that afternoon partly to thank Charlie[6] for the beautiful appearance of the book which everyone who has seen it comments upon, and partly to thank you again for the unceasing help and stimulation you gave me toward it, from the very first reading in *The Virginia Quarterly*.

Yours
Stark

771 | To Samuel A. Bowman, Exeter, New Hampshire

Jennymead
Waccabuc, New York
Saturday [September 29, 1951]

Dear Sam,

I am in bed with broken bones[7] but would like to see my nephew, whom I hope is already settled and happy in Exeter. It is certainly a

---

3. Joseph Wood Krutch reviewed *The Pavilion* in "Mr. Young Seeks Out His Early Years," *New York Herald Tribune Books,* September 9, 1951, p. 5. Krutch devoted much of his review to justifying Young's interest in his family at a time when "in present-day society . . . only principles, forces and classes are supposed to be really important." Krutch wrote that "Southerners may have been fanatically concerned with social classes but the class to which a man belonged was not the only thing which interested them. . . . It was not enough to say that a man was or was not a gentleman. You had also to add that he took after his mother's side of the family and that his cousin was the hardest drinker in the county." Although Krutch's comments were favorable, Young believed that they did not indicate his most important achievements in the work.

4. Young was successful in his efforts to get additional coverage of *The Pavilion.* See below, Letter 771 and n. 9.

5. Young appeared on her radio program. In a note written after his appearance, she said, "You were the perfect guest, as charming and delightful as your book."

6. Charles Scribner.

7. Young had broken his arm and injured his shoulder in a fall from a folding ladder.

very elegant and distinguished place and I like to think of your being there.

I am glad I saw that pretty frame with your father's picture and the medals.[8] Think of having *seven* of them. He was a remarkable man and I am very sorry that I never had a chance of knowing him better. I saw him only briefly and but a few times, such is life. He was a wonderful father to you and if he were alive I am sure he would be proud of you. No one can take his place, of course, but at least I love you and get much pleasure out of your company. I have known, as you know, many people and have, I hope, a sense of who's who and what's what, and I can truly say that I value your friendship. As time passes and occasions arise I want you to meet my most interesting friends and I want them to meet you. One of the best ways to get educated is by contact with the best people. This house is your home so long as you want it to be.

You would be pleased to see the reviews coming in from all over the country of my book. I hear a piece will be in the *Herald Tribune* Sunday[9] and if so I will send you a copy—that's tomorrow. They have telephoned out from New York about it. Yesterday there was a radio [program] about the book that went over the whole country—that ought to help the book in general. I am writing this scrawl in bed, pardon the scratchiness.

I hope everything goes well for you. Love to you

Uncle Stark

8. Samuel Andrew Bowman; see above, Letter 277 and n. 6.
9. John Hutchens, "Stark Young," *New York Herald Tribune Books,* September 30, 1951, p. 2. This account of an interview with Young emphasized the aspects of *The Pavilion* which Young felt had not been mentioned in Joseph Wood Krutch's earlier review of the book. See the preceding letter.

772 | To Robert Penn Warren, London, England

Waccabuc, New York
October 12, 1951

Dear Red:

I don't think I put myself very aptly in my letter [1] for I had no idea of asking you for a comment. This was not because I don't value anything you would say but rather because as a general habit I don't believe in using comments with individual signatures, unless it is a reprint of something published, otherwise it has always seemed to me a suggestion that there was a request behind it rather than necessarily an impulse. It goes without saying that whatever you would say about my book would mean a great deal to me, and that I shall live in a considerable hope that you will care about this book. You are the kind of person that I wrote it for. So I will not crowd a copy upon you in Europe, but since you are coming back in December or January we can see whether or not the copy is waiting for you here. If not, I will have another one for you.

I imagine your mind is taken up with so many things over there that it will be a relief for you to let this rest for awhile.

I read about your divorce and feel a great delicacy about mentioning the matter. But my regard for you is such that I want to say at least that these things on both and all sides have their cost, and that I hope it will all turn out for your best happiness in the end. If that much is an intrusion please forgive me.

Let me know when you come back so that we may meet.

Affectionately
Stark

1. In August, Young wrote Warren about *The Pavilion.* After having been sent to France by mistake, the letter finally reached Warren in September; and by September 19, when Warren replied to Young, the book had still not arrived. In his reply, Warren readily agreed to make a comment and expressed his appreciation over being requested to speak in behalf of the book.

773 | To Allen Tate, University of Minnesota, Minneapolis, Minnesota

320 East 57th Street
New York
Saturday [November 17, 1951]

Dearest Allen,

I have just replied to this letter,[2] which arrived this morning.

By the way I sent John[3] one of the first copies of *The Pavilion,* some weeks before the publication date but have never heard anything from him.

I enclose a review from the NR and the letter I sent the reviewer.[4] My letter is certainly dignified and mild. The review sounds both idiotic and malicious. Don't bother to return these. I thought maybe you don't see the NR.

There was a review of Caroline's book in the *Commonweal* for November 16.[5] I cut it out to put in this letter but Warren, our boy, has stuck it somewhere and I can't find it.

When I told Dan Mebane on the telephone that Mr. Henry Wallace was absorbed by my book, sat down and went through it, and I have a

---

2. In a letter written November 15, 1951, Robert Daniel had requested Young to support the nomination of John Crowe Ransom to receive an honorary degree from the University of the South. Daniel noted that Tate and Robert Penn Warren had written such letters. Young enclosed Daniel's letter.

3. John Crowe Ransom.

4. Gerald Sykes reviewed *The Pavilion* in "The Archetypal South," *New Republic,* CXXV (October 22, 1951), 19–20. Sykes viewed the book as a "running, interlinear debate" between "the code of embattled gentility" and "the urban traditionlessness that New York represents." He concluded his brief notice with the judgment: *"The Pavilion* suffers from concretism, an almost adolescent incapacity to abstract realistically from experience, and it also suffers from self-congratulation, but it invokes traditional graces and hard-headed classical insights that no one with culture or imagination would wish to see vanish from the world. Those who have been uprooted socially and wish to be rerooted will not get much of practical value from it, but it is well turned in a way that nowadays only an anachronism can be, and it may serve as a corrective to uncritical modernism."

5. Both *The Pavilion* and Caroline Gordon's *The Strange Children* were reviewed by Anne Fremantle in "Books," *Commonweal,* LV (November 16, 1951), 155–57.

fine letter from him, Dan was greatly surprised.[6] It shows how little they know about him.

I hope you and Caroline are getting on happily out there. Wales sends his love.

Love to you both
Stark

774 | To Sarah McNeil Lockwood,[7] Bedford Hills, New York

320 East 57th Street
New York
Sunday [November 18, 1951]

Dear Miss Sally,

I thanked you voluminously at the exhibition, for your very lovely letter, which I still treasure, about *The Pavilion*. It was written for people like you, and I was so very much gratified that you liked it so warmly and discerningly. The reviews keep coming in—over 150 by now, and all but two of them most laudatory indeed.[8] The second edition came out two weeks ago. In the *Times* next Sunday Scribners has a fine advertisement of quotes.[9]

6. Young sent Wallace a copy of the *New Republic* review and his letter to Sykes. In reply, Wallace wrote: "Dan Mebane is a dear and I was closer to him than anyone else in the New Republic. I can see why he would express surprise. But then Dan knew only one part of me. Yes, Stark, I did like it and I did think well of you after reading it. I will not say better because that would imply that I thought ill of you."

7. Sarah McNeil Lockwood (Mrs. Franklin Lockwood, b. 1882) has written *Antiques* (1925), *New York, Not So Little and Not So Old* (1926), *Decoration, Past, Present and Future* (1934), *The Man from Mesabi* (1955), and *The Elbow of the Snake* (1959).

8. In addition to the review in the *New Republic* (see above, Letter 773 and n. 4, Young had in mind the brief, unsigned and unflattering notice in the *Nation*, CLXXIII (September 22, 1951), 246. In this review, the writer complained that "the prose is less substantial than it is meant to be" and continued: "Sentences which at a first reading are pregnant with wisdom sometimes turn out on a second to be merely cloudy. . . . If the general tone is suitably elegiac, it also makes of Mr. Young's evocations a series of forlorn shadows."

9. The three-column advertisement, in the *New York Times Book Review*, November 25, 1951, p. 10, included quotations from reviews in nine newspapers.

I hope you are on another book. I enjoyed your last very much. You are a sweet lady, Miss Sally, and no fool.

Love to you
Stark

775 | To John Davis Williams,[1] University of Mississippi, Oxford, Mississippi

[320 East 57th Street]
[New York]
November 19, 1951

Dear Mr. Williams,

Mr. Bishop may have told you of the very serious accident I had to my arm and shoulder. It has put me out of the running for some time, otherwise I would have replied to your kind invitation to the dedication of the new Library. In many ways indeed it would have been a great pleasure to me.

My friends up here give their MSS. and letters of varying interest to Princeton, Yale and Harvard. If you want these I should prefer giving them to my own university. In that case I will send the MS. of *The Pavilion* when I hear from you about it. I have letters from Gosse, Sherwood Anderson, Ellen Glasgow and a good many others, but those I would send somewhat later on.[2]

My arm still makes my typing less than perfect, as you see. I hope life treats you kindly and that the new Library will bring you many desired things. Please remember me to Mrs. Williams.[3]

Yours sincerely
Stark Young

1. John Davis Williams (b. 1902), university administrator, was chancellor of the University of Mississippi from 1946 until he retired in 1967.
2. Eventually Young sent an early draft of *The Pavilion* to the University of Mississippi library; the collection of letters he subsequently directed should be given to the library of the University of Texas.
3. The former Ruth Margaret Link.

776 | To Samuel A. Bowman, Exeter, New Hampshire

320 East 57th Street
New York
Saturday [January 19, 1952]

Dear Sam,

I got back from Texas about a week ago and have still a pile of stuff to write, answering letters etc. But I must write to my nephew a little just the same, to tell him what a pleasure it was to have you here even for that short time and how proud I was of the reading you had done this fall term, and of how much you had learned of such historical matters as Alexander—B.C. 336 for his coming to the throne, 323 for his death and all that—and of the Ptolemy succession and other matters. And besides your other reading I was especially delighted with your having read the *Oedipus Rex* and the *Antigone*. A great many of my friends who go in for culture and the arts have never in their lives read either one—which seems unbelievable. So here are some notes on the *Oedipus* which I hope you will digest well, even if you have to run through some of the text again. This play is regarded universally as the greatest of all extant Greek plays, and many think it the greatest of plays written in the Western world. However that may be—for there is Shakespeare—please go at it thus:

1) The theme of *Oedipus* is in general *the mystery of justice*. For example, how can it be just that a man who has done nothing to deserve it should be made to suffer? Through no fault of his own a man may, for instance, suffer some terrible physical punishment all his life. You remember from the Prologue or rather preceding introductory note that we read that when Pelops in a rage threw Myrtilos headlong from Cape Gerestos [4] to his death, Myrtilos as he died put a curse on Pelops and this was the beginning of all the evils that befell that house. It was this curse that through his father, Laios, Oedipus inherited and paid for. Oedipus was a great, brave, warm hearted man.

2) But in a work of art the effect would have been too harsh and disturbing if there had been nothing at all that might to some extent

---

4. Perhaps Cape Geraistos on the southern tip of Euboia, off the east coast of Greece.

make some of the fault belong to Oedipus, that is to say would seem to excuse the harsh fate dealt out to him. So he is given the element of rashness, the fight with Laios—whom he had no way of knowing was his father and his killing Laios, a cursed act since Laios was his father. This means that the fated injustice remains but that the pattern of it is to a softening extent balanced by this defect in Oedipus himself. Mind you the curse was working nevertheless, and there was no escape from it for Oedipus. The *Book of Job* in the Bible has the same theme, but the effect is much hurt by some later hand making it all end happily after all—Job came out richer than ever etc.—which lowers and cheapens the whole thing. (In the next play, *Oedipus at Colonus,* Sophocles shows Oedipus turned into a mystic and saint through his suffering and wandering etc.; but that has nothing to do with the play we are talking about.)

3) Greek tragedies fall into the exposition, the climax and the catastrophe. Oedipus is struggling against fate, we see the story progress. Finally there is the turning point, the climax, the highest point in the struggle, where we see that Oedipus has lost. After that we descend to the final tragic end, which is the catastrophe.

The whole thing, of course, will depend for its greatness on the elevation and power that are created and maintained. Here Sophocles is supreme.

This play is considered the finest case of what is called *dramatic irony,* which is that the audience knows the situation long before the hero does. We watch the hero as he struggles within the tragic net, without knowing what it all means. In sum we are somewhat in the position of the gods, who see what is going on for a mortal man where the man himself is mocked by his own blindness or helpless mortality.

I wish you would go over the play in your mind or in your hand and know that it is and always will be one of the greatest things you can ever experience. Think of being able to open one single book and find all that!

I am sorry this is messy and hasty and badly expressed, but I have not the time right now to do it any better. But as I said I was very proud of your having taken up this play.

I enclose a pole vaulting note that may interest you. Also the note about the proposed Art Museum at Exeter—very swanky that sounds.

Thank you for your nice letter. I am glad the Chinese box was pleasing to you. Can you see those small hands setting those semi-precious stones into that brass? The war has probably been stopping all that.

What are you reading now?

Love to you
Uncle Stark

777 | To Norman Dello Joio, New York

[320 East 57th Street]
[New York]
Monday [February 4, 1952]

Dear Norman,

I hope we can hear about your *Psalm of David*[5] when you come to dinner Saturday. Wales and I have talked a lot about it. We were profoundly moved by it. In the deep-hearted parts of it I kept thinking of Racine's line—de quelle amour blessée—with what love art thou wounded?—that heavenly line! I thought the *Times* review very stupid—there would be no sense and no talent or inspiration in writing the liturgical form over again etc.—that would—or might be—learned but not much else.[6] Basta. We can talk of this face to face.

The party was a great success—the banquet table and the hostess. Grace miraculously got around to everyone. I hope she is alive today.

All around us, dear Norman, the atmosphere after your number was triumphant. I was so very glad and proud.

Love to you both

Stark

5. On February 3, the first New York performance of Dello Joio's *Psalm of David* was given as part of the Choral Masterwork Series in Carnegie Hall. Helen Hosmer conducted the Crane Chorus from the State University Teacher's College at Potsdam, New York, which had commissioned the work and presented its first performance at the Potsdam Spring Festival in 1951. Dello Joio's piece, the final number on the program, followed works by Hindemith, Brahms, and Des Pres.

6. In "Upstate Students Give Concert Here," New York *Times*, February 4, 1952, p. 14, Harold C. Schonberg noted that Dello Joio seemed to be dealing with "emotional elements that were alien to him" and concluded: "In ecclesiastical music it is hazardous to substitute calculated intellectual effects for what should be an expression of spiritual value. Only too often the result is neither especially good music nor especially good liturgy."

778 | To Lavinia Gadsden Dimond, San Francisco, California

320 East 57th Street
New York
Friday [February 15, 1952]

Dearest Lavinia,

When I got home after New Years I found your lovely card and letter, and did appreciate them both very much. That is fine of you to be giving away so many of my books at Christmas, and to be willing to stand behind them. It goes without saying how much I value your opinion, as I value and honor all your lovely qualities and fine consciences. And so thank you so very much.

Not long ago two quail arrived, sent from a Berkshire farm through Hammacher and Schlemmer. There was no card and so I stopped by there and asked if they had a record. They had no record of this parcel but the ORDER number on the wrapper was yours, they said. Thus we concluded that you had been bothering to spend your money on us and your thought and good wishes. There was an excellent little pamphlet on how they should be cooked, so Wales undertook that with loving hands. There was even a bit of stuffing in each bird and in the package there was a jar of currant jelly. It all seemed very luxurious indeed. Thank you again, dear Lavinia.

I am sorry to say my beloved friend and believer and backer, Charlie Scribner died suddenly at noon Monday, no previous warning except a pain in his vitals during the night. He went to Medical Center and was gone before they even made an examination. He was most reserved, but most tenderhearted, and gifted with distinguished taste and judgement. He took great pride and interest in *The Pavilion* and made that fact known widely. His son, young Charles,[7] will probably take over soon, as soon as the Navy releases him from his job in Washington. His father has been grooming him for several years and was very proud of his ability and anxious to turn over more to him. One has no idea how complex a great publishing house is, the many departments, not merely the publishing of literary output newly

7. Charles Scribner, Jr. (b. 1921), son of Charles and Vera Scribner, began his career with Charles Scribner's Sons in 1946 as advertising manager; he became vice-president in 1948 and president in 1952. In 1949, he married Dorothy Joan Sunderland.

written. A rich old firm like Scribner's has many standard authors in their store, many thousands a year in series of books and in educational books. Also art books. The public knows little of most of this. The tone at Scribners is very simple and high-bred and honorable. I could not be more fortunate [with] them as friends and publishers.

You will be glad to know that *The Pavilion* is still going well. The other day I got from Rome a two column article about me and it by their leading critic Prezzolini,[8] whom I do not know personally.

Wales is busy getting up a garden to hold pieces from the exhibition of the Sculptor's Guild.[9]

Please give my love to Doug and the children. Much love to yourself, you are a wonderful friend.

                                             Stark

779 | To John Hall Wheelock, Charles Scribner's Sons, New York

                                  320 East 57th Street
                                  New York
                                  Wednesday [March 5, 1952]

Dear Jack,

I had hoped that Miss Stark[1] could notify the right person and so clean up the money note.[2] The man who does my taxes has been hounding me, and so the note is welcome. It is a shame you had to write me about it.

I am sure you are indeed overwhelmed.[3] I am one author and friend

8. Giuseppe Prezzolini (b. 1882), Italian critic and editor, founded the Italian review *Voce* in 1908, emigrated to the United States in 1930, and became professor of Italian literature at Columbia University.

9. In a letter written several days later to Caroline Charlotte McGehee, Young remarked that "Bowman was finishing up an artificial garden, all high green walls and tulips and white birches and dogwood, in the Museum of Natural History, a part of the exhibition of the Sculptors' guild. His work was a great success and much complimented." Margaret Breuning reviewed the exhibit, called "Sculpture in Time and Place," in "Sculpture in Situ," *Art Digest*, XXVI (March 1, 1952), 16.

1. Fidelia Stark, Wheelock's secretary.

2. Young had requested from Scribner's a statement of his income for the preceding year; Wheelock had sent the information the preceding day and explained that illness in the cashier's department had caused the delay.

3. The death of Charles Scribner had placed additional work upon Wheelock.

that you don't have to worry about, not just now. What I want to say only, and now, is that there must be some MS. reading, of minor importance perhaps, that I could help you with, or some proof, though, as you know I am not proof's white haired boy—and who is these days?—Anything however modest that I could do to help you through this immediate time I'd be glad to do. And this requires no answer of thanks. Try not to kill yourself, for everything else aside, where then should all of us, Scribners included, be?

I am reading a play that Eugene O'Neill has done recently, more or less.[4] Perfectly without himself, nothing that could interest anybody. Lost and sick and always neurotic from the start. I have always had a very gentle and right relation to him and a genuine fondness, but there we are—and such is life.

Thank you again and there is nothing that needs a reply in this.

Affectionately
Stark

780 | To Ella Somerville, Oxford, Mississippi

320 East 57th Street
New York
Wednesday [March 5, 1952]

Dearest Ella,

You'll see I wrote Mr. Dodd[5] about ES's book.[6]

The plum pudding is finished,[7] but the memory of it is still rich in my mouth and warm in my heart.

I wish I could come in and see you all.

Love to you
Stark

4. Probably *A Moon for the Misbegotten.* O'Neill finished the play in 1943, deposited for copyright a typescript of it in 1945, and published it in August, 1952. Young probably read an advance copy of the published version.

5. Edward Howard Dodd, Jr. (b. 1905), publisher and author, then vice-president of Dodd, Mead and Company. On February 29, Dodd had replied to Young's letter in praise of Elizabeth Spencer's book that his remarks would be helpful for publicity.

6. *This Crooked Way.*

7. A Christmas present to Young from Miss Somerville.

781 | To Hudson Strode, University of Alabama,
Tuscaloosa, Alabama

320 East 57th Street
New York
Friday [April, 1952]

Dear Hudson,

Your generous and thoughtful letter gave me the greatest feeling of pleasure and gratification. I am sure your praise will help extend the appeal of *The Pavilion*. I have had a great many letters from people I know or don't know to tell me how much they felt about this book. There were more than two hundred reviews of various lengths and only two or three unfavorable. The one in the New Republic was stupid and malicious.[8] But most of them dwell on the first part, the Southern records and portraits, the rest they pay no heed to. So long as they like the book so much that is something to be grateful for, but it is disconcerting on the whole. That latter section is the finish of the pattern of the culture that I had come into by the time I was of age. Not in any flattering sense, but as you understand, of course, the definition and nourishment of one's self and the line or pattern of that process.

This reflection makes difficult the tone or treatment to follow in any record of later years and people; it cannot possibly have as much of that lyric tone, or that element of simple perfection, at least in intention, that this earlier book or period in my life has. If I can't find a tone to suit me I just won't finish or publish the book. Endless labor and time went on *The Pavilion* and that effect that so many people speak of—that you can open the book anywhere and begin reading with pleasure.

Not long ago somebody or other was speaking of the wonderful opening of Chapter Nineteen. I said yes, thank you, and for one sentence in it, for example, it took me about an hour to get that tortoise across the road.

Sometimes a tortoise with a air of lowly indifference crossed my path and moved steadily on to where he had chosen to go.

8. See above, Letter 773 and n. 4.

The *sometimes* is how they appear, any old time, not regular—the *lowly* is as you look down on him, the *indifference* is part of his character and comicality. They always seem to be *crossing* the line ahead of one. They *move* rather than walk and with a droll steadiness. They seem to [be] going to no place you can guess but, at that, they have evidently *chosen* to go there.

And then when we get through with it the sentence seems easy and casual almost.

Those remarks of yours in various places have I am sure done a great deal directly and indirectly for my book. I am glad to hear Lon Tinkle's [9] good opinion. I have seen him twice only but liked him very much.

Among nowadays novels have you seen that by Goyen—of Texas—called "The House of Breath" ? [1] A poor title, though in the book you can find what it means to convey. A morbid and remarkable talent. I'd like to know what you think of it.

Your words about yours and Therese's place make me homesick in my heart. It is full spring there now, I suppose, and what that means there in that far South I know very well.

I wish I could see you and my beloved Thérèse. The world seems indeed thwarted these days and I have the sense that few people feel any direction in themselves; *I often feel lost, and sit down and read more about St. Augustine.* I must get to painting soon, when we go to the country. I have the technical thing, but at present seem without ideas. Most painting like most writing should never happen. I have a large painting in the Art Institute of Chicago, and the brilliant Director, Daniel Catton Rich, has written me several times about it and urged me to paint. Before I met him he was a great devotee of *So Red the Rose* and my criticism etc. and he wrote me a beautiful letter saying of *The Pavilion* that he had never read a book that "moved" him so much. [2]

9. Lon Tinkle (b. 1906), professor of French and comparative literature at Southern Methodist University and literary editor of the Dallas *News.*

1. William Goyen (b. 1915), born in Trinity, Texas, published his first novel, *The House of Breath,* in 1950. Subsequently he has written *In a Farther Country* (1955), *The Fair Sister* (1963), and several plays.

2. Young may have had reference to a letter from Rich, September 20, 1951, in which he wrote: "I don't know when I have read anything which moved me as it [*The Pavilion*] has done. I keep returning to a thought, an allusion, an insight here and there."

I must say that finishing *The Pavilion* and looking after it since its appearance took a great deal out of me. I suppose we all begin to unwind with the years.

Bowman sends greetings.

My best love to you and Therese, and thanks

Stark

---

782 | To Robert Penn Warren, Yale University, New Haven, Connecticut

320 East 57th Street
New York
April 16, 1952

Dear Red,

I must thank you at least, that is the least I can do, for your letter and for the good things you say about my book.[3] It goes without saying how much I value your opinion. I don't have to say what an old—by now—admiration and affection I have for you. There is something in you that I saw when I met you first—something generous, lyric, gentle and highly gifted—*basta*—but I mean it, as you know.

You would be surprised at the number of times I think of those period passages—so to speak—those inventions in a by-gone style—that are in your last book.[4] They have their own magnificence indeed—I keep wondering if you can't apply, or employ, or impress, that style and effect somewhere, somehow, in some other writing. I am myself always astonished at the force with which somehow those passages remain in my memory.

In about a week I am off to the country—for the summer. I hope to see you again out there.

Yours
Stark

---

3. On March 30, Warren had written to express his admiration for *The Pavilion*.
4. *World Enough and Time.*

783 | To Susie Gibert Knowlton,[5] Perthshire, Mississippi

320 East 57th Street
New York
April 17, 1952

Dear Mrs. Knowlton,

Your letter was so generous and charming—for which I thank you—that it seems a shame I cannot make you win that bet. Even the utmost gallantry could not do that, since the Miles McGehee house is against me, in all its solid reality.

The truth is that in such minor details I did not try to stick to accuracy but wanted to get an effect without too much explaining. Miles McGehee[6] was my great-grandfather's brother, I never heard his wife's name but Cousin Blanche, the daughter, used to visit in Como before she married Mr. Stokes. I knew or met once her son, McGehee Stokes, and it was he who told me about holding the man with a pistol, his mother, Cousin Blanche, that was. My Cousin Henry Stewart of Feliciana Parish—Edward McGehee's grandson, Uncle Miles' great nephew—told me about the money lost, he said two million, in banks here and there and the records all lost, burned and what not, during the War. He told me about the nineteen people being shot etc. The burning of the house I just transposed from an account I read of Sherman's soldiers burning the house of Reverdy Johnson—Sherman mentions that house in his memoirs, though I don't know whether he mentions its being burnt by his men—a few lies in his memoirs he cheerfully admitted.[7]

5. Susie Gibert Knowlton (Mrs. Sam Dove Knowlton, 1884–1970), born in Gallman, Mississippi, attended the University of Mississippi in 1903–1904. After her marriage in 1905, she lived in Perthshire, Mississippi, where, with her husband, she participated actively in community affairs. She supplemented her lifelong interest in literature and history with an extensive personal correspondence. Young's letter replies to her questions about the historicity of the events narrated in chapter 6 of *The Pavilion* and chapter 49 of *So Red the Rose*.

6. Miles Hill McGehee (1813–65) was not the brother of Young's great-grandfather Hugh McGehee. Miles McGehee's father, John Scott McGehee (b. 1789), was the brother of Hugh McGehee. Miles McGehee's daughter by his second marriage (to Mrs. Mary Crouse Porter) was Ida Blanche McGehee (1849–89), who married James F. Stokes. Their son was Miles McGehee Stokes.

7. Passages in chapter 49 of *So Red the Rose* closely parallel incidents recounted in *The Memoirs of General William T. Sherman* (pp. 320–21). In the novel, Sherman, the fictional character, describes the burning of Hard Times Plantation, owned by Mrs.

Various things in *So Red the Rose* are composite,[8] since I wanted to get certain motifs expressed and embodied in the most efficient and complete way. The main thing about such a book is the final content. Only in this profound sense is it history.

I advise you to make your bets in Confederate money after this, or to give winners over you some poisoned gloves.

Thank you again, you must be a very lovely lady.

Yours sincerely
Stark Young

784 | To Ella Somerville, Oxford, Mississippi

320 East 57th Street
New York
Monday [May 5, 1952]

Dearest Ella,

Your lovely letter came shortly after Mr. Bryant's [9] and I was made so warm in my heart by all you said. I'd have answered sooner but have been having a mild case of our town flu—which I have escaped up till now. I have to send this to Oxford only, but if it reaches you it will be doing no more than letters to Phil Stone, who dictates letters about coming to see publishers etc.—he means very generously by all that, do. Your pages have no Fifth Street address on them and my address book was stolen in a suit-case along with some old silver et cetera last Friday while I was waiting next door to the garage. There

---

Reverdy Johnson, on Lake St. Joseph, Louisiana. In his memoirs, Sherman refers to the burning of the mansion of "Mr. Bowie, who was the brother-in-law of . . . Mr. Reverdy Johnson," that is, Dr. Allen Thomas Bowie, whose sister, Mary Mackall Bowie, was the wife of Reverdy Johnson. Bowie's plantation was known as Franklin Plantation, while Hard Times Plantation was owned by Dr. J. Y. Hollingsworth.

8. For an account of another burning of a house, which may have entered into the "composite" description in the novel, see above, Letter 336.

9. Bryant, then chairman of the English department at the University of Mississippi, had written Young inviting him to return to the university either to deliver a series of lectures or to teach for a semester.

were a lot of city workmen around, on a large new building, and no wonder they did quick work. I had scarcely turned my back on them.

I have written Mr. Bryant that my commitments and modest affairs here make it impossible to promise anything for the future. A great deal of what I do is tied up here in this town. I don't even know whether I can fly over for a short stay in Europe in August. It all seems very silly, since my doings are most modestly involved with anything.

It was a real honor for my university to want me to come, and it gives me even more pleasure to think my old friends would like me around. Of course I should be so pleased and touched with all their sweetness that I would never get to a class.

You are very sweet to say you would do all in your power to make my stay happy. I am sure you would and that you could contribute a great deal in that direction, I consider you always one of my most distinguished and beloved friends.

Please give my love to all the family—it seems a shame I am always so far away, and nothing much to my existence at that. What you report to me about *The Pavilion* pleases me very much, doubly so because I wrote mostly about what I love and believe in, and also because such endless labor went into the book. People have been wonderful about it. I still get letters several times a week telling me how much it has meant to this person or that, some of them people who have worked in the arts on their own. The brilliant Director of the Art Institute of Chicago wrote me that he had never been so moved by a book as by this, etc.[1]

I must close and get the boy—cook and houseman he is—to post this. Your list of helpers sounds dazzling. A neighbor of ours has just been paying $2.50 an hour for a man spading up her ground.

Thank you again for your letter, dear Ella.

Affectionately
Stark

1. See above, Letter 781 and n. 2.

785 | To Norman Dello Joio, New York

320 East 57th Street
New York
Tuesday [May 6, 1952]

Dear Norman,

I don't want you to go off for two weeks without my telling you that I forgot to say this morning, or rather just now, that it is not entirely that I like hard liquor so much—except Bourbon of course—but that often I want a drink because I want to be eased of what is going on inside of me, the problem of life, especially these days, and the sense of my own futility, and the shortcomings of my imagination in contact with experience and with other people. That need is worse than just wanting a good drink, and that is all the more reason I had better go on the wagon for a while.

Basta. I hope you have a fine trip and get something done that you really want to do. The idea of these trips you take is excellent and separates you from the silly business that most of the New York people in the arts are milling in.

Tell Grace I will come to see her and see my goddaughter and give her my dear love.

Best to you
Stark

786 | To Norman Dello Joio, New York

320 East 57th Street
New York
Tuesday [May 13, 1952]

Dear Norman,

I was so sorry to hear from Grace of your mother's death. It is at least better than months of torture such as two of my friends endured.

But that is a very poor comfort at such a moment. The only comfort is perhaps what I know. The beloved people of mine whom I have lost are with me still, strangely real and close. In my dreams sometimes I see them—always gentle, always their most precious selves.

One of the things you can at least do for your mother's love through these years is to go on writing beautiful and sincere music.

I am glad you have that sweet and wonderful Grace. And now the daughter too.

I suppose your copy of *The Pavilion* is in the country. Otherwise I wish you would read at such a time as this those pages on my father and my mother. There was a great deal more I could have set down, but after much thought and labor this was what I wanted. Many people have written me about it.

Affectionately
Stark

787 | To Bedford Thurman, Ithaca, New York

320 East 57th Street
New York
Thursday [June 5, 1952]

Dear Bedford,

You may have seen in the TIMES the column last Friday about the suicide of Herschel Brickell. He was one of my oldest and best friends and a champion always of my work. I knew him first in 1906 when I was beginning teaching at the University of Mississippi, and toward 1920 when I came to the NR he was a famous literary editor of the old NYPOST, later a Holt editor etc. Always a fine friend to me, and his wife one of my dearest and most admired friends, a wonderful creature, completely devastated by this blow. So last week-end was terrible and there have been things to do this week. They lived, when in this part of the world just a few miles from me in the country.

This accounts for my not having written you definitely. We are going out this afternoon and I will try to help her tomorrow.

As to plans we will be in town well before noon Monday and through Wednesday at least. Any of those *days* you would be most welcome. Not at night. At night I am always too tired just now to be of any use. I just go to bed and read a while and try to sleep.

Next Thursday, perhaps in the afternoon we are going to the country for good, permanently till autumn. So it will have to be during those first three days of next week, or some time later in the country. Here in town would have its advantages, for I have here a file of letters and comments and books that might—or might not—be of use or interest to you.[2]

You can call there as you have done. S. Salem 3–3547, or just save money by sending me a line here. Or you can telephone Betsy and I will call her any way when I get to town Monday.

Any time during the day on Monday, Tuesday or Wednesday then, or else later on in the country.

My best love to you and Jorita—I advise the town if possible, you would look through a good deal here that I can't take to the country.

Lovingly
Stark

788 | To Donald Davidson, Bread Loaf, Vermont

Jennymead
Waccabuc, New York
Friday [July 4, 1952]

Dear Donald,

I was delighted to have your letter[3] and would have replied sooner but for the task and complications of moving to the country and getting settled.

I will answer your points as best I can. I do think, however, that the

2. For his doctoral dissertation at Cornell University, Thurman was beginning work on a bibliography of Young's writings.

3. So early as January 9, 1952, Davidson had written that Scribner's had requested him to write an introduction to a new edition of *So Red the Rose*. On June 3, Davidson had written that he hoped to begin the work while in Vermont during the summer. Young is responding to this letter.

best plan would be a talk if possible or else you send me your pre-
liminary draft and I will make what suggestions I think might be of
use to you. If you have your car with you, you and Mrs. Davidson
might run down and spend the night with us here—I live with an
architect, Princeton, a good friend of Allen's and Caroline's—Bowman.
(Please make allowances for these blemishes, they will be worse than
usual because I am writing in the loggia of the garden and the house a
good jaunt up hill, and the heat something indeed when in the sun.)
It would be so very good to have you all here. Allen and Caroline and
Menotti [4] and Stravinsky and Dame Edith Evans, and others have been
here to visit and find it peaceful and lovable. I wish you would consider this. I may go to Europe but not till September.

First. I feel indeed that SO RED THE ROSE belongs in the "general pattern of my fiction." [5] It sums it all up, and carries the Southern
theme as far as I can carry it. That is why I never followed up—as
would have been wise commercially, the success of SO RED THE
ROSE. The Mississippi end of all this is partially incidental. I am not
really thinking of Mississippi but of the whole Southern cultural idea.
I used Mississippi because that is the scene I know but you will note in
this novel no particular reference to Deep South characteristics as diverse, or as parallel to the rest of the South. I might have done that, of
course, but it would have changed the theme somewhat in my own
mind and sympathy.

Various historians like Freeman (Lee) and Tomlinson [6] if that is the
right form of his name (Jeb Stuart) and Princeton and other places
etc. had the highest praise for the historical accuracy and value of SO
RED THE ROSE—Allan Nevins for one, he had great praise for it,
and Henry Commager. The Natchez side of it is purely because I
wanted a scene still standing, so that people like John Chamberlain
could not say it never existed, it was "the South of Tom Wolfe" that
they believed. It was something to be able to show a photograph and
say see for yourself. I visited Natchez and had the advantage of a series
of newspaper articles in the local paper, collected for me by a friend
there—I have not the papers nor the writer's name at hand. Natchez

4. Gian Carlo Menotti (b. 1911), composer of cantatas, operas, and ballets, whose
Amahl and the Night Visitors had received wide acclaim from television audiences in
1951.
5. Davidson had asked how Young felt *So Red the Rose* "fits or 'belongs' in the
general pattern of your fiction."
6. Thomason.

is interesting to look at, otherwise save for three or four friends there I don't care about it at all, in fact I find it very boring. I was really talking about Woodville farther south and St. Francisville and other Delta places where my own kin lived. I made some good enemies in Natchez, it seems, because the people like Mrs. Byrnes that I took up with were on the opposing side in the famous Garden Club row or feud. What's more several of the families are not mentioned in my book. My cousins and family, the McGehees and Stewarts and so on thought very poorly of Natchez people. The house in my novel is directly, and known to be, Rosedown, two miles from St. Francisville, the Bowman plantation.

The frontier idea is very interesting.[7] I think if we could have talk it would all be much forwarded, the whole discussion. I mean I have no car, but hope you have and can come, you and Mrs. Donald, to see us here. The telephone is South Salem 3–3547. Under the name William McKnight Bowman.

The program of the opera[8] is very interesting to me. I wish I might see it or have seen it, or heard some records from it. I have had a good deal of contact one way or another with Gian-Carlo Menotti and that gives me a little more insight into such endeavour. I am very glad to hear of the success, the real success you speak of.

You may have seen of Stravinsky's triumphs in Paris and elsewhere lately. But his beginning fame was back in 1913. That is a comment of sorts on what art means and does and takes out of us.

Please forgive a very dull letter. I am here in the garden, after a roasting in New York yesterday, and am duller than ever.

Affectionately yours
Stark Young

7. After remarking that he had never understood *So Red the Rose* until he visited Natchez, Davidson asserted his belief that the Southern frontier in the Deep South had never been understood or even described. "What is not realized," wrote Davidson, "is that what might be called the New World principle brought about, in the South, a kind of reestablishment of 'European' tradition at the moment when Europe was engaged in repudiating tradition. So, in a sense, the true Britain, the true France, etc. were on these shores. Only thus . . . can the paradox of 'elegance' (so-called) and 'crudity' (so-called) be adequately explained. And Natchez, a special place, was 'frontier' too. . . ."

8. Davidson enclosed a program for *Singin' Billy,* an opera, which he had written in collaboration with Charles Faulkner Bryan, a member of the faculty at the George Peabody College of Music. Davidson wrote that he believed Bryan was doing in the "American vein . . . what such artists as Stravinski are doing in their vein."

This letter does look disgraceful.

This house is near Katonah and near Ridgefield, a not too long drive from Middleburg.

S.

789 | To Mary Hartwell Bishop, Oxford, Mississippi

Waccabuc, New York
July 14, 1952

Dear Mary Hartwell,

I left the announcement card in town—55 miles away—so I must content myself with writing you instead of Martha—since I don't re-call her new name or address.[9] So please give her much love from me and every good wish for her happiness all her life long—in so far as such a thing may visit our all too human lives. I remember her with much pleasure and admiration.

I have ordered from a shop in Texas a modest present; let's hope she will enjoy a little possessing it.

I have no news—a *quiet* summer here in the country. Many thousands of flowers. I may go to Europe in the fall. Italy, France and London—largely visiting friends. It will doubtless be my last trip.

I hope you didn't see that silly-sounding "interview" in the *Commercial Appeal*.[1] The young reporter was very nice but what I really said was that writing about people I have known was made more difficult by the fact of my knowing too much about them personally. I also said that in so many cases the people I would speak of sought me out first, because of what I had written about them, but that if I kept saying this it would sound as if I were the world's sweetheart. Et cetera.

9. Young refers to the wedding of Mrs. Bishop's daughter, Martha Somerville Bishop, and the Reverend Mr. Willis Ryan Henton, June 7, 1952. When Young wrote this letter, her address was Besao, Luzon, where her husband was rector of an Episcopalian church.

1. In her article, "A Southerner in New York—Mississippi Critic, Stark Young, Knows Too Much and He's Sad," Memphis *Commercial Appeal*, May 4, 1952, Sec. 6, p. 5, Rhea Talley had quoted Young as saying: "'I know too much about people.'"

I usually decline interviews but the circumstances around this one made that awkward or impossible.

I hope you and Mr. Bishop and the whole family keep well. I still remember the chance to see you all—it warmed all my heart.

Lovingly
Stark

790 | To Lawton Campbell, Bronxville, New York

Waccabuc, New York
Friday [August 22, 1952]

Dear Lawton,

Your note came yesterday with the enclosure.[2] As you will see by this letter you have what often happens to me: people supposed to be doing research want their work done for them. They nearly always give a close deadline. I wrote a few words on this machine, signed Warren Powell, Secretary, and saying I was in Canada.

No reason to bother with this dullish person. I have known Bobby longer and probably better than most people, but what I suggest is that you write your man and say that in *The Flower in Drama* and especially in *Immortal Shadows* he will find criticisms of many of Bobby's important works, and more still in the files of the [NR]. You will have done your share then. You can add that REJ likes what I have written about him better than any other criticism.

It was fine seeing you all. I hope the news for the play continues to be promising.

We are leaving this morning for Rochester, to drive Gertrude Newell up, stopping overnight at Cooperstown to see the sights, and coming home Monday.

Love to you every one.

Stark

2. Campbell had received a note from Louisette Roser, July 15, 1952, enclosing a letter she had received from Eugene Robert Black, then a graduate student at the University of Wisconsin. Black had asked a number of questions about Robert Edmond Jones. Black's dissertation, "Robert Edmond Jones: Poetic Artist of the New Stagecraft," was completed in 1955.

791 | To Donald Davidson, Ripton, Vermont

Jennymead
Waccabuc, New York
Friday, September 9, 1952

Dear Donald,

Your letter [3] was very welcome and very much absorbed by my dull heart and mind. For some time I have felt that I was not any too necessary in this hasty world today and that there was small need for me to write anything else. Your generous remarks are at least some indication that I might amount to something however small in the day's productions. I have read your letter carefully and talked it over with that sympathetic and stimulating friend of yours and mine, Tom Walsh, and have tried to think out some comments on the general subject of the introduction to SO RED THE ROSE.

There are various points in your letter that I think ought to be kept and that will be splendidly in line with the whole intention. Please know that these are suggestions only.

Quote your sentence, "There is no other 'Civil War' novel that even approaches So Red the Rose; it is *sui generis,* absolutely, unique, and remarkable as a novel, entirely aside from any reference to the War, because it presents some very remarkable people with faithful, loving—and also sufficiently grim—insight." I return your letter with the Weaver reference, [4] good to include in your introduction if you think best.

I have conceived a plan to send you a copy of SO RED THE ROSE with transcriptions from my original copy, as to various people, incidents, technical intentions, writing these matters in the margins as I have done in that copy of my own. To save you trouble this would be excellent.

3. Throughout the summer Davidson had been trying to arrange a meeting with Young at Waccabuc. On September 2, Davidson wrote that the visit seemed impossible. Young here replies to Davidson's letter.

4. In his letter, Davidson had quoted extensively from Richard M. Weaver's "Aspects of the Southern Philosophy," *Hopkins Review,* V (Summer, 1952), 5–21. Davidson had been impressed by Weaver's argument that the Southerner rebelled against the "idea of analysis," a Northern characteristic, because his philosophical and intellectual tradition "tells him that this is not the way to arrive at the kind of truth he is interested in." Weaver had concluded that "analysis is destructive of the kind of reality which he [the Southerner] most wishes to preserve."

I have thought also that I might send a few quotations from various reviews, including those in England, where the book had a real following.

I have studied Red Warren's introduction to FAREWELL TO ARMS very closely.[5] I admire and like Red very much, and for this particular book he may have done the right thing. To my mind, if we are thinking of SO RED THE ROSE, no such detail of biography or general criticism would be right. I have already sensed from your letters that you have what to me seems the right approach to the book. And I get the impression that you won't boggle up what you feel and think, in such a way that theories are in the air and never get out of it, and clichés unconsciously pop up, supported by a lot of silly slants that have become the bosh and business of criticism.

I think it should be positively mentioned that SO RED THE ROSE, unlike many novels, has gone on selling. After eighteen years it still sells, and quite fairly every year. That ought to mean something. SO RED THE ROSE was translated into Danish soon after its publication.

Two years ago it was translated into German and received excellent reviews on the Continent.

The landed society depicted has caused the book to be found to be most familiar to Austrian, Russian, Italian readers of the same class as the characters in the novel; there have been evidences of this and quite often.

Margaret Mitchell when interviewers asked her about her novel, GONE WITH THE WIND had a practice of saying "Why do you talk about my book, you should talk about SO RED THE ROSE." This happened many times that I have had reported to me. This might to popular minds, our general mash of newspaper impressions, influences, etc. mean something that might prove to be quite significant. And there is Ellen Glasgow's comment—the best novel about the South in the war—or something like that—see the jacket—but considering her own works she couldn't quite take that and so put the *Deep* South.

Granville-Barker, nothing if not exacting in his critical taste, re-

---

5. In an earlier letter, dated August 4, Davidson had remarked that he would prefer that the biographical material about Young not be so formal and detailed as that in Robert Penn Warren's introduction to *A Farewell to Arms* in Scribner's Modern Standard Authors edition (1949).

marked to various persons that "most novels are full of holes, SO RED THE ROSE is practically perfect."

Almost all the characters in the novel are *composites,* very much so, made up of details from various actual persons or else created entire. Miss Mary Cherry comes closest to being an actual portrait. The events in the book are either invented or are transcripts of things that actually happened, not merely history or tales or portraits, as some have thought. The historical side of the novel is carefully rendered and was highly praised by such authorities as Douglas Southall Freeman, the famous biographer of Lee. Allan Nevins likewise. And also Henry Steele Commager in his—I can't locate his book [*The American Mind*]. The point was that of all the Agrarians—the title was unfortunate—I most truly expressed the Southern etc. idea.

When Henry S. Canby, editor at the time of The Saturday Review of Lit. inquired of Julia Peterkin as to what novelist she considered most truly representative of the Southern, she said to his surprise, "Stark Young of course."

My play THE COLONNADE was produced by the London Stage Society, at which time the leading critic Walkley wrote that it was an absorbing play and gave it high praise.[6] This play was to be produced by the Provincetown Theatre in 1924 but I withdrew it because of casting difficulties. I then used it to make my novel RIVER HOUSE.

In my opinion you might dispose of my performance as dramatic critic, on the *New Republic,* then for a year on the *Times,* in a short passage. If you have not seen my last book of criticisms—and the last —I can get it sent to you. The quotations on the cover would serve any purpose you might have.

I struggled through about ninety items for a title, and finally one day I took up FitzGerald's *Rubaiyat* saying to myself I will this day find a title here or die. I struck the two quatrains used in the book, on an opening page, and they seem to give a very happy suggestion of what the book is about. You might quote them

"I sometimes think that never blows so red" etc. that blood-stained soil, that flowering of the heart and pride and soul.

Natchez was chosen for this reason: people like John Chamberlain, whose head has so many holes that his hair is practically an air plant,

6. See above, Letter 194 and n. 4.

would say, AS HE DID SAY, this is not the real South, the real South is in such writers as Tom Wolfe. I said, granting all Tom's genius, he was scarcely Southern. He was a German family from Pennsylvania transplanted to N.C. on the wrong side of the tracks so far as the people in my book are involved, I chose Natchez, I said, only because the houses are still standing and people like you, John, do perhaps recognize photographs. Good strong wooden houses—wood to the wood, I said, sourly, meaning such thinkers as John. You could hardly say, therefore, that my locale pictures were mere romance. Natchez is nothing to me, but I don't think we need go into that. It would only confuse the Southern issue in the book.

Caroline Tate told me that in her course at Columbia on the novel she always pointed out SO RED THE ROSE as a book where everything is "realized." She hit there what was one of my basic intentions in the book. Instead of jabber and chatter and analysis and pretentious psychology or unintentional muddling I tried always for images that would convey the idea that underlay the moment. To my mind most things can be understood elementally at least by an average person, even sometimes a simple person—in a good sense. The business of the creative writer in such a case is to find what can express his idea, as a circle expresses circularity even in the moon or an orange; he is not able to rest till he finds a body for the soul of his matter. I always remember, and try never to forget, Spenser's line

"For soul is form and doth the body make"[7]

which is good Greek as well.

A good example of this in SO RED THE ROSE is on page 355, where a very complicated matter is rendered into something seemingly simple, and at least graspable.

Since this is one of the most important points about my book I think a genuine definition of what it means in an art to "realize" a content, you might write a really luminous paragraph as to what that means.[8] I hear you are a magnificent teacher in your classrooms, and thus I feel sure you can do this definition and exegesis wonderfully well.

7. Edmund Spenser, "An Hymne in Honour of Beautie," line 132.
8. In his Introduction to the Scribner's Modern Standard Authors edition of *So Red the Rose,* Davidson wrote: "The complete artist, neither romanticist nor realist, dramatizes the ethical conflict in its own terms, without imposing special views upon it. He strives to reveal it, to evoke it, to 'realize' it in a full-bodied fiction that implies in every part that whole of which it is a symbolic rather than a merely pictorial or argued representation" (p. vii).

Your teaching experience and teaching powers ought here to be of great service to the cause of the book.

Following on that thought is one that seems to me important. Your introduction is to a book that is intended, at that price and in that EDITION to be for university and college and such students. That seems to me a very worthy end in itself, instead of their parents and their parents' reading of reviewers in the papers and magazines. I have a great interest in the young and a great pity for them. That made me a fine teacher and ended my career in that field, for I decided *if,* as I said to President Meiklejohn, I was good enough for Amherst I was too good. That, however, does not alter the point here, which is that you will be able in your introduction to offer what is rich and wonderful for the young or the student, for I feel sure you have an attitude that is, as it were, always young in heart. My book must surely have some of that if it is worth anything at all. That last is quite a remark, and bears on the perennial freshness of the saints and the poets and people with minds and natures like yours.

A few critics have complained that SO RED THE ROSE is too lush with descriptions, and one has spoken of its "jewelry-laden belles." [9] It will pay one to look through the book with this in mind. The actual number of lines devoted to description of places or nature is amazingly small. On page 210, for example, there is really a small amount of description and yet the effect is of a much greater amount of it. One New England comment said the book was all too heavy with the scent of camellias etc.; I said that was indeed an effect, since camellias have no fragrance. The word *chivalry,* if I remember right, is used in the book only once, and that by an old windbag. The word aristocracy is scarcely used at all. There are none of the clichés—or so they are often thought to be—regarded as especially SOUTHERN.

The *rhythm* of the Southern speech cost me a lot of work. The tone of that is very elusive; I had to write it by ear, saying the things as soon as they came to me, not waiting and fooling with them. After that I did a lot of cutting or moving the position of words. Take lines 10-11-12-13 on page 199. I wanted them to break one's heart. Or the end of Chapter XLI pages 202-203—note the Southern *tone* of the lines and speeches, that final sentence and its rhythm.

I have travelled a good deal in Europe and made acquaintances often

9. See above, Letter 492 and notes.

with the express purpose of learning about the landed society and codes, so that I might compare them with, or use them to verify, my inherited society. In this way I hope I have avoided the silly, outside stuff about grandeur and mansions and aristocrats and so on; I wanted whatever effect there was to be that of taking whatever there was as a matter of course.

One of the tests of what happens—it has often happened evidently—in one's experience with *So Red the Rose*—it is that the reading of it aloud is something. The effect is quite noticeable.

From the remarks in these pages please, dear Donald, quote anything you see fit. I think, for example, that the Margaret Mitchell item is of real convincingness for some of our simple, colonistic cultures in various U.S.A. people's individuals—that is to say the average birds we are in contact with.

There might be said to be a general melancholy hanging over the whole of *So Red the Rose*. But this is not so. It is true that it has no booby optimism, sugar-coated rot that can be quoted and that is to be sold easily for the proper public, the expedient buyers of such crap. But this book of mine is safe from depression first by warmth of the heart, which is all through its pages and especially in the tenderness of its concluding pages. That end was taken by one reviewer as propaganda for war. The lasting optimism of *So Red the Rose* in so far as optimism is required is that life rests in the individual heart and soul, along with an inclusion with the social general in which this soul and heart exists and finds its human expression; for the young I do think that optimism—not underscored or heavily sold to them—is the right thing. But this is not to mean that silly individualism, producing boresome freaks in New England and Harvard asses, who planned to be interesting cases or burst—this is to mean a certain strength or character of soul in an individual, by which he will bless his single and profound self. If that sentence does not say it, I, at least, cannot say it, nor will Mrs. Roosevelt understand it—even her belches must be extrovert —a large fart into the general avid void.

Dear Donald, please remind yourself that all this is largely to be of use to you. Take what you want of it, let the rest go.

Yours as ever

Stark

Please make allowances for my typing.

792 | To John Mason Brown, Saturday Review, New York

Jennymead
Waccabuc, New York
Monday [September 22, 1952]

Dear John,

I am flying to Rome on October 3rd, if all goes well, and my conscience will trouble me if I don't tell you before I go that lately in my going through some books in my apartment, for some quotes, I found myself caught in those two war books of yours[1] and dropped everything to go on reading. I wrote of one of them,[2] I remember, but it occurs to me now that with all the praise I gave it I may not have done it justice, or at least expressed sufficiently my admiration and enjoyment of it. I am very much impressed with the abundance of the sense of life, the easy gift that it shows for style, the capacity for excitement in your responses to the world you encountered, and the tenderness that appears from time to time. I do indeed congratulate you.

Your ears must have burned several times this past season when I was at the Delanos'. They are great admirers of yours; and she still delights in the fact that she proposed you to the *Post*. I remember when the editor[3] asked me who I would propose, I said Mrs. Delano has already proposed him, unless, that is, the *Post* minds its critic's being educated.

Well, if he reads one or another of some of the pieces that pass for criticism these days, he won't think I was merely pulling his leg.

I hope those books had the wide sale that they deserved.

Give my love to Cassie.

Affectionately
Stark

1. Young refers to Brown's *To All Hands: An Amphibious Adventure* (1943), and *Many a Watchful Night* (1944).

2. Young had reviewed *Many a Watchful Night* in "Watch and Ware," *New Republic*, CXII (January 1, 1945), 26–27, and praised "its intensity, its acuteness, its lucid rightness of response to what is experienced." In reply to this letter, Brown remembered that Young had found Brown's remarks about the British "much more intelligent, far less colonial and certainly less fulsome-fumbled" than what Emerson wrote on the subject in *English Traits*.

3. Julian Starkweather Mason (1876–1954) edited the New York *Evening Post* from 1926 to 1933; John Mason Brown joined its staff in 1929.

793 | To Pauline Goldmann, 26th W. and Salado,
"Any Fool Would Know," [4] Austin, Texas

320 East 57th Street
New York
Friday [September 26, 1952]

Dear Tiny Cousin,

I must thank you for being so sweet as to write me about Ben. Since then, too, I have heard from my sister. It was enough to set her crazy, poor child. I was worried sick myself till I called last Sunday and found that he was out of danger. To lose Ben would be a loss indeed. Of all the men I ever knew I'd rather have him for a brother-in-law.

Bowman and I fly off in the afternoon of October 3rd. He has had some heavy work on big jobs and this will be a rest for him. I don't feel as fresh as a daisy myself—a dead brain—and so going off to a beautiful country won't do me too much harm. I was with Mr. Henry Wallace for hours last night and we talked of many things, but oftenest of these Latin countries. He is a lovely, warm-hearted wonderful man.

I hope Cousin Mamie [5] is entirely well by now. She probably looks more outrageously young than ever, bless her heart. If you find where she hides her monkey glands, steal some for me. I am fading fast.

I don't know when exactly we'll be back from Europe—but when I do, one of the pleasures to look forward to will be seeing my cousins on 26th Street, not 24th, 23rd, or 22nd. You see how careful I am—so don't move.

Thank you again, so take care of yourself. Love to you all three.

Stark

4. Young included this message for the postman because a recent letter to the Gold-manns had been returned to him for improper address. Since the family had lived at this address for more than forty years, Young felt the postman should have delivered a letter addressed to them on an adjacent street.
5. Mrs. Paul Herman Goldmann.

794 | To Anne Sharkey,[6] Snedens Landing, Palisades, New York

American Express Rome
October 13, 1952

Dearest Miss Annie,

We were 33 hours delayed in reaching Lisbon, having been sent home again and resting, if you call it so, in Sidney Nova Scotia from Friday midnight till four next morning (Sunday) and so got to Lisbon 33 hours late. We left Lisbon on the plane the following Saturday, 17 hours late—etc. We got here before dinner last night and Ernest de Weerth[7] gave us a fine evening—the Forum and St. Peters lighted, a great dinner and so on. So today I wanted to write you a line and stopped on the way home—after Frascati—to buy some airmail paper —then on the way went to the American Express and there was your very sweet note. You beat me to it therefore, bless your heart.

I wanted to say that ever since we got to Rome we keep saying

6. For many years one of Young's best friends, Anne J. Sharkey began her career in 1931 as a managerial associate in the advertising and manufacturing enterprises of Henry B. Sell. In 1962, she became administrative assistant to the director of the Cultural Exchange Series of the American National Theatre and Academy, and, in 1963, she took charge of the New York office of the U.S. Department of State's Cultural Presentations Program. Since 1968, she has been executive secretary and administrative assistant to the director of the American Federation of Arts.

7. Ernest de Weerth (1897–1967), stage and costume designer, born in Paris, came to the United States after attending Oxford University and became assistant stage manager and designer at the Neighborhood Playhouse. Young and de Weerth became friends in 1921. In addition to his costume designing for Broadway productions and motion pictures, de Weerth became closely associated with Max Reinhardt, especially in the New York production of *The Miracle* (1924) and *A Midsummer Night's Dream* (1927) and the Vienna staging of *King Lear* (1925). Although Young praised his friend's work in the *New Republic*, he probably made his most considered evaluation in the presentation copy of *Immortal Shadows* which he sent to de Weerth in 1953: "For Ernest de Weerth—whose beautiful spirit and marvelous gift for design, and fine passion of Faith in the splendor and flower of art, and whose generous response to others, has been one of the most admirable and blessed contributions to the theatre of our time." Writing of their friendship, Ernest de Weerth has said that Young's criticism became "the most valuable asset in our friendship and I began to cherish it beyond all others. We both loved the theatre and we both loved music. We had another bond in common which over a period of many years grew ever deeper: our mutual love for Italy. We both enjoyed the same places, the same forms of art, and my friends became his." De Weerth lived in Rome for many years before his death on March 28, 1967.

Annie and Janie [8] must have liked this and how nice if they could drop in. We have two rooms on the top floor at The Marini—a bath between—opposite us a large terrace with willow chairs and flower pots, overlooking a fine lot of Rome—straight ahead is the campodoglio, the Victor Emmanuel monument (!) and lovely roofs and golden-brown walls. The other thing I wanted to say was that I hope your own news is better, whatever that might happen to be. Life does keep books and you are paying the due price for being a fine, deep-feeling loyal person —qualities I do stand by and like, and am apt to love the holder of them. Please send at least a note sometime telling us your news and about your housing problem as it were—what you are doing about an apartment and all that.

I don't know how long we are to be here. I leave and have left as much as possible to Wales—he has had so much on his hands, worked so hard, these last many months, that this trip ought to be to a good extent his, so to speak. Give Zue [9] and Janie my love—and thank you again for writing me.

Affectionately,
Stark

795 | To Louis Kronenberger, Brandeis University, Waltham, Massachusetts

Rome Italy
October 18, 1952

Dear Louis,

When a book appears from a friend [1] you have an old affection and admiration for you feel a trifle of nervousness for fear it will not be quite his very best sort of achievement. This feeling left me the very first page of your book. The very first paragraph indeed went off to

---

8. Jane Wasey.
9. Anne Sharkey's sister, Margaret A. Sharkey.
1. Shortly before leaving for Europe, Young had received a copy of Kronenberger's *Thread of Laughter: Chapters on English Stage Comedy from Jonson to Maugham.*

perfection. I took time out of my midnight hours to read it through. Getting ready to come to Europe put a pressure on everything, but I did board the plane at last. I don't know just how long I'll be over here.

Louis, I do indeed congratulate you on a book of so much real distinction—in range and in the general background of reading and experience, and in the fine distinction of the style itself. We have few books nowadays that even approach all of that, usually not any of it, God help us! Remember me with love to Emmy [2] and to yourself, and thank you again.

> Affectionately
> Stark

796 | To Ella Somerville, Oxford, Mississippi

> Rome Italy
> October 25 [1952]

Dearest Ella,

I have thought of you often when I see so many wonderful things. But marvellous as it is, Rome is horribly, really horribly, overcrowded and noisy. The main streets almost impossible to traverse. Give all the family my love—love to little Spencer—I will send a card—not a note like this—soon to the Stones—

> Affectionately
> Stark

2. Mrs. Kronenberger.

797 | To Fiammetta Innocenti,[3] "The Studio," Long Island

Hotel Luna
Venice, Italy
November 17, 1952

Dear Miss Fiammetta,

People were so kind to us in Rome that the days flew past, and a friend there at the Excelsior with a car took us on trips to Frascati, Cori, Circeo, Ravello and so on, and thus the visit was longer than we had quite thought of, though we had no definite plans except to shine on Paris and London briefly and get back to the house of a friend down near Pau and the Spanish border by Christmas. But Rome shortened our stay in Florence and Venice. And Florence in spite of the ruin was as wonderful as ever—such distinction in so many directions, not least in the peoples' faces. All my old admiration and love of that city was kindled anew—not that anything but time had ever dimmed it. It is unique in the world.

This is especially to thank you for that fine letter and the trouble you took with introductions for us. We called your mother's house [4] but she was not well enough at the moment to receive visitors and your sister [5] was in America. We sent your mother a bouquet of lilac chrysanthemums mixed with white and were sorry indeed not to have the pleasure of meeting her. Your whole list of people must have been warned, for all have been absent from town, including Miss Garth [6] here in Venice. Nevertheless, we do indeed appreciate your kindness and characteristic thoughtfulness.

In spite of the Louvre, the Chateaux and what not, I feel if I confess the truth as silly in leaving Italy for any other country as if I were go-

---

3. Fiammetta Pecori-Giraldi Innocenti (b. 1906) and her husband, Umberto Innocenti (1895–1968), were both friends of Young and Bowman. After coming to the United States in 1925, Innocenti formed a partnership with the landscape architect Richard K. Webel. They designed landscape projects for the New York world's fairs in 1939 and 1964, Wellesley College, the Frick Museum, and the Belmont and Aqueduct race tracks. Although born in Naples, Fiammetta Innocenti lived mostly in Florence before coming to the United States in 1950 for her marriage.
4. The home of Contessa Eleonora Pecori-Giraldi in Florence.
5. Contessa Franca Pecori-Giraldi.
6. Violet Garth, then owner of the Casetta Rossa on the Grand Canal in Venice.

ing to New Jersey. That would be heresy to many of my New York friends and they would at least burn me with their cigarettes, since the stake is too strong for modern hands.

Until the last few days we have had marvellous weather always, and it has added to my delight in seeing how the Italians in spite of everything have accomplished so much in coming back after such ruin and wasted destruction in every direction.

Please remember me most cordially to your signore, he is a very lovely person.

With love to you both, I am

Yours sincerely
Stark Young

P.S. We were not in Florence long enough to manage the trip to Grassina [7] and were awfully sorry. To meet the brother would have been very nice indeed and a touch of farm life, a podére, a world of vines and olive trees, would have been a fine experience along with Donatello,[8] Piero di Cosimo [9] and the Pitti [1] and the Uffizi [2]—and so on to numberless sweet things.

S.Y.

7. Umberto Innocenti owned a farm and villa at Grassina, on the southeastern outskirts of Florence, where his brother, Giuseppe Innocenti, and family lived.

8. Donato di Niccolo di Betto Bardi (*ca.* 1382–1466), Italian sculptor.

9. Piero di Cosimo (1462–1521), Florentine painter.

1. A reference to the Italian Renaissance palace in Florence built for Luca Pitti about 1485, now an important painting gallery.

2. The Uffizi Palace in Florence, begun in 1560 and finished in 1581, for Cosimo I de' Medici, now a painting gallery.

798 | To Anne Sharkey, New York

Hotel Luna
Venice, Italy
November 20, 1952

Dear Annie,

I had your lovely letter this morning, with its sad news.[3] In a way, of course, it is all for the best, but that is only an indirect comfort. You and Zue[4] have at least the satisfaction of knowing that you have been wonderful and always in the deeper sense right, not to say careful, right and conscientious and loyal. We may all take comfort in the fact that these very things, the fine qualities, don't exist to themselves alone, in a vacuum. They radiate through the entire character and personality, and it's something to remember that we all think you are one of the finest people, the most loyal, serious and to be loved, that could be found anywhere. I am answering your letter at once because at such times as this in your life one needs all the reassurances available, one needs support for all the sinking heart and shaken soul. In this case of your mother you will have nothing to regret and many beautiful things to remember, more and more as time goes on.

I am glad to hear of the kin up there and their goodness and cordial nearness. I am sure—from your own family if nothing else, that they are fine people, as well as distinguished and well-bred in the true sense. This will renew a section of your life and will warm your many memories.

We have had until lately very fine weather and have seen and enjoyed many fine things. Italy is far more difficult than it used to be, more crowded, much more expensive, more noisy and so on, but it still makes all other countries [sentence unfinished at end of page].

Rome was impossibly pressed with traffic scooters and bicycles and people, but was inexhaustibly absorbing. We kept saying I wonder if

3. Young refers to Anne Sharkey's mother, Mrs. Alice M. Sharkey, retired executive director of the Whitney Museum of American Art. Born in Glasgow, Scotland, she became a resident of New York in 1908. In 1920, she was made assistant to the director of the Art Center, and, from 1926 to 1933, she served as executive director of the Art Alliance of America. Subsequently, she translated articles from French and German for *The Arts* and *Art in America*. From 1936 until her retirement in 1948, she was executive secretary of the Whitney Museum. She died in 1954. See below, Letter 850.

4. Margaret A. Sharkey.

Janie [5] and Annie saw this and hoping that you did. Ernest de Weerth was in Rome and kept taking us here and there into the country, to various towns and finally to Ravello, by way of Naples. And various other people were kindness itself to us. We were there October 12th and stayed on for about five weeks. We leave here the 23rd and go by Cannes on a job Wales has to inspect, then Paris and London and back to Pau-Bas Pyrénnées for Christmas, with Gertrude Newell, then very likely to Morocco and finally *sail* from Italy I don't know just when. We both couldn't bear the thought that our last sight of Europe would be Liverpool and an English boat—we want to leave from Italy and on an *Italian* boat. So I don't know when we'll sail. We miss you and Zue and Janie. She wrote us, Miss Janie did, a very sweet (restaurant—I leave that to make you smile—Wales interrupted by saying he wondered where the Colombe was) letter, bless her heart.

Today is the festa of Santa Maria della Salute—the shops are closed, the streets are packed with all Venice, all talking when there were at least two together—the place hums and as the dark comes there are countless lights. Have you seen *The Skin* (Le Pelle) Malaparte's last book? [6] Very tiresome in places but full of interesting and pressing matters. I won't read this over—forgive the errata—Wales sends love—and give Zue my love and Janie.

Affectionately,
Stark

799 | To John Hall Wheelock, Charles Scribner's Sons, New York

Paris
December 5 [1952]

Dear Jack,

This is only to send love and good wishes to you and Phyllis, Christmas and New Years. Bowman asks me to send his greetings. He has

5. Jane Wasey.
6. Presumably Young refers to David Moore's translation of Curzio Malaparte's *The Skin* (1952). The volume was originally published in Rome in 1950.

the offer to do a house for some rich American outside Madrid, so I don't exactly [know] our dates. If there is a tiny sum from Scribners please ask the Business Manager to hold it till my return.

People have been so overwhelmingly kind to us with their hospitality, motors etc., that I am beginning to think I'll break a leg or something surely. Europe can be very warm and responsive or whatever one wants to call it.

We are going to London for a week only, about the 14th % American Express Co., if you care to send me your news—how you and Phyllis are and so on. I hope the fall season hasn't worked you to death. I hope Phyllis got the clipping about Croce.[7] Bless her heart!

From London we fly down to Bordeaux for Christmas and some while after with an old friend, Gertrude Newell, who has an old house[8] we've never seen—13 stairs in it and I don't know what else. I'm anxious to see it.

Paris has been rainy and cold most of the week we have been here but our little French Hotel on the river opposite the Louvre is warm and kind. The Louvre for a wonder is heated! I'm not looking forward too hotly to London, and we changed our whole plans—and expense!— to sail from Italy not some damned Protestant Northern climate port. I'll be a pauper when I return, but this is apt to be my last trip abroad —I'm too old, too unrich and too exhaustible to try it again, though after many years of absence it is all more wonderful than ever. So many sides of Italy were so incredibly rich and deep and beautiful, despite the war. If we have peace and some sort of renascence in the western world, it may come from Italy, though I doubt if we have any for years, and that we do have may come from the East again. Nostradamus says as much, or did in 1550. Certainly it won't come from our America, for all the advantages in scientific things and so on, and our real kindness of heart—not always full of light—and our resources— not always too profoundly good for us perhaps.

7. On November 21, Young had written to Mrs. Wheelock: "I was very proud of Italy yesterday. The newsboys were crying the death of Croce in the streets as we would cry that of Henry Ford. I enclose a clipping, from the Corriere d'Informazione." When making the comment, Young doubtless recalled her admiration for the work of Benedetto Croce (1866–1952) and her translation of his "Commedia dell'arte" in *Theatre Arts Monthly,* XVII (December, 1933), 929–39.
8. Planterose, near Moumour, in the Basses Pyrénées; see above, Letter 278 and n. 9.

Give your Charlie my love—I hope the burden of the new office won't break him down. Love to your Phyllis and to you.

Affectionately
Stark

800 | To Norman Dello Joio, New York

London
December 16 [1952]

Dear Norman,

I wrote you the other day but forgot to tell you that I finished *Christ Stopped at Eboli*[9] last week. I had been doing some other reading and so got to this later than I expected. Thank you for the chance to read it. It is as a whole monotonous because he approaches every place, incident and character in the same way. He evidently does not see that each is a separate problem—you study the way to introduce each in the way most engaging etc. Some of the monotonous impression may come from the translation, which is perfectly competent but sounds always the same. But nevertheless I should hate to have missed reading this book. It has many valuable reflections in it, apart from the regional and racial material. I know something at least about the southern part of Italy, and I feel now that I learned a great deal on the subject from this account of Levi's. I read some of it for the second time.

By the way, soon after I got to Lisbon I remembered saying to you something about the author's going to pot, sporting around, Don Juan etc. after the success of this book, and it came over me that it was [not] Levi at all—it was the author of *Christ in Concrete*—an Italian American.[1]

I have also read Malaparte's *The Skin,* it came out in English not so long ago. Very unequal—not always making clear what is fiction in the grim or grotesque vein and what is truth. But it has a lot of matter

9. Carlo Levi, *Christ Stopped at Eboli* (1947), translated by Frances Frenaye.
1. Pietro di Donato, *Christ in Concrete* (1939).

in it that is remarkable, and some that is impressive, some that's exciting, and so on. It is vastly different from the *Eboli*—more talented, less reliable, more (at times) absorbing. A great deal of it is in Naples or the surrounding country. He must be an intense, sometimes brilliant, sometimes unreliable neurotic, semi-creative, semi-journalistic, without good taste at times. Basta.

I heard a Pergolese opera in Rome and a Monteverde—done with spirit and entertainingly, but by no means with musicianship on the part of most of the singers. In Paris I went to a concert of Nadia Boulanger's[2]—one of her pupils with B. at the piano. That evening she came to dinner with friends of hers who also asked Wales and me. B. asked us to her place next afternoon partly to hear a young pupil of hers play. A Turkish little girl of eleven—she knows nine concertos, B. said, and pages of Bach and others. She played a longish and very difficult Bach piece and as maturely as any pianist I ever heard. She has had offers to USA, Berlin etc. but B. won't let her start as a child, says she is already too fine a musician to spoil that way. The Turkish Government has passed a law to provide for this child as long as she studies. Isn't that quite thrilling, civilized—it almost made me cry when I heard that she is kept at 2 hours a day, one piano, one solfeggio. Otherwise is a happy, normal child, much beloved and not at all self-conscious.

Well, Merry Christmas, again to you all and love. Wales sends his love.

Stark

I won't read this over.

2. Nadia Boulanger (b. 1887), teacher of music and conductor, became teacher of composition at the École normale de musique in 1935. She has also won fame for her performances as an organist and conductor of choral works.

801 | To John Hall Wheelock, Charles Scribner's Sons, New York

Meknes, Morocco
January 25, 1953

Dear Jack,

This is largely to send greetings to you and dear Phyllis, from a long way off it is indeed. We have been in Morocco two weeks, a little over, and go from here this afternoon by bus—they have the most splendid looking buses here in this French colony that I ever saw, and at many hours of the day—few train departures—to Casablanca to take the plane to Tunis—about two hours instead of two days—then to Rome in two hours, instead of a boat trip and then the railroad. It's not just a foolish matter of saving time, we have seen various places already that we will fly over; it's that you have longer time in marvellous places like Rabat, Marrakech, Fez, etc. People have been so terrifically kind to us—dinners, theatres, motors lent and so on that I don't know how we'll settle down when we get home. If we hadn't been often to London, Paris and Rome all this would have been too silly, but there are many sides to life as you know, and Christmas in a chateau is an experience in itself as you know, and dinner with a famous Monsignore, a canon of the Vatican, vying with us in risqué stories, is another experience—a good man at that—far inside, and useful in Catholic policy—I have sense enough to know that. It's one reason why the Church and I get on so well. (over)

This gives me more room, what with the fussy French methods of weighing, writing details, endless trivia, which is one reason a friend of mine says who has lived here for years, they have no great light in their eyes. Every moment, to change 72 cents worth of coins for example, at the bank, you show your passport and all that. I got a little even on this point—I said I regretted not being able to give anything to the blind beggars in Marrakech—they couldn't read my passport. They laughed at that crack—the Latin mind—just as the priest in San Moise in Venice—the church freezing, my head bared, horrible, so I said, "Father, I wish you talk less of this world and more about Hell, or aren't you cold?" He laughed at that—Also the tailor in Venice—

the church front outside his windows covered with cupids, naked Renaissance figures and so on—I said, Signor Canellia, what a bad setting for a tailor, evidently clothes are not needed to get to heaven. I like saying such things to Italians—there is something brittle in their minds—they have minds that respond.

In Biarritz we were invited with our hostess to lunch—about twelve people. One was General Conte de Chaumont—Lafayette's great grandson as he told me at once, patting my hand, eighty, now in the stage of limericks. His wife is a celebrated Shakespeare scholar, I was told, I was too ignorant to know about that. But in conversation she told me that she was a Scribner author, shame on me. She is Nicholas Longworth's sister, I knew that long ago, from the General's angle— and it was very pleasant to see that she looks still like a lady American style, very well-born looking, and not a battered imitation of French— Some of the chateau people I was taken to see were quite well battered, but looked the real thing, whereas it was a superchic in the Countesse to look well-bred American. Could you send me a line in care of the American Express Co., Rome, telling me how things are going, how you are and how Phyllis is, and what about the Chaumont—her books and all that?[3] I'd like to know and I am ashamed of my ignorance. At the same dinner was a Mr. Prince,[4] it seems one of the top rich men in America—94—beat that, a pink shirt with black evening tie, a grey sweater, striped trousers, white spats, skin like a pink baby, hair parted in the middle, *two men on the box* of his Rolls Royce, and everybody's darling and a self-conscious pet, a real dear, I must admit. I was two

---

3. On January 30, Wheelock replied: "The Countess and the General whom you refer to by the charming name of 'de Chaumont' are General and Countess de Chambrun—he being the great-grandson of Lafayette, and she born Clara Longworth, sister of the late Nicholas Longworth who married Alice Roosevelt. Countess de Chambrun is a most delightful, as well as intelligent, lady who, as you point out, has the character and the good sense to remain an old fashioned American. She is a high-minded—at times even perhaps a strong-minded—woman of scholarly attainments and even achievements. We have published a number of books by Countess de Chambrun— *Shakespeare Rediscovered* and her autobiography in two volumes: *Shadows Like Myself* and *Shadows Lengthen,* to mention only three of her books published by Scribners. She has also had some success with her plays in French, some of which had a good run in Paris. She is a graduate of the Sorbonne, a Ph.D.—but that's nothing against her. I understand that she had her examiners there overawed by her learning and overwhelmed by her almost too ready answers to their inquisition. Phyllis and I are very fond of her and of the General also."

4. Frederick Henry Prince (1859–1953), banker, owner of Prince and Company, president of Chicago Stock Yards, director of Armour and Company and various other enterprises. He died on February 2, 1953.

people away from the head of the table, given over to him. I could vaguely hear that he was talking about the Bible, and so when he turned to me and asked if I didn't think so? I said I hadn't heard exactly what he had said, I was sorry, but I must remind him of what Colbert said to Louis Quaterze, a propos of *Tartuffe*—"You may say what you like about God but you have to be careful what you say about his ministers." After lunch when we were leaving, he called me to his place on the sofa, held my hand and said, "Ah, you are so brilliant. And you are a sweet man." This in English—life does have its surprises. I am so simple and country Southern that I thought only that Countesse de Chaumont was a very gracious and nice woman, giving us a lift, and I would have thought nothing more of it had not the barber shop, barbet et cie received us with such elegant point, style and expedition (a good hair cut at that).

I was sorry to see that harsh review of Rawling's book in *Time*. I don't know the book, but a good deal in the review seemed unnecessary. If it is that bad why put that much space and energy on it?[5]

Wales Bowman, much overwhelmed with the subtle intellectualism and air of fine mystery in the best of the Arab things, the arches, ceilings, ornament, reserve, the resources of light and shadow, sends you and Phyllis most cordial greetings—he is a real admirer of you both. Please forgive this scrawl, if I read it over I might tear it up. I shudder to think what the postage will be. Please tell me about La Chaumont.

Love to you both—

Stark

5. See "Ase's Agonies," a review of Marjorie Kinnan Rawlings' *The Sojourner,* in *Time*, LXI (January 5, 1953), 74. After noting the "hangnail character sketches and hangdog attitudes," the reviewer characterized the novel as "a sententious smudge compared to her famed, finely drawn 1938 novel, *The Yearling*."

802 | To Donald Davidson, Vanderbilt University, Nashville, Tennessee

[Rome]
January 31, 1953

Dear Donald,

I got here a few days ago from Morocco and was very much pleased to find your good letter and the MS. of the *Introduction*. I am delayed getting this—the letter was written Jan. 14—but I have been on the loose so to speak since January 8, in Marrakech, Meknes, Fez, Tunis, Rabat, Tiflet etc. and only by the grace of God did any letters—except my sister's one letter, which I had advised her to send to Marrakech and let wait for me whenever—I have most carefully read the introduction, a great deal of it amounts to brilliance, I think, (I rarely use that word) and some of it is very beautiful in feeling and very moving. Some suggestions I have made and so questions—nothing overwhelming. In *two* days I will return certain pages or all to you, with indications. No use now blundering into concrete points and so on. I will do that in a letter with the MS. I do thank you, Donald, I don't know anybody who could have done this difficult task better or rather as well. I hope your flu is entirely gone. There seems to be an epidemic on the Continent—Mrs. Davidson's work turned out well I feel pretty sure, I'd like to have seen it. Excuse this seemingly flattering letter. I do very profoundly appreciate your real interest in your subject.

Affectionately
Stark

p.s. I see in a letter dated Jan. 21 from Tom Walsh [6] where he says, "Donald Davidson has just sent me the Introduction to *So Red the Rose*. He said in his accompanying letter that he was sending you a good copy of it in care of the A-E. Co. in Rome."

So perhaps your MS was sent later than the date of your letter and so didn't wait so long here. At any rate thank you many times.

6. Thomas J. B. Walsh, member of the editorial staff of Charles Scribner's Sons.

803 | To Donald Davidson, Vanderbilt University, Nashville, Tennessee

American Express Co.
Rome
January 4⁷ [February 4, 1953]

Dear Donald,

I wrote you how much I was made happy by your Introduction and promised to send any suggestions I could conjure up. I have put about two days' work on it—for it seemed to me that if you could do all that work you did, I at least might do what I could. I have so much admiration and confidence in you that [I] take you at your word, and have approached it very carefully in the hope that this outside criticism, plus inside familiarity with the subject, will be of practical use. To me, for example, and the average reader—not specialist—the Sherman passages could be shortened in the light of the article's general emphases. No need to say more here, the comments are on the sheets. But one thing, please feel entirely free to accept or dismiss any or all my suggestions—I'm merely trying to be useful. There is nothing in your whole article that *per se* I don't find of marked interest, often wonderfully penetrative, and often in itself creative. I'd like to keep the MS. if you'll let me. Just put it by when you have done with it, and post it to me to Tom Walsh—I'll ask him to keep it. I'm writing him today how delighted I am with your essay. Jack Wheelock has just written me how thoroughly he admires it.

I hope your flu is long since past—it's a mess indeed. I sail March 9th on the Doria—Forgive this fancy pen—it seems on the skids, though not very old. My address will be here up to about March 5th, or 4th, they will forward mail till then, wherever I'll be—it's not definite just where—somewhere south of here in Italy—or else in Rome. With grateful affection.

I am yours
Stark

7. The sequence of Young's letters establishes the date as February 4.

804 | To John Hall Wheelock, Charles Scribner's Sons,
New York

Hotel de la Ville
Rome
January [February] 4 [1953]

Dear Jack,

I am writing smack off after reading your lovely poem[8] a number
of times. It is convincing and haunting—I like it very much—thank
you for sending it. The rhyming finally threatened to outdo me so I
had to write out the scheme—as you see by the enclosed. It will make
you laugh. That last "things" with no rhyme to go with it gets a curiously right effect—that of the bird seeming to be there singing without
end, forever, and if not in the tree, in your mind.[9]

I smiled over the Chaumont[1]—It's a wonder I didn't write Cham-
bord, the restaurant. I know that it's Chambrun, and if I hadn't I
would have—since he told me so as he shook my hand at the start. I
didn't tell the Countess so, of course, but on a visit to Cincinnati some
years ago I sat by her sister at dinner—Nan may have been her name—
She was tight as a tick. A few nights later or lunch perhaps—she was
there again, but so sober that she couldn't remember at all the festivities
with me and Bowman. Such is life. But you didn't *dictate* any marked
judgement of the Countess' achievements—I'll ask you that when I
get home.[2]

I was relieved to hear that my endless letter would at least get by. I

8. Wheelock had sent his poem "Wood-thrush."
9. On February 9, Wheelock replied: "I'm naturally very much pleased that you
like 'Wood-thrush.' The fact that you so carefully worked out the rhyme scheme is
flattering. Could one do anything to-day more unfashionable than to write a poem
with a complicated rhyme scheme, in which the rhymes answer each other like the
voices in a fugue. To me the effect produced when such a poem is read aloud—and,
again, to me every poem should be read aloud—is enormously exciting. You got every
rhyme except 'Golgotha' which does, in a bastard way, rhyme with 'are' and 'earlier.'"
1. See above, Letter 801 and n. 3.
2. In reply Wheelock commented: "As for our friend, 'the Chaumont,' concerning
whose literary achievements you ask my judgment, she writes fluently, is a cultivated
woman, and has had an interesting life. Anything beyond that I shall reserve to tell
you when we next meet. She is a magnificent, warm-hearted friend and an indomitable
woman."

wrote it the day we left Meknes and suddenly had to leave off for lunch and the taxi—so it went unreread.

I liked Donald Davidson's introduction very much, but put about two days more or less working on it, he requested any suggestions possible—etc. I'll tell you about them when we meet. We sail March 9, the Doria. Bowman sends very cordial greetings. Love to you and Phyllis.

Stark

805 | To John Hall Wheelock, Charles Scribner's Sons, New York

[Rome]
February 15 [1953]

Dear Jack,

Despite orders and secret agreements I'll go right on and say I like this poem, Bonac,[3] very much. What a finely built line, for example

And the owl's tremolo and the firefly

Anybody can thunder but such verse as that is quite another matter. From "now the bird song fails us"—to the very end I think moving and beautiful—the call for the surcease and so on, and then the alert spirit listening to the rumors and so on. "With all its waters" is especially right somehow. But I must say no more evidently.

Your line about not letting Countess Chambrun's sister getting turned upside down and spilling[4]—made me laugh. She was a most agreeable souse but not a Shakespeare scholar.

The only suggestion I'd make about your poem is that the title

3. In replying to Young's letter of February 4 (see the preceding letter), Wheelock enclosed his poem "Bonac." He sent the poem, he wrote, "on the distinct understanding that you do not write me about it, or even bother to acknowledge it."

4. In his letter to Young, Wheelock had remarked: "I like your story about the lady you sat next to at dinner. 'Hold up your head or you'll spill it' might perhaps have been good advice."

would mean nothing to most people—me for example,—unless explained,[5] and I'm not sure that costs the poem's effect rather more than the place is worth, as poetry. However, how should I know?

I'm looking forward to seeing you and Phyllis—sweet people. Bowman sends very cordial greetings.

Love to you both
Stark

806 | To John Benjamin Robertson, Austin, Texas

Andrea Doria
Monday [March 9, 1953]

Dear Ben,

I sent a card in Naples, left with an official to be posted. I hope it was and reaches you. It was quite fine to have a cable, I never thought of that. The ship left Genoa Saturday, went by Cannes and arrived in Naples at eleven Sunday morning. We went aboard at three and were due to sail at 5, but there were delayed passengers from somewhere and we got off after six. The boat is not showy, but the last word in luxury, every imaginable device and comfort. The only thing is that it is air conditioned, and I'd like to open a window the first thing in the morning; even for a little. (The pen scratches the paper but I won't stagger to my room for my patented pen—the ship is rolling so— though the sun is very bright.) The only darkish spot is special to me —when we went to the head steward for our places last night for dinner, he recognized my name at once—"Count de Weerth told me to be sure, etc." So we got a table at a quiet end, next to the table of some ambassador, such eccelenza—and had various special attentions—and so on. All that means to me—some people love it—is clean shirts and

5. Wheelock had explained the title: "The local people on the southeasterly end of Long Island call that area 'Bonac,' and my poem was written about our countryside at East Hampton, where I have spent some part of almost every summer for the past sixty-four years. At the time the poem was written I thought I should have to sell our place there."

a fat extra tip—the headwaiter as well as the table waiter. Ernest de W. loves this world, has been about in it enough, and meant to do me a kindness, alas, such is life.

Julia wrote that your head was doing all right, it was evidently a close call. I try more and more to be careful. I don't want to end up as a broken old fool. In Rome but for Wales I wouldn't have dared cross the street often for fear of slipping or being run over—it makes me feel old indeed. I am writing this on the chance that it gets posted at Gibraltar, where we stop a little to take on passengers. I hear the boat is jammed on the return trip. It means that tourism is already starting, 6,800,000 in Italy last year—this year promises many more. Wales sends love.

Love to you both
Stark

Sorry about this pen.

807 | To Donald Davidson, Vanderbilt University, Nashville, Tennessee

320 East 57th Street
New York
Wednesday [March, 1953]

Dear Donald,

I spent some hours studying the introduction [6] only to find it more and more worth the trouble all around, to find it richer and richer in content, statement and implication. My book is indeed fortunate, and I am very very appreciative. These things are hard to say, but my heart is in the right place, and you will understand.

I am enclosing a sentence that seems to me to be rich in significant meaning but not easy to follow in the reading. You can study it and do what you think best.

6. Young refers to Davidson's Introduction to Scribner's Modern Standard Authors edition of *So Red the Rose*.

p. 26 bottom—p. 27 top

For the scene, brief though it is, reveals not only the gross violation which ultimately implies (as Hugh McGehee says later on) the collapse of civilized society, but also the plight of the Confederacy, symbolized in the futile skirmishing of the little Confederate detachment for which the McGehees have been cooking a hasty breakfast, as well as, in the details of the ravaging, the nature of the defeat that the McGehees and the South are experiencing and must continue to face.[7]

At the end of the references for my books I cut out the *Kenyon Review* and put Eric Bentley's book *just out*—it repeats the same material and enlarges it, so there's no need to send anyone to the magazine, unless you decide that both should be referred to, that was a good break for the book to appear just as this juncture.[8]

I am mailing you a little Renaissance volume I picked up at a Rome dealers. It will at least serve to remind you of my grateful thoughts, dear Donald.

Affectionately
Stark

808 | To Ernest de Weerth, Rome

Jennymead
Waccabuc, New York
Saturday [March, 1953]

Dearest Ernest,

We didn't half tell you how wonderful it was to see you again. Nor could I quite express my appreciation of the things you said about

7. The sentence, as it appears on p. xxvi of Davidson's Introduction, has been divided into two sentences. The first ends with the word *breakfast,* and the second begins, "It discloses, in the details of the ravaging. . . ."
8. *In Search of Theater,* listed in *Publishers Weekly,* March 14, 1953. See above, Letter 731, n. 4.

Immortal Shadows.[9] Considering your great talent in music and décor and your understanding of so many things in the theatre, your praise means all the more in every way. And I value and cherish your affection and always note your great, unfailing generosity of mind and heart.

We hope to see you soon.

Affectionately
Stark

809 | To Ella Somerville, Oxford, Mississippi

320 East 57th Street
New York
Sunday [March 22, 1953]

Dearest Ella,

We got back Monday from six months in Europe and have been struggling through a mountain of mail and what not ever since—six months makes quite an absence, as you might well guess. I brought you a modest little present—I hope the model hasn't got to America yet—I didn't see it in Paris or London, so I'm hoping that Master Jeweller Pestrelli in Florence was not kidding me when he said this was a specialty of his house—at any rate I only hope that every lady in Oxford hasn't got one already—that's the way of the world these days—ladies in Thibet may have gone in for smelling like Chanel #5 instead of rancid butter—however—Not that Oxford is Thibet—I only meant to imply distance. At any rate this little silver bit is sent you as a reminder of kind thoughts of you in far-off lands and of an old affection and admiration.

I have not seen my dear family since Christmas 1951—so am going next week to Austin, then back here by May 1st and to the country till November.

9. Shortly after returning to New York, Young sent Ernest de Weerth a copy of *Immortal Shadows* with an inscription dated March 16, 1953. See Letter 794, n. 7.

Europe was wonderful to us—people putting car and chauffeur at our service in Rome, Paris, Basses Pyrrenees, doing all sorts of lovely things for us—very fortunately we had seen before and not seldom, Italy, Paris, London etc. So could spend the time with interesting or dear people. It was off season of course with all the discomfort, cold and the devil knows what of winter in Europe. But it had no tourists to speak of—that is to say no crowds and bookings ahead and all that. Such marvels we saw—sometimes never seen before, sometimes more wonderful when revisited. But travelling in Europe is not what it used to be!!! No velvet carpets laid down and if that only at great expense. I wouldn't advise you or any one to try a trip alone in Europe, not unless you have a great deal of money, patience and genuine interest. A party would be another matter—not that I could stand one. We went also to Morocco—what a marvellous world that is! What fine, elegant people the Arabs!

I had a lovely note of thanks from that sweet Bishop child—blood will tell—about a wedding present.[1]

If you see the Stones give them my love—I can't write countless letters but my heart is in the right place. Give my love to all the family. I wish I could drop in and seize my room there in your house. But no—such is life. I shall not forget what a perfect visit I had with you.

Lovingly
Stark

810 | To Roane and Ferriday Byrnes, Natchez, Mississippi

320 East 57th Street
New York
Friday [March 27, 1953]

Dear Roane and Ferriday,

I got home a few days ago from Europe, six months' absence, and it was a very sweet item to find in my pile of mail your lovely Christ-

1. See above, Letter 789 and n. 9.

mas card. It made me very sick to see you all—you are old friends and very much beloved. Time passes, we grow older, and to what end? The world, eternity, skies, moon and stars leave me behind; I can't cope with any of it, but I do remember the people I love. Bless you.

Affectionately
Stark

811 | To Edmund Wilson, Princeton, New Jersey

320 East 57th Street
New York
March 27, 1953

Dear Bunny,

I got back just a few days ago from six months in Europe and found your book here on my desk, sent in October.[2] So please understand and forgive the delay in this reply. I saw some notes on the book in some Paris columns—the *Herald Tribune*, I think it was, and a copy of *Time*, and since then have looked forward to a chance to read it. I am delighted to have this copy and from you.

I have not had a chance to read the entire book, but at least three-fourths of it I have already read, I mean since getting the book, and with great interest. Some of the pieces and various passages I, of course, already know and have remembered very happily; but no little of these pages is fresh or new for me. I must say I don't know anybody writing who can present as you do the combination of mind, persuasive temperament, if I may put it that way, and a constant shimmer and incredible ease of effect. One needs only to pick up most critical writing and most biographical et cetera accounts to see the terrific difference between them and your pages. It grows on me every year the conviction or feeling that most writing shouldn't be done at all—in many cases it is not even writing. All that is obvious of course. I must add, how-

---

2. Edmund Wilson, *The Shores of Light* (1952).

ever, that the variety of subjects and the variety in your approach is very impressive. For a book of this nature to be called exciting may sound odd, but I find it very exciting, very absorbing and very rich.

I have to go for a few weeks to Texas to see my sister and then I'll settle in the country till frost. So far I haven't got myself at all balanced in mind or nerves after all that time in Rome, Paris, London, Morocco, and all the great kindness extended to me.

I hope your lovely lady is well and happy and that things are going to suit you. These days that's a large order.

Thank you again and congratulations.

Affectionately,
Stark

N.B. The stupidity and chaos of this letter shows how scattered I still am.

812 | To the Reverend Anselm Strittmatter,[3] O.S.B., Rome

320 East 57th Street
New York
March 31, 1953

Dear Father Anselm,

We have been back two weeks yesterday—already our national rattlebrain seems to have set in—I seem to have little of value to say or

---

3. The Reverend Anselm Strittmatter, O.S.B. (b. 1894), born Eugene John Strittmatter, first met Young in the late summer of 1912 at the Villa S. Girolamo in Fiesole. Young soon afterwards returned to teach at the University of Texas, and Father Strittmatter continued his studies at the North American College in Rome before entering Columbia University in 1917. After graduation from Columbia in 1919, Father Strittmatter took his master's degree at the University of Chicago and later studied at Harvard. In 1925, he entered the novitiate of St. Benedict's Abbey, Fort Augustus, Scotland, and in 1927 returned to the United States to become a junior member of St. Alselm's Priory, Washington, D.C. He was ordained priest in 1930. In 1932 and 1937, he received Guggenheim fellowships; and, in 1950, he was appointed a member of the Liturgical Institute in the Collegio S. Anselmo in Rome. In 1955, he returned to Washington to serve as novice-master at St. Anselm's Priory, which became St. Anselm's Abbey in 1961. From that date until 1967, Father Strittmatter was Prior of the Abbey. From January to June, 1963, he was a member of the Institute for Advanced Study at Princeton, New Jersey; and since that time he has continued his research related to the history of Christian worship and other religious and scholarly activities.

to think. My country is dear to me, of course. My ancestors in these parts began with Emma White of the Lost Colony in Virginia, the time of the Armada—1580—and after the turn of the century began to come early and stay later, so that I am really more American than Irving Berlin.[4] But what we are all at these days I don't know. At any rate the divine scenes we saw during those six months remain in our minds. I think of that loveliest of travel poems:—Catullus: *Iam uer egelidos refert tepores* [5]—and the line in it *ad claras Asiae volemus urbes*—and ask myself where now are these famous cities and where am I? Where is Stark Young? Where is his loved friend, Father Anselmo? Where the bells over the great Rome at twilight, the fading sounds of the busy day, the gradual coming of night? Alas, alas!

Bowman and I often speak of you. We do hope that God or the Pope—or both, in case they are in agreement this summer—for you know the great John Knox's remark when they quoted the Bible as against his desire for war—"these are very singular notions of Almighty God"—will bring you to see us in the country, for as long as you can stay. We have a guesthouse, which for practical purposes is better than the *Cuisine des Anges.*[6]

I so often think of things I wanted to ask you or want to ask you: the Assumption of the Virgin for instance.[7] I understand well enough the demand from many persons that this ancient legend be fulfilled, or rather confirmed. The paintings on the subject did not decrease the convictions of this event. But the questions arising are obvious enough. Do we mean shooting up through the neighboring atmosphere? To where? for one's contadino friends—or Irish—that might be—Or is this a *glorification* of a human being, a deification in light? A rise through the conscious mind into the splendor of some super-knowing? You could hardly go into this, but I am thus letting you know of the great regions into which my thoughts of you may wander.

4. Irving Berlin (b. 1888), perhaps the most popular American song writer and composer of the twentieth century.

5. The first line of Carmen 46.

6. Young had in mind the painting by Bartolome Esteban Murillo (1607–82). In a letter to his sister, April 24, 1953, Young wrote: "I like the idea of Murillo's big picture *La Cuisine des Anges.* It [is] a convent kitchen—something went wrong and the angels have come down to do the cooking. It's in the Louvre."

7. Apparently Young recalled the paintings he had seen on the subject and the definition by Pope Pius XII on the feast of All Saints, November 1, 1950, of the dogma of the Assumption of the Virgin Mother of Christ. See below, Letter 831.

Dear Father Anselm, you were a great blessing to us in Rome, showing us things we might not otherwise have seen—not to speak of seeing them in your company.[8] You are very kind and lovely and gentle in spirit—all human qualities these are and all to be kept—as in St. Luke—ἐν τῇ καρδίᾳ αὐτῆς[9]—in one's heart. Such things as you know, easily and by study and best of all by living them, are what, as, again, you know I am sure, lie at the bottom of my thoughts, despite my seeming irreverence and dispersion.

I have just had sent you a copy of my last book—*The Pavilion*. It had some very fine reviews. At any rate it took me two years to get it to suit—the style above all—I sought a perfect casting, as if it were inevitable, of the thought; the tone, the emphases must all be right. I hope you feel something about it that you care about.

Bowman asks to be most cordially remembered.

Affectionately
Stark Young

813 | To Julia Young Robertson, Austin, Texas

[320 East 57th Street]
[New York]
Wednesday [April 29, 1953]

Dearest Sister,

You will have to excuse worse typing than usual even, I am astonished how seven months away from this dear machine have messed up my inadequacy. But later on I want to quote some from the new version of the Bible that I borrowed from Elsie.[1] Somebody gave it to her for Christmas and I gather that like most Christians she will

8. Through Gertrude Newell, who had met Father Strittmatter earlier, Young and Bowman learned that he was in Rome. Father Strittmatter recalls that he took them to see the thirteenth-century cloister attached to the nunnery by SS Quattro Coronati, S. Giovanni al Pozzo by the Latin Gate, and perhaps to the treasury of St. Peter's.
9. From Luke 2:19.
1. Elsie Baskin Adams (Mrs. Huntington Adams).

wait a few Christmases before opening it. Going to hear every Sunday a weakminded sermon and not reading the source of it, supposedly, is still a mystery to me. I am returning the check or the remains of it because the extra baggage was largely my fault.[2] I used the third suitcase and put in things I could have carried by hand. I had it weighed here, the man there charged five pounds more than the weight here—$2.50. I did not take the matter further there, though I realized it was all heavier than coming down because that type of small-mouthed, extra-self-respecting virile bore makes me tired to look at him. So I just left the question on the table, that the baggage was not that heavy.

Thank you for the recipe. We had a turkey last night because for one thing you can be sure it is good meat and for another that it is cheaper than other meats all told. Warren roasts it very well indeed. We had a guest, the man in Rome—about 35—whom we met at a party at the Baron Manheim's, in the Orsini Palace, he had four floors from one wing of it, has arrived in New York, called up at once and we asked him to dinner. A very clever man. Lawton Campbell came too. We plan to have the turkey to take to the country tomorrow. We will stay at Elsie's, but this will give us food for lunch the three days, and for Lou Saturday. He does not know it yet but he will be given the neck and lower wings to enjoy. We will try the Mornay recipe tonight chez nous and see how Warren gets it. Mornay is a well known sauce it seems. But the combination might be excellent and we want to try it before Diane[3] comes Monday night for dinner.

Coming from the dentist's, tell Ben, I passed a restaurant where there was a sign steak, with potato and lettuce-tomato salad, $2.50. From the look of the place I shouldn't say the steak was apt to be a masterpiece. At the Newport, Wales says, a steak is 4.50 to 6. I think with fondness of those steaks at the Irving, and I don't think I thanked Ben half enough for them. By the way I don't think I really got expressed what a good job I thought that was in the Manhattan club. Very clever and very effective and also workable. I looked bored but that was because I thought we should be at home and let you get to bed. It did make me sad, however, to think that Austin would fall for that same common business that we get here in New York, the dim

2. A reference to the airline's charge for overweight baggage.
3. Diane Tate.

lights and the nigger singers etc. But that is all over the country. But if we are going to have that place at all it is lucky that it is so cleverly done.

I have a wire this morning, somebody in Oregon has made a little opera out of The Twilight Saint and they want to broadcast it.[4] That's that.

Please don't think any more about my saying you are bull-headed. That word seems to have stuck. Of course you are bull-headed and so am I, and is nearly everybody else. So what? I must say to see you scalding a glass because you have picked it off the shelf makes me want to murder you, but in time I was getting used to the idea. Penicillin might conceivably be good for tuberculosis but I doubt if it would help this hot water mania, so there is no use talking about it. I am sure if I dropped dead there the first thing you would do would be to pour a kettle of boiling water on me. That might make some sense, since I don't propose to die till I am good and ready and rotten. (Aren't old men funny when they try to be witty!)

I'll wait till the next letter to quote those Bible changes.

I just talked with Margaret[5] on the telephone, she is not certain when she will leave, wants to stay and yet is homesick, etc. That's human of course. She says she has been to a doctor recommended by Dr. Goddard, and thinks he has helped her, a matter of diet was the way she seemed to take it. I passed her hotel coming from the dentist's, it looked very nice indeed. Narrow and high, a handsome building. That auto bump in Rome that I told you about finally came to a conclusion, as I expected it to. That whole front of teeth, bridge and all, just fell out. Dr. Oeder is now making another plate, will take out two stumps of tooth and will doubtless charge a good sum. Wales sends his love.

Love to you both
Stark

Seven months and no typing certainly shows as I whack at this machine.

---

4. On March 24, 1953, Sister Mary Teresine had requested permission to perform *The Twilight Saint* at Marylhurst College, Marylhurst, Oregon. Miss Lou Stears had written a libretto for the work.

5. Probably Margaret Robertson.

814 | To Maurice Sterne, Mount Kisco, New York

320 East 57th Street
New York
Monday, May 11 [1953]

Dearest Maurice,

I got back from Europe a few weeks ago and went down to Texas to see my sister. In a pile of magazines, catalogues et cetera on my table I found just now a brown envelope with your article on Cezanne.[6] I don't know when it came—whether a long time ago or rather lately. The only indication is that this is from the winter issue of *The American Scholar*. At any rate I am delighted to have it and have read it very closely, and parts of it several times over, and have profited very profoundly, as well as derived a great amount of pleasure.

My pleasure and comprehension of the things you say are both heightened by my recollections of that walk around and around with you and Vera at the Cezanne Show.[7] That was a genuine blessing for me, to be with you at such a time.

It is good to find that your writing itself moves with complete ease, there is no dry effect either, nor is there the effect of silly exaggeration and the reckless use of words, terms, clichés, half-baked ideas and theories and so on, such as is to be found in so much writing about art, most of it a waste of time. The over-all sense that what you say comes from a profound artist is the deepest satisfaction that lies in your article—one reads with profound intensity and determined alertness. I don't know when your book will be finished, but I am glad you went ahead and published this. Thank you indeed for sending it to me.

Wales and I had a very wonderful six months in Europe—great kindness everywhere, and since we knew most of the places already we could see more of various people—all of whom rose manfully to the occasion.

6. Maurice Sterne, "Cezanne Today," *American Scholar*, XXII (Winter, 1952–53), 40–59.
7. Sterne began his article with a reference to the great Cezanne show at the Metropolitan Museum of Art, April 4 through May 18, 1952. The exhibition of more than a hundred and thirty Cezanne paintings representative of his entire career was assembled from collections in the United States, Europe, North and South America, and South Africa.

Margaret,[8] I hear, is in Europe. I have no news of you and Vera,[9] or of anybody else almost—to get settled back into life here seems a slow process.

We have been week-ends working in the country, and will be settling out there soon. I could gladly be in Morocco again instead. Wales sends his love to you both. I'd like to know how your book comes on. Bless you and Vera.

Affectionately
Stark

You see I wrote the wrong address. By the way I suppose by now you are tired of people telling you that it was not Alexander who cut the Gordian knot, was it?

Just the same there are many brilliant things you manage to say—to my eternal benefit.

S.

815 | To the Reverend Anselm Strittmatter, O.S.B., Rome

"Andrea Doria"
[Jennymead]
[Waccabuc, New York]
May 12, 1953

Dear Father Anselmo,

This paper may astonish you, but it is part of an envelope sent most courteously to all our cabins on the Doria, and its air mail properties may enable me to overwhelm you with more words and without ruining myself with postage.

I am glad you read *The Pavilion* with pleasure, and am indeed grateful for the word *pietas*—I know the meaning you give to it, or rather understand in it—It is a quality that by inherited tradition and

8. Margaret Seligman Lewisohn (Mrs. Sam A. Lewisohn).
9. Vera Segal Sterne (Mrs. Maurice Sterne).

by whatever culture I may possess, I want my book to have. The *style* of *The Pavilion* took me about fifteen months of work to achieve. I threw away a good deal more than I finally included in the volume. The last paragraph about the crazy old man (p. 99) took many writings before the arrangement of the phrases seemed to suit me, or the rhythm in the words and in the ideas. The final paragraph in the book (p. 194) was written, rewritten, recast, considered when read aloud, etc.[1] For example it was a long time before I came to the idea in line 6, which is an essay in itself "but what I did know *I shall never know so well again.*"

That business about the first-born can be found in Exodus xxii,28. also Exodus xiii,1, also Ezekiel xx,25.[2] The "redeemed" change is Exodus xxxiv,20, also Genesis xxii. These are doubtless old primitive matter taken over from some old Torah. The point, dear Father Anselm, does not so much concern the Bible—which manages to be about everything, savage, civilized, or transcendent—my point is only to marvel that such gentle saints as the Hensons could read and read again such fierce matter and never seem disturbed by it.[3] To change the angle—to my mind the general Protestant attitude toward the Bible—I mean those who have taken it intensely, has been full of various disasters. (You can see why Aristophanes and the solid classic Greek world thought Socrates a menace.)

I am sure you are pulling my leg about Tertullian.[4] He is a kind of foil to Origen,[5] who brought Christianity and Greek culture into a luminous relationship. I fancy roasting—in case he was burnt—did not even improve the flavor of him. At least he stuck by his guns however.

We have been several week-ends in the country—bad weather—try-

---

1. See above, Letter 750 and n. 9.

2. Young probably meant, respectively, Exodus 22:29–30, 13:2, and Ezekiel 20:26.

3. In *The Pavilion,* chapter 17, Young recalls his experiences during the summer of 1906 in Canton, North Carolina. At a nearby settlement he met Mr. and Mrs. Henson, who seemed to know the Bible but to ignore all of its harsh aspects, particularly passages of the kind represented by Young's references in this paragraph.

4. Father Strittmatter writes: "In a previous letter to Stark Young I had probably said that Tertullian died in heresy, and Stark Young decided that this meant that he died at the stake. Tertullian died at an advanced age something after 220, and we have no evidence which might indicate that his death was a violent one." Young referred to the same subject in *The Pavilion,* p. 165; see also, below, Letter 821 and notes.

5. Origen (*ca.* 185–254), Greek writer and teacher, one of the three or four greatest names in the history of Christian literature, lived first in Alexandria and later in Caesarea.

ing to get the pruning done and various tasks, if we are to have anything right this summer. Wales and I are both very happy at the idea
that you are coming over and that we may see you. We'd like to drive
you out to this little place of ours and to remember afterward your
having been there.

Affectionately yours,

Stark Young

(You don't have to promote my full name—the first one ought to
serve.)

816 | To Ella Somerville, Oxford, Mississippi

320 East 57th Street
New York
May 13, 1953

Dearest Ella,

I have your sweet letter and shall be glad to write **Little Spencer**
something that might warm her spirit at least a little. She is a remarkable person and I am very glad for her that she has you for a friend;
you know how to be a friend—something that takes brains, heart and
profound good breeding, if it is going to be satisfying.

I should say by Spencer's eyes that she might get herself into some
intense situation such as you describe. I hope her writing will divert
her mind, but these things often make a vicious circle.

I suppose you are getting up steam for your trip abroad. You will
have plenty of company. I wish you were—perhaps you are—going on
the Andrea Doria—straight to Italy. If so, please introduce yourself to
Marchesa Antinovi—a great Florentine family—she is the *hostess* on
the boat, and makes it all another matter from most boats. If you are
going thus, let me know and I'll give you a note to her—proudly.

Julia has not been very well, so that my visit was always anxious, but
she is much better now and if she keeps up her regimen ought to

manage well enough. Please give my love to all the family—it would be good to drop into Oxford.

The enclosed [6] seems to fit other references I have seen to Bill Faulkner's television—these highly popular arts and crafts have their own strict demands. I didn't see this piece of his—alas, I don't see any television.

Love to you, dear Ella
Stark

817 | To Elizabeth Spencer, Oxford, Mississippi

320 East 57th Street
New York
Wednesday [May 13, 1953]

Dear Little Spencer,

This is a great world. I meant to write you yesterday and had the envelope addressed, when I was interrupted. And this morning comes your letter with the highly welcome news of the Guggenheim. I was going to write that I hope the spring warmths—*iam uer egelidos refert tepores* [7]—had not slowed down too greatly your inspiration and impulse to write. There are few young writers that I know of who have anything like your degree of talent. Certainly very few indeed who

---

6. Young enclosed a newspaper clipping of Jack Gould's column, "Television in Review," from the New York *Times,* May 13, 1953, p. 40. While reviewing Robert Montgomery's production of John O'Hara's *Appointment in Samarra,* Gould wrote: "Coming so soon after William Faulkner's abject and disheartening surrender to silly taboos on another drama program, the achievement of Mr. Montgomery . . . is truly a cause for renewed faith in the video medium." In his column on April 12, 1953, Sec. 2, p. 11, Gould had reviewed the Lux Video Theatre performance of Faulkner's "The Brooch." Gould characterized the production as a "synthetic and diluted Faulkner of the worst sort. What originally was a bitter study of a man caught in a fatal mother complex turned up on the screen as a soap opera that dutifully met all the provisions of television's purity code." Gould maintained that "the irony is that even under the television industry's purity code there was no reason for Mr. Faulkner to capitulate so completely to the video mores."

7. See above, Letter 812.

could have written some of your scenes, with their vividness, convincing touch and passion of mind. Since I have told plenty of others this I may as well tell you to your face.

And now this very exciting year opens up to you, what a dream that must be! I hope you go straight to Florence or Rome—get a place to live that is warmed well—and settle down. My advice is to take pension or demi-pension—which means you have breakfast and then either lunch or dinner—the other meal eaten out or in the hotel, as you wish. You don't even have to tell them which meal you'll take. In Rome there is a Pensione Rubens—in the telephone book—near the Piazza de Spagna and the Keats house—a good many writers and artists stay there. I have never been in it. In Florence there are very nice pensions. You can start at the Hotel Berchietti—no meals but breakfast—and from there find a pension to suit you. At any rate to write in Europe one must settle down. The Hotel Residenza in Rome is very attractive, not fussy. I hope you work some on Italian—even a mild amount of it makes many things so much easier. I have no tips— just take your money in American Express checks, and change it as you need it. I can well believe this will be a marvellous year for you. Italy with all the marvellous mind and tradition behind it and the boundless expression of our human experience that is to be found in the life and the art around one has a way of smoothing many things out for us, and what seemed urgent and most pressing and intense may find itself seeming less so indeed. We can think more readily of Wordsworth's line that the gods approve the depth and not the tumult of the soul.[8] Tumult may sound interesting, but is apt to be largely a waste. But every heart hath its own sorrows—that's one of the loveliest lines in the Bible.

Just the same, nobody knows better than I do what a blind alley life can be. Well, you have your great talent and your already step forward—indeed yes—so I can believe you and Italy will bless each other.

Thank you for your sweet letter. I have been able to do very little for you—the best thing I have done is to recognize your quality and to foresee something of what you can give to life.

Well, as Hamlet says, something too much of this—so I had better

---

8. Wordsworth's "Laodamia," stanza 13, lines 74–75.

stop. That is fine, very fine, about the Guggenheim and what it can promise Little Spencer, bless her trembling heart!

Affectionately yours,
Stark Young

I won't read this over, lest I tear it up.

S. Y.

818 | To Harrison Smith,⁹ Saturday Review, New York

320 East 57th Street
New York
Thursday [June 4, 1953]

Dear Mr. Harrison Smith,

I enjoyed very much seeing you again after so long a time, and I must say that so far as I am able to judge, all your comments on Bill Faulkner were sympathetic and also sensible, including your remark about his going home before long, "where he ought to be."

I will send the article soon. Not any attack on Bill, of course, but mostly about Sherwood, with some comment on their relationship and its unfortunate end—from Sherwood's side of it; the reaction that he expressed to me—not in detail—more than once. It seems to me that readers interested are entitled to know this.¹ And I think that some of the personal things about Sherwood would be diverting to various admirers of his.

With best wishes, I am

Yours sincerely
Stark Young

9. (Oliver) Harrison Smith (1888–1971), editor, publisher, and magazine executive, known primarily for his long association with the *Saturday Review*. After assuming direction of the magazine in 1938, Smith is said to have increased its circulation from 30,000 to 650,000 at his retirement in 1966. Earlier, as a partner in the publishing firm of Jonathan Cape and Harrison Smith, he published several of William Faulkner's novels, including *The Sound and the Fury,* and formed a lasting friendship with the Mississippi novelist.

1. Young's conversation with Smith about Faulkner and the subsequent article Young wrote about the relationship between Sherwood Anderson and Faulkner may have been prompted by Faulkner's article "Sherwood Anderson: An Appreciation," *Atlantic Monthly,* CXCI (June, 1953), 27–29.

819 | To Harrison Smith, Saturday Review, New York

320 East 57th Street
New York
June 15, 1953

Dear Mr. Harrison Smith,

I finished my article on the Sherwood Anderson-Faulkner subject about a week—it came easily in the writing—ago and have taken the time to let it rest and restudy it.[2] It seems quite good and I seem to have said what was in my mind, though mildly at times. But thinking it over I have decided, not without some self-denial on my part, that it would serve not the best ends to publish it, not now at least. I feel sure of this, and so I just put into my files these pages of mine.[3]

I hope I have in no way inconvenienced you, and I appreciated your offering me the chance to write it.

The trip to Texas was rewarding, I trust. Letters from my sister in Austin speak of a terrific heat there.

With regards, I beg to remain

Yours sincerely
Stark Young

820 | To Juliette Huxley, London, England

Jennymead
Waccabuc, New York
June 15, 1953

Dearest Juliette,

I must thank you for your lovely letter, with your kind words about the Bentley book[4] and your taking me into the very presence of the

2. See the preceding letter.
3. Unfortunately, Young's article cannot be found.
4. Eric Bentley, *In Search of Theater.*

coronation. Bentley is an Englishman who has been in many theatres by now and in many countries; he is now on the New Republic—which has lately been revamped, with very different policies. It is more the way it was in Croly's day, long ago now. Your judgement of him seems to me pretty just. Brecht is something of an idol of his, far more than your Frenchman. I have forgotten what German I ever knew, and have seen more of everybody, I suppose, than I have of Brecht. I saw one play, in English, here in New York, but the leading role—an excellent German actor was lost to me because of this actor's very unintelligible English.[5] Eric Bentley is not afraid to rush in anywhere, and is not at all overawed by Broadway or a mere success per se.

I saw the coronation on a vague television and much better on General Motors, but all too small. I expect to see it in the technicolor film soon—they speak of it very glowingly. The young queen kept herself in hand to a remarkable extent—if we know what that means in pageantry or in a ballet even. Some of the words were marvellous— what a language the English language at its best can be! I should have liked especially to have seen the emotional response of the British crowd, that mass emotion—not just loud excitement—that they can have.

I have heard a good deal about Elizabeth and Philip from Oliver Messel, who made his lovely house—two thrown into one—[available to us] when Bowman and I were in London. Oliver's Scarf[6] [?] was a great event, I have read. It was two-thirds done when I was there. Another London friend of mine John Gielgud, whom I saw but twice in New York—once when he invited me to lunch with him and again when he invited himself to lunch with me and came from Philadelphia and stayed for a good long visit. Then I was at his house in London for lunch. That's all, but he sent me books when I was there, books to

5. Young had seen Bertolt Brecht's *Galileo* (see above, Letter 678) and *The Private Life of the Master Race* translated by Eric Bentley. In his review of *Galileo*, Young complained that almost all the speech was unintelligible. Wrote Young: "Albert Basserman . . . is an actor with a fine technique . . . but what difference can that make in this latest effort, when he himself speaks none too distinctly and the lines he replies to are unintelligibly yapped by Frau Basserman?" "Nazi Privacies," *New Republic,* CXII (June 25, 1945), 871; see also above, Letter 731, and n. 9.

6. The first two words of this sentence cannot be read with any certainty. In some manner, Young seems to be referring to the decor executed by Oliver Messel for the ballet, *Homage to the Queen,* produced by the Sadler's Wells Ballet, at the Royal Opera House, Covent Garden, London, June 2, 1953, in honor of the coronation of H. M. Queen Elizabeth II.

Rome, to New York et cetera, and quite remarkable letters, and just before Christmas a book entirely about him in divers roles,[7] with extraordinary make-ups—as varied and expert as the Russians—and so on—a friend with the English gift for friendship—well, the point of all that is to say it was splendid to see that he was knighted—he should have been long before most of them who are knighted had that honor given them.

Another pleasing item was that Richards, the jockey who was knighted,[8] is the nephew of old Bill, one of our elevator men here for years—and very proud he is.

I think that psychologically shall we say, it was a fine piece of wisdom for the Government to have the coronation so grand and elaborate. After the years of discipline, uncertainty and all, such a gesture was splendid for them and for outside peoples to see. There are many people here who think Churchill's, Atlee's and various others' attitude of the U.S., Korea, Asia et cetera is well taken. Such are the affairs of the wide world just now.

Julian is inexhaustible in his possibilities. Imagine Australia for three months! As soon as the voyage is straightened out, its method and the rest he will be among the first to look into Mars. I hope you can go to Australia with him. The thought of seeing you both last Christmas still warms my heart.

Affectionately
Stark

821 | To the Reverend Anselm Strittmatter, O.S.B., Rome

320 East 57th Street
New York
June 15, 1953

Dear Father Anselm,

Your letter was very welcome, especially with the good news that Tertullian is in hell.[9] I got my note about his unholy glee from a cita-

---

7. Hallam Fordham, *John Gielgud: An Actor's Biography in Pictures* (1952).

8. Gordon Richards (b. 1904), jockey, knighted in 1953, began his career as a stable apprentice, became a jockey, and broke the world record for the number of winning horses ridden. In 1953, he rode the winning horse in the Derby.

9. See above, Letter 815, n. 4.

tion from Justin or somebody De Spect XXX.[1] I don't know a spoonful about the early writers. There is another quotation from Tertullian— in Justin: *Apol.* 1.16[2] where he says that Socrates' guardian Demon "doubtless distorted his mind from the Good"![3] I got these from a learned book *Jew and Greek Tutors Unto Christ,* by MacGregor of Glasgow and the Hartford Theological Seminary and A. C. Purdy of the Hartford T. Seminary.

As to the Catullus, thank you. I had it wrong. But it does give me a chance to tell you what you doubtless already know, that [my] knowledge of the classics is about nil. The only way I can really get anything satisfactory out of a Greek or Latin passage is to *memorize* it and then the meaning I get, not spoiled with translation, which the older I am the more I see is never really possible. For the simplest of examples take

Paene insularum, Sirmio, insularumque[4]

no possible translation in English can get all that it contains as it stands.

But as for my scholarship—what a small scandal! Writing myself and teaching English Literature don't give a full chance to real scholarship unless one gets it early, and when I was in an early stage I was taught practically nothing—village rumors in the Deep South! That was about all it was.

I envy you seeing Fiesole and San Miniato—they seem far away indeed.

1. Father Strittmatter comments: "Certainly not from a passage in Justin Martyr. . . . The final chapter of Tertullian's *De Spectaculis* (*On the Public Shows*) depicts with delight the torments of the damned. It is a perfect illustration of the overzealous mentality which eventually led this brilliant theologian into heresy and finally into founding a sect of his own, the Tertullianists, whom St. Augustine later brought back into Catholic unity."

2. Father Strittmatter's note: "There is serious confusion here. Since Justin suffered martyrdom about 165 A.D. and Tertullian wrote his famous *Apology* in the year 197 A.D., there can be no question of Justin's quoting Tertullian. . . . As for the reference to Justin, *Apol.* 1.16, this may be based on a misprint or misreading of 1.46. Here indeed, i.e., *Apol.* 1.46, Justin in a striking passage says that all who (before Christ) led 'rational' lives (literally, lived with 'logos'), even though they were considered atheists, are Christians, as among the Greeks, for example, Socrates and Heraclitus; among the barbarians, Abraham, Ananias, Azarias, Misael, and Elias, and many others. . . ."

3. Tertullian's derogatory remark about Socrates' *daimonion* appears in his *Apologeticus,* XXII. As Young implies in the following sentence, he is quoting the translation in *Jew and Greek: Tutors unto Christ: The Jewish and Hellenistic Background of the New Testament,* by G. H. C. MacGregor and A. C. Purdy (1936), p. 197.

4. The opening line of Catullus' Carmen 31.

I'm sorry we must delay the pleasure of seeing you till the Autumn. June 25 we shall be living in the country. In fact we are there now, with only a day or two now and then in town. The apartment is not really running. We motor in and out. It's in the country we were and are hoping to see you anyhow—town will be very stale—even in season New York has sadly declined.

I hope you find your family well and what plans Washington provides both stimulating and agreeable.

Wales would send messages if he were here at the moment.

Yours sincerely
Stark Young

I should copy over this untidy letter but today I am not in any perfection of anything. Make kind allowances, please.

S. Y.

822 | To Juliette Huxley, London, England

Jennymead
Waccabuc, New York
Friday, September 4 [1953]

Dearest Juliette,

Julian came to lunch at the Gladstone with me Wednesday. I was delighted to see how fit he seemed. Young looking, fresh looking and with that astonishing brain of his clicking away like blazes. He is all lit up about his travels—even New Zealand!—and happy that you will join him in Java, when November comes. He is very proud of you of course; I daresay he likes skies, flowers, jewels and what not also.

On the telephone the hostess he is visiting sounds like a very charming person. What a talent Julian has, a genius for friends: it is partly his gentle, rich heart, and partly his vastly responsive mind and range of interests. I have at least sense enough to get out of the rain, as they say—though we have had such a drought lately that even an idiot enjoys comparative safety, as the song says of the hedgehog among the

Harvard pederasts. But I could never imagine myself living through the innumerable contacts and varieties of human nature that Julian takes in his gracious stride. You, dear Juliette, have been a miracle of light and strength for him.

It was odd—when your letter came I had just acquired a box in which to pack some little napkins—tea or cocktails that I got for you in Mexico, when I journeyed to Texas after my return here. They are of no value but are made on small looms out in the country places and are of a delicious pink that I never saw from anywhere but Mexico. Some of their dyes are old vegetable recipes that I never saw explained, their varnishes are often so too. At any rate you can do something with these nothings.

I was also clipping out a piece about food experiments with algae—for Julian—I gave that to him at lunch.

I was seeing the recent acquisition at the Metropolitan lately—twice. Another copy of the Praxiteles—as is the Venus de Medici. On the whole more beautiful—the brow, the upper chest, the right leg, the suspension in the torso—weight. And less restored (not restored at all) if less complete. The hands, tip of the nose etc., 17th century, on the Venus de Medici, are a great mess. I looked at her well on this last trip, studying really my own mind in sculpture and my memory. It's not my favorite quality in sculpture or style, but is something at that.

Since I had never seen even a kodak of your work, it was new to me—and I must say I was delighted with it—it had real *volume* and a beautiful elimination and completeness. I must say sculpture except in gardens or monuments is for me all too often a bore. And yet at its best how marvellous and exciting and final.

My dear Oliver Messel did, I am told the most marvellous things here and there and everywhere for the coronation. I'd think they'd have given him a knighthood. At any rate Philip and Elizabeth had him called first thing next morning to come and go over it all with them and explain etc. Very charming and lovable—imagine that right on top of the coronation day! Oliver has a painting from the *Midsummer Night's Dream* that Philip wanted to buy some time ago for a birthday present to Elizabeth, but Oliver kept it. A very lovely picture over the mantle of his drawing room. He has two houses turned into one (rich parents) and [in] a very sweet way made that our home while we were in London—we declined to stay there, he was too busy and by no means well—arthritis, and a shame that is. I thought you'd like to hear that lovely gesture of Elizabeth and Philip's.

I have been reading carefully Stendhal,[5] with admiring astonishment. No wonder Gide[6] studied him—he is far better than Gide's autobiographical work—intellectually not in the same class I should say.

I must close. Bowman asks to be remembered. He has three jobs going and since he insists on doing all the designing itself he is quite busy. Two more in the offing.

I know you miss Julian—but Java is not far away.

Affectionately
Stark

823 | To Ella Somerville, Oxford, Mississippi

Jennymead
Waccabuc, New York
Monday [September 14, 1953]

Dearest Ella,

It was fine to hear from you, but I was indeed sorry to learn that you were not coming by New York. It would have been a great pleasure to see you. I hope what you say is true and that you will be coming up here before long.

Lawton and Booth went down to the funeral of Miss Margaret.[7] Great honors were done her, police parades and what not. The whole thing moved them deeply, they would like to think most of it personal mourning for Miss Margaret, but it was not quite so simple as that.

5. Young had been reading Stendhal's *Le rouge et le noir*.
6. André Gide (1869–1951).
7. Margaret Booth (1880–1953), Lawton Campbell's aunt, was born and reared in Montgomery, Alabama. After graduating from Agnes Scott Institute and Mount Holyoke College, she became principal of the high school at Demopolis, Alabama. In 1914, she established the Margaret Booth School for Girls in Montgomery, which she operated until her death. From 1909, she conducted guided tours of Europe for young women. She died in London, August 14, 1953, while traveling abroad with a party of girls.

You speak of Bill Faulkner—he was up here quite a long time, he may be still. He never looks me up and I can't say I blame him. All I have heard about his visit is what his host, Harrison Smith, editor of the *Saturday Review* told me—he said he wished Bill "would go on home where he belonged." [8] That and what Saxe Commins [9]—deputed by the publishers to look after Bill. He said Bill nearly drove him crazy—never read a book or a paper—drank and just sat. None of that matters, however, if he is writing some that is really good. His talent can't be disputed. Its results depend for their lustre on the individual reader.

I sent the Stones a copy of the new college edition of *So Red the Rose*. They *were most kind to* me when I broke my arm etc. and I can never seem to do anything nice for them.

I do hope we see you up here, dear Ella—Love to all the family.

> Lovingly
> Stark

824 | To Robert Penn Warren, Fairfield, Connecticut

> Jennymead
> Waccabuc, New York
> October 5, 1953

Dear Red,

I thought I'd be writing you a blazing letter, so profound, so notable; but the truth is that reading your book,[1] marking the devil out of it— the wonderful spots—and then rereading today a lot of it, has taken rather the wind out of my sails. I feel quite modest really and by no means competitive as to brains.

The whole scheme of the book seems to me quite dazzling—all those

8. See above, Letters 818, 819, and notes.
9. Saxe Commins (1892–1958), editor at Random House, and friend of such authors as Eugene O'Neill, Irwin Shaw, Budd Schulberg, William Faulkner, and Adlai Stevenson.
1. Robert Penn Warren, *Brother to Dragons: A Tale in Verse* (1953).

voices—and the author himself speaking—and often so very beautiful—see the second stanza on page 161—or the first on page 163!—for example. There are plenty of other places. Really, dear Red, some of the web of motifs—analyses, are very impressive. Some of Jefferson's speeches—as at the bottom of page 134 and following—they have a cadence and tragic reflection that I can't get over, truly. Aunt Cat and the mother are extraordinary—the tenderness and acumen in such places is remarkable. The movement in many of the lines is fresh and compelling—even in certain simple places:

"The snow lies thin and pure, and I stand

Amid the brown leaves and snow. I lift up my eyes"

If I say those lines—which are indeed simple compared to most of the book, I hear something in the mere form of them that arrests me. "that heartbreaking new delicacy of green—" for another example. I could keep this up, going into the subtle places and the highly cerebral effects. But I don't seem to be getting very far—so I had better stop. It is absurd to talk in a letter about a book of such a lyric and intellectual passion and such complex and ranging motifs and asides, as it were.

(I wondered how you'd get by with the killing scene—you hit it off excellently—bravo.)

Well, I'll memorize some of the lines from the book, and let it go at that. What is most impressive about it is the poetic mingling of highly subtle motivations—terrible readings of the soul now and then—Et cetera. Basta, Stark.

The one thing lacking in the whole book is a certain firm outline by which all of it could be held in mind. I have thought a good deal about this and can see clearly that this is impossible given the treatment you follow. Such subtlety and such a weaving of voices, from the dead and from the living RPW precludes the other possibility. If one made a study of this book the number of nuances, motifs, analyses and highly imaginative reactions would be astonishing. We can't have everything. At any rate this is one of the most profoundly original books I ever read.

This postscript seems likely to go on forever and me with it. And it looks a dreary mess. I am reminded of the story of a GI that a girl tried to pick up in Piccadilly. He declined, saying you girls are never clean. She said she was clean, to come with her and see. When they opened her door they saw a dead horse in the middle of the floor. You see! he said, what did I tell you. She said—No, I said I was clean, I didn't say I was tidy.

Maybe that seems a poor story, but with the cockney accent it seems to me funny.

Thank you again for the book.

Yours
Stark

I hope the daughter[2] is thriving and you are happy at the thought of her. And that Miss Eleanor[3] is writing for us.

Thank you again, dear Red, and pardon so poor a reply to such a book.

Yours
Stark

P.S. That first paragraph on page 90 is very lovely and perfect. How many times that sort of thing exactly has been tried, how very rarely it has come off!

825 | To Hudson Strode, University of Alabama, Tuscaloosa, Alabama

320 East 57th Street
New York
October 5, 1953

Dear Hudson,

I found myself out of paper—so far as this place goes—and all I have—plenty of it—in the country—such is life. But this morning I got here before they had forwarded your lovely letter to the country which is what they usually do, and I want to write you almost by return mail. Such a sweet letter and so characteristic. It carries me back over the

2. Rosanna Phelps Warren, whose birth Warren had announced to Young in a letter written August 25, 1953.
3. Eleanor Clark Warren (Mrs. Robert Penn Warren, b. 1913) had published *Rome and a Villa* in 1952, the year in which she married Warren. Earlier, she had written *The Bitter Box* (1946).

years when you have unfailingly bucked me up and helped me to believe—in the face of a good deal of very different trends in novels—
that it is worthwhile to do it my way. At any rate it's the only way I
can do it. It is interesting that so quiet a book as *So Red the Rose* has
the record it has. It went through four printings the first week of its
publication, stayed at the top of the best-seller list for six months or
more, and then was in the list for many months, and unlike novels in
general it has never gone out of print. It still sells quietly. I hope this
college edition [4] will have some chance—who knows?

The years fly past. I was nearly six months in Europe—every one
most kind with their cars and their dinner tables—I should almost be
afraid to try it again—one could hardly expect all this to happen again.
Can you imagine a Monsignore at the Vatican when I was introduced
to him, saying "Stark Young, why I had breakfast with you in 1912,"
and their taking Bowman and me to various convents, old churches et
cetera that we might have missed. I won't drop any titled name, I'll
just say people were heavenly to us, in Rome, Paris, Lisbon, Bas
Pyrenées, London, and so on. In Morocco we didn't know any one
who was there at the time, so I made friends with Coco, a monkey,
about the size of a cocker spaniel. His mother, about 14, carried him
over town gathering in pennies. So at lunch on the terrace every day
Coco came and sat on my knee, looked in my ear for fleas, threw his
arms around my neck and had an order of fruit salad. I really have
missed him.

I am delighted that the Jefferson Davis ventures turned out so well.
Is the book scheduled for any particular date? [5] My old friend Miss
Elizabeth Cutting, editor of the North American tried a life of him,
but as I remember it she never got said even what she wanted to get
said. She was a lady born—as Vermont goes—but was afraid of this,
that and the other—which ends in the bourgeois, doesn't it?

I had a lovely note from that beloved Therese—it would be very nice
to see you both again.

I myself have no plans beyond some *journals*—not in the tone of
The Pavilion of course, which has a high tone something like Yeats.

4. Young refers to Scribner's Modern Standard Authors edition of *So Red the Rose*
with an Introduction by Donald Davidson.
5. The first volume of Strode's biography, *Jefferson Davis: American Patriot*, was
published in 1955.

But much of what I might put down couldn't be in that style, obviously. If I don't like it when I have done some of it I'll just throw it in the wastebasket. Thank you again, dear Hudson—love to you both

Stark

826 | To Eileen Heckart Yankee,[6] New Canaan, Connecticut

320 East 57th Street
New York
November 23, 1953

Dear Eileen,

I do indeed thank you for a most engaging evening and understand very well that a large part of it was due to your performance. I'm still wondering who in blazes you "supported." (I'd say the audience.) It seems that since then I have been *Picnic* conscious or something, for I have run into a good many people who spoke of, or answered concerning, *Picnic*. In every case it would seem that it is your role that made impression.

I will say again that I was much impressed with a definite line, edge, style—what does one say?—that is in your acting. (It is partly in your feet.) That line, edge, style, is hard to define, for it is both an inner and outer thing.

Well, you have two good press-agents at the above address. We shall hope to see you after the holidays subside.

Please remember me to that very nice man at the box-office.

Love to you, good wishes for your next venture.

Yours sincerely
Stark Young

6. Eileen Heckart Yankee (Mrs. John H. Yankee, b. 1919) began her career as an understudy and supporting actress during World War II. Later she appeared in such plays as *The Traitor, Hilda Crane, In Any Language,* and *Butterflies Are Free.* In William Inge's *Picnic,* she played the role of Rosemary Sidney, and the cast included Kim Stanley, Ruth McDevitt, Peggy Conklin, and Ralph Meeker. Directed by Joshua Logan, with settings by Jo Mielziner, *Picnic* opened at the Music Box on February 19, 1953, and closed on April 10, 1954.

XI

In Place of Memoirs
1954–1962

A DEDICATED letter writer for more than half a century, Stark Young wrote some of his finest letters during the last years of his life. Now liberated from the pressures of weekly deadlines, relaxed by the leisure that he enjoyed after he finished *The Pavilion,* and mellowed somewhat by advancing age and the praise of his friends, Young could pour into his correspondence an abundance of the witticism, observation, and anecdote that characterized the best of his earlier writing. As the informal writing of a man whose knowledge covered just about every aspect of the fine arts but whose primary concern remained the theatre, the letters after 1953 reflect his humanism, but, as might be expected, they lack the clear-cut patterns evident in his earlier correspondence. Nevertheless, during these years, Young's memoirs, his publications, his interest in the Chekhov productions at the Fourth Street Theatre, and his European trips provide focal points and continuity for the reader. Young's remarks about his reading, attendance at plays, lectures, and friends add variety to the letters of this period.

In *The Pavilion,* Stark Young confined the account of his own life to the first twenty-one years because he expected eventually to write a continuation of the autobiography. In a second volume, he originally planned to write about famous persons with whom he had been associated during his career. His tentative list, consisting almost wholly of persons known in the theatre, included such names as Eleonora Duse, Charlie Chaplin, Jacinto Benavente, Luigi Pirandello, Eugene O'Neill, Sherwood Anderson, Doris Keane, and, perhaps, the Lunts. Probably he would have added, depending upon limitations of space, Robert Edmond Jones, Maurice Sterne, Jacob Ben-Ami, and John Gielgud. Throughout 1954 and 1955, Young made notes, wrote drafts of tentative sections, and told friends he was working on a journal. By the spring of 1956, however, Young admitted that he had not made much progress and did not feel "very much inspired." So late as August, 1958, he wrote that he was presently "trying a kind of journal memoirs," but his remarks indicate no advance and little enthusiasm. Since his extant letters contain no further comment, one infers that gradually he lost interest in the project and that the illness which was soon to follow prevented him from bringing the work to anything like completion.

Even if Young had wished to make substantial progress on his memoirs during 1955 and 1956, he would probably have been prevented by several rewarding but confining projects which occupied much of his time. In the spring of 1955, Scribner's decided to reissue *The Flower in Drama* and *Glamour* in a single volume. Young took the opportunity to review and slightly revise both books. About the same time, with the prospect of a publisher for a new edition of his translation of Machiavelli's *Mandragola,* Young felt that he should also reconsider this work. He had scarcely finished revising *Mandragola* when he decided with Bowman to accept a friend's offer to permit them to rent an apartment in Venice for three months in the summer of 1955. Young had no time to write while he was enjoying Venice and taking short trips to Rome, Athens, Corinth, Eleusis, and the islands of Greece. Finally, just before he was to return to New York, he received a tempting offer to translate Chekhov's *Uncle Vanya.* Young accepted and became involved in months of first pleasure and then frustration over the affairs of the Chekhov revivals at the Fourth Street Theatre off Broadway. Before the long Chekhov episode ended, Young took time to translate Pirandello's *Vestire gli ignudi,* though the version has remained unperformed and unpublished.

Stark Young's letters contain an almost continuous account of the four productions of Chekhov's plays presented by David Ross at the small Fourth Street Theatre. The correspondence begins with a reference to *The Three*

Sisters, which, in Young's translation, enjoyed a successful run of more than a hundred performances from February 25 to May 22, 1955. Although many reviewers commented favorably, Young was irritated by an article in which his translation was characterized as a "satire" upon Chekhov. Even though Ross maintained that he lost money on the production, he was so encouraged by the reception accorded *The Three Sisters* that he made plans for an entire Chekhov season. On October 18, shortly before Young returned from his European trip, *The Cherry Orchard,* in his translation, began a successful run at the same theatre. Before leaving Venice, Young had agreed to translate Chekhov's *Uncle Vanya,* and, by late November, he had completed the work. *The Cherry Orchard* closed on January 15, 1956, and, on January 31, Ross presented Young's translation of *Uncle Vanya,* starring Franchot Tone, whom Young had persuaded to play the leading role. It proved to be the most successful of all the Chekhov plays which Ross directed. During the summer, however, Ross decided to save expense by producing *The Sea Gull* in the Garnett translation instead of Young's, because the Garnett translation, by then in the public domain, required no royalty payments. The play opened on October 22 and closed, after twenty-five performances, on November 22, the least successful of the four Chekhov plays which Ross produced. Meanwhile, Young's translations of the Chekhov plays, with his introduction, had been published by Random House in the Modern Library.

In 1957 and 1958, personal and literary affairs kept Stark Young from accomplishing any significant work on his memoirs. In 1957, the illness of his sister in Austin caused him great anxiety, especially during the spring and summer; and in the fall he devoted much of his time to reconsidering *The Theater,* which was being reissued in paperback. Most of what he had to show for his work on the memoirs consisted of the "diary" piece of Eugene O'Neill. Throughout 1958, Young continued to worry about his sister's condition, and he made several trips to Austin to give what help he could. In April and May, he made his last trip to Europe. In the summer and fall, he had no energy for serious writing. In April, 1959, at Wellesley and Harvard, he delivered his last public lectures. A month later, he suffered a severe stroke that prevented any further creative work.

Although Young made a temporary recovery, he failed rapidly at the end of 1959. He was too ill in 1960 to receive in person the distinguished service award from the South Eastern Theatre Conference and unable to respond as he would have wished to a book of tributes presented to him in honor of the occasion. From this time until his death, Young tried at intervals to correspond with his friends, but the words in his handwriting are often illegible and the letters written for him by someone else are stiff and uncharacteristic. The last months of his life, he spent in a nursing home. On December 20, 1962, his sister, Julia McGehee Young Robertson, died in Austin. Two weeks later, on January 6, 1963, Stark Young died in New York. His friend, William McKnight Bowman, who had taken care of him since the first stroke, took the body to Como, Mississippi, for burial in the family plot between the graves of his aunts, Frances and Sarah Starks, and near those of his mother and father. Later, Bowman placed a marble slab above the grave of Stark Young.

827 | To Maurice Sterne, Mount Kisco, New York

Monterrey, Mexico
January 2, 1954

Dearest Maurice,

I was talking with Margaret[1] just before I left New York, nearly three weeks ago, and she told me you had been unwell. I was going to write but had to scuttle off and then have been in Texas and then in Monterrey, most of the time with my sister who had not been in a good condition for some time. Largely hypertension. She is some better now.

This is to wish you and Vera, that dear Vera, happy things in the new year just beginning.

I often think of you, Maurice, and of the fact that you are the only painter I have ever known that I really call great. The landscape of Anticoli is one of the most profound and beautiful I know of anywhere, and there are the drawings and many other paintings—but you must know that. Among authors I have met and known briefly Yeats, Pirandello, Benavente and others, but none of them well, so that I have never known a great author. Among those in music Stravinsky is the only friend I ever had who would be called great, by me at least. In the theatre Duse and Charlie Chaplin. Your range and depth have long been a delight, an emotion and a stimulating sum of technical and cerebral content. Not to speak of our old affection, which I have never doubted for a moment. "Something too much of this" perhaps, as Hamlet would say.

I am flying back home the 4th and must settle down to the book I am trying to write.

Give Vera my love, bless her heart.

Affectionately
Stark

---

1. Margaret Seligman Lewisohn (Mrs. Sam A. Lewisohn).

828 | To Julia Young Robertson, Austin, Texas

[320 East 57th Street]
[New York]
Saturday [January 16, 1954]

Dearest Sister,

I had yesterday your sweet letter and the Adams clippings,[2] which Wales was interested to see. There was also for him a very nice letter about the tie, from Ben. Wales said how nice it was, and for Ben how long. So that's that. You are sweet to think of me as a wonderful brother. I am never what I'd like to be—I so often now wish I could do more to make your days brighter. Nerves are a mess. Ben is so good and generous for you and you think so much of him that that in itself is far more than most people ever have in life. The physical strain gets us all down to a point that does not do us justice, but there's little to be done about it. The constant references in Time Magazine to this man or that as the old man of 72 or 75 ought to get me down—but the only thing I know is to try to stick to the great people in books and history, and when I read at the end of Plato's *Phaedrus* Socrates' prayer —"Beloved Pan, and all ye other gods who here abide, grant me to be beautiful in the inner man, and all I have of outer things to be at peace with these within," I don't feel anything very much at all about age. I feel sorry for our poor countrymen who are harried about what's prosperous or new, and our poor countrywomen whom our salesman-ship methods have driven to gadgets and novelties. But meanwhile I know that such is life, and who am I? You'll be interested and glad to know that one of the young editors at Scribners came up to me yester-day and said *So Red the Rose* is a great book, and *The Pavilion* is a haunting book—I have found that it keeps coming into my mind—it haunts me.

That, however, doesn't help me as to what tone to take for the next memoirs. If they are not good, the MS will go to the fire. And so—

Monday there is the to-do at Columbia—an exhibition of their pro-

2. The Austin *American-Statesman*, January 10, 1954, Pt. D, p. 1, published a full page of photographs of various rooms in Wayman Adams' home in Austin and in the same issue (p. 10) a feature article by Lois Hale Galvin, "Wayman Adamses Live in Museum Treasures."

duced authors [3]—I have a panel of MSS and must go to the opening, by invitation et cetera.

I have written the Adams a note of thanks. Scribners may use his portrait [4] for their press department if he sends a photograph—it won't do him any harm. They have made a wide use of the Abram Poole portrait, now belonging to the U. of Miss.

I fear I don't blame you for the Albanese event [5]—I heard her on the radio or in the opera or something a year or so ago. Quite good, and I didn't care anything about it.

Jane Wasey at the symphony Tuesday night had a close string of large pearl beads around her neck, plus a slim string of beads in a gold nest above, it was very becoming, and made me understand what you meant by regretting your larger pearl beads. On the way from Scribner's this afternoon I'll stop and see what they have. I couldn't get over how well they helped to make Jane look. I wish I could sit down a bit with you and Ben.

Lovingly
Stark

829 | To Ella Somerville, Oxford, Mississippi

[320 East 57th Street]
[New York]
Monday [January 18, 1954]

Dearest Ella,

I find myself out of paper—the weather is about ten above zero, so I sit here in a warm apartment—flooded with sun and use my old MS. scratch paper.

3. The Brander Matthews Dramatic Museum and the department of music of Columbia University sponsored an exhibition, "Columbia and the Theatre," in the Low Library, January 18, 1954.

4. Adams' portrait of Young was soon to be featured at an exhibition of Adams' work in the Art Gallery of the Texas Federation of Women's Clubs, opening February 8, 1954. See also above, Letter 688 and n. 5.

5. Licia Albanese (b. 1913), soprano, best known for her singing of roles in operas by Puccini and Verdi, sang a program of arias from *La Traviata, La Boheme, Carmen,* and *Madame Butterfly* in Austin on January 10, 1954.

The big news is that we have about half of the fruitcake left. Wrapped tight in the tinfoil it is as wet and marvellous as ever. We have had a number of more or less distinguished people to dinner, but I say to Wales Bowman—"No, if they can eat what they buy here, let's let them eat it. Not gobble up this Mississippi marvel." It makes me feel very proud to talk thus, especially just after a good morsel of the cake. I can't thank you enough, you dear Ella.

Life goes on here the same—I struggle trying to get the tone for memoirs, for which I have copious notes. That will be my last book. I'll try after that to read specially and learn something. I do wish I had been educated, however solitary that might make me in this vague and lost world today. And yet I wouldn't say I should want to live my young years over again—it all costs too much. Of course it is really a question of whether one wants to pay what it costs, whatever is involved. There is so much love, pain, longing for fine things, so much realization of what life has cost the people who have glorified or enriched it, or have led it beautifully and lovingly for those about them, that one must think twice as to experiencing it again. History repeats to such a terrifying degree that one must think before encountering life again. I must say that people like you, dear Ella, make life more reassuring, make it seem more responsive and rewarding. You and Hartie and my darling sister represent to me—who we must admit have known and often been liked or loved by people like Charlie Chaplin, Dame Edith Evans, Printemps, Duse and whatnot, who should therefore have a right to some scale of values by which to judge and by which to live, and who are so far as is judged the top of our world of poor mortals—well, as I started to say, you and Hartie and Julia represent to me things I greatly value in life, things I must face and live by, things for which I seek the evidence of what we must all long for.

My God, I sound like St. Paul, that learned, meddlesome improving Jew that has set Protestants especially to biting the drippy nose of one off another. (Shades of Mr. Bishop and the Choir of the Methodist church there in Oxford, with its grunts and groans and in my day of the organ and Miss Carrie Dunlop [6]—doubtless now intoning for St. Peter, let's hope so).

6. Identification not established.

My, my if the good little consecrated, (constipated) Christian at College Hill who baked that cake, could have read all this she would be
sorry she had not put hellbone (Shakespearean) or rat-poison—(Oxford) into her dough. So what?

Frank Lyell came in lately—a nice London tie for a present to this
patriarch and said he had seen Elizabeth Spencer a good many times in
Rome—spoke beautifully of her. I hope she gets some writing done
in Italy—very hard, since there is so much to absorb or respond to—
and will forget some of the effects she was imitating that were not her
style or character. She has a very real talent.

I won't read this over—or might tear it up. Thank you. One thing
I would ask of you and that is some information as to the organization
and personnel involved in the Buie Museum—I have some beautiful
things to bequeath, but don't want them to be lost among people who
don't know the difference. Dear Ella, I wish I could see you.

Lovingly
Stark

830 | To Julia Young Robertson, Austin, Texas

[320 East 57th Street]
[New York]
Friday [February 5, 1954]

Dearest Sister,

I had your very elegant pages of letter—sorry you troubled with its
looks etc. but delighted to hear from you and to know the elevator is
a success. They certainly seemed superior workmen. Don't worry about
the cold here. It sounds impressive in the papers and no doubt cost the
city several millions (literally) but except for a few days of overshoes
it was no bother to us. The pavements outside are clear and my ex-
cursions are brief. Wales' office is not far away. We go Sunday up to
see the man about the new roof on the house, then by the Campbell's—
then leave at six and go to dinner at Eric Bentley's—where it seems

Faubion Bowers [7]—(who told me at lunch with the literary editor of Harpers, when he suddenly got my name said, "Stark Young, why you've been my god for some years.") And so on. He had been several years in the Orient, and had been MacArthur's adviser on what to do about the national theatres in Japan. Last year a big book on the Japanese theatre—appalling amount of knowledge he has. I don't know how much of a real mind. However—

His wife of two years is quite known as an author etc.[8] Her father is the Indian head of the delegation to the United Nations, her uncle Ambassador to Japan. Said to be very beautiful. She'll be at Eric's too. Such is life. Her name is Rhama-Rau—or something like that. Her best known book had quite a success—*West of Home.*

You made a smart crack bringing up Cousin Jennie and the inferiority whine she had—largely a form of egotism. I have no inferiority complex in the sense that I feel inferior to most people. What I feel inferior about is mainly this: I have imagination enough to know that I so very often have not the imagination to be, do or say what would be what I'd like, what, too, would make other people feel happier about themselves, et cetera. I get so many fine things said to me or reported to me—with people coming across the theatre or concert hall to see me etc. that I sometimes think they must think me a silly old fool. At any rate I don't think I'm all that. Caroline Tate writes from Rome that Father Anselm [9] talks about me a lot. Well, at any rate I made an impression to that extent at the Vatican—what I did for Father Anselm is to think a lovely saint as well as a great scholar. Allen has a Fulbright scholarship and he and Caroline have an apartment—through the American Academy—for a year—until August. They can't get over how wonderful that city is. I bet they regret the many months in the past that they spent in Paris. But that was before they were converts to the Catholic Church.

Billy Baldwin [1] is decorating the new country club in Houston and

7. Faubion Bowers (b. 1917) studied piano at the Juilliard School of Music, taught in Japan, and served in the Pacific area as aide to General MacArthur and during the Occupation as civilian censor of the Japanese theatre. In 1952, he published *Japanese Theatre* and in 1953 *Dance in India.* In 1951, he married Santha Rama Rau (b. 1923); the marriage was subsequently dissolved.

8. Using her maiden name, she wrote *Home to India* (1945), *East of Home* (1950), *This Is India* (1954), and others.

9. The Reverend Anselm Strittmatter, O.S.B.

1. William Baldwin, interior decorator, in the New York firm Baldwin and Martin.

some rich man's house in Dallas—He's done a few jobs in Houston already. You can see from Mrs. Wallace's letter that she liked that little brooch from Sanborn's—sort of like that [drawing]—a piece of obsidian in the middle. You may remember it. I wish you and Ben could meet the Wallaces—they are really lovely people. She is a real darling —very sweet looking, unaffected, delicate—you'd love her and she'd love you. The medicine spoons seem to have gone very well with Diane and Marian.[2] I'm glad of that. Wales sends his love. Is still planning glass for his silver thing—hopes for some palish blue glass—not so easy.

I must stop—

Love to both

Stark

831 | To the Reverend Anselm Strittmatter, O.S.B., Rome

320 East 57th Street
New York
[February 9, 1954]

Dear Father Anselmo,

Bowman and I speak of you often, as a matter of course, and in two letters Caroline Tate has spoken of their pleasure and great privilege in seeing you. That goes as a matter of course, or else I should never have brought you all together. The visit with you to the miniatures was especially worthwhile.[3] Well, why not? I regard my friendship with you as one of [the] great blessings of my life; there is some fine flower in it of the mind and heart and soul that I value beyond words.

I don't know how much your South German affiliation with the

---

2. Diane Tate and Marian Hall.

3. Father Strittmatter's note: "A reference to the magnificent exhibition of illuminated manuscripts which under the auspices of the Italian Ministry of Public Information opened in the Palazzo Venezia in December, 1953, and continued for some months in the year following. A very handsome catalogue, *Mostra Storica Nazionale della Miniatura* (Sansoni [Firenze], 1953), describing the 808 objects exhibited, contained besides 522 pages of text, 104 plates in black and white, and 5 in color."

American scene brought you into an understanding of all the under-currents of *So Red the Rose;* but it does seem to me that the devotions, the irrational devotions, the subtle exchange between person and person, would have touched your heart. I hired an actor for six weeks to read aloud over and over the chapters to me, so that I might get the sounds right.

As to some of the questions I might ask you, I don't think they fit well into most correspondence these days. People have less time, shall we say, for the Holy Ghost than they have for the virtues of the Mercury or the Cadillac. But questions like that for instance when Gertrude Newell asks, or discourses, about the Assumption of the Virgin [4] —she chooses to think it all important to think that The Virgin was lifted out of her tomb and borne away, so that there might be no pollution of her flesh after the birth of Jesus. Where does she get that? What becomes of Matthew in the 24th verse of the first chapter, where he says that Joseph "took her but knew her not till she had borne a son and he called his name Jesus?" You could tell me the orthodox opinion of such things.

I have lately been reading a great deal of Plato, and there are often places that I might read aloud to you for your comment. But that is only another way of saying how very nice it would be to see you and talk over things with you. I solicit your gentle thoughts and should like to add your profound goodness to all I think.

> Yours affectionately
> Stark Young

Wales would send messages if he were here.

> S.

4. See above, Letter 812, n. 7.

832 | To Maurice Sterne, Mount Kisco, New York

320 East 57th Street
New York
Friday [March 12, 1954]

Dearest Maurice,

I have been having a minor spell of the virus flu or would have written you sooner to say how sorry I am to hear that Vera is not well. Margaret told me on the telephone. Life seems crowded with unhappy things these days.

Margaret said you were writing away. I hope it comes well, writing is a perilous art, alas. I am on a book, a kind of journal, but don't know yet whether what I have written is any good. I threw away at least half of what I had written for *The Pavilion.*

Just think, this time last year I was on the Andrea Doria, sailing back from Italy. It all seems like a dream. I have been reading much in Gide, and some in Plato and Tolstoi. The book on Tolstoi by his devoted daughter[5] has much detail about him that is very interesting, but is written with enough economy or selection, which does seem a shame, considering that she knows more about him than anybody else. He is a trying, changing, tormented creature, devoted to others but often entirely absorbed in itself. His mind as such could be called negligible, but the fact remains that when it comes to fiction he is unforgettable. I never knew before what tortures he went through with one of his books, each one a prolonged torment.

I hope you have some pleasant days, dear Maurice.

Affectionately
Stark

5. Alexandra Tolstoy, *Tolstoy: A Life of My Father,* translated from the Russian by Elizabeth Reynolds (1953).

833 | To Julia Young Robertson, Austin, Texas

[320 East 57th Street]
[New York]
Thursday [March 18, 1954]

Dear Sister,

Your voice has seemed far away on the telephone and evidently mine does since you have me "exhausted" and nearly at death's door. I am entirely recovered, and please stop thinking up horrors. There are enough cases and operations in Austin to furnish plenty of messy thoughts. I am sorry you and Ben feel tired—I think everybody in America does except Mrs. Roosevelt.

I am invited tonight to see the **T. S. Eliot** play—*The Confidential Clerk*.[6] There are various opinions about it. I am asked to go because of a meeting of the American theatre at which the play is to be discussed—it is to be compared—on a hint from Mr. Eliot with Euripides' *Ion*. I hope they haven't figured it around so that I have to go on the stage and join in. You have to watch your steps in this theatre—they put you forward before you know it.

The enclosed booklet may interest you. They have just asked permission to include my three Russian translations of Chekhov. French & Co. have them but I am told the contract includes only the amateur field, in which French is king and does a tremendous business.

I don't think I told you about Betsy's mother [7]—a great reader. Since her stroke not able to read—I sent her to Dr. Beshner[?]—she is thrilled—his analysis and prescription for glasses enable her to read now as much as she likes. Betsy is delighted of course, it takes some of the burden off her—her mother is there in the apartment and confines Betsy a lot, poor creature. The father [8] is careening around in his Florida camp—that's some relief for them all. He is in the late 70's and wild and fresh as a hornet.

6. The play opened on February 11, 1954, at the Morosco Theatre.
7. Edna Patterson Farrar (Mrs. Preston Cooke Farrar, 1876–1956).
8. Preston Cooke Farrar (1870–1967), author, lecturer, and academic administrator, taught courses in English literature and education at the University of North Carolina from 1927 until his retirement in 1947.

I sent you a letter last week-end—and another last Tuesday—you must have got them by now.

It's fine your car turns out so well. I wish I could advise you about the summer. I don't blame you for not liking the Waccabuc summer with its changeable heat, cold and dampness. I can't speak for Maine. There is something to be said for having a nice cool house, and good car, and staying at home except for trips. Perhaps a few weeks visit in New York, toward the autumn months would be a diverting change. What a comment on America that the places one goes to are so flat or trying etc. except for people who swim, play bridge, or swim. Europe is to be a nightmare—every boat is full. The hotels are horrors with the tourists—every passage here for some months seems taken. Thank goodness Wales and I, though we nearly froze to death at times, escaped that.

I have been deep in Gide, Tolstoi, Euripides, Stendhal, Van Wyck Brooks, and some poetry from Greek, and seem to have some fair things for my book. Thank God, my last! I wish I were really convinced there is any need for it. But look at the mess that has been published. A loving letter from Pierre Fresnay and Yvonne Printemps, saying they wished there were somebody in France who could write such criticism as mine. So what? They mean to be sweet at any rate.

Wales has to go to Maine tonight, till Saturday night I am sorry to say. The houses are to be ready about May 1st, the three of them.

Another invitation to lecture in Washington—I have not decided about that yet—the subject etc.

Try to rest up—both of you. I find nasty things like spinach help me to feel rested.

I'm glad about the bed-jackets. Fine.

Love to both
Stark

834 | To Ella Somerville, Oxford, Mississippi

320 East 57th Street
New York
Friday [April 9, 1954]

Dearest Ella,

I have your last letter here before me in my desk-rack—what a lovely, friendly letter. I do appreciate and value it. The invitation to Oxford is tempting enough; I can only hope that I will get there again before too long. The longer I live and the more I see of the world the more I appreciate fine people, especially those who, like you, add great charm to character, brains, loyalty and heritage. The delay in my thanking you for the letters about the museum is largely due to some bouts with the virus plague in this town. I have had just enough off and on to make me worthless; so forgive me. You took a lot of pains to give me the situation there and I appreciate that fact and the most valuable data that you set down.

I have no invaluable things, but I have a few beautiful things that almost any museum would be glad to own.

This letter was begun several days ago, but meanwhile I have somewhat crippled the ligaments of my right arm and to write is not a torment, but is anything but pleasant—so forgive this look of a mess.

As for Spencer I wrote one of the Guggenheim reconnections for her name and I hope it will work out.

The house in the country is having a good deal done to it, but we hope to move out the first week in May. I can see how you'd like to go to Europe, though the crowding there is to be terrific and the passage on lines or planes are [*sic*] almost unobtainable. With what pleasure I look back on the trip last year. I don't imagine that so many people could ever be so kind or interesting again. This writing has to be on my lap and lack diversion. I'll hope to try again soon with better bones.

Love to you
Stark

835 | To Lavinia Gadsden Dimond, San Francisco, California

320 East 57th Street
New York
Monday [April–May, 1954]

Dearest Lavinia,

We have been in the country for two stays, trying to get the repairs nearer an end, so that we can move out. Otherwise I'd have written sooner to say how lovely it was to see you, how much I appreciated your visit in these far quarters and how those mangoes were given an ovation. We let them wait a day or so and get even more fully ripe. Wales likes them as well as I do, so that for two separate occasions, when we screeched and gobbled [*sic*]. I will tell Wales that I conveyed his thanks indeed and say that he can wait a little before writing you. He is over his head with those three houses in Maine, with having to go up there every other week—the three rival lady clients going after him with a vengeance. I have made him promise not to take any more jobs this summer or for a good while, else he will have a real break-down.

I am glad you will take to the Stendhal.[9] I have really studied it—when you think what poor stuff almost all memoirs are! He has been a tremendous influence—people like Gide. It seems ironical that with the exception of Voltaire and Napoleon more has been written about him in French than any other Frenchman. I don't admire him whole-heartedly, but can't get past the originality and freshness of his mind and method. It was even more astonishing in his own time, though it all faded and almost vanished till it was revived again toward the end of his century, as he said it would.

It was nice to hear news of your family and that you get so much pleasure out of them. It's a shame California is such a long way off. I doubt if I ever see it again.

---

9. Young had recently given Mrs. Dimond a copy of *Memoirs of Egotism* by Stendhal (Marie Henri Boyle), translated by Hannah and Matthew Josephson (1949).

Please give my love to Doug and the boys.
Forgive this scrawl.

Lovingly,
Stark

Thank you for telling me about painting. We'll hope for the best.

836 | To Dorothy Coit,[1] New York

320 East 57th Street
[New York]
Friday [May 14, 1954]

Dear Miss Coit,

I stayed quite a while after the play[2] yesterday but never succeeded in finding you and Miss King—both busy with your stars very likely. I must thank you—before setting out for the country—for a very delightful occasion. My old enthusiasm for your venture in the theatre I found on this revisiting to be as lively as ever. I don't know anything in the Broadway theatre that is as lovely as your production. "Quaint" is all very well, and since—as Talleyrand said, "Parents of children are capable of anything," we'll have to let that pass, but there must have been a good many present who didn't entirely realize what exquisite taste and what variety of invention were exhibited. I shall never forget how enchanting some of the little figures were and how enchantingly posed. I do congratulate you. Those children can learn for life a lesson

1. Dorothy Coit (b. 1889), dramatic coach and author, had been associated with children's theatre groups since 1922. In 1935, Young reviewed with approval the production of *Nala and Damayanti,* staged by Dorothy Coit and Edith King, in "Kindness, Flying and Flowers," *New Republic,* LXXXII (May 8, 1935), 370.

2. The performance had been announced earlier: "A 'resident' children's theatre has been established by Edith King and Dorothy Coit in the ballroom of the Sutton Hotel, 330 East Fifty-sixth Street. The initial bill, opening May 5 and running through May 21, will be the Hindu classic 'Nala and Damayanti.' The performance on May 17 will be a benefit for the Monastery of Mount Savior. Students of the King-Coit school, ranging in age from 5 to 12, will participate"—see "Resident Children's Theatre Set up by D. Coit and E. King, Sutton Hotel," New York *Times,* April 22, 1954, p. 37.

on the difference between style and the obvious reality—and this might then extend to many styles. In very frequent spots the writing seemed quite lovely, and in places the wit in the rather old-fashioned wording was delightful. Great tact often appears in the management of sheer words.

I must congratulate you on your press connection, Miss Bennett and Mr. Pleasant. They were most courteous and thoughtful and well-bred. This is a side of our New York theatre that is all too often neglected.

Please excuse a dull letter. I have an army of carpenters, plasterers, and what not awaiting me on the house in the country. There has been so much virus X and various illnesses that the old house suddenly decided evidently that it was its turn to decline.

With thanks and every good wish and a genuine delight in your (you and Miss King's) unwearying desire for perfection, I am

Yours sincerely
Stark Young

837 | To John Benjamin Robertson, Austin, Texas

[320 East 57th Street]
[New York]
Wednesday [May 26, 1954]

Dear Ben,

I have been glad to hear from Julia that you are improving well. I hope by now you can get out and move around. That will make you sleep better perhaps. Dr. Wolf gave me some of the nembutal once, I took it twice but it had very slight effect. Some people take it every night. Jack Wheelock at Scribner's says he has taken it every night for forty years, varying it with Seconal, which is stronger.

I often wish I could do something nice for you just now. You have done me so many kindnesses that I feel ungrateful just sitting here. I can't think of anything I could send you.

I'm glad you and Julia saw the *Julius Caesar.*[3] Of course it is not authentic, as Julia says. Neither are the stage productions, but of course they are much nearer to the authentic than the movie. You just have to take the movie as it stands—even though nobody knows how to read the verse except Louis Calhern as Caesar—he is a bore however, and John Gielgud, who does wonders in the emphases and rhythms and the sense involved. He worked with Brando I hear teaching him the reading. Brando has no training or experience, but in an amateur young sort of way he is quite convincing, as Julia says. Not as Shakespeare's Antony by any means and certainly not the historical Antony —the general and lover. The funeral speech was written for a small theatre for a crowd of perhaps a dozen people on the stage, and is full of shadings, crescendos for the delivery, sarcasm, tears, etc. which can't be yelled. That's not Brando's fault. James Mason had a certain honest effect, but doesn't know how to read the verse. Having Caesar a big man, instead of the actual Caesar, small, baldheaded and an epileptic— accords with some of the play's lines or slants—bully, arrogance, egoist etc.—all obvious, though the actual small Caesar could have the same quality only more poisonously ingrown.

Wales left for Maine last night, flies back for dinner tonight, and we go Friday afternoon to the country to get to work. Rain has stopped us so often.

There are still quite a lot of lilacs, six or seven varieties, blue and white wood-hyacinths, spirea, pale pink wild azalea—much prettier than the familiar garden kind.

I hope Diana's boy's eyes will be all right now, it's bad luck.

Wales asks every letter if Julia says anything about you all's coming up.

Love to both
Stark

---

3. Young had reference to the motion picture version of Shakespeare's *Julius Caesar,* directed by Joseph Mankiewicz and produced by Metro-Goldwyn-Mayer. Louis Calhern appeared as Julius Caesar, John Gielgud as Cassius, Marlon Brando as Mark Antony, and James Mason as Brutus. Young's opinion of their performances generally agrees with the comments of Parker Tyler in "Et tu, Mankiewicz," *Theatre Arts,* XXXVII (June, 1953), 84, 86. Young saw the production twice in November, 1953.

838 | To Julia Young Robertson, Austin, Texas

[320 East 57th Street]
[New York]
Wednesday morning [June 2,
1954]

Dearest Sister,

We are leaving this afternoon for the country, spend the the night—
to shorten the drive to Maine—and then go on next day. We are getting there in about five ½ hours. I'll be glad of the trip and glad to
see Wales' houses.[4] The people are much delighted with them and he
thinks they came off beautifully. He is worn out with the clients, the
trips etc. and I hope soon will get a complete rest. He ought to be
cheered up by his Irish sweepstakes. He bought ($3) a ticket from the
Irish Bill on the elevator, and though he didn't get the main prizes, he
was one of about 20 to whom they give just general notice, of policy
etc. So he has $4400 coming in. Not bad at all. The men on the elevator
and down stairs are quite excited about it. They are really lovable in
their fraternal excitement. Frank, the sup included. He was at the
street door when we got in yesterday morning, waiting to tell Wales
before anybody else could. Bill had telephoned him. Wales got back—
unexpectedly—$5000 on the last year taxes, paid in 1953, so he is quite
rich, not to speak of his houses being built etc.

Yesterday as a favor to Mr. Strasberg,[5] the leading trainer, student of
theatre etc. in New York I had to make a so-called lecture in the small
rehearsal theatre in the Actor's Studio offices. I talked about various
stage events in the past and what they represented etc. meaning theatre
principles, theories illustrated etc. Over an hour, impromptu, just talking. The applause went on so long that I felt like a fool. I never knew
the Strasbergs except by reputation until about two months ago, but
they have done my reputation great profit. And he introduced me,

4. At Prouts Neck, Maine, Bowman had designed the exteriors and interiors of
houses for Ranald MacDonald, Mrs. Melville D. Truesdale, and Mrs. Irving M. Day.
5. Lee Strasberg (b. 1901), drama coach, director, and actor, began his career in the
1920s as a stage manager and supporting actor. In the 1930s he became a prominent
director with the Group Theatre which he helped to found. Later he became an acting
coach and director of the Actor's Studio Theatre.

after commenting on the theatre as an art and saying that ultimately the only way it existed (as to its qualities and merits—he meant after some years had passed) was in the writings of perceptive and creative critics who felt the theatre art as a part of life, and that since he had known the New York theatre—that goes back before 1915—I was the only critic he knew who had stood for all this etc. plus other handsome remarks. All I know how to do is to stand there like an idiot and smirk. It seems the thing now among many younger workers in the theatre to speak of me as their "idol"—to whose writing they can turn etc. I don't know when that word got going. There are few things now, however, to review seriously in the theatre just now, so it may be a blessing that I am out of it and left as their "idol" and so on.

All this is all very well. I can use the applause and so on, but what I value most is having the affection of you and Ben. I suppose you are trying to decide just what to plan.

The garden and the grounds have peonies, syringa, several kinds of lilacs yet, wood hyacinths, yellow casia, yellow lilies, rugosa roses, climbing white roses (by the front door) bugle, snow drops, several kinds of daisies, columbines, ageratum, quince, beauty bush, sweet rocket, valerican and some other—I wish you all could be here to have it. I must close.

Love to both
Stark

We get back here Monday, 7th.

839 | To Mary Goldmann, Austin, Texas

Portland, Maine
Saturday [June 5, 1954]

Dear Mary,

Julia wrote me about your losing Skippy, the sweet little dog you loved so much. It has to be finally with animals and all pets except swans, which live forever; but that doesn't make it very much easier.

Animals just break your heart, love you and depend on you and that ties you all the more to them. In the last fifteen years I have lost two. First a beautiful little grey cat with the sweetest, prettiest face. I had to leave him one winter in a kennels—an excellent one—trying to shut him up in a New York apartment had proved impossible and unkind —and he had a run of his own at the kennels and all that. But one night all the inmates were killed by gas leaking from a heater. At least it was a much less painful death than most, but it still makes me sick to think of it all. The other was a larger and more matter-of-fact cat but very lovable and sound. He got hold of some poison—rat and after a fairly long sickness and two vets died. So no more pets for me, how-ever selfish that may be. We have a gray cat now that was discovered living under the house. Very practical, has managed for himself on rats, squirrels, rabbits and so on. We feed him when we are there, but he depends not so much on us, and we don't depend on him in the other way. The first cat had the eyes of a poet, this one's eyes are like a manager in a store or a business boy. But bless his heart, just the same.

Well, I just thought I'd write and let you know how sorry I am about Skippy.

This comes from Maine because I have driven up here with Bowman for a few days to see three houses he has built here—they are a great success, right on the shore, with pine trees behind them, and are much admired.

I hope you are having a pleasant summer and your garden a success. We have many many kinds of flowers and more to come.

Give Pauline messages for me. She is a dear cousin.

Affectionately
S.Y.

840 | To the Reverend Anselm Strittmatter, O.S.B., Rome

320 East 57th Street
New York
June 15, 1954

Dear Father Anselmo,

I have enjoyed keeping your letter and have read it over at various times. As to the church as a mystery I think I at least have some idea of what is meant by that, having lived in all about five months in a convent, visited often in the Franciscan monastery at the top of Fiesole, where Ventura Dei,[6] a young monk my own age at the time, a divine spirit and a scholar (he was editor of the Revista Francescana)—was one of my closest friends. I spent eight entire days—literally, from nine till dinnertime with Cardinal O'Connell crossing the Atlantic to Boston[7]—sat all day everyday talking with him—(asking questions) went to see him in Boston—had as a good friend during my Texas days Father Carey, director of the Newman Society (is that the right name?) and having read no little in the early Fathers, St. Augustine, etc. A long sentence, as difficult as the mystery to a Presbyterian perhaps. But at any rate the point is not that correction of St. Matthew that delights me in this case. It is the fact that this is the best example I have seen of the Catholic way with the Bible. The Protestants taught me that the Catholics don't know anything about the Bible; the Church doesn't want them to read it. It is to be assumed that the Protestants are different. They "believe every word is inspired" (not to mention the 2000 and more mistranslations in the St. James version). But when for example it comes to divorce they let the Bible roar and pay no attention—the Episcopalians alone excepted. I side with the Church—it is absurd to turn Tom, Dick and Harry loose to read the Bible any way they like, that mélange of Jewish, Oriental, Greek and other cultures, not to say the exact meaning of words, which change often in meaning or shading with the years.

I should be honest with so valued a friend as you about myself and the Bible. To me in its relation to our fellowmen, to histories etc. it is

6. See above, Letter 26 and n. 7.
7. See above, Letter 93 and n. 7.

absorbingly interesting. In the King James it is marvellous as literature. Otherwise I read it precisely as I do Plato or Virgil or Shakespeare. But I do read it, which is more than most Christians have ever done, either in itself or in whatever essence of it the Church gives out. And though I find the Protestant churches most unsympathetic—to put it mildly (as a rule they make me sick and bored) I feel at home with the Catholic world, especially the non-Irish. What would I do if a loved friend like you were a Baptist? A foolish question. You wouldn't be you if you were a Baptist.

Caroline Tate telephoned me from Princeton—her daughter seems about well. She has sold the house and bought a large but uglier one for her daughter and her family. Allen is coming back soon. They always seem to land in some trouble or crisis—bless their hearts! My present crisis is that I am too stupid and can't get the writing done as I want it to go. Mediocre writing is insufferable, distinguished writing is difficult to attain, and to give it all a remoteness and fineness of soul is still more rarely likely.

Just think it is two years this October since we left for Italy. Rome seems a dream—so wonderful and so inexhaustible.

I have read with much interest the accounts of Pope Pius X's elevation.[8] Cardinal O'Connell knew him intimately and talked to me a good deal about him, about his holy nature (and of the Vatican in relation to him, not always by any means in a complimentary manner. The Cardinal had no timid hesitations about knocking heads off.)

I wish you might have paid us a little visit in the country during these last few months—heavenly flowers! Perhaps there is a chance of your coming to these shores this summer. I hope so. Bowman has been busy with three houses in Maine—but soon he hopes to settle into a rest. He would send messages to you if he were here. We often speak of you.

Affectionately yours
Stark Young

8. Pope St. Pius X was canonized by his third successor, Pius XII, May 29, 1954.

841 | To John Arthos, University of Michigan, Ann Arbor, Michigan

320 East 57th Street
New York
June 16, 1954

Dear Mr. Arthos,

I came home from a short stay in Maine and found at my country address a copy of the review with your article;[9] and then yesterday when I came to town for two or three days I found the copy you sent, together with a very kind note.

It is a difficult matter to thank you properly. To say your article is excellent criticism may suggest a degree of self-complacency, I had better say it is a triumph of beautiful appreciation and of understanding of at least what my intentions were and what I should like to express or convey.

You could never have written such an article if you had not had the insight and lovely penetration to know how I should value all you said. Basta. I'll only spoil your wonderful effect if I go stammering on. I must, however, go on at least to mention the evidences of care and knowledge and style that are everywhere in your pages.

I see in the page of authors that you have had a book of poems just published by the press there.[1] I know what it is to have books begged of one, people think a writer can get the whole edition for nothing if he wants to give it away; but I should greatly like to have a copy.

My address now is Waccabuc, New York, where my country house is, but I'll be back in this apartment with the first frost—November—and if you chance to be in town perhaps you'd find time to look me up. The telephone is not in the book—Plaza 5,6493. Meanwhile thank you again—I have but lamely expressed my appreciation.

Yours sincerely
Stark Young

9. John Arthos, "In Honor of Stark Young," *Shenandoah,* V (Summer, 1954), 14–27.
1. The note called attention to John Arthos, *On a Mask Presented at Ludlow Castle, by John Milton* (1954).

842 | To Paul Green, University of North Carolina, Chapel Hill, North Carolina

Waccabuc, New York
July 8, 1954

Dear Mr. Paul Green,

When they wrote me from Theatre Arts about doing the review of your book,[2] I said I was not writing any theatre articles but that I'd "do this for Mr. Paul Green." Then I thought it over and since it was limited to five hundred words I decided that instead of detailed citations that might make us *both* shine somewhat I would make it general and in broad strokes as the best way to further the book itself. I meant to write you explaining this and may have done so, though I think not. At any rate I appreciated your writing me and hope the little review really gave you some pleasure or satisfaction.

And I do value and appreciate the kind things you said of me. I am quite a long way off in the country and so will not have a chance to see your one-act plays at the Theatre de Lys. I regret that very much.

Your work is going well I hope and your summer pleasant. You certainly cover enough ground in that book to deserve as much vacation as you find it in your heart to take. Nobody could wish you more good fortune than I do.

Yours cordially
Stark Young

2. Young reviewed Paul Green's *Dramatic Heritage* in "All the World's His Stage," *Theatre Arts*, XXXVIII (June, 1954), 12. Young mentioned Green's most important plays by name, acknowledged his scholarship, and praised his essays dealing with the theatre of foreign countries and the plays of Shaw.

843 | To John Arthos, University of Michigan, Ann Arbor, Michigan

Jennymead
Waccabuc, New York
July 13, 1954

Dear Mr. Arthos,

Your study of *Comus* [3] came to me and I read most of it at once and then took it on a trip to Maine. I suppose every one of us has a degree of pedantry in him; at any rate I had a peculiar delight in all that learning and scholarship and discernment and felt for the moment ashamed of myself for ever doing anything but blow myself up with shining details and fine flowers of knowledge. I am no judge when it comes to *Comus*—which I find I have always accepted with an innocence almost the equal of any professor's when it comes to art. All that may sound like a back-handed something or other, but I mean it as a great compliment. For once at least somebody did a fine thing in Italy on the Fulbright bounty. I will value owning your study, believe me, and am only too sorry not to write a more worthy letter about it. (And I haven't just glanced it over, believe me.)

Yours cordially
Stark Young

844 | To Juliette Huxley, London, England

320 East 57th Street
New York
July 22, 1954

Dearest Juliette,

I wrote you a long, flat letter the other day, about various things, you, Julian and writings and what not, and was so taken up with

3. See above, Letter 841 and n. 1.

Julian's book that I even forgot to remember that I had forgotten to mention—even mention—the remarkable photographs that do so much for the whole book.[4] Well, I mention them now with a bang. I have looked at them many times and wished I might see the whole batch that he took. The color helps greatly with such blue-sky scenes. All his architectural comments show his old concern with that field of art and this world of our living.

I wonder if you saw Eliot's *The Confidential Clerk* when it was played in London.[5] It evidently went better there than in New York[6] —it was played more farcically I gather—and since it is a poetic farce— farce in the technical sense of an arbitrary connection between the characters and the dénouément, that was the happier way to go at it. Here they had the same director[7]—Mr. Eliot's friend and choice for the job—but here the result was very poor. Partly the actors if you like, but by no means wholly so. Ina Claire returned to the theatre for it but got a sad reward. She is a brilliant player of high comedy—much the best I know, but found it very disappointing as an experience, though she had seen it twice in London and thought it might be a good ve- hicle for her. You might read it some time if you haven't already done so. Shockingly banal and boring in spots—very nearly always in the New York version.

Mr. Eliot, it seems, has said that it was suggested to him by Euripides' *Ion. Ion* is one of Euripides' poor, rather conscienceless pieces—though not so bad as the *Helen.* But it is at least better than *The Confidential Clerk.* And it is rather pompous to imply the derivation—many later Greek novels also had the theme of *identity—Twelfth Night,* for exam- ple, truly descends from them. I am sorry Mr. Eliot wrote this piece.

John Gielgud sent me his mother's autobiography[8]—at 86—a re-

4. Young seems to have in mind two of his recent letters to the Huxleys. On July 14, he wrote to Julian Huxley primarily about his book, *From an Antique Land: Ancient and Modern in the Middle East* (1954). Although Young briefly mentioned the volume in his letter July 19, he dealt mainly with Huxley's review of J. Robert Oppenheimer's *Science and the Common Understanding* in the *New Republic,* CXXI (July 19, 1954), 18–20, and with Young's resignation from the *New Republic.* Huxley's book contained sixty-six photographs.

5. T. S. Eliot's play opened in London on September 16, 1953, at the Lyric Theatre.

6. The play opened at the Morosco Theatre on February 11, 1954, and closed May 22, 1954.

7. E. Martin Browne (b. 1900) has produced all of Eliot's plays and many of those by Christopher Fry.

8. Kate Terry (Lewis) Gielgud, *Kate Terry Gielgud: An Autobiography* (1953).

markable document of English life in the last century and its continued practice and flavor into the earlier part of our own time. She seems to be going full sail still. But I must stop.

Love to you both—
Stark

845 | To William M. Kethley, Delta State College, Cleveland, Mississippi

Jennymead
Waccabuc, New York
Wednesday [September 8, 1954]

Dear Mr. Kethley,

I appreciated your letter very much, and was interested indeed in what you say about the Yazoo River author.[9] He deserves much credit. But what a pity he could not have written in some of the Indian civilization, some of the settlers' culture and ideals and destinies and so on. I should never know, for example, that such a man as you would ever be a product of the region. When he speaks of *So Red the Rose* celebrating the glories of the old South it is sickening.[1] Of all things I avoided just that slop. It is about that land civilization with its responsibilities and the life of the affections, et cetera—as you, of course, would know.

I am afraid that writing in the rush of getting off on the motor trip

9. Frank E. Smith, *The Yazoo River*, in *Rivers of America*, edited by Carl Carmer (1954). Smith (b. 1918), born in Sidon, Mississippi, was a member of Congress from the third Mississippi district from the 82nd to the 87th Congress. Since 1962, he has been director of the Tennessee Valley Authority. Smith has written *Congressman from Mississippi* (1964), *Look Away from Dixie* (1965), and *The Politics of Conservation* (1966).
1. Smith mentioned "the McGehee brothers" as examples of the westward movement of planters who left worn out lands on the eastern seaboard to move westward. According to Smith, the last of the McGehee brothers to migrate built a log house near Como, on the Tallahatchie River. His grandson, Stark Young, born in Como, as a boy "heard enough stories of ante bellum glory" to inspire the novel *So Red the Rose*. See Frank E. Smith, *The Yazoo River*, p. 45.

in Maine I was not very clear about the card. It was not for Christmas, I wanted you to see this—though greatly reduced—reproduction of my painting,[2] and I should have told you that it was now coming on sale at 20 cents a card at any card shop or may be ordered direct from the publishers—American Artists Group—106 Seventh Avenue, N.Y.C. (one of the leading companies in this country).

You speak of your problem of retiring from office[3] and not retiring. It touched my heart what you said. The time comes to every man when he must face that. There is the question of whether in character, state of mind and moral health one can endure the changed life. And then whether one has the means to live without the salary. And then this that and the other. I have had to face it, and know very well that in a very few years I will still have to face it but more and more gravely. It makes me feel weak and sick to think of it—partly for other people's sake. But sometimes Fate takes it all out of our hands and not always unhappily. Or if unhappily, it is a good thing we don't know it yet. I know, however, that anything I can say on the subject is worthless in any other person's case.

I hope you and Mrs. Kethley will find a fair solution, though I know too well that what you will want must have the glow and luminous rightness that such spirits require. I am sure that in the end you will do what is wise and truly basic, but that need not make the process of doing it any more easy or comfortable. I feel this for you but am saying it poorly.

Let the college bookshop get some of the cards and choke them down the throats of the wrong people.

Thank you again for your letter. Remember me to Mrs. Kethley,

Affectionately yours
Stark Young

2. A reproduction of Young's painting, *Madonna and Child*, appeared on the card.
3. Kethley was president of Delta State College.

846 | To Ella Somerville, Oxford, Mississippi

Waccabuc, New York
Monday [September 20, 1954]

Dearest Ella,

I have only a few minutes ago received your most welcome letter telling me that that sweet Nina[4] was improving. How that must fill your heart with gratitude. Let's hope the faculty of speech will come back rapidly. When she is ready to smile at a silly remark tell her from me not to smother herself with any regrets for not being able to talk much for a while; nobody nowadays wants to hear what anybody else says; they want to talk themselves. I read the other day of a woman who will make a business for herself; she asks $5 an hour for *listening*. Already she has a lot of clients. Somebody has commented already that in some cases $5 would be a very low rate. So Nina for a while can put by something to help pay the doctor's bills or something. If that doesn't entertain her—I mean my advice—tell her that an old lady in the 80's was here yesterday—Mrs. Maud Rogers—she ate carefully. But, I said, "you don't have to diet, you could easily put on a few more pounds." "Yes," she said, "if I could only be sure I'd gain in the proper places." "But," I said wittily, "I thought the proper places were improper." She went right on with her thoughts however.

Then I told her of Toscanini and Milanova[5]—who is vastly upholstered in the bosom. He was much annoyed at the way she had just sung in a concert of his, and seeing her afterward went up by way of greeting and shook her breasts—"Oh, if they were only full of brains!"

You were very sweet to bother about the cards just at this time. I'm glad they give you some pleasure.

The summer here has been much broken up with various matters and people, and there have been hot days, mostly in the city not out here—and cold nights that slowed things up sadly in the garden—and

4. Miss Somerville's sister, Mrs. John C. Culley.
5. Zinka Milanov (b. 1906), operatic soprano, made her debut in 1927 in Yugoslavia and afterwards sang in Hamburg and Vienna. She was soloist in Verdi's *Requiem* under the direction of Toscanini in 1937 before coming to the United States to make her American debut at the Metropolitan Opera House, December 17, 1937, where she continued her distinguished career until her retirement.

now rains lately that make tomatoes et cetera resort to the blight. The storm played much havoc, as you have read in the papers, but we were spared in this neighborhood except for some broken trees.

I made a new friend not long ago. I met Joan Fontaine,[6] she asked me to see her play *Tea and Sympathy* again and advise her, which I did. So we said she'd better come out to see us, which she and her husband did last week-end—after the play Saturday night and stayed till Monday afternoon. Very sweet and very full of sense and humor and very responsive when she likes you. I had not seen her husband before —he proved to be a very likeable and intelligent man—in the early forties—devoted to her and very good company. Well, I have chattered enough—I hope it takes your mind off your troubles. I haven't seen the New Yorker piece about Bill Faulkner,[7] but saw a quote from it. I'm afraid I won't try the *Fable*. There are too many good books otherwise —such is life.

Lovingly—
Stark

Bowman sends you messages, is very glad Nina is better he asks me to tell you.

6. Joan Fontaine (b. 1917), actress, played leading roles in numerous motion pictures in the 1930s and 1940s before coming to New York to succeed Deborah Kerr as Laura Reynolds in Robert Anderson's *Tea and Sympathy*. She first appeared in the role on May 31, 1954. In 1952, she married Collier Hudson Young, film producer.

7. Brendan Gill reviewed *A Fable* in "Fifth Gospel," *New Yorker,* XXX (August 28, 1954), 70–72. Gill characterized the novel as "a calamity," "a bad small novel, absurdly distended," "neither very interesting in itself nor very important." After providing a "partial summary" of the plot, whose "vulgarity reflects the underlying vulgarity of the novel," Gill advised readers to leave the resurrection story to the Biblical writers who had already "told it better than anyone is ever going to tell it again."

847 | To Thérèse Strode, Tuscaloosa, Alabama

Jennymead
Waccabuc, New York
Tuesday [October 5, 1954]

Dearest Thérèse,

I was on the point of writing to thank you for your sweet note about the card[8] when this second little letter came, so lovely and generous and characteristic of you. I was sorry my card didn't reach you in better time, but they will be good another year. I was so very glad that you liked it. The picture is quite sizable—about 2 feet by 15 inches—and they did an excellent job in reproducing it, considering the smallness of the card itself. Jensen, Scribner's Bookshop et cetera have it, so I hope it will be seen by various people.

I hope Hudson is entirely well again, he deserves to be. These days people like you and Hudson are more needed than ever, in every sense, for one's own heart and for the world in general.

I saw his note on the envelope about the essay in *Shenandoah* magazine.[9] The fact about that is that the first copy came to me last June. I sent a check to the business manager asking that four copies be sent to me and one to you and Hudson. I suppose the student manager was on vacation by then, so that only a few weeks ago the copies came, as you know by yours arrival.

I had a very fine letter from the author, who is evidently a highly cultivated young professor of Greek descent and various scholarship abroad and so on. I have never met him, but hope to.

I have been piling up notes for a *Journal*—something of a continuation of *The Pavilion* but dealing with later material. It has thus to be in a different tone, and when I return to form I am planning to set to work getting some of the book written. If I can't get it to suit me, I'll just throw it away.

Joan Fontaine and her husband spent the weekend here in the country with me recently and Norman Dello Joio and his wife happened

8. See above, Letter 845 and n. 2.
9. See above, Letter 841 and n. 9.

in. He has a new 20 minute song that Leonard Thomas[1] is singing and will do on his concert tour. Norman spoke very enthusiastically of his meeting you all, said many lovely things. He is a remarkable fellow and has done some beautiful music. He and Joan Fontaine—who is very sensitive and intelligent—had some happy exchange.

Bowman and I remember our visit in Bermuda with much pleasure, the best part of which deals with the visits with you and Hudson, and meeting your mother. He sends most cordial messages. His career in architecture has been kept quiet by his preference, but he has done a good many beautiful things—the last—just finished, three "cottages" on the Maine coast—each different from the rest, and each a fine success. They are the kind of "cottages" where the linen alone costs three to four thousand, and the little porcelain stove $1800. (These people here do make me smile, with their simple needs.)

Your camellias sound divine. The alba plena is my favorite flower. Where my cousins live in Louisiana and Mississippi is said to be ideal for them. No bother at all—they just grow. Some are there that my great great uncle set out about 1830. At times on one tree there are about 300 flowers in bloom at one time. I found them in full flower on each of my two visits to St. Francisville. Enormous bushes. I almost went out of my mind. It's fine that you and Hudson have them. Weeks Hall[2] tried to send me a big box with many varieties from his place on the Teche—but they arrived in fairly poor shape, ravishing but really distressing. We have marvellous lilacs here et cetera, but I will take camellias. I don't know where the Garden Club ladies got their pronunciation: Cam-aýlias. That would be partly Spanish, partly nothing. The first form is Camĕllas—(from Kamel the botanist) but

1. Young refers to Leonard Warren (1911–60), the leading baritone in the Italian repertoire of the Metropolitan Opera Company during the 1950s. Warren sang Dello Joio's *Lamentation of Saul* at its first performance at the chamber music festival in memory of Elizabeth Sprague Coolidge at South Mountain near Pittsfield, Massachusetts, August 21–22, 1954. Dello Joio wrote the work for Warren, who continued to sing it on concert tours until the end of his life.

2. William Weeks Hall (1895–1958), art critic, photographer, and painter, was born on the Shadows-on-the-Teche Plantation of his great-grandfather, David Weeks, near New Iberia, Louisiana. After living his childhood on the plantation, Hall studied art in Paris until 1920, when he returned to New Iberia to spend the remainder of his life restoring The Shadows, which David Weeks had built in 1830. Early in his career, Hall showed promise as a painter, but, in 1937, an injury to his arm forced him to abandon the art. Subsequently, his color photographs brought him widespread recognition.

that sounds ugly and I never heard it in this country. Cameēllias is a very sweet word.

Enough of this running on and on. I do wish I could see you and Hudson. You'd like this place we *own* now in the country—about nine miles from the rented place that Hudson saw, bless his heart. My beloved Henry Wallaces live about three miles away. He was used for their own ends by the wrong people, but all that is shaken off. Just plants and animals and experiments. He is a kind of saint that man.

Lovingly
Stark

848 | To Hudson Strode, University of Alabama,
       Tuscaloosa, Alabama

320 East 57th Street
New York
Sunday [November 21, 1954]

Dearest Hudson,

Ever since your review of Miss Glasgow's book[3] came out I have been interesting myself in trying to think out just how you approached it with such taste and tact and persuasive tone, and have meant to write you my compliments on your success. It was a most difficult problem, especially to a man of your delicate responses.

I knew Miss Glasgow so well that I have heard these things that are in the book (many times I heard her say them and have her write them in letters) (from the part of it I have had a chance to read so far and from what I have heard cited, or read cited too, from it.)

I put a lot of time on the proofs of her book of prefaces, changing a good many passages that were said in a manner defeatingly antagonistic in effect, and uselessly so, bless her heart.

I was very fond of her, and was only too sorry to feel how mixed up

3. Hudson Strode reviewed Ellen Glasgow's *The Woman Within* in "The Secret Places of a Heart," *New York Times Book Review,* October 31, 1954, pp. 1, 42.

she was—wanting to eat her cake and have it too. She never got entirely over her early years of writing with its drive to say what she
wanted to say and her resentment of anything but admiration. She
watched the exact space of advertising that her publisher gave each
book, and read every review and was almost never satisfied. I told her
once that I had found that the simplest way was just to say she was
greater than Dostoievsky. Bless her heart—She was a wonderful
woman. I certainly owe a lot to her.[4]

Again compliments on your achievement of such an article on such
a subject.

I hope you and Thérèse are well and happy and wish I could see you
both there in your own garden and light.

Lovingly
Stark

I can't seem to write this morning—too many things went on this
week—last week it is now.

S.

849 | To Julian Huxley, New York

320 East 57th Street
New York
Wednesday [November 24, 1954]

Dearest Julian,

Here is a little box—not too big to carry—for Juliette, bless her heart.
It's many years since I bought these objects in Venice.

4. Late in January, 1955, in a letter to Ella Somerville, Young again commented
upon Ellen Glasgow and *The Woman Within:* "Miss Glasgow was one of my best
and most loyal and most helpful friends, but the book—*entre nous*—by no means does
her justice. The English visits have none of the wit, observation and bite or warmth
that she might have put into them. I had stacks of letters from her through the years
and some parts of them are capital stuff in various directions. Her best book—of those
I have read—seems to me *The Sheltered Life.* As a woman writer she would have
been a happier person if she had come along fifteen or twenty years later. That remark
could be greatly extended."

I was sorry to belabor you with my *New Republic* saga.[5] I cut it very short indeed. I am glad you know this little of it and also that Michael[6] urged me not to leave the paper. Bruce Bliven was already in possession and wrecking the latter half—in my case it was an old resentment of Croly's attitude and indulgence, plus an antagonism toward nearly everybody that was ever on the paper and toward me especially. The variations of pettiness and plotting to get me off were endless—I won't go into them. You should see the collection I have of yellow slips that had been sent around the office for initials—he could never get a complete endorsement and has no idea that they all came in the end to me.

The anniversary number of the NR has just come. I note that for all my part in its past my name is not listed among the contributors on the cover.[7] That seems pathetically small rather than something for me to resent. Such is life.

I have thought several times with the warmest pleasure over the success of your book,[8] the things you told me really delighted me. The book of course deserves all that, but deserts are not always fulfilled.

I hope your trip home is a fine rest. Remember me to the Zieglers.[9] I have just written Juliette.

Affectionately
Stark

5. Huxley had been in the United States to lecture at several universities and to receive an honorary degree from Columbia University. During Huxley's visit, Young had described the circumstances of his resignation from the *New Republic*. Huxley was about to sail for England as Young wrote this letter.

6. Michael Straight.

7. Although omitted from the list of contributing authors on the cover, Young was represented by his article "The Spiritual Audacity of Duse," a reprint of an article published June 20, 1923. See the *New Republic,* CXXXI (November 22, 1954), 103–104.

8. See above, Letter 844 and n. 4.

9. Huxley had stayed with his friends, Dr. and Mrs. James E. Ziegler. A native of California, Ziegler has been a professor of microbiology at the New York University School of Medicine since 1949.

850 | To Anne Sharkey, New York

[320 East 57th Street]
[New York]
Friday [December 17, 1954]

Dearest Annie,

I am sending you and our dear Zue[1] just a greeting on the card, but this letter means at least to say a great deal more. I know that, whatever one may think and decide to think about or put out of the mind, this Christmas season will be crowded at times with old memories, and things that will not fade easily from the heart.

You can reflect always that you were a very wonderful daughter to your dear mother,[2] I am sure she was proud of you. She was indeed a great thoroughbred, an aristocrat, she looked every inch of that and her actions were that. I'll always remember her as a lady who never let one down, a dear and lovely person. All words get nowhere however.

You may wisely think on yourself, dear Annie. I don't know anybody with more depth of character, more loyalty, more of a beautiful gift of friendship. I said one day in Rome to Wales, "Do you know who if I were counting over friends and supposed friends to me at home who I'd say first?" He said without a pause "Annie."

I was proud of that lack of pause and also at the discernment.

I wish I could say something of use, but words are very poor instruments when one's need for them is strong—such is life.

Bless you, Annie—Love to you and Zue.

Stark

1. Margaret A. Sharkey.
2. Mrs. Alice M. Sharkey died December 3, 1954.

851 | To Charles Scribner, Jr., Charles Scribner's Sons, New York

320 East 57th Street
New York
Wednesday [January 12, 1955]

Dear Charlie,

I have just seen—yesterday it was—a notice that Eric Bentley is editing a collection of Bernard Shaw's musical criticism for the Anchor series.[3] You no doubt know this series, and better than I do. I got the idea that my first two drama books—*The Flower in Drama* and *Glamour*—might be treated likewise by him. So I telephoned him and he professed to think it a capital suggestion, said for me to take it up with you and he would take it up with the Anchor publishers. Since both books have been out of print and unavailable a long time now, and since there is of course no argument for your publishing them again, but are in a genuine if limited demand among actors, drama schools and others interested, this cheap way of republishing would seem to be a solution.

It might surprise you to know how many people have asked me or written me as to the possibility of getting hold of them—a letter yesterday, for example, from Eileen Eckhart [*sic*] of the new hit, *The Bad Seed*,[4] asked what I could suggest. She has had her bookseller for months looking for these books and even a friend in London is trying to find chance copies there. Carnegie Tech says they have only a very few copies and yet all their theatre students—several hundred perhaps —are set to read them at their very beginning.[5] A Mr. Lumianski from Michigan State has just been here—or just before Christmas—to go over the thick MS. of a thesis-book he had done about me.[6] We had two days of it! He said I was the only critic of drama that the faculty

3. *Shaw on Music: A Selection from the Music Criticism of Bernard Shaw*, edited by Eric Bentley (1955).

4. Eileen Heckart played the role of Mrs. Daigle in *The Bad Seed*, which opened at the 46th Street Theatre, December 8, 1954.

5. Early in December, 1954, Young had lectured at the Carnegie Institute of Technology.

6. In 1955, Robert M. Lumianski wrote a doctoral dissertation at Michigan State University on "Stark Young and His Dramatic Criticism."

would consent his taking on this serious thesis basis. Also a man at Cornell has done some sort of elaborate bibliography thesis about me [7] —et cetera. John Gielgud announced that there was only one dramatic critic in America—me—and Hobson—dramatic critic, now editor of the Sunday Times of London, said of *Immortal Shadows* that they had never had a dramatic critic in England like me [8]—and so on. I am boring you no doubt, but all this seems to me a reason for having Bentley get the books into the Anchor series—since they are for most practical uses, as good as dead. That does seem a kind of farce.

If you think well of this idea (and if Bentley can get the *Anchor* publishers interested) I hope you will consider letting me know. [9]

I am struggling with many notes for the next book—some time ahead, that's certain—and have pages written, but not continuously, and have yet to find in what tone I must write it. That must be different from the tone of *Encaustics* in many ways, since so much of *Encaustics* is rooted in a kind of nostalgia. I know you wish me well in this and it is wonderful to have a publisher, and friend, to whom I can talk of it all—the essential problem to be solved in this instance.

Affectionately
Stark

852 | To the Reverend Anselm Strittmatter, O.S.B., Rome

320 East 57th Street
New York
January 26, 1955

Dear Father Anselmo,

I don't want to wait too long before I express my sympathy with your losing your beloved Rome. [1] However loyal you may be to your

---

7. In 1954, Bedford Thurman completed his doctoral dissertation at Cornell University on "Stark Young: A Bibliography of His Writings with a Selective Index to His Criticism of the Arts."

8. See above, Letter 705 and n. 3.

9. Although Scribner expressed willingness to cooperate, the proposed volume was never published.

1. At the call of the prior of St. Anselm's Priory, Father Strittmatter left Rome, where he had been a member of the Liturgical Institute in the Collegio S. Anselmo, to return to Washington to assume the post of novice-master in the priory.

own country it is obvious that Rome is so glorious and inexhaustible and to all your inclinations so sympathetic that nothing could ever take its place for you. Perhaps in not too many years you will be assigned to it again.

Wales Bowman and I have some vague, dim plans for coming to Europe again this year—it's all on the lap of the gods so far—and if we do, it is easy to imagine how we should miss seeing you in Rome. If we do go we plan to spend a good deal of time in Venice. But who knows? The state of the world, the trouble in the Orient, and plenty of other conditions make everything very heavy with black turns of fortune and threaten the loss and destruction of many of the most profound and valued things in life.

I spent Christmas with my sister and brother-in-law in Austin, Texas; but my sister had broken her ankle two weeks before so I sat upstairs in her room with her almost the entire day and into the evening every day for the two weeks I was there. It was nevertheless, a great pleasure and privilege to be within her lovely influence and loving, sweet presence. I have told her and my fine brother-in-law a great deal about you.

Bowman would send messages if he were here and not absent on Grand Jury duty. He has finished his three houses in Maine and has three or four lesser jobs on hand at present. He has had one client who almost drove him frantic with highly unreasonable fault-finding with the execution of a house with which she is inwardly delighted— that is indeed tiresome.

I have been buried in some heavy reading—and enjoyed it deeply. You didn't say whether you'd be in Washington or New York or where when you do come over to stay.

Affectionately yours
Stark Young

853 | To Frank H. Lyell, University of Texas, Austin, Texas

320 East 57th Street
New York
Thursday [February 10, 1955]

Dear Frank,

I finished the book[2] two or three days ago and since then have read in parts of it again, partly to see how some of the remarkable impression of an understanding of Italy is so definitely achieved, though with no apparent effort. In the most elusive manner the characters are established from the start, and this rightness about Italy appears often in one phrase, one verb, one omission of what would not be true. I know the subtle problem of trying to convey the Italian temperament and the easy and certain reactions to life et cetera that are to be found among that people. Take the portrait of Gino—with complete rightness and sound truth that very complex-simple nature and habit is conveyed—and no Anglo-Saxon rot involved, not superiority, not moral reproof, not social theory, not over-sentimentalizing. Wales and I read the opera scene over, aloud. It is very delicious and all the more satisfying by being so really Italian (and without implying that it is soundly Italian). One race about another is usually apt to be asinine, however interesting to attend to, listen to, agree, object, scorn et cetera.

The one part of that very true and skillful book that doesn't quite come off, I think, are the final pages. They have the awkward self-consciousness of many writers in English when they are trying to express some idea or theme or reaction that may be lofty, psychologically sound or what not, but ends by being too explicit to be deeply expressive. What is needed of course is the discovery or creation of some image or what not, something the characters do, by which the idea is what is called "realized."

I will say for myself that I did some of this in *So Red the Rose*. I tried always for it. For example the complicated aspects of the relation between the Negroes and their masters is completely present in the

---

2. Aware that Young read little fiction and wishing to send him a novel which he would admire and yet not have already read, Lyell chose E. M. Forster's *Where Angels Fear to Tread* (1905).

scene of the old colored man and the little boy, when the Negro stops the carriage—"Uncle Phil, why don't you come to see me?" and the old man's response—the way so many things are said in that scene.[3] With all the various departures in that novel every single one is different, in order to express the particular thing to be expressed, and not just talk about it as most writers do. But I wander.

The suspense in the Forster book of the interest, the light, bright touch plus the darker notes—all that is certainly remarkable and I am very grateful, dear Frank. Your quoting the talkative goose bit, on the fly leaf, is duly noted—great and lovable tact.

Please remember me to Mr. Fearing.[4] I remember his pictures with great distinctness and admiration.

Wales sends warm messages to you.

Affectionately,
Stark

854 | To Julian Huxley, London, England

320 East 57th Street
New York
February 21, 1955

Dearest Julian—

I have still your very good letter from the Queen Mary[5]—it was somewhat Homeric evidently at times, but you read, slept and rested, so that I imagine you were very much alive when you stepped ashore in your England, and in many ways very happy to see it again—as who would not be that had any sense?

3. *So Red the Rose,* pp. 355–56; see above, Letter 791.
4. Kelly Fearing (b. 1918), painter, born in Fordyce, Arkansas, professor of art at the University of Texas.
5. On December 9, 1954, while on his return voyage to England, Huxley had answered Young's earlier letter (see above, Letter 849). This letter should be compared with Young's other correspondence dealing with his resignation from the *New Republic;* see especially above, Letter 674.

What you say about the *New Republic* does you credit both as a loyal friend to Michael[6] and to me. Michael was entirely warm and friendly in the matter of my leaving, urging me to stay on et cetera. Meantime, however, he had let that whole part of the paper go to the dogs under Bruce Bliven and lose all the distinction it ever had. My part was persistently cut down, with lies and excuses as to lack of room and tampering with the MS. until I merely quit with no row of any kind. Immediately a new man—a playwright—came on and went into very lengthy pieces, then was evidently bored and quit.[7] They tried Harold Clurman, a good man, a frank blower of my horn, who presently quit. Finally Eric Bentley—who, also, has always frankly said in print that I was the leading dramatic critic in America. He writes as he pleases but Bruce is not there any longer to muddle things up. Bruce is in fact well off the NR, since Mr. Harrison[8] came on. Now and then a sop of a review thrown to him, even that very rarely. The fact remains that after I was off a rotten, completely stupid and misleading review of my book *The Pavilion* came out—quite unbelievable.[9] If Michael were more alert he would at least [have] written me his regrets, but I doubt if he ever read it. If I had any spiteful feelings I'd say that of late the NR seems very thin and flat both materially and as mind or literature. I'm really sorry, for I have a deep feeling for that paper and for Leonard and Dorothy.[1] You are very generous, like your beloved self, to speak of "the feeling of guilt, for being rich, which has also hampered Dorothy's activities." That is well observed, but it is also well to note that this same business has given Dorothy (I can't speak for Michael) many occasions for slipping out of what she didn't care for at that moment—such, to take a petty instance, as not coming to a dinner where she was expected and not even sending an excuse. She backed many charities, bless her heart, but some of them she got executed through another, or one way or another, in order to be rid of a nui-

6. Michael Straight.
7. Young refers to Irwin Shaw.
8. Gilbert Avery Harrison (b. 1915), editor and publisher, served in the Army Air Forces during World War II. At the close of the war, he helped to found the American Veterans Committee and became its national chairman in 1948. In April, 1953, he joined the staff of the *New Republic* as publisher; in May, 1956, he became editor and publisher; and since February, 1963, he has been editor-in-chief. In addition to editing the *New Republic,* Harrison is president of the Liveright Publishing Corporation.
9. See above, Letters 773 and 781.
1. The reference is to Leonard K. Elmhirst and his wife, Dorothy Straight Elmhirst.

sance plaguing her for help (or for a fat trip and visit in some august place). It seems that my projection from the *New Republic* has greatly added to a pathos of prestige—all sorts of praise, responses from new playwrights and younger actors et cetera. That puts the *New Republic* farther than ever from their respect—of which they often had little enough before. I see all that as just too bad, the *New Republic* will always be to me what Croly and people like Dorothy and Leonard wanted it to be. (Though I must say it is many years since Dorothy or Leonard bothered in any real or serious sense about the contents of the paper.)

Your Bridges reading[2] sounds exciting enough, at least when you tell of it. A "practical critique of gluttony and epicury" sounds like something indeed.

That is miraculous news that you and Juliette might come over, and even get to Waccabuc. You can have it very peaceful there. Bowman and I may go at least to Venice this summer, who knows? When I know about that I will write you. Meantime my thoughts of seeing you and Juliette there in London in 1953 are very sweet and warm in my heart.

Affectionately
Stark

I have been told from the newspapers of Maria's death[3] and have just written Aldous. He is such a lovable, fine man—and this seems uselessly cruel.

---

2. Huxley had written that on shipboard he was reading Robert Bridges' *Testament of Beauty* (1929).

3. Maria Nys Huxley (Mrs. Aldous Huxley, 1900–55) died February 12, 1955, in Los Angeles; Young probably saw the account of her death in the New York *Times*, February 13, 1955, p. 86.

855 | To Juliette Huxley, London, England

320 East 57th Street
New York
February 21, 1955

Dearest Juliette,

I have just written Julian,[4] a dull letter to his much alive account of his sea-shaken cerebrations—(I sometimes wonder if his brain ever takes a nap). I hope he arrived at home all aglint—(that sounds like Coleridge). At any rate that is wonderful news that there is a chance of you two dear people coming over here in the summer of '56. Imagine that!

One matter—of the 1¾ pence left from my cheque you have already sent two books—for heaven's sake be generous and do as I intended: on the pittance left get some flowers. Surely your garden will need something. There are so many flowers in England to love with all one's heart. And there are other flowers to love discretely, somewhat dully, as if something elegiac was to be noted in the air.

I am delighted that you have already found *Hadrian's Memoirs*.[5] But I am also glad to say that your conclusion that it was for "rare spirits" may well be qualified. You will see by the enclosed list, from the Sunday *New York Times*,[6] that for several months it has been one of the national best sellers, and is now 6th on the list of sixteen. That's quite something to think over. The author is now an American citizen, was once a professor at Sarah Lawrence College, whose president is one of my friends,[7] and I mean to ask him more about her. The book has gone into about six or eight languages, has taken prizes here and there, and goes into edition after edition here in this country. I am indeed sorry Julian "couldn't read it." And Aldous only half of it. (But first one thing must be said: Chapter I and Chapter II don't quite come off or measure up to the rest of the book. I have not been able yet to discover why, after various rereadings.) The story of the meeting with

4. See the preceding letter.
5. Marguerite Yourcenar, *Memoirs of Hadrian,* translated from the French by Grace Frich in collaboration with the author (1954).
6. *New York Times Book Review,* February 20, 1955, p. 8.
7. Harold Taylor (b. 1914), president of Sarah Lawrence College, 1945–59.

Antinous; the youth with his solemn unity of mind and passion; the complete tremor and tension and nobility of his response and devotion; the finality, super-knowledge Hadrian could bring to bear on given situations; the creation of the chain of motives for and meanings behind the death, are remarkably done—worth the repeated readings I have given them.

I have seen Hadrian's Villa several times and there is the unequal but clever book of two years back—*Rome and a Villa* by Eleanor Clark. But I'd hoped Julian would find this elaborate recreation of the great Hadrian full of comments on Plato's *Phaedrus* for example, on the Greek Anthology, on the marvellous account in Appian's *The Anabasis of Alexander* of the death of Hephaestion and Alexander's grief—Appian belonged to Hadrian's epoch—and on great love as seen in two diversely great natures—regardless of the homosexual aspect. The weakness of the book, when there is to be found a sense of weakness or fault—there are those who would certainly find it so at times—lies, I think, in a certain almost monotonous handsomeness of style or discourse. In my case I rarely found that objection.

I have just written Aldous—it seems very brutal of fortune. I always liked Maria—a certain almost passion of style inwardly—perhaps lonely at bottom.[8] What a life! *Cosi la vita.*

[unsigned]

Excuse this unsatisfactory paper. Don't read it against a light surface—it's clearer against dark or none.

8. See the preceding letter, n. 2.

856 | To Katharine Cornell,[9] New York

320 East 57th Street
New York
Thursday [February 24, 1955]

Dear Kit,

I was aching to go behind and tell you last night what a beautiful evening I had had, but there was such an army of people that it seemed an imposition.[1] You must have felt somewhat exhausted already sustaining a role so abundant and so complex.

That Countess is unbelievably elaborate, both modern and Elizabethan in her lines and the great variety of her motifs and images and moods. You humanized her by simplifying and making more lovely and lyric the whole portrait. It was a triumph of graciousness and a noble heart. And you kept those very difficult scenes together so that the audience seemed to me always held. I do congratulate you. Edith Evans is a great friend of mine but I had left London when she did this play and so can't make any comparisons, and so must content myself in the writing her how beautifully it all came off.

I think Guthrie outdid himself in the directing. I had read the play three times, and marvelled all the more at the clear outlines and the vivid movement that he achieved.

Oliver Messel's setting was the finest baroque I ever saw on the stage, very stunning to look at and very inventive and ingenious in the boundless detail. I stayed on and looked at it very closely. He works with more genius and *con amore* than any designer I know of. When

9. Katharine Cornell (Mrs. Guthrie McClintic, 1893–1974), actress, made her first New York appearance in 1916 with the Washington Square Players, and from that time she had a distinguished career as the star of many successful Broadway productions. Her most famous roles include Jo in *Little Women,* Candida in *Candida,* Ellen Olenska in *The Age of Innocence,* Elizabeth Barrett in *The Barretts of Wimpole Street,* Juliet in *Romeo and Juliet,* Jenifer Dubedat in *The Doctor's Dilemma,* and Masha in *The Three Sisters.* In 1921, she married Guthrie McClintic (see above, Letter 585, n. 7).

1. On the preceding evening, Christopher Fry's *The Dark Is Light Enough,* with Katharine Cornell playing the role of the Countess Rosmarin Ostenburg, had opened at the ANTA Theatre in Lincoln Center. Produced by Katharine Cornell and Roger L. Stevens, the play was directed by Guthrie McClintic, and the settings were designed by Oliver Messel.

he got back from seeing the play in Ohio he was enchanted with the whole event.

I could go on and on, but should stop and spare you a little.

Congratulations and thanks, and love to you and Guthrie.

> Yours affectionately,
> Stark Y.

857 | To Lillian Foote,[2] Nyack, New York

> 320 East 57th Street
> New York
> Wednesday [March, 1955]

Dear Lillian:

Excuse a hasty letter—I must get this off and Wales is about to leave for his office and can post it.

I can write the introduction to the play[3] with genuine pleasure as well as affection for the author, but have to see the ms. first. It would be stupid to try it from the mere memory of the performance. I will promise to get the ms. to the publisher in a day or two,[4] whether it comes from him or direct from you. Or mail it back to you. I'll give Wales your messages.

It does seem a long time since I saw you loved people, bless your hearts.

Jack Lord[5] wrote me from your address there. Please give him my warm wishes for his success out there.

Lovingly—in haste

Stark

2. Lillian Vallish Foote, wife of Horton Foote (b. 1916), playwright and novelist. Horton Foote was born in Wharton, Texas. In 1945, he married Lillian Vallish. Foote's plays include *The Chase* (1952), *Trip to Bountiful* (1953), and *The Traveling Lady* (1954). In 1962, his film version of the novel *To Kill a Mockingbird* received the Motion Picture Academy Award for the best screenplay based upon material from another medium.

3. Foote's *The Traveling Lady* opened at the Playhouse Theatre on October 27, 1954. Young had been requested to write a foreword to the published version.

4. Young's foreword appeared in the volume which was released later in the year.

5. Jack Lord made his Broadway debut as Slim Murray in Foote's *The Traveling Lady.*

858 | To Irita B. Van Doren, New York Herald Tribune, New York

320 East 57th Street
New York
Thursday [March 10, 1955]

Dear Irita,

I have been absent in Baltimore with two silly lecture events[6] or would have written you sooner. I was afraid that you—as a true and dear friend of mine through the years—might have been worried to think that that very inane review of *The Three Sisters* at the 4th Street Theater might have blasted my state of mind and left me sadly disgruntled.[7] But not at all. *I had nothing to do with the occasion except to* [corner of page missing] *the translation.* That, according to your reviewer, "seems at times almost a satire on Chekhov" etc. If Miss Crist will compare the translation (French & Co.) with her Russian text, she will see that I follow Chekhov's lines more closely than any other translations so far as I know. As compared, however, with her conception of Chekhov's play in her next two paragraphs (about ½ the article), the translation may be satire or what not, since the whole conception expressed hardly fits Chekhov at all. What grieves you and Mr. Kerr,[8] I am afraid, is that the *Herald-Tribune* should at this late date be expressing a crude and vulgar public attitude toward the plays of this Russian dramatist, now over fifty years old and regarded as among the classics of the modern theatre. All that kind of lively humor was not so bad before 1920, but these days it is only embarrassing. Don't really bother about it. The people I have heard comment were just as if they had hit on grandpa's opinion of "opery."

6. At the request of Richard G. Fallon, professor of speech and theatre, Young had lectured to theatre classes and met informally with students at the Maryland State Teacher's College at Towson.

7. Young has in mind Judith Crist's "Off Broadway: Chekhov's 'Three Sisters' Revived at 4th St. Theater," New York *Herald Tribune*, February 26, 1955, p. 7. The play opened on February 25.

8. Walter Kerr (b. 1913), drama critic, wrote criticism for *Commonweal* magazine before becoming in 1951 the drama critic for the New York *Herald Tribune*. Kerr's books include *How Not to Write a Play* (1955), *Criticism and Censorship* (1957), *Pieces of Eight* (1957), and *The Decline of Pleasure* (1962). In 1943, he married Jean Collins (b. 1923) and with her wrote the revue *Touch and Go* and the script for *Goldilocks*. Kerr has taught courses in the drama at Catholic University. Jean Kerr has written *Jenny Kissed Me*, *Please Don't Eat the Daisies*, and *Poor Richard*.

I wish you would congratulate Mr. Kerr for me on the very fine review of the Christopher Fry play.[9] In a short time he has made a big niche for himself in our theatre forum—or whatever we might call it.

I hope everything goes well for you, dear Irita. I appreciated your reply to my Glasgow note. Bless your heart. Please remember me to Mr. Gaworth[?].

Affectionately
Stark

859 | To Bedford Thurman, Kent State University, Kent, Ohio

320 East 57th Street
New York
Tuesday [April 5, 1955]

Dearest Bedford,

You are a sweet fellow to think of that book. A man[1] of great learning etc.—assistant to Roger Stevens[2]—has something of the same thought—he was thrilled, by the way, with your bibliography, and fired to greater projects. But what has happened is that Scribners has decided to reissue *The Flower in Drama* and *Glamour* in one volume —as *Revised*.[3] There has been a considerable demand for these books

9. Walter Kerr reviewed Christopher Fry's *The Dark Is Light Enough* in "Miss Cornell in Fry's Daring Winter Comedy," New York *Herald Tribune*, March 6, 1955, Sec. 4, p. 1.

1. In January, 1955, William Becker suggested to Charles Scribner, Jr., that he publish a collection of Young's articles about the drama.

2. Roger L. Stevens (b. 1910), real estate broker, producer, and governmental official, produced a large number of Broadway shows, including *West Side Story, Cat on a Hot Tin Roof, Bus Stop,* and *Tea and Sympathy.* During the 1960s, he was prominently associated with such projects as the National Endowment for the Arts, the John F. Kennedy Center for the Performing Arts, the Metropolitan Opera Association, and the American National Theatre and Academy.

3. On March 25, Charles Scribner, Jr., wrote Young that Scribner's had recently "put in hand" a new edition of Young's *The Flower in Drama* and *Glamour.* The volume was published later in the year.

long out of print. And so I have told Mr. Becker—he's also Roger Stevens' right hand man—that we'll just wait a bit on this newer project—see what follows the book coming out in the fall—though the promotion begins earlier. I'll see that one of the first copies is sent to you.

Meanwhile thank you indeed for the microfilm,[4] dear cousin.

There seems to be a great wave among the young actors, playwrights etc. toward me. I should like to be of use to them. You can't believe how many even loving instances there are.

Mr. Ross,[5] who is producing *The Three Sisters* is a great believer, through the influence of the Actors' Studio. The production is at least better than any I have ever seen in New York—and the attendance is remarkable. The theatre is very small, and that cripples matters. He wants to keep it going for a long time yet. We shall see what we shall see.

Don't forget entirely any plan about a book of things hitherto unpublished. Just let it wait.

The MS, bound, of the thesis on my dramatic criticism, has come, from Michigan State. Much labor, much very worthy seriousness of approach, much detail. It can do no harm. By Robert Lumianski.[6]

My love to Joreta,[7] bless her heart. I hope things go well for you all.

Lovingly
Stark

4. Microfilm copy of Thurman's dissertation; see above, Letter 851, n. 5.
5. David Ross (1922–66), director and producer, produced a number of plays by Chekhov and Ibsen, including *The Three Sisters, The Cherry Orchard, The Sea Gull, Hedda Gabler,* and *A Doll's House.*
6. See above, Letter 851, n. 6.
7. Mrs. Bedford Thurman.

860 | To Caroline Charlotte McGehee, Baptist Hospital, Memphis, Tennessee

320 East 57th Street
New York
Tuesday [April 5, 1955]

Dearest Cousin Cad,

Robert's sweet wife [8] has written me that you have gone at last to the hospital in Memphis, and I am hoping that you will speedily find yourself improving. Really you will enjoy the hospital with all the variety of people it affords; you will find an excellent chance to study the human comedy. And I am sure many of them will be delighted to know such a witty and wise and human-souled person as you are.

If you ask me they are infernally lucky to get a chance to know you. I have been a great deal at the American Ambassador's in Rome, where I saw all sorts of people from all over the world, princes, ex-rulers, prelates from the Vatican and the fine ladies that might be expected with such men, plus literary charmers and what not. And I have seen few people as attractive, magnetic and lovable as my Cousin Cad. So there you are, young lady!

Bowman and I have tickets on the plane for Switzerland June 30 en route to Venice. We have an apartment of four rooms, bath, kitchen and so on (with a cat in residence) beginning July 1st and running to October 1st. From Venice we'll make some side trips to the Greek Isles and elsewhere. There is a cook who comes for breakfast, stays till in the afternoon, markets, does the laundry and so on, about $15 a month. The apartment completely furnished costs us about what we pay the colored man in the country, our one servant, $200 a month about. At that I am living on my modest savings and count on leaving this world before they give out. I hope I don't get stung on that.

Dearest Cousin Cad, hurry and get better. You are too wonderful to waste time being sick.

Bowman sends his love—he still talks about how delightful you are.

Lovingly
Stark

8. Mrs. Robert W. Lipscomb, Como, Mississippi, had written Young about the illness of Miss McGehee. On April 8, Mrs. Lipscomb wrote that Miss McGehee's health had greatly improved and that she had returned to her home in Como.

861 | To Catherine Alexander Burland, Washington, D.C.

320 East 57th Street
New York
April 8, 1955

Dear Katya,

I ought to tell you that Miss Salisbury, my agent, has agreed to give Mr. Ross a change from the contract—not the increase as the gross receipts increased but a fixed $75 a week. I know she knows her business, so this is all right. The reason for it is that Mr. Ross is anxious about making ends meet. The theatre is so small[9] that he can't take in much, though it is sold out on many nights. The chance to keep the play going longer naturally depends on this. The longer it runs the better in every way, since he wants to do *The Cherry Orchard* next season—has made me promise. The attention *The Three Sisters* has gotten from real people—many editors, critics, producers et cetera— have gone! So I hope he can keep it going for some months, as he hopes greatly to do. Next season if he gets a larger theatre the whole situation might be changed. Miss Salisbury will make things go as they should as far as the money is concerned. The $150 (minus her 10%) is all I have received so far. It opened February 25th so that will make eight weeks this Friday, April 8th. I don't know what the theatre custom is as to when payments are given the author of a play, but I know Miss Salisbury will keep all that straight. Mr. Ross has carefully shown her his books already. She told me that when discussing the change from the contract.

I know it is "occupy myself with science" for one meaning. But *nauka* means *knowledge* or *learning* as well as *science*. The sense here is not *science* as we use the word in English. We know from Andrei's speeches that he is in the literary direction, is translating a book from English, reads languages et cetera. I will have the actor change tomorrow to *knowledge* or *learning* or whatever sounds well for the actor to speak. I think *learning* will have to do. *Scholarship* is too stuffy.

I think my Italian had something to do with my keeping it *science*.

9. On March 24, 1955, Young had written Mrs. Burland that the theatre seated only 188 persons.

Their *scienza* you use widely, as we say the science of cooking, or remembering things exactly, et cetera. But Andrei is talking about a university, where *science* has the one meaning of the sciences.

I haven't looked at German for thirty years and never studied it much and never intend to again—I haven't seen Russian for seventeen years and never learned it with any thoroughness of course, and I am horrified to see how much I have forgotten, when I go over lines in Chekhov and the dictionary. Well, well. I know more Greek and Latin and French and Italian at least, though none too much. It takes a lifetime to know English with any choice distinction for that matter. I often despair of the depth of our wonderful language.

Your travel news is most impressive. You and Tommy [1] are true citizens of the world. (I must say very attractive ones.)

Wales sends love to you both.

Love to you
Stark

I hope Granville [2] is entirely well.

862 | To Catherine Alexander Burland, Washington, D.C.

320 East 57th Street
New York
May 2, 1955

Dear Katya,

I'm glad the cheque [3] went to your heart—Lord knows we need money these days. As to more translating, for me it is over fifteen years since I took the six translations of *The Sea Gull* and decided to dig it out myself in the Russian dictionary.

The Three Sisters and *The Cherry Orchard* are simpler to translate —more truly Chekhov they also are—and with your translations and

---

1. Thomas Burland, husband of Catherine A. Burland.
2. Mrs. Burland's son.
3. Division of royalty payments for *The Three Sisters*.

the other translations I had, it was of course a less intense job than I had on *The Sea Gull*. But lately when studying lines in *The Three Sisters* to see what I wanted to do with them—change words if necessary—I found the use of the dictionary much harder. I'd rather put my time on my own writing than ever try any translating in any language again. I have been going over my translation of Machiavelli's *La Mandragola*, to be reprinted in a collection of classic comedies.[4] I find that Renaissance Italian an awful bore to fool with again. Such is life.

Mr. Ross has various plans, and needs money to go on. He has lost $27000 on this year's ventures, he says, *The Dybbuk* and *The Three Sisters*. Theatre expenses are terrible as well as silly. He talks in various directions—I don't intend to mix up with it all. The theatre world can get your time and plans all in a mess, and very often a waste. I have some writing under way that is as much as I can carry in my head, without getting stewed up with the theatre.

That's fine news about Granville. He struck me as a gifted and witty fellow and I see no reason why he could not go on and up. Please congratulate him for me.

Lavinia[5] has been here, looking very lovely. We spoke of you of course. She has probably gone back now, but I think she misses this part of the world.

Tommie's quest of millions certainly takes him into wild places. Give him my love when you write.

Wales and I will be highly delighted to see you.

Yours as ever
Stark

4. The project, mentioned in several of Young's letters, seems never to have materialized.

5. Lavinia Gadsden Dimond (Mrs. Douglas M. Dimond), then living in San Francisco.

863 | To Louis Kronenberger, Brandeis University, Waltham, Massachusetts

320 East 57th Street
New York
Tuesday [May, 1955]

Dear Louis,

My proper instinct was to write at once to thank you for the book [6] and the lovely inscription, and say that at the earliest moment I would give myself the pleasure of reading it. And then like a fool I read the last piece in *The Republic of Letters*—that on Tom Wolfe [7] and that ruined me. My sister was here in New York to see the doctor and I had the final revising of my translation of *La Mandragola* to finish, for a new collection in which it is to be republished [8] (this will be the third time it will be in print) and I had to go to the country for the week-end and whip things toward some better shape (we do that every week-end). But the Wolfe piece ruined me, as I said. The fact always remains that many people take all his stuff seriously—or so they say— and I am not the kind to ride rough-shod over that fact—the young especially, I am told, swallow him whole. Your article is by far the best discussion I have ever read or heard about Tom Wolfe—so complicated the whole matter is, so many side-comments et cetera. Point by point you express and dispose of all the items in my mind about him. By some quite dazzling process you have included all the points. Tom essentially had no intellect—but the first novel seemed to promise God knows what. [9] (I admired the good places in it, I never swallowed it whole.) But to set him down as you have is something out of class with anybody else I could think of. I can't say this in a letter thus with any

6. Louis Kronenberger, *The Republic of Letters* (1955).
7. "The Autobiography of Thomas Wolfe."
8. Young's translation of Niccolo Machiavelli's *Mandragola* was originally published in 1927 by the Macaulay Company. In 1953, the translation was reprinted in *A Renaissance Treasury*, edited by Hiram Haydn and John Charles Nelson. The plan to include the work in a collection of classic comedies seems never to have materialized; see the preceding letter and n. 4.
9. In Kronenberger's estimation, Wolfe lacked "cerebration" and wrote always as an amateur and an adolescent.

satisfactory coherence. I have read the article four times, point by point.

The *Wolfe* got me into a maze—so then came one piece after another—and this morning at 5.30 I was on the *Gibbon*—with what tact done as a person and a life, not only as a writer. I knew only splashes of his life and places. The *Mencken* is deadly and astonishingly final. I met him once—he was very gentle and warm—said I must write for him et cetera. Fortunately I had more sense than to get into that, having one's writing corrected into Menckenise and so on. You summed up the whole amount of him, then and now. I have read all of Byron, including the letters, and I think you said at least what I should want said about him. But on page 144 you imply that his limp was affected —where do you get that?[1] Trelawney's disgusting testimony about the tendon of Achilles would seem to mean quite the contrary. Of all the complicated creatures Byron almost leads. I know in Italy some of the Countess Guiccioli's family—the Gambas—the confusion at that end is just as great. It is a lot for me in this particular instance to say that I heartily agree with your article—your conception, your gentle depths.

You take my beloved La Rochefoucauld at a respectful depth greater than it happens that I ever took him. It all seems to me the aristocratic, cool regard of people around him, in his world. It does not depress me or elevate me either, it nudges me into many happy recognitions. A part of its perfection lies in his staying within his own world, and in our knowing he does. If one has had contact with the French this self business, the ego number one, this criticize first and then thank when one gets a present, this thinking you have said a lot because in your language you said it so *concretely*—that leaves a cool surrounding atmosphere very often.

My God, Louis, I must stop—I have a job on hand—that Machiavelli revision—but I must say that your summation of the Henry Adams book is precisely what I have kept these many years as a recollection of its effect. And the Chekhov—if I had known this essay before I read your letter about *The Three Sisters* I would have been impressed even more than I was, which was a great deal. Everything you say seems to me right, but of course there is more to be said, and I thank Heaven I haven't got to say it. He eludes us, or does me when I come down to the end you have essayed. I wonder if you have my translation of *The*

1. Kronenberger asked: "If one is a lord and romantically handsome, need one also walk with a limp?"

Sea Gull—I can send it to you. But with all this familiarity with him I doubt if I could add anything of value to your essay.

Your Shaw is full of right things about him. The *Showman*[2] you speak of is the key word to him. Look at *Candida*—the poet is *safely* an earl's son, Candida *stays* in the end with her husband—imagine taking all that seriously as social comment and so on. The one thing I disagree with in the book is that about Shaw's as the "most *searching*" of modern dramatic criticism—etc.[3] I should say that Shaw is effective and often brilliant reading; as to the art of the theatre he very rarely sees the point. He wished to do-in the Irving school[4] and make way for his own conceptions, works et al. No tongs were spared, though Irving had his virtues, now out of date if you like. But where Shaw gives himself away is in the famous Duse-Bernhardt pieces.[5] They read effectively. At bottom they are absurd considering the nature of the theatre art. That they are most persuasive is another matter, as you imply in your article. In these Duse-Bernhardt articles Shaw gives support and plausibility to some of the worst mistaken conceptions of the young workers in our theatre today. More anon.

If I don't stop you'll wish you had never sent me the book, dear Louis. At any rate it only confirms my old appreciation, sense of congeniality of mind and love of you, and that's a pleasant thought.

Please give my love to Emmy. Bowman and I hope to see you soon.

Yours
Stark

2. Kronenberger wrote that "most of all . . . Shaw was a showman of ideas."

3. Without using precisely this phrase, Kronenberger had emphasized the depth and comprehensiveness of Shaw's grasp of all human activity and the difficulty of pronouncing judgment upon the critical content of his work.

4. Young refers to Henry Irving (1838–1905), English actor and theatre manager, whose style of acting provoked controversy and harsh criticism as well as great admiration from actors, critics, and audiences.

5. Presumably Young had in mind Shaw's articles which he contributed to the *Saturday Review* from January, 1895, to May, 1898. In a number of them Shaw compared the acting of Duse and Bernhardt. The essays have been collected as *Our Theatres in the Nineties by Bernard Shaw* (3 vols., 1932); see especially I, 144–54, 162; II, 39, 55, 145–47; III, 186–88.

864 | To John Arthos, University of Michigan, Ann Arbor, Michigan

320 East 57th Street
New York
May 25, 1955

Dear Mr. Arthos,

I hope you will forgive me for not writing sooner to acknowledge your Comédie Francaise article.[6] I have been much engaged in getting the copy ready for an edition of my theatre books, *The Flower in Drama* and *Glamour,* that Scribner is bringing out again in one volume, after many years out of print. And then there has been the final revision of my translation of Machiavelli's *La Mandragola,* which is to reappear in a volume of classic comedies—it too has been out of print a long time, until recently there was a Renaissance volume with it included.[7] So all that has been burning me up and making me wish I had never seen a book. At last today I took up your article. In most cases I would have run through it and written a perfunctory acknowledgement long ago, but in your case I knew better.

But I didn't know ENOUGH BETTER, I am typing this solely because I want to keep a touch of my reaction in my files for future reference. The essay is remarkable and because of its inner beauty is very moving. Under it is the assumption that all the Theatre Francais represents is very fine, but at the same time it is not our thing—we could profit by it but would not repeat it, nor could we. Your points are all made with much grace and delicate poetic cerebration—what a rotten phrase I did then!—and one has constantly the sense of profound culture as a base for the whole reaction you express. I have read the essay three times, but seem unable to express anything I want to express, and so will wait till in the morning and try again, else I shall be saying frustrated, fascinating and " 'til" before I know it.) Not that the words apply here, but just to use them and be in the vogue. Thursday

6. John Arthos, "The Excellence of the Comédie Française," *Michigan Quarterly Review,* LXI (1955), 146–51.
7. See above, Letter 862 and n. 4.

To start again.

I must be bold and ask if I can get three copies of the essay. I want to send one to my dear friend John Gielgud, he will see points in what you say about *The Winter's Tale*. He is the most remarkable director I know of in English—as well as the most laborious—and is always sending me books about Shakespeare and what not—the last one was the first night of Twelfth Night book, by Hotson,[8] which you doubtless have seen by now. He has, I have heard before I even knew him, the bad habit of saying flatly in New York that there is only one dramatic critic in America et cetera. I want to send another to Pierre Fresnay, he and Yvonne Printemps I have seen not often but we are profoundly devoted—it seems to me we have nobody in this country that touches them. I think what you say will mean a great deal to him —he is educated in more races than his own French, and he is a darling of a person, loving, loyal, generous and profoundly technical. There are few people I have ever felt—and at once—so free with and happy with and warm in the heart as I do with him and Printemps.

I also want to give a copy to my publisher and loved friend Charlie Scribner, who is one of the most delicate and really learned people I ever knew. He has the firm going excellently and is headed for the position of the leading publisher in English. I don't know whether you have books already published or not, but I should like to think of Charlie Scribner having a connection with you. He is one of the handful of thoroughly distinguished people that I know. His father died about three years ago and he has led things straight along and ahead with a high and thorough scholarship and fine perceptiveness. I am not expressing very well something that deserves the most exquisite exactness.

I feel very proud to be sending such an essay as this of yours to such people as these.

I am now asking for even a fourth copy. I want Lee Strasberg to read it. If you have not got that many I will lend him mine and probably never see it again. His position in the theatre here is unique, however quiet. The number of new people, writers and actors and directors, that have come from his studio is very impressive, somewhat overwhelming.

8. Gielgud had sent Young a copy of John Leslie Hotson's *First Night of Twelfth Night* (1954).

Your concluding paragraph on *The Winter's Tale* seems to me full of useful imagination—in this case much needed—and has a great many shadings and overtones. I rarely use the word, but I should call that a brilliant paragraph. The comment on *Tartuffe* contributes a real point. I know the play very well but I should not have thought of "splendor of spirit,"[9] I should have thought mostly of Moliere's sanity and sweet reasonableness. But the other goes further in meaning where Moliere is concerned.

The whole final column, page 151, is very close and fruitful and spacious. And the very last about the perfect intelligibility and the something less than it can mean, is necessary and deep and right.[1] It's a long time since I read anything that gave me the satisfaction that this essay gives me, and so I had better stop here and not be ploughing myself under.

If I were a more calculating personage I would delay all this till I get more rested from my recent labors and dull spirits, but that might be a long time, and so I will send this on.

I was delighted to see your promotion to a full chair of English.[2] That speaks well for the University of Michigan.

I have no secretary at present and I never type if I can avoid it, and you will forgive this messy letter, I hope—*que dois—je faire encore?*

Cordially yours
Stark Young

9. Arthos had written: *"Tartuffe* is given with all the effort due to Shakespeare and Racine—all the care possible in order to reveal the splendor of spirit that alone can make that terrible story endurable."

1. After remarking that in the Comédie Française production of *Othello* "the glory of Shakespeare's language was lost" and "the conception of certain passions was also deficient," Arthos wrote: "All was perfectly intelligible, and this is why the play meant something less than it can mean."

2. In a note to the article, the editor mentioned Arthos' promotion to full professor.

865 | To Catherine Alexander Burland, Washington, D.C.

320 East 57th Street
New York
Wednesday [June 1, 1955]

Dear Katya,

So endeth the first lesson—this is the last alas of the checks. If Mr. Ross does get a theatre proper I imagine he might revive *The Three Sisters*. Let's hope so.

As to any more translating I am myself through with it. I have lately done a lot of work on my translation of Machiavelli's *La Mandragola,* for the third printing of it[3]—in a new series now. It originally came out about 1923. Then lately was reprinted in a Renaissance collection. Now with an annotated edition in Italian I have done a laborious re-study all through. I was *younger* when I did *The Sea Gull*. I remember I began with five or six translations and a Russian dictionary. I took all the lines to pieces and tried for a real stage style. Then delivered that act to the Lunts and they were delighted with the result in rehearsal. Then I delivered the other acts to them and showed the whole to you and you made very helpful suggestions, bless your Rooshian heart! with the other two plays I began with your translation and two others and picked my way line by line. Well, lately I have looked up a good many lines in the Russian of *The Three Sisters* and it is boring how much I have forgotten even in the use of the dictionary. Small wonder—it has been about fourteen years since I was working in it. *I was younger then.* Some one often suggests that I translate this or that—from French or Italian. Never again—never again—*Le Légataire Universel* of Regnard's, and *La Mandragola* of Machiavelli's are enough, though I must confess that if the copyright was not badly sewed up I might be tempted to try Benavente's *La Malquerida*—though English does poorly by Spanish. The Lorca translations that I have seen are pretty inadequate. The classical verse in Latin or in Greek seems to be entirely untranslatable, unless you are an insensitive castrate cow of a professor who does the translating.

---

3. See above, Letter 862 and n. 4 and Letter 863, n. 8.

Let's hope Mr. Ross gets a theatre. Then he can do *The Cherry Orchard* and perhaps *The Three Sisters* again.

Love to you all

Stark

866 | To Walter Kerr, New York Herald Tribune, New York

320 East 57th Street
New York
June 2, 1955

Dear Mr. Kerr,

I am not in the habit of writing to critics and don't often indulge in long letters, but you must make allowances for this one, if only because I am so interested in writing it. I still have your review of Tennessee Williams' play[4] and have read it a number of times. It should have taught me that your book would be of great interest to me. That review is very easily one of the best I have seen in many seasons, very often brilliant and not without the penetration of the poetic insight as well as the rest of the critical judgement. The only point in it that I didn't follow is that at the end. I think the uncertainty you imply is due largely to the vague meanings of the word *homosexual*. Without doubt Brick is homosexual, but that leaves a wide margin as to the extent and the in practice et cetera. All the way from St. Augustine naked in the summer-house with his naked boys teaching them about

4. Walter Kerr, "Cat on a Hot Tin Roof," New York *Herald Tribune,* March 25, 1955, p. 12. Kerr had criticized Williams' "tantalizing reluctance . . . to let the play blurt out its promised secret" and the "evasion on the part of its principal character" of the precise nature of his feelings. Even in the scene of confession, wrote Kerr, "the truth still dodges around verbal corners, slips somewhere between the veranda shutters, refuses to meet us on firm, clear terms." To Kerr's criticism, Tennessee Williams replied in "Critic Says 'Evasion,' Writer Says 'Mystery,'" New York *Herald Tribune,* April 17, 1955, Sec. 4, pp. 1–2. "I still feel," wrote Williams, "that I deal unsparingly with what I feel is the truth of character. I would never evade it for the sake of evasion, because I was in any way reluctant to reveal what I knew of the truth." Williams insisted that "some mystery should be left in the revelation of character in a play, just as a great deal of mystery is always left in the revelation of character in life." He wished to give the audience "clews, but not certainties."

religious reason and esctasy to Byron's fainting when after many years he saw Lord Clair, to Whitman and the street car conductor in Brooklyn, to Whitman nursing and kissing the dying soldiers in the hospital, to the silly degeneracy of Oscar Wilde at the trial—to the highly proper men who can't bear to have the barber touch their cheeks even —obviously there is no end to the implications, compulsions and so on. Then there is the bi-sexual, but enough. I am not saying that the play would not be clearer, if you like, by having Brick more of an out-and-out case; but that would have started a discussion as to right and wrong and what Tennessee thought of the matter. You astutely perceived that he was not going to do that, and so we go.

Well, that too long remark was leading to my saying that your book, which Simon and Schuster sent me,[5] I have found of great persuasion and often very fine content. (I do sound prissy, please make allowances.) I agree with you about the musical comedy's being the best thing our theatre has produced. The only dissent may be, or may not, from your implications is that most—not all, of course—of the none too many musical comedies that I have seen are so damned dull and without skill as wholes, though good in part. The *fun* seems to have gone out of our theatre pretty much. Please say why, if you can, in some article where are the healthy spirits and the bright joy? Perhaps you can say something about this.

I don't know how much you simplify the case of the larger public. Only the other day a leading publisher told me that there was no pleasure in bringing out a book nowadays—he meant the lack of close response, talk, discussion and all that that goes with a civilized society. I agree with your theory, however; though I think it is well to stress keeping up the older things; I mean there should be some place in the theatre for the interest of cultivated people who remember things past as well as present. (Such as one has in Paris.) But the point here might easily be that, for lack of technique and any continuity, our theatre does not know how to do the plays of older schools as a rule. For instance, before your day, the Guild did Molière's *L'École des Maris,* leaving just Broadway; they turned entirely around the famous first act exposition, and with the theme that to keep your wife faithful you should make her a friend etc., they took from another play scenes with the theme that a young woman cannot be expected by an old husband

5. Walter Kerr, *How Not to Write a Play* (1955).

to be faithful—a direct contradiction. Not a critic bothered to notice that. The efforts at Lorca are hopeless because we cannot get Lorca into either English or our theatre routine, and Olivier's Oedipus was merely collegiate. A silly, leggy costume, changes in costume at the wrong time, a thin voice, a witch-like chorus and so on. As for Shakespeare and Congreve you, Mr. Walter Kerr, know when they are good, when they are all wrong, etc. In sum I do heartily agree with you that the large popular base is the one hopeful thing to talk about, and I also agree with Eric Bentley that what you call the minority theatre[6] has a very important place. You of course would agree with this, or you could not write so shiningly and accurately as you often do in your book about this past detail or style or what not.

I agree with you about the Ibsen and the limitations of that method or school, once so stimulating to some people at least. But the thing about Ibsen that has always stumped me is that the translations are evidently rotten and dead, according to all the Norwegians that I know. On the subject of words your chapter Seventeen is more effective than anything I can say here; that whole discussion is very fine. So I must not be too firm about Ibsen, since a good percent of it is not Ibsen. Ibsen provided some lively imitations however. I remember how excited I was as a student when I saw Mrs. Campbell in her Tanqueray —of course there was Mrs. Campbell and of course I was just getting the drama under my skin. And Pinero was slick enough.

I am sure you are right about the ill effects of Chekhov in many cases. About that we must say that not so much of it is Chekhov's fault. In the first place most of his followers, if you like, don't understand what he is doing; his terrific intensity on the values, the underlying quiver and emotion of life. In the second place you rarely see an even decent production of Chekhov. The Cornell production[7] that you men-

6. According to Kerr, the "minority theatre," modeled upon the work of Ibsen and Chekhov and consciously fashioned to appeal to the intelligentsia, has never produced a great play. He deplored the fact that much of the American theatre tradition in the twentieth century had been shaped by Ibsen and Chekhov. Even Tennessee Williams' *The Glass Menagerie* was "quasi-Chekhovian in both method and content." Kerr repeated his criticism of the Ibsen-Chekhov tradition in "Killing off the Theater," *Harper's Magazine,* CCX (April, 1955), 55–62, mentioned below by Young.

7. Kerr recalled Katharine Cornell's production of *The Three Sisters* which opened on December 21, 1942, at the Ethel Barrymore Theatre. In his review of the performance, Young had declared that six months of playing would bring the entire cast "nearer to the content of 'The Three Sisters' and to the infinite variety of reactions, moods, dramatic transitions, etc., that are there to be explored." See above, Letter 585 and notes.

tion proves nothing about Chekhov. It was appalling from start to finish, a dull translation and a company of what you call stars—the more stars the worse it was. And Guthrie afraid of the real effects and motifs. The first principle of Chekhov playing is the mutual rapport, not these creatures standing about each intending to register his own. This is one of the few holes in your splendid book, not to record this fact. The third point about Chekhov is the translations. In a way they are so wrong that they often give a quite unusual effect. This does not mean that we should try to be Chekhov's type etc. But it is worthwhile to see what he is really like, however bad or good his influence. D'Annunzio is a less important and more inexorable case. His best effects depend too much on his native language to be possible in an English transference.

That fine end to your Harper article[8] leads me to a further feeling that the *Herald Tribune* review of *The Three Sisters* must have distressed you. That is why I wrote my beloved Irita that she must not think me distressed, I was sorry for the paper to be so callow, since it was yours and hers.[9] The remarks about Chekhov were merely kidding in the style of the twenties, and to say my translation was in the nature of satire was incredibly stupid and ignorant except when it was seen beside the reviewer's idea of Chekhov. *You* would never, evidently, have striven for that smartish—*vieux jeu*—estimate, my God! Compared to the other translations mine is very close indeed. It is not that they don't know the Russian far better than I do, it is that they don't see the point Chekhov is making and they can't write lines that have the emphasis etc. for speaking in the theatre. The lines themselves in Russian are really very simple, it is the *combinations* and all that from which the complexity and excitement arises.

I am taking the liberty of sending you a copy of my translation of *The Sea Gull* that the Lunts did. If you read the Russian of Chekhov you may merely glance at it. But if not, I think you might find the preface of some interest.

I want to wish the book every prosperity, and to congratulate you again on that extraordinary review of *Cat on the Hot Tin Roof*. I have

---

8. Kerr concluded his article appealing for a theatre which through activity would interest "a crowd."
9. See above, Letter 858.

seen the play well twice, but must confess I could never have written a review to equal that of yours. Now in my file, and to be reread.

With best wishes I am

Yours sincerely
Stark Young

I hardly ever type, and always badly, this is to spare you my hand-writing.

867 | To Ella Somerville, Oxford, Mississippi

320 East 57th Street
New York
[June 17, 1955]

Dearest Ella,

I have so much on hand before flying away June 30 to Venice that I can't write a decent letter—out of my heart and mind. But I do hope to hear that that sweet Nina is doing well, better even. And I must tell you that Monday after I got to town from the country I was to lunch with Frank Lyell and Eudora Welty. She and I talked of you much and warmly. I liked her for that. I said you added to other Somerville fine qualities something masculine. She said no, feminine. I said then I'd meant womanly. At any rate, I said, I meant something very special, intelligent, wise, witty and fine—as she could take it or leave it —She seemed inclined to take it. Your ears must have burned. I liked her very much—not only her great talent—we all know that—but something unaffected, cerebral, and lovable. And very Southern in a real sense, not the usual rat, tat, tat.

Tell Nina this story for me: Some little dogs were walking along and saw a lot of new coin slot parking stands, "Look, buddie, at the new pay-toilets."

Dear Ella, bless your heart.

Lovingly
Stark

868 | To Walter Kerr, New York Herald Tribune, New York

320 East 57th Street
New York
Friday [June 24, 1955]

Dear Mr. Kerr,

I am not one to correspond the hell out of people, but must tell you before I get off to the country how delighted I was with your letter. I agree entirely with all you say about what seems to be called the "minority theatre," point by point I agree with you.[1] My beloved Louis Kronenberger may see it a bit differently: with all his culture and deep insight he is not, so far as actual theatre goes, a child of the theatre, as it were, and so he admits, bless him!

I evidently read your book without enough perception on my part; at any rate how sound you are about the theatre proceeding first from the popular theatre![2] Molière knew that, and yet there's nobody can take a more sophisticated and civilized audience more roundly and soundly than he can. (Not on our stages however.) Et cetera. All you say in your letter about this warms my heart with its soundness and right intuition and rapport with the stage. The thing that bothers me is that so very often our theatre that might be called the popular theatre is as far removed from the public as Broadway is from the fields of Kansas. It has not even the integrity of the whorehouse. What you say is so succinct and good that I feel like returning your letter so that you can use some of those passages directly in various articles or pages. I hope you have a carbon of your letter, if not I'll return it for you to copy out the various fine, clear statements and use them. Otherwise my intention is to paste the letter into my copy of your book.

As to *The Three Sisters* I wish more than ever that you had seen it.

1. Although Kerr's letter has not survived, his attitude towards the minority theatre is clear from his book *How Not to Write a Play;* see above, Letter 866 and n. 6.

2. Kerr had argued in *How Not to Write a Play* that the masterpieces of Sophocles, Shakespeare, Molière, and other great dramatists had been made possible because of their ability to appeal to the popular as well as the intellectual audience. The presence in the audience of the nonintellectual mass, whose support the dramatist must capture, is, he asserted, an essential prerequisite for great drama.

If I [had] read your book then or this letter, I'd have prodded you. The number of interesting or distinguished people that went is astonishing, some of them more than once. As to the performance it was far better at least than most, and the actors themselves were spellbound with the ease of intention and feeling that was implicit in the translation of their speeches. Louis[3] may have told you of the effect. I hope so.

As for the *Cat on the Hot Roof* etc. I will say that a number of people whose opinions we respect have made that objection about the final solution, very much as you—though much better said—put the case.[4] Not to compare the play with *Hamlet,* I must say, nevertheless, that I find the case parallel. In *Hamlet* it is admitted even by scholars who want to be authors that Shakespeare could not find the solution, as the Quarto and Folio edition might seem to indicate. The profound appeal of the play is related to that of course. Tennessee Williams' Brick is not Hamlet, obviously, but he seems to me to remain in the unsatisfactory and poignant region—he is what he is, see it as you will, and so is the family around him—and the distinct desire for a husbandly screw in the young wife is only one of the waves that beat against all this in him. It is a pity that the word *mendacity* was introduced. The impossibility of everybody in the play so far as exact communication goes, the shaken relationships, et cetera, are what the play ends by being about. In a Southern family that means a great deal. I don't say that Tennessee did it so very well (But neither did Shakespeare.) By the way, after the White Barn and Williams, Mildred Dunnock took me to see Arthur Kennedy[5] and others. There was a discussion of your book, which I crowned blissfully by quoting your fine letter, and all ended greatly to your credit. I think your one thing to watch is not to be adopted by the saucy smarties. You are much too good for that. Please forgive so many words on my part. As Pascal said I didn't have time to write a shorter letter.

I am flying next Thursday to Venice, have an apartment, a cook and

3. Louis Kronenberger.
4. See above, Letter 866, n. 4.
5. Arthur Kennedy (b. 1914), actor, has appeared in such plays as *Death of a Salesman* (1948), *The Crucible* (1953), and *Becket* (1961) and in a number of motion pictures, including *The Glass Menagerie* (1950), *The Man from Laramie* (1955), *Peyton Place* (1957), *Elmer Gantry* (1960), and *Lawrence of Arabia* (1962).

a cat (I haven't seen any of them). But at least I won't see Noel
Coward at the Lido, undressed as Gandhi. I do wish you well.

Cordially yours
Stark Young

P.S.

I think you should show this letter to Irita Van Doren. She has led
the Herald-Tribune book portion into what I think is the best in this
country. (Other people think so too. The pap of the Sunday *Times*
grows weaker and weaker—but has a public doubtless. Can you imagine how lovely it is in Garden City or Bedford Village to find that you
have understood Cervantes in fifteen minutes!)

Please don't let ideas of Philistine stupidity make you rebound
further than you really feel and think, dear Mr. Kerr. Again, what a
very wonderful and exciting [*sic*] your Chapter XVII is! [6]

S.Y.

869 | To Anne Sharkey and Jane Wasey, New York

[Venice]
July 6 [1955]

Dear Miss Annie and Miss Janie,

Since we are five hours ahead of you we had a good deal of figuring
to do in order to tell just what you were doing at various times during
the week-end of the Fourth. "Now they are just awakening and having
coffee," "now"—et cetera. We thought with so much pleasure of your
being there and hoped the flowers were bursting out gloriously for
you—the rhododendrons especially. Here we have been having brilliant mornings and then toward evening it clouds up and rains. That is
not so good as I hope fell to your lot.

Ada, the cook, turns out to be mild and pleasant and modest as to

6. Chapter 17, "Worst Foot Forward," presents a commentary upon the use of verse
and prose in the stage and motion picture media during the past thirty years.

her cooking. That means only breakfast and lunch. We have just had a good breakfast, with ham, yogurt, jam and tomatoes—to Ada's astonishment. Madame R.[7] quietly consumed Wales' cigarettes. She would be a nightmare if you had her around. Fortunately when she does turn up again—she has a room in the apartment below—we can always have an engagement to go out to meals. She has told the owner of the house that we are friends of Mr. Sell's,[8] to whom she is so indebted that she is glad to let his friends have her place. Thus she "gets no rent," to a great advantage in papers, stamps etc. She wanted to show she had been to Paul Bourget's[9] house and so quoted a remark of his —a simple one—and said that she was going to quote his words and that if I didn't know French she would translate it for me. I said modestly that I could understand the French at the Theatre Français but hadn't heard hers yet. We all three got on sweetly however, and let's hope she stays in England. Please tell Henry that I am delighted with having the apartment. Wales is writing to thank him and so on, since he had all the dealings with Henry and Reuch in the matter. We think we are very fortunate.

Zue[1] wrote of a roaring happy time and that she would be in Trieste the tenth instead of the seventh. She will telephone us. I think her library room here will be comfortable all right. It will be very nice to have her. Please remember not to make yourself a chore of the place, don't bother to keep things on the grounds as if we were there and bothering with it. Just be as happy as you can.

Lovingly
Stark

7. Young and Bowman had rented the apartment of Mrs. Alice Reuch and her brother, Rudi Reuch, a photographer for *Town and Country* magazine.

8. Henry Blackman Sell (b. 1889), editor of *Town and Country* and president of Sell's Specialties, Inc., a food products company, had an apartment in the building where Young and Bowman lived and was associated in business with Anne Sharkey. Earlier Sell had been an editor of *Harper's Bazaar* and president of Vitamins Plus, Inc.

9. The reference is to Paul Bourget (1852–1935), French critic, poet, and novelist, born in Amiens.

1. Margaret A. Sharkey.

870 | To Julia Young Robertson, Santa Monica, California

Athens
July 22 [1955]

Dearest Sister,

We had a fine flight from Venice to Rome—got there around ten. Lunch with Father Anselmo, my scholar friend from the Vatican—plane to Athens from 4—really got in from NYC & Paris late and left at six. Clear, beautiful weather. Rome hot, noisy and crowded. This country here comes back to me as so like around Austin and in Mexico, though with more things that are lovely—olive groves, shrines, pine trees, temple columns—that was the trip yesterday afternoon to Sunion—dinner there—home by 9.30—left here 4.30. The auto bus put it all under a reasonable fee. $3.70 including dinner.

Today we go to the museum for the morning, then a trip from 3.30 on to see the many points in Athens. It's hot exactly like San Antonio and Austin (though very lovely in the shade) and walking all over the city with the sights wide apart would about kill anybody. The trip will be $1.70. My new suit in Venice ($80) turned out well—some retouching when I get back. Very fine stuff, very thin, grey with small stripes.

You all will be starting for Santa Monica tomorrow. I hope it turns out a success for your whole stay. And will last till good weather in Austin.

We may and probably will get back to Venice by Aug. 3—in which case I'll invite Mary R.[2] and her friends to Florian's at tea time. I'll send her a card from here.

My ink is giving out—the flight (Wales' writing thing now) at 17000 ft. made the ink ooze out of the pen—as it did on the flight from NYC.

There were miles of oleanders on the road to Sunion—in full bloom, thicker than I have ever seen. We leave Monday on that five day cruise of the Islands that Wales bought in New York—I imagine we'll fly to Rome about August 1. Very different from the old days on trains and boats—which when it is as hot as this would be something to take.

2. Mary C. Rice.

Wales says give you all some messages from him. He is enjoying himself greatly—more so too because he has a fine job waiting for him when he gets back.

I hope this finds you happily settled—

Love to both
Stark

871 | To Julia Young Robertson, Santa Monica, California

866 San Vio
Venice
August 2 [1955]

Dearest Sister,

We are settled here again, as I wrote you yesterday, and feel very much repaid for our Greek trip. The scenes, the art, the guide's talks were very fine. I think I told you that. But I must tell you about a young Englishman,[3] about 23–24—just graduated at Durham University—mad about the Greek thing—art and country. In Mikonos, living in a fisherman's house by the Aegean Sea. In the morning he had come over to Milos—nearby—to hear and see with the guide— Madame Alexandrya—whom he admired for the great knowledge, etc. I met up with him, talked a bit, on various good subjects—so then he stuck by me all the time we were seeing the place—explaining, keeping my Dr. Watts knee from making me stumble etc. It was very rough going. After lunch on the boat the tour was to go to Mikonos— nearby—he lived there—said he'd be back in the afternoon and see me. So he took me in charge again—insisted I see some things I would not have seen—meet some of the simple people he knew, etc., and finally put us in the row boat long after the other passengers had gone to the ship, and so told me a devoted goodbye. A lovely, fresh spirit and I enjoy thinking of such a person. I'd have been flattered by all this at-

3. Although he mentioned the young Englishman several times in letters, Young never identified him by name.

tention but with such a person that would be too cheap a response. Such is life.

He seemed to know all the temple ruins, mosaics, shrine and so on by heart, and kept me quite alive to take it all in. Talked about the metres of *Oedipus Rex,* the English attempts at the prosody of Greek poetry, the adaptations of Chaucer and other things that nobody seems to think about any more. And very fresh and modest and candid. I was lucky.

Dee Nelson had written me that Cousin Cad would soon leave them—a very sweet letter. Thank you for my share of the flowers. Cousin Cad besides loving us had an immediate appreciation of Ben that always pleased me very much.[4]

Mary Rice is due tomorrow. I have left a note at the Europa—a lovely hotel—asking her to set aside a time—in the late afternoon—for coming to a little party at Florian's for her and her friends.

I am glad your apartment is nice. You are lucky to find one these days, it seems. I will look up the brocade or brocatelle or velvet soon and send samples. You are one of the fortunate–unfortunate people who have brains enough to know what you want.

My new suit seems quite promising. If you see the rather recent book—*The Wilder Shores of Love* [5] I think you and Ben would enjoy it. Anne Sharkey gave it to me when I was leaving. Elsie gave me a delightful new book, Boswell's Journal and note on his tour in Europe, 1765–1766.[6]

Wales sends his love—he is loving Venice more than ever.

Love to both
Stark

4. Young's "Cousin Cad," Caroline Charlotte McGehee, died July 23, 1955.
5. Lesley Blanch (Mrs. Romain Gary), *The Wilder Shores of Love* (1954).
6. Mrs. Huntington Adams had given Young a copy of *Boswell on the Grand Tour: Italy, Corsica, and France, 1765–1766,* edited by Frank Brady and Frederick A. Pottle (1955).

872 | To Anne Sharkey and Jane Wasey, New York

866 San Vio
Venice
August 3 [1955]

Dearest Annie and Janie,

It's a very pleasant thought to imagine at least that you can escape some of that heat we hear of in New York. In the sun Greece was as hot as the worst Texas, in the shade delightful. Zue[7] has come and gone—a most perfect guest—we enjoyed seeing her—and what an intrepid traveller! I believe she'd set out alone at midnight across the Sahara if the idea appealed to her! She looked very pretty and very well, though some of her travel must have been a beating.

I'm sorry that stove bothered you. I offered to show how to work it, but Janie said she knew and I grew calm. I always think she can do anything she sets out to do. The whole thing is letting it catch on well before adding a lot of coal. I put a gallon jar of kerosene there to start the fires with. Just pour it from a can however. The bottle might have enough evaporated gas to explode a bit.

I hope the raspberries had enough rain to be good, and the numberless blackberries. The grapes ought by now to be in perhaps. The cherry tomatoes are God's blessing, even as salad.

You wouldn't know the apartment if you saw it, with the small mess taken out, off the wall et cetera. The furniture seen thus is quite dignified. Alice[8] seems to be still in England. Ada[9] is doing very well indeed and the cat is very cosy and gentle (and lonely). That's good to hear about Gide[1]—I know he'll prefer you all to us, but who doesn't? The stove doesn't matter, the furnace I mean; we left it merely to burn papers in. As to its seeming indecent now that makes little impression on me. It seems that everybody is taking off everything possible this year—its gets quite tiresome, so much back, legs, arms, bosoms!!!

7. Margaret A. Sharkey.
8. Mrs. Alice Reuch, owner of the apartment rented by Young and Bowman in Venice.
9. The cook.
1. Anne Sharkey and Jane Wasey, vacationing at Young's and Bowman's house in Waccabuc, were taking care of Young's cat, Gide.

I hope your days go happily and that Janie will get some fine work done. She'd be surprised to know how often this summer I've wished she could be looking at some piece of sculpture with me, and that Miss Annie were along with us. It seems sad that the Apostles were the only people we know of who could be in two places at once.[2]

Love to you both
Stark

873 | To Charles Scribner, Jr., Charles Scribner's Sons,

866 San Vio
Venice
August 9 [1955]

Dear Charlie,

It seems a long time since I was at your office for a little visit—so many things happen that the calendar is stretched. For one thing Bowman, my architect friend, and I have been to Greece, Athens, Eleusis and so on, plus a week's tour of the Isles. Thanks to the Romans, Turks, Christians and goats the remains on Greece are ruins indeed, but there is still plenty to fill your mind and days to come. Thanks to my old friend Pausanias many places come alive—I have not owned those six volumes for nothing.[3]

The theatre at Epidauras was no longer so beautiful, but practically, it was astonishing.

You can stand in the middle of the orchestra—on the spot of the altar to Dionysus—and strike a match or tear a piece of paper, and in the farthest reaches of the seats it is completely audible, and that means to all the audience of 14,000 to 16,000 who go now to productions there at certain times. The Plymouth in New York holds a thousand, sixteen times that is quite an audience.

2. Young was fond of this quotation; see above, Letters 537 and 560 with notes.
3. *Pausanias's Description of Greece,* translated by J[ames]. G[eorge]. Frazer (6 vols., 1898, 1913).

I heard a French lady say an amusing thing on the steps just below the maidens on the other side of this. The guard had cautioned her to keep away from those steps. "He must think I'm English," she said, a nice crack at Lord Elgin—the third maiden you see takes the place of the one now in the *British Museum.*

Charlie, I do always value and think with deep pleasure of your consideration and friendship.

I hope your summer is a happy one.

Stark

874 | To Julia Young Robertson, Santa Monica, California

866 San Vio
Venice
August 10 [1955]

Dearest Sister,

I went to Rubelli's yesterday, saw all the samples they had of satins— the green nice greens, but nothing of the tan in them that you want— I can see you are right for that room. The brocade I sent yesterday— both Wales and I think it looks very fine and it has a good deal of tan in it. But a hotel manager told me of a place where they get their curtains, upholstery, etc.—linens. Some of them may be good. I have seen some stunning pieces in windows. I have also seen some heavenly bedroom curtain stuff—thin and summery. Nothing is cheap anymore—except compared with NYC and not always then. I don't need much, but I don't even ask prices at the antique shops. The Venetian glass prices are crazy if one remembers the past. I'll see if the linen place has anything and if so will send you samples. We have plenty of time fortunately.

The crowds of tourists just now are terrific, but they don't touch us here. In Spain, Portugal, Strasburg and all over Europe there is the same situation—no hotel space etc. Ernest de Weerth has written that all that Wagner part of Germany is appalling, and he is known there, has cousins there, etc. Most of the tourists here are French and German, but there are plenty of Americans. One sees all these most in Piazza San Marco and the cafes there—the other night there were about 10,000 people in the Piazza, using some of them the chairs from a municipal concert the night before. Lots of these were of course Italians.

We went last night to *Madame Butterfly,* given in a large piazza with house wall, church walls, and palace wall all round, and the moon coming out. About 5000 people—the best seats 1200 lire—$1.80. The woman who sang Madame Butterfly was very touching and lovely. She was a delicate figure to see and her voice was very sympathetic and moving. The opera is too much drawn out and pulls at your heart-strings to a degree and with an immediacy that is certainly not the finest art. But it does floor you. I'll never see it again, even stupidly done at the Metropolitan. I was sunk afterward of course. Thought of the sad things in our family, and of Stark, and you and Ben, and how you have made it into something worthy of him and of you. But at what a price! Even though it makes you more deep and wonderful, but again at what a price! I thought of Papa—You told me at Mr. Travis Taylor's [4] to look at him, he looked "so pretty," you said. I had looked at him but have never said so. He looked white and proud and beautiful. Poor Papa, great, rare virtues and character, great faults, naked impulses often, and all in all in the end helpless. One of the fine things about Cousin Cad—she really appreciated Papa. Said people talked of Cousin Fannie and Cousin Sallie getting us educated so far as was in their power—what about Dr. Young? He had struggled to keep us from being just like the rest of the Como young people, etc.

Edward's wife [5] asked for my address. Said there was a library to be built in Como and they talked of naming it for me, and that's that. It took me a long time and much desuetude to have any patience with Como. I know only too well what Cousin Cad meant.

It has turned cool here—cooler than Wales and I prefer it, but will doubtless warm up right off. I hope your cool weather keeps up. Wales sends his love to you both.

Lovingly
Stark

4. Prominent landowner and businessman in Como, Mississippi.
5. Mrs. Albert Edward Nelson, Jr.

875 | To Norman Dello Joio, New York

866 San Vio
Venice
August 19 [1955]

Dearest Norman,

How often I have thought of you! And of Grace! And that adorable Vittoria.[6] Venice is unbelievably jammed with tourists but having an apartment, and in a not too foreign-filled part of town, has made us very fortunate. And the cook and housewoman, Ada, who came with the apartment has proved a treasure indeed. You could be very rich in America and not get such service. We have breakfast and lunch here and go out for dinner—and usually sit afterwards in Piazza San Marco—very fair music at Florian's—for a long time. This place is inexhaustibly beautiful, the walks in the numberless side streets with their canals—at night especially, are wonderful. The men sweep the stone streets twice a day. I have never seen a city half as clean. Lately we had a short trip in Greece—Athens, Sunion, Mycenae, Corinth, Eleusis and so on, and then a six day and seven nights tour of the Isles, living on the boat the while. So many incredible things, such memories, such haunting moments in history—all very much up my street. I wish you could have been along, at Rhodes especially.

I met by chance a young Englishman,[7] just out of Durham University, who was there last summer also—that was in Delos—and is mad about the whole thing and the simple Greek people. He took me in hand—went everywhere our leader-lecturer took us—then came to the next island that afternoon and was with me till nine o'clock, when I had to go back to my boat. Such a fine quality, so warm and bright and full of the poetry of the place and the people! How fortunate I was! How sweet people can be, sometimes! I'll doubtless never see him again, but the mind and heart will always be with me in recollection.

Wales is constantly happy at just being in Venice. He has a very fine job with a young Rockefeller branch—Mrs. Tate[8]—for a manor

6. Norman Dello Joio's daughter.
7. See above, Letter 871.
8. Probably a reference to Mrs. H. Clinch Tate for whom Bowman subsequently designed a house in Southern Pines, North Carolina.

house in Maryland when he gets back, so that's an ease to his mind. He has another job underway now. He sends his love to you and Grace.

I hope you have been able to write some fine things this summer, and that the place you rented has proved entirely satisfactory. The number of cities where your piece with the Philadelphia orchestra went, in Europe, is quite dazzling. I delight in the thought of it for your sake, and all our sakes, dear Norman. I hope Grace[9] and the children keep fit—bless their hearts!

Affectionately,
Stark

876 | To Allen Tate, University of Minnesota, Minneapolis, Minnesota

866 San Vio
Venice
August 26 [1955]

Dearest Allen,

As you see by the enclosed from Bowman's secretary, who is looking after our mail, we had an inexplicable delay with some of our mail, so that your fine letter of June 29 reached me only yesterday. I don't have to tell you how welcome it was. I will keep it, and it will give me at times a sense of life much needed and an assurance of your affection, which I don't have any doubts about that stay with me very long.[1] But

9. Mrs. Norman Dello Joio.
1. The background of this letter is supplied by Tate's comments in a letter to Young, June 29: "I am saddened by it [an earlier letter from Young], and even a little shocked that you should imagine for an instant that my old and deep devotion to you has abated one jot in these more than thirty years. I don't write many letters, and I scarcely write them at all to my dearest friends. You, my dearest Stark, are the dearest, in a most special sense that we both understand. I have seen you and me, over many years, sharing a kind of secret about the world in which we live—partly a Southern matter and partly the sense of the high style in life and art, opposed to the degradation of the sensibility and the *conscience* in this present world. I hope you will ponder these matters, and will return from Greece perfectly secure in your feeling for Caroline and me."

St. Paul's remark that we are all of one flesh, with its profound meaning has a close application to people especially who love each other. I don't have to tell you any more; but only that I value your letter beyond words, and bless you.

The summer in Venice has been very fine, plus a brief trip to Greece. I was there for a short visit years ago—and a week's cruise of the Isles. That speaks for itself. On the way there we had several hours over in Rome, and Father Anselmo came to lunch in Trastevere with us. A gentle, lovely man. He is not happy about having to leave Rome and come home in a few weeks. We talked of you all.

I hope Nancy is all right and Percy still prospering. It will be fine some day to see you and my beloved Caroline again. Wales sends love to you.

Lovingly
Stark

877 | To Leah Salisbury, New York

866 San Vio
Venice
September 3, 1955

Dearest Leah,

I thought when I finished the new version of Machiavelli's *La Mandragola*[2] this spring that I was through for life with translating. But as usual I take your sweet advice—the idea of a whole Chekhov season in my translation is good.[3] I can see that. I expect to be home soon after the middle of October, and can finish the translation by the

---

2. See above, Letter 862 and n. 4.

3. In anticipation of presenting an entire season of Chekhov plays at the Fourth Street Theatre, David Ross had started negotiations with Leah Salisbury for the rights to Young's translations. Having already translated *The Sea Gull, The Cherry Orchard,* and *The Three Sisters,* Young was confident he could finish *Uncle Vanya* in time to meet Ross's schedule.

middle of November, you can tell Mr. Ross, perhaps a week earlier. I'll get a copy here. Bowman sends greetings.

Lovingly
Stark

878 | To Julia Young Robertson, Austin, Texas

Spoleto
October 9, 1955

Dearest Sister,

I wrote you of our plans of going to Rome with stops at great places like Ravenna, Rimini, Fano etc.— and so now after a day in Assisi, which is more beautiful than after 20 years I remembered it, we get to Rome tomorrow and fly from there Friday the 14th on the only 1st class plane that week—one a week—but we have changed our plans about Spain. Europe has turned into a cold spell—here in a very nice hotel there is no heat—it's about like Christmas often in Austin, and Spain, except in some good Madrid hotel, will be worse. We want especially to go to Santa Maria Compostela [4]—far off in northwest Spain—and it will be deadly—so it all seems foolish, for somewhat over exercised people to take that on, and tomorrow in Rome if we can get the space on the plane, we plan to go straight to New York instead of to Madrid, that would mean New York on the 15th instead of the 29th. We ought to be grateful for the wonderful trip we have had. It seems almost incredible that we should have had it.

I'll start finishing up the translation of *Uncle Vanya* when I get back. *The Cherry Orchard* opens on the 17th, for a run of six or eight weeks. I don't know how effective *Uncle Vanya* will be as an acting play. It is famous enough of course.

4. Young and Bowman may have wished to see the renowned, twelfth-century church, the Colegiata de Santa Maria la Real de Sar, whose interior columns are not set perpendicular but tilted at such an angle that spectators often believe the pillars are about to fall into the aisles.

I hope everything goes well for you and Ben. Wales sends his love—he hates to leave Italy.

Love to both
Stark

879 | To John Hall Wheelock, Charles Scribner's Sons, New York

Hotel de la Ville
Rome
October 11, 1955

Dear Jack,

This morning by way of a birthday present I got a lovely little letter from Phyllis. In it among many kind and gentle things she told me of your book of selected poems that you are soon to give us.[5] And so I must write you and say how pleased I am and how proud that life and fortune rule thus. I know you are having fits choosing and perhaps retouching, though I don't remember places where that was very much needed. I'll look forward, as you can imagine, with much anticipation to such a volume of yours. And I take real pride in this one more instance of what a fine and discriminating man Charlie Scribner is. I'd hate to be any other publisher that I know of.

Wales has a call to go to Paris to do some advising on a very grand Louis Quinz house,[6] so that we fly home by that way instead of by Spain, as we had planned. Whatever happens we'll be home by the end of the month—before the 29th. I don't look forward very much to

5. Wheelock was preparing his *Poems Old and New* (1956).
6. Writing to his sister, Julia Young Robertson, on this same date, Young commented: "Arthur Sachs has written asking Wales to come by Paris and advise him about the house. . . . Sachs plans some alterations in his grand house so that when he feels like it he can cut off the two upper stories into another dwelling. There will be room left in plenty, Goodness knows."

New York, but I do look forward to seeing such beloved friends as you and Phyllis.

Thank Phyllis for her very sweet letter.

Affectionately
Stark

Please remember me to Charlie. Wales sends his love to you both (how much better and more usable our Southern you all is!)

880 | To Leah Salisbury, New York

320 East 57th Street
New York
November 26, 1955

Dearest Leah,

So that's that as to French and *Uncle Vanya*.[7] Working on it I have realized more and more what a fine play it is—his best in many respects—and it may do well at the Fourth Street Theatre. There will be some requests at least concerning it, but they can be heaped on your kind shoulders.

Thanks for this last check. I have seen a number of performances of *The Cherry Orchard,* and the response from the audience is often quite remarkable.

There was some misunderstanding about the date of publication of my new book [8] at Scribner's—a revised edition of the first two books of criticism—long since out of print. I was in the country, after being in Europe, and so only these last few days have had access to my book. So naturally I am sending one to you, with much love and appreciation. Charlie Scribner himself was interested in the book sufficiently to take entire charge of the issue, even putting it all into new type. That

7. Since his return from Europe, Young had been preparing his translation of Chekhov's *Uncle Vanya* for Ross's production. Meanwhile, *The Cherry Orchard* had opened on October 18 at the Fourth Street Theatre. Ross was using Young's translation. Leah Salisbury was negotiating with Samuel French and Company for publication rights to Young's work.

8. Scribner's single volume reprint of Young's *The Flower in Drama and Glamour.*

was indeed a compliment. And the result is a very fine, choice volume, jacket, the pages, the frontispiece, that last quite a dazzling design in print. I was fortunate.

Bless you, Leah

Love to you
Stark

881 | To Richard Hayes,[9] New York

320 East 57th Street
New York
December 1, 1955

Dear Mr. Hayes,

I have just read your very beautiful and remarkable review of *The Cherry Orchard* at the 4th Street Theatre.[1] If you read Chekhov in Russian the points you establish would still be most valuable and important. If you don't read Chekhov in Russian the discernment and sense of him is just about brilliant. If it were not for that fact and your kind reference to the reissue of my two books of theatre pieces, I doubtless would not be troubling you with this letter, and especially in my scrawl—I am lately back from Italy and my typewriter is at the cleaner's.

This is to speak of the fact that you didn't mention the translation. I am sorry I have no copy of the Scribner *The Sea Gull* to send you, but the edition is long since out of print, and the French & Co. edition I have no copy of. The preface to that play would be an easier way for you to read what I have done with Chekhov.

On the copy of *The Cherry Orchard* I have marked a passage about the bookcase; it illustrates how they can miss Chekhov's real meaning, and how impossible for the actor to say such writing is, not to mention

9. Richard Hayes, teacher, writer, and drama critic, has written criticism for several publications and taught at Hunter College. In October, 1952, he became drama critic for the *Commonweal* magazine.

1. Richard Hayes, "The Stage: The Cherry Orchard," *Commonweal,* LXIII (December 2, 1955), 223–25.

its making Chekhov sound fuzzy-headed or "profoundly subtle" etc.

If you will trouble to run over the prefaces a little I think you will see what I am not going to heap upon you.

I have called up some of the actors and told them to hurry out and get the *Commonweal*. They have worked very hard, and they will tell you to a man what they are constantly saying: "how happy they are in the speeches" et cetera.

I have just finished the last touches on *Uncle Vanya* for the 4th Street Theatre. And as well as I know what the translators have done to the other plays, I was amazed at the renderings of *Uncle Vanya,* turgid lines, missed Chekhov's *theatrical* point in certain words, such, for instance, as turning Chekhov's

"Men will not remember but God will remember"
into
"Man is forgetful but God remembers."

Keep that sort of thing up and you kill many things in Chekhov without anybody's suspecting it.

I could give you many many instances, especially in the longer speeches where Chekhov has a rough time, but will refrain.

I send you the paper copies of *The Cherry Orchard* and *The Three Sisters* in case you'd care to have them. *The Sea Gull* I haven't even a paper copy of.

Lately I was reading in a Gide journal and saw a translation by a British scholar that I can't resist quoting in this translation business. The famous lines from Racine's *Phèdre.*

> Ariane ma soeur, de quel amour blessée
> Vous mourûtes aux bords òu vous fûtes laissée!
> You die on the shores where you were left—

This became

> You succumbed on the shores where you were abandoned.[2]

Apart from translations I would have written you anyway about so extraordinary an article on so misunderstood a subject.

> Yours sincerely
> Stark Young

2. See *The Journals of Andre Gide,* translated by Justin O'Brien (1948), 2, 239. The passage occurs in Racine's *Phèdre* (1.3.253–54).

882 | To Louis Kronenberger, Brandeis University, Waltham, Massachusetts

Monterrey, Mexico
December 30, 1955

Dear Louis,

I brought your lovely letter with me and will take it back with me for my files. It goes without saying that I do indeed value your judgment and opinion. I think of you always as a man of a very fine and warm distinction.

Charlie Scribner took a direct interest in my book and saw it himself into its present form.[3] I am very proud the volume as a book materially speaking, [*sic*] partly because it is a beautiful piece of book-making and partly because Charlie Scribner's opinion means a great deal to me. He seems almost too good to be true, when you know him really and have a genuine relationship with him. I am very fortunate.

I liked very much the chance to see you at the theatre and your stopping by for a moment, necessarily brief. The review of *Six Characters* in *Time* seemed to me excellent.[4] I think the analysis was capital and that final point sadly right. I think Mr. Guthrie took the sharp cerebral edge off the play, very sadly so, and the evening didn't therefore add up. I hope you wrote that review; we are always happy when some one we love comes off shining.

I am sorry to hear about your mother's accident, and hope things have been mending as well as may be. These things break your heart.

Please give my love to Emmy. Bowman and I will hope to see you all soon.

Affectionately
Stark

3. *The Flower in Drama and Glamour.*
4. [Louis Kronenberger] "The Theater: Old Play in Manhattan" [review of *Six Characters in Search of an Author,* by Luigi Pirandello], *Time,* LXVI (December 26, 1955), 30. In the concluding paragraph of his article, Kronenberger observed that Tyrone Guthrie's direction "enlivens the evening more than it illumines the play."

883 | To Leah Salisbury, New York

320 East 57th Street
New York
Monday [January 16, 1956]

Dearest Leah,

You are sweet to bother with my pygmy affairs—I do appreciate it. Franchot tells me on the telephone that the rehearsals of *Uncle Vanya* are going well.[5] He likes having Signe Hasso.[6] Mr. Ross of course doesn't know what he thinks in general. I went last night to the final performance[7]—Fair, just fair. Mr. Ross has been neglecting them for Uncle Vanya, and he is really tired and wants now only laurels. You are right, he has things for the theatre, but I told him if he went in for the way he was annoyed at you and the way he acted about the contracts, he'd ruin himself in the theatre which I said he didn't know enough yet to realize.

Lovingly
Stark

5. Young had finished his translation of *Uncle Vanya* early in December and had urged Franchot Tone to play the leading role. Late in December, Young wrote to Leah Salisbury: "As to Franchot I asked him and wrote him that this might be a milestone in his career, which had not always gone to his credit, considering his great value, in which I have always believed. I would not have wanted him to try this experiment if I had not believed that it would be fine for him in many directions. Outside of some letters and telephone talks I certainly left him to his own considerations. He evidently did a lot of thinking, with the translation in hand, and took his time, while Mr. Ross kept telephoning me and asking if I had heard from him, why didn't I call him and soon. Evidently the first consideration in Franchot's mind is that it is a wise thing for him to do—certainly on the plane of excellence. He and I have always been pretty high-minded friends, and each trusts the other. I have often grieved over his turns of fortune, reckless climaxes etc., and have many times defended him."

6. Signe Hasso (b. 1918), actress, made her first appearance in New York as Judith in *Golden Wings* (1941). Subsequently, she has appeared in such productions as *Edwina Black* (1950), *Glad Tidings* (1951), and *The Final Moment* (1959). She has also appeared in motion pictures and on television.

7. Young refers to the final performance of *The Cherry Orchard*, which closed, after 104 performances, on January 15, 1956. *Uncle Vanya* opened January 31, 1956.

884 | To Norma Long Brickell, Jackson, Mississippi

320 East 57th Street
New York
February 6, 1956

Dearest Norma,

I was delighted to hear your news (and thank you for the Glasgow clipping). Frank Lyell told me Christmas in Texas that you were expected in Jackson, had some of your things in your quarters there, in the house of people who loved you very much.

I had a lot of letters from Miss Glasgow but gave them to a friend [8] some time ago who wanted them for a collection he has. I don't suppose he'd give them back to me. He lent some of them to a man in some college who is doing some sort of book.[9] They were safely returned. I'm sorry to hear about Mr. Cabell.[1] I never met him but Miss Glasgow seemed devoted to him.

My translation of Chekhov's *Uncle Vanya* is turning away hundreds every night, I am told. I have just finished the translation of a long Pirandello play for Roger Stevens.[2] Wales is busy with a house in Greenwich and another—a very fine, large one—near Warrenton, Virginia.

He sends you his love.

Bless you, dear Norma.

Affectionately
Stark

8. Lawton Campbell.
9. With Young's permission, Campbell had sent the letters to Blair Rouse, at Emory University, who was then preparing for publication a volume of Ellen Glasgow's letters.
1. James Branch Cabell (1879–1958), novelist, author of *Jurgen* (1919) and many other novels chronicling life in the imaginary land of Poictesme, had been in failing health since the spring of 1955.
2. Stevens had commissioned Young to translate Pirandello's *Vestire gli ignudi* so that Kim Stanley might determine whether she wished to appear in it. Although Young delivered the translation to Stevens and Kim Stanley on March 2, the project was later abandoned.

885 | To Julian Huxley, London, England

320 East 57th Street
New York
February 6, 1956

Dearest Julian,

Your essay[3] came just before I left for Texas Christmas. I took it
with me and read it twice there, and since I came home once again—
(and it's not short). Obviously some of it is out of my range but the
major part of it is not. I was filled with admiration. The whole project,
as it were, and progression of it shows the effect of practice in speaking
to audiences one way or another. That means a very fine exposition
and a clear and compelling movement from section to section in the
thinking. These qualities in the essay get to the point where they are
really quite thrilling—(as they might be in art). I am lending my
copy to Charlie Scribner—the head now of that fine firm and a really
educated man—(a thesis on Lucretius, a friend of Einstein's and
student of logic and great books et cetera, and a modest, remarkable
person). I think he will be greatly impressed by this essay. Thank you
indeed for sending it.

I'd have written sooner but have been tied down tight doing a
translation of *Vestire gli ignudi* of Pirandello's—a commission from
Roger Stevens,[4] who owns the Empire State Building and backs a good
many stage events. It remains to be seen whether we go on to try an
adaptation, for use by one of our best younger players. In any case I
get paid for this literal translation—the only other translation into
English is very free and fancy and a long way from the Pirandello. If
they decide to adopt something out of it then I can be in on that if I
want to do it. That's in the lap of the gods.

My translation of Chekhov's *Uncle Vanya* has made a great im-

3. On October 18, 1955, Huxley delivered the first Alfred P. Sloan Lecture, "Cancer:
A Cross-roads of Biology." The lecture was later expanded as "Cancer Biology: Com-
parative and Genetic," *Biological Reviews,* XXXI (1956), 474–514; and "Cancer
Biology: Viral and Epigenetic," *Biological Reviews,* XXXII (1957), 1–37. In 1958,
Huxley published the essays in book form as *Biological Aspects of Cancer.*
4. See the preceding letter and notes.

pression. The public knew only things like Mrs. Garnett's,[5] which is not only stuffy but often misses the point. Anybody with fair brains and a stage sense can straighten much of Chekhov out from the dictionary. Russians especially are raving about the Russian quality of my lines. After all Chekhov's Russian as such is as simple as language can be made to be. They are turning away hundreds of people every night. This is something new indeed with Chekhov. I asked Franchot Tone to do it—instead of Broadway or $4000 a week in Hollywood. He did so, and is having a sort of triumph. I hope it will be a new mark in his career—a very fine quality, but he has in a sense got lost.

I have a fine letter from Juliette—and do agree with her about the Museum of Modern Art![6] It's very fine to have you and Juliette like my book. John Gielgud wrote me a fine letter about it—says he has bought fourteen copies to give here and there, et cetera.

I hope your flight toward the Mediterranean has been a great success. A picture I saw from Cannes with the snow and all didn't look promising. Perhaps you went on to Italy, really to the south part of it. Cosí la vita. Bowman sends cordial regards—he is very busy with a fine house in Virginia. I wish I could see you.

Affectionately
Stark

Thanks for the card from Orange—how I envy you two sweet people!
S.

5. Constance Black Garnett (1862–1946), wife of the British author David Garnett, began to publish English translations of major Russian authors in the 1890s. Her translation of *Uncle Vanya* was included in *The Plays of Tchehov* (2 vols., 1923).

6. In a letter to Young, January 4, 1956, Juliette Huxley expressed disapproval of an exhibition at the Museum of Modern Art. She characterized much of what she saw as "tripe and rubbish in expensive paints" and concluded that she was no follower of "blind ugliness."

886 | To Ella Somerville, Oxford, Mississippi

320 East 57th Street
New York
February 7, 1956

Dearest Ella,

I think the enclosed costly ad from the *New York Times* Sunday will please you.[7] My translation seems to have given New York another conception of Chekhov. At any rate they are turning away literally hundreds every night. Can you beat that! The cast is unusually good. Franchot Tone gave up Broadway and $4000 a week in Hollywood when I asked him to be in this fine play—for the play's sake and for his.[8] We are all rewarded, for his performance has turned out to be a triumph for him.

I wonder if a silly little reminder of Venice that I sent you some time before Christmas ever got to you. (It was really made in Vienna they said.) At any rate it was of no importance—just sort of pretty for travelling—and a kind of little message from me to a beloved friend.

I hope Nina is going as well as may be. Julia's hip that she broke at New Year's has just let her leave the hospital—in a chair till March—then crutches a while. A rotten shame that these people we love can't escape these ills. It makes so little sense.

Please give my love to all the family.

Stark

7. Young enclosed a two-column advertisement for *Uncle Vanya* from the New York *Times*, February 5, 1956, Sec. 2, p. 2. Below the heading "Unanimous Raves!" appeared comments from Brooks Atkinson, Walter Kerr, William Hawkins, and others, praising the production.
8. See above, Letter 883 and n. 5.

887 | To Lucy Kroll,[9] New York

[320 East 57th Street]
[New York]
February 19, 1956

Dearest Miss Lucy,

Here we are, before I get my letter written thanking you for that evening,[1] comes the telephone to the theatre. I was pleased indeed. With all you have to think of, this flower of remembrance comes out —I do thank you.

As to Horton's evening it was all done so sweetly and fully, and with so much loving care behind it. (Not to mention that real food.) Such sweetness in an atmosphere can come only from sweet people who will to have it so. Which you may guess means you and Nathan. You both have it in your faces, which is nice too.

Thank you again. Miss Barry[2] has nearly finished the last act of VESTIRE GLI IGNUDI so I'll be sending you this close or almost literal copy soon. You can see what the play is really like—and then—

Affectionately,
Stark

9. Lucy Rosengardt Kroll (Mrs. Nathan Kroll), literary and talent representative, was graduated in 1933 from Hunter College and in 1939 married Nathan Kroll, musician and film producer. She served as coproducer of the American Actors Company from 1937 to 1942 and as literary analyst for Warner Brothers studios from 1942 to 1945. After teaching drama for two years at Hunter College, she established the Lucy Kroll Agency in 1945. Her clients included Kim Stanley and Horton Foote.

1. Lucy Kroll had given a party to celebrate the publication of Horton Foote's *Harrison Texas.*

2. Typist.

888 | To Horton Foote, Nyack, New York

[320 East 57th Street]
[New York]
Wednesday [March 7, 1956]

Dearest Horton:

I told that sweet Lillian [3] about the picnic I have had with the ms.—
bad carbons et cetera—Very stupid of me really. So I asked Miss Lucy [4]
about an agency, she said Hart—I went over Monday morning with
the ms.—was greeted bloomingly by Miss Sara, the lady manager—
who said she had been indebted to me for years—in print, lectures and
so on. Mr. Hart, the boss, said the place had been all excited ever since
I telephoned. Well, well—an old crow like me—people are very kind
indeed.

The Pirandello [5] read at a sitting in this cleaner form seems very often engaging and then you wonder what about it. The *mentality* in it
repeats a lot in effect, if you see what I mean.

Some of the words would be changed of course. The very last line
of the play—che questa morta—ecco qua—non s'e potuta vestire . . .
"that this dead woman—here—could not clothe herself" is very bad.
Livingston [6] translated it "that I am dead—yes, and that I died naked."
That's where the "naked" comes from—it's bad all right. These matters
will no doubt be taken over. All through the translation are words
that follow exactly—but could of course be eased into.

Words like impediments, humiliated, etc. They are too often said,
but it would be all right in Italian, where these formal sounding words
are taken as ordinary talk.

My Chekhov pages are worn to a frazzle looking up words to get just
what he says, but this formal-sounding Latin business is more elusive.
I have suggestions to translate *Ivanoff*—not for me—I don't really care
about the play and I have had enough grinding over those Russian
speeches.

3. Mrs. Horton Foote.
4. Lucy Kroll.
5. See above, Letter 884 and n. 2.
6. Arthur Livingston (1883–1944), professor of romance languages at Columbia,
translated the work of Pirandello and many other Italian authors.

The preface for the four plays [7] is in at Random House—nice people there.

I am bursting to tell everybody I see about the movie, of *The Chase*.[8] I am reading it tonight—my first good chance at it. Love to you and Lillian.

Stark

889 | To Catherine Alexander Burland, Washington, D.C.

[320 East 57th Street]
[New York]
Monday [March 12, 1956]

Dear Cattia,

I have so many letters to see to that this is only a scrawl—with a desirable check.[9] Mr. Ross thinks *Uncle Vanya* may run all summer. Of course Franchot won't keep it that long—and should not,[1] but Louis Edmonds—who was Gayeff in *The Cherry Orchard* is the under-study and this week-end they say did an excellent performance—he speaks beautifully and is very fine looking when made up on the stage. From Louisiana, near my cousins down there—very well born and bred.

When you write Tommy [2] tell him I had a sweet little letter from him at Montevideo—but no address on it. But no *Ivanoff* [3] for me—For one thing I want to do some painting again. Best to you.

Stark

The checks go through the week ending 2/26.

7. In January, editors of Random House decided to publish a volume of Chekhov's plays translated by Young and requested him to write an introduction for them. The book was published later in the year in the Modern Library Series as *Best Plays by Chekhov.*

8. Horton Foote originally wrote *The Chase* in 1952 as a play. In 1956, he made the play into a novel with the same title, but the motion picture version, produced by Samuel Spiegel, directed by Arthur Penn, and starring Marlon Brando and Jane Fonda, was not released until 1966.

9. Young and Catherine Burland divided royalties from the translation.

1. On June 11, Alfred Ryder replaced Tone as Astroff in the play.

2. Husband of Catherine Burland.

3. Mrs. Burland had suggested a translation of Chekhov's *Ivanoff.*

890 | To Charles Edward Eaton,[4] Woodbury, Connecticut

> 320 East 57th Street
> New York
> March 22, 1956

Dear Mr. Eaton,

I have had to delay reading *The Greenhouse in the Garden,* which you so kindly sent me, till I had done with a translation of Pirandello's *Vestire gli ignudi* for Roger Stevens. I have been rewarded at last, for your book gave me much pleasure.

I am not at all versed in recent poetry, but the effect of your poems impresses me with a certain uniqueness, surprising, original figures, very delicate and elusive images—plus an almost shameless amount of imaginative invention, as if you didn't care at all whether or not there was any of that rare substance left for other poets. Well, let them heed you.

That final poem [5] is particularly happy coming at the very last heart beat of the book. I have gone back to this poem several times.

The jacket says you are at Woodbury and so I am trying that instead of the publishers.

Thank you again.

> Cordially
> Stark Young

4. Charles Edward Eaton (b. 1916), poet and teacher, was professor of creative writing at the University of North Carolina from 1946 to 1952. In addition to *The Greenhouse in the Garden,* his volumes of poetry include *The Bright Plain* (1942), *The Shadow of the Swimmer* (1951), *Countermoves* (1963), and *On the Edge of the Knife* (1969).

5. Young refers to "Sense in the Darkness the Purple Jet."

891 | To Roane Fleming Byrnes, Natchez, Mississippi

320 East 57th Street
New York
Thursday [March 22, 1956]

Dearest Roane,

As the enclosed note from Mr. Miller will show you, I have just heard of Ferriday's death.[6] I have never met with Mr. Miller but have only talked with him on the telephone and this was very kind of him —and I must write at once to send you my love and sympathy, and tell you how sorry I am to hear of Ferriday's death. He was a sweet fellow, intelligent, warm, generous and loyal. It was impossible not to love him. I wish I could say something that would be of any use.

How long it seems since I saw you all! And your mother, what an aristocratic lady, I remember her as if I had seen her yesterday. Life gets less and less shining for us with the years.

My only news is that the translations I did of Chekhov's *The Three Sisters, The Cherry Orchard* and *Uncle Vanya* have had a very distinguished reception. *Uncle Vanya* opened soon after New Years and they turn away people by hundreds and will do so for some time. In the autumn they will do *The Sea Gull*. The four translations are coming out in the Modern Library, a very fine place for them to be. Well, that's that.

Dear Roane, forgive a dull, almost useless letter, but I do send you my love and sympathy, and I shall by no means forget Ferriday.

Affectionately
Stark

6. Earl Hart Miller had written Young a brief note to tell him about the recent death of Ferriday Byrnes in Natchez, February 3, 1956.

892 | To Robert Penn Warren, Fairfield, Connecticut

320 East 57th Street
New York
March 22, 1956

Dear Red,

They never did find the copy of your book you so kindly sent me, so I bought one for myself. (I know what it is for authors to be obliged to buy their own books to give away!) And with some work on translating Pirandello's *Vestire gli ignudi* for Roger Stevens done at last, I could settle down and read *Band of Angels*—from which I got much more pleasure.

The central freedom idea seemed to me most originally developed, and with its own emotional power—which increased as the story went on. The amount of history you had got hold of and used is something terrific. There are so many highly effective characters that the book suggests a remarkable movie, if somehow so delicate a subject can be handled just now. There are enough incidents to select from and settings that would be highly—I just said *highly,* didn't I?—effective, some of them very haunting. The book is astonishingly full and rich. I can thank you for the pleasure and even excitement I had from reading it.

I still of course remember my visit to Yale.[7] It revived my sense of a university, that it still could be a happy place. Much of this is due to you and Eleanor. I was looking into various chapters of her Rome book[8] not long ago and found them still very absorbing.

This has been a short winter—in some ways rewarding. The distinguished reception of my Chekhov translations has been heartening. *Uncle Vanya* was produced in January and is still turning away hundreds and can run a long time if they choose to keep it on. Imagine that with Chekhov! I don't think I'll do any more translating—I'll try to turn to my own writing—a journal that would parallel *Pavilion* but would deal with more contemporaneous material. It's on the lap of the gods. At the moment I don't feel very much inspired.

7. Early in December, 1955, Young lectured at Yale.
8. Eleanor Clark [Warren], *Rome and a Villa* (1952).

Spring will soon be making your place even more attractive and lovable. *Iam uer egelidos refert tepores*[9]—

My love to you both
Stark

893 | To Leah Salisbury, New York

320 East 57th Street
New York
Friday [March 23, 1956]

Dearest Leah,

I turned up the enclosed aged letter, but I may as well pile it on you. You doubtless say you don't mind being bothered, that's how sweet you are.

That article about the miracle man in last Sunday's Times was most regrettable.[1] I have done my best, on endless telephone occasions when Mr. Ross calls about this or that, to slow up this greed he has for public attention; I merely ask him to go slow, not want everything at once. He evidently put it over the young man at the *Times,* Mr. Gelb. He says he expected some space for translator and actors—I know him well enough to know how much there is to that. I told Brooks[2] a bit of sequence like this: Ivanoff, Strindberg, Pirandello, Cadillac. He [Ross] never saw a copy of *Ivanoff* till somebody mentioned it and I lent him my copy a fortnight ago, he knows nothing of Strindberg's, the Pirandello he got a notion of from learning that I was to do *Vestire gli ignudi* for Roger Stevens. The Cadillac at the end of the article—it would be nice to have a Cadillac, etc.—not to sacrifice for art is the idea[3]—I told Brooks that ever since I first knew him Mr. Ross has had

---

9. Catullus, Carmen 46.

1. Young refers to Arthur Gelb, "4th St. Miracle Man," New York *Times,* March 18, 1956, Sec. 2, pp. 1, 3. Gelb referred to David Ross as the "miracle man" of the Fourth Street Theatre.

2. Brooks Atkinson, critic for the New York *Times.*

3. In the concluding paragraph of the article, Ross was quoted as saying: "I, too, would like to ride around in a Cadillac. Who wouldn't? But the main thing is the performance. If that's bad, what good is a gold-plated theatre?"

the biggest white Cadillac I ever saw, lined with green and gray leather, and he has a good-sized apartment in a new apartment-house at No. 2 Fifth Ave. It was not very fair to act out that effect of denial etc. I'd think Mr. Gelb would feel like a fool. I'm sorry to see this greedy, completely devious way of getting on, since he [Ross] has good traits of course and ability pulling things together with the play, though he himself knows nothing about the acting elements, technique etc. Franchot Tone and Signe Hasso think he knows nothing. He knows something but it is not exactly in their medium. He has a personable slant indeed and in a pet has said nasty things by now about everyone connected with the occasion there at the 4th—sometimes highly obscene, and then when something smoothes him down he gets pathetic and thinks all should be forgotten. It is quite out of class for people like you and me. At the moment he constantly says how it upsets him to be so famous. Time alone will have to settle some of this.

Love to you
Stark

894 | To Richard Hayes, New York

320 East 57th Street
New York
Monday night [April 23, 1956]

Dear Mr. Richard Hayes,

I came in at noon today from the house in the country, where we had been working to repair a host of damages that recently some storm had done. Your very lovely letter and the distinguished and beautiful review of *Uncle Vanya* [4] have come and have been read with such grati-

---

4. Early in April, Young wrote Hayes to praise his review of *The Cradle Song* by Martinez Sierra in *Commonweal*, LXIII (February 3, 1956), 457–58, and to agree with his estimate of the Tyrone Guthrie production of Pirandello's *Six Characters in Search of an Author* in *Commonweal*, LXIII (February 10, 1956), 483–84. On April 21, Hayes expressed his pleasure over Young's approval; in addition, Hayes enclosed a copy of a review of *Uncle Vanya*, "The Stage: The Expense of Spirit," *Commonweal*, LXIV (April 20, 1956), 75–76.

tude and appreciation, and the deepest good hopes for your future, which for some reason you seem to enjoy a degree of modesty about—the next time we meet we must talk about that, for I confess I don't really see what you mean. Honestly you must know how your words startle and shine, or move the reader so profoundly in their happier instances. That last paragraph in this article [5]—for which obviously I am very grateful indeed, you know that or you could not have written such lines, and such brilliant sequences of words as "release their potency through their own *vibrant, exact and accessible* language" and "fidelity and love"—that paragraph carries and persuades and delights.

(Here I was interrupted by a visitor.)

Tuesday night . . .

There are various points in your article that are all right of course, but they suggest a good many things about the whole venture and Mr. Ross et cetera that it would be good for us to talk about. Such inside points lead to more and more theatre understanding, and are often diverting as well. Many of our critics know little of the inside of the theatre and have only more or less slight or vulgar connections with actors and their minds. Intelligent actors—and born actors—know the difference, however much they may be pleased at any sort of "good notice."

My friend Bowman, the architect, and I have begun the week-end trips to the house in Westchester, trying to get things straightened out preparatory to going for good, with only occasional visits to town and labors here. We go out Friday afternoon and return Monday morning —to avoid the terrific Sunday traffic. I have nothing in mind for next Monday evening and if you are free it would be very nice if you could come over and we could have dinner together and a talk.

I must close, this is a flat document, but I send you very special thanks and appreciation.

Yours sincerely
Stark Young

5. The final paragraph of Hayes's review dealt with Young's translations: "I have not, in these notices of the Chekhov cycle at the Fourth Street Theatre, sufficiently honored Mr. Stark Young's translations, which are the firm and beautiful base upon which Mr. Ross' productions rest. The voice of Chekhov has been so clouded and obscured in our theatre . . . that Mr. Young's translations, which release its potency through their own vibrant, exact and accessible language, stand uniquely as creative and reconstitutive acts of the highest fidelity and love."

895 | To B[ernard]. H. Haggin, New York

320 East 57th Street
New York
May 16, 1956

Dear Bernard,

I ought to feel somewhat absurd writing you about such a book as yours,[6] since I know so little about music and can take only a certain amount of it—it can bore me as Muncsh[7]—how do you spell it? sometimes does, or it can leave me half broken-hearted as Mozart can do, or in the seventh heaven, half antique, half the eternal sighing heart, as Gluck can do. All that does not mean anything that is too worthy of such a book as yours, which delights me with its attention to the point and the accurate record even when I don't follow the special thing you are talking about.

I take refuge in a compliment I heard said of me by Stravinsky: *Il sent tout.* I like that better than any thing I ever heard said of me.

But that is a long way from *knowing.*

I may not always follow you where I do know what you are discussing. For instance Puccini. I don't see why *La Boheme* is not a strangely perfect combination of the story and the opera as a whole. It does not try to do things that are far above or outside it, so far as I know. And the *Vissi d'arte* seems to me ravishing, especially for what the voice can do with it. I would like you to say more about Verdi's singability—how even a bad singer can turn on something worthwhile instead of fighting it.

Otherwise how I did feel relieved in what you said of Brahms. I never cared enough to be sorry, but he from the very start sounded to me like a professor writing for serious thinkers. I have no right to speak in this however. I do love the *Sapphic Ode,* provided the *form and the classic repetitions* et cetera are allowed to do the expressing, and not the ovaries of the she-singer, which is what happens in most records.

Page 64 did delight me, what Tovey, for example, says of the lan-

6. B. H. Haggin, *The Listener's Musical Companion* (1956).
7. Charles Munch (1891–1971) was then conducting the Boston Symphony Orchestra and directing the Berkshire Music Center.

guage of comedy as expressing tragedy.[8] The Berlioz observations are quite dazzling to me at least, page 102![9] bless you for that. Those Rimsky passages,[1] as on page 144 and elsewhere, seem to me very sound and fine, even if I had never heard any of the music I should sense that the writer here is the real thing. I was very much pleased with what you said about the *Four Saints*.[2] Norman Dello Joio in the midst of praise for *Immortal Shadows* has always sat on me for liking the music.

But regardless of opinions in any given case, what I sense about the whole book is that this is the only way, really, to do criticism and interpretation. I respect everything I read in it, and I know that this is the real thing. It makes our other musical criticism such crap really, breakfast twiddling.

I wondered when I saw a jacket photograph that was not a mere mess, then I saw it was Walker Evans.[3] I have never been able to explain to myself why his photographs make all the other photographs I know look like mostly nothing. In the Museum of Modern Art he could do a little thing of a window with a cotton lace curtain and make that whole huge Steichen show about all mankind turn into mere offal mostly.[4]

8. In his discussion of Mozart's *The Marriage of Figaro* and *Don Giovanni*, Haggin, indirectly quoting Donald F. Tovey, wrote: "One often, he [Tovey] says, finds the language of comedy the only dignified expression for the deepest feelings."

9. A reference to Haggin's comments about *Harold in Italy, Symphonie fantastique,* and *Romeo and Juliet.*

1. Haggin here objected to Rimsky-Korsakov's changes in Musorgsky's scores.

2. Haggin wrote that Virgil Thomson was "brilliantly successful with music organized around words—specifically the words of Gertrude Stein" in *Four Saints in Three Acts,* and added: "His music separates, differentiates, articulates the endless repetitions, gives them point, structure, climax, and achieves something unique, delightful, often very funny, sometimes very moving" (pp. 177–78).

3. Walker Evans (1903–75), photographer, served on the editorial staffs of *Time* and *Fortune* magazines and taught at the Yale School of Art and Architecture. Examples of Evans' work had been on display in an exhibition arranged by Edward Steichen at the Museum of Modern Art during February and March. A photograph of Haggin, taken by Evans, appeared on the dust jacket of *The Listener's Companion.*

4. Young has reference to the exhibition, "The Family of Man," arranged by Edward Steichen for the Museum of Modern Art, January 26 through May 8, 1955. According to the museum's statement, Steichen (1879–1973), the most famous of American photographers, assisted by Wayne Miller, "spent more than two years selecting the pictures after seeing more than two million photographs." The show included more than five hundred pictures taken by 257 photographers from many different countries. Evans' work was not included. For a review of the exhibition, see Edwin Rosskam, "Family of Steichen," *Art News,* LIV (March, 1955), 34–37, 64–65.

You must make allowances for this typing. I do it rarely and hate it. But a screed this length would be impossible.

I have not half expressed my admiration of your book and the sense of some security in knowledge and taste that it gives me. Not to speak of the many keen points and the many genuinely imaginative images.

> Affectionately
> Stark

I was interested in what you said about *Uncle Vanya*. It is a remarkable play, and counts heavily as a sum, but it comes some years before *The Three Sisters* and *The Cherry Orchard* and before Chekhov had developed the ensemble method they exhibit. Some people definitely prefer *Uncle Vanya,* but I think my own response is due to the other two plays—his last. They seem really different from the whole Continental drama before them, profoundly original, and never forced.

> S.

However tedious this letter, I owe its *length* to such a book.

> S.

896 | To Walker Evans, New York

> 320 East 57th Street
> New York
> June 5, 1956

Dear Walker,

I must admit that I have been haunted by those photographs at the Museum of Modern (often crap) Art [5] and though I wrote you an uninspired letter of appreciation, I am obliged to write and tell you again what you have often heard no doubt—that the quality and mood of these little photographs in that exhibition just beats Hell. I have, of course, seen many beautiful photographs, in Europe especially, the subjects being beautiful of course. But as I have told you before, the impact

5. See above, Letter 895, n. 3.

of your photographs is unique. That great distinction within very often an astounding plainness—that strange, secret accuracy in the whole effect—I suppose I might as well shut up. But this morning for some reason as mysterious perhaps as this mystery in the photographs themselves, I have been absorbed in the thought of your works.

Please remember me to your lady, whom I know only on the telephone.

Yours affectionately
Stark Young

897 | To Horton Foote, Nyack, New York

Waccabuc, New York
August 30, 1956

Dearest Horton:

Thank you for your sweet letter, recalling a very lovely visit to us from you all.

I tried to telephone you about this mess with the 4th St. Theater and "The Sea Gull." I will try to tell you a few items about it with the very urgent request that you tell Miss Lucy and Kim,[6] and if you see them Bill Becker [7] and Roger Stevens.

1. When he first came to me about producing my translation of Chekhov Mr. Ross had to do a lot of pleading, arguing et cetera for me to agree. By comparison he could not tolerate Mrs. Garnett's translations.

2. At the beginning of "Uncle Vanya" he tried to argue and wheedle Leah Salisbury into giving him a lower royalty. He was getting the minimum for such productions Off-Broadway, et cetera. Said he could get other translations for nothing! They evidently had quite a hot

6. Lucy Kroll and Kim Stanley, respectively.
7. William Becker (b. 1927), writer, actor and director, has acted in a number of plays at the Brattle Theatre (Cambridge, Massachusetts), which he helped to organize, and served as stage manager for the Internationale Theatrefestspiele at Salsburg. In 1954, he joined the Roger L. Stevens Productions in New York as Stevens' assistant.

scene. (He took it out partly on me by giving me the worst, back of the stage seats for the opening.) A month ago they asked again for a reduction. Miss Salisbury told them that she had had no box office reports for several weeks, when she got them she would consider whether the reduction was "legal" etc. A message came back—the request withdrawn. Then came later on a discussion of "The Sea Gull," introducing this minimum royalty. He said he could save $200 a week if he used Mrs. Garnett's. The end of that was his decision to change.

What burnt me up was the Times giving the notice of the change—on the first drama page, with that stuff Mr. Ross said about being told in London that Mrs. Garnett's was the finest translation. He had got the rights the week before.[8] All lies—so far as I can find out the Garnett is in the public domain[9] so the reason for the change is the lack of royalty. He puts in that stuff about an experiment of using another "adaptation." To change is one thing but this crooked plausibility is nauseating. That's what I want to spread right and left. Vincent,[1] Miss Lucy, Everybody.

I never thought I would be in this lying, dirty mix-up and it has had a very bad effect on me.

I hope the family are enjoying the country—they all deserve it, bless their hearts. Give them my love.

Affectionately,
Stark

8. Young refers to Arthur Gelb's column, "Rialto Gossip," in the New York *Times,* August 12, 1956, Sec. 2, p. 1. In a paragraph entitled "Switch," Gelb reported that Young's translation of *The Sea Gull* would not be used for the forthcoming production; instead David Ross would use Mrs. Constance Garnett's version. According to Gelb, Ross explained that when he was recently in London "he discovered that Mrs. Garnett was regarded in many circles there as perhaps the finest translator of 'The Sea Gull.' 'I decided it'd be interesting to experiment with a different kind of adaptation,' said Mr. Ross, who obtained the rights to the translation last week."

9. Presumably the translation of *The Sea Gull* first published in London by Chatto and Windus in 1923; see above, Letter 885 and n. 5.

1. Vincent Donehue (1915–66) began his career as an actor but achieved greatest recognition as a director. In addition to Horton Foote's plays, *The Trip to Bountiful* (1953) and *The Traveling Lady* (1954), Donehue directed *Sunrise at Campobello* (1958) and *The Sound of Music* (1959), as well as the television productions of *Annie Get Your Gun* (1957) and *Peter Pan* (1960).

898 | To Walter Kerr, New York Herald Tribune, New York

Jennymead
Waccabuc, New York
Tuesday, September 11, 1956

Dear Mr. Walter Kerr,

I hope this won't be too great a nuisance, but I not only should be looking forward to the pleasure at last of knowing you, I'd like very much to have your advice in a troublesome matter.[2] Could you meet me for a little visit next week on Monday, Tuesday, Wednesday or Thursday? Either lunch or for a drink, anywhere you say. I am going to town on tedious business tomorrow and will be there till Friday morning. I'll take the liberty of calling your office at the *Herald-Tribune* and seeing when I can speak with you.

I read your article about the public and the theatre (plus Granville-Barker) for Sunday, September 2.[3] I entirely agree with you, as I so often do, and know you are writing from inside the theatre—art, as it were. I keep thinking what word Mr. Granville-Barker could have used that would have been useful in the discussion instead of his "lacking taste" motif—*taste* yes, but there must be some other word that would be both less obviously inevitable and at the same time more genuinely expressive. On exactly that theme I think you could write a useful article, also useful and engaging.

I was reading in your "How Not to Write a Play"[4] the other day, and was struck again with the fact that it was never outside the theatre as most theatre books are. There must be somebody who reads them—

2. Young probably wished to discuss with Kerr the difficulties over the Fourth Street Theatre productions of Chekhov's plays. See the preceding letter.

3. Walter Kerr, "Public Is Hungry for Stage Fare," New York *Herald Tribune,* September 2, 1956, Sec. 4, pp. 1–2. In his article, Kerr quoted a remark by Harley Granville-Barker about audiences that thronged into the Elizabethan playhouse: " 'Its public, like our own—but like every public, I suppose, anywhen and anywhere, had been more remarkable for appetite than taste.' " Kerr used the remark to support his contention that audiences support both first- and second-rate productions because "appetite outruns taste."

4. See above, Letter 866 and n. 5.

in the same sense that for stupid actors—in the French proverb—God made stupid spectators.

Yours sincerely
Stark Young

899 | To Walter Kerr, New York Herald Tribune, New York

610 West Lynn
Austin, Texas
December 21, 1956

Dear Mr. Walter Kerr,

I write this instead of an amiable Christmas card because I want to add some remarks independent of the season.

One is that I am afraid I agree with you about *Candide*. It was disastrous, as you say,[5] as well as generally intangible and boring. I read three reviews besides yours. They seemed to me incredible, to put it mildly.

I wanted also to mention your very fine review of the O'Neill play. That whole passage beginning "It is a mistake to think of the theatre as absolute illusion" et cetera is a notable statement of that basic point in the theatre,[6] and you express it all with words that count profoundly, and so bless you!

---

5. In his review, "Theatre: 'Candide,'" New York *Herald Tribune,* December 3, 1956, p. 10, Walter Kerr wrote: "Three of the most talented people our theatre possesses—Lillian Hellman, Leonard Bernstein, Tyrone Guthrie—have joined hands to transform Voltaire's 'Candide' into a really spectacular disaster."
6. In "'Long Day's Journey,'" New York *Herald Tribune,* November 18, 1956, Sec. 4, pp. 1, 3, Kerr wrote: "It is a mistake to think of the theater as absolute illusion. . . . In every theatrical experience there is both contact and detachment. . . . The player knows perfectly well that there are customers . . . and the audience is equally aware that the figures it is watching with such fascination are also, and just as importantly, living human beings. To acknowledge this duality is to sharpen every response; the best theatrical experiences are those in which both kinds of knowledge shimmer simultaneously, each at its maximum intensity." A large part of Young's drama criticism was based upon this premise.

Many people have spoken to me about that shining *tour de force* of Mrs. Kerr's [7]—the French young lady needed just that.

With best wishes for your holiday season, I am

Yours sincerely
Stark Young

900 | To B[ernard]. H. Haggin, New York

320 East 57th Street
New York
Sunday [January 27, 1957]

Dear Bernard,

You'll have to forgive me—it's ages since I had your good letter. I had various disturbing things, and Christmas I stayed longer in Texas than I usually do—my sister—all the family I have—was not well and I stayed as long as I could to be of any use I could.

No trouble between Mr. Ross and me—he tried to get the royalty— already the minimum cut or cut down, Miss Salisbury refused. He got Garnett's for nothing. What I do object to is the lies he told Mr. Gelb at the *Times,* about hearing in London that she was the finest transla- tor et cetera. "He obtained the rights" last week. John Gielgud has written me that "nobody here cares to use the Garnett versions any more." As for the "rights" there are no rights. Everybody knows the translation of *The Sea Gull* by Mrs. Garnett is in the public domain.[8] Well the venture was a flop all right.

The new owner and manager of the NR wrote me a most compli- mentary letter asking me to come back and do dramatic criticism. But I declined. These past few months the NR, with this Mr. Harrison and without Bruce Bliven, has vastly improved.[9]

7. The incident to which Young alludes cannot be explained.

8. See above, Letter 897 and notes.

9. Young's remark, one of the last comments he wrote about the *New Republic,* reflects his optimism about its future. In a letter to Harrison, written in May of the preceding year, Young expressed his satisfaction in the improvement he noted in the magazine since Harrison had become editor. Young remarked that if he amounted to anything as a writer he owed a great part of it to the *New Republic,* and that his love, interest, and loyalty to the paper had never essentially diminished.

I feared it would be like that with Mr. Hatch.[1] He is really a squirt. That sounds promising—the Yale Review job.[2] I'm sure you can do it better than anybody else. Your book[3] gave proof of that, overwhelmingly.

I'll have a copy of the Random House Chekhov—my four translations, and will keep it till I see you. I'd like you to have it.

I hope now to see you soon. Thank you for writing.

Affectionately
Stark

901 | To Robert Liddell Lowe, West Lafayette, Indiana

320 East 57th Street
New York
May 17, 1957

Dear Bob,

Thank you very much for that Tintoretto card Christmas—I still have it—and now for a lovely letter. I didn't see the copy of the *Tribune* with the quote from Illinois—too bad. You are very good to mention it however.

That's very fine news about the song based on your "All Foxes."[4] You doubtless have other things hidden away that would be just as admired. I hope so.

MacGregor[5] and this house have become great friends, though we don't see him often. Whatever the treatment was, or whatever his mind

---

1. See above, Letter 671 and notes. Haggin felt he was being harassed by Hatch and in April, 1957, resigned from the *Nation*.

2. Haggin had begun to write a quarterly survey of new recordings for the *Yale Review*.

3. *The Listener's Musical Companion*.

4. See above, Letter 333, n. 5.

5. Frank Silver MacGregor (1897–1971), editor and book publisher, in 1924 became head of the college textbook department of Harper and Brothers, now Harper and Row Publishers. In 1935, he became vice-president of the company, president in 1945, and chairman of the board in 1955.

changed toward, have been most noticeable. He is most affectionate and responsive and an attractive man. I am glad that this could be so.

I wrote the editor how much I was impressed by those two articles of Bernard Haggin's.[6] He is far above any other critic in our town, in knowledge and in a high-minded generosity and desire to explain, etc.

By the way the NR editor when he took over and got things going wrote a most complimentary letter, asking me to do the dramatic criticism again. But I have no impulse in general ever toward going back, and don't want to start criticism again, especially since the theatre field is now so middle class compared to what it was when I went on *The New Republic*.

Thank you again, Bob, for thinking of me. I hope all your plans go well.

Affectionately
Stark

902 | To Vera Segal Sterne, Mount Kisco, New York

Waccabuc, New York
Monday [July 29, 1957]

Dearest Vera,

I have been meaning to write you to say how sorry I am to know of Maurice's death.[7] You know how much affection I had for him, and admiration for his great work—the best in America—and how much I appreciated his friendship and valued his opinion.

I can only say now that I hope life will treat you as kindly as may be possible. Time is the only thing, I suppose, that can help at all, and that is only wearing down the sharp edge of grief and loss.

---

6. On May 16, 1947, Young wrote Gilbert Harrison, editor of the *New Republic,* to express admiration for Haggin and his two articles, "Schnabel's Beethoven Sonatas," *New Republic,* CXXXVI (April 8, 1957), 22, and "Singers and Players" (May 6, 1957), 21.

7. Maurice Sterne died July 23, 1957.

My affection for you, dear Vera, is the same as always. Wales Bowman asks me to give you his love and sympathy.

Affectionately
Stark

903 | To Robert Penn Warren, Fairfield, Connecticut

Waccabuc, New York
August 8, 1957

Dear Red,

The other day I saw at Mildred Dunnock's,[8] who lives near me here in the country, a copy of your *Dragons*. She had just read it with much enthusiasm, and of course I had a chance to sing its praises and to show off with how much I remembered of it. *Brother to Dragons* is a shining name to remember it by.

I have been here in the wilds and only heard lately, incidentally and by chance, that you all were home again from Italy. I thought of you Christmas and of my little plan to get something entertaining to go into your very lovely house, to keep you all from forgetting the pleasure I had in being there, in that whole visit to Yale in fact. But my Christmas in Texas was flattened out by my dear Sister's illness. For the whole time and a long while afterward. So I never got to Mexico—we usually go there Christmas, drive down to Monterrey. I sat most of all day everyday with my sister. We didn't even get to San Antonio; from Austin.

But I still cherish the idea that I will find something that will be happy in a house with so special a style. I admired it greatly—most houses are a mess.

It seems to me my dear friend Red is very well set up. With such a

---

8. Mildred Dunnock, actress, began her New York career in 1932 and since that time has appeared in a succession of plays and motion pictures, including *The Corn Is Green, Death of a Salesman,* and *Cat on a Hot Tin Roof.* In 1933, she married Keith M. Urmy.

beautiful wife and two such children. Tell Eleanor I kept thinking of her when I saw pictures of the new passages out at Hadrian's—which I saw partly myself the last time I was there—and I hoped she was writing some more Roman memories et cetera. The *Rome and a Villa* is among the few books I have two copies of, one in town and one out here. I don't expect her to be overpowered by that fact; I overpower myself by realizing how one can return to it so often and with so much pleasure.

Affectionately yours, Red,

Stark

904 | To Robert Penn Warren, Fairfield, Connecticut

Waccabuc, New York
Monday [August 19, 1957]

Dear Red,

I had to go into town last Tuesday, and at my apartment I read two acts of the play [9] before I went to bed. Then I read them over next day and the rest of the play, and since then I have re-read lots of it more than once. I feel that for a play with so much beautiful matter in it I could not do less, not to mention its being the work of an old and good friend.

I never read a MS. with a greater number of beautiful things in it, beautiful and subtle motivation, nuances and moving ideas and reactions.

I began a letter to you, but couldn't get it what I wanted it to be, and so never finished it. This one won't satisfy me either, but I must try it, I won't be able to do it better next time. I think I have never seen a MS more admirable and more difficult to write about.

I am at a double disadvantage. The first and most important one is

---

9. Warren had sent Young the manuscript of the unpublished play *Brother to Dragons,* based upon Warren's earlier work of the same title.

that having read and read well the first form of the people and story, I can't for the life of me tell how much or how little of it all I could get from this form of it. In sum I don't know how much anyone coming to the play first would get of the vast content you have put into it, or even the more or less plain narrative behind it, the characters and plot in any genuine comprehension or definiteness. For an audience that would be a fatal shortcoming. Obviously I may be mistaken of course. I got an intelligent young actor to begin it, but he gave up after the first act. Said he was at a loss and hopeless in it. None of that proves anything of course, but that is the point I should in any worthy candor make.

The other point is that if a great deal of it is intended to be produced as pantomime, no little of it is not expressible in pantomime, though very fine and subtle. A marvellous company for a special audience might get a great deal of it expressed in pantomime, but even then many of the finest motivations are not for pantomime and some of them are not even theatre writing except in some very special case, in treatment, in such audience-reaction et cetera.

For example, on page 6, Act One, the lines about actuality, Eden and so on, and its innocence, seem to me quite grand. I would say that is all quite risky as theatre—one has to react very rapidly and subtly, not to say pay completely absorbed attention, which is likely or even possible in the theatre for more or less limited periods. Your play is full of fine things that might be discussed under this head.

No use to go on with that point. Perhaps you don't intend the piece to be anything but high and original poetic thinking.

I must say one more thing, which is that the presentation of Isham's love for his brother is very beautiful as tragic poetry and as passionate dramatic motif.

I rarely type and am no good at it, and, what's more, this letter very likely gets nowhere.

Thank you for the book of poems, I am anxious to read it.

And thank you for your good letter. My best to Eleanor and all of you.

Finally no matter what, your play is a very lofty and beautiful thing.

Affectionately
Stark

905 | To Robert Penn Warren, Fairfield, Connecticut

320 East 57th Street
New York
Monday [August 19, 1957]

Dear Red,

I had left your letter in town, where I find it today and have just read it. I might have written less stupidly if I had had the letter on hand when I wrote.[1]

If a Broadway producer thinks he can handle even half-adequately such a fine dream as that play is, I take it all back and think somewhat better of Broadway. It requires marvellous technical assets in director, actors and audience. But who knows?

So take my comments as the result of real study of the play and at least well intended.

Best to you
Stark

906 | To Robert Penn Warren, Fairfield, Connecticut

Waccabuc, New York
September 3, 1957

Dear Red,

It was tactless of me to use that old French envelope, it looked as if I had been to a lot of trouble. But I had nothing out here in the country to use otherwise and wanted to send the MS back.[2] Why throw it away? So many fine things in it.

Thank you for the poems.[3] I read them last week with a surprised

1. See the preceding letter.
2. See the two preceding letters.
3. Young refers to Warren's recently published *Promises: Poems 1954–1956.*

pleasure. I have not read widely in recent poetry, but these seemed to me different and fresh. All woods, flowers, lights and young hearts in young breasts. I think one of those I like best is *The Hazel Leaf.*

I hope Eleanor's mother is better.

We are in transition here now. No cook any more and no boys to help with the grounds even an afternoon a week. So it won't be long before we are in town again. A strange summer it has been. Well, I won't go on griping. Thank you again for the poems and the generous letter.

Love to you both.
Stark

907 | To Maud Morrow Brown,[4] Oxford, Mississippi

320 East 57th Street
New York
September 9, 1957

Dear Miss Maud,

I have been busy preparing a re-issue of *The Theater*—a book of mine first published some years ago—or I would have written sooner. I was delighted to have the inquiries about Miss Isom.[5] It gives me a chance

---

4. Maud Morrow Brown (Mrs. Calvin S. Brown, 1877–1968), historian, born in Brazil, Tennessee, was graduated from the University of Mississippi in 1897, the year Young entered the university, and received her master's degree in 1902, the year after Young was graduated. In 1905, after teaching Greek and Latin at Mary Conner College and Agnes Scott College, she returned to Oxford and married Calvin S. Brown (1866–1945), a member of the faculty at the University of Mississippi. Active in educational and historical organizations, she contributed articles about Mississippi history to various journals and wrote *The University Greys,* an account of the company of students at the University of Mississippi who left the school to join the Confederate army.

5. Maud Morrow Brown was preparing a paper on Sarah McGehee Isom (*ca.* 1854–1905). Born in Oxford, Sarah McGehee Isom studied at the Augusta Seminary (now Mary Baldwin College), Staunton, Virginia; the University of Mississippi; and the Philadelphia School of Expression. She continued her studies in speech in Boston with George Riddle (see below); and in 1885, when she accepted the chair of elocution and oratory at the University of Mississippi, she became the first woman to join its faculty. In *The Pavilion* (chapter 14), Young had already paid tribute to the high quality of her teaching. A condensation of Mrs. Brown's paper written about Miss Isom but never published appears in "The First Woman Faculty Member," *Ole Miss Alumni Review,* II (April, 1958), 8–9.

to say a thing I have intended to say in my memoirs, on which I am now, by the way, working, God help me!

Apart from the usual kind of anecdotes about such a person as Miss Isom was—you will have plenty of them—I am glad to point out something that is to her credit, let us hope, and that she would like to hear. It is this: When I gave up my professorship at Amherst and went to New York to take up writing as a profession I wrote a few reviews of plays for *The New Republic* and was then asked to come on the board of that distinguished magazine as one of the editors and as dramatic critic. My articles began to be reprinted very soon, and quoted and presently my books of criticism were received with very high praise, and presently were reviewed abroad and were known in China and Japan and India, among special people interested in the theatre, and it was asked where I had studied about the theatre and what was the background of these criticisms. The only reply I had was my experience in that and arts in general, my reading and at the final base of it all my work with Miss Isom. It came to me slowly how much I owed to her, especially in the reading of lines and the rhythm of words. I have heard most of the great actors of the last forty years, in English, Italian, French, German and Russian. I can truly say, and with the great emphasis, that Miss Isom was the finest reader I have ever heard, of prose especially. I might also speak of her interest and acquaintance as concerns the great literary works, those belonging to the taste of her epoch that is.

This is markedly important to state in Miss Isom's case in view of the fact that she was on the faculty of a small university in the country provinces and most of those around her never had had the advantages or the taste to comprehend the high plane of her capacity. It took me a good deal of experience in the world theatre before I realized her superb qualities and what I owe to her. It is by comparing her with great stage reading as I have seen it that I have come to realize this.

The great teacher, George Riddle,[6] forgotten now almost but supreme in his day, said that if Miss Isom had gone on the stage she would have been the greatest actress of her time. And why did she

---

6. George Peabody Riddle (1851–1910) enjoyed a brief but remarkable success as actor and reader from 1874 to 1876 in New York and Canada. From 1878 to 1881, he taught elocution at Harvard College and published two books, *George Riddle's Readings* (1888) and *A Modern Reader and Speaker* (1900).

choose to become a professor in her home university? There must be a good many answers to that, more or less true. She was a woman of her generation when all was said and done; there was no world of art or the theatre around her in the University of Mississippi or even in the South generally; and she was Southern herself, with all that that might imply.

It is only because my theatre criticism has been so widely accepted and often followed that I myself can feel any confidence in the above statement; it is hard even for me to believe.

Sir John Gielgud, Duse, Doris Keane, Gordon Craig, Charlie Chaplin, the great Chinese actor Mei Lan-fang would bear me out in this; and The Actor's Studio in New York would do the same, and the two leading directors in the New York theatre, Elia Kazan and Harold Clurman, would do the same.

Dear Miss Maud, I don't know how to put what I have said above, but it has little point unless the reader knows some of it. Otherwise it might be mere loyal enthusiasm and provincial opinion.

You don't have to use any of it. But mere anecdotes about such a remarkable and almost improbable person would not serve the fuller purpose.

I wish you every success with your article. And it is a long time indeed since the days I used to see you and Calvin Brown; I have always thought of you as good friends.

I wish this letter could have been more worthy of Miss Isom.

With many cordial good wishes, I am

Yours sincerely
Stark Young

You can see I am no typist and have no secretary.

S.

908 | To Morgan Farley, Twenty-nine Palms, California

Waccabuc, New York
September 10, 1957

Dear Morgan,

Your letter gave me a surprise and a deep pleasure. I intended to answer it at once, but was interrupted, and then, too, I was much occupied with studying over my small volume *The Theater,* published years ago—when I used to see you—and now to be re-issued in a series by a young firm—very ambitious and choice—in a paper volume—not the fifty cent type. It comes out around the first of January.[7]

Your letter shows me you are a long way from dead or finished. There is the same old sweet and generous quality, the same gift of real affection, the same warm, speaking heart, and so far as art goes the same delicate and acute perception. How well I remember your *Fata Morgana,* very fresh and beautiful that was! And how right you were in *The American Tragedy.* Your chief limitation in the theatre —insofar as you had any—was that you were not pig enough. Pig is exactly what I mean.

Bobby Jones is to have a memorial volume of his designs [8]—the editor is Ralph Pendleton at Middleton University—I don't know him personally. There are various contributors. I was asked to do the introductory—or opening article. It was a statement of Bobby's that I was the "only critic who understood what he was trying to do." At any rate the volume appears in January.

I think you sound very wise and profound to settle in the desert, and I understand somewhat your meaning in what you write about it.

Well, one point in this letter is to say that we move back to the apartment in town about the first week in October, and so I can look forward to the chance of a visit from you. It is 320 East 57th and the telephone is Plaza 5-6493. It is not in the book in my name but under

7. Young's *The Theater,* originally published in 1927, was reissued in paperback by Hill and Wang in 1958.
8. *The Theatre of Robert Edmond Jones,* edited by Ralph Pendleton (1958). Young wrote the initial essay in the volume "Robert Edmond Jones: A Note." The other contributors were Mary Hall Furber, Lee Simonson, Jo Mielziner, Donald Oenslager, Kenneth Macgowan, Ralph Pendleton, and John Mason Brown.

William McKnight Bowman—in case you lose the number. He, by the way, has done beautifully in architecture—the real thing, not the game so publicly practiced and so tiresome as a rule. He has just finished on a big house in Virginia [9]—with incredible ancient box in a multitude that have prospered in the grounds and can be moved to a design closer to fine taste and the old poetry. He asks to be remembered cordially to you. Bless you, dear Morgan, for being yourself, and not losing what you are, and don't fail to look me up very soon after you get to New York—not the day before you are to leave for California.

I'm so glad you liked the Gene O'Neill piece.[1] I had no diary, of course—the form was an experiment. But I covered most of the main points about him, not too obviously I hope.

Love to you
Stark

909 | To B[ernard]. H. Haggin, New York

Waccabuc, New York
October 10, 1957

Dear Bernard,

I have been intending to write you how very much pleased I am to see your name on the regular list of The New Republic.[2] Not so long ago I saw an article by some other critic [3] on music or records and feared there had been some sort of mix-up. But now I see your name in the place where I wanted very much for it to be. (That other man's article by the way was so flat that I read only a little of it.)

9. Bowman had designed the house at Heronwood, the country estate of Rear Admiral and Mrs. Neill Phillips, near Upperville, Virginia.

1. Stark Young, "Eugene O'Neill: Notes from a Critic's Diary," *Harper's Magazine,* CCXIV (June, 1957), 66–74.

2. Haggin had begun to write in the *New Republic* a monthly column about records.

3. Probably Paul Hume, "The Off-Beat Repertory," *New Republic,* CXXXVI (June 24, 1957), 22.

I met recently a young instructor from Harvard [4] but did not get his name clearly. Dover or something like that. He was with the drama director from M.I.T. He said fine things about you and seeing my response went on with more. He has been four years at Harvard and was an Amherst man.

I have one suggestion to make.[5] It has nothing to do, as to the judgements, but is a matter of tact on occasion. I think your criticism is to me the most satisfying done in America, though in the matter of music I make no claims, not in any exact sense. The suggestion is merely this: now and then when you are going to say something good and also something bad about some person's performance or some music, consider putting the good remark *last* instead of the unfavorable. I have studied this as a critic of the theatre, because I know it worthwhile to have a warm reaction from the reader and not have some silly reaction that asks if this critic "ever likes anything." In many cases this change in the order would not in any sense affect the point or the judgement. That suggestion I make in all admiration and affection. I am constantly anxious for as many people as possible to respond readily to this remarkable and distinguished criticism. At any rate you can consider this suggestion. I say again that I feel a satisfaction from an article of yours that I can't describe—the core of it is so right and the approach so genuine and noble.

Forgive this typing, I am no performer and besides just now I am trying to recover from a virus cold that is taking the town.

Affectionately

Stark

4. Richard Poirier received his doctorate in English from Harvard in 1959; since 1963, he has been professor of English and chairman of the English department at Rutgers University.

5. Young's comments, writes Haggin, were prompted by his review in the *New Republic,* CXXXVII (July 1, 1957), 22, of "some recorded performances of Mozart sonatas by Landowska, which began with favorable comments on certain performances and ended with unfavorable comments on others." In his reply, October 13, to Young's letter, Haggin recognized the validity of the principle but explained that in this instance he had been unable to arrange his points in accordance with it.

910 | To Charles Clayton Harbour, Oxford, Mississippi

320 East 57th Street
New York
November 14, 1957

Dear Mr. Harbour,

Thanks for your good letter and the information about your plans.[6] As to the Lumianski thesis[7] I had in mind only the much studied bibliography. But I have also the Thurman bibliography (Cornell)[8] and so there would be small advantage in your seeing the other, a bulky volume of typing at that.

Your words about the kind former friends and minor biographers made me smile, to recognize the names and remember the kind hearts. I have heard from Mrs. Brown and written her a short note on my great indebtedness to Miss Isom. As to my background the real essence of that is in my books. SO RED THE ROSE came out one Tuesday in 1934 and went through three printings by Friday and was at the head of the best seller lists for a long time and then on the list for months and still sells—which Scribner's is very proud of. You will have seen some of that, as you mentioned in your readings. And so you can take it easy and not kill yourself. Teaching is a mountainous business, I saw I had to quit it if I wanted to do anything else, though I loved teaching and the fine contacts.

As to I'LL TAKE MY STAND, there seems no good reason why you should bother much with it, certainly not with an eye of me and the theatre; I worked hard on my contribution to that volume, which was more than some of the contributors did, but I would not do it again.

You mention Eric Bentley—in one of his books he has a very long section about me, published originally in THE KENYON REVIEW.[9]

6. Harbour was beginning his research on his master's thesis, "Criteria for Stark Young's Dramatic Criticism," University of Mississippi, Department of Speech, 1959.

7. In an earlier letter, Young had mentioned Robert M. Lumianski's doctoral thesis, "Stark Young and His Dramatic Criticism," Michigan State University, 1955.

8. Bedford Thurman's doctoral dissertation, "Stark Young: A Bibliography of His Writings," Cornell University, 1954.

9. See above, Letters 731 and 733 and notes.

Very laudatory, and in some points not right. He is a sweet, wild fellow and a great friend of mine. He and Mary McCarthy [1] would very likely agree on Eugene O'Neill. Both are good friends of mine, but neither would be likely to see his final, deep quality though they might easily see his shortcomings, not hard to do. My piece about O'Neill [2] in the June *Harper's* though seemingly simple and a diary mildness—though the diary form here was entirely invented for the occasion—is full of truths about him and his work.

You are entirely right in not choosing my plays for a thesis. They had many qualities but I gave up that field when I saw that my play *The Colonnade* would be slaughtered by the actors available. That only shows that I was not the man to struggle in that field. I am glad you are sticking to the criticism and essays.

I am going to Texas the middle of December and return here by January 1, but perhaps you will still be on hand.

Yours sincerely
Stark Young

Please make allowances—I am no typist!

911 | To Juliette Huxley, London, England

320 East 57th Street
New York
February 16, 1958

Dearest Juliette,

I was in Texas and didn't know about the knighthood [3] or would have sent Sir Julian and Lady Huxley a cable. Julian sent a very sweet

---

1. Mary McCarthy (Mrs. James Raymond West, b. 1912) served as drama critic for the *Partisan Review* from 1937 to 1948. She has written novels, autobiographical works, and essays on the theatre.

2. See above, Letter 908 and n. 1.

3. On January 10, 1958, Huxley had written to say that he had been "made a Knight in the New Queen's Honors."

reply to the letter I did finally write. Bless his heart! I am glad he is fit again.

I think Lady Juliette will sound like a quotation from Shakespeare. The Lady Juliet he has it. You won't be any lovelier and no more charming. Just the same I am delighted with the honor.

I was profoundly impressed and very often moved by Julian's book.[4] As I told him, I think there was all through it a fine spiritual tact, which can only derive from far within. I can't imagine a more searching compliment. Bowman sends cordial regards. He has just been doing some very distinguished and choice work for Mr. Alfred Vanderbilt and for Mr. Paley—head of CBS—the fabulous radio or television chief.[5] But one would never know such things from Bowman himself.

John Gielgud writes me that he has just made a lecture at Cambridge using my *Immortal Shadows* as criticism, to great applause et cetera.[6] These things are pleasant to hear. He sent me the *Hamlet* records, the play entire, which he headed The Old Vic Company doing. Very fine. I hope you have seen it, or rather heard it.

Lovingly
Stark

912 | To Catherine Alexander Burland, AID Mission, U.S. Embassy, Ankara, Turkey

320 East 57th Street
New York
February 24, 1958

Dear Katya,

It was good to hear your news. Somehow I think it would be pleasant to be among Turks. I saw a lot of them on a Greek boat years ago. The

---

4. Julian Sorell Huxley, *Religion without Revelation* (1957).

5. William S. Paley (b. 1901), chairman of the board of the Columbia Broadcasting System and trustee of various educational institutions.

6. On December 2, 1957, Gielgud wrote Young: "I gave two lectures recently, one at Cambridge University to the Marlowe Society, and one to an amateur group at Leicester, on actor and producer. I used your last book of essays for both talks extensively, reading extracts from your admirable surveys on the subject, to great enthusiasm. . . . So you see you are much in my thoughts and a continual inspiration to me and my work."

quality was very human and easy. You are having an adventurous life with that millionaire you married.

I have no news to tell you about the film of *Uncle Vanya*[7] except that it seems to me quite moving and original. The premier was last month in Baltimore, in a very attractive small theatre whose owner and manager loved the film. The notices were long and good. Very. Franchot is in Hollywood for another week now I believe. Then I can know more of the film's career. Dolores Dorn-Heft[8] or whatever it is came in for the movie. She is quite lovely and intelligent. She may be married to Franchot. At any rate she lives in his house—her own apartment joins his. She gives a good performance and can look quite lovely.

The only money I have had since I saw you last is for amateur performance—French & Co. Your percent on *The Cherry Orchard* and *The Three Sisters* came to $56. I enclose check. On the film, I have of course had nothing yet since it started. I had at first about $750 by the terms of the contract, but that all went to the expert who worked out the contract with Miss Salisbury. It seems a terrible sum but she wanted the top man in that line. I have the receipt from him of the sum paid. I hope the film makes some money. You have probably heard of the movie-television etc. situation, though it remains fairly problematical and confusing.

I hope everything goes well for you and Tommy. Wales sends his love.

Best to you
Stark

7. Operating with what the reviewer for *Time*, LXXI (May 12, 1958), 98, called a "shoestring" budget, Franchot Tone, with help from Marion Parsonnet, produced an "art" film version of Young's translation which David Ross had produced in 1956 (see above, Letter 883). Except for the substitution of Dolores Dorn-Heft for Signe Hasso, the original cast was used. Although reviewers disagreed about the merits of the work as a motion picture, virtually all agreed upon its value as a record of a splendid Chekhov stage production. For the comments of Franchot Tone about the film version, see Lewis Funke, "Uncle Vanya," *Theatre Arts*, XLI (October, 1957), 28–29, 84.

8. Dolores Dorn-Heft (b. 1935), stage, film, and television actress, made her New York debut in 1956 when she succeeded Signe Hasso as Elena in *Uncle Vanya*. Later Dolores Dorn-Heft appeared in such plays as *Hide and Seek, Between Two Thieves,* and *Critic's Choice*. Besides the film version of *Uncle Vanya*, she has had roles in *The Bounty Hunter, Phantom of the Rue Morgue,* and *Underworld USA,* and numerous appearances on television. On May 14, 1956, she married Franchot Tone; the marriage was dissolved in 1959.

913 | To Paul Flowers, Memphis, Tennessee

320 East 57th Street
New York
Wednesday [March 19, 1958]

Dear Paul,

I am much disappointed not to have seen you. On the 9th I was obliged to go to Texas because of my sister's illness, in Austin, I have just got back to town. Our houseman here says nobody called, no Mr. Flowers, while he was here. And my friend here in the apartment says you didn't call at his office. So perhaps you changed your plans and have not yet come. At any rate I am flying to Rome in a few days. Perhaps in the fall you will come again, I hope so.

Thank you for the clippings, they should be deadly if people are not determined to think their own way and everything else be damned. I am going to remember your remark in the ballroom. When an idiot told me that in his home town of Boston they thought the punishment in the South for rape was excessive, five years ought to be enough penalty, I simply said "But rape is more appreciated in Boston."

I'll hope to be seeing you & do regret this hasty trip to Texas.

Affectionately yours
Stark

The *Greenhouse* is quite a little treasury of good things. Thank you.
S.

914 | To Julian and Juliette Huxley, London, England

Dublin, Ireland
Monday [May 5, 1958]

Dear Juliette and Julian,

It was very wonderful to see you two even for that short visit—and my French box sits here very charmingly. I did like the gift of it and the sweet thought and love that went with it. And it was—I mean the sight of you—fine to see you both so rested and well.

I think of our fiery argument about the *Pieta*. No, Lady Huxley, you are wrong. It has always been highly polished.[9] I have long loved and revisited that statue—not this year—it was covered the day I was in St. Peters. But that high polish suits—and was a part of—that work of so much complexity—too much in certain folds and so on for a final grandeur, but, nevertheless, so deeply poignant with feeling of a young artist of twenty-three.

I used to think that nothing was so great as the Sistine Chapel, I used to go back to the hotel and cry sometimes after staying in the chapel a long time, and with nobody with me to talk about it to. Now the word *greatest* no longer comes into my mind about any one thing in art. Et cetera, Et cetera.

It was silly of me to pop out like that about *Santa Maria della Pace* church of Bramante's [1]—after all it is almost hidden in the Rome of today. After all I might have lit out about the Sansovino [2] facade on the Library of San Marco and various other things of course.

I hope the flowers were in good shape when they arrived Sunday. We bought them Saturday at a fine shop and were promised a choice and careful delivery on Sunday.

The Chicago news is fine.[3] For one thing we'll get to see you. And I was delighted to hear of the painting. I admired your sculpture so very much. The painting was news.

Julian, you may receive a copy of *The Texas Quarterly*. It may have been delayed because it is the first issue, and the magazine sold out entire the initial printing of 2000. As you will see it will be most exceptional as college magazines go. It will pay much better than most

9. Unlike most of Michelangelo's work the *Pietà* is polished.
1. The Santa Maria Della Pace was built in Rome near the end of the fifteenth century perhaps by Baccio Pontelli. About 1500, Donato Bramante (1444–1514) built for the church a square cloister on two levels.
2. Jacopo Tatti, called Sansovino (1486?–1570), architect and sculptor, designed many of the finest Venetian buildings of the sixteenth century; his most celebrated work is the Library of San Marco (1536–1548), with its façade of two superimposed orders of columns.
3. Huxley was already engaged in helping to plan the Darwin centennial celebrations organized by the University of Chicago. In the fall of 1959, Huxley went to Chicago to open the Darwin Symposium with an address entitled "The Evolutionary Vision."

magazines. How much I don't know. I did an article for that first number [4] and got $500 for it, plus another $500 for some meetings and consultations the week before. I chose that time because it paid my expenses for my annual visit to my sister and brother-in-law. The new president (really the vice president, but he is regarded, justifiably as president) [5] seemed to me a most congenial and exceptional man. The U. of T. is now over 20,000 students, with many distinguished men on the faculty. There is a new building started, one of the so-called University Centers [6]—headquarters for student studies, reading and so on. The main room is to be named for me I am told. A bust of me there and so on. At any rate it was all very kind.

Oliver Messel's brother-in-law—Lord Rosse [7] and Lady Rosse have invited us to lunch today, and offers of having Wales see some of the famous Georgian houses and to spend the week-end at his castle—Birr. In Offaly—150 miles from here, on the way to Shannon. I don't know what we'll do about that last. People in the British Isles have killed us with kindness, and the worst of that is that we like and admire them and can't see enough of them. Lord Rosse has some office in the Georgian Society. [8]

The friend (Gertrude Newell, whose house near Pau we visited our last Christmas [9] who insisted on joining us here, in spite of our vague efforts to discourage her) took sick with ptomaine but especially pleurisy the day she arrived and has been shut up in bed ever since. We'll have to stay a few days at least longer than we intended, which does [not] fit in exactly with what would be best in general. But such is life.

4. Stark Young, "From a Notebook: Italy," *Texas Quarterly,* I (February, 1958), 68–76.

5. Harry Hunt Ransom (b. 1908) was then vice-president and provost of the University of Texas; in 1960, he became president of the university. In 1958, Ransom was also editor of the *Texas Quarterly.*

6. A reference to the University of Texas Academic Center Library.

7. Sir Laurence Parsons, sixth earl of Rosse. Sir Laurence (b. 1906), vice-chancellor of the University of Dublin and later chancellor, married Anne Armstrong-Jones (Mrs. Ronald Owen L. Armstrong-Jones), Oliver Messel's sister.

8. Since 1947, Lord Rosse had been chairman of the Georgian Group, founded in 1937 to awaken public interest in Georgian architecture and to save from destruction or disfigurement Georgian squares, terraces, streets, and individual buildings.

9. Young meant to say "our last Christmas abroad," that is, 1952. See above, Letter 799.

Say what you like I think Sir Julian and Lady Huxley sound handsome and deserved.

Bowman sends his best.

Love
Stark

915 | To Julian Huxley, London, England

Waccabuc, New York
August 3, 1958

Dear Julian,

I do apologize for a thin letter about your last book.[1] But we were having weather both hot and cold and very humid, and I was a poorer fish than usual. I read over again yesterday the two concluding chapters in *New Bottles for New Wine*. My scientific opinion is of course, highly unimportant, but there are very fine elements and pages in the chapters. Taken as teaching or lecturing they are very impressive for the expository technique, the human conveyance to other human beings of your matter, and the pattern of development. All that in the pages 260–272[2] for example, seems to me superbly done—and to me quite deeply moving, partly because of the noble progression of the points or ideas, and partly because they sink deep into the sense of the writer's personality. If that means what I felt and am trying to say.

I read Robert Graves' review of the Bertrand Russell book and the *New Wine*.[3] He sounded as lively as he could but I do believe that if he hadn't called the name of your book I should not have been sure of

---

1. On July 27, Young had written Huxley about his *New Bottles for New Wine* (1957).

2. Young refers to Huxley's chapter on "Knowledge, Morality, and Destiny," in which he discusses "the unitary approach" to human destiny, morality, and religion.

3. Young is somewhat mistaken. Robert Graves reviewed Huxley's reissued *Religion with Revelation* and Bertrand Russell's *Why I Am Not a Christian* in "Two Studies in Scientific Atheism," *New Republic*, CXXXVIII (April 28, 1958), 13–17.

whatever book he was talking about. And that end with bringing Nell Gwyn and her delicious remark about being the Protestant whore [4]— though it's one of my favorite stories in history, along with Charles' remark that it all comes down to the question of who will have the blackest asse (ass) at doomesday—but I didn't think his bringing it in the way he did was anything of point or wit in Mr. Graves.

If you get to America in time to drop by here and see us—before the frost drives us to town—I trust we give better service than the last time. I didn't tell you that since you could come only on that date the cook-man, who had never been here except for about two hours before we arrived had to scuttle around [to] make the best of things. Such is life.

I have no air mail stationery on hand. But if you don't have white paper under this the other side won't show through.

My love to my dear Juliette. What a short visit that was with you sweet people in London!

Affectionately
Stark

Make allowances, please, for all this blotted effect and untidiness. The air is so damp, the paper so damp *et cetera,* what with my curses at it —that the result is what you see.

S.

916 | To Huntington Cairns, National Gallery of Art, Washington, D.C.

Waccabuc, New York
August 19, 1958

Dear Huntington,

Sometimes the Bollinger Press sends me a book, sometimes not. At any rate I got home some weeks ago from a stay in Europe—mostly

4. Graves concluded his review with a reference to Nell Gwyn, who, when her sedan-chair was mobbed, looked out and "cried with spirit: 'Let me be, good people! I am the King's *Protestant* whore.' English ruling-class conditioning has made both Huxley and Russell . . . Queen Elizabeth II's *Protestant* atheists."

Rome but a little each of Paris, London and Dublin—and found a copy of Friedländer's *Plato* with a chapter by you.[5] As soon as I had a moment to settle down and try to catch up with my wits, I began the *Plato,* read a good deal of it, but most, of course, your essay on *Plato as Jurist.* I have read it twice in fact with increasing humility at my glaring ignorance and admiration for the great range and precision of your pages. The pages were so full that I'll have to go over them some more to get at least a part of what they contain. The section on the *Theory of Legislation,* for example, seems to me very fine—though I have to admit I have small right to any opinion—and that on the *Penal Code* and that on *Lawyers.* It seems hard to believe that right here on my deskshelf is a book of the poetry of the world edited by this same Huntington Cairns.[6] I can only thank you and express an old admiration and affection.

I am indebted to you for many acts of friendship and encouragement, and I never have forgotten that for a moment. Life flies away from us and it seems to me ages since I was at your house in Washington and Florence[7] was so cordial and fine. I hope she is well and that she has not forgotten me.

I am at present trying a kind of journal memoirs but don't know whether they will turn out anything but average, in which case they will go in the wastebasket. There is enough mediocrity already in print.

I am here in the country till frost—my old house is very gentle and pleasant. If you are in New York this season I wish you'd let me know and we could have lunch together.

Affectionately
Stark

5. Huntington Cairns, "Plato as Jurist," in Paul Friedländer, *Plato.* Vol. I. *An Introduction,* translated from the German by Hans Meyerhoff (Bolingen Series, 59, 1958), 286–313.
6. *The Limits of Art;* see above, Letter 699 and notes.
7. Mrs. Cairns.

917 | To the Reverend Anselm Strittmatter, O.S.B.,
Washington, D.C.

Waccabuc, New York
August 21, 1958

Dear Father Strittmatter,

You were very thoughtful correcting your mistake about Gertrude Newell. But the fact is she was determined for some reason to join us in Ireland, it was May 3rd. That was Sunday. She left the table during the first meal, saying she felt unwell, went to her room and to her bed and said she'd not see anybody till a few days and she felt well again. On the insistence of some lady she knew at the consulate—by telephone she was told that she must have a doctor. On Tuesday afternoon the doctor came. He notified us through the manager that our friend was very ill. Wednesday morning we tried to see Gertrude, but she said please wait. Thursday morning we went up to see her. She had had the last rites et cetera, and at about 11 o'clock the doctor carried her to the nursing home nearby. While we were at lunch he came to tell us that she was dead. I have a notion that states of mind and medicines used had something to do with it all, but have no way of knowing any more. The American consul took over and was in every way efficient and considerate. Her niece came to Paris and the burial—in her village, Moumour, where she had a lot ready in the cemetery, a tiny peasant place.[8] The niece we have seen in New York when she passed through going home. She said her aunt had left half a million dollars, most of it to that home two very admirable foreign priests, Father Gregory and another, run near Elmira—for bums, scholars and what not.[9] So that's that, and it all remains—as Gertrude wanted everything in her life to be—half inexplicable. I had met those fine, scholarly men and

8. Gertrude Newell's niece, Charlotte Newell Connolly (Mrs. Patrick L. Connolly), assisted with the funeral arrangements in the small village of Moumour on the Vert River in the Basses Pyrénées.

9. Father Gregory Borgstedt, O.S.B. (a native American), and the Reverend Dom Damasus Winzen, O.S.B. (1901–71, a native of Germany), together with Father Placid Cormey, O.S.B., and Father Bernard Burns, O.S.B., founded in 1951 the Priory of Mount Saviour, at Pine City, near Elmira, New York. A close friend of Father Winzen, Gertrude Newell gave the chapel bell, as well as her house and its furnishings at Moumour, to the monastery.

know of their sacrifice and Catholic devotion. So that's that, and meantime the whole incident did little good to my state of mind and response to life. In a sense Gertrude was thus extremely selfish, even in
death, bless her heart! Your note was characteristically considerate and
genuine. I hope we may see you in New York later in the fall. Wales
sends greetings.

Affectionately
Stark Y.

918 | To Horton Foote, Nyack, New York

Waccabuc, New York
September 5 [1958]

Dearest Horton:

Life is mocking us all. I got home from Europe and settled here just
as your plays came.[1] But when I went to Katonah for *The Times,* to
see what the review was,[2] I got that *morning* edition and the reviews
were not in it. We have seen a few people, and nobody could tell me
about the plays—they seemed to have closed. I telephoned twice to
your house but got no answer. From something Miss Millie Dunnock
said I gather, or guess, you may have been at Williams, or perhaps in
Texas. I'd love to hear how everything is going for you all, sweet
people, and next week I'll try telephoning again. If I'd been living in
town, I'd have been less ignorant. If you'd like me to see the plays I'd
be delighted. Meantime, I hope you are all well and Wales sends his
love.

Affectionately,
Stark

1. Two plays by Horton Foote, *John Turner Davis* and *The Midnight Caller,*
opened at the Sheridan Square Playhouse, July 1, 1958, and ran for seventeen performances until July 12.

2. Brooks Atkinson reviewed the productions in "Theatre: Foote Twin Bill," New
York *Times,* July 2, 1958, p. 25. Atkinson praised *John Turner Davis* as "an idiomatic
idyl touching, decent and alive," and found Foote's "leisurely" method not so well
adapted to *The Midnight Caller.*

919 | To Jane Wasey, New York

Waccabuc, New York
September 5, 1958

Dearest Miss Janie,

I took a taxi there and back to see your show,[3] so as to be ready to talk it over with you when you came out here. But then you had your rotten luck when the big piece was dropped and broken,[4] and didn't get here. I tried telephoning but you were somewhere out. Then I heard you were at the cape. I told Miss Anne[5] messages for you, I hope she remembered when she saw you. And now you have been absent with the family, and now you are in Maine or Canada. So I'll just send a few lines to catch you. I stayed a long time looking at your work and was much impressed and delighted. I really think you have grown still further in what I have to call the sculpturesque, for lack of a better word. I mean of course, as you know, that power to give the sense of volume or pressure from within, to stabilize and create and justify the outer line—both together are the final quality or work of art. That small animal[6] whose name I had never seen before—on the right, just past some metal work and the exit—he was in a gray marked dark stone—the hair scratched into a paler color. I did think he came off wonderfully—and some of the cats, and especially that big black snake that got broken. I really studied him and thought him very very fine and mysteriously impressive. I hope the mending will conceal any defect of the breakage. It's a truly rotten shame. You certainly mopped

---

3. With Rhys Caparn and Thomas Hardy, Jane Wasey had presented an exhibition called "Animals in Sculpture" at the American Museum of Natural History, April 2 through June 8. In a review of the exhibition in *Arts,* XXXII (May, 1958), 53, Margaret Breuning noted that "in varied media, of metal, stone and wood, they have seized the vital essence which informs the motivation and gesture of these creatures." After praising Rhys Caparn's *Stalking Cat* and Thomas Hardy's *Hairy Goat,* she noted that Jane Wasey's sculptures were "remarkable in their smooth articulation and intrinsic suggestion of life. . . . It is difficult to play favorites, but a few pieces may be cited—the latent power of the horrendous, coiled serpent; the palpable gliding of a large fish through the water."
4. The movers accidentally dropped a large granite serpent.
5. Anne Sharkey.
6. A basalt bandicoot or Australian rat in the exhibition on loan from Katharine Cornell.

up the show, Miss Janie. The other woman [7] was too soft, every now and then a real moment, but very rarely indeed.

The metal is all right, if you like it. I didn't worry to think much for or against it.

I do congratulate you.

Your mother and father I hope will profit by Hot Springs. Long ago, after a month there, it cured me of a very acute sciatica.

We'll hope to see you when you get back.

Again congratulations.

Love to you
Stark

920 | To John Arthos, University of Michigan, Ann Arbor, Michigan

320 East 57th Street
New York
October 28, 1958

Dear Mr. Arthos,

I am at last settled again in town and find a letter here that I began to you too long ago—unfinished. Perhaps I wrote otherwise to thank you for the Firenze reprint. I am not at all sure because I have been broken up by the very grave illness of my sister—the only family I have left, and a very special and profound relationship between us— but no use talking of that. I am only trying to say that there has been so much uncertainty and confusion in this case and other minor ones that I am not sure of many things and one of them is this thanking for sending the article. I have it filed away and value it, and greatly appreciate your sending it. It made me homesick for Florence. My last stay there was short—the terrible changes in a town I knew so well were to me very depressing. Most of all the Lungarno and the far side

---

7. Rhys Caparn (b. 1909), whose *Stalking Cat* was characterized by Margaret Breuning as "a brilliant epitome of feral instinct."

of it, and the Trinita bridge gone. I understand the restoration is excellent, but having stood long minutes and memorized it like music I know it can't be the same—despite that Italian genius at restoration.

But I did enjoy and treasure the article, and your sending it. I do hope when you are next in New York that you will come by to see me. The telephone, not in the book, is Plaza 5–6493. Please excuse this untidy letter. I am jittery and no mistake.

Cordially yours,
Stark Young

921 | To Ella Somerville, Oxford, Mississippi

320 East 57th Street
New York
December 14, 1958

Dearest Ella,

This is only a silly letter written before I leave for Texas the 16th, and to send you all lots of love and good wishes for Christmas and the New Year, and you especially—a valued friend indeed through the years. And to beg you not to try to send me a Christmas present. Nothing is worth the money asked these days and the money we can get together buys nothing and so to hell with it all, don't you think so?

My sister after about two years of hopeless states of health seems to be somewhat better. I hope indeed to find her so. Ben is an angel or Julia would have been dead by now, poor child!

I hope you can give me good news of Nina and the rest of the family. Life does fall away from us! I am getting old and dull, but not quite dead yet, I trust. I'm sure you are as fine and brave a person as ever, and I hope life treats you according to your deserts.

My very dearest love and devotion to you

Stark

Bowman asks to be cordially remembered. He is a profound admirer of yours.

S.

922 | To Allen Tate, Oxford, England

320 East 57th Street
New York
December 15, 1958

Dearest Allen,

Your letter was indeed welcome and the assurance doubly so that the love between us for so many years has never changed and I am sure will never change.

I am sorry of course to hear about you and Caroline,[8] but there is nothing I can say. I realized seeing her in Rome more than ever what a wonderful person she is, and I got her novel from my bookseller here and, despite some lapses, thought [it] an astonishing piece of work and wrote her so. But all this proves to me nothing, there is nothing to suggest. I should [think] reading some of your poetry would break her heart at not being with you, but that proves nothing either. Nessun major dolore che ricordarsi [9]—and so on. Poor human creatures.

Wales sends you very cordial messages. I send my old love and do bless you, Allen,

Yours
Stark

8. Although Tate and his wife had separated, they were not divorced until the summer of 1959.

9. Young quotes a passage from Dante's *Inferno* (5. 121–23), "Nessun maggior delore / che ricordarsi del tempo felice / nella miseria"; as translated by Harry Morgan Ayres in *Casa Italiana Library of Italian Classics,* "There is no greater grief than remembering a time of happiness in midst of misery" (p. 52).

923 | To Ruth Ford and Zachary Scott, New York

> 320 East 57th Street
> New York
> Sunday [February 1, 1959]

Dearest Ruth and Zack,

I must not wait longer to tell you what a distinguished evening that was. There seemed to be no break in it, everything was along the lines intended. I went out and bought all the reviews. The one that seemed to get anywhere was Kerr's,[1] I am writing him a note about it. That is his due for taking trouble with his article and saying something.

I felt proud of many of the details in the course of the evening, and, incidentally I felt very little Motley[2] in it. The setting I mean. Much more you two had determined that economy and dignity. See you soon.

Wales sends his love and congratulations.

> Lovingly
> Stark

924 | To Walter Kerr, New York Herald Tribune, New York

> 320 East 57th Street
> New York
> February 1, 1959

Dear Mr. Kerr,

I am an old friend and appreciator of William Faulkner, but not a raging admirer; I say that before telling you that your review of his

1. The stage version of William Faulkner's *Requiem for a Nun* opened at the John Golden Theatre, January 30, 1959. On the following day, Kerr reviewed the performance in the New York *Herald Tribune* (see the following letter). In the play, Ruth Ford took the part of Mrs. Gowan Stevens (née Temple Drake) and Scott appeared as her husband's uncle, Gavin Stevens.

2. Elizabeth Montgomery, Audrey Sophia Harris, and Margaret F. Harris designed together under the name of Motley. As Motley, they designed the London production of *Requiem for a Nun*, which opened at the Royal Court Theatre, November 26, 1957, as well as the American version cited above.

play was admirable, careful, very much thought out and engagingly written.[3] Some of the other reviews suffered badly by comparison. It must have been hard to write. Congratulations.

This is warm praise, modestly offered but most cordially meant. I hope everything goes well for you.

Yours sincerely
Stark Young

925 | To Robert Chapman,[4] Harvard University, Cambridge, Massachusetts

320 East 57th Street
New York
February 14, 1959

Dear Mr. Chapman,

It was very happy to see you again and talk a little about *Billy Budd,* which I remember very vividly, and now to have your invitation. I make very few lectures indeed, but without coquetry I may say that I'd be delighted to come to Harvard for the Spencer lecture.[5]

The subject I should like to try is the production of foreign plays— you can word that as you choose—I mean from Greek, French, Spanish, Russian *et cetera*. As to the date would Sunday, April 12, be pos-

---

3. Walter Kerr reviewed the stage play, *Requiem for a Nun,* in "First Night Report: 'Requiem for a Nun,'" New York *Herald Tribune*, February 1, 1959, p. 10. Except for brief praise of Bertice Reading's performance as Nancy Mannigoe, Kerr said little about the acting; instead, he characterized the play as one "of language, of speeches that are meant to be speeches." Although aware that Faulkner's rhetorical phrases at times "seem to be evading and even forestalling the action," Kerr concluded that the play was a "wholly valid experiment," even "an original and stimulating achievement."

4. Robert Harris Chapman (b. 1919), professor, director, and playwright, had been a member of the Harvard faculty since 1950. With Louis Coxe, he wrote an adaptation of *Billy Budd,* which opened in New York at the Biltmore Theatre, February 10, 1951. Since 1960, Chapman has been director of the Loeb Drama Center at Harvard.

5. Chapman had invited Young to deliver the Theodore Spencer Memorial Lecture. On April 16, Young spoke on "The Production of Foreign Plays in America."

sible for you? If that is not possible would Sunday, April 19, be possible? Either one of them would be excellent so far as I am concerned.

It will be a great pleasure to see you again, dear Mr. Chapman.

Cordially yours
Stark Young

P.S.

It is Sunday and I find I am completely out of the right envelopes, so please make allowances.

S.Y.

926 | To Gilbert A. Harrison, New Republic,
Washington, D.C.

320 East 57th Street
New York
February 24, 1959

Dear Mr. Harrison,

I came in from the country last night and found here your beautiful, warm letter. You could never have written it if you hadn't known what such a letter would mean to a writer. I do indeed appreciate it and am putting it in a file along with a very few others that I value so much with all my heart. I find myself blocked in trying to thank you adequately. The picture conclusion of that first paragraph is coming to just the right man, for pictures mean so much to me.

I take great pride in the advance of *The New Republic,* it is resuming no little of its old tone and approach, most of that due to such editorship as yours. That seems almost too good to be true. For a while I despaired of that. It was like someone who has been very close to me and is dying. But now that feeling has left me, has been leaving me for some time.

Your letter follows several that have come from universities et cetera with high praise and cordial invitations, but none like your letter—to be able to write that was, or is, a special gift.

I'll go off into gibberish if I keep on, and so had better stop. And I feel that I have not answered your letter at all. At least I can keep it and be moved and blessed by it.

Yours as ever
Stark Young

927 | To Alexander Meiklejohn, Berkeley, California

320 East 57th Street
New York
March 19, 1959

Dear Mr. Mickiejohn,

I was delighted, of course, to get your lovely letter.[6] It is already in my files to be in excellent company, some thin and flat, some rich and warm. I will look forward to seeing you and that goes without saying.

My only definite engagements of the year—to take me out of town —are April 13—to 17th when I am to lecture at Wellesley and do the Spencer lecture at Harvard.[7] I have had numerous invitations to lecture here and there in colleges and universities, but these are the only ones that I have accepted. On the whole I have a feeling that a lot of lecturing would make me glib. More of that anon. Well, there's no need for me to sit writing when it is so more than obvious that I look forward to the chance of seeing you for a fact, not a hope.

6. Earlier Meiklejohn had written about the possibility of his coming to New York. Although Young's reply has been lost, something of its contents may be inferred from Meiklejohn's comments in his letter to Young, March 16, 1959: "Nothing could have given me greater pleasure than this letter which you sent, with its treasuring of the days when we were together and its promise that, for a little while at least, we may be together again. You have always, since that first day at Dartmouth, done for me good things which no one else could do, and I have kept the sense of our friendship as one of the best things of my life." Meiklejohn and Helen, his wife, expected to come East in May.

7. Early in October, 1958, Paul R. Barstow, director of the Wellesley College Theatre, had invited Young to deliver a series of lectures as part of the celebration of the opening of the Jewett Arts Center, comprising an art gallery, music building, and theatre, at the college. Young had agreed to lecture. For the Harvard lecture, see above, Letter 925.

That is certainly good about Helen's recovery.[8] I'm sure she was very game about it all, but I'll miss something of that charming voice nevertheless. At any rate she will have her smile still.

Love to you both
Stark Y.

928 | To Paul R. Barstow, Wellesley College Theatre, Wellesley, Massachusetts

320 East 57th Street
New York
April 2, 1959

Dear Mr. Barstow,

First, the delay in this reply to your very good letter[9] is due to the fact that all the photographs I have are too old to send, so I had some taken yesterday and am supposed to have them today or tomorrow and will send them right off. You are, of course, welcome to one of them, but had better reserve your acceptance till you see them.

Two. Please let me know if the evening talks there need *black tie plus* or just the dark suit I will wear in the afternoon. A friend[1] is going to drive me up, if not too awkward could you reserve a bed for him and invitations to the dinners and the luncheon? He is an architect, Princeton man, and was the president of their dramatic—is it the *Triangle?* Club, I forget, and he is not here for me to ask.

Thank you for that expense cheque. It is not necessary but is most thoughtful. I think we should if nothing happens be in town by [*sic*] but I will telephone you from some place around an hour from town, or you can just drop me a note and tell me where to come.

8. Meiklejohn wrote that his wife had recovered from a throat operation which had slightly reduced "the timbre of her voice."

9. On March 26, Barstow had written to confirm plans for Young's four appearances. Young's lecture on the evening of April 14 was to be an "all-college" occasion; the other talks were scheduled for students and faculty members primarily interested in the drama.

1. William M. Bowman.

As to the lectures:

I appreciate your trying to suggest the order for them—yesterday I spent all day trying to work out with the plan I have already made, the inclusion of the order of subjects. I don't want to use the title of *Plays and Playwrights*. For example, for one lecture it sounds too general and too ambitious, too like a lecture for a Chatauqua. But I understand that you intended these titles to give me some guiding suggestions. I am to stretch any suggestion in the direction of the topic desired.

I. (Tuesday, 4.40) Golden Fires—the world in which a play moves; that is to say décor in the theatre.
II. True Sources—People, personally remembered, who are great sources from which theatre art has drawn.[2]
III. The director and the theatre. The kind of knowledge the director should have. Technical points needed. Et cetera. Translations.
IV. Producing and acting foreign plays, Oedipus Rex, Racine, Spanish plays, Chekhov, for the producer and actor. Translations.

I have put some thought indeed on these four plans and do hope they will reward us. Please change wherever you think best.

As to recording please use your own judgment.[3] I am not sure they will be worth recording, I mean that sincerely.

Yours sincerely
Stark Young

P.S.

Thinking it over I realize how inadequately I thanked you for all the fine courtesy and consideration in your letters. Just the same I do appreciate it. Cordially

S.Y.

2. Young's principal address which he delivered as the Wellesley Speech Department's Annette Finnegan Lecture. According to the *Wellesley College News*, April 16, 1959, p. 1, Young, described as the "dean of theater critics," spoke of "the extraordinary sensitivity of Eleanor Duse, the private tragedy of Pirandello, the comicmasked bitterness of Charlie Chaplin," as well as the "brilliance and sweetness" of Doris Keane and "the instinct of perfection" of Mei Lan-fang.
3. Barstow had requested permission to record the lectures on tape.

929 | To Charles Scribner, Jr., Charles Scribner's Sons,
New York

> 320 East 57th Street
> New York
> July 9 [1959]

Dear Charley,

I have often thought of you, and, as you know, have valued you as a friend. But in the middle of May I had a turn of sickness which prevented me writing a letter, and which is only partially over now.[4] I only want to tell you why I have not written to you. My doctor claims that the whole thing will be over soon.

Not long ago someone in my house told me that you had called about a visitor from England. But I was never told of this again.

I am entirely out of bed, and hope to be fully recovered soon.

> Affectionately,
> Stark

930 | To Leah Salisbury, New York

> Jennymead
> Waccabuc, New York
> August 14 [1959]

Dearest Leah,

I went to town on Tuesday, and on the way found a sweet note from you.[5] I got home last night and this morning found another note with

---

4. Although Young was recovering from a stroke suffered, as he says, about the middle of May, he was still unable to write. This letter was written by someone else but signed by Young.

5. On August 11, Leah Salisbury had written to inquire about Young. This letter, though signed by Young, is not in his handwriting.

the check—the check is worth something of course, but the little note with your interest and love is dear to have.

I began with this sickness in the middle of May, and since then have been at a disadvantage as far as writing and reading are concerned. I am getting somewhat better and before so very long I hope to be completely well. I wish I could send some more useful and interesting news, and now I can only hope to send it soon. It will be wonderful to see you again when I am better.

Lovingly,
Stark

931 | To John W. Gassner, Yale University, New Haven, Connecticut

320 East 57th Street
New York
November 2, 1959

Dear John,

I am recovering so I am told, but my management of writing remains bad and that leaves me still in rather a mess. To have your lovely letter brought me a great deal of pleasure and reminded me of the enjoyment your work has always given me, and of the long years of friendship between us.

Your ascent in your work must be a source of great pride to you and Mollie [6]—her gentle heart, so warm and gracious has always remained vivid to me.

This is a very dull letter but it is meant to express all the warmth and affection I feel for you.

Cordially,
Stark

6. Mollie Kern Gassner (Mrs. John Gassner).

932 | To Alexander Meiklejohn, Berkeley, California

320 East 57th Street
New York
November 16, 1959

Dear Mr. Mickiejohn,

It's been a long time since I had your letter, and thank you for it, it touched me very much. You wrote and said you would look me up when you came to town.[7] I looked forward to it very much, but then I went to Europe from the country. This year after I came back I settled again in the house in the country and absurdly enough, had a stroke. It was not terrible but it did cut out writing, for a time. I had to get some help to do the actual handwriting.

This all began early in the summer and even now that I have mostly recovered, I can only write in my own hand with a great deal of effort. I came back to town several weeks ago and this is one of my first letters. A good friend helps me by taking my dictation.

I am writing this to tell you I hope that sooner or later you will be coming to New York, Miss Helen with you. If you do, please be sure to let me know so that I may get a chance to see you. I shall be leaving New York in the middle of December for a two or three week Christmas visit to Texas, otherwise I shall be here in New York.

I'll have things to tell you, but they can wait until I see you. I have had numerous invitations to lecture, from universities, and many flattering expressions of gratitude and good will. One I most appreciate is from the University of Texas which is now the richest University in the world. Mr. Ransom who wrote to me, is a remarkable man and a distinguished figure in many respects.

The University is erecting a new main building and there is to be a large room in it that has been given my name.[8] Various books and manuscripts of mine will be placed in it.

I'm looking forward to seeing you.

Stark

7. Compare above, Letter 927 and n. 6. Young, however, may have had reference to a letter from Meiklejohn written before Young's journey to Europe in April, 1958. During Meiklejohn's trip East in 1959, Young was ill.
8. See above, Letter 914 and n. 6.

933 | To Leah Salisbury, New York

[320 East 57th Street]
[New York]
November 19, 1959

Dear Miss Leah,

Thank you for the check and your very sweet note which I valued greatly. I'm looking forward to seeing the play. It will mean a great deal to me to see, and to remember.

I am looking forward to your seeing *Cheri*.[9] Many of the limitations of the first act are due to the director and producer. But most of the play, in Cheri's own rooms, is effective. As far as Kim's playing goes, I know of not a single actress now playing whom she does not very much indeed excel. It was interesting to know that last season in London, of all the players, including both foreign and American, she was given for her work, the top award.

Among our players, she faintly reminds me of Pauline Lord; but her range and versatility, and imagination are easily greater. I must say again it is a shame that the producer and the director allowed numerous points that detract from the first act.

Bless you again, and love.

Stark

934 | To Robert Penn Warren, Fairfield, Connecticut

320 East 57th Street
New York
November 27, 1959

Dear Red,

You have already heard of my infernal illness which has for the past few months messed up my whole existence.

9. Produced by the Playwrights' Company and Robert Lewis, *Cheri* opened at the Morosco Theatre, October 12, 1959, and closed November 28, 1959. Robert Lewis directed the play and Kim Stanley acted the part of Léa de Lonval.

I was very much delighted to receive your book [1] so soon after it was published, and though I did attempt to read the book on my own it turned out that the attention I was physically able to give it was by no means satisfactory or worthy of it. So it waited on my desk.

A good many weeks ago, I got to the point where I am almost entirely recovered, but I still cannot read on my own in any full or completely satisfactory way. I now have a friend who helps me with this and with letters and general typing. So it happens that I am now able to express my delight in your book and my full appreciation of it.

If I may mention one place in the book which is developed in a manner most admirable to me, I should mention the place where the Greek meets his wife, and the story of their relationship begins. It is a most remarkably developed section. However, I am sure these remarks are no great news to you. Let me again express my gratitude and admiration.

I must say too, that the whole meaning of the title—The Cave, is very clear as one comes to the final pages. Every character and every action is in some way or other led to, by the thought of the cave.

I trust Eleanor is well along with the writing of her next book. I am looking forward to it.

By the way, I saw at dinner the other evening, my old friend Horton Foote and he spoke of your book of verse [2] with much admiration. I was delighted to hear it, for I genuinely value his judgment.

With great affection and admiration for you both,

Stark

1. *The Cave* (1959).
2. *Promises: Poems 1954–1956* (1957).

935 | To Burnet M. Hobgood,[3] Catawba College,
Salisbury, North Carolina [telegram]

New York
April 21, 1960

Dear Hob your remarkable book of quotations [4] and etc. arrived a few hours ago and I am overwhelmed with its contents. I can't here express my affection to you and yours. Am trying to write a letter to express a little of this to you.

Love
Stark Young

936 | To Edith Evans, London, England

[New York]
[February, 1961]

Dear Cousin,

My friend is writing a little note to go along with this to show my good intentions to write you in spite of my accident. The truth is, it is

3. Burnet McLean Hobgood (b. 1922), teacher, editor, and director, was then chairman of the drama and speech department at Catawba College, where he had been teaching courses in theatre since 1950. In 1964, he joined the faculty of Southern Methodist University and since 1965 has been chairman of its department of dramatic arts and theatre.

4. In 1959, the South Eastern Theatre Conference awarded Young its first distinguished service award, although Young was too ill to receive the award in person. Professor Hobgood, chairman of the organization's honors committee and a friend of Young, compiled a book of letters from himself and other admirers, including Charles Scribner, Jr., Louis Kronenberger, George Freedly, Brooks Atkinson, John Mason Brown, John W. Gassner, Francis Fergusson, Henry W. Wells, Eric Bentley, Bedford Thurman, Paul Green, Horton Foote, Rosamond Gilder, Mildred Dunnock, Katharine Cornell and Guthrie McClintic, Edward G. Robinson, John Gielgud, Maurice Evans, and others.

almost impossible to tell you how much I was impressed with your work in *Time Remembered.*[5]

Wales would send you much love, too if he were here.

Lovingly,
Stark

937 | To Edith Evans, London, England

[New York]
[February, 1961]

Dearest Cousin,

This is the first effort to write out a letter since my bad accident. I am trying to say that your first [part] in that play was the finest to see that I think I ever saw in our theatre.[6] That seems strange to say so, but what very beautiful and complete playing, so extremely complete and beautiful—I can't tell you enough. Do forgive this writing, I'm still trying to write.

Love indeed
Stark

5. Unable to write in his own hand, Young's memory apparently failed him in his effort to convey his affection and admiration to Dame Edith Evans. Helen Hayes played in the American production of *Time Remembered,* which opened on November 12, 1957, at the Morosco Theatre. Earlier Margaret Rutherford had appeared in the English version, adapted by Patricia Moyes from Jean Anouilh's play *Léocadia,* for the British Broadcasting Company. Young may have had in mind Dame Edith's performance in the motion picture, *Look Back in Anger,* released in 1959, but the identification is conjecture.

6. The play cannot be identified; see the preceding letter and note.

938 | To Julia Young Robertson, Austin, Texas

320 East 57th Street
New York
May 4, 1961

Dearest Sister,

My head is acting a little slower than usual so instead of messing things up I am asking Betsy[7] a favor to scratch this off for you. I have been quite occupied but not very brilliant and have written you a score of letters you probably can't read. You probably would like to have some better.

One of the things I asked you no doubt was, did those little neck things reach you which I sent you and thought were quite pretty.

I wish you had been here to hear the beautiful performance of Kim Stanley[8] greatly to the credit of Texas. Many people have admitted that she's the best actress in the country. Wales and I had dinner with her after the theatre at Sardi's. I am devoted to her. She said it to people in the theatre at some special session elsewhere. She got it off very well. "Just one critic I'm afraid of and that's Stark Young. The most important performance was when Stark Young was in the theatre." She is a quite dazzling person. My God she's smart. I suppose you know she came from Texas and went to the University.[9]

I wish I could come and see you all for a little bit and then come back and go to work, but I can't do all that traveling. I hope to God this rheumatism will be better so that I can get to work.

Someone tells me that Dr. Wolfe always sings my praise and hopes I will come to see him. So I am going next Tuesday. I love that man.

I have spent so many hundred dollars at the hospital and I know that some of it has helped me some.

---

7. Mrs. Beverly Thurman.

8. Kim Stanley was playing the role of Elizabeth von Ritter in Henry Denker's *A Far Country,* which opened at the Music Box Theatre, April 4, 1961, and closed November 25, 1961.

9. Although Kim Stanley was born in Tularosa, New Mexico, and attended the University of New Mexico, she was graduated from the University of Texas in 1945 with an academic major in psychology.

Wales would send his love if he knew we were writing and it is very pleasant for me to have my little cousin do this writing.

[unsigned]

939 | To Julia and John Benjamin Robertson, Austin, Texas

320 East 57th Street
New York
April 2, 1962

Dear Sister & Brother,[1]

A day or so [ago] I sent you a not too clear letter and so I am asking my friend to follow that one up with a clearer one.

I just wanted to acknowledge the fact that I had received your letter which I enjoyed so much. As always I want to add how much I love you both. Many pleasant things have happened to me but putting them into a written form is not easy for me though I understand them easily. This letter is really to say that and to extend dearest wishes to you both.

Love,
Stark

1. Although this letter is not written in Stark Young's autograph, his signature appears at the end.

Index